Did you get ALL your learning resources?

Each NEW copy of *Human Motor Development: A Lifespan Approach* comes with a free registration code to access premium resources found on the Online Learning Center (www.mhhe.com/payne6e). The Online Learning Center includes tools to help you succeed in your course and in your future career. Resources include self-quizzes and glossary puzzles for review, lab activities, and links to key Internet sites. The password also provides access to PowerWeb articles, current news, guidelines for Web research, and information on career paths.

If you purchased a used copy of *Human Motor Development: A Lifespan Approach*, you can purchase access to the premium content on the Online Learning Center separately; visit the Online Learning Center (www.mhhe.com/payne6e) for more details.

IMPORTANT

HERE IS YOUR REGISTRATION CODE TO ACCESS MCGRAW-HILL PREMIUM CONTENT AND MCGRAW-HILL ONLINE RESOURCES

For key premium online resources you need THIS CODE to gain access. Once the code is entered, you will be able to use the web resources for the length of your course.

Access is provided only if you have purchased a new book.

If the registration code is missing from this book, the registration screen on our website, and within your WebCT or Blackboard course will tell you how to obtain your new code. Your registration code can be used only once to establish access. It is not transferable.

To gain access to these online resources

1. **USE** your web browser to go to: **www.mhhe.com/payne6e**

2. **CLICK** on "First Time User"

3. **ENTER** the Registration Code printed on the tear-off bookmark on the right

4. After you have entered your registration code, click on "Register"

5. **FOLLOW** the instructions to setup your personal UserID and Password

6. **WRITE** your UserID and Password down for future reference. Keep it in a safe place.

If your course is using WebCT or Blackboard, you'll be able to use this code to access the McGraw-Hill content within your instructor's online course.

To gain access to the McGraw-Hill content in your instructor's WebCT or Blackboard course simply log into the course with the user ID and Password provided by your instructor. Enter the registration code exactly as it appears to the right when prompted by the system. You will only need to use this code the first time you click on McGraw-Hill content.

These instructions are specifically for student access. Instructors are not required to register via the above instructions.

The McGraw-Hill Companies

Mc Graw Hill **Higher Education**

Thank you, and welcome to your McGraw-Hill Online Resources.

0-07-297400-1 t/a
Payne
Human Motor Development, 6E

GZFE-92VA-5ACM-S4P9-WXQI

REGISTRATION CODE
REGISTRATION CODE

The McGraw-Hill Companies

Mc Graw Hill **Higher Education**

Human Motor
Development

Note: The authors' names appear side by side on the title page to denote an equal contribution to the production of this textbook.

Higher Education

HUMAN MOTOR DEVELOPMENT: A LIFESPAN APPROACH, Sixth Edition
Published by McGraw-Hill, a business unit of The McGraw-Hill Companies, Inc., 1221 Avenue of the Americas, New York, NY 10020. Copyright © 2005, 2002, 1999, 1995, 1991, 1987 by The McGraw-Hill Companies, Inc. All rights reserved. No part of this publication may be reproduced or distributed in any form or by any means, or stored in a database or retrieval system, without the prior written consent of The McGraw-Hill Companies, Inc., including, but not limited to, any network or other electronic storage or transmission, or broadcast for distance learning. Some ancillaries, including electronic and print components, may not be available to customers outside the United States. The Web addresses cited in this text were current as of April 2004, unless otherwise noted.

2 3 4 5 6 7 8 9 0 DOC/DOC 0 9 8 7 6 5

ISBN 0-07-285169-4

Editor-in-chief: *Emily Barrosse*
Publisher: *William Glass*
Sponsoring editor: *Nick Barrett*
Director of development: *Kate Engelberg*
Development editor: *Kirstan Price*
Marketing manager: *Pam Cooper*
Production services manager: *Jennifer Mills*
Production service: *Hal Lockwood,*
 Penmarin Books

Manuscript editor: *Molly Roth*
Art director: *Jeanne M. Schreiber*
Design manager and cover designer:
 Preston Thomas
Interior designer: *Adriane Bosworth*
Art manager: *Robin Mouat*
Illustrator: *Joan Carol*
Indexer: *Joy Isaacs*
Production supervisor: *Randy Hurst*

The text was set in 10/12 New Caledonia by ColorType and printed on acid-free, 45# New Era Matte by RR Donnelley, Crawfordville.

Cover image: © Ariel Skelley/Corbis

Library of Congress Cataloging-in-Publication Data
Payne, V. Gregory
 Human motor development : a lifespan approach / V. Gregory Payne, Larry D. Isaacs. —6th ed.
  p. cm.
 Includes bibliographical references and index.
  ISBN 0-07-285169-4
  1. Motor ability in children. 2. Child development. 3. Human mechanics. I. Isaacs, Larry D.
(Larry David) II. Title.
RJ133.P39 2005
155.4′123—dc22
                                                        2004046546

www.mhhe.com

To my children, Brooke and Timothy, and my wife, Joy. No words could ever adequately express my love for each of you. To my feline companions, Lucy, Burt, Ernie, Elmo, Ginger, and Oliver, whose motor skills I always observe with amazement. And to the loving memory of my parents, Linwood and Gracie Isaacs.
–L. D. I.–

To Luke, Linda, my parents, and a good life.
–V. G. P.–

Brief Contents

Contents

PART IV   Movement Across the Lifespan

10   Infant Reflexes and Stereotypies   247

Preface

Our longstanding and established emphasis on covering well-founded undergraduate level information related to human motor development remains the focus of the sixth edition of *Human Motor Development: A Lifespan Approach.* As with our previous editions, the approach of our book continues to be unique in many ways.

SPECIAL FEATURES AND ORGANIZATION

Traditionally, human motor development has been studied and presented as a process that ceased at the onset of adulthood. Our book approaches the topic as a lifespan proposition recognizing the dramatic changes in our population's demographics and the increasing need and popularity of studying people of all ages, including those in early, middle, and late adulthood.

This book is also influenced by the philosophy that movement affects and is affected by social, cognitive, and physical changes in our development. Therefore, separate chapters are allocated to each of these areas of development and how they interrelate with human movement.

The organization of the sixth edition remains straightforward. Part I provides an overview of human development and includes chapters on many of the developmental aspects just mentioned. Part II covers factors affecting development, including effects of early stimulation and deprivation. Part III, Physical Changes Across the Lifespan, and Part IV, Movement Across the Lifespan, present the book's core concepts. Part V, the culminating section, addresses assessment in motor development and implementing a motor development program.

Chapter 15, "Youth Sports," and Chapter 18, "Planning and Conducting Developmental Movement Programs," present information that is commonly omitted in traditional texts for motor development courses. In addition, Chapter 18 provides information necessary for those interested in establishing their own developmental movement programs.

Several features assist both the student and instructor. For example, the book has been written with the undergraduate student in mind. We have made every effort to explain concepts in a manner understandable to the motor development novice. In addition, each chapter concludes with a list of key terms, related Web sites, questions for reflection, and complete references by chapter. New instructor teaching tools and student study aids have been added for the sixth edition; these are described later in the preface.

KEY CHANGES FOR THE SIXTH EDITION

Chapters have been updated and modified to reflect up-to-date thought and theory and to improve the book's readability for students. Numerous new photos have been added in every chapter of the book, and new illustrations have been added to aid in student learning. Following are some of the more significant chapter-by-chapter modifications in our sixth edition:

Chapter 1, "Introduction to Motor Development"

- Thorough updating
- Significant reorganization for reading ease
- New photos

Chapter 2, "Cognitive and Motor Development"

- Thorough updating
- New photos

Chapter 3, "Social and Motor Development"

- Thorough updating
- Seven new photos

Chapter 5, "Prenatal Development Concerns"

- New and expanded coverage of the three stages of prenatal development
- Expanded coverage of alcohol-related neurodevelopmental disorders
- New and expanded coverage of rubella and congenital rubella syndrome
- New coverage on the value of assisted treadmill walking in children with Down syndrome
- New coverage of sickle-cell trait and sickle-cell disease with new interpretative illustrations
- New coverage of triple marker screening during pregnancy

Chapter 6, "Effects of Early Stimulation and Deprivation"

- Thorough updating
- New photos
- Expanded section on deprivation or psychosocial dwarfism

Chapter 7, "Growth and Maturation"

- Thorough updating
- New photos
- Incorporation of new growth data based on the most recent NHANES data
- New coverage on the measurement of and developmental changes in head circumference

- Updated descriptive anthropometric reference data for older Americans

Chapter 8, "Physiological Changes: Health-Related Physical Fitness"

- Expanded coverage of the epidemic of overweight and obesity
- New coverage of the use of the Bod Pod in determining body composition
- Ethnic, racial, and socioeconomic status group comparisons of overweight and obesity
- New coverage on the treatment of overweight and obesity

Chapter 9, "Movement and the Changing Senses"

- New section on auditory development

Chapter 10, "Infant Reflexes and Stereotypies"

- Thorough updating
- New photos

Chapter 12, "Fine Motor Development"

- Thorough updating
- New photos

Chapter 13, "Fundamental Locomotion Skills of Childhood"

- New table reporting average run velocity (ft/sec) for individuals 2.5 through 17+ years of age

Chapter 14, "Fundamental Object-Control Skills of Childhood"

- New report of ball-throwing velocity based on a 20-year cohort comparison of 13-year-olds

Chapter 15, "Youth Sports"

- Updated figures on the number of youth sport participants
- New recent data on youth football injuries
- New discussion on background screening (criminal and child sex offenses) of youth sport coaches

Chapter 16, "Movement in Adulthood"

- Thorough updating
- New photos
- New section, on sports-related injuries to baby boomers and older adults

Chapter 17, "Assessment"

- Updated information on ordering the assessment instruments presented in the chapter
- Expanded coverage of the Test of Gross Motor Development–2
- Expanded coverage of the FITNESSGRAM/ACTIVITYGRAM
- Expanded coverage of the President's Challenge Youth Physical Fitness Program, including tables that report qualifying standards for both the Presidential Physical Fitness Award and the National Physical Fitness Award

SUPPLEMENTS

A comprehensive package of supplementary materials designed to enhance teaching and learning is available with the sixth edition of *Human Motor Development: A Lifespan Approach.* Contact your local McGraw-Hill sales representative to receive these supplements, including the password to access PageOut and the instructor materials available on the Online Learning Center, and to obtain additional information on using the Online Learning Center resources with other course management systems.

Instructor's Resource CD-ROM (ISBN 0-07-294463-3)

New to the sixth edition, the Instructor's Resource CD-ROM features many useful teaching tools:

- ***Instructor's Manual to Accompany Human Motor Development: A Lifespan Approach:*** Updated for the sixth edition, the manual includes a sample syllabus, a test bank with more than 500 multiple-choice and short-essay questions, suggested assignments for each chapter, and extended assignments. The extended assignments include such details as expected length, criteria for evaluation, and problems the student may encounter in completing the assignment. These assignments are in ready-to-use format or are easily adaptable to the instructor's own course or preferences.
- **PowerPoint® Slides:** A complete set of PowerPoint slides is available on the CD-ROM and for download from the book's Online Learning Center (see next section). Keyed to the major points in each chapter, these slide sets can be modified or expanded to better fit the instructor's lectures. The PowerPoint slides were created by Roberta Pohlman, Wright State University.
- **Computerized Test Bank:** New for the sixth edition, the test questions from the instructor's manual are available with test generation software. The computerized test bank software from Brownstone provides a powerful, easy-to-use test maker to create a print version, a computer lab version, or an Internet version of each test. The CD-ROM includes the Diploma program for Windows users and Exam VI for Macintosh users. The Diploma program also includes a built-in grade book.

Online Learning Center (www.mhhe.com/payne6e)

The Online Learning Center provides many resources for both instructors and students. For instructors, there are downloadable versions of the *Instructor's Manual* and PowerPoint slides found on the Instructor's Resource CD-ROM; in addition, there are links to professional resources. For students, there are a variety of study and learning tools:

- Self-correcting quizzes and crossword puzzles for review of key concepts
- Lab activities focusing on important aspects of motor development
- Links to key motor development Web sites
- Access to PowerWeb resources, including articles, study tips, links, a daily news feed, and guidelines for conducting Web research

Many of the lab activities were created by Martin Block, University of Virginia.

PageOut (www.pageout.net)

PageOut is a free, easy-to-use program that enables instructors to develop Web sites quickly for their courses. PageOut can be used to create a course home page, an instructor home page, an interactive syllabus, Web links, online discussion areas, an online grade book, and much more.

ACKNOWLEDGMENTS

Special thanks are extended to Kirstan Price of McGraw-Hill. As our developmental editor, she capably, carefully, knowledgeably, energetically, and successfully guided us through the process of revising and updating. She was most helpful and pleasant in working with us and assuring us that our book is as useful as it can be to our readers. We also appreciate the reviews that were solicited by McGraw-Hill. The input provided by these conscientious experts was integral to helping us adjust the quality and content of our book, as well as update, modify, and generally meet the needs of instructors and students. We are particularly grateful to the following reviewers of the sixth edition:

Kelly J. Cole, University of Iowa

Kim A. Duchane, Manchester College

Deborah A. Garrahy, Illinois State University

Louis Harrison, Jr., Louisiana State University

Melanie Hart, University of Northern Iowa

Yuhua Li, University of Memphis

Shannon D. R. Ringenbach, Arizona State University

Last, we would again like to continue to extend our gratitude to Dr. John Haubenstricker, Dr. Vern Seefeldt, and their colleagues at Michigan State University for providing us with research data and supporting studies pertaining to the "total body approach" for describing developmental sequences (presented in Chapters 13, 14, and 17). Dr. Joy Kiger produced the film tracings for this work. Joy is a former doctoral student at Michigan State University and is currently a member of the faculty at Otterbein College in Westerville, Ohio.

ABOUT THE AUTHORS

V. Gregory Payne is a professor and Chair of the Department of Human Performance at San Jose State University. Dr. Payne is a specialist in human motor development, with interests ranging from aging and physical activity to children's sports and fitness. He received a B.S. degree from Western Illinois University and was presented that institution's Distinguished Alumni Award in 1995. He earned an M.A. from the University of Iowa and a P.E.D. from Indiana University. Dr. Payne lived and worked in

Venezuela for two years as a Peace Corps volunteer assigned to the Venezuelan Ministry of Education. He has produced more than 150 publications, including numerous refereed articles and ten editions of four books. In 2000, Dr. Payne was elected to fellowship in the prestigious Academy of Kinesiology and Physical Education (AAKPE), generally regarded to be the top tier of leaders in the discipline who have made long-term contributions primarily through research and scholarship. He was also a member of the task force that developed the physical education national standards published in 1995 and has made nearly 300 presentations at conferences throughout the world. Dr. Payne was the first Distinguished Honorary Professor of the Shenyang Institute of Physical Education in China. He also received the Distinguished Service Award from the California Governor's Council on Physical Fitness and Sports, the Southwest District AAHPERD Scholar Award, and the AAHPERD Honor Award. He received the prestigious *Research Quarterly for Exercise and Sport* Research Writing Award for work involving children's physical activity and VO_2 max. Dr. Payne is a former president of the 22,000-member National Association for Sport and Physical Education (NASPE); former president of the California Association for Health, Physical Education, Recreation, and Dance (CAHPERD); former

chair of the National Motor Development Academy of AAHPERD; and fellow of the Research Consortium of AAHPERD. He has chaired two editorial boards and reviews for many journals. Dr. Payne resides in San Jose with Linda and Luke.

Larry D. Isaacs is a professor and directs the activities of the Exercise Biology Program, Department of Biological Sciences, College of Science and Mathematics, at Wright State University. Since receiving his doctorate in 1979 from the University of Maryland, Dr. Isaacs has served as a reviewer for many scholarly journals. In addition, he has published numerous scholarly articles and has written 15 textbooks. Throughout the past 20 years, his writings have been recognized by many organizations, including AAHPERD, where he was awarded the status of fellow by the Research Consortium. Dr. Isaacs holds international certifications with the American College of Sports Medicine. Presently, Dr. Isaacs's research focuses on the physiological basis of muscular strength development for prepubescent and elderly individuals. Additionally, his research examines the physiological changes that accompany resistance training in cardiac rehabilitation. Dr. Isaacs currently lives in Dayton, Ohio, with his wife, Joy. His daughter, Brooke, and son, Timothy, attend the University of South Carolina.

Introduction to Motor Development

HUMAN MOTOR DEVELOPMENT

Human motor development is both a process through which we pass during the course of life and an academic field of study. As a human process, motor development is defined as the changes that occur in our ability to move and our movement in general as we proceed through the lifespan. Defining motor development as a field of study has been a bit more controversial. This controversy may have begun as early as 1974, when six motor developmentalists met to "delineate the focus of research in motor development" (Notes from Scholarly Directions Committee, 1974, p. 1). Though several attempts were required, the group eventually generated a definition of motor development as "changes in motor behavior which reflect the interaction of the maturing organism and its environment" (p. 2).

This definition, the committee believed, melded the two main opposing views of those in attendance. One group, who primarily conducted research to generate predictive data on motor skills, was most interested in the movement product. The other group, who manipulated underlying process variables to better understand movement responses, was most interested in the movement process. One member of the 1974 committee, Vern Seefeldt, believes this definition has "stood the test of time," according to his article entitled "This Is Motor Development" (1989, p. 2). As Seefeldt explains, this definition includes the phrase "changes in motor behavior" to incorporate developmental differences that occur with time. The phrase "interactions of a maturing organism and its environment" was included to recognize the contributions of genetics and the environment to the process of development. This, Seefeldt states, was important to "defuse" the historical debate over nature versus nurture (genetics or the environment) and the magnitude of their effects on human development (1989, p. 2).

Despite Seefeldt's views, not all motor developmentalists support this definition. Keogh, for example, suggested this definition in a 1977 article: [Motor development can be defined as] "changes in

movement competencies from infancy to adulthood and involves many aspects of human behavior, both as they affect movement development and as movement development affects them" (p. 76). Clark and Whitall state that the "overwhelmingly" prevalent current definition of motor development is "the change in motor behavior across the lifespan" (1989, p. 183).

Clark and Whitall's definition has had considerable support. Roberton (1989) states that this is her view of motor development as well as the one proposed by the first textbook in the field, Espenschade and Eckert's *Motor Development* (1967). However, Clark and Whitall contrast that original definition with one supplied by Haywood and Getchell in their text, *Lifespan Motor Development* (2001): "the sequential, continuous age-related process whereby an individual progresses from simple, unorganized, and unskilled movement to the achievement of highly organized, complex motor skills and finally to the adjustment of skills that accompanies aging" (p. 7).

The major difference between these last two definitions is that the former only recognizes the efforts of developmentalists to study change, the product of development, whereas the latter emphasizes the process of development. Using historical information to support their case, Clark and Whitall argue that both the product and the process of motor development have been examined throughout the history of the field of motor development and should be reflected in the definition. Therefore, they propose the following definition of motor development: "the changes in motor behavior over the lifespan and the processes which underlie these changes" (1989, p. 194).

Because a definition must be current, accurate, and relatively simple and succinct to be practical, we support Clark and Whitall's definition as the most useful. However, we also recognize that an examination of all the definitions presented here enables a more thorough understanding of the thinking of different motor developmentalists and subsequently a more thorough understanding of the field.

With a working definition of motor development, we can now define it as a field of study:

_____

Motor development is the study of the changes in human motor behavior over the lifespan, the processes that underlie these changes, and the factors that affect them.

_____

We obviously added "the study of" to our original definition of motor development. We also added "and the factors that affect them" because we believe the field of motor development encompasses more than the examination of the products and processes of motor development. It also encompasses the study of related or affecting factors. For that reason, in later chapters we shall examine such topics as the effects of early motor programs on motor development, children's physical fitness, youth sports, and the effects of physical activity on the aging process.

Finally, Roberton (1988) has further clarified the role of motor developmentalists by stating that we attempt to improve understanding in three general areas. First, we try to understand present motor behavior, both what is happening and why it happens. Second, we strive to understand what this behavior was like in the past and why. Finally, we seek to understand what the behavior will be like in the future and why. As we shall discuss later in the chapter, motor development research is often interdisciplinary; we team with experts from other areas of study to do our research. However, what makes us unique is that we do not stop with understanding the present motor behavior; our primary interest drives us to understand what it was, what it will be, and why.

THE IMPORTANCE OF MOTOR DEVELOPMENT

Human development is a diverse, complex area of study in which we cannot consider ourselves completely educated until we understand all aspects of the changes that occur throughout the lifespan. We must strive to understand the movement changes that we commonly experience with age and its accompanying intellectual, social, and emotional changes. Our knowledge of all aspects of human development is valuable because it contributes to a general body of knowledge that enables us to better understand ourselves and the world we live in. However, although knowledge gained purely for the sake of knowledge is important, there are other, more practical applications for our knowledge of motor development.

For easy communication and more efficient organization, we divide the study of human development into the cognitive, affective, motor, and physical domains. Because these domains of human behavior are constantly interacting, a complete understanding of any one domain requires knowledge of the domains with which it interacts. Full understanding of motor development therefore requires knowledge of the cognitive, affective, and physical domains because they so profoundly affect movement behavior. Conversely, full understanding of human development in the cognitive, affective, and physical domains requires a knowledge of motor development. As discussed in upcoming chapters, motor development has profound effects on the development of cognitive, social, and physical behaviors throughout the lifespan.

Knowledge of motor development has other applications. For example, understanding the way people normally develop movement skills throughout the lifespan enables us to diagnose problems in those individuals who may be developing abnormally. Consider an infant who does not exhibit a particular reflex at the expected time of appearance. As discussed in greater detail in Chapter 10, certain reflexive movements normally occur at certain ages. Any significant deviations from the expected timeline may indicate the need for special treatment.

Understanding human motor development is also important for helping individuals perfect or improve their movement performance, which can yield many benefits. For example, an improved self-concept enables a person to become more emotionally stable and satisfied. Also, because there are links among all domains of behavior, improvement in the motor domain may indirectly lead to improvements in intellectual or social development. Activities can therefore be devised to assist in the development of movement potential. To accurately create such a movement curriculum, we must have a knowledge of normal motor development. With that knowledge and the subsequent structuring of developmentally appropriate movement tasks, we can challenge individuals relative to their levels of achievement. Developmentally appropriate movement curricula lead to more effective learning of motor tasks because the participants seldom become frustrated or bored by tasks that are too difficult or too easy.

For these reasons, knowledge of motor development is important for movement specialists working with "normal" children. This same knowledge can be applied when working with special populations. Although many conditions lead to a developmental lag in an individual's movement performance, the sequence or pattern of development generally remains similar to the normal development pattern, making comparisons among differing populations useful. For example, in recent research examining children with Down syndrome, Jobling (1999) stated that, compared with normally functioning children, Down children have specific motor impairments, though progress can be made with age and intervention. Jobling also noted that the degree of impairment is generally related to the individual's mental, rather than chronological, age. Furthermore, a wide range of proficiency was noted in children with Down syndrome at the same age level, with the most significant delays being detected in the area of balance. Gender differences within Jobling's sample reflected the trends often noted in nondisabled populations, with boys performing better on gross motor tasks and girls performing better on fine motor tasks.

Similarly, Lefebvre and Reid (1999) found that children with developmental coordination disorder (DCD) showed a developmental trend from young to older age though they tended to show considerable delays when compared with children who are more normally functioning. Generally, children with DCD improved performance in a ball-catching task as they gained experience and knowledge. This enabled them, according to the researchers, to better predict ball trajectory with less information (Lefebvre & Reid, 1999).

In their research examining children with mental retardation, Shapiro and Dummer (1999) noted that mental retardation can interfere with one's ability to learn and perform physical activity. Specifically, "cognitive delays may influence reaction time, movement time, acquisition of fundamental movement patterns, physical fitness, and complex motor skill development" (p. 179). From infancy, children with mental retardation may progress more slowly than children with average intelligence. These differences often become more apparent as the child ages (Shapiro & Dummer, 1999).

Clearly, the study of motor development offers many benefits. See Table 1-1 for a summary of the importance of such research and knowledge.

THE DOMAINS OF HUMAN DEVELOPMENT

Nearly a half century ago, Benjamin Bloom (1956) devised a taxonomy (method of classification or organization) to categorize educational objectives. In his taxonomy, he created three categories of educational objectives and deemed each a "domain." His three major domains were the cognitive, the affective, and the psychomotor. Though our focus in this book is not educational objectives, Bloom's domains, with one significant change, work very nicely in categorizing the study of human development. The significant change is to add one domain, the physical domain.

These four domains enable us to neatly organize our study of human development. The cognitive domain, which concerns human intellectual development, has been the main focus of developmentalists throughout history. Jean Piaget, the most prominent developmentalist of all times, emphasized intellectual development. His work in relationship to motor development is examined in Chapter 2. To understand cognitive development in a practical way, imagine a third-grade girl sitting at her desk at school. If our focus is on her cognitive

Table 1-1   Why Should We Study Motor Development?

1. Human development is multifaceted. In addition to changes in human movement, intellectual, social, and emotional changes occur. Because these domains of human development are in constant interaction, we can never fully understand ourselves until we fully understand each of these domains, including the motor domain.

2. Knowledge of the way most people develop in their movement enables us to diagnose cases that are sufficiently abnormal to warrant intervention and remediation.

3. Knowledge of human motor development allows the establishment of developmentally appropriate activities that enable optimal teaching/learning of movement skills for people of all ages and all ability levels.

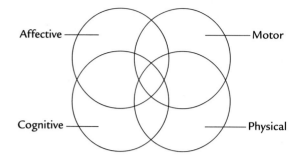

Figure 1-1 The four domains of human development are useful for categorizing our study of such areas as motor development. However, we must remember that these domains are not discrete; they are in constant interaction with each other.

development, we would be most concerned with her reading, problem solving in math, pondering facts in social studies, and other similar activities.

The affective domain is primarily concerned with the social and emotional aspects of human development. Thus, we often refer to this domain as the social-emotional domain, a term more recognizable to most. Now, in considering our third-grader, we would focus on aspects such as her feelings of self-worth, her ability to interact with her peers in the classroom, and how she feels about their interaction with her.

The psychomotor, or motor, domain is the main focus of this book. Here, we emphasize the development of human movement and the factors that affect that development. In this domain, for our third-grader, focus shifts to examinations of her handwriting ability; her movement technique and level of maturity in running, throwing, and jumping; and her rhythmic ability in dance activities.

As mentioned, the fourth domain involves physical change. Often included with the physical domain, we believe this domain deserves separate recognition. Here, we include all types of bodily change. To illustrate, imagine our third-grader. We are now concerned with bodily types of change such as her increases in height or weight. Has she in-

creased or decreased in body fat? What about her range of motion around joints, or her cardiovascular endurance? Though these factors all impact the other domains, they can also be clearly distinguished.

Finally, though these domains are extremely useful in organizing our study of human development, we must remember that this organizational schema is also a bit artificial. When we think in terms of discrete categories of development, we imagine our third-grader switching into and out of domains of development based on whether she has been given a math worksheet or the recess bell just rang. In fact, these domains constantly interact with each other. Each influences all of the others and, in turn, is influenced by all others (see Figure 1-1). For example, has your performance on a written exam (cognitive domain) ever been influenced by your emotional state (affective domain)? Does your muscular strength (physical domain) impact your athletic performance (motor domain)? Or, have you ever been affected emotionally (affective domain) by having too much body fat or too little muscle mass (physical domain)?

Because the interaction of domains is so prevalent in human development, isolating any one area of development can be difficult. Thus, though our primary intent in this book is to emphasize changes in human movement throughout the lifespan, we often examine the interactions just described, with special focus on human movement. Specific examples include Chapters 2 and 3, where we examine movement in relationship to cognitive and social development, and Chapters 7, 8, and 9, where we examine the interrelationship between the physical and motor domains.

DEVELOPMENT, MATURATION, AND GROWTH

Development

The term ***development,*** as it applies to human beings, is generally considered to refer to changes we experience as we pass through life. Though this book focuses on human movement, people obviously develop intellectually, socially, and emotionally as well. The term *development* has become more popular over the last decade in part because of the publication of a position statement and guidelines on developmentally appropriate practice for early childhood programs. Composed by the National Association for the Education of Young Children (NAEYC), this document was meant to "describe developmentally appropriate practice in early childhood programs for administrators, teachers, parents, policy makers, and others who make decisions about care and education for young children" (Bredekamp & Copple, 1997, p. 1). Its authors believed that many programs for very young children failed to consider the "basic developmental needs of young children." "Programs should be tailored to meet the needs of children, rather than expecting children to adjust to the demands of a specific program" (p. 1). In other words, programs should be ***developmentally appropriate.*** According to the NAEYC, this term has two dimensions: age appropriateness and individual appropriateness. *Age appropriate* refers to the predictable sequences of growth and development through which most children pass. Knowledge of these sequences provides a basis from which we can begin to provide optimal instructional experiences for children. *Individual appropriateness* refers to the uniqueness of each child. Though predictable developmental sequences exist, children have individual patterns and rates of growth as well as unique personalities, approaches to learning, and home experiences. One must consider all such matters when composing any learning activities for children, regardless of the domain of human behavior under consideration.

As a result of the increase in their popularity, terms such as *development* or *developmentally appropriate* have come to be misused or abused, taking on many meanings according to individual agendas. Development must be clearly defined and understood if the concept is to be optimally integrated into programs for children and youth. In this book, development is about the changes that all human beings face across their lifespan. Such changes result from increasing age as well as one's experiences in life, one's genetic potential, and the interactions of all three factors at any given time. Therefore, development is "an interactional process that leads to changes in behavior over the lifespan" (Motor Development Task Force, 1995, p. 2).

According to a position statement prepared by the Motor Development Task Force of the National Association for Sports and Physical Education (NASPE), there are six elements or components of developmental change. It is qualitative, sequential, cumulative, directional, multifactorial, and individual (see Table 1-2). "Qualitative" implies that developmental change is "not just more of something." So, in addition to jumping farther or throwing more accurately, one's actual technique changes, enabling the pattern to become more efficient. For example, when throwing, children may begin to take a step with the leg opposite their throwing arm, whereas before they took no step or stepped with the leg on the same side as their throwing arm.

"Sequential" implies that certain motor patterns precede others and are orderly in their appearance. For example, we leap (e.g., an extended running stride used to cross a small stream) before we run or we reach before we grasp. Sequences of development have been identified in motor development, and knowledge of these sequences is crucial for the optimal teaching of movement skills.

"Cumulative" suggests that current behaviors are additive. Current behaviors are built on previous

Table 1-2 Elements of Developmental Change

Development is

- Qualitative
- Sequential
- Cumulative
- Directional
- Multifactorial
- Individual

Understanding the elements of developmental change is essential to attaining a developmental perspective: looking at current behaviors with an interest in what preceded them and what will follow, and understanding that development is "age-related but not completely age-determined" (Motor Development Task Force, 1995, p. 5).

SOURCE: Position statement of NASPE prepared by the Motor Development Task Force (1995).

ones. The early behaviors are, therefore, stepping stones to more mature movement. For example, unassisted standing evolves from the ability to stand with a minimum of support or a handhold from a parent.

"Directional" suggests that development has an ultimate goal. We generally tend to think of development as progressive, but it can also be regressive. In other words, skills become less mature. This can happen as a result of ceasing training or practice or through the long-term effects of aging or disease.

Developmental change is also "multifactorial." This means that no one factor directs such change. Factors that can impact developmental change include physical characteristics such as strength, flexibility, and endurance or emotional factors such as motivation. Environmental effects can also impact change. These include such factors as having supportive parents or having ample equipment for practicing throwing or striking. Clearly, all these factors, both internal and external, affect developmental change.

"Individual" implies that the rate of change varies for all people, though the general sequence of development remains relatively similar. While one child may exhibit a relatively mature pattern for running at 4 years of age, another may remain quite immature. Change is the result of many factors that interact in

unique ways. Factors that make development individual include the individual characteristics of each body and the equally unique environmental circumstances surrounding each person (Motor Development Task Force, 1995).

Understanding these elements of developmental change is critical to gaining a **developmental perspective,** in which we consider not just today's behavior but what preceded the behavior and what will evolve from it. For example, given this perspective, we would not consider age alone in assessing development. Though age is important, development is "age-related but not age-determined" (Motor Development Task Force, 1995, p. 5). In other words, most 7-year-olds use a mature technique in handwriting. However, because one is 7 does not insure such a level of development. Furthermore, when a 4-year-old takes no step in batting a ball, the pattern is not incorrect. It may be quite appropriate for the developmental status of the child. Though this technique would not indicate a mature performance, the child may be well on his or her way to a mature pattern of throwing (1995).

Maturation and Growth

Two other terms important to our understanding of human development are **maturation** and **growth.** In daily conversation, these terms can be used interchangeably. For example, a student may comment, "I really grew during last semester's course." "Developed" or "matured" could be inserted for "grew" without changing the intended meaning. The idea is that there was a significant positive change as a result of the course.

Although the terms *development, maturation,* and *growth* used synonymously are acceptable in casual conversation, we must use them carefully and use specific definitions for the purposes of study and research. In this textbook, *development* includes both maturation and growth. The qualitative functional changes that occur with age are collectively known as *maturation. Growth* refers to the quantitative structural changes that occur with age (see Figure 1-2). Although both terms indicate

Figure 1-2 *Development* is a general term referring to the progressions and regressions that occur throughout the lifespan. *Growth* is the structural aspect of development; *maturation* deals with the functional changes in human development.

specific aspects of a metamorphosis from childhood to adulthood, *maturation* refers to organizational changes in the function of the organs and tissues. The individual's behavior is subsequently modified as a result of these qualitative changes. An example of maturation is the neurological organization of the brain during childhood. Virtually all anatomical parts are present from very early in childhood, but qualitative change in brain function continues to occur, enabling children to achieve ever higher levels of cognitive ability.

Growth can be simply described as an increase in physical size. This physical transformation primarily involves hyperplasia—an increase in cell number; hypertrophy—an increase in cell size; and accretion—an increase in intercellular matter (Malina, Bouchard & Bar-Or, 2004). Although these processes are gradual, generally imperceptible phenomena, they are increasingly evident when a human being is observed over a long time. One of the most noticeable examples of growth occurs at the onset of adolescence: Both male and female individuals experience a growth spurt. During that time, an increase in height of several inches over a single year is not unusual. That increase in height, independent of any simultaneous changes, is growth.

Maturation and growth should be separately defined for facilitating our understanding of development, but they are related aspects of the developmental process. Growth and maturation are intertwined because, as the body grows, functions improve. However, most people's rate of growth (other than increase in body fat) often slows greatly when they are about 20 years old. In contrast, maturation proceeds until the end of the lifespan.

GENERAL MOTOR DEVELOPMENT TERMS

As discussed earlier, there are important reasons why we need a general understanding of human motor development. Although many of us pride ourselves on the characteristics that make us unique, the general motor development of all human beings is remarkably similar. Several terms are used in motor development to depict the general growth and maturation trends that occur throughout the population.

Developmental Direction

Cephalocaudal and *proximodistal* are frequently referred to as the developmental directions because they indicate the direction in which growth and movement maturation proceeds. **Cephalocaudal** literally means "from the head to the tail." Specifically, this term refers to the development of the human being from the top of the body, the head, downward toward the "tail" or the feet. This phenomenon is especially noticeable as it applies to growth. The head of a human fetus or infant is much larger than the head of an older child, adolescent, or adult relative to the body. The head experiences greater growth earlier than the rest of the body.

The cephalocaudal concept can also be applied to the maturation of human movement. The development of walking is an excellent example. When children first learn to walk, their legs are stiff and their feet flat. This awkward but typical walking technique is partly caused by cephalocaudal development. Control over the muscles that govern the hip joint enables the infant to swing the entire leg, but the child has not yet achieved similar ability at the knee or the ankle. With time, the child will gain comparable control at the knee and then the ankle, eventually achieving the mature walking technique.

Proximodistal, the second developmental direction, literally means "from those points close to the body's center to those points close to the periphery, or farthest from the body's center." This phenomenon is evidenced by human prenatal growth. The human evolves from the neural groove, a tiny elongated mass of cells that eventually forms the central portion of the body, the spinal column. From that central portion of the body, all else will evolve until the fingers and toes have been completed.

A similar process occurs in the acquisition of movement skill, such as an infant's early attempts at reaching and grasping (prehension). Initially, the infant's arm is controlled by the muscles that are predominantly responsible for shoulder movement. Gradually, dominance over the elbow also evolves, which allows much greater accuracy of movement. Finally, control over the wrist and then the fingers concludes the normal progression in prehension.

Interestingly, as a person ages and movement ability begins to regress, the cephalocaudal and proximodistal processes reverse themselves. The most currently acquired movements of the lower body or periphery will be the first to exhibit signs of regression. The process of movement regression slowly evolves in a "tail to head" and "outside-in" direction. However, as discussed in upcoming chapters, people can prevent or reduce such regression throughout most of their lives.

The cephalocaudal and proximodistal concepts are useful tools in our efforts to gain a general understanding of motor development. These processes generally apply to human growth and motor development, but there are a few exceptions. For example, in the case of prehension, a child normally acquires control of the fingers before control of the thumb. This is an exception to the proximodistal rule, because the thumb is closer to the body's center than are the fingers.

Differentiation and Integration

Two other terms useful for describing general motor development are *differentiation* and *integration*. **Differentiation** is the progression from gross, immature movement to precise, well-controlled, intentional movement. Our previous walking example also illustrates differentiation. Whereas early in the development of the walking pattern the leg swing is predominantly under the control of the large muscles surrounding the hip joint, eventually each segment of the leg becomes differentiated. That is, each segment of the leg develops a unique duty or specialization in the walking pattern, and thus the

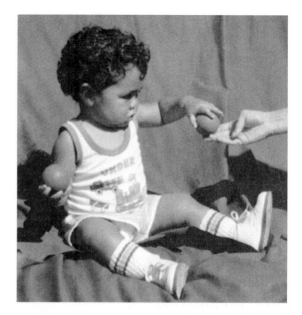

Figure 1-3 A young child handed a succession of toys may exhibit integration of the hands and arms by receiving the toy with one hand and storing it in the other. This storage process frees up the receiving hand for additional receptions.

stiff, inconsistent gait that characterizes immature walking evolves into a more efficient movement pattern as the segments of the leg begin to function as individual units rather than as a unified block.

Integration is a related, similar change that occurs as an individual's movement ability gradually progresses. As just described, various muscle systems develop or change duties as movement skill improves. As the muscle systems become differentiated, they also become more capable of functioning together. For example, a young child handed one toy may hold on to it using only the hand closest to the toy. If the child is immediately handed a second toy on the same side, she will place the first toy in the other hand for safekeeping if she is capable of integrating the use of one hand with the other. The child incapable of such integration or coordination will simply discard the first toy in favor of the second one, freeing the receiving hand to take the new toy (see Figure 1-3). This movement may represent the hands' or arms' lack of integrative ability for this particular task.

Like the cephalocaudal and proximodistal processes, differentiation and integration reverse when movement regression occurs later in life. In other words, the improved motor ability acquired as a result of differentiation and integration gradually returns to a lower level of functioning. The coordination achieved between body parts and the parts' ability to perform highly specific duties during movement activity return to a lower level of functioning. Individuals can allay such regression, however, by maintaining certain habits and attitudes throughout life. Adulthood and movement regression is discussed in Chapter 16.

GROSS MOVEMENT AND FINE MOVEMENT

The terms *gross movement* and *fine movement* are generally used to categorize types of movements; however, they can also generally describe motor development. **Gross movements** are primarily controlled by the large muscles or muscle groups. One relatively large muscle group, for example, is in the upper leg. These muscles are integral in producing an array of movements, such as walking, running, and skipping. Such movements, primarily a function of large muscle groups, are considered gross movements.

Fine movements are primarily governed by the small muscles or muscle groups. Many movements performed with the hands are considered fine movements because the smaller muscles of the fingers, hand, and forearm are critical to the production of finger and hand movement. Therefore, such movements as drawing, sewing, typing, or playing a musical instrument are fine movements.

Although movements are frequently categorized as gross or fine, very few are completely governed by either the small or the large muscle groups. For example, handwriting is normally considered a fine movement, but as in most fine movements, there is a gross motor component: The large muscles of the shoulder are necessary for positioning the arm be-

fore the more subtle movement the smaller muscles create can be effective.

A combination of the large and small muscle groups is often responsible for the production of gross movements as well. Throwing, for example, is considered a gross movement, a logical categorization because upon casual observation the most significant muscle involvement appears to emanate from the shoulder and the legs. A throw, however, is normally initiated with a certain degree of accuracy intended. The large muscles of the shoulder and the legs contribute greatly to the desired accuracy, but minute, subtle adjustments of the wrist and fingers are imperative for optimal precision. Therefore, although throwing is considered a gross movement, an important fine motor component is critical to perfection in throwing. In fact, the degree of fine motor control is a reasonably good indication of movement perfection. An individual may be capable of performing the necessary gross motor aspects of a movement, but the skill may not be honed until the person acquires the fine motor components.

The terms *gross motor* and *fine motor* therefore can be used to categorize movement or to describe general progression or regression in motor development. As a person matures in a particular movement, the fine components of the skill become increasingly significant; the person becomes increasingly adept at both fine and gross motor aspects of the movement. During movement regression, which often occurs from lack of activity in later life, the reverse occurs: The performer initially loses the ability to incorporate the fine motor aspect of the movement. After extreme regression, even the gross motor components of a movement begin to diminish.

THE PROCESS-PRODUCT CONTROVERSY

As described in the previous section, movements can be observed and usefully categorized by simple and general means. Often, however, movement specialists require more specific measurement. As we saw in our earlier discussion of the history of motor development, depending on the objective of their investigation and their philosophical stance, researchers generally use a ***product*** or a ***process approach.*** In the product, or task-oriented, approach (Pew, 1970, 1974) to measuring movement, the end result, the outcome, of the movement is the focus. For example, for a child's catching performance, the product-oriented approach analyzes the child's control of the ball.

The process-oriented approach emphasizes the movement itself, with little attention to the movement's outcome. In our example of catching, the researcher using the process-oriented approach focuses on the technique the child uses to attempt to receive the ball accurately rather than the amount of ball control. In some cases, the movement product and process are the same. Although the process or product can be easily distinguished in a movement like catching, the process involved in many gymnastics-related movements is also the product. In a movement like a forward roll (as in catching), the process is the technique used to perform the movement. However, in the forward roll, the technique can also be the desired product because in competitive situations such movements are judged on level of perfection.

The process orientation has grown more popular in recent years because researchers believe that compared with outcome, it unveils more information about the underlying processes critical to understanding human movement. However, the product orientation, criticized for its lack of concern for the underlying movement processes, can be valuable in movement research designed to have educational implications. For example, there has been considerable research to determine the factors that most significantly affect the outcome of certain movement skills. Children's success in movement outcome is widely accepted as an important factor in keeping children interested and motivated in the activity. Product-oriented research can determine that certain variables negatively or positively affect movement outcome, thus potentially hampering the child's likelihood of further pursuing the movement activity. Although the process approach was derived from a dissatisfaction with the product ap-

proach, both means of analyzing movement have potential value in motor development. But to profit fully from the research, the investigator must first closely examine the intent of the study and on that basis determine which approach is the most satisfactory for the specific situation.

TERMS FOR AGE PERIODS THROUGHOUT THE LIFESPAN

As depicted in Figure 1-4, specific terms are applied to the various age periods throughout the lifespan. These terms vary slightly from source to source in the ages specified but otherwise are generally accepted for use in the study of human development. These terms are *not* used to suggest that everyone in a particular age range will possess the same movement characteristics. The terms are helpful in organizing our discussion and communicating statements about persons at a particular time of life. Because these terms are frequently used throughout this book, we now briefly discuss them in the order of their occurrence.

The first age period is the prenatal period, which spans the time from conception to birth. This period was once considered insignificant for human development but is now believed to be one of the most influential periods in the entire lifespan, particularly during the first 8 weeks of the prenatal period, which is known as the embryonic period. During the embryonic period, the developing human is known as an embryo. At the conclusion of the first 8 weeks of gestation, the fetal period begins. The onset of the fetal period is often described as the point at which the individual has become recognizable as a human being. *Organogenesis,* the formation of the vital organs, has occurred, although considerable growth and maturation have yet to take place. The individual is referred to as a fetus until the fetal period culminates at birth.

The first 22 days following birth make up the neonatal period. These 22 days are included in the period known as infancy. Therefore, a baby younger than 22 days can be called an infant or, more specifically, a neonate. Infancy lasts from birth throughout

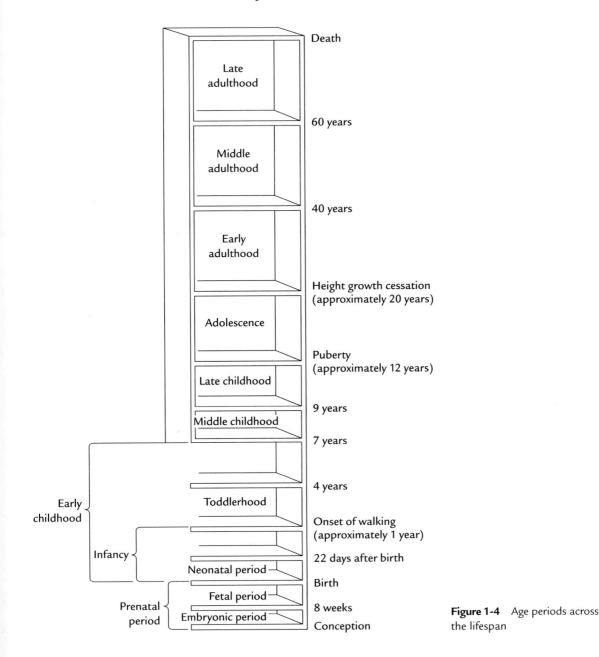

Death

Late
adulthood

60 years

Middle
adulthood

40 years

Early
adulthood

Height growth cessation
(approximately 20 years)

Adolescence

Puberty
(approximately 12 years)

Late childhood

9 years

Middle childhood

7 years

4 years

Toddlerhood

Onset of walking
(approximately 1 year)

22 days after birth

Neonatal period

Birth

Fetal period

8 weeks

Embryonic period

Conception

Early
childhood

Infancy

Prenatal
period

Figure 1-4 Age periods across
the lifespan

the first year of life, to the onset of independent walking.

Once children have begun to walk alone, they are considered toddlers. The approximate mean age for this landmark occurrence is 1 year; toddlerhood culminates at 4 years. This upper range for toddler-

hood has been determined rather arbitrarily, because no abrupt nor immediate behavioral change is associated with the transformation from toddlerhood to early childhood.

Arbitrary limits have also been established to distinguish early childhood, which follows toddlerhood, from middle childhood. Early childhood begins at approximately age 4 and ends when the child is 7 years old. Middle childhood ceases at 9 years and precedes the last preadolescent period, late childhood. Late childhood spans approximately 3 years and, as with all the periods discussed here, does not necessarily indicate an abrupt transformation to a new mode of behavior. An individual in the late childhood period is normally quite different in many respects from a person in middle childhood. However, the transformation is gradual, with the newly emerging behaviors often imperceptible. In fact, the transition from the first to the second year of late childhood may involve behavioral change as profound as that in the transition from the last year of middle childhood to the first year of late childhood.

Again, the establishment of these periods is often arbitrary. Nevertheless, dividing the lifespan into age periods helps organize the study of it and promotes efficiency in examining the enormous span of time. Studying the lifespan as a whole would be exceptionally cumbersome!

The next age period, adolescence, is marked by a significant landmark of life. According to most developmentalists, the process known as puberty begins adolescence. *Puberty* is a time of radical hormonal releases that are directly and indirectly associated with many of the behavioral changes accompanying adolescence. This phenomenon is more thoroughly discussed in later chapters dealing with human physical changes and their effects on motor development. This important developmental landmark commonly occurs in girls around age 11 and in boys around age 13. For this reason we should declare separate times of onset for adolescence based on gender. Although the onset of adolescence is signaled by puberty, the offset is often more arbitrarily determined. To determine the offset, some experts rely on such sociocultural factors as graduating from school or reaching voting age. Others simply assume that completion of the teen years indicates attainment of adulthood. The most common indicator, however, would be the achievement of maximal height. Adulthood is typically achieved by young women at around age 19; young

men usually require 2 additional years (Malina & Bouchard, 1991).

Adulthood typically spans a much greater time than do any of the preceding periods of life. In fact, adulthood commonly encompasses more than 60 years. To organize our discussion, we divide this lengthy block of time into early, middle, and late adulthood. Early adulthood begins at age 20 and continues until age 40. Middle adulthood encompasses the subsequent 20 years, ending at age 60. Finally, late adulthood begins at 60 and ends at death. Because the behavioral changes in the adult are particularly gradual and subtle relative to the changes in the child or adolescent, all the adult age periods have been established arbitrarily for organizing the discussion of adult motor development.

STAGES OF DEVELOPMENT

The age periods we discussed in the previous section could all be termed **stages,** or age stages. *Stage* is one of the most frequently encountered words in the study of human development, often used interchangeably with *phase, time,* or even *level.* Use of the term *stage* implies that there is a particular time in the life of a human being that is characterized by unique behaviors. Such behaviors are not evident prior to the onset of the stage and may not be evident in the same form when the stage ends. The premise of the "terrible twos" stage, for example, is that it is common for children at or about 2 years to exhibit disruptive behavior. Furthermore, this behavior was not present before age 2 and will cease or become modified before the child passes into the next stage of behavior.

Do stages such as the terrible twos really exist? There is a major controversy among developmentalists as to whether or not such abrupt beginnings and ends of behavioral states really occur. The continuity-versus-discontinuity debate poses the question, Does life proceed smoothly and continuously from birth to death? Or is life discontinuous, with occasional, relatively abrupt behavior changes occurring throughout?

Most of us find it difficult to accept the possibility that stages do not exist. The popularization of such terms as *terrible twos* and *teenager* has led us to believe that periods of unique behavior are a fact of life. Nevertheless, the existence versus nonexistence of stages remains an ongoing controversy among developmentalists. There is no absolute evidence to substantiate either viewpoint conclusively.

This controversy also prevails in the field of motor development. Roberton (1978) suggests that for stages to exist, a hierarchical, qualitative change must occur in the human movement behavior. In other words, one stage of behavior flows into a subsequent, qualitatively different stage. Furthermore, each stage must be unique from all others but must possess traits that link it to the preceding stage. The ordering of these behavior states must be invariant and universal. Therefore, a person would not progress through the stages in reverse or mixed order, and everyone would experience these stages. Researchers have tested these and other criteria to determine if stages are present in motor development. However, to this date, the research remains inconclusive regarding the existence or nonexistence of stages in human motor development.

Even though this controversy remains unresolved, it is extremely useful to organize the study of human development into stages. Capsulizing aspects of human development into stages or manageable portions of information facilitates our attempts to study the human being. Therefore, despite a lack of documentation for the existence of stages, we refer throughout this book to stages, phases, or periods. We do not, however, suggest that these stages or periods are times of unique, hierarchical, or universal behaviors.

THE HISTORY OF THE FIELD OF MOTOR DEVELOPMENT

Many brief histories of motor development have been published over the years (Clark & Whitall, 1989; Keogh, 1977; Roberton, 1988, 1989; Smoll, 1982; Thelen, 1987; Thomas 1997; Thomas & Thomas, 1984). Keogh (1977) and Thomas and Thomas (1984) suggest that the study of motor development was begun around 1920 to 1930 by physicians who were interested in creating scales to note the developmental progress of infants. Roberton (1988, 1989) has indicated a much earlier starting point. She believes motor development may have begun with the work of the "baby biographers" of the late 1800s through the early 1900s. Included in this group were Darwin (1877) and Shinn (1900), who wrote "A Biographical Sketch of an Infant" and *The Biography of a Baby,* respectively. Clark and Whitall (1989) cite an even earlier starting point. They agree that Darwin and Shinn were influential but that Tiedemann's (1787, as cited by Borstelmann, 1983) observations of his son's first 2 1/2 years mark the beginning of what Clark and Whitall have named the precursor period of motor development, the first of their four historical periods of motor development (see Table 1-3).

The precursor period of motor development lasted from 1787 to 1928. That, according to Clark and Whitall, was followed by the maturational period, 1928–1946. The third period, the normative/descriptive period lasted from 1946 to 1970. Finally, the process-oriented period covers the years of 1970 to the present.

In the ***precursor period*** of motor development, descriptive observation was established as a method for studying human development. As mentioned earlier, Tiedemann's observation of his young son marked the beginning of this era. Tiedemann discussed common sequences in movement behavior and examined the transitional period from, for example, the grasp reflex to voluntary grasping. Over a century later, Preyer (1909, as cited by Clark & Whitall, 1989) wrote *The Mind of a Child,* which was a major impetus for the emergence of developmental psychology. However, the most significant influence of the period, according to Clark and Whitall, was such works of Darwin as "A Biographical Sketch of an Infant," which led to a greater understanding of human behavior and its causes. Though these early researchers, like Darwin, were generally less interested in motor development than in the function of the mind, motor development as a field of study later benefited from their research.

Table 1-3	Clark and Whitall's Periods in the History of Motor Development

1787–1928   Precursor Period

Descriptive observation was established as a method for studying human development. The most significant influence was Darwin's "Biographical Sketch of an Infant." Early researchers were most interested in the function of the mind, though their research benefited the motor developmentalists who followed.

1928–1946   Maturational Period

Motor development as a primary interest began to emerge, and the maturational philosophy predominated. This philosophy held that the biological processes were the main influence in shaping human development. Work by Gesell and McGraw yielded valuable product- and process-oriented information concerning human movement. Bayley's scales of motor development, still used today, were a product of this period. These norm-referenced scales charted motor behavior across the first 3 years of life.

1946–1970   Normative/Descriptive Period

In the mid-1940s, interest in motor development became "dormant" (Keogh, 1977). In the early 1960s, however, a revival began. This revival was led by physical educators who were interested in children's movement and developed norm-referenced standardized tests for measuring motor performance. Kephart's publication of *The Slow Learner in the Classroom* (1960) was also an influence. Kephart maintained that certain movement activities enhanced academic performance. Though never well supported by the research, Kephart's theory still influences professional practice today.

1970–present   Process-Oriented Period

The most recent period was characterized by a return to studying the processes underlying motor development rather than simply describing change. Interest grew in information-processing theory, which suggested that the human mind functioned much like a computer. This theory may have contributed to many psychologists' returning to study motor development. A second era of this period began in the 1980s when work by Kugler, Kelso, and Turvey (1982) prompted interest in dynamical systems theory. This theory deviated substantially from information-processing theory and posited that systems undergoing change are complex, coordinated, and somewhat self-organizing. Thus, a movement pattern can arise from component parts interacting among themselves and the environment though the pattern was never "coded" in the central nervous system.

SOURCE: Clark and Whitall (1989).

Around 1930, motor development as a primary interest area began to emerge. Because the study of maturation was the main focus, Clark and Whitall have chosen to name this second historical period the ***maturational period.*** The maturational philosophy argued the significance of the biological processes on the development of the individual to the near exclusion of the effects of the environment. Clark and Whitall believe this period was initiated by the publication of Gesell's *Infancy and Human Growth* (1928). Myrtle McGraw (1935), along with Gesell, was particularly influential in espousing the maturational viewpoint. Her classic work with the twins Johnny and Jimmy and her ideas concerning critical periods are discussed in more detail in Chapter 6. While McGraw and

Gesell clearly sought to determine the processes underlying changes in motor behavior, they have also become known for their descriptions of changes in motor behavior in infants and children. Thus, they not only emphasized the movement process but also uncovered valuable information concerning the movement product.

Another highlight of the maturational period of motor development, according to Clark and Whitall, was the publication of Bayley's scale of motor development (1936). This scale charted normative motor behavior across the first 3 years of life and, in modified form, is still in use today.

Though this was a critical period in the history of motor development, interest in human movement began to wane in the early to mid 1940s. In fact, in his brief history of motor development, Keogh calls the period from 1940 to 1960 "dormant"(1977, p. 77). Clark and Whitall, however, suggest that a revival of motor development was occurring prior to 1960. They state that renewed interest in motor development began toward the end of World War II and was prompted by researchers in physical education. Keogh, though, believes an increased interest in studying children with disabilities prompted a resurgence around 1960. The newly emerging interest in mind-body relationships and Kephart's *The Slow Learner in the Classroom* (1960) are specifically cited by Keogh as agents in increasing interest in motor development. Kephart's theory suggests that academic improvements could be brought about by involvement in specific types of movement activities. This theory, which was never well supported scientifically, had a substantial impact on the course of history because of its emphasis on movement activity. Many professionals still employ teaching techniques based on Kephart's theory. For that reason, it is discussed in greater detail in Chapter 4.

Despite Keogh's claim that the resurgence in motor development did not occur until around 1960, Clark and Whitall's ***normative/descriptive period*** encompasses the years 1946–1970. They specifically attribute the revival to physical education researchers such as Anna Espenschade, Ruth Glassow, and G. Lawrence Rarick, who focused primarily on children's motor skills rather than their cognitive abilities. Though few significant motor development studies emerged in the 1950s, an increased focus was seen on measuring children anthropometrically (bodily measures), testing their strength, measuring performance on such skills as running and jumping, and making gender comparisons on various motor performance measures (Keogh, 1977). As a result, standardized tests for evaluating children's motor performance were created. Overall, the emphasis was on developing standardized norms and describing children anthropometrically. Little emphasis was placed on understanding the processes underlying changes in motor behavior. Thus this era derived its name, the normative/descriptive period.

According to Clark and Whitall (1989), the 1960s brought more biomechanical analysis of movement and the emergence of ***perceptual-motor theory.*** Many researchers began to study the efficacy of perceptual-motor theory, which generally renewed interest in motor development. As mentioned earlier, Keogh (1977) believes that perceptual-motor theory was of greater impact historically and, perhaps, should be attributed with the "rebirth" of motor development.

The period from 1970 to the present was labeled the ***process-oriented period*** as a result of the return to studying the processes underlying motor development rather than simply describing the change (products). Clark and Whitall believe this new focus was brought about by Connolly's *Mechanisms of Motor Skill Development* (1970), which was a summation of a meeting by a small group of psychologists. This publication seemed to mark psychologists' return to the study of motor development. Many of these psychologists pursued understanding the processes of motor development by using ***information-processing theory,*** thinking of the brain as functioning much like a computer.

Clark and Whitall also believe the increased number of published motor learning texts during this period increased interest in information-processing theory and motor development. The new interest in information processing was partially responsible for more researchers attending to the underlying processes of motor development. At the same time, however, some researchers continued to study the products of movement change as a carryover from the previous historical period.

As we discussed earlier in this chapter, several motor developmentalists met in Seattle, Washington, in 1974 to discuss research directions in motor development. Their goal was to determine the actual focus of research in motor development (Seefeldt, 1989). Clark and Whitall believe this meeting reflected the diversity between two prevalent views of the time, process and product orientations. One view expressed was to study children's change in such underlying processes and functions as perception, memory, and attention. Much of this same type of research had already been completed using adult subjects. Others, according to Clark and Whitall, saw a need to continue the product-oriented line of investigation seeking to achieve such ends as ordering and classifying fundamental motor patterns.

The second half of Clark and Whitall's last period of motor development history began in the 1980s. This era was initiated, they say, by a paper published by Kugler, Kelso, and Turvey (1982). This publication presented an innovative theoretical perspective for the study of movement control and coordination and sharply contrasted information-processing theory. This theoretical approach, known as the ***dynamical systems perspective,*** is an important contribution to our study of human motor development as it seeks to examine movement control and coordination as well as seeking explanations to the process of development. This perspective will be explained more thoroughly in the next section.

CURRENT TRENDS IN MOTOR DEVELOPMENT

Over the last two decades, two prominent trends have arisen in the study of human motor development. As we discussed in the last section, Clark and Whitall (1989) believe one of these trends to be the emergence of the dynamical systems perspective. The other, despite its equally profound effect on the study of motor development, was not acknowledged by Clark and Whitall in their history of motor development. This is the trend toward studying human motor development from a lifespan perspective. Both of these trends are explained in the following sections.

Dynamical Systems Perspective

Over the years, many theoretical perspectives have been proposed in an attempt to explain the development of human movement. However, many of today's experts believe that these theories do not adequately address the full range and complexity of human motor development. For example, the neural maturation concept dominated the thinking of motor developmentalists for years. This theory posited that the nervous system is the main control element in human movement. It was believed to be the "switch" that initiates movement. As mentioned earlier in the chapter, in more recent years, the way in which the brain organized the nervous system for movement was compared to a computer in what is often referred to as information-processing theory. Because little attention was paid to other contributing factors in these theoretical approaches, some current experts believe they were too limited to enable a complete understanding of how human movement is generated and how it evolves throughout the lifespan (Scholz, 1990).

Today, we recognize that a variety of systems interact with our nervous system to create human movement. Gravitational forces are an easy example. As we move, their impact on our neurological, muscular, and skeletal systems is constantly altered as the body or body part in question changes position. Similarly, the effect of one body part's movement alters the process of moving another. So, movement is a product of an entire system comprising numerous components or subsystems that are constantly interacting and changing. The nervous system, originally thought to be the sole determinant of movement, is a part of this system and must also dynamically change and interact with all other components if movement is to be coordinated and efficient (Kamm, Thelen, & Jensen, 1990). For example, the initial voluntary attempts at reaching and grasping are under the influence of the relevant joints, muscles, and nerves as well as the arm's weight. Gravity and numerous contextual factors like children's level of motivation, their body position, and the height and weight of the object for which they are reaching also interact. One of the main attractions of dynamical systems perspective of human movement is that it allows for explanations that include the interacting subsystems.

A major impetus in the shift to dynamical systems perspective was the work of Haken (1983). In his work, Haken discussed ***synergetics,*** the study of physical, chemical, and biological systems. Synergetics, according to Haken, is an attempt to establish principles governing pattern generation that would be common to a variety of systems though independent of the structure producing the behavior. In synergetics, relatively simple systems are often studied because they are easier to understand. However, even "simple" systems can be difficult to understand. So, researchers often select *order parameters* within these systems. **Order parameters** are a relatively small number of carefully selected variables that have been chosen with the intention of narrowing the study of the more global system (Kamm et al., 1990).

The work of Kugler, Kelso, and Turvey (1982) further advanced interest in dynamical systems perspective as they began to adapt the idea of synergetics to human movement. Though we discuss dynamical systems perspective for the purposes of more clearly understanding human motor development, many scientists in other disciplines are using the same theoretical approach to learn more about a variety of natural phenomena ranging from weather systems to cardiac physiology (Kamm et al., 1990).

Regardless of the discipline in question, many fundamental features underlie dynamical systems theory. For example, systems are believed to be complex, multifaceted, and cooperative. No one component is thought to have priority or ultimate responsibility for the overall behavior of the system. In addition, the system is believed to be **self-organizing.** This suggests that the components cooperate and interact in an almost infinite number of ways to yield a movement the outward appearance of which remains relatively stable. Additionally, the complex system is believed to be nonlinear in terms of its change over time (Magill, 2001).

So, the dynamical systems perspective posits that a movement pattern can be created as a result of a near infinite combination of interactions of component parts. However, proponents of this theoretical perspective also acknowledge that one set of interactions is more easily achievable than others because it requires less energy. This particular combination of interactions of variables is called an **attractor,** the preferred or stable behavioral state (Magill, 2004). An attractor can be relatively strong or weak depending on how readily the system re-

turns to it. A strong attractor is said to have a deep **attractor well.** An attractor that is less commonly "sought" by the interacting system is said to have a shallow attractor well.

Another basic tenet of the dynamical systems perspective is that motor development is discontinuous or constantly changing. This aspect of the systems perspective makes it particularly attractive to developmentalists because it offers an explanation for human motor development, unlike previous theories. According to the systems perspective, motor development would occur as any one component or subsystem changes. In fact, the development or emergence of one or more new subsystems could cause the previously existing ones to disappear. As a subsystem changes, it may alter the depth of the existing attractor well. For example, as infants increase in weight because of normal growth, their stepping rate may decrease to a point that the stepping ceases. The factor believed to be primarily responsible for the system change, in this case the weight increase, is known as a **control parameter.** The dynamical systems perspective maintains that during a period of change the whole system becomes vulnerable to more change to the point that normally insignificant factors can become control parameters. Though development usually progresses as a series of phase shifts between varying degrees of stability, an exceptionally deep attractor well can cause such phase stability that development is impeded. After several phase shifts, the contributing subsystems may be almost entirely different than they were at an earlier developmental point.

Our ability to employ more complex theoretical perspectives, such as the dynamical systems perspective, has been facilitated by improved research technology. For example, technology in kinematic analysis is far superior today than in years past. Improved **kinematics,** "the science of mechanics . . . that deals solely with describing the nature of motion" (Hay & Reid, 1988, p. 114), allows more detailed quantification and, therefore, a more complete understanding of the details of the organization and development of human movement. We can now accurately track the motion of a limb throughout its range of motion. The entire movement time

Table 1-4   Percentage of U.S. Population by Age Group (Years), 1900–2000

Year	Total Population (thousands)	<5 years	5–14	15–24	25–34	35–44	45–54	55–64	65+
2000	276,059	7	14	14	13	16	14	9	13
1990	248,710	7	14	15	17	15	10	9	13
1980	226,546	7	15	19	16	11	10	10	11
1970	204,879	8	20	19	12	11	11	9	10
1960	180,671	11	20	14	13	13	11	9	9
1950	151,684	11	16	15	16	14	11	9	8
1940	132,122	8	17	18	16	14	12	8	7
1930	123,077	9	20	18	15	14	11	7	5
1920	106,461	11	21	18	16	14	10	6	5
1910	92,407	12	21	20	17	13	9	6	4
1900	76,094	12	22	20	16	12	8	5	4

SOURCE: Calculations are based on United States Department of Commerce (1975, 1983, 1992, 2001).

can be calculated and the relative position of the component parts can be recorded repeatedly within each second of movement. Additional details such as joint angles, movement accuracy, velocity, and acceleration can be determined. When combined with other advancing technologies, such as electromyographical analyses, entirely new and different views of motor development are possible. Such detailed analyses allow researchers to determine which segment of the limb may have initiated the movement and the sequence in which each became involved. Thus, enhanced scientific ability has freed researchers from their dependence on past theories that were strictly neural based and has allowed greater exploration of multiple interacting factors in theories like dynamical systems (Kamm et al., 1990).

Motor Development as a Lifespan Perspective

Over the last decade, several new motor development textbooks have emerged (Gabbard, 2004; Gallahue & Ozmun, 2002; Payne & Isaacs, 2005). Unlike many of their predecessors, the authors of these books adopt a *lifespan perspective* for the study of motor development. The orientation of these texts and the increasing amount of research concerning movement in adulthood indicate that a "lifespan concept of motor development is emerging" (VanSant, 1990, p. 788). This is a relatively drastic deviation from earlier approaches that seemed to assume that when height growth ceases, behavior also stops changing or that human development peaked at adolescence or early adulthood (Lefrancois, 1999). The authors of the most recent motor development texts have most likely been influenced by the dramatic shift occurring in our population. This shift is illustrated in Table 1-4, where the percentage of the total U.S. population by age group is presented by decade back to 1900. This table was created by determining the total U.S. population by decade and the total for each age group. The percentage of the total population for each age group was then computed. This table clearly illustrates the rapid increase in the relative number of people over age 65 in our population. As indicated, that group has increased approximately 1 percentage point each decade since 1940 except during the 1980s. During those 10 years, a 2 percentage point increase occurred. According to *Healthy People 2000* (U.S. Department of Health

Table 1-5   Our Population Since 1900

In the United States, we have

- 3 times more people over age 65
- 8 times more people age 65–74
- 16 times more people age 75–84
- 31 times more people over age 85

SOURCE: American Association of Retired Persons (AARP) (1998).

and Human Services, 1992), people reaching the age of 65 can expect to live well into their 80s.

As recently as 1997, the older population (people over age 65) numbered 34.1 million or just under 13 percent of the total population. During the twentieth century, the percentage of U.S. citizens over 65 years of age more than tripled while the actual number of people aged 65–74 increased 8 times and the number aged 75–84 increased 16 times. The number of people over age 85 increased by 31 times (American Association of Retired Persons, 1998)! (See Table 1-5.) In 1997 alone, approximately 2 million people in the United States reached their 65th birthday, while 1.7 million people over age 65 died. In other words, during that year we experienced a net increase of 325,000 people over 65. Included in the over-65 population were approximately 20 million women and 13.9 million men (145 women per 100 men), a gender ratio that increases with age.

These trends have continued with some slowing because of fewer babies born during the years of the Great Depression. A rapid increase is expected between 2010 and 2029 when the "baby boomers" begin to celebrate their 65th birthdays.

The dramatic increase in the number of older citizens is no doubt a testament to scientific and medical efforts designed to maintain health and prolong life. Nevertheless, with increasing numbers of older U.S. citizens, we will need to increase special services, such as nutritional services, housing arrangements, medical care, and recreational and educational opportunities (Siegel, 1996). Therefore, our need to study and understand this sector of our population also continues to increase.

Academically, adopting the lifespan approach offers the opportunity to examine a broader range of change processes, as the individual is studied through both the progressive and regressive phases of development. This obviously enables the examination of many intrinsic and extrinsic factors (like a variety of cultural phenomena) that have not regularly been considered in our traditional approach to studying motor development (VanSant, 1990).

AN INTERDISCIPLINARY APPROACH TO MOTOR DEVELOPMENT

Considerable interaction occurs among the three subareas of motor behavior. Although we presented specific examples of topics of study within each motor area, these topics often overlap. For example, the motor learning expert may seek information about the acquisition of movement skill and the differences in that acquisition as a child ages. Therefore, this effort is not simply research into motor learning but also research into motor development because a change occurring as a result of aging is also of significant concern in the investigation. Obviously, there can be similar overlap between motor development and motor control: The underlying neurophysiological factors would be examined as they change with aging. Such research could involve comparisons of children of various ages or even of children with adolescents and adults.

Motor development also interacts with many of the other subdisciplines in the study of human movement. Motor developmentalists once were satisfied to use simple visual observation to assess movement change that occurs with aging, but advanced technology has made other techniques more valuable. Today, motor developmentalists often can evaluate movement more accurately by working with specialists from other fields; subtle movement differences can then be detected and analyzed using current technology from those fields. In biomechanics, for example, movement differences between various age groups can be assessed and analyzed by computer using biomechanical techniques that far surpass human capabilities to discern change visually. For instance, accurate developmental differences in body-fat levels, lung capacity, or level of electrical stimulation in specific muscles can be determined through collaboration with exercise physiologists. As technology advances, motor development continues to depend ever more on cooperative efforts with other related fields, making interdisciplinary efforts to enhance our knowledge increasingly common.

DESIGNING RESEARCH IN MOTOR DEVELOPMENT: CROSS-SECTIONAL, LONGITUDINAL, OR . . . ?

Generally, two research designs have been employed for studying motor development. In a **cross-sectional design,** subjects from the various treatment or age groups are examined on the same measure once and at the same time (Baltes, 1968). For example, to examine the development of handwriting technique between childhood and adulthood, three groups of subjects might be employed. One group would include children, aged 7–9, a second group would be adolescents, aged 13–15, and a third would include adults, aged 25–27. All subjects would be examined and measured on the specified handwriting task, with the differences between groups being noted. In a **longitudinal design,** one group of subjects is observed repeatedly at different ages and different times of measurement (Baltes, 1968). So, in our hypothetical handwriting study, we would now start with our child subjects and periodically examine their handwriting technique until they reach adulthood.

Commonly, researchers select a cross-sectional design because of its administrative efficiency. It offers the advantage of time efficiency because it can be completed in a short period. Despite these advantages, the cross-sectional design requires the researcher to assume change has occurred because

of age difference. The cross-sectional design allows age differences, but not behavioral changes, to be observed. In addition, if the correct age groupings are not chosen initially for the cross-sectional design, an important part of a developmental sequence might be missed entirely (Roberton, Williams, & Langendorfer, 1980).

Though the longitudinal design requires considerably more time, the change in the subjects' motor behavior can be observed and not just assumed to have occurred. However, some problems may arise. One of the most critical is subject mortality, as subjects drop out more often than in the cross-sectional situation. This is a particular problem if subjects drop out in a nonrandom fashion. Subjects who perform poorly on the behavior being examined are often more likely to drop out. Therefore, the overall findings may be positively biased. Another potential problem with the longitudinal design is that the same subjects are retested periodically, which "practice" may result in an inflated score on successive attempts (Baltes, 1968).

In addition to these potential problems, both designs have three components that are difficult to separate for the purposes of accurate interpretation of research findings (Thomas 1989). The first component is simply the subjects' chronological ages. The second is known as the *cohort,* the set of experiences a group of subjects brings into the study because of the generation in which they were reared. The third component is time of measurement. This refers to the unique situation that existed at the time measurements were made. In the cross-sectional design, problems exist with confusing age and cohort (Lefrancois, 1999). For example, in our hypothetical cross-sectional handwriting study, the children differed from the adolescents and adults by age and by cohort. Any resultant differences in handwriting technique would likely be attributed to age but might have been due to the experiences the subjects had as a result of when they were reared. Similarly, a longitudinal design confuses age and time of measurement. Obviously, all of the subjects are similar in terms of age and cohort, but years may have passed since the last examination of their handwriting. The unique situation surrounding the

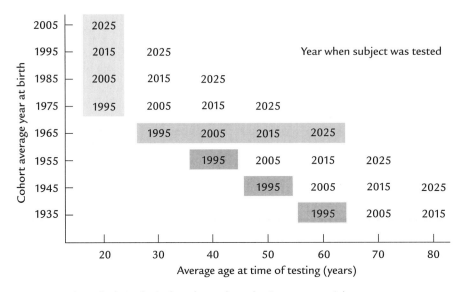

Figure 1-5   A representation of a hypothetical study conducted using a sequential research design

previous handwriting analysis may have been sufficient to cause differences in handwriting. Unfortunately, these differences will often be attributed
to age.

To help avoid some of the potential confounding of results in research, two different experimental designs are often employed, the **time-lag** and
the **sequential** or **cohort designs.** In a time-lag
design, different cohorts are compared at different
times. For example, subjects who are 10 years old
in 1995 can be compared with subjects who will be
10 in 1997, 1999, and 2001. In such a design, age
remains the same while the cohort varies (Lefrancois, 1999). Thus, the potential confounding of age
and cohort is reduced.

Researchers can also employ a sequential or
cohort design. This design integrates the cross-
sectional, longitudinal, and time-lag designs within
one study. In the cross-sectional portion of the
study, different cohorts are tested each year. In the
longitudinal portion, the same cohort is followed
for an extended period. Meanwhile, in the time-lag
portion, different cohorts are compared with each
other at different times when subjects are the same
age (see Figure 1-5).

Though the time-lag and the sequential designs
offer resolutions to some problems inherent in cross-
sectional and longitudinal testing, they also present
unique problems. Most notably, these designs often
require considerable time, effort, and money. In addition, they are very difficult to analyze accurately
using current statistical techniques (see Table 1-6).

Figure 1-5 is a representation of a hypothetical
study in which the effects of age on functional flexibility (neck rotation and lateral trunk and neck
flexion) are examined. The effects from age 20 to
age 80 are studied using a sequential design to reduce cohort effects. The sequential design includes
components of time-lag, longitudinal, and cross-
sectional research designs. A section of the study
that examines time-lag differences (different cohorts at different times but at the same age) is indicated with a light screen. A section that examines
longitudinal (same cohort at different times) differences is indicated with a medium screen. A section
that examines the cross-sectional (different cohorts
at the same time) differences is indicated with a
dark screen.

Clearly, research design selection in motor development research is a problem. Considerable care

Table 1-6   Pros and Cons of Various Research Designs Used in Developmental Research

	Pros	Cons
Cross-sectional	• Administratively efficient • Quickly completed • Age differences can be observed	• Cannot observe change (it must be assumed) • Premium placed on accurate determination of age groups • Age and cohort are confounded
Longitudinal	• Change can be observed across ages	• Administratively inefficient • Age and time of measurements are confounded • Subjects may be influenced by repeated testing • Subjects may drop out
Sequential (Cohort)	• Accounts for generational (cohort) effects	• Administratively inefficient • Financially costly • Subjects may drop out • Difficult to analyze statistically

must be taken in the design of our research because scientific progress in developmental research "is contingent largely upon the quality of its methodology" (Baltes, 1968, p. 167). As Thomas (1989) concludes in his article on motor development research, the currently available research designs cannot completely separate chronological age, cohort, and time of measurement, making valid research in motor development particularly difficult. Rarick (1989) notes, however, that cross-sectional research may be useful, within limits, as it can provide norms and predict behaviors. But a longitudinal design is more useful if the researcher is specifically interested in development and the factors affecting it. Table 1-6 shows several pros and cons of various research designs.

SUMMARY

Motor development, the focus of this book, is the study of changes in motor behavior over the lifespan, the processes underlying these changes, and the factors affecting them.

Motor development is an important area of study because it helps us understand all aspects of human development. Practical applications from this field of study include detection of motor abnormalities, which facilitates early intervention and remediation of problems, and through our knowledge of motor development, the creation of more valid, efficient, and scientifically based programs for teaching movement skills to people of all ages.

Human development is often categorized into motor, cognitive, affective, and physical domains. The motor domain refers to human movement. The cognitive domain refers to human intellectual change; the affective domain refers to social-emotional change. The physical domain refers to actual bodily changes such as height or weight. All of these domains are in constant interaction. Motor development strongly influences, and is strongly influenced by, cognitive and affective development.

Human development is the progressions and regressions that occur within human beings as they age.

Developmental change is characterized by six elements. It is qualitative, sequential, cumulative, directional, multifactorial, and individual. Understanding these elements is essential to attaining a developmental perspective: looking at current behaviors with an interest in what preceded them and what will follow and understanding that development is "age-related but not completely age-determined" (Motor Development Task Force, 1995, p. 5).

Maturation is a specific aspect of development involving the qualitative, functional changes that occur with aging. Growth, another aspect of development, concerns increases in physical size—that is, quantitative, structural increases occurring with aging.

Cephalocaudal, proximodistal, differentiation, and *integration* describe general motor development trends. All people follow the general progression these terms describe but vary considerably in their rate of change.

The terms *gross motor* and *fine motor* refer to movements created by the large and small muscle groups, respectively. These terms are useful because they help us generally categorize movements and describe movement progressions and regressions throughout the lifespan.

Process- and product-oriented approaches are used to evaluate or measure movement performances. The process approach emphasizes the technique of the movement; the product approach examines the outcome or end product of the movement.

An age-period approach is useful for facilitating our study of motor development throughout the lifespan. We use common terms to refer to various age periods, such as infancy, toddlerhood, or early adulthood. This approach is particularly useful, but we do not suggest that these age periods are characterized by specific behavioral traits of the individuals included within the periods.

The history of the study of motor development, according to Clark and Whitall (1989), can be divided into four periods: the precursor period, 1787–1928; the maturational period, 1928–1946; the normative/descriptive period, 1946–1970; and the process-oriented period, 1970 to the present.

Two important trends prevalent in recent years are the increased interest in the dynamical systems perspective and the lifespan approach to studying motor development. Dynamical systems posits that a variety of systems, not just the nervous system, constantly interact and adjust to each other to create human movement. Improved kinematics, our ability to describe the nature of motion, have facilitated the advancement of this approach. Increased interest in the entire lifespan has resulted from a rapidly aging society and the opportunity it offers for studying progression and regression as well as exploring many new and different explanations for how we develop.

Motor development research is generally conducted using a cross-sectional or a longitudinal design. The cross-sectional design selects subjects from various age groups for observation on a given motor behavior. They are all measured or observed at approximately the same time. The longitudinal design selects only one age group of subjects and observes them for an extended period. While the cross-sectional design can detect differences between age groups, the longitudinal design can actually detect change. Both designs offer advantages but also have disadvantages that make research in motor development particularly difficult. Because of these disadvantages, the time-lag or sequential (cohort) designs were created. The time-lag design examines different cohorts at different times. The sequential design incorporates the time-lag, cross-sectional, and longitudinal designs in one study. Thus, some of the disadvantages of the other design types are avoided, though this design is difficult to analyze statistically, less efficient administratively, and potentially costly.

KEY TERMS

attractor
attractor well
cephalocaudal
cohort design
control parameter
cross-sectional design
development
developmental perspective
developmentally appropriate

differentiation
dynamical systems perspective
fine movement
gross movement
growth
human motor development
information-processing theory
integration
kinematics

lifespan perspective
longitudinal design
maturation
maturational period
normative/descriptive period
order parameters
perceptual-motor theory
precursor period
process approach

process-oriented period
product approach
proximodistal

self-organizing
sequential design
stage

synergetics
time-lag design

QUESTIONS FOR REFLECTION

1. Why is our knowledge of motor development important? Give at least three specific examples of how this information can be practically employed.

2. What do we mean by *developmentally appropriate?* What are the two dimensions of the term as discussed in this chapter? Can you define each?

3. List and describe the six components of developmental change.

4. Explain the terms *differentiation* and *integration*. Provide an example of each.

5. Some controversy exists as to whether stages really exist in motor development. Take a stand. What do you think? Provide some rationale for your position.

6. According to Clark and Whitall, what are the four historical periods of motor development and what characterized each?

7. Generally explain what we mean by *dynamical systems perspective*. What is its purpose? What do we mean by *order parameter?*

8. List and explain four key points from the dynamical systems perspective.

9. What is a lifespan approach to studying motor development? Why would we consider taking such an approach? Does it have any practical value?

10. What are the differences between longitudinal, cross-sectional, and cohort research designs? Give an example of each and explain some advantages and disadvantages of each.

INTERNET RESOURCES

American Academy of Pediatrics   **www.aap.org**

American Alliance for Health, Physical Education, Recreation, and Dance   **www.aahperd.org**

American College of Sports Medicine   **www.acsm.org**

American College of Sports Medicine Current Comments   **www.acsm.org/health%2Bfitness/comments.htm**

Centers for Disease Control   **www.cdc.gov**

Centers for Disease Control Morbidity and Mortality Weekly Report   **www.cdc.gov/mmwr/mmwr_wk.html**

Motor Development Academy of NASPE (National Association for Sports and Physical Education)   **www.aahperd.org/naspe/ specialinterest-motordev.html**

North American Society for the Psychology of Sports and Physical Activity   **www.naspspa.org**

ONLINE LEARNING CENTER (www.mhhe.com/payne6e)

Visit the *Human Motor Development* Online Learning Center for study aids and additional resources. You can use the study guide questions and key terms puzzles to review key terms and concepts for this chapter and to prepare for exams. You can further extend your knowledge of motor development by checking out the Web links, articles, and activities found on the site.

REFERENCES

American Association of Retired Persons. (1998). *A profile of older Americans*. Washington, DC: AARP.

Baltes, P. B. (1968). Longitudinal and cross sectional sequences in the study of age and generation effects. *Human Development, 11,* 145–171.

Bayley, N. (1936). *The California infant scale of motor development*. Berkeley: University of California Press.

Bloom, B. S. (1956). *Taxonomy of educational objectives: Handbook I. Cognitive domain*. New York: McKay.

Borstelmann, L. J. (1983). Children before psychology. In W. Kessen (Ed.), *Handbook of child psychology: Volume 1. History, theory, and methods*. 4th ed. New York: Wiley.

Bredekamp, S., & Copple, C. (1997). *Developmentally appropriate practice in early childhood programs*. Revised edition. Washington, DC: National Association for the Education of Young Children.

Clark, J. E., & Whitall, J. (1989). What is motor development: The lessons of history. *Quest, 41,* 183–202.

Connolly, K. J. (1970). *Mechanisms of motor skill development*. London: Academic Press.

Darwin, C. (1877). A biographical sketch of an infant. *Mind, 2,* 285–294.

Espenschade, A., & Eckert, H. (1967). *Motor development*. Columbus, OH: Merrill.

Gabbard, C. P. (2004). *Lifelong motor development*. 4th ed. Dubuque, IA: Addison-Wesley.

Gallahue, D. L., & Ozmun, J. C. (2002). *Understanding motor development: Infants, children, adolescents, adults*. 5th ed. Boston: McGraw-Hill.

Gesell, A. (1928). *Infancy and human growth*. New York: Macmillan.

Haken, H. (1983). *Synergetics, an introduction: Nonequilibrium phase transitions and self-organization in physics, chemistry, and biology*. New York: Springer-Verlag.

Hay, J., & Reid, J. (1988). *Anatomy, mechanics, and human motion*. 2nd ed. Englewood Cliffs, NJ: Prentice-Hall.

Haywood, K. M., & Getchell, N. (2001). *Lifespan motor development*. 3rd ed. Champaign, IL: Human Kinetics.

Jobling, A. (1999). Attainment of motor proficiency in school-aged children with Down syndrome. *Adapted Physical Activity Quarterly, 16*(4), 344–361.

Kamm, K., Thelen, E., & Jensen, J. L. (1990). A dynamical systems approach to motor development. *Physical Therapy, 70*(12), 763–775.

Keogh, J. F. (1977). The study of movement skill development. *Quest, 28,* 76–88.

Kephart, N. C. (1960). *The slow learner in the classroom*. Columbus, OH: Merrill.

Kugler, P. N., Kelso, J. A. S., & Turvey, M. T. (1982). On the control and coordination of naturally developing systems. In J. A. S. Kelso & J. E. Clark (Eds.), *The development of movement control and coordination*. New York: Wiley.

Lefebvre, C., & Reid, G. (1999). Prediction in ball catching by children with and without a developmental coordination disorder. *Adapted Physical Activity Quarterly, 15*(4), 299–315.

Lefrancois, G. (1999). *The lifespan*. 6th ed. Belmont, CA: Wadsworth.

Magill, R. A. (2004). *Motor learning: Concepts and applications*. 7th ed. Boston: WCB/McGraw-Hill.

Malina, R. M., Bouchard, C., & Bar-Or, O. (2004). *Growth, maturation, and physical activity*. 2nd ed. Champaign, IL: Human Kinetics.

McGraw, M. (1935). *Growth: A study of Johnny and Jimmy*. New York: Appleton-Century-Crofts.

Motor Development Task Force. (1995). *Looking at physical education from a developmental perspective: A guide to teaching*. Reston, VA: National Association for Sports and Physical Education.

Notes from Scholarly Directions Committee of NCPEAM and NAPECW. (1974, Nov.). Seattle, WA.

Payne, V. G., & Isaacs, L. D. (2005). *Human motor development*. 6th ed. Boston: McGraw-Hill.

Pew, R. W. (1970). Toward a process-oriented theory of human skilled performance. *Journal of Motor Behavior, 2,* 8–24.

———. (1974). Human perceptual motor performance. In B. H. Kantowitz (Ed.), *Human information processing: Tutorials in performance and cognition*. New York: Erlbaum.

Rarick, G. L. (1989). Motor development: A commentary. In J. S. Skinner, C. B. Corbin, D. M. Landers, P. E. Martin, & C. L. Wells (Eds.), *Future directions in exercise and sport science research*, 383–391. Champaign, IL: Human Kinetics.

Roberton, M. A. (1978). Stages of motor development. In M. V. Ridenour (Ed.), *Motor development: Issues and applications*. Princeton, NJ: Princeton Book Company.

———. (1988). The weaver's loom: A developmental metaphor. In J. E. Clark & J. H. Humphrey (Eds.), *Advances in motor development research 2*. New York: AMS Press.

———. (1989). Motor development: Recognizing our roots, charting our future. *Quest, 41,* 213–223.

Roberton, M., Williams, K., & Langendorfer, S. (1980). Prelongitudinal screening of motor development sequences. *Research Quarterly for Exercise and Sport, 51*(4), 724–731.

Scholz, J. P. (1990). Dynamic pattern theory—Some implications. *Physical Therapy, 70*(12), 827–843.

Seefeldt, V. (1989). This is motor development. *Motor Development Academy Newsletter, 10,* 2–5.

Shapiro, D., & Dummer, G. M. (1999). Perceived and actual basketball competence of adolescent males with mild mental retardation. *Adapted Physical Activity Quarterly, 15*(2), 179–190.

Shinn, M. (1900). *The biography of a baby*. Boston: Houghton Mifflin.

Siegel, J. (1996). *Aging into the twenty-first century*. Washington, DC: Administration on Aging.

Smoll, F. L. (1982). Developmental kinesiology: Toward a sub-discipline focusing on motor development. In J. S. Kelso & J. E. Clark (Eds.), *The development of movement control and coordination.* New York: Wiley.

Thelen, E. (1987). The role of motor development in developmental psychology: A view of the past and an agenda for the future. In N. Eisenberg (Ed.), *Contemporary topics in developmental psychology.* New York: Wiley.

Thomas, J. R. (1989). Naturalistic research can drive motor development theory. In J. S. Skinner, C. B. Corbin, D. M. Landers, P. E. Martin, & C. L. Wells (Eds.), *Future directions in exercise and sport science research,* 349–367. Champaign, IL: Human Kinetics.

———. (1997). Motor behavior. In J. D. Massengale & R. A. Swanson (Eds.), *The history of exercise and sport science,* 205–292. Champaign, IL: Human Kinetics.

Thomas, J. R., & Thomas, K. (1984). Planning kiddie research: Little kids but big problems. In J. R. Thomas (Ed.), *Motor development during childhood and adolescence.* Minneapolis, MN: Burgess.

United States Department of Commerce: Bureau of the Census. (1975). *Historical statistics of the United States: Colonial times to 1970.* Washington, DC: U.S. Government Printing Office.

———. (1983). *1980 census of the population: General population characteristics.* Washington, DC: U.S. Government Printing Office.

———. (1992). *1990 census of the population: General population characteristics.* Washington, DC: U.S. Government Printing Office.

———. (2001). *National estimates by age group and sex: Selected years from 1990–2000.* Online: http://eire.census.gov/popest/archives/national/nation2/intfile2-1txt.

United States Department of Health and Human Services: Public Health Service. (1992). *Healthy people 2000: National health promotion and disease prevention objectives.* Boston: Jones and Bartlett.

VanSant, A. F. (1990). Life-span development in functional tasks. *Physical Therapy, 70*(12), 788–798.az

2

Cognitive and Motor Development

Digital Vision/Getty Images

As mentioned in Chapter 1, the four domains of human development are the affective, cognitive, motor, and physical. This system of categorizing human behavior into domains evolved because it is useful for organizing and simplifying the study of human development. Although these domains of development are usually studied as individual units, we must remember that they are in constant interaction with each other (refer back to Figure 1-1). Everything we do in the motor domain is affected by our emotions, social interactions, and cognitive development. Furthermore, all behavior in the affective and cognitive domains is strongly influenced by motor behavior (see Figure 2-1). Can our emotional state affect weight gain? Does our physical state (percent body fat, muscle mass) impact self-esteem? Of course! In short, all domains affect all others.

This chapter examines several important specific interrelationships between the cognitive and the motor domains. How does our gradually changing motor ability affect our cognitive development? How does our evolving cognitive development affect our motor development? What are some significant areas of integration?

PSYCHOMOTOR OR MOTOR?

For this book we deliberately chose to use *motor* as a general term to refer to any form of human movement behavior, rather than using the more common **psychomotor.** *Psychomotor* is particularly useful for referring to the domain of human development that involves human movement. Although generally used synonymously with the term *motor, psychomotor* actually refers to those movements initiated by an electrical impulse from the higher brain centers, for example, the motor cortex. Most human movement is the result of such stimulation. However, because there is a form of movement behavior—reflexive movement—that is initiated in the lower brain centers or the central nervous system, we use the more general term *motor* so as not to exclude the reflexes from the movement-related domain, the motor domain.

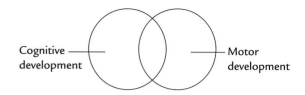

Figure 2-1 Cognitive and motor development interact continually throughout the lifespan as they reciprocally inhibit or facilitate each other.

Nevertheless, the term *psychomotor* deserves special attention in this chapter. This word was created in recognition of the interaction between the mind (psycho) and human movement (motor). The mind is a critical component of the production of almost all human movement. This interactive relationship is thoroughly examined in the remainder of this chapter. We also study the equally important effects of human movement on mental or cognitive development.

JEAN PIAGET AND COGNITIVE DEVELOPMENT

Unquestionably, developmentalists have paid more attention to cognitive development than to any other domain of human behavior. And no one wrote more about cognitive development than the most famous developmentalist, Jean Piaget. Piaget is generally accepted as one of the most innovative, accurate, informative, and prolific developmentalists (Sigelman, 2003). He wrote over 40 internationally acclaimed books and was labeled a genius by such people as Albert Einstein.

Piaget's interest in human intellectual development emerged after years of study in related fields of interest. When he was 10 years old, he published his first biology-oriented article and gradually increased his interest in biology throughout his childhood, adolescence, and early adulthood.

Eventually, Piaget became interested in examining how we "know"—that is, the process of thinking. According to Piaget, this process is a critical function in life that enables us to adapt to our environment. Of particular interest to Piaget were children's incorrect responses to questions or problem-solving situations. By observing these responses, Piaget found that children demonstrated varying impressions of the world relative to each other and to adults. This system of inquiry evolved into what is now known as Piaget's **clinical method,** a system of collecting data by question-and-answer sessions to understand more fully the process of thinking (Newman, 2003). Piaget questioned children and carefully noted their mode of approaching problems and issues. By including children from several age groups in his interviews, Piaget was able to categorize similar behaviors into the four stages of development that constitute his famous theory of cognitive development.

Piaget's Theory of Cognitive Development

Between 1925 and 1931, Piaget's wife gave birth to three children. The births were a particularly important impetus for Piaget to understand the changing cognitive processes. During those years, he developed the basis of what is still the most widely accepted theory of cognitive development. In fact, Piaget's theory of cognitive development is the most detailed, systematic interpretation of any aspect of human development. This theory, although largely based on Piaget's observations of his children rather than on formal scientific inquiry, is a guideline for understanding the changing thought process throughout childhood and adolescence. Furthermore, this theory has given cognitive developmentalists a specific basis from which to begin their investigating. An awareness of this theory is critical to a thorough understanding of motor development, because cognitive and motor development constantly interact. Cognitive development strongly depends on the movement capabilities the individual has acquired; similarly, motor development depends on intellectual capabilities. This interactive process is apparent in Piaget's theory.

The four major stages in Piaget's theory of cognitive development are sensorimotor, preopera-

Table 2-1 Major Stages of Piaget's Theory of Cognitive Development and Approximate Ages of Periods of Occurrence

Stage	Age/Period of Occurrence
Sensorimotor	Birth to 2 years
Preoperational	2 to 7 years
Concrete operational	7 to 11 years
Formal operational	Early to midadolescence (11 to 12 years)

tional, concrete operational, and formal operational (see Table 2-1). The ages Piaget cited for each stage are only guidelines. Individual variation is expected, although it is believed that most children approximate the course of development Piaget suggested. Furthermore, not everyone achieves Piaget's highest level of cognitive development, formal thought. But children do follow the same sequence through the stages regardless of the level of cognitive ability they eventually attain. In other words, the stages are always experienced in the same order, and no stage is ever skipped, although the rate and degree of completion vary with each child. Also, each stage is increasingly more complex than its predecessor and builds on the cognitive abilities gained in the previous stage.

ADAPTATION According to Piaget, cognitive development occurs through a process he called adaptation. **Adaptation** is the adjusting to the demands of the environment and the intellectualization of that adjustment through two complementary acts, assimilation and accommodation. **Assimilation** is a process by which children attempt to interpret new experiences based on their present interpretation of the world (Shaffer, 1999). This process of perceiving experiences relative to a past mode of thinking is exemplified by an infant who with one hand attempts to grasp a ball slightly too large for the small hand (Figure 2-2). The one-handed "plan" to grasp the ball was in the child's cognitive repertoire as a result of previous experiences with rattles or smaller objects. Thus, the infant tries to incorporate

Figure 2-2   An example of assimilation. The infant is trying to grasp a large ball by using a one-handed reaching and grasping technique. This new experience is being incorporated into the child's cognitive repertoire by an existing mode of thinking.

Table 2-2   Piaget's Work on Cognitive Development

Some criticisms of Piaget's theory of work and his theory of cognitive development include the following:

1. Piaget's clinical method lacked sufficient scientific control.

2. Much of Piaget's work was conducted using his own children as subjects.

3. Piaget's examination of cognitive change did not have a lifespan orientation.

4. Piaget may have underestimated children's capabilities.

5. Piaget did not discern well between competency and performance.

6. Piaget placed too little emphasis on the influence of motivation and emotions.

7. Piaget's stages of development were too broad.

8. Piaget described, but did not clearly explain, development.

the ball, the new experience, using an already established mode of thinking.

In *accommodation,* the second facet of adaptation, the individual attempts to adjust existing thought structures to account for, or accommodate, new experiences. In the case of the infant trying to obtain the large ball, accommodation could occur when the child recognizes that the ball is larger than the more familiar rattle. The infant then modifies the approach to obtaining the ball by either adapting the one-handed grasp or by using the other hand to help. Therefore, the child has made an adjustment to accommodate the ball. A new experience or environmental event has altered the child's behavior and past understanding or interpretation of the event.

According to Piaget, assimilation and accommodation always work together. Assimilation suggests that the individual always experiences new events according to what is already known; accommodation infers that the environment always challenges the individual to modify actions relative to the spe-

cific situation (Sigelman, 2003). As we saw in the earlier example of the infant trying to get the large ball, both components of adaptation highly depend on the individual's movement, especially during Piaget's first stage of cognitive development, the sensorimotor stage. Adaptation and its two facets, assimilation and accommodation, are basic to Piaget's theory of cognitive development and emphasize the importance he placed on the role of the environment in human development.

CRITICISMS OF PIAGET'S THEORY   Jean Piaget's theory has been amazingly well accepted by experts throughout the world. It has profoundly influenced theory and practice. As a result, it has also been the subject of considerable examination, scrutiny, and criticism. Some aspects of these criticisms are worth consideration (see Table 2-2). First, although Piaget became adept at his clinical method of gathering data concerning children's thought processes, this method has been criticized for lacking scientific control during the collection process. In addition, much of Piaget's observation centered on his own children, which of course leads to concerns about his potential bias in interpreting the thought processes of people so dear to him. Nevertheless, Piaget's theory of cognitive development has withstood considerable scrutiny for many years and continues to be the most significant guide in our efforts to understand human development more fully.

Perhaps the most strongly contested aspect of Piaget's theory is his proposal that the highest level of intellectual development is formal operational, a stage he claims is often achieved by children as young as 11 years. Although Piaget stated that some children may never achieve formal operations and some may not achieve them until as late as 20 years, a significant portion of the lifespan still remains unaccounted for. Strong proponents of Piagetian theory support his notion, but subsequent interest in adult development has led to speculation that there is continued development beyond adolescence (Sigelman, 2003). Undoubtedly, cognitive behavior continues to develop long after early adolescence, despite Piaget's relative omission of this time of life. Several of the important cognitive changes that occur during adulthood and their relationship to motor development are discussed later in the chapter.

Still others have criticized Piaget for his underestimation of the true capabilities of children. More recent efforts have revealed that children may possess hidden competencies that remained unknown to Piaget. Furthermore, Piaget may have not fully recognized the distinction between competency and performance. In other words, if a child performed poorly on one of Piaget's tasks, the assumption was that intellectual competence was lacking. In fact, the child may have been completely competent, but as a result of the child's emotional state; lack of motivation; verbal ability; memory; lack of familiarity with the task; or nature of social influences from parents, peers, teachers, and siblings, poor performance resulted. This assumption could have affected the age guidelines that Piaget provided with each of his stages (Sigelman, 2003).

Other critics have noted that Piaget's stages of development may be too encompassing or broad. This criticism arises out of recent research that indicates that intellect may be mainly content specific rather than existing in a certain mode across a wide range of problem-solving areas as Piaget suggested. Still other critics have noted how well Piaget described development but lament his apparent inattention to explaining the process. For example, how do specific intellectual changes evolve anatomically, and how do life experiences contribute to this whole process (Sigelman, 2003)?

INFANCY: THE SENSORIMOTOR STAGE AND MOTOR DEVELOPMENT

The interaction between motor and cognitive development is a lifelong process particularly evident during the first 2 years. This is acknowledged in Piaget's theory and his decision to call the first stage of cognitive development sensorimotor. In the **sensorimotor stage,** intelligence develops as a result of movement actions and their consequences. According to Piaget, movement is critical to the thought process.

The sensorimotor stage, which normally lasts throughout the first 24 months of age, is a time of creating a foundation for all subsequent understanding that hinges on a child's ability to perform bodily movement. An infant's experience of being able to grasp and hold with certainty simultaneously influences the development of cognition. In the sensorimotor stage, knowing and thinking emerge as a result of action that occurs via bodily movement. Of particular importance in this stage are the environment and motor development.

The sensorimotor stage is subdivided into six substages (see Table 2-3), making this stage the most detailed of Piaget's four major stages. The first substage is called *exercise of reflexes* and lasts from birth through the first month of age. This substage is characterized by the earliest form of movement behavior, the infant reflexes, and their repetition. According to Piaget, the repetition of the reflexes helps the child explore the world through movement and forms the foundation for cognitive understanding. This earliest form of movement behavior facilitates the development of intellectual behavior

Table 2-3   Substages of the Sensorimotor Stage of Development and Their Approximate Ages of Occurrence

Substage	Age of Occurrence
Exercise of reflexes	Birth to 1 month
Primary circular reactions	1 to 4 months
Secondary circular reactions	4 to 8 months
Secondary schemata	8 to 12 months
Tertiary circular reactions	12 to 18 months
Invention of new means through mental combinations	18 to 24 months

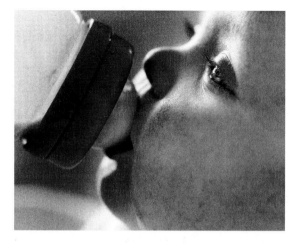

Figure 2-3   The sucking reflex is gradually modified to become a completely new behavior. This is an example of learning by doing.

Digital Vision/Getty Images

and may be the impetus for all future intellectual development. The infant reflexes are apparently innate forms of movement behavior that occur without stimulation from the higher centers of the brain. Reflexive movement is discussed in detail in Chapter 10; for now, we simply emphasize the role of this form of movement in the development of intellectual behavior. Reflexes help us adapt and modify our behaviors by experience. Gradually, reflexes are modified to produce a completely new behavior. For example, the nipple of the mother's breast stimulates the sucking reflex in the infant. As another example, by accident, or by repetition of other reflexive movements, the child's hand may come into contact with the mouth. By trial and error and as a result of modifying existing reflexive behavior, infants may learn to find the mouth with the hand, thus becoming capable of the gratifying act of sucking the thumb: They learn a new behavior (see Figure 2-3).

The second sensorimotor substage is known as *primary circular reactions.* Lasting from the end of the first month until approximately 4 months, this substage is characterized by the onset of increased voluntary movement. Infants now can consciously and capably create certain movement behaviors. Whereas in the first substage repetition occurred solely by accident, now the infant makes conscious efforts to repeat desired acts. By repeating actions, infants come to realize that certain stimuli allow

them to repeat an activity voluntarily when the same stimulus is presented in the future. These repeated actions are known as circular reactions and are considered primary because they always occur in close proximity to the infant.

Movement therefore plays an integral role in the development of thought processes. However, the relationship is reciprocal, because the increasing cognitive abilities facilitate such movement concerns as eye-hand coordination and early reaching and grasping.

Secondary circular reactions is the third substage of the sensorimotor stage of development. Generally, this substage, which lasts from about 4 to 8 months, is a continuation of primary circular reactions but incorporates more enduring behaviors: Movement behavior is intended to make an event lasting. The infant repeats the primary circular reactions. Examples of behaviors common in this substage are persistent shaking of a rattle and banging a toy to make noise. Such behavior familiarizes the infant with the environment and its forces.

During this substage, the infant's interaction with the environment gradually expands. In fact, two or more movement forms may be incorporated to enable more thorough interaction with and manipulation of the environment. For example, infants may make visual contact with a rattle, which stimulates them to obtain and shake the rattle. Such action is further evidence that the infant learns the stimuli and actions necessary to initiate certain behaviors through interaction with the environment via bodily movement. Furthermore, once the child can integrate vision, hearing, grasping, and certain movement behaviors, imitation, a major characteristic of secondary circular reactions, is possible. However, like most events or objects in the life of an infant of this age, there is no sense of permanence. Objects last only as long as they are viewed. Once a rattle is removed from the view of infants in this substage, they cease to seek it because they assume it no longer exists. Imitation can be performed only as long as the source of imitation is immediately present.

From approximately 8 to 12 months, the fourth substage, *secondary schemata,* takes place. Movement is still critical in the continued development of the intellect. Past modes of movement, designed to interact with the environment, are now applied to new situations, enabling many new behaviors to emerge. These new behaviors are facilitated by increasing movement capabilities such as crawling and creeping, which allow greater exploration of the environment and more contact with new objects and situations.

Particularly noteworthy in this substage are the increasing repetition of experimentation and the continued trial-and-error exploration. Through these learning processes, infants develop an ability to anticipate actions or situations that may occur in their environment; they can predict potential occurrences beyond their immediate activity. This ability, according to Piaget, is the onset of intellectual reasoning, and it allows infants to pair objects with their related activities and prepare to act on the basis of that determination. For example, when a ball is rolled to infants 8 to 12 months old, they can crudely return it. More important, the infants then prepare for their turn at receiving the ball be-

cause they realize the ball will once again be returned to them. They have associated the ball with playing catch.

The secondary schemata substage is followed by the *tertiary circular reactions* substage. This fifth substage, which covers the first half of the second year, is characterized by the discovery of new ways to produce desired results through active experimentation. In fact, active experimentation now consumes a major portion of the infant's time. Results of experimentation are incorporated into existing intellectual frameworks to create entirely new knowledge. Piaget believed that reasoning is fairly well developed in this substage and is necessary for the cyclical repetition of activities, which is characteristic of this substage, to occur.

Additionally, there is an intensified interest in the surrounding environment as well as constant attempts to understand it. Therefore, the various sensory modalities, especially vision, become extremely important in furnishing valuable information concerning the child's surroundings. Piaget noted that children in this substage realize that the discovery of a new object and the actual use of the object are separate entities. For example, children recognize that a ball can be thrown to create an enjoyable activity, but they know they do not have to pitch the ball at that time, because they have developed the capability of delaying the act until later, with the assurance that the ball will not lose its valuable property. This ability is one of the first signs of a child being capable of visualizing an object beyond its immediate use. However, in this substage, immediate relationships are still the only relationships clearly understood.

People become increasingly important in tertiary circular reactions as they become potential sources of resolution of the child's "problems." According to Piaget, this event may be a function of children's improving ability to recognize that they are different from other people. Distinguishing the self from others facilitates the development of the ability to create action through others. For example, children can seek help for their problem-solving situations from parents or older siblings. Piaget claimed that this was a critical skill in the establishment of social development and such important human factors as emotion, competition, and rivalry. We can thus see that cognitive and motor development considerably affect development in the affective domain as well as in each other's.

Invention of new means through mental combinations is the last of Piaget's substages in the sensorimotor stage. Lasting from 18 months to 24, this substage is a period of metamorphosis from active involvement in movement interactions with the environment to an increased reflection about those movements. This substage is often considered the climax of the sensorimotor stage and a transitional phase into the preoperational stage.

In this substage, children clearly recognize objects as independent from themselves and as possessing unique properties. Similarly, children recognize themselves as one object among the many existing in the environment. The child's interaction with environmental objects has been almost completely manifested via movement activities and has allowed to develop an understanding of the properties of objects such as size, shape, color, texture, weight, and use. However, the child may require a separate cognitive ability for each property. This fact is illustrated by children who respond to statements concerning their yellow ball but who do not understand when the ball is called the "big" ball. In fact, they may often refute such statements by noting that the ball is yellow, not big, when it is actually yellow and big.

Perhaps the most important characteristic of this substage is the development of the cognitive ability to consider the self and an object in simple situations in the past, present, and future. This cognitive skill allows contemplation of activities and may be the onset of what Piaget termed *semimental functioning.* By the end of this substage, "thinking with the body" has been gradually replaced by thinking with the mind. A new skill is made possible. Children can now recall an event without physically reenacting what happened. Furthermore, they can ponder alternatives and predict potential outcomes to situations without having to perform the acts

first. The following list summarizes the major developments that occur in the sensorimotor stage:

1. Increasing awareness of the difference between the self and others

2. Recognition that objects continue to exist even though they are no longer in view

3. Production of the mental images that allow the contemplation of the past, present, and future

The individual, after experiencing all facets of the sensorimotor stage, now enters childhood.

CHILDHOOD: PREOPERATIONS AND MOTOR DEVELOPMENT

Piaget's second major stage, the **preoperational,** begins at around 2 years and spans the next 5 years. This stage builds on the skills learned earlier in life as the child becomes more imaginative in play and recognizes that everyone views the world from a slightly different perspective. Furthermore, the child begins to more capably use symbols to represent objects in the environment. This capability enables one of the most important of all cognitive skills, verbal communication, to emerge.

Language development is the most important characteristic of preoperations and is strongly linked to rapidly improving motor abilities. The child becomes particularly adept at verbal communication very soon after learning to walk upright unassisted. Walking enables the child more thoroughly to explore and therefore understand the environment, and the rapidly expanding repertoire of new concepts gained from this increased exploration facilitates language. By the middle of the preoperational stage, most children have a highly efficient ability to communicate verbally as a result of this important interaction between motor and cognitive development.

Although Piaget generally focused on the cognitive attributes gained in each of his stages of cognitive development, in the preoperational stage he emphasized the limitations. In fact, the term *preoperations* was coined because at this stage children still do not have the ability to think logically or operationally. This second major stage of Piaget's theory is subdivided into two substages: preconceptual (from 2 years to 4 years) and intuitive (4 years to 7 years).

As mentioned, during the *preconceptual* substage, an ability to use symbols to represent objects in the environment emerges—for example, having a rock represent a turtle or the word *Dad* represent a certain person. Obviously, this new skill is critical to language development, but it also enables the child to reconstruct past events more easily and facilitates pretend play. During pretend play, children role play; they pretend they are other individuals and use props to symbolize objects to supplement their play. This play often focuses on various movement activities and contributes significantly to all areas of child development, including motor development. It is believed that movement is enhanced by a child's pretend play, which may include such acts as imitating a parent or other role model engaged in a favorite movement activity.

Piaget believed that the preconceptual substage was characterized by a level of cognitive ability that is primitive relative to adult capabilities. Piaget said that during this stage children's thinking is flawed by their tendency to animate inanimate objects. For example, children may refer to the emotional state of a drooping flower by saying, "The flower is sad!" This is a fun and interesting way to perceive the world, but it is also unrealistic and usually erroneous.

Transductive reasoning is another characteristic of the preconceptual substage. In this form of flawed reasoning, the child assumes that there is a cause and effect between two events occurring simultaneously. For example, a child who has missed breakfast may declare it cannot be morning because breakfast has not been prepared; obviously, the preparation of breakfast does not cause the onset of morning. Transductive reasoning often leads to incorrect assumptions.

Perhaps the most serious deficiency of this substage of preoperational thought is egocentrism. Children 2 to 4 years old view the world from a very narrow perspective. They have difficulty visualizing the perspective of others and do not adapt their rapidly developing language skills to facilitate the listener's understanding. Motor activities help in this regard because they increase a child's capability to interact socially by providing a means of locomoting to other children, thereby creating an outlet for social activity and enhanced social awareness. Increased social interaction expands the child's sensitivity to the needs and feelings of others and generally reduces the egocentrism characteristic of this stage of cognitive development.

The *intuitive* substage, an extension of the preconceptual substage, is characterized by reduced egocentrism and continued improvement in the use of symbols. Piaget called this substage "intuitive" because the child's understanding of the ways of the world are based on the appearance of objects and events that may not accurately depict reality.

As in the first substage of preoperations, Piaget continued to characterize cognitive development by the child's limitations. In both substages, the preoperational child is incapable of an ability Piaget called **conservation.** Conservation is realizing that certain characteristics of something may remain the same when the appearance is rearranged (Shaffer, 1999). The concept of conservation is exemplified by Piaget's classic test involving a ball of clay. When the ball is manually transformed into an elongated sausage, the child incapable of conservation responds that the elongated clay weighs more. The child capable of conservation knows that the spatial transformation of the clay has no effect on the weight of the clay.

The inability to conserve results from the child's difficulty in attending to more than one aspect of a problem-solving situation at one time. Preoperational children cannot "decenter" their attention from one particular component of the problem. Once they attain this ability, they can concentrate on more than one aspect of that problem. In the ball of clay example, the child with conservation ability can ponder the weight, length, and even the width of the clay rather than being restricted to one aspect of the clay. Inability to decenter attention can also have significant implications in motor de-

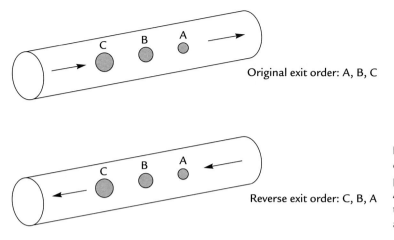

Figure 2-4 Demonstration of reversibility. The child can predict the sequence of balls A, B, and C as they exit the tube in both the original and the reverse order.

velopment. By this time in a child's life, many new motor activities, such as games, have become popular. The inability to simultaneously consider multiple aspects of a problem inhibits the child's efforts at games or activities involving complex strategies or multiple movements for each child. Consider young children involved in a game of soccer: Their attention becomes so focused on their objective of scoring a goal that they are impervious to the possibility of passing off to a teammate.

LATER CHILDHOOD AND ADOLESCENCE: COGNITIVE AND MOTOR DEVELOPMENT

Toward the end of childhood, most individuals enter Piaget's third stage of cognitive development: concrete operations. First we focus on this stage, and then we examine formal operations, the last stage of cognitive development, which is considered to begin for many at early adolescence.

Concrete Operational Stage

Piaget's third major stage of cognitive development, the **concrete operational,** generally spans ages 7 to 11. Many experts believe that children attain concrete operations once they have gained the ability to conserve. Thus, a major characteristic of this stage is the enhanced ability to decenter attention from one variable in a problem-solving situation. As mentioned earlier in the discussion of conservation, this ability to decenter attention can have important implications for motor development.

Also in this stage of development, children and young adolescents gradually attain the ability to mentally modify, organize, or even reverse their thought processes. A characteristic such as reversibility is exemplified by rolling balls A, B, and C through a small tube (Figure 2-4). We ask the child, "What order will the balls be in as they exit the other end of the tube?" Both the preoperational and the concrete operational child can correctly answer "A, B, and C." However, if we immediately roll the balls back through the tube without altering the order in which they exited, and ask, "What will the order of exit be this time?" only the concrete operational child can correctly respond "C, B, and A."

Piaget used the term *concrete operational* because the child at this level of cognitive development faces a major limitation. Although this stage is a major advancement over the preoperational one, the concrete operational child is still limited to pondering objects, events, or situations that are real or based on experience. This of course impedes efforts to examine hypothetical or abstract situations mentally.

On the positive side, the child who has attained this level of cognitive ability is now capable of mentally representing objects or a series of actions or events. This mental capability has obvious implications for motor development. For example, the child can facilitate many movement activities by formulating strategies for or expectations about an opposing player's or team's possible intent. By being able to ponder probable events or actions, the child can anticipate and, hopefully, successfully counter the opponent's tactics.

Piaget considered *seriation* another characteristic common to children at this level of development. **Seriation** is an ability to arrange a set of variables by a certain characteristic. For example, teammates can be arranged by height, and the relative relationships among these individuals can then be discerned. In other words, if a group of concrete operational children are informed that the basketball center is taller than the forward and that the forward is taller than the guard, they can determine that the center is also taller than the guard.

As emphasized throughout this chapter, there is a constant, reciprocal, mutually beneficial relationship between cognitive development and motor development. Piaget indirectly referred to this phenomenon throughout his theory; the concrete operational stage is no exception. In this stage (as well as others), Piaget stressed that learning can be facilitated by doing or by actions. That is, such cognitive skills as seriation can best be taught by having children manipulate objects of various lengths and widths into series. Piaget recommended that one of the best modes of teaching such concepts as space or distance was having the child "do" by instructing the child to move through the space or the distance under consideration. In Piaget's mind, movement in the form of doing, or action, was a critical component in the development of cognitive ability.

Formal Operational Stage

According to Piaget, the highest level of cognitive ability begins at about age 11 to 12 and is known as the **formal operational stage** or, simply, formal operations. The main accomplishment in this final stage is the ability to consider ideas that are not based on reality; that is, the individual is no longer confined to observable objects or experience-based thoughts. Abstract ideas are possible, which enables young people to resolve problems that violate their concept about reality in the world. Children in the concrete operational stage may be completely baffled by questions concerning abstract or nonexistent events or objects. In fact, the children may respond that there is no possible response because the concept under consideration is nonexistent. Formal operators, however, are challenged and enjoy the opportunity to ponder the new concept. According to Piaget, many individuals never achieve this stage of development. In fact, people who score below average on intelligence tests most likely have not achieved formal operations (Shaffer, 1999).

Formal operators are also capable of performing what Piaget called *interpropositional thought*. This enhanced level of cognitive ability allows children to relate one or more parts of a proposition or a situation to another part to arrive at a solution to a problem. To illustrate, if confronted with the statement "The ball is in my left hand or it isn't in my left hand," the child in concrete operations may need to inspect his or her hands visually before responding. The young adolescent in formal operations, however, can determine that the statement, although somewhat unusual, is correct. By simultaneously considering the two propositions within the statement, the formal operator determines that the ball is either in the hand or it is somewhere else, which indicates that the statement is correct.

This ability to perform interpropositional thought can be useful in many situations. In complex movement situations, this capability could enhance one's success strategically. In many team activities, the positioning of two or more players, each a "movement proposition," may indicate the onset of a particular play. A defender who can "read" the interrelationship between these movement propositions can prepare accordingly and help the team counter the play.

An additional product of formal thought is what Piaget referred to as *hypothetical-deductive reasoning*. This term indicates a problem-solving style in which possible solutions to a problem are generated and systematically considered. This rational, systematic, and abstract form of reasoning facilitates the selection of the correct solution. Piaget believed that this new form of reasoning, which allows consideration of the abstract, has dramatic effects on the child's emotional development, including the development of new feelings, behaviors, and goals. Newly emerging values may result from this enhanced cognitive capability. Frequently, young adolescents become increasingly idealistic as they ponder such magnanimous concepts as world peace or the search for the perfect energy source. Resolution of these problems may seem fairly simple to a young formal "operator" who can now think about what presently appear to be unrealistic situations.

The changing values that Piaget believed emerge as a result of formal operations may also affect the young adolescent's decisions concerning participation in movement endeavors. Because of increased idealism, the adolescent may decide that the competition common to many adolescent movement activities is not mutually beneficial to all involved and therefore choose not to participate. Or the adolescent may begin to become aware of the potential benefits of participation and learn to cherish the possibility of being exceptionally fit or successful in a movement endeavor. The extent and direction of the individual's new values are also functions of the current trends among peers and society; this topic is more thoroughly discussed in Chapter 3.

ADULTHOOD: POSTFORMAL OPERATIONS

Like his predecessors in development and the developmentalists of his day, Piaget did not specifically consider adulthood in his theory of cognitive development. We now clearly recognize that development is a lifelong process and seek to understand all age groups. Therefore, cognitive developmentalists have speculated as to the nature of intellectual change throughout the adult years. As early as 1975, Arlin proposed a so-called fifth stage to Piaget's

work. This fifth stage was considered a higher level of ability because it involved larger quantities of information.

Others (Rybash, Hoyer, & Roodin, 1986), however, have suggested that *postformal operations* involves more than dealing with larger quantities of information. It is characterized by discovering new questions instead of simply attempting to determine logical, well-defined solutions to a given problem. In formal operations we can become consumed by our newfound logical capabilities and assume that logical answers exist for all problems. As we continue to develop beyond formal operations, we see answers as more relative and less absolute. In advanced levels of thinking, we thrive on detecting paradoxes and inconsistencies in ideas and try to reconcile them. We develop the ability to think logically about abstract concepts and can manipulate whole systems of ideas. These advanced capabilities, however, are thought to exist in a minority of adults and mostly among those with advanced education who reside in a culture that embraces new ideas and freethinking. This reinforces the idea that cognitive development, like other aspects of human development, does not depend on age. Rather, it is tied to life experiences and demands to think at home, at work, and throughout our communities (Sigelman, 2003).

ADULTHOOD: GENERAL THEORIES OF INTELLECTUAL DEVELOPMENT

Today, consensus among the expert community asserts that certain forms of intellectual decline occur with age during adulthood. These claims are made on the basis of a flood of research over the last two decades on the topic of intellectual development and adulthood. Much of this research has shown that many older adults learn more slowly and sometimes less well than younger folks. Other older adults may drop much more precipitously. However, specific analysis is required because some forms of intellect show no decline, and several factors could cloud our examination of aging and intellect (Craik, 1999). The following sections examine some major findings from recent research on this topic.

The Notion of Total Intellectual Decline

One of the most traditional views of aging and intellect posits that a gradual, consistent, and pervasive decline occurs in overall intellectual ability throughout the adult years. This theory, which lacks strong scientific support today, gained early support from results yielded from the Wechsler Adult Intelligence Scale (WAIS). This scale measures 11 components of intellectual ability, 6 concerning verbal ability and 5 concerning performance ability. The WAIS has been particularly valuable in clinically assessing adults with various forms of psychopathology and has been shown to be highly reliable in older persons, though the reliability between its two scales, verbal and performance, has been questioned. Nevertheless, the scale has often been used as a measure or estimate of intellectual decline (Schaie, 1996). Though declines have been seen in WAIS performance across adulthood, recent, more specific evidence indicates a consistent improvement in WAIS performance for adults from 18 years to 54 years of age. In addition, one of the most intensive studies of intellectual change across adulthood, the Seattle Longitudinal Study, examined six primary mental abilities that are meaningful in daily work and life activities. Subjects ranged in age from 25 to 88. On average, these subjects increased performance until the late 30s or early 40s before plateauing by the mid-50s or early 60s. Starting in the late 60s, 7-year increments of study showed statistically significant declines in performance. Researchers concluded that, for some, a decline may begin as early as the 50s, but it remains small until the mid-70s. The change also tends to occur in those abilities that are less central to one's life and less practical to daily function. By the age of 60, nearly all subjects in the Seattle Longitudinal Study declined on at least one of the six intelligence variables tested; however, by age 88, no one declined on all six. In short, though clear reductions in intel-

lectual capacity occurred for most by their late 80s or early 90s, few subjects showed a global decline in intelligence (Schaie, 1996).

Partial Intellectual Declines

Currently, the most widely accepted view on aging and intellect posits that cognitive decline occurs in some areas but not others. This notion is well supported by current research, and is generally much more positive emotionally. Societal stigmas regarding old age and "senility" are often criticized for leading to a self-fulfilling prophecy; that is, if we think it will happen, it will. Clearly, aside from age, many other factors can contribute to a decline. For example, if we have negative thoughts about memory, confidence can diminish. This, in turn, hampers performance. Studies on Chinese elders, who are much more respected for their wisdom and experience, and therefore less negatively stereotyped than their U.S. counterparts, have demonstrated less intellectual decline when compared with younger Chinese adults. One's knowledge base has also been found to be a factor. A greater base of information may help offset losses in processing efficiency (Sigelman, 2003). Knowledge really is power!

The recognition of factors other than age, and their effects on intellectual change across time, is often referred to as a ***contextual perspective.*** This simply means that learning and memory depend in part on factors like culture, as we saw in the study of Chinese elders. Noncognitive, situational factors can strongly affect the degree to which any decline occurs (Zacks, Hasher, & Li, 2000). Factors like one's own goals, motivation, social activities, modifications of daily routines, changes in emotions, and ability related to the task in question can also affect performance. Even one's own optimistic or pessimistic self-appraisal can affect performance (Schaie, 1996). Thus, the decline we often see in intellectual abilities is not convincingly universal and not completely a function of inevitable biological decline (Sigelman, 2003).

However, biological effects are clearly involved. Changes like declining neural systems, slower neural activation, and less efficient vascular or circulatory processes are thought to contribute (Prull, Gabrieli, & Bunge, 2000). Though highly variable, the brain also decreases in size with age, though neuronal losses are gradual in normal aging, and the greatest loss of neurons occurs during the prenatal period. The overall longevity and adaptive capacity of our nervous system is generally remarkable, with most neurons maintaining strong adaptive capacity throughout life (Scheibel, 1996).

Though there appear to be "no simple rules about when age differences in memory will and will not occur, and if they do, whether differences will be small, modest, or large" (Zacks et al., 2000, p. 342), considerable recent research has centered on *implicit* and *explicit memory* and learning. Some researchers have concluded that "nowhere is there a trend more salient than in research on implicit memory" (p. 305). Implicit memory is unintentional, automatic, or without awareness. It is tested, therefore, without the subject being aware of being tested. Explicit memory is deliberate and effortful, and is tested by traditional tests of recall or recognition. These two types of memory are believed to follow quite different developmental paths. Explicit memory improves from infancy to adulthood and then shows decline. Implicit memory also improves from infancy but does not change much at all during adulthood, with elders performing no worse than young adults (Sigelman, 2003). This difference in developmental trends is so notable it has been deemed a "striking dissociation" (Zacks et al., 2000, p. 306).

Many other trends have been noted in research on aging and intellect. For example, memory on information learned earlier, rather than later, in life is superior in older adulthood. If the information is well established early in life, it will be easier to retrieve. An age-related decline on "new learning" related to "old learning" appears to be clear-cut (Prull et al., 2000; Zacks et al., 2000).

Another clear trend is the tendency for older adults to respond more slowly. When time restrictions are placed on intellectual tasks, the performance of older adults is more likely to be negatively impacted (Sigelman, 2003). In fact, the decline in speed of processing may be the most obvious, well-established decline with age. It contributes to a large part of age-related declines on many cognitive tasks (Zacks et al., 2000). Obviously, this decline in speed of mental processing has clear ramifications for motor development. Many movement activities require fast, even split-second decision making. Thus, motor ability may decline with increasing age. This phenomenon will be more thoroughly discussed in Chapter 16.

Although declines in intellect are often noted during later adulthood, much can be done to allay their onset. A lifestyle can be designed that optimizes the cognitive attributes. When cognitive abilities are practiced, declines are often delayed or avoided altogether (Sigelman, 2003). Cognitive training has been shown to be effective in enhancing capabilities of older adults (Schaie, 1996). In addition, movement plays an important role in this effort to maximize cognitive ability. Heart-diseased or hypertense individuals have been shown to perform more poorly on many cognitive performance tasks (Birren, Woods, & Williams, 1980); an active, movement-oriented lifestyle helps combat such conditions. Furthermore, it is believed that maintenance of an active, movement-oriented lifestyle heightens cognitive sensitivity and responsiveness because cerebral blood flow increases and neural tissues undergo positive alterations. In addition, physical activity increases the size of motor neurons while decreasing the density of neural synapses—both factors are considered critical to inhibiting the slowdown of cognitive and motor responses that commonly occurs with old age. Reaction time and cognitive performance improve in both uninstitutionalized aged people and institutionalized geriatric patients who are placed on an exercise program (Powell & Pohndorf, 1971). Clearly, maintenance of an active, movement-oriented lifestyle into and throughout adulthood can affect cognitive as well as motor development. And, as discussed in Chapter 3, the effects are even more pervasive because social development is also strongly influenced by an individual's motor development.

KNOWLEDGE DEVELOPMENT AND SPORT PERFORMANCE

Most of the early research examining the processes that ultimately lead to skilled motor control and performance have been conducted in laboratory settings. The assigned movement task used to experimentally explore movement control and learning factors has generally involved some simple and novel movement. While such an arrangement is scientifically sound (in part, this arrangement controls for differences in past experiences), it does present problems regarding external validity. No doubt, this line of research has successfully led to better understanding of the underlying memory processes that are employed during novel skill performance. Unfortunately, we do not know whether these theories adequately explain performance as it is encountered in a real-world setting.

Thomas and colleagues (1988) have produced convincing evidence that improvements to the task-specific knowledge base may lead to better task-specific sport performance (see Figure 2-5). It is believed that children's motor performance deficits can be attributed to their inexperience (lack of a sufficient knowledge base) and to their inefficient use of control processes. These control processes are needed to store, retrieve, and effectively use information. Indeed, some studies have shown that when novice adults are compared with more experienced children, the children can perform as well as or better than the adults (cited in Thomas et al., 1988). These children probably outperformed the novice adults because of their greater depth of task-specific knowledge.

According to Anderson (1976), knowledge can be represented in two forms: declarative knowledge and procedural knowledge. **Declarative knowledge** can be thought of as "factual information," while **procedural knowledge** can be thought of as a "production system" or "how to do something." Research comparing expert and novice performers has clearly shown that the expert performer has more knowledge of task-specific concepts (Charness, 1979) and has better problem-solving abilities (Adelson, 1984).

To appreciate fully the strong relationship between cognitive abilities and sport-specific performance, it is important to realize that raw athletic ability does not necessarily ensure athletic success. Let us illustrate this point with a real-world example from basketball. There are only 7 seconds left in the game and the offensive team trails by one point. The ball is in the hands of the team's best ball handler. As time is about to expire, he looks to his right and quickly executes a perfect behind-the-back pass to a teammate located on the left side of the court. Unfortunately, this perfect pass has been directed to the team's worst ball handler and worst shooter. Time expires without a final shot being attempted. This situation is unfortunate because the team's leading scorer, who was located on the right side of the court, was also open for a shot. Because the ball handler used poor judgment, his superior skills did not translate into athletic success. In short, an incorrect cognitive decision was made (whom best to pass the ball to), which probably cost his team the game. If successful athletic performance is to occur, then there must be a strong link between sport-specific knowledge and skilled movement execution. In our example, the ball handler should have known that the team's strategy was to get the ball into the hands of the best shooter.

French and Thomas (1987) conducted a series of two experiments that point out the strong relationship between the sport-specific knowledge base and athletic success. In their first study, these researchers studied the relationship between knowledge development, skill development, and development of expertise in basketball among children aged 8 to 10 and aged 11 to 12. Participants in both age-group leagues were administered a 50-item multiple-choice test to assess basketball knowledge, as well as two basketball skills tests that were adapted from the AAHPERD basketball skills test (speed shot and control dribble). An observational instrument was also developed for the purpose of assessing individual basketball performance during an actual game. This observational instrument was used to code the young participants' behaviors during one quarter of play. Behaviors were coded according to the following categories: control, deci-

Figure 2-5 Researchers have found that improving task-specific knowledge of a skill may lead to improved performance of that skill.

Keith Brofsky/Getty Images/Brand X Pictures

sion, and execution. *Control* refers to the child's ability to decide what to do with the basketball once it was caught (shoot, pass, dribble, etc.), while *execution* refers to whether the child performed the skill of shooting, passing, or dribbling in an appropriate manner. Coaches were also required to fill in a questionnaire for the purpose of rating their players' basketball ability. In addition, an open-ended basketball interview was conducted with the players. During this interview, players were asked questions regarding how they would respond to various basketball situations. For example, one question asked them to list appropriate offensive strategies for a two-on-one fast break.

The results from this first experiment indicated that the child experts (in both age groups) practiced longer, had more years of basketball experience, and participated in more sports than did the novices. In addition, on average the child experts made correct decisions (85 percent) more frequently than did the novice performers (51 percent). Furthermore, the child experts scored higher than the novices on both skills tests and basketball knowledge. The authors concluded that "development of sport-specific

declarative knowledge is related to the development of cognitive decision-making skills or procedural knowledge, whereas development of shooting skill and dribbling skill are related to the motor execution components of control and execution" (French & Thomas, 1987, p. 24).

In their second experiment, French and Thomas (1987) wanted to determine the influence of changes in basketball skills improvement and basketball knowledge on game performance during the course of one season. Subjects were 14 child novices and 17 child experts who had participated in the first experiment. To control for maturational effects, a control group of 16 children who had no previous organized basketball experience was utilized. The basketball participants were administered the control dribble test, the speed spot-shooting test, and the basketball knowledge test at the beginning and at the end of the basketball season. The control group also was administered these same three tests two times, 7 weeks apart. Assessing playing performance involved coding behaviors during one quarter of play for each of three games. More specifically, the three games in which behaviors were coded included the first game and the last two games of the season.

In general, the findings from this second experiment found that game performance improved over the course of the season. However, this improvement was the result of being able to make more appropriate cognitive decisions during the course of a game and also being able to better catch the basketball. It was not due to improvements in basketball skill execution. In fact, during the course of this 7-week season, no significant changes were found to exist among dribbling and shooting test scores

or the execution component that was coded during game performance. Thus, it appears that task-specific knowledge is acquired faster than motor skill development. In other words, children in this study learned "what to do" in a given situation before they acquired the physical skills to carry out their strategic plan successfully. The researchers (French & Thomas, 1987) point out that additional research is needed before we can recommend the best combination of motor and cognitive instruction and the timing of each for the purpose of maximizing sport-specific performance.

SUMMARY

As motor and cognitive abilities develop, they uniquely facilitate or inhibit all other aspects of development. These abilities reciprocally interact at all times throughout the lifespan, significantly affecting motor and cognitive behavior.

Jean Piaget was the most famous and prolific of all developmentalists. His theory concerning cognitive development—the most widely accepted theory in that area—proposes the sensorimotor, preoperational, concrete operational, and formal operational stages.

The interaction between motor and cognitive development is particularly evident in the sensorimotor stage, which spans the first 2 years of life. This stage is characterized by "thinking by bodily movement," which suggests that actions created by the body enhance the cognitive process.

Major accomplishments during the sensorimotor stage include the ability to differentiate between the self and others and to recognize that objects continue to exist even though they are no longer in the visual field. Also, the child becomes capable of producing mental images that allow contemplation of the past and future as well as the present.

The main cognitive achievement during the preoperational stage is acquisition of language. This process is facilitated by rapidly improving manipulation and locomotor skills. These skills enable the child to explore more and to understand the environment better, contributing to the child's ability to express related concepts verbally.

The concrete operational stage is reached when the child has developed the ability to decenter attention from one to two or more aspects of a problem-solving situation. This decentering skill is important in accurately planning and executing many movement activities.

Piaget believed that the formal operational stage was the highest level of cognitive ability. In formal operations, the major cognitive landmark is the acquisition of the ability to think hypothetically—that is, ponder the unreal. New cognitive abilities such as interpropositional thought may continue to enhance an individual's ability in strategic movement situations.

Many experts disagree with Piaget's view that formal operations is the highest level of cognitive ability. These experts believe that cognitive development continues throughout adulthood, although they debate the specific nature of the change. Adulthood (postformal operations) is traditionally and stereotypically viewed as a time of cognitive decline, but current evidence suggests that cognitive development is not only age dependent; it is also affected by life experiences and demands.

The decline in split-second decision making seriously impairs performance in many movement activities. However, maintenance of an active, movement-oriented lifestyle may delay the onset and slow the rate of cognitive decline, because movement activity increases cerebral blood flow and causes other helpful physiological effects.

Researchers are just beginning to examine the relationship between sport-specific knowledge and sport performance.

KEY TERMS

accommodation
adaptation
assimilation
clinical method
concrete operational stage
conservation

contextual perspective
declarative knowledge
explicit memory
formal operational stage
implicit memory
postformal operations

preoperational stage
procedural knowledge
psychomotor
semimental functioning
sensorimotor stage
seriation

QUESTIONS FOR REFLECTION

1. What do we mean by the terms *adaptation, assimilation,* and *accommodation?* Define each and distinguish the differences.

2. Though Piaget's theory has been widely accepted, explain three criticisms one might wage against it.

3. In order, what are the substages of Piaget's sensorimotor stage of development? Characterize each.

4. What are the major developments of the sensorimotor stage of development?

5. What does Piaget mean by "semimental functioning"?

6. What are some potential relationships between motor development and children's cognitive ability in the preoperational stage of development?

7. What does Piaget mean by "interpropositional thought," and how is this concept important to development? How might it be important for motor development?

8. Name two theories that attempt to explain cognitive change throughout adulthood. What are the major characteristics of each? Which would you subscribe to and why?

9. What are the differences between explicit and implicit memory?

10. What are some differences between declarative knowledge and procedural knowledge, and how do they relate to sports performance?

ONLINE LEARNING CENTER (www.mhhe.com/payne6e)

Visit the *Human Motor Development* Online Learning Center for study aids and additional resources. You can use the study guide questions and key terms puzzles to review key terms and concepts for this chapter and to prepare for exams. You can further extend your knowledge of motor development by checking out the Web links, articles, and activities found on the site.

REFERENCES

Adelson, B. (1984). When novices surpass experts: The difficulty of a task may increase with expertise. *Journal of Experimental Psychology: Learning, Memory, and Cognition, 10,* 483–495.

Anderson, J. R. (1976). *Language, memory, and thought.* Hillsdale, NJ: Erlbaum.

Arlin, P. K. (1975). Cognitive development in adulthood: A fifth stage? *Developmental Psychology, 11,* 602–606.

Birren, J. E., Woods, A. M., & Williams, M. V. (1980). Behavior slowing with age: Causes, organization, and consequences. In L. W. Poon (Ed.), *Aging in the 80's: Psychological issues.* Washington, DC: American Psychological Association.

Charness, N. (1979). Components of skill in bridge. *Canadian Journal of Psychology, 33,* 1–16.

Craik, F. I. M. (1999). Memory, aging, and survey measurement. In N. Schwartz, D. Parker, B. Knauper, and S. Sudman (Eds.), *Cognition, aging, and self-reports.* Philadelphia: Psychology Press.

French, K. E., & Thomas, J. R. (1987). The relation of knowledge development to children's basketball performance. *Journal of Sport Psychology, 9,* 15–32.

Newman, B. M. (2003). *Development through life: A psychosocial approach.* 8th ed. Pacific Grove, CA: Brooks/Cole.

Powell, R. R., & Pohndorf, R. H. (1971). Comparison of adult exercisers and nonexercisers on fluid intelligence and physiological variables. *Research Quarterly, 23,* 70–71.

Prull, M. W., Gabrieli, J. D. E., & Bunge, S. A. (2000). Age-related changes in memory: A cognitive neuroscience perspective. In F. I. M. Craik and T. A. Salthouse (Eds.), *The handbook of aging and cognition,* 91–153. Mahwah, NJ: Erlbaum.

Rybash, J. M., Hoyer, W. J., & Roodin, P. A. (1986). *Adult cognition and aging.* New York: Pergamon Press.

Schaie, K. W. (1996). Intellectual development in adulthood. In J. E. Birren and K. W. Schaie (Eds.), *Handbook of the psychology of aging,* 266-286. San Diego: Academic Press.

Scheibel, A. B. (1996). Structural and fundamental changes in the aging brain. In J. E. Birren and K. W. Schaie (Eds.), *Handbook of the psychology of aging,* 105–128. San Diego: Academic Press.

Shaffer, D. R. (1999). *Developmental psychology: Childhood and adolescence.* 5th ed. Pacific Grove, CA: Brooks/Cole.

Sigelman, C. K. (2003). *Life-span human development.* 4th ed. Pacific Grove, CA: Brooks/Cole.

Thomas, J. R., French, K. E., Thomas, K. T., & Gallagher, J. D. (1988). Children's knowledge development and sport performance. In F. L. Smoll, R. A. Magill, & M. J. Ash (Eds.), *Children in sport.* 3rd ed. Champaign, IL: Human Kinetics.

Zacks, R. T., Hasher, L., & Li, K. Z. H. (2000). Human memory. In F. I. M. Craik and T. A. Salthouse (Eds.), *The handbook of aging and cognition,* 293–358. Mahwah, NJ: Erlbaum.

Social and Motor Development

While the somewhat arbitrary classification of the human being into the cognitive, affective, motor, and physical domains facilitates discussion of human development, it does not produce a realistic portrayal of the person. Human behavior is *not* compartmentalized; there is a complex system of constant, reciprocal exchange among an individual's cognitive, affective, motor, and physical aspects. That which affects an individual in one domain is bound to have a subsequent effect in all other domains as well. For example, Chapter 2 emphasized the strong relationship between human intellectual function and movement: Any intellectual change is also accompanied by a change in motor function. Many of these changes are so slight that they are of no obvious consequence in a person's life. But other changes produce tremendous effects and may have lifelong implications for human movement as well as social, emotional, and physical well-being.

This chapter examines another reciprocal relationship of particular importance to human motor development: social behavior and movement. Social behavior affects a person's movement behavior; conversely, motor behaviors equally affect an individual's social development.

SOCIALIZATION

Socialization is a "dual process of interaction and development through which human beings learn (1) who they are and how they are connected to the social worlds in which they live, and (2) the orientations used as a basis for the individual behaviors and group life in the same worlds" (Coakley, 1993, p. 571). Though generally associated with learning that occurs through social interactions, socialization can include any means by which a person gathers information about society, and it generally includes the entire process of becoming a human being. Common means of socialization include observation, inference, modeling, and trial and error, but the most important is social interaction. The influence of others around us is extremely important in determining how and when persons acquire certain

movement abilities. They are also integral in determining which movement activities we choose. The amount of social support supplied by significant others in our lives is positively associated with the extent of our participation in physical activity. Researchers have determined that parents, siblings, teachers, coaches, and friends can all have varying amounts of influence on the choices we make concerning physical activity. In turn, the movement activities we choose affect our ability to "fit in" socially based on the compatibility of our choices with the dominant social values. Our movement choices also affect our self-identity, social mobility, educational achievement, attitudes concerning masculinity and femininity, and even our moral development (e.g., attitudes about cheating and fair play) (Coakley, 1993).

Although generally associated with development during childhood, the socialization process is lifelong, facilitating a person's function within society throughout childhood, adolescence, and adulthood. Furthermore, even though the term is commonly associated with the learning that occurs through social interaction, socialization can include any means by which a person gathers information about society. Nevertheless, the most important means of learning societal rules and expectations is through social interaction, which is also true for learning human movement. The influence of others around us is extremely important in determining how and when persons acquire certain movements as well as what movements.

The process of socialization teaches the members of society their social roles. A *social role* is the behavior that members of a particular social group expect in a particular situation (Kaluger & Kaluger, 1984). There are many social roles in any society. Occupational roles of, say, a professor or a police officer are exemplified by specific expected behaviors. Family roles can be illustrated by a mother or a father, who are expected to exhibit certain behaviors relative to the rest of their family and their society. Society's role expectations tremendously influence human motor development. Movement may or may not be acquired, depending on whether individuals believe that movement to be role appropriate. In other words, is it a movement that individuals assume appropriate for what they consider their role in society?

This set of expectations about behavior is formally called a **norm.** Societal norms can facilitate or inhibit people's movement development, depending on the individual's perspective of the norms. For example, in many areas of the United States, the norm is to expect less of older adults, so many older adults indeed do expect less of themselves. They are inhibited or constrained by the societal norm concerning their age group. As another example, the norm for the male adolescent regarding physical activity is vigorous involvement in movement pursuits, to the extent that his social success may depend on his athletic prowess. Both of these examples are examined more thoroughly later in this chapter.

SELF-ESTEEM DEVELOPMENT AND PHYSICAL ACTIVITY

One extremely important human characteristic affected by social interaction and physical activity is *self-esteem,* defined as how much we believe ourselves to be competent, successful, significant, and worthy, or how much we like ourselves. Other terms often used interchangeably with self-esteem include *self-concept, self-worth, self-acceptance, self-like, self-love, self-respect,* and *self-regard* (Donnelly, Eburne, & Kittleson, 2001). Simply stated, self-esteem is the value we place on ourselves as individuals (Gruber, 1985; Harter, 1988). Self-esteem is one of the most important aspects of self-development. It generally emerges in early childhood (Berk, 2004). This is not to be confused with *self-concept,* which is simply our perception of self (Gruber, 1985). Self-esteem and self-concept have been widely studied, with most researchers finding them to be affected significantly by involvement in physical activity. So much research has been done on this issue that Gruber (1985) was able to conduct a meta-analysis, a quantitative review of literature (see Chapter 4). In his review, he found 84 articles reporting studies of the effects of physical activity

on self-esteem or self-concept. Of these studies, 27 offered sufficient data for use in his meta-analysis. Of those 27 studies, 18 found physical activity to affect self-concept or self-esteem significantly. Overall, Gruber determined that 66 percent of the children in physical education or directed-play situations exceeded the self-concept or self-esteem scores of the children in non-physical activity settings. Physical activity programs with physical fitness objectives were found to be particularly beneficial for the children studied.

Gruber also determined that emotionally disturbed, trainably mentally retarded, educably mentally retarded, perceptually disabled, or economically disadvantaged children who were physically active exhibited a mean self-concept score much higher than the scores of all other groups. Gruber suggested that those subjects, in particular, begin to feel important when allowed opportunities for involvement in programs of motor enrichment that are conducted by trained and supportive professionals. The greatest gain in self-esteem was, therefore, found in those who most needed it, though normal children also exhibited an improvement.

In conclusion, Gruber states that involvement in directed play or physical education can enhance self-esteem in children though it is not clear why. Perhaps, the simple distraction is sufficient to increase self-esteem, or some have hypothesized a physiological change. The physical activity could also affect endorphins or monamine (a brain neurotransmitter), which, in turn, would alter the child's affective state. In general, Gruber (1985) believes these findings to be critical because improving one's self-image greatly affects future behavior.

In other research, Harter (1988) determined that self-esteem evolves developmentally in a series of somewhat predictable steps (see Table 3-1). Young children, for example, are incapable of making meaningful and consistent judgments about their *global self-worth,* the overall value that one places on oneself as a person. They can, however, make reliable judgments about such elements of self-worth as cognitive and social competence and their own behavioral conduct, though they cannot accurately distinguish between them. Harter also

Table 3-1	Self-Worth Development
Early Childhood	Though young children can make reliable judgments concerning their own cognitive and social competence and behavioral conduct, they cannot distinguish between them. In addition, they cannot make judgments about their global self-worth, and they have difficulty discerning between cognitive and physical skills. Because of limited cognitive capabilities, they also have difficulty expressing their own sense of self-worth.
Mid to Late Childhood	Because of enhanced cognitive ability, children begin to verbalize self-worth and make judgments about it. Ability also begins to emerge in distinguishing between scholastic and athletic competence, peer social acceptance, physical appearance, and behavioral conduct. As in all other age groups, physical appearance and social acceptance are the most important elements contributing to global self-worth.
Adolescence	By adolescence, increased capability emerges as adolescents articulate and discern between the elements of global self-worth. In addition to the elements they could articulate earlier, they can now distinguish feelings concerning friendship, romantic appeal, and job competence. In addition to physical appearance and social acceptance, friend and teacher support is a major contributor to global self-worth.
College Age	By college age, the ability to make more distinctions becomes apparent. In addition to global self-worth, the elements of scholastic competence, intellectual ability, creativity, job competence, athletic competence, physical appearance, romantic appeal, peer social acceptance, close friendships, parental relationships, sense of humor, and morality can be articulated. In addition, clear distinctions are made between scholastic competence, intellectual ability, and creativity. Global self-worth becomes a function of the individual's perceived self-worth in the areas that have become most important personally. Intimate relationships and adequacy as a provider also become increasingly important in young adulthood.
Adulthood	By adulthood, a need has developed for further distinction between elements of self-worth, including intimate relationships, nurturance, adequacy as a provider, and household management in addition to all of those mentioned earlier.

SOURCE: Harter (1988).

contends that young children cannot distinguish between their competency in cognitive and physical skills. This does not mean that young children do not have a sense of self-worth. Rather, they simply have difficulty expressing it verbally because of their limited cognitive capabilities.

Harter believes this changes at midchildhood because of increased cognitive capabilities. At around 8 years of age, children can begin to verbalize their feelings of self-worth and make judgments about their self-esteem. Furthermore, between ages 8 and 12, children develop the ability to distinguish among scholastic and athletic competence, peer social acceptance, physical appearance, and their own behavioral conduct.

Adolescents are capable of even greater articulation and discrimination concerning the elements of self-worth. They can distinguish all the same elements as before, with the addition of close friendships, romantic appeal, and job competence. This process of development continues with college students, in whom more distinctions are exhibited. In addition to global self-worth, Harter believes the college-age individual can differentiate and articulate 12 elements of self-worth: scholastic competence, intellectual ability, creativity, job competence, athletic competence, physical appearance, romantic appeal, peer social acceptance, close friendships, parent relationships, sense of humor, and morality. Interestingly, Harter indicates that this age group clearly distinguishes between scholastic competence, intellectual ability, and creativity.

The adult has developed a need for distinguishing additional elements of self-esteem or self-worth. Specifically, these include intimate relationships, nurturance, adequacy as a provider, and household management in addition to those mentioned for younger age groups. This need for new elements with each additional age group implies, according to Harter, a developmental change in one's self-esteem.

Harter also notes that, for each age group, certain elements of self-esteem contribute more or less to global self-worth. Physical appearance and social acceptance, respectively, were the most important elements contributing to the global self-worth of elementary schoolchildren. Surprisingly, these two elements of self-worth were the two most important for all age groups. For adolescents, parent and classmate support were also major contributors to global self-worth, followed by friend and teacher support. Harter expressed some surprise at the contribution of parent support in adolescents, who are generally believed to be gradually evolving to increasing reliance on peers and decreasing reliance on parents.

In college students, self-worth was a function of the individual's perceived competence in the areas that had become most important to him or her personally. As was the case with all age groups, athletic competence was not found to be a high-ranking contributor to most students' formation of global self-worth. This may seem to contradict Gruber's finding that we discussed earlier. However, we must distinguish between involvement in physical activity and athletic competence. While Gruber found physical activity to improve self-esteem significantly, Harter believes that athletic ability is a fairly low-ranking influence in global self-worth. "Physical activity" as examined by Gruber implies involvement in movement, whereas "athletic competence" implies a perceived level of success in competitive sporting activities. These are clearly distinguishable and, apparently, vastly different in the effect they exert on self-esteem.

Like all other groups, the young adult's global self-worth was most affected by physical appearance and social acceptance. These elements were followed by intimate relations and sociability. Intelligence and adequacy as a provider were also found to be important contributors in young adults. The two lowest elements of self-worth were household management and athletic ability.

In general, the developmental changes noted in self-worth include an inability to express a concept of global self-worth during early childhood. This ability evolves in midchildhood, however, as we see an increasing ability to articulate global self-worth as well as differentiate some of its elements. With age, we also see the changes in the nature of social relationships being reflected in the elements influencing global self-worth. For example, while peer acceptance and romantic appeal are important to the adolescent, intimate relations and nurturance are more highly valued by the adult.

Like Gruber, Harter believes findings relative to self-worth or self-esteem to be significant. She specifically notes the pervasive effect of self-worth on one's mood or affective state. Individuals with higher levels of self-worth are more cheerful and exude higher levels of energy, whereas low self-esteem has a depressing effect on behavior. No doubt, these mood alterations could have, at least, an indirect effect on motor development. Lack of desire to participate and subsequent lack of participation would inhibit the practice necessary to develop certain movement skills. In turn, successful attainment of certain levels of motor development likely has a reciprocal effect on self-concept. The feeling of accomplishment in movement or the simple act of participation, as illustrated by Gruber's research, can positively affect the self-concept.

SOCIAL INFLUENCES DURING INFANCY

The first year of life is often considered egocentric or asocial (Kaluger & Kaluger, 1984). Although the infant becomes increasingly social through that first year and on into adulthood, the baby's first few months of life involve only limited social interaction (see Figure 3-1). Because the baby totally relies on the caregiver(s), any social interactions at this time

Figure 3-1 Infants have very few social ties, but the strong family relationship created during infancy can significantly affect their motor development.

Digital Vision/Getty Images

depend on the caregiver's whims. Some social ties form early in infancy. One form of social attachment is the infant's attempts to maintain some form of contact with the object of the attachment, such as by visual exchange or through reciprocal touch. Another form of early attachment is the distress the baby often expresses when the object of the attachment leaves or is absent. A third form of early social attachment is the infant distinguishing and differentially responding to the caregiver (Thompson, 1998).

According to Newman and Newman (2003), the formation of social attachment occurs in four stages. These stages are particularly worthy of our examination because of movement's apparent role in facilitating the social attachment. According to these researchers, initially the infant grasps, sucks, roots, and performs numerous other infant reflexes. The infant also visually tracks, gazes, cries, and smiles in an effort to initiate and maintain close social contact with the object of attachment. These behaviors are all prominently involved in the social attachment process up to the age of approximately 3 months and are critical elements in the formation of the bond between the child and the caregiver.

For the next 3 months, the baby rapidly progresses in distinguishing between strangers and fa-

miliar human figures. In the third stage, from around 7 months to 2 years, the baby becomes increasingly adept at locomotion; this newfound ability enables the baby to actively seek close physical proximity with the object(s) of attachment (Thompson, 1998). In the fourth stage (Figure 3-2), the baby gradually learns to control the use of the arms and hands, allowing him or her to pursue and manually respond to social touches.

Thus the newly developing movement activities facilitate and expand social interaction; the increasing social sophistication promotes and stimulates greater motor activity. The expanded social repertoire allows the baby to be more actively involved with the environment, further enhancing motor abilities as well as intellectual and emotional behaviors.

SOCIAL INFLUENCES DURING CHILDHOOD

Although social interrelationships during infancy are limited because babies lack social, intellectual, and motor abilities, the social influences expand throughout childhood. Many specific forces contribute to the child's social development and, there-

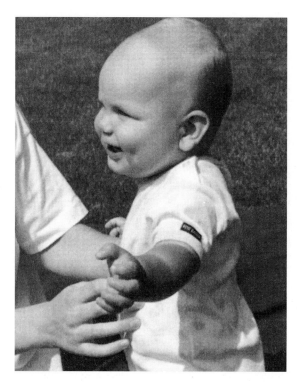

Figure 3-2 Gaining control of the arms and hands enables infants to respond manually to social touches.

Figure 3-3 Play is crucial to learning the rules of society and many skills critical to functioning in that society.

Keith Brofsky/Getty Images/Brand X Pictures

fore, motor development. The family, for example, is the primary socializing agency during childhood. Although the magnitude of the family's effect may be diminishing because of present cultural trends, the family still exerts more influence on a child than does any other force. Increased television viewing and the use of babysitters and preschools at earlier ages have lessened the impact of the family but have not overtaken this institution.

Play, whether done alone or in the presence of others, is also a major socializing force during childhood (see Figure 3-3). Pleasurable activity is considered important to the development of such skills as problem solving, creativity, language, and many movements in general.

Another major socializing agent, although generally not a factor until the child is 4 or 5, is the school, where teachers and coaches play an im-

mediate role in the child's "learning of the culture." In fact, the school can overtake the family as the major socializing agency as the child approaches adolescence. The school also allows the establishment of a peer group, which can be a tremendous influence on the socialization process. Children's relationships with peer groups become increasingly important as they approach their adolescent years.

Play

The term **play** is commonly associated with children. People of all ages engage in play, but the word often inspires images of children engaged in some pleasurable, generally movement-oriented activity. Garvey (1990) describes play as an activity that is always pleasurable and that the participant always cherishes. Furthermore, the motivation to play is intrinsic—play has no other objective. According to Garvey, play is inherently unproductive, spontaneous, and voluntary. Another important element of play is that it involves active participation by the player and "has systematic relations to what is not play." In other words, this seemingly insignificant act is actually a crucial part of learning the rules of society as well as many skills critical to functioning in that society.

The effect of play on overall child development was demonstrated in a study of 30 children from an orphanage in India. The children, ranging in age from 65 months to 2½ years, were assessed for motor, mental, and physical characteristics as well as social maturity. They were then exposed to a "structured," daily play program that was incorporated into the routine of the orphanage. After three months, all children were reassessed to determine the impact of the play program. Children improved in their motor, mental, physical, and social maturity measures, and the overall environment in the orphanage was believed to have improved as the children increased their activity levels, were more playful, and even became more independent. As children became more responsive, the workload of the attendants dropped. In general, in settings like this, child development can be positively affected by daily play sessions (Taneja et al., 2002).

This notion was supported in a 2003 Clinical Report of the American Academy of Pediatrics (AAP), which said play was an "essential" element in a child's learning. Generally, parents and guardians are the ones who create or mold the play experiences for very young children. Often, this is done with the help of toys. According to the AAP, toys should be carefully selected, because they can be so instrumental in the child's development. Though toys can provide a nice supplement to the parent–child interaction leading up to or within play, they should never substitute for warm, caring, loving attention from the parent or caregiver. The right toy, however, can create a bond between the child and the caregiver by creating a means for more social interaction. These relationships are instrumental in early brain development, mastery of play activities, self-esteem, and the development of play-related skills (AAP, 2003).

Play is often based on movement. When movement, such as running, jumping, or even clapping or laughing, is involved, the pleasurable aspects of play are most clearly visible. In fact, one of children's first forms of amusement may involve being jostled or hoisted by the caregiver. Gradually, children become more involved with other children and expand their play experiences. Group play becomes particularly evident at early school age. However, play appears to evolve through a series of increasingly more social stages before it reaches a point of group involvement. According to Cratty (1986), play remains rather unsocial for young children even when social opportunities exist. When children are between 24 and 30 months old, their most common type of play is often solitary. Two children playing side by side pay little attention to each other and make few, if any, attempts at social interaction. They are generally so engrossed in their own activity that their companion's activity is of minimal consequence. This behavior soon evolves into what is known as parallel play. By the time children are 2½ to 3½ years old, they will still make few attempts to socially interact, but they may begin to display an awareness of each other and may even subtly copy each other's play behavior through observation and imitation. Nevertheless, the children are not likely to interact to any greater extent.

Approximately 1 year later, when they are 3½ to 4½ years old, children will begin to display the interaction missing in their previous levels of play behavior. When involved in associative play, two or more children exhibit an awareness of each other and begin to exchange toys; however, there is no group goal. This lack of a group goal is the major difference between associative play and the final level of play during early childhood, cooperative play. Cooperative play generally occurs when children are around 4½ to 5 years old and is evidenced by purposeful, group-oriented play activities involving games and even group leaders.

As a function of cooperative play, larger social units are formed. The movement activities selected for use within the larger group enable children to develop leadership skills as well as learn to compete, cooperate, and form a sense of need for greater social recognition. As children's social skills develop, group activities become more attractive and are more commonly sought out. Increased participation in popular group movement activities subsequently facilitates a child's motor development. Thus a positive, reciprocal relationship can develop between social and motor development; in fact, to a surprising extent, one form of development may depend on the other. Even at the young age of 5 or 6 years, group leaders are likely to be those who are superior in performing such physical activities as running, throwing, and balancing (Cratty, 1986). This is an expected phenomenon during early to late adolescence, but such a relationship between movement and social success is surprising at such a young age.

Family

As mentioned, the family is the most important socializing force in the lives of most children. The family is also the earliest and, in most cases, greatest determinant of a child's movement choices and movement success, because it strongly influences the child's attitudes and expectations about movement. Furthermore, the family is largely responsible for the role that children envision for themselves. Depending on the family's views concerning physical activity, a child may or may not assume a role that is movement related. In fact, a child can even acquire many movement characteristics that are reminiscent of those of the parent. The parent of the same sex as the child has the greatest influence on such movement acquisition, although both parents remarkably prevail in shaping the child's movement idiosyncrasies involving, for example, gesture, gait, or posture (see Figure 3-4). The child can acquire these movement habits from

Figure 3-4 Although both parents help shape a child's movement repertoire, the same-sex parent is often the more influential.

Keith Brofsky/Getty Images/Brand X Pictures

long-term observation of the caregiver (Birdwhistell, 1960).

In a study on the determinants of exercise among children, DiLorenzo and associates (1998) sought to identify the social factors that affected children's likelihood of being physically active. Over 100 families were studied, with data being drawn from mothers, fathers, and fifth- and sixth-grade male and female children of these parents. Major predictors for involvement in exercise differed for boys and girls. Major predictors for girls tended to be their own knowledge about exercise, their mother's physical activity level, and the child's social support. For boys, their own self-efficacy (feeling capable of being successful) in physical activity, enjoyment of physical activity, and interest in sport media were important factors. Generally, these researchers concluded that socialization within the family exerted a "tremendous influence" on participation in physical activity (DiLorenzo et al., 1998).

As discussed, the family's approval or disapproval of the child's movement endeavors is also crucial in determining future movement habits. If the child behaves motorically in a way that is rewarded, either overtly or subtly, he or she is likely to reproduce that movement behavior. However, ignoring the child's motor behavior or responding negatively may cause the behavior to subside. The family therefore can consciously or subconsciously shape their children's movement behavior and become one of the most potent of socializing institutions.

Greendorfer and Lewko (1978) studied the specific role of family members in their children's sport socialization. In this research, 95 children 8 to 13 years old were surveyed. Greendorfer and Lewko conclude that sport socialization begins during childhood and continues into adolescence. They further state that the role of certain family members is significant in this socialization process. Specifically, parents were found to significantly influence the child's involvement in sport activities. Siblings, however, were not found to have a particularly critical effect on either boys' or girls' choices concerning involvement in sports. Also, the father is an important predictor of sport selections for both boys and girls. Generally, however, boys receive greater exposure to more sport socializing agents than do girls, and such agents tend to encourage boys more than girls to participate. This fact was particularly evidenced by the finding that the father, the peers, and the teacher were all significant influences for the boys, whereas only the peers and the father significantly influenced the girls. More generally, this research substantiates the traditional view that boys have had more opportunity for socialization into sport and that gender differentiation does exist in this area.

The importance of the family is further reinforced by Greendorfer and Ewing's (1981) investi-gation. These researchers agree that the family can be an important predictor of involvement in sports. However, Greendorfer and Ewing also found that this process of socialization can affect children differently, depending on the children's race and gender. The researchers particularly emphasize these two factors in their paper "Race and Gender Differences in Children's Socialization into Sport" (1981). To examine these factors, Greendorfer and Ewing distributed questionnaires to hundreds of children, male and female, African American and white, from 9 to 12 years old. The questionnaires were designed to determine what factors influenced children's decisions to become involved in sport activities. Based on an analysis of the results, these researchers determined that children of different genders and of different races socialized into sports differently. Among white children, boys were more influenced by their peers and their fathers; the greatest influences for girls were their teachers and their mothers. Among African American children, the boys were most greatly influenced by their peers; the girls were more likely to be influenced by their teachers or sisters. These findings somewhat contradicted Greendorfer and Lewko's findings that girls were not significantly influenced by their teachers or their sisters. That apparent contradiction may, however, add support to Greendorfer and Ewing's (1981) final conclusion that a great deal of variability occurs in the ways that children are introduced to games and sports.

Based on the research discussed to this point, the family is obviously integral in the sport socialization process. A child's decision to participate in movement activities and the kinds of activities selected appear to be important functions of the family. The role of the family may have other motor-related ramifications as well. Lee (1980) examined the effects of child-rearing practices on the motor performance of both African American and white children. Lee studied lower socioeconomic children from both races. The children ranged from slightly over 7 years to approximately 9½ years and were grouped according to their mothers' attitudes

Figure 3-5 As a child approaches adolescence, the peer group usually emerges as a powerful force in life.

Digital Vision/Getty Images

concerning child rearing. The children's mothers were categorized as authoritarian or nonauthoritarian based on the results of a specially designed inventory. According to Lee, authoritarianism is associated with the parent's demand for obedience and the firm enforcement of the parent's expectations of the child. The nonauthoritarian mothers were more likely to exhibit permissiveness and grant their children independence. From this research, Lee determined that the children reared by the nonauthoritarian mothers had superior jumping and running skills. Lee concludes from such findings that the nonrestrictive environment may be a more ideal setting for a child's motor development because increased independence may enhance his or her opportunity to be physically active. Furthermore, Lee states that she found the more permissive, free atmosphere more likely to be present in lower socioeconomic areas common to many African American children. Lee postulates that this atmosphere and its resulting independence are why the African American children in this research performed the motor tasks significantly better than the white children.

SOCIAL INFLUENCES DURING OLDER CHILDHOOD AND ADOLESCENCE

As the child approaches adolescence, the family's influence generally begins to diminish and the peer group becomes an increasingly important social force. The parent, teacher, and other adults in the child's life slowly lose their power of persuasion over the child as a need for peer approval becomes particularly powerful. This new social force, the **peer group,** is less structured than adult social groups but considerably more structured than the groups in the child's previous social environment (see Figure 3-5). The peer group is also characterized by its transitory nature because it may vary from the neighborhood to the school as well as from day to day. It also has the capability of shaping the mode of children's dress, speech, or actions and their decisions concerning participation in movement activities. For example, members of the same peer group may often share similar gait or speech patterns (Bandura & Kupers, 1964). Furthermore, the relationships created in the peer group give the child or young adolescent friendship, support, companionship, and fun in ways that could not be achieved with the family. Peers strongly influence each other by interacting as equals, a situation unique from the family structure, which generally has a primary authority figure. The peer group therefore often has a strong influence on decisions older children or adolescents make concerning involvement in movement activities.

This gradually evolving independence from the family enables children to shed the egocentrism so common during their earlier childhood. A person's daily interaction with peers also provides considerable learning experiences. For example, youngsters develop an increasing appreciation of many points of view, because members of the same peer group often express diverse opinions. Additionally, young adolescents become increasingly aware of social norms and pressures. In fact, adolescents' social acceptability may be based on how they conform to the expectations of their social group. Two of the most common determinants of social acceptability, particularly for boys, are athletic ability and willingness to become involved in athletically oriented activities. Other determinants of social acceptability, as defined by the peer group, are appearance, academic achievement, career expectations, ethnicity, and special talents. Many of these characteristics, such as appearance and special talents, may, again, reflect the extent to which the person is involved in a movement endeavor. These characteristics are not, however, generally announced as qualifiers for status in a particular peer group, but such consistent standards are frequently used to include and exclude members.

As mentioned, movement ability partly determines peer group association but can also be molded within the group. Association with new and diverse opinions may promote participation in new versions of old games or completely new and different attempts at previously untried movement endeavors. The peer group applies pressure toward conformity, although the type of conformity varies tremendously from one peer group to another. However, if the peers consider participation in movement activities an accepted norm for their group, they pressure the members to be active in that pursuit. Gaining respect and approval becomes increasingly important to members of the peer group and depends on their adherence to the group's expectations. This often means that the peer group guides the individual into, or away from, participation, and perhaps achievement, in an athletic activity.

Research has indicated that adolescent girls are particularly at risk for physical inactivity and resultant factors, such as obesity. Thus, researchers have tried to determine the barriers that prevent young girls from being more active. For example, Robbins, Pender, and Kazanis (2003) studied an ethnically diverse sample of adolescent girls, aged 11–14 years. The girls were surveyed to determine what they thought were the most significant barriers to their participation in physical activities. The most important factors included feeling self-conscious when engaged in exercise and a lack of motivation. This led the researchers to conclude that new strategies need to be formulated to help these girls improve motivation, reduce self-consciousness, and overcome the barriers to exercise (Robbins et al., 2003).

A similar study sought to identify factors that lead to changes in patterns of physical activity among adolescent girls. Over 200 high school girls participated. The two strongest predictors of changes in physical activity were limited amount of time and support from their social circle, including friends, teachers, and parents. As expected, too little time was expected to decrease levels of participation while support from the social support group was expected to increase it. Like the research conducted by Robbins and colleagues (2003), this study concluded that interventions designed to increase physical activity among adolescent girls should include programs to increase social support while addressing time constraints in the lives of young girls. Improving the confidence level of young girls in physical activity was also seen as a critical factor (Neumark-Sztainer et al., 2003).

Team Play

During later childhood and adolescence, youngsters encounter an increasing sense of team or club participation. This factor is particularly important

Figure 3-6 Team play teaches the value of co-operative efforts to achieve group goals, an important lesson for children who may still be overcoming their childhood egocentrism.

Digital Vision/Getty Images

for influencing the types of movement activities the older children or young adolescents may select. Whereas during earlier childhood youngsters are content to play alone or in a small group, the emphasis changes as children approach adolescence. Because of increasing social capabilities and their relationship with the peer group, adolescents often actively seek group or team activities. Those who do decide to participate in a team movement experience devote much energy to trying to ensure the team's success (Newman & Newman, 2003).

Movement participation through team membership can greatly affect children's or adolescents' development. Through team participation, youngsters learn to work toward achieving group or team goals while subordinating personal goals, a major developmental stride for children who may still be overcoming the egocentrism so prevalent earlier in their lives (see Figure 3-6). The team concept also teaches children the importance of the division of labor. Gradually, youngsters learn that every

member of the team has a duty and a responsibility and that the team's goals are most likely to be accomplished through sharing these duties and responsibilities. Also, team membership often makes greater intellectual demands than do the more unstructured group or individual activities of young childhood. More rules, strategies, and responsibilities tend to occur in team activities than in childhood group play.

In team play, the youngster also assumes greater social responsibilities. If people do not carry out their assigned duties, they may be ostracized or ridiculed. On the other hand, tremendous individual recognition is possible for those who are particularly successful in carrying out their duty to the team. Ideally, the more proficient participants should, and often do, assist the less capable, which is to the team's advantage. However, too frequently the less capable are scorned and their inability to perform is blamed for the team's failure.

Although it is unpleasant to think of a child or young adolescent boy scorned or ostracized in team play, in many ways the team is a model for life in general. In one respect, team participation teaches the child about failure and success as well as such common emotions as shame and embarrassment. For more successful participants, team play is an avenue for expressing humility or modesty. Experiencing these emotions personally and witnessing them in others is an important lesson that may help youngsters deal with more difficult situations later in life.

Gender Role Identification and Movement Activity

In addition to all the functions discussed previously, the peer group serves another critical developmental purpose: It facilitates interaction with the opposite gender. Adolescence is when dating generally begins, and gender roles become increasingly apparent. The degree to which adolescents identify with the role ascribed to their gender depends on several factors. The peer group influences the level at which young adolescents may identify with their gender, but *gender role identity* begins much earlier in life. The expectations for behaviors based on gender start early in childhood and often depend on the quality of a child's association with the parent of the same sex.

Even though many behaviors once commonly accepted for only one gender are now acceptable for both, many human characteristics are still considered masculine or feminine. For example, 50 percent of college students asked to describe the ideal sex role for children in their care responded by citing dominance, aggressiveness, achievement for boys, and deference, nurturance, abasement for girls (Hamilton, 1977). Similarly, Michael (1970) states that aggressive behavior is acceptable in boys and men. In fact, they may be scorned if they are excessively dependent, whereas the opposite is true for girls and women. This gender typing often produces rigid concepts regarding individuals' abilities and behaviors and no doubt affects decisions concerning their involvement in movement activity. Gender role conflict is often experienced by girls who seek

to participate and boys who do not. Unfortunately, both cases can lead to emotional distress and limit potential by inhibiting the development of self-selected talents and skills (Oglesby & Hill, 1993).

Gender stereotypes can have major implications in an adolescent's decision to participate in a movement activity. The activity may seem enticing, but the gender role associated with that activity may conflict with the role adolescents deem appropriate for themselves. If an adolescent decides to participate anyway, a *role conflict* may be created. That is, an emotional trauma of varying proportions may evolve concerning the sex role that the adolescent considers appropriate versus the sex role that the relevant society views as appropriate.

The negative sentiment expressed by society concerning girls and women in physical activity and sport may also affect the *attribution* of the participant. Girls and women tend to attribute positive performances to external sources and negative performances to internal ones. Boys and men attribute their positive performances to internal sources, demonstrating greater self-appreciation. According to Eccles and Harold (1991), these findings may be linked to the social view that women are unsuited for success in sports.

Anthrop and Allison (1983) examined this phenomenon. They assessed the level of role conflict in female high school athletes via their questionnaire, which they administered to 133 female high school athletes. One half of the athletes surveyed cited little or no role conflict; 32 percent cited little problem with role conflict; 17 percent believed they had a great problem with role conflict. The authors state that although they believe games are critical to the total socialization process and help people learn gender roles, the games are predominantly masculine. In other words, participation for boys and men is regarded as positive, whereas female participation can more frequently cause gender role conflict. Anthrop and Allison say this is a function of a so-called *Victorian influence,* whereby sports are perceived as potentially dangerous, particularly for "the female," who is considered more delicate and thus prone to impeding her childbearing capabilities. Should the female impair her ability to bear children, she would greatly decrease her attractiveness to men. This belief, although not as prevalent today, continues to exist, according to Anthrop and Allison.

From a social standpoint, however, male involvement in a movement activity is more likely to be an exclusively positive undertaking. The stereotypical male characteristics of aggression, toughness, dominance, and strength are further reinforced by lively male involvement in many movement activities. Thus, whereas a girl's participation may cause slight to severe role conflict, a boy normally avoids the emotional strife of role conflict. The girl who experiences role conflict through participation in sport can attempt to ignore the expectations of others or abandon her sport-oriented role. This problem, which Anthrop and Allison (1983) describe as being particularly discouraging for girls involved in non-socially accepted sports, is actually less widespread than hypothesized. Anthrop and Allison suggest the possibility, however, that the relatively low levels of "great or very great problems" with role conflict may be due to an aversion to sports by those who anticipated the role conflict. Or, perhaps others who suffered role conflict had already ceased participation.

Ostrow, Jones, and Spiker (1981) performed similar research to determine if there were role expectations for 12 selected sporting activities. In this research, 93 subjects completed an activity appropriateness scale and a sex role inventory. From an analysis of the completed surveys, the researchers determined that boys are more easily socialized than girls into sport activities for two reasons. First, the relatively small number of female role models is believed to reduce the number of female participants. Second, of the 12 sports examined in this research, 10 were considered to be "masculine." The authors assume that this reduced the likelihood of female participation, because the level of role conflict, discussed earlier, would likely be elevated for many female participants. Only ballet and figure skating were deemed more appropriate for female participants.

The stigma concerning women's role in sports may be declining. Title IX, a 1972 federal mandate designed to reduce gender discrimination in education, equalized the number of athletic and physical education programs for boys and girls. This mandate has greatly increased the number and quality of programs available to female participants in the United States (Anthrop & Allison, 1983). Before 1972, girls were not allowed to participate during their school years; now they are. In fact, in 1972 only 7 percent of all high school athletes were female; more recent evidence shows that number to be 35 percent. Additionally, the number of college athletic scholarships available to women has increased nearly 10 times from the 1972 level of 16,000 (*NEA Today,* 1985, p. 10). The opportunities for girls and women to participate in a higher level of movement activity have increased, and presumably this increase has subsequently enhanced the likelihood of women and girls achieving a higher level of motor performance in an athletic endeavor.

SOCIAL FACTORS OF ADULTHOOD

Adulthood begins when adolescence ends. Although experts disagree about the actual time of the onset of adulthood, as discussed in Chapter 1, we are assuming that adulthood begins at age 20. Unfortunately, as we age during adulthood, our involvement in movement activities or sports begins to decline. In fact, in research conducted by Rudman (1984), age was the prime determinant of sport involvement when compared with social class, level of education, and income. This age effect was also found to be most powerful in team sports, as older individuals were more likely to continue participation in individual sports.

At adulthood, three major social factors affecting human movement have their greatest negative impact on adult motor behavior, significantly affecting lifestyles and generally contributing to a tendency toward decreased participation in movement activity. These social forces are leaving school/going to work, taking a companion with the intent of a permanent relationship (usually marriage), and having children.

Brown and Trost (2003) studied this phenomenon in over 7,000 young adult women (late teens and early 20s) to determine the effects of key events in their lives on their physical activity levels. The participants self-reported their physical activity and life events during the time of involvement, body mass index, and sociodemographic information. For many of these young women, no change was found in physical activity levels across the 4 years of participation in the study. Nevertheless, even though only 4 years of early adulthood were examined, nearly 20 percent of the participants moved from being physically active to physically inactive. These participants were most likely to have also reported getting married, having a first or subsequent child, or beginning paid work. The researchers concluded that these life events are associated with decreased levels of physical activity in young women. Thus, programs and ideas are needed to promote physical activity during this time of life when women most often experience such important life events (Brown & Trost, 2003).

Many people experience all of these key factors early in adulthood. However, there is a trend toward postponing marriage and starting a family, or not marrying at all. According to U.S. Department of Commerce data (1975, 1983, 1992, 2003), the number of men and women choosing to marry decreased significantly between 1960 and 2000. In 1960, 69 percent of men and 66 percent of women were married. That number decreased gradually through 1990, when 57 percent of men and 52 percent of women were married. By 2000, only a slightly larger percentage of women were choosing to marry. As illustrated by Table 3-2, a substantial decrease in married people was noted between 1970 and 1980, and the percentage gradually declined after that. For many, this trend will avert the negative effects marriage often has on an individual's level of physical activity and, subsequently, his or her overall motor behavior.

Table 3-2   Percentage of Married Men and Women in the United States Since 1960

	Men	Women
2000	57	53
1990	57	52
1980	59	54
1970	66	61
1960	69	66

SOURCE: U.S. Department of Commerce (1975, 1983, 1992, 2003).

Once an individual begins regular employment, marries or takes a relatively permanent companion, and/or has children, the tendency for physiological regression and its ensuing decline in motor performance increases greatly. For example, strength, cardiorespiratory endurance, and flexibility may all begin to decrease. This decline is much more difficult to predict than many of the motor changes that occur in children or adolescents, because there is much greater individual variability among adults (Kausler, 1982). Thus, although a decline in motor performance usually occurs when a person experiences the three major social factors, some individuals may actually improve. If an individual can overcome the normally prevailing social forces by staying involved in movement activities, the person can decrease the rate of the regression. In fact, adults can progress in movement endeavors until much later in life if they continue to participate in those activities regularly. Unfortunately, though, these social factors commonly mark the onset of a regression in motor development that will extend throughout the remainder of the lifespan.

The reasons why these factors stabilize or regress motor development are somewhat controversial. For example, although occasionally a moderately active person marries an exceptionally active person and is motivated to increase involvement in movement pursuits, this is not the norm. Typically, both partners are compelled to reduce activity levels as they become increasingly satisfied with staying at home in the company of each other. This negative effect is particularly strong between ages 18 and 34 (Rudman, 1984). This increasing inactivity causes a decline in fitness levels and a subsequent plateauing or regression in motor development.

Many people believe that having children, for example, increases parents' overall level of activity, but generally this is not the case. Initially, having children may induce fatigue or even exhaustion because of the lack of sleep, the new responsibilities, and the rearrangement of the schedule. The children also reduce the parents' freedom or spontaneity, which enabled them to participate in movement activities more regularly. Even if the parents had not been regular participants in some movement endeavor, their lifestyle becomes much more restricted and sedentary, which leads to the aforementioned decline in the physiological abilities, causing a subsequent decline in motor ability. We must recognize, however, that having children may occasionally have the reverse effect. Having children may have a strong positive influence on parents' participation in certain sports between ages 35 and 54. This is particularly true of such sports as football, which tend to be more "family oriented" (Rudman, 1984).

For most people, beginning full-time employment, depending on the type of employment, produces similar long-term effects. Work ordinarily creates a relatively permanent lifestyle change by structuring or limiting the time a person has for participation in the activities that were once a regular source of recreational pleasure. Furthermore, the worker normally has few coworkers with similar movement interests. Unless the worker participates alone in the movement or has friends with the same interest outside the workplace, he or she may decrease or discontinue an activity. This situation contrasts considerably to school, where the person was surrounded by same-age peers with similar interests. Leaving school therefore often decreases the number of available people with whom one can interact socially in a movement activity. A high school student can easily locate nine friends for a basketball game, but an adult may have a difficult time finding one partner for racquetball.

Social Learning and Ageism

The three major factors just discussed critically affect motor development early in adulthood. These factors, however, are not the only social elements that inhibit the level of involvement in active movement over the remainder of the lifespan. **Social learning** is the act of acquiring new behaviors by modeling the actions of others (K. S. Berger, 2001).

Although this type of learning is important for motor development throughout the lifespan, it is often expected to occur only in childhood and adolescence. Actually, social roles and expectations are learned in adulthood, just as they are earlier. These roles and expectations arise from the common beliefs that members of a group or a society jointly hold (Colarusso & Nemiroff, 1981). If the adult does not conform to such expectations, a role conflict may result. One such conflict may concern the adult's attempt at maintaining an active lifestyle. The individual may be well aware of the need to continue vigorous movement to avoid regression both motorically and physiologically, but society expects adults to become increasingly sedentary with age. In fact, society is often exceptionally protective of the older adult.

Ostrow, Jones, and Spiker (1981) address this issue. From their research, they have determined that age barriers "blatantly exist" concerning societal expectations toward active participation in adulthood. They also found that the subjects surveyed deemed participation in the 12 sports included in the investigation decreasingly appropriate as one ages. The degree of appropriateness, as determined by the respondents, decreased as the adult aged from 20 years to 80 years for such movement activities as swimming, jogging, tennis, and basketball. The only exception was bowling, which was considered as appropriate at 40 as at 20. Ostrow and colleagues have determined that this stereotyping based on age is "much more severe than sex stereotyping" concerning the appropriateness of these sports. Furthermore, this severe stereotyping no doubt contributes greatly to the "disengagement" from movement activity.

The findings of Ostrow and associates (1981) are somewhat substantiated by a recent article on age grading. **Age grading** is the idea of determining the level of perceived appropriateness of certain age groups being involved in movement activity.

Unfortunately, stereotypes concerning the aged in the United States are often negative to the extent that they can be referred to as **ageism.** Ageism is based on a person's relatively old age rather than race or gender. Like racism or sexism, ageism can lead to discrimination that can become so severe that some members of society avoid or exclude the older adult. Ageism may indicate society's aversion to the aging process and subsequent death of older adults. This form of discrimination obviously inhibits the older adult's attempts at becoming an active participant in society. Many older adults are "forced" into a life of inactivity despite attempts to interact; as a result, their movement capabilities as well as many other behaviors continue to regress.

Figure 3-7   Retirement often frees individuals for active pursuit of movement activities; unfortunately, active movement after retirement frequently decreases.

PhotoLink/Getty Images/PhotoDisc

Other Social Situations Likely to Affect Motor Development

Besides leaving school/going to work, marriage, and parenthood, many other conditions, usually occurring in middle to late adulthood, also significantly create a relatively permanent change in motor behavior. This change is normally a regression, but in less typical cases, depending on the individual involved, there may be a reestablishment of interest in a movement, which could lead to an improvement of the movement status. Three of the most important of these situations are the children leaving home, retirement, and the death of a spouse.

When children leave home, many people think the parents are now "liberated" to pursue their own personal interests and activities, which may have been repressed in favor of the children's interests. Indeed, some parents actually do rediscover movement activity, which of course benefits their movement in general. However, the norm is actually a tendency toward a more inactive lifestyle. The children's presence at home has a somewhat positive effect on the parents in that it helps keep them at least minimally

active. In addition, a child's departure is a reminder that the parents are no longer youthful. As mentioned earlier, our society generally expects the older adult to avoid movement activity. When this expectation is coupled with the emotional crisis of a child leaving home, the likelihood of a more sedentary lifestyle is enhanced.

Retirement can have a similar effect. Today more people are living past age 65 than ever before, which means that more retirees will go through what will become a major shift in their life cycle. Retirement begins a period of leisure that has the potential for giving the retiree time to pursue movement endeavors (see Figure 3-7).

Research conducted by Kelly and Wescott (1991) found that most retirees are quite content with their retirement. In particular, they enjoy their new "freedom" and leisure time. More specifically, Atchley (1989) found that a positive retirement is a function of at least four major conditions: the retirement was unforced, the work experience was not the most important aspect of the individual's life, the retiree's health and financial condition was sufficient to enjoy the free time, and adequate planning and preparation had occurred for and prior to the retirement.

Unfortunately, retirement too frequently marks a significant decline in standard of living, causing financial, transportational, and even nutritional problems. Retirees may also lose their social status and sense of usefulness. Furthermore, retirement may bring the first realization that an individual has reached "old age," which can be an emotional trauma leading to depression and inactivity. As a result of these sentiments and social considerations related to retirement, older adults may not be sufficiently motivated or capable of seeking the movement activity that their leisure time would allow; the increased or continued inactivity in turn contributes to the individual's regression in motor development.

If they live long enough, most Americans will experience retirement and its accompanying social implications. If married, they may also experience the death of their spouse. This tragic experience usually causes depression and involves a long period of mourning; both factors contribute to the decrease in overall activity level. Generally, this experience occurs during late adulthood. After retirement, the loss of a spouse can have a particularly grave impact, because the bond between the two companions increases as they begin to spend more time together. Therefore, at a time when individuals might find the emotionally uplifting effects of movement activity especially beneficial, they are most likely to withdraw from such exploits.

Four other, more general, social problems associated with aging deserve examination, because their ramifications pervade all areas of human behavior, including movement. These problems, all of which become increasingly severe with age, involve income, transportation, health, and nutrition. Many other considerations could be added to this list, but these factors are among the most critical for older persons, especially as related to their attempts at being active participants in society.

Retirement may impede the financial status of retirees. Whereas they once had a regular income from employment, retirees now have to rely on Social Security and/or pension payments. Opponents of the Social Security program argue that it provides too little financial assistance to enable older adults to live satisfactory lifestyles. In many cases, the postretirement years are a struggle for economic survival. Minority groups suffer the consequences of poverty in old age more severely than do nonminority older adults. But no matter what the retirees' ethnic background or gender, a poor economic condition can lead to severe emotional trauma that, as discussed earlier, may indirectly affect individuals' desire or ability to become involved in movement activities. The resultant lack of movement facilitates the physiological and subsequent motor decline generally associated with aging. In other words, a vicious cycle is created: As older adults are less active, they become less able to be active.

The financial struggle that frequently accompanies retirement is the basis of a series of associated problems. Insufficient finances often impede individuals' ability to acquire transportation. If retirees have cars, maintaining the automobile in satisfactory condition becomes an additional burden. Other forms of travel, such as taxi or bus, may be too costly or cumbersome for an older person. Fortunately, many communities provide transportation, but where it is unavailable or unknown, the likelihood of retirees actively interacting with society decreases, which increases the level of disengagement and causes older adults to finish their lives in a sedentary, depressed, and lonely fashion.

Decreased finances and transportation may also have nutritional ramifications. Without sufficient money and transportation, older adults may find buying food a significant burden, so rather than shop, they may attempt to go without proper nourishment. A poor diet obviously affects an individual's ability to engage with society and in fact may cause serious health problems that further devastate the older adult's attempts at staying active. The isolation that indirectly results from lack of funds, transportation, and nutrition also creates an attitude that impedes any desire on the part of the adult to participate in movement activities. This lack of participation contributes to the gradual decline in overall motor function that begins at the onset of early adulthood.

THE EXERCISE-AGING CYCLE

As indicated in the previous section, a number of sociocultural factors contribute to the declining levels of physical activity and fitness that often occur across adulthood. Foremost among these is the phenomenon of ageism discussed earlier. Ageism contributes to increasingly undesirable views of people as they age. Too often older individuals are inaccurately labeled as being poor, frail, unhealthy, forgetful, and physically incapable. As illustrated by the poem "The Little Boy and the Old Man," we often treat older adults like children because of our reduced expectations for their capabilities.

THE LITTLE BOY AND THE OLD MAN

By

Shel Silverstein

Said the little boy, "Sometimes I drop my spoon."
Said the little old man, "I do that too."
The little boy whispered, "I wet my pants."
"I do that too," laughed the little old man.
Said the little boy, "I often cry."
The old man nodded, "So do I."
"But worst of all," said the boy, "it seems
Grown-ups don't pay attention to me."
And he felt the warmth of a wrinkled old hand.
"I know what you mean," said the little old man.

SOURCE: Reprinted with permission of HarperCollins Publishers from Silverstein, S. (1981). *A light in the attic.* New York: Harper & Row, p. 95. Copyright © 1981 Evil Eye Music, Inc.

Thus, the prevalent attitude that physical activity becomes less appropriate the older we become is not surprising. These attitudes commonly begin as early as preschool and continue through older adulthood. This notion, known as age grading for exercise, is an obvious deterrent to exercise for adults as they begin to believe the societal attitudes, leading to what may become a self-fulfilling prophecy (B. G. Berger & Hecht, 1989; B. G. Berger & McInman, 1993). When the negative attitudes concerning adulthood and involvement in physical activity are coupled with the growing responsibilities and lifestyles of adulthood, the pursuit of physical activity may become a very low priority. Increasing work and family responsibilities are perceived as limiting time for "frivolous" endeavors like exercise. Particularly "at risk" are young adult working women with children who may find they have very little time to themselves. Later in adulthood, factors like retirement and the corresponding decrease in financial status and transportation inhibit efforts to be active. The combination of these factors creates a sense of diminished self-expectancy, a low valuation of exercise, and few physically active role models. Many adults may have become so poorly skilled that physical activity is perceived as being embarrassing.

Figures from *Healthy People 2010* (*Healthy people 2010,* 2002) support the idea that few adults receive adequate physical activity. Only 15 percent of adults performed the recommended amount of physical activity, and 40 percent participated in no leisure time physical activity at all! The report also found that 23 percent of adults over 20 in the United States were obese. This condition was found to be more common among Mexican American and African American women than white women. In addition, by age 75, a third of all men and half of all women did not engage in any regular physical activity. Thus, a cycle appears to exist—the older we get, the less active we become (*Healthy people 2010,* 2002).

This cycle, called the ***exercise-aging cycle*** (see Figure 3-8), illustrates the trend that normally occurs. Early in adulthood, in part because of the factors discussed earlier, we tend to gradually disengage from physical activities. As a result of this disengagement, physical changes become apparent. For example, our physical ability declines, fat levels increase, muscular atrophy occurs, and energy declines. We then begin to feel "old" and "act our age." Stress levels and depression increase, and

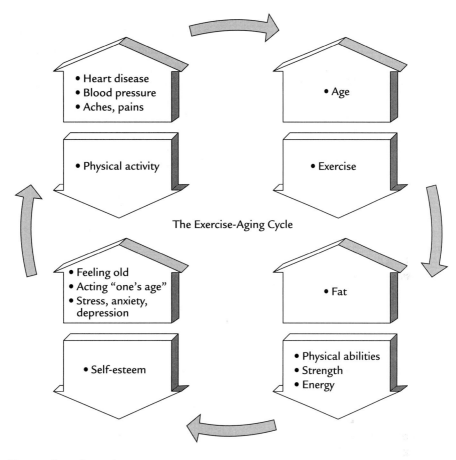

Figure 3-8 The exercise-aging cycle
SOURCE: Berger and Hecht (1989).

self-esteem declines. All of these factors further decrease our interest in being physically active. In turn, the cycle becomes even more severe (B. G. Berger & Hecht, 1989; B. G. Berger & McInman, 1993). This is not to suggest that sociocultural phenomena are exclusively responsible for a decline in physical ability. However, according to B. G. Berger and McInman (1993), as much as 50 percent of the decline associated with aging may actually be related to a phenomenon known as disuse atrophy rather than the process of aging. ***Disuse atrophy*** is a wasting away of muscle mass that is the direct result of physical inactivity. See Table 3-3 for numer-

ous examples of physiological and functional changes with age.

AVOIDING THE EXERCISE-AGING CYCLE

The exercise-aging cycle discussed in the previous section is all too common in today's society. However, one's depth of involvement in this cycle is often largely a matter of lifestyle. Though the effects of aging cannot be completely overcome, choosing to engage in an appropriate level of physical activity

Table 3-3   Physiological and Functional Changes Associated with Aging

	Decreases	Increases
Cardiovascular	Cardiac output Maximum heart rate HDL cholesterol	Systolic and diastolic blood pressures Total cholesterol Vascular resistance
Respiratory	Vital capacity Chest wall compliance Maximum ventilation Alveolar size	Functional residual capacity
Musculoskeletal	Muscle mass Elasticity in connective tissue Synovial fluid viscosity Muscle fiber length	Osteoporosis
Central nervous system	Nerve conduction Number of neurons Motor responses Brain mass	

SOURCE: Reproduced with permission from Barry, H. C., Rich, B. S. E., and Carlson, R. T. (1993). How exercise can benefit older patients: A practical approach. *The Physician and Sports Medicine, 21*(2) 124–140. Copyright © 1993 The McGraw-Hill Companies. All rights reserved.

Table 3-4   Some Functional Adaptations to Exercise in Frail Elderly Patients

	Increases	Decreases
Cardiovascular	Work capacity HDL cholesterol Maximum oxygen capacity	Resting heart rate Total cholesterol Blood pressure
Respiratory	Minute ventilation Vital capacity	
Musculoskeletal	Bone density Flexibility Muscle tone and strength Coordination	
Miscellaneous	Mental outlook Socialization Fat and carbohydrate metabolism Insulin receptor sensitivity Plasma volume Maintenance of lean body mass Weight control Metabolic rate	Loneliness Idle time Anxiety Symptoms of depression Appetite

SOURCE: Reproduced with permission and adapted from Barry, H. C., Rich, B. S. E., and Carlson, R. T. (1993). How exercise can benefit older patients: A practical approach. *The Physician and Sports Medicine, 21*(2) 124–140. Copyright © 1993 The McGraw-Hill Companies. All rights reserved.

can greatly lessen the regression that occurs as a result of the sociocultural effects discussed earlier. Regression does not have to begin so early in adulthood or be so severe. Individuals who are aware of the potential that results from decreased physical activity through adulthood and who are motivated to do something about it can play an active role in the quality of the rest of their life. Though societal attitudes frequently suggest that, at some point, we may be too old to engage in a physical activity program ("He's too old to do aerobic dance!"), the information presented in Table 3-4 suggests otherwise. When frail, elderly patients were given appropriate levels of physical activity, remarkable results were seen. Work capacity and bone density increased. They became more flexible and improved in muscle tone and coordination. Perhaps most important, their mental outlook improved as anxiety and depression, the most common psychiatric disorders among older adults, declined (Barry, Rich, & Carlson, 1993). In short, a well-designed training program for any age group in adulthood can increase muscle strength and endurance, increase cardiovascular endurance, halt bone decalcification, improve joint flexibility, and generally improve life satisfaction, enabling us to overcome, and even temporarily reverse, the exercise-aging cycle. "Exercise seems to reduce many of the ravages of older age, resulting in younger appearance, and increases in energy, and enhanced physical capabilities" (B. G. Berger & Hecht, 1989, p. 129). Thus, the probability of a healthier, happier adulthood can increase considerably (see Figure 3-9).

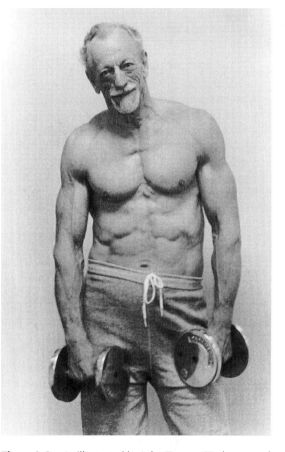

Figure 3-9   As illustrated by John Turner, 67, the normal movement regression through adulthood can be slowed or delayed. Turner lifts weights, jogs, and walks.

SOURCE: Reprinted with permission from Clark, E. (1986). *Growing old is not for sissies.* Corte Madera, CA: Pomegranate.

SUMMARY

Socialization is one of the most dominant facilitators of movement acquisitions throughout the lifespan. Because this process of learning society's expected roles, behaviors, rules, and regulations greatly influences an individual's decisions concerning movement participation, it is a major force in human motor development.

Self-esteem, or self-worth, which is greatly affected by social interactions, has also been found to be significantly influenced by involvement in physical activity. Self-esteem also follows a predictable developmental pattern, evolving through increasing levels of ability to articulate and differentiate the elements of self-esteem. With age, the nature of social relationships and their effects on self-esteem also change as such elements of self-worth as peer acceptance and romantic appeal decline in importance. Intimate relationships and nurturance increase in importance in adulthood. Interestingly, throughout the lifespan, physical appearance and social acceptance have been found to be the most important elements influencing global self-worth, while athletic competence has been found to be one of the least influential contributors.

Infancy is a relatively asocial period. The interaction that does occur is greatly facilitated by the baby's movement ability. Similarly, social interaction offers the baby an opportunity to practice and expand movement opportunities.

School, television, and play are important social influences that contribute to motor development throughout childhood. Play is particularly significant because it tends to depend greatly on bodily movement.

During the latter part of childhood, the peer group becomes more socially important to the child, and the family gradually becomes less significant. By adolescence, the peer group is generally the dominant social force and critical to the establishment of movement-related interests.

During later childhood and adolescence, team play becomes common. This type of social interaction allows the child to perfect movement skills and develop new social, cognitive, and emotional behaviors.

Of particular interest during later childhood and early adolescence is the increasing opportunity to interact with the opposite gender. This interaction assists in the creation of a gender identity. However, there can be problems if the gender role ascribed to individuals does not conform to the gender role associated with the chosen movement activity. Role conflict, which is particularly common for the female participant, can lead to emotional trauma or dropping out of an activity.

The three most significant social influences affecting motor development in adulthood are leaving school/going to work, marriage, and having children. All of these factors tend to increase sedentarism and inhibit the forces that facilitate motor performance. A gradual, consistent decline in motor performance often begins surprisingly early in adulthood and continues until death.

Research has shown that elementary schoolchildren through adults consider the need for physical activity to decrease in importance as people age, contributing to an exercise-aging cycle. This cycle suggests that we exercise less with increasing age, resulting in decreased physical ability and feelings of inadequacy. These feelings impair the incentive to be physically active, which further proliferates the cycle. Fortunately, with more positive attitudes and increased knowledge about aging, the negative cycle can be reduced and even reversed.

Ageism, the negative view of aging and of older people, can lead to an avoidance of older adults. This attitude, common in the United States, inhibits older adults' attempts to engage with their society and impedes their efforts at maintaining an active lifestyle. Additionally, research has shown that there are stereotypes that view movement activity as increasingly inappropriate as one progresses through adulthood.

In later adulthood, many social forces contribute to a decreasing activity level. Children leaving home, retirement, and death of a spouse typically lead older adults away from societal interaction and movement experiences.

Despite the common social pitfalls and their effects on motor development, the early onset of movement regression can be allayed and the severity delayed if a person maintains an active lifestyle.

KEY TERMS

age grading
ageism
attribution
disuse atrophy
exercise-aging cycle
gender role identity

global self-worth
norm
peer group
play
role conflict
self-concept

self-esteem
social learning
social role
socialization
Victorian influence

QUESTIONS FOR REFLECTION

1. What is play? List and describe five elements of play.
2. What is the difference between self-concept and self-esteem?
3. According to Harter (1988), what are the five steps of self-worth development? Describe each step.
4. What effect does one's family have on socialization into sports? List some specific examples for each

gender, and cite some research discussed in this chapter to support your claims.

5. How many benefits does team sport participation offer during adolescence? Provide some examples for each benefit you list.

6. In general, how can participation in team sports resemble life itself?

7. What is meant by the term *Victorian influence?* What is its effect relative to team sport participation?

8. What social factors could contribute to declining fitness levels in early to mid adulthood? Give specific

examples of where you have seen this in real-life situations.

9. List three to five physiological and functional changes that are associated with increasing age. Why do these occur? Can one offset these changes?

10. What is the exercise-aging cycle? Do you think this really happens to most people? Is there anything that can be done to offset the effects of this cycle? Does it have to happen to everyone?

INTERNET RESOURCES

Healthy People 2010 **www.health.gov/healthypeople**

National Association for Self-Esteem **www.self-esteem-nase.org**

ONLINE LEARNING CENTER (www.mhhe.com/payne6e)

Visit the *Human Motor Development* Online Learning Center for study aids and additional resources. You can use the study guide questions and glossary flashcards to review key terms and concepts for this chapter and to

prepare for exams. You can further extend your knowledge of motor development by checking out the Web links, articles, and activities found on the site.

REFERENCES

American Academy of Pediatrics. (2003). *Selecting appropriate toys for young children: The pediatrician's role.* Online: www.aap.org/policy/cr030129.html.

Anthrop, J., & Allison, M. T. (1983). Role conflict and the high school female athlete. *Research Quarterly for Exercise and Sport, 54,* 104–111.

Atchley, R. C. (1989). A continuity theory of aging. *Gerontologist, 29,* 183–190.

Bandura, A., & Kupers, C. J. (1964). Transmission of patterns of self-reinforcement through modeling. *Journal of Abnormal Psychology, 69,* 1–9.

Barry, H. C., Rich, B. S. E., & Carlson, R. T. (1993). How exercise can benefit older patients: A practical approach. *Physician and Sportsmedicine, 21*(2), 124–140.

Berger, B. G., & Hecht, L. M. (1989). Exercise, aging, and psychological well-being: The mind-body question. In A. C. Ostrow (Ed.), *Aging and motor behavior.* Indianapolis, IN: Benchmark.

Berger, B. G., & McInman, A. (1993). Exercise and the quality of life. In R. N. Singer, M. Murphey, & L. K. Tennant (Eds.), *Handbook of research on sport psychology.* New York: Macmillan.

Berger, K. S. (2001). *The developing person through the lifespan.* 5th ed. New York: Worth.

Berk, L. E. (2004). *Development through the lifespan.* 3rd ed. Boston: Allyn and Bacon.

Birdwhistell, R. L. (1960). *Kinesics and communication: Explorations in communication.* Boston: Beacon Press.

Brown, W. J., & Trost, S. G. (2003). Life transitions and changing physical activity patterns in young women. *American Journal of Preventive Medicine, 25*(2), 140–143.

Clark, E. (1986). *Growing old is not for sissies.* Corte Madera, CA: Pomegranate.

Coakley, J. (1993). Socialization and sport. In R. N. Singer, M. Murphey, and L. K. Tennant (Eds.), *Handbook of research on sport psychology.* New York: Macmillan.

Colarusso, C. A., & Nemiroff, R. A. (1981). *Adult development.* New York: Plenum Press.

Cratty, B. J. (1986). *Perceptual and motor development in infants and children.* 3rd ed. Englewood Cliffs, NJ: Prentice-Hall.

DiLorenzo, T. M., Stucky-Ropp, R. C., Vander Wal, J. S., & Gotham, H. J. (1998). Determinants of exercise among children: II. A longitudinal analysis. *Preventive Medicine, 27*(3), 470–477.

Donnelly, J. W., Eburne, N., & Kittleson, M. (2001). *Mental health: Dimensions of self-esteem and emotional well-being.* Boston: Allyn and Bacon.

Eccles, J., & Harold, R. (1991). Gender differences in sport involvement: Applying the Eccles expectancy value model. *Journal of Applied Sport Psychology, 3,* 7–35.

Garvey, K. (1990). *Play.* Cambridge, MA: Harvard University Press.

Greendorfer, S. L., & Ewing, M. E. (1981). Race and gender differences in children's socialization into sport. *Research Quarterly for Exercise and Sport, 52,* 301–310.

Greendorfer, S. L., & Lewko, J. H. (1978). Role of the family members in sport socialization of children. *Research Quarterly, 49,* 146–152.

Gruber, J. J. (1985). Physical activity and self-esteem development in children: A meta-analysis. *Academy Papers, 19,* 30–48.

Hamilton, M. L. (1977). Ideal sex roles for children and acceptance of variation from stereotypic sex roles. *Adolescence, 12,* 89–96.

Harter, S. (1988). Causes, correlates, and the functional role of global self-worth: A life-span perspective. In J. Killigian & R. Sternberg (Eds.), *Perceptions of competence and incompetence across the life-span.* New Haven, CN: Yale University Press.

Healthy People 2010. (2002). Data overview. Online: www.health.gov/healthypeople/Data/dataover.htm.

Kaluger, G., & Kaluger, M. F. (1984). *Human development: The span of life.* St. Louis, MO: Times Mirror/Mosby.

Kausler, D. H. (1982). *Experimental psychology and aging.* New York: Wiley.

Kelly, J. R., & Wescott, G. (1991). Ordinary retirement: Commonalities and continuity. *International Journal of Aging and Human Development, 32,* 81–89.

Lee, A. M. (1980). Child rearing practices and motor performance of black and white children. *Research Quarterly for Exercise and Sport, 51,* 494–500.

Michael, M. (1970). Sex typing and socialization. In P. H. Mussen (Ed.), *Carmichael's manual of child psychology.* Vol. 2. New York: Wiley.

NEA Today. (1985, Mar. 10). School yard . . . daring to be great.

Neumark-Sztainer, D., Story, M., Hannan, P. J., Tharp, T., & Rex, J. (2003). Factors associated with changes in physical activity: A cohort study of inactive adolescent girls. *Archives of Pediatrics and Adolescent Medicine, 157*(8), 803–810.

Newman, B. M., & Newman, P. R. (2003). *Development through life: A psychosocial approach.* 8th ed. Pacific Grove, CA: Brooks/Cole.

Oglesby, C. A., & Hill, K. L. (1993). Gender and sport. In R. N. Singer, M. Murphey, & L. K. Tennant (Eds.), *Handbook of research on sport psychology.* New York: Macmillan.

Ostrow, A. C., Jones, D. C., & Spiker, D. D. (1981). Age role expectations and sex role expectations for selected sport activities. *Research Quarterly for Exercise and Sport, 52,* 216–227.

Robbins, L. B., Pender, N. J., & Kazanis, A. S. (2003). Barriers to physical activity perceived by adolescent girls. *Journal of Midwifery and Women's Health, 48*(3), 206–212.

Rudman, W. J. (1984). Life course socioeconomic transitions and sport involvement: A theory of restricted opportunity. In B. D. McPherson (Ed.), *The 1984 Olympic scientific congress proceedings: Volume 5. Sport and aging.* Champaign, IL: Human Kinetics.

Silverstein, S. (1981). *A light in the attic.* New York: Harper & Row.

Taneja, V., Sriram, S., Beri, R. S., Sreenivas, V., Aggarwal, R., & Kaur, R. (2002). Not by bread alone: Impact of a structured 90-minute play session on development of children in an orphanage. *Child: Care, Health and Development, 28*(1), 95–100.

Thompson, R. A. (1998). Early sociopersonality development. In *Handbook of clinical psychology: Volume 3. Social, emotional, and personality development* (pp. 25–104). New York: Wiley.

United States Department of Commerce: Bureau of the Census. (1975). *Historical statistics of the United States: Colonial times to 1970.* Washington, DC: U.S. Government Printing Office.

———. (1983). *1980 census of the population: General population characteristics.* Washington, DC: U.S. Government Printing Office.

———. (1992). *1990 census of the population: General population characteristics.* Washington, DC: U.S. Government Printing Office.

———. (2003). *Marital status 2000.* Washington, DC: U.S. Government Printing Office

Perceptual-Motor Development

*P*erceptual-motor is one of the most commonly used terms in motor development and education in general. Almost all motor development or elementary physical education texts contain extensive information concerning this concept. However, there is tremendous confusion about the exact meaning of the term. The perceptual-motor concept, which first began to affect education nearly a half century ago, has since been misused and overused until it has been drained of much of its intended significance. More than 25 years ago, Seefeldt declared that the "term has been rendered worthless in representing specific methodology, programs, or content" (1974, p. 266). To help clear the confusion and examine the controversy, this chapter discusses the significance of the perceptual-motor concept and several important related concepts.

WHAT IS PERCEPTUAL-MOTOR DEVELOPMENT?

Regardless of how it is specifically defined,

The perceptual-motor concept refers to movement activities, usually involving children, performed with primary intent of improving cognitive or academic skills.

The term refers to programs involving children because most perceptual-motor development occurs during the preschool and primary school years (Gallahue & Ozmun, 2002). It is common practice in perceptual-motor programs to supplement or replace academic activities with movement activities to improve such academic concerns as reading, writing, and problem solving (see Figure 4-1). If the movement activities are designed specifically to improve movement ability, they do not constitute a perceptual-motor program (Seefeldt, 1974).

Other Interpretations of Perceptual-Motor

Although we believe that the concept Seefeldt suggested accurately describes perceptual-motor, others have approached the concept from a different per-

Figure 4-1 Perceptual-motor activities are designed to enhance cognitive or academic performance through the performance of movement activities.

spective. Many discussions of perceptual-motor include a statement of the movement activities considered perceptual-motor. According to the Perceptual-Motor Task Force Summary of the Perceptual-Motor Survey (Haslinger, 1971), the vast list of movements that various experts claim are perceptual-motor activities leads one to believe that *all* human movements are perceptual-motor. This statement is supported by those who believe that all voluntary movement is perceptual-motor and all physical education programs are perceptual-motor programs. We prefer to assume that the term *perceptual-motor* was not created simply to replace the term *physical education;* perceptual-motor may be an entity encompassed within physical education, but physical education programs and perceptual-motor programs are not synonymous. The objectives of a physical education program can be more diverse than the relatively narrow ones of a perceptual-motor program.

Perceptual-motor is also frequently explained as that which concerns the relationship between human movement and perceptions. Some would interchange the term **perceptions** with *sensations.* However, we differentiate by noting that sensations have specifically to do with the senses (touch, taste, smell, hearing, and vision) and the fairly passive process of our receptors detecting an environment stimulus (Berk, 2001). Thus, one gains direct knowledge that a sound, for example, just occurred (Adam, 1998). Perceptions, on the other hand, involve the "integration of the sensory events in the organism's external world, especially as a function of expectations derived from past experiences and serving as a basis for or as verified by further action" (Adam, 1998, p. 8). This is a much more active process whereby we compare incoming information from the senses with stored information compiled from our past.

The interrelationship between perceptions and movement is unquestionably important. Without perceptions, such as those received through our sensory processes, even the simplest movement would be difficult if not impossible. This has been demonstrated in studies conducted with children who have various forms of sensory deprivation. Blind children, and even children with limited light perception, for example, have frequently been found to show significant developmental delays in their motor performance. Similarly, children with hearing impairments often score below average on eye-hand coordination tests while demonstrating less coordinated movement than do their hearing peers (Eichstaedt & Lavay, 1992). In children with a serious disability, these age gaps often widen over time, making early intervention imperative (Jansma, 1999).

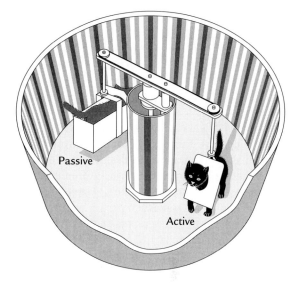

Figure 4-2 Held and Hein involved kittens in active and passive movement. The researchers concluded that the active movement benefited the kittens' development of depth perception, whereas the passive movement did not.

There has also been considerable discussion about the importance of active movement for optimal development of the perceptions. Perceptual-motor programs sometimes have been justified on the basis of their value in enhancing the child's perceptual abilities. This argument is frequently substantiated by the findings of Held and Hein's 1963 study.

In their research, Held and Hein raised kittens in a completely dark environment for 8 to 12 weeks. The kittens were then separated into two groups: active and passive. A kitten from each group was attached to a cartlike device that rotated around a central axis in a lighted carousel. The active kitten propelled its cart around the axis via its own legs; the passive kitten was simply a passenger because its legs were prevented from moving. The passive kitten's cart also rotated around the central axis, but the cart was propelled by the leg movement of the active kitten, because the two carts were connected (see Figure 4-2). Kittens from both groups spent up to 3 hours per day in this lighted situation. On being posttested, the active kittens showed signs of having acquired normal depth perception, whereas the passive kittens exhibited impaired depth perception, which eventually improved markedly when they were exposed to light. Held and Hein concluded from this research that active movement plays a vital role in the development of visual-spatial skills such as depth perception. And, as mentioned, this research has also been used to justify perceptual-motor programs. These programs often involve children in movement activities designed to improve skills like depth perception to in turn enhance an academic ability such as reading, which normally depends on visual proficiency.

The Held and Hein research has been criticized because those kittens actively involved in producing movement most likely were also required to maintain greater visual attentiveness (Shaffer, 2001). Therefore, the active kittens may have achieved better depth perception than the passive kittens because they had more visual experience and practice rather than higher levels of actively produced movement, as the original researchers suspected.

Related research by Walk (1981) supports this critical view of Held and Hein's research. On the basis of much more recent research, Walk suggested that active movement may be an essential element in development, but the movement does not need to be self-produced, only viewed. As Held and Hein did, Walk researched kittens to reach these conclusions. The kittens in Walk's research were kept in total darkness for a time following their birth. Then one group of kittens was removed from the darkness and allowed to move actively around the environment and examine the available visual stimuli. A second group of kittens was inhibited from actively moving but allowed to examine passive stimuli. A final group of kittens, also inhibited from movement, viewed active, interesting stimuli.

Following exposure to these varying situations, all kittens were tested for depth perception. The kittens that could not actively interact with the environment and that watched the passive stimuli had the poorest level of depth perception. According to Walk, this was most likely due to the tendency of these kittens to become bored and fall asleep. However, the kittens that watched the active stimuli remained attentive despite their inability to move actively through their environment. As a result, these kittens developed depth perception comparable to that of the kittens that were allowed to move actively through the environment.

Walk's research and similar investigations have led to the **motion hypothesis,** which is the idea that individuals must attend to objects that move in order to develop a normal repertoire of visual-spatial skills (Shaffer, 2001), such as depth perception. Contrary to early research, such as in the Held and Hein study, and considerable popular opinion, self-produced movement may not be as critical as once believed in the development of such important abilities as depth perception.

The Perceptual-Motor Process

Like Held and Hein and Walk, Williams (1983) and others have theorized about the role of perceptions in movement production and correction. However, these authors' intent was to delineate the steps in a so-called **perceptual-motor process** rather than specifically determine the role of active movement in the development of the perceptions.

Generally, the first step in the perceptual-motor process (in this case, also known as information processing) is the reception of environmental information vital to the production of the movement. Imagine a young boy who has just visually perceived a ball being tossed in his direction. By focusing on the ball, the child receives information concerning the speed, trajectory, weight, and texture of the ball—information critical to the production of a successful catching movement. The initial step in the perceptual-motor process is therefore the reception of pertinent environmental information.

Once that information has traveled to the brain via the afferent or incoming nerves, it is perceived and processed. Included in this processing is the integration of the new information with that from similar past experiences. This **sensory integration** involves a comparison of information from the present movement with that stored in the long-term memory concerning previous similar movements.

This process of integrating the "new" information with the "old" enables a more accurate and complete analysis of the present movement situation and improves the chances of more successful movement production.

After information concerning the present movement has been integrated with pertinent past information, the movement selection is made. The efferent, or outgoing, nerves then send a command to the muscles, creating a movement. However, the process is not yet complete, because once the movement begins, information is fed back to the performer, to enable an ongoing monitoring of the movement process. This feedback is facilitated by information from the senses. Vision, hearing, touch, and proprioception play a particularly important role in the feedback process. For the young boy we mentioned earlier, seeing, hearing, or feeling the ball rebound off his own chest might cue him to modify his catching movement in future catching attempts. The sensory information therefore assists in making judgments about the movement and affects the way that movement or similar movements will be made in the future. If the information from the original motor prescription does not compare favorably with the information fed back, a correction may be made on similar movements in the future. However, if there is a close match between these two sources of information, and the movement proved successful, attempts will be made to reproduce that movement in similar movement situations in the future.

This process, although theoretical and somewhat simplistically described, appears to be generally well accepted and has no doubt led to the following related definition of ***perceptual-motor development:***

> Perceptual-motor development is that part of a child's development that is concerned with changes in the movement behavior, changes that represent improvement in sensory-perceptual motor development and reafference processes that underlie such behavior. (Williams, 1983, p. 9)

Therefore, perceptual-motor development, as Williams viewed it, is the child's changing, generally improving ability to utilize the perceptual-motor process that we just described and that is summarized as follows:

1. In the perceptual-motor process, environmental stimulation that is relevant to the movement in question is recognized.
2. The brain receives the information through the afferent (input) nervous system.
3. The information is processed at the brain, which organizes and integrates the new and the old information concerning previous similar movements.
4. A decision is made to move.
5. The appropriate movement information is efferently (through output) transmitted to the muscles to create the desired movement.
6. The movement is performed.
7. The movement is observed, and relevant information is stored for integration with information concerning similar future movements.

Is All Movement Perceptual-Motor?

Earlier we mentioned that *perceptual-motor* has been considered an alternate term for *physical education.* We do not subscribe to this use of the term, because it implies that perceptual-motor involves all the kinds of movement that one would expect to see in a physical education program. Our view is that perceptual-motor activities are movements created through the process of sensory integration that we discussed earlier; this includes all voluntary movement, such as the activities in a physical education class. However, we also stated that the intent of perceptual-motor activities is to enhance cognitive function. Although the performance of all voluntary movement activities may contribute slightly to this effort, certain movements are most commonly acclaimed for their contribution to this effort and can therefore be considered perceptual-motor activities.

In determining which movements would be considered perceptual-motor, we found an examination of the Perceptual-Motor Survey to be particularly useful (Haslinger, 1971). This survey, conducted many years ago, was devised by a perceptual-motor task force that was created to allay confusion surrounding the term *perceptual-motor*. To attain this goal, the task force solicited definitions of perceptual-motor from numerous individuals across the country who were considered experts on this topic. The task force attempted to determine the nature of perceptual-motor activities by having respondents list those movement activities they believed were perceptual-motor. An examination of the results revealed clear disagreement among the experts. No doubt there is still a comparable lack of agreement, but certain categories of movement do tend to appear on most responses to the perceptual-motor survey: balance and spatial, temporal, body, and directional awareness, among others. These types of movement activities are also commonly cited in discussions of *perceptual-motor* in many related texts (Gallahue & Ozmun, 2002). Also, these types of movements were among those frequently prescribed by Kephart (1964), who is regularly cited for his role in originally initiating interest in the term *perceptual-motor*. Kephart and his perceptual-motor theory are discussed in greater detail later in the chapter. Now we briefly discuss the movement-related concepts commonly associated with the term *perceptual-motor*.

BALANCE

Balance, or stability, is traditionally defined as "a state of equilibrium maintained between opposing forces" (Burton & Davis, 1992; p. 14). It is an "integral part of almost every movement task" (p. 14) and is frequently called **postural control,** which is "an ability to maintain equilibrium in a gravitational field by keeping or returning the center of body mass over its base of support" (Horak, 1987, p. 1881). In light of the contemporary emphasis placed on ecological considerations and dynamical systems, Burton and Davis have defined balance as being "not a state, skill, or ability but rather the aspect of a particular action involving a variety of processes that allow for the orientation of the body that is necessary to carry out the functional task at hand" (1992, p. 16).

Though research is divided on the topic, balance appears to be quite task specific. It also depends greatly on the form and structure of one's body, as factors affecting the size of the base of support, such as foot length or width, have been found to affect postural responses. Balance is also inversely proportional to the height of the body's center of mass above the base of support (Burton & Davis, 1992). Given the obvious changes normal growth makes in body dimensions, balance is clearly influenced by developmental changes.

Balance, in the form of postural change, is exhibited quite early in life. In fact, the fetus has been known to change position by rotating along the longitudinal axis of the body. This motion is typically initiated by a turn of the head or the hips. The fetus also changes position by alternate leg movements. This often results in a "somersault" when the legs are positioned so they can push against the uterine wall. These postural changes occur as often as 20 times per hour during the first 6 months of pregnancy and decrease in incidence during the remainder of the gestational period. This somewhat surprising decrease in the rate of postural change may be a function of the declining space available for movement as the fetus increases in size (Woollacott, Shumway-Cook, & Williams, 1989).

Following birth, babies less than 3 days old are often capable of orienting their bodies and heads relative to a visual stimulus. At 9 months, children can activate the postural muscles in the trunk in association with reaching movements of the arms. In general, though children from 15 months to 3 years exhibit organized leg muscle responses when balance is perturbed, the number of postural adjustments is more variable and slower than in adults. Children at this age also appear to rely primarily on visual information in decisions concerning balance. From 4 to 6 years, a slight regression in postural organization occurs and may indicate a period when the child is attempting to integrate various other forms of information with vision so as to achieve postural control.

By the age of 7 to 10 years, postural responses are similar to those of adults, though slightly longer latency periods following a balance disruption are common for children. During this time, the leg muscles have usually achieved adultlike balance responses, though the upper body continues to improve in function (Woollacott et al., 1989).

Balance is commonly subdivided into two types: static and dynamic. **Static balance** is the ability to maintain a desired body posture or position when the body is stationary. **Dynamic balance** is the ability to maintain a desired body posture or position when the body is moving. Both static and dynamic balances are used in many movement activities. For example, a diver uses static balance as she stands poised and relatively motionless on the tip of the diving board prior to the dive. However, once the dive has been initiated and the body is experiencing various rotations, dynamic balance helps maintain the desired body position.

For greater awareness of the characteristics and underlying mechanisms of balance, both forms of balance have been scientifically investigated. In a study of static balance in children, researchers sought to determine the relationship between body characteristics and balance in children who were nondisabled and who ranged in age from just under 2 years to just under 13 years of age. Participants were asked to stand on two different measurement devices designed to measure static balance. Not surprisingly, the younger children were found to exhibit less consistency in their balance than did the older children, who demonstrated relatively similar sway patterns among themselves. According to the researchers, the degree of postural sway and the reliability of the measures were affected by the participant's age (Baker et al., 1998).

Clark and Watkins (1984) investigated the static balance of 6- to 9-year-old children. The children attempted balancing tasks in various body positions. While balancing, the children were asked to maintain a normal stand, stand with their hands on their hips, fold their arms across their chests, or bend over at their waists. In addition, the balance tasks were performed on both the left and right feet, with the eyes open and closed, and using bases of various sizes. The children were timed on all balance tasks from the time their nonsupport foot left the floor until it returned. Developmentally, the older children in this research were not found to be significantly more successful on balance tasks than were the younger children. However, using a larger base of support and keeping the eyes open significantly improved balance performance. Body position was also found to be a significant factor, but only when the stock used as the base of support was in a lengthwise rather than a crosswise position. Finally, the foot selected for support in the balance task was not a significant factor, although Clark and Watkins speculate that it may be critical in the way it interacts with the other variables examined. One of the most important conclusions of this research was that static balance is a multidimensional task that is affected by a multitude of variables; it therefore cannot be accurately assessed by any one test of balance.

In a recent investigation of both static and dynamic balance in children, researchers studied 11- to 13-year-old participants' balance and its relationship to specific perceptual and motor skills. Balance was measured in relationship to simple, visual, choice, and discrimination reaction times. It was also measured in relationship to attention, visuomotor coordination, kinesthesis, and depth perception. Static balance was found to be strongly related to the ability to perceive and process the visual information that is believed to be critical for balance control. For dynamic balance, strong associations were found between balance performance and response speeds. In general, the authors concluded that participants in this age group could select and use various balance strategies, depending upon the type of balance task necessary (Hatzitaki et al., 2002).

In yet another examination of static and dynamic balance, researchers administered the Bruinincks-Oseretsky balance test to 10- to 21-year-old boys. Interestingly, balance performance was found to correlate negatively with several measures of body fat: body weight, body mass index, percentage fat, and total fat mass. The researchers concluded that this study supports the notion that overweight performers often have poorer balance than do healthy weight participants (Goulding et al., 2003).

Streepey and Angulo-Kinzler (2002) focused exclusively on dynamic balance in children relative to the difficulty of the balance task. Specifically, the researchers required participants to reach in varying directions and at various distances requiring greater challenges to their balance as measured by center of pressure. Participants ranged in age from 6 to 10 years of age. Results indicated that minimal differences resulted between younger and older participants on the least and most difficult tasks; however, for the tasks of moderate difficulty, the older participants were found to have a level of balance control similar to children on some tasks and similar to adults on others. These findings led the researchers to conclude that balance control is a function of both age of the performer and difficulty of the balance task at hand (Streepey & Angulo-Kinzler, 2002).

Beam walking has often been the focus of research designed to investigate dynamic balance. For example, DeOreo (1974, 1975) examined the technique her 3- to 5-year-old subjects used to walk across a beam. She instructed children to cross beams of varying widths by walking forward and backward. DeOreo noticed that beam walking could be categorized into two distinct patterns. Younger subjects tended to use a "mark time" or shuffle-step pattern in which one foot stayed in front at all times and was simply shuffled along across the beam. Older subjects seemed to have developed the more mature pattern of striding with both the left and right legs. DeOreo also noted that more than 25 percent of the 3-year-old subjects were incapable of balancing well enough to cross the beam. In addition, this task became more difficult for all children as the width of the beam decreased, resulting in subjects of all ages tending to resort to the more immature shuffle-step technique. This type of research has been valuable for determining the progression children use to perform specific dynamic-balance tasks. Chapter 16 addresses several important concepts relative to balance in adulthood.

Researchers have also studied balance by using a stabilometer. With the stabilometer, the subject must balance on a platform suspended on a single axis across its midline. The subject places one foot on each side of this axis, similar to attempting to balance on the center of a seesaw. Certain evidence

implies that stabilometer performance may not increase with age, unlike most movement skills. In fact, Bachman (1961) studied people aged 6 to 26 and found that there was a tendency for balance ability on the stabilometer to decrease with age, perhaps a function of the older performer's increasing weight, which causes faster fluctuations in the position of the base of support (Keogh & Sugden, 1985). The increasing height of the older subjects' center of gravity may also contribute to this atypical developmental trend, because the height of an individual's center of gravity can increase the difficulty of this type of balance task.

SPATIAL AWARENESS

Spatial awareness, like balance, is a movement-related concept frequently emphasized in perceptual-motor programs. As the name implies, **spatial awareness** is an understanding of the external spaces surrounding an individual and the individual's ability to function motorically in and through that space. Children evolve from an immature form of spatial awareness known as egocentric localization to the more advanced objective localization. *Egocentric localization* is an immature and limited spatial awareness in which all or most aspects of a child's understanding of the surroundings are noted in reference to him- or herself. *Objective localization* is the more advanced capability of referencing objects in space relative to objects other than the self (Gallahue & Ozmun, 2002).

Children often divulge their localization status when asked directions to a specific location in their surroundings. Those children who highlight landmarks other than themselves when giving the directions have developed the more advanced objective localization, whereas children who give directions with the self as the point of reference are exhibiting egocentric localization. Many experts believe that spatial awareness can be facilitated through involvement in movement activity. Unquestionably, movement often requires an acute understanding of the surroundings, such as that often exhibited by tennis players, who have developed such a high level of spatial awareness that they do not have to look at the lines surrounding the court during play to know that their opponent's shot is going to land in or out of bounds. Thus, spatial awareness is not only beneficial in many movement endeavors but can be improved by participation in the movement activity. However, numerous claims that this movement-related ability can be enhanced through movement activities in a way that will help the child academically remain unsubstantiated.

Using children 4 and 9 years old, Thomas and colleagues (1983) investigated the developmental differences in a form of spatial awareness. Of specific interest to these researchers were the strategies their subjects used to remember locations and distances in their environment while jogging. As we would expect, the 9-year-olds recalled both locations and distances better than did the 4-year-olds. However, both groups found distances difficult to recall accurately. When subjects were assisted by various cues, they recalled locations better but still poorly remembered distance, leading to the conclusion that recalling specific distances requires a sophisticated strategy, such as counting steps. This was a strategy approximately 30 percent of the 9-year-olds used; generally, the 4-year-olds did not use the technique.

Additional research by Thomas and colleagues has determined that older children become increasingly likely to use a strategy to recall distances and are typically more successful than their younger counterparts in remembering accurately. However, according to this research, children 5 to 12 years old can be taught to use a strategy to recall jogging distances. In fact, 5-year-olds who were taught to count steps learned to recall distance as well as did 9-year-olds and slightly less effectively than did 12-year-olds who were not given instruction.

In one example of a specific form of spatial awareness, Rosenbaum and Chaiken (2001) examined perceptual motor learning in a blind manual-positioning task. Using a computer screen and a joystick, participants were asked to move a cursor to specified targets on the screen. As soon as the cursor began to move, the cursor disappeared until the participant indicated that they had arrived at the target location. Participants improved their spatial awareness with practice, but when conditions were changed, performance suffered. Researchers also found that there was little difference in performance based on hand use, but when both the hand and target positions were changed, the most significant disruption in performance occurred. The researchers concluded that this type of perceptual-motor learning required both a sense of the spatial environment as well as intrinsic body positioning.

TEMPORAL AWARENESS

Temporal awareness involves the gradually evolving understanding of time relationships, such as understanding the characteristics of a rapidly approaching ball. In this case, temporal awareness is an ability to predict the projectile's time of arrival, based on such characteristics as the speed, trajectory, and weight of the ball and the distance the ball has been projected. This specific form of temporal awareness is also known as coincidence-anticipation timing and has been acclaimed as one of the most important aspects of bodily movement (Bartlett, 1958). Specifically, coincidence-anticipation timing is a person's ability to predict the arrival of a moving object at a certain point in space and to coordinate a movement with that arrival. Batting a pitched ball or attempting to intercept a soccer pass both require coincidence-anticipation timing ability.

Dorfman (1977) used subjects 6 to 19 years old to investigate the development of coincidence-anticipation timing in children and young adults. To intercept an approaching target dot, subjects were instructed to move a slide to control a cursor dot appearing on a monitor. Dorfman determined a typical developmental trend: The older subjects consistently performed more proficiently and exhibited a faster rate of learning than did their younger counterparts.

In two additional studies, Haywood (1980, 1987) extended research on coincidence-anticipation timing to include adults of varying ages. Initially, Haywood examined four age groups: 7–9, 11–13, 18–32, and 60–75 years. Each group was administered

60 trials on a Bassin Anticipation Timer. This device projects a stream of lights in a predetermined direction. The subjects were required to press a button when they anticipated the light stream would reach a designated location. No gender differences were determined in coincidence-anticipation accuracy. The youngest group was the least accurate and least consistent. Accuracy was better in the older children and, according to Haywood, appeared to plateau thereafter. Older adults were highly variable in their responses and significantly less accurate than younger adults (Haywood, 1980).

In similar research using a longitudinal rather than cross-sectional design, Haywood (1987) sought to determine if coincidence-anticipation timing performance continued to decline in the later years. Using 10 older adults ranging in age from 62 to 73, Haywood repeatedly tested the subjects over a 7-year period. Interestingly, these subjects showed improvement over that time. As the author suggests, this could have been a function of increased confidence and familiarity with the task rather than a typical age-related phenomenon.

While both of Haywood's investigations are interesting from a developmental perspective, the findings should be interpreted cautiously. Few subjects were involved, and all older adult subjects in both studies were participants in physical activity programs, which may have affected their performance on the timing task. More sedentary subjects may have performed differently.

Coincidence-anticipation timing is one particular form of temporal awareness. However, temporal awareness can occur independently of such external objects as an approaching ball. Coordination of various parts of a person's own body in a planned, synchronous fashion relative to another body part is critical to success in most movement, such as the popular jumping jack exercise. The jumping jack requires considerable temporal awareness to keep the arms and legs properly synchronized. Movement participants often become extremely adept at this form of temporal awareness.

In a relatively large study on timed performance from 5 to 18 years of age, researchers examined performance on several types of timed performance involving repetitive finger movements, hand and foot movements, alternating hand and foot movements, and sequential finger movements. Timed performances improved up to and through prepuberty, but they varied somewhat by when the subjects seemed to reach an improvement plateau, usually around the time of puberty. Socioeconomic status and gender did not yield clinically relevant differences in timed performance. In general, the researchers concluded that timed performance led to a "long-lasting developmental change" with considerable variation by individual (Largo et al., 2001, p. 435).

BODY AND DIRECTIONAL AWARENESS

Body awareness, also referred to as body image, is a gradually developing ability to know and understand the names and functions of various body parts. Body awareness is the ability to understand the body's potential in movement performance as well as how to produce various movements. It is unquestionably important to optimal movement performance and has been closely linked with a related concept, directional awareness.

Directional awareness is the understanding and application of such concepts as up and down, front and back, and left and right. Directional awareness is often subdivided into laterality and directionality. *Laterality* is the understanding of various directional concepts; *directionality* is the application of that information (Cratty, 1986). Because we constantly make directional decisions while involved in movement activities, laterality and directionality can be improved through participation in the kinds of movement activities that are commonly included in perceptual-motor programs. However, directional awareness is also important for such academically related tasks as reading. Obviously, reading depends on the ability to discern letters on the basis of their direction. For example, a child with a poorly refined or underdeveloped sense of direction easily confuses a *b* and a *d*. However, although directional awareness appears to be improvable as it is related to the specific movements in a perceptual-motor program, there is scant evidence as to the value of involvement in specific movement activities for improving reading achievement or other related academic concerns. Yet, claims continue to be made and programs devised with the intent of involving children in specific movement activities for purposes of direct cognitive or academic gain. Some of the research that has examined the effectiveness of such programs in improving academic or cognitive ability is examined later in the chapter.

PERCEPTUAL-MOTOR THEORIES: KEPHART AND DELACATO

As mentioned, the concept of perceptual-motor has been in existence for almost 50 years. Numerous programs developed by many innovators throughout this time have sought to improve academic performance through involvement in some form of movement activity. However, two theorists have particularly affected the evolution of thinking relative to the perceptual-motor concept. Kephart (1960, 1964) developed a perceptual-motor theory in which he stated that cognitive development could be enhanced through movement. Delacato (1959, 1963) also advanced a theory about enhancing cognitive ability through movement. However, the theories differ considerably. Each has had a major impact educationally and both continue to generate tremendous controversy.

Kephart's Perceptual-Motor Theory

Kephart is generally credited with initiating the emphasis that educators tend to place on movement for improving students' academic performance. Kephart believed that learning deficiencies were a result of poor sensory integration of present stimuli with the stored information concerning past stimuli. Sensory integration, discussed earlier, is a critical step in the perceptual-motor process. Kephart also believed that the feedback process, necessary for

correcting errors in movement and perfecting future movements, was faulty in children with learning difficulties. Kephart therefore theorized that participation in basic forms of movement would help these integration and feedback problems and consequently improve the child's learning of such academic skills as spelling and reading. In fact, Kephart emphasized the interrelationship between perceptions and movement by stating that we must not "think of perceptual activities and motor activities as two different items; we must think of the hyphenated term, perceptual-motor" (1960, p. 63). On the basis of Kephart's theory, children were frequently advised to participate in activities that involved several general areas of movement. Kephart believed that balance, eye-hand coordination, laterality, directionality, temporal and spatial awareness, and form perception enhanced cognitive as well as motor function.

Notice that the movements Kephart prescribed are similar to the movements we suggested earlier as being perceptual-motor activities. Our list is not intended to be an exhaustive inclusion of all possibilities or a replica of Kephart's recommendations; we merely include the most commonly mentioned activities in response to the Perceptual-Motor Survey (Haslinger, 1971) briefly discussed earlier. This survey, which requested that experts write what they considered perceptual-motor activities, yielded a list of activities very similar to Kephart's recommendations, which had been prescribed years before the survey.

Kephart's impact on movement experts throughout the country is obvious. This impact is still evident today, as perceptual-motor programs continue to involve many of the kinds of movements Kephart prescribed. Kephart selected these general movement categories on the basis of his belief that children with learning difficulties frequently displayed deficiencies in these movement-related abilities. Although remnants of Kephart's ideas still pervade education today, his theory has become extremely controversial. Some educators believe that perceptual-motor programs based on Kephart's theory are educational panaceas, but others oppose them because there is too little substantive evidence to support such programs. The ending section of this chapter discusses some of the research into perceptual-motor programs.

Delacato and Hemispheric Dominance

Although perhaps less encompassing than Kephart's perceptual-motor theory, the theory Delacato (1959, 1963) proposed has certainly contributed to the controversy surrounding the term *perceptual-motor.* Like Kephart, Delacato believed that involvement in certain forms of movement behavior facilitates intellectual development. Delacato specifically believed that a critical element in optimal cognitive functioning is the development of **hemispheric dominance.** In other words, one hemisphere of the brain must maintain control, or dominate the other, for certain behaviors to occur optimally. Gaining this hemispheric dominance is part of a process. Delacato theorized that children who had not experienced and "perfected" certain infant movements faced an increased likelihood of intellectual problems later in life because of a lack of neurological organization. Delacato also believed that many intellectual problems could be overcome by recapitulating the early movement that was thought to be imperfect or omitted. To enable the child to experience or reexperience the infant movement, Delacato recommended a process known as patterning. Through patterning, an individual simply practiced the movement, usually crawling, to accommodate the need for the neural organization that Delacato believed was imperative to the child's enhanced cognitive functioning. Children who were incapable of actively recapitulating this movement were passively assisted through the movements. This process frequently involved numerous assistants and was often maintained for prolonged periods.

Although patterning has become the most widely publicized aspect of Delacato's prescription for enhanced cognitive function, other techniques are also involved. For example, reducing fluid, sugar, and salt consumption and reinspirating expired air were also believed to enhance efforts to improve the cognitive functioning of children who, according to Delacato, exhibited a lack of hemispheric dominance as a result of omitted or "improper" infant movement (American Academy of Pediatrics [AAP], 1999).

Some proponents of Delacato's theory are still around, but many experts agree that his techniques are unsubstantiated and extremely questionable (AAP, 1999). Critics of Delacato's theory cite cases of children who failed to crawl during infancy but still functioned at a normal cognitive level. The critics also noted children who were patterned, as prescribed by Delacato, yet failed to exhibit intellectual improvement. Some children, however, showed improvements when following patterning. But these cases are considered suspect because these children might have caught up via a naturally slower rate of maturation rather than from patterning. Intellectual improvements in children who were patterned have also been attributed to the social contact that is an inevitable part of patterning. In other words, the child was believed to benefit from the regular social interaction and attention as much as or more than from the passive or active action of the patterning.

The American Academy of Pediatrics (AAP, 1999) sufficiently opposed Delacato's recommended treatment of neurologically impaired children that they developed and published a position statement expressing their opposition. They cite several specific reasons for concern. For example, the AAP claim the means employed to promote the treatment make it hard for parents to reject treatment for fear of appearing inadequate as parents. In addition, the regimen of the program is extremely demanding and inflexible, which may cause the parents to feel stressed and possibly neglect other family members. Further, proponents claim that rapid improvements are generally noted on the basis of assessments administered using their own developmental profile. Unfortunately, research validating the profile, according to the AAP, is lacking. Most important, the AAP notes that they are aware of only one scientific investigation in over 20 years that has indicated small improvements in the functioning of the patients receiving the Doman-Delacato patterning treatment. This is reason to doubt the extensive claims for the patterning (AAP, 1999).

RESEARCHING THE EFFECTIVENESS OF PERCEPTUAL-MOTOR PROGRAMS

In a classic, large-scale **meta-analysis,** Kavale and Matson (1983) integrated the findings of over 180 scientific investigations designed to research the efficacy of perceptual-motor programs. This process of statistically integrating numerous sources examining the same topic is an intensive, scientific alternative to the more common narrative discussions of research studies. Over 60 percent of the investigations Kavale and Matson examined had been reported in research journals, with the remaining research coming from dissertations, books, and such sources as conference proceedings. The average study included in this meta-analysis involved children from the third grade at just less than 8 years of age. The average length of involvement in a perceptual-motor program was 19 weeks. It was found that, cognitively, children in this meta-analysis yielded a minimal gain. Specifically, the average subject gained 0.1 standard deviation and was performing better cognitively than only 54 percent of the control subjects, who received no perceptual-motor training. These findings support the reviews we reported earlier that stated that perceptual-motor intervention appears relatively ineffective. In fact, according to Kavale and Matson, the effects of perceptual-motor training are negligible compared with other forms of educational intervention and may even be harmful because considerable time, energy, and money frequently are wasted on these types of programs.

The authors of this meta-analysis were clearly opposed to intervention through perceptual-motor programs. As mentioned throughout this chapter, many sources concur with Kavale and Matson by objectively and subjectively questioning the value of these programs. The programs Kephart and Delacato recommended received particular scrutiny. Nevertheless, we must also remember that the research that has failed to substantiate these programs has also been widely criticized. One of the most common problems encountered in investigations examining the efficacy of perceptual-motor programs is the brief period of treatment. Even programs that last nearly 5 months, which was the average time in the meta-analysis, may not be long enough. Many educators believe that a perceptual-motor program must be initiated very early in life and last for years rather than months (Williams, 1984). In addition, although many experts agree that perceptual-motor programs are not the cure-all they once were believed to be, they may be an important indirect mode through which academic concepts can be introduced, reinforced, and developed (Gallahue & Ozmun, 2002). Direct improvement in academic abilities such as reading will not occur as a direct result of the kinds of perceptual-motor involvement Kephart or Delacato suggested. These programs typically do not incorporate academic concepts into the movement activity. However, when academic concepts are creatively interspersed throughout a movement activity, movement may be an excellent medium through which reading, spelling, math, social studies, or problem-solving concepts can be facilitated.

SUMMARY

Although *perceptual-motor* is one of the most commonly used terms in physical education, it is also one of the most confusing. Perceptual-motor refers to movement activities used to enhance academic or intellectual performance.

Perceptual-motor also implies a relationship between the perceptions and human movement. It has been purported that active participation in movement enhances

such visual skills as depth perception. However, Walk's movement hypothesis states that optimal development of depth perception can occur from simply watching active, interesting stimuli.

Perceptions are important for movement to occur optimally as implied in the perceptual-motor process. This process facilitates movement behavior by accommodating the input and output of appropriate stimuli to and from the brain and includes the processing and integration of movement information within the brain. In addition, future movement correction is possible because there is a feedback process. After the movement is completed, information about the outcome is stored for future analysis and comparison.

Although most human movement occurs via the perceptual-motor process, only certain movements are popularly believed to be perceptual-motor activities. Among the movements most often cited for value in improving cognitive or academic performance are balance and spatial, temporal, body, and directional awareness.

Kephart and Delacato proposed theories that have significantly affected education for almost 50 years. Both theorists claimed that specific movement activities can improve cognitive or academic performance. However, both theories have been heavily criticized because of a lack of scientific substantiation. Nevertheless, both theories still have many proponents and therefore continue to impact contemporary educational theory.

Research on perceptual-motor intervention in education indicates that perceptual-motor programs may yield a negligible educational effect and actually may be harmful in some cases because they waste money, time, and energy. Kavale and Matson used meta-analysis to examine 180 studies on the effects of perceptual-motor programs. The subject receiving average treatment performed better cognitively or academically than only 54 percent of the control subjects, who had no comparable training.

A direct cognitive or academic benefit from perceptual-motor programs has not been substantiated scientifically, but the research in question has been heavily scrutinized and criticized. Many experts support the idea that perceptual-motor programs are not the panacea they were once purported to be. However, movement programs that incorporate academic concepts with the movement activities may be an excellent indirect way to supplement a child's education.

KEY TERMS

balance
body awareness
directional awareness
dynamic balance
hemispheric dominance
meta-analysis

motion hypothesis
perception
perceptual-motor
perceptual-motor development
perceptual-motor process
postural control

sensory integration
spatial awareness
static balance
temporal awareness

QUESTIONS FOR REFLECTION

1. What is a perceptual-motor program? How would it differ from a physical education program?

2. What is the motion hypothesis, and what are some research findings that led to its creation?

3. What is balance? What is the difference between static balance and dynamic balance?

4. List and describe five movement-related concepts that Kephart emphasized in his perceptual-motor theory. How and why did he think these concepts were helpful?

5. Typically, what happens to our balance as we age? Give two possible explanations as to why this phenomenon occurs.

6. What is directional awareness? Give two subdivisions of directional awareness and explain each.

7. What was the basis for Kephart's perceptual-motor theory? Is it well established, well accepted, or controversial? Explain your answer.

8. What are the steps of the perceptual-motor process? Explain each step. Are there any practical applications of this process?

INTERNET RESOURCES

Buros Institute–Sensory Motor Classification
  www.unl.edu/buros/index15.html

Johns Hopkins Center for Hearing and Balance
  www.bme.jhu.edu/labs/chb

Mayo Clinic Vestibular Rehabilitation Program
  www.mayoclinic.org/ent-rst/vestibular.html

Vestibular Disorders Association   **www.vestibular.org**

ONLINE LEARNING CENTER (www.mhhe.com/payne6e)

Visit the *Human Motor Development* Online Learning Center for study aids and additional resources. You can use the study guide questions and key terms puzzles to review key terms and concepts for this chapter and to prepare for exams. You can further extend your knowledge of motor development by checking out the Web links, articles, and activities found on the site.

REFERENCES

Adam, G. (1998). *Visceral perception: Internal cognition.* New York: Plenum Press.

American Academy of Pediatrics. (1999). The treatment of neurologically impaired children using patterning. *Pediatrics, 104*(5), 1149–1151.

Bachman, J. C. (1961). Motor learning and performance as related to age and sex in two measures of balance coordination. *Research Quarterly, 32,* 123–137.

Baker, C. P., Newstead, A. H., Mossberg, K. A., & Nicodemus, C. L. (1998). Reliability of static standing balance in nondisabled children: Comparison of two methods of measurement. *Pediatric Rehabilitation, 2*(1), 15–20.

Bartlett, F. C. (1958). *Thinking.* New York: Basic Books.

Berk, L. E. (2001). *Development through the lifespan.* 2nd ed. Boston: Allyn and Bacon.

Burton, A. W., & Davis, W. E. (1992). Assessing balance in adapted physical education: Fundamental concepts and applications. *Adapted Physical Activity Quarterly, 9,* 14–46.

Clark, J. E., & Watkins, D. L. (1984). Static balance in young children. *Child Development, 55,* 854–857.

Cratty, B. J. (1986). *Perceptual and motor development in infants and children.* 3rd ed. Englewood Cliffs, NJ: Prentice-Hall.

Delacato, C. H. (1959). *Treatment and prevention of reading problems.* Springfield, IL: Thomas.

———. (1963). *The diagnosis and treatment of speech and reading problems.* Springfield, IL: Thomas.

DeOreo, K. O. (1974). The performance and development of fundamental motor skills in preschool children. In M. Wade & R. Martens (Eds.), *Psychology of motor behavior and sport.* Urbana, IL: Human Kinetics.

———. (1975). Dynamic balance in preschool children: Process and product. In D. Landers (Ed.), *Psychology of sport and motor behavior II.* Proceedings of NASPSPA, Pennsylvania State University, State College.

Dorfman, P. W. (1977). Timing and anticipation: A developmental perspective. *Journal of Motor Behavior, 9,* 67–79.

Eichstaedt, C. B., & Lavay, B. W. (1992). *Physical activity for individuals with mental retardation: Infancy through adulthood.* Champaign, IL: Human Kinetics.

Gallahue, D. L., & Ozmun, J. C. (2002). *Understanding motor development: Infants, children, adolescents, adults.* 5th ed. Boston: WCB/McGraw-Hill.

Goulding, A., Jones, I. E., Taylor, R. W., Piggot, J. M., & Taylor, D. (2003). Dynamic and static tests of balance and postural sway in boys: Effects of previous wrist bone fractures and high adiposity. *Gait and Posture, 17*(2), 136–141.

Haslinger, L. W. (1971). Perceptual-motor task force summary of perceptual-motor survey. In American Association of Health, Physical Education, Recreation, and Dance (Ed.), *Foundations and practices in perceptual-motor learning: A quest for learning.* Washington, DC: AAHPERD.

Hatzitaki, V., Zisi, V., Kollias, I., & Kioumourtzoglou, E. (2002). Perceptual-motor contributions to static and dynamic balance in children. *Journal of Motor Behavior, 34*(2), 161–170.

Haywood, K. M. (1980). Coincidence-anticipation accuracy across the lifespan. *Experimental Aging Research, 6*(5), 451–462.

———. (1987). A longitudinal analysis of anticipatory judgment in older adult motor performance. In A. C. Ostrow (Ed.), *Aging and motor behavior.* Indianapolis, IN: Benchmark.

Held, R., & Hein, A. (1963). Movement-produced stimulation in the development of visually guided behavior. *Journal of Comparative and Physiological Psychology, 56,* 872–876.

Horak, F. B. (1987). Clinical measures of postural control in adults. *Physical Therapy, 67,* 1881–1885.

Jansma, P. (1999). Defining serious disability. In P. Jansma (Ed.), *Psychomotor training and serious disability* (pp. 4–9). Lanham, MD: University Press of America.

Kavale, K., & Matson, P. D. (1983). One jumped off the balance beam: Meta-analysis of perceptual-motor training. *Journal of Learning Disabilities, 16,* 165–173.

Keogh, J., & Sugden, D. (1985). *Movement skill development.* New York: Macmillan.

Kephart, N. (1960). *The slow learner in the classroom.* Columbus, OH: Merrill.

———. (1964). Perceptual-motor aspects of learning disabilities. *Exceptional Child, 31,* 201–206.

Largo, R. H., Caflisch, J. A., Hug, F., Muggli, K., Molnar, A. A., Molinari, L., Sheehy, A., & Gasser, S. T. (2001). Neuromotor development from 5 to 18 years: Part 1. Timed performance. *Developmental Medicine and Child Neurology, 43*(7), 444–453.

Rosenbaum, D. A., & Chaiken, S. R. (2001). Frames of reference in perceptual-motor learning: Evidence from a blind manual positioning task. *Psychological Research, 65*(2), 119–127.

Seefeldt, V. (1974). Perceptual-motor programs. In J. H. Wilmore (Ed.), *Exercise and sports sciences reviews.* Vol. 2. New York: Academic Press.

Shaffer, D. R. (2001). *Developmental psychology: Childhood and adolescence.* 5th ed. Pacific Grove, CA: Brooks/Cole.

Streepey, J. W., & Angulo-Kinzler, R. M. (2002). The role of task difficulty in the control of dynamic balance in children and adults. *Human Movement Science, 21*(4), 423–438.

Thomas, J. R., Thomas, K. T., Lee, A. M., Testerman, E., & Ashby, M. (1983). Age differences in use of strategy for recall of movement in a large-scale environment. *Research Quarterly for Exercise and Sport, 54*(3), 264–272.

Walk, R. D. (1981). *Perceptual development.* Monterey, CA: Brooks/Cole.

Williams, H. G. (1983). *Perceptual and motor development.* Englewood Cliffs, NJ: Prentice-Hall.

———. (1984). Problems in research in perceptual-motor development. Presentation at the National Conference of the American Alliance for Health, Physical Education, Recreation, and Dance, Anaheim, CA.

Woollacott, M. H., Shumway-Cook, A., & Williams, H. (1989). The development of posture and balance control in children. In M. H. Woollacott and A. Shumway-Cook (Eds.), *Development of posture and gait across the lifespan.* Columbia: University of South Carolina Press.

Prenatal Development Concerns

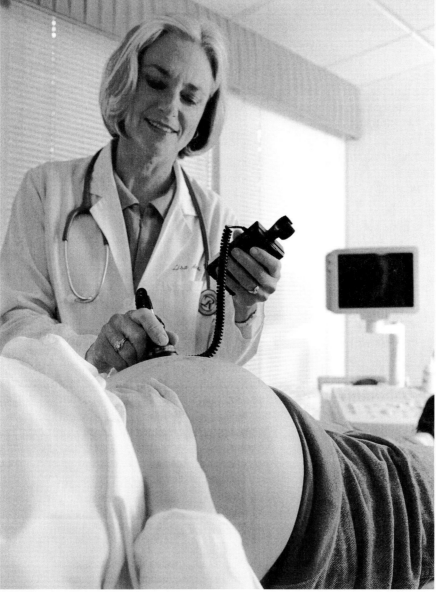

All human beings are unique, varying in appearance, personality, and movement abilities. Nevertheless, the normal growth and development process of all human beings is predictable. Although normally everyone attains the same mature human behaviors, the *rate* and ultimate *level* of achievement may vary considerably. Unfortunately, uncontrolled factors occasionally negatively influence the growth and development of the human organism. Such factors can emerge at any time throughout the lifespan; here, we discuss those that are particularly influential during the prenatal stage of growth and development. Because there are far more prenatal factors than we can discuss in this chapter, we have limited our coverage to those that are particularly timely, devastating, or important for the study of motor development.

The negative factors influencing prenatal life are believed to be a result of genetic or environmental misfortune. An environmental agent that causes harm to the embryo or fetus is known as a **teratogen.** The extent of damage caused from a teratogen is a function of such factors as the amount of exposure, the baby's genetic makeup, and the time of exposure. To better understand how time of exposure can influence a baby's development, let us first examine the anticipated course of human prenatal development.

PRENATAL DEVELOPMENT

Development of the human organism can be described in three major phases: the germinal period (fertilization and implantation), the embryonic period, and the fetal period.

The First 2 Weeks: Germinal Period

As illustrated in Figure 5-1, the first 2 weeks consist of the release of the oocyte from the ovary into the uterine tube where fertilization is accomplished. During the next 3 days the zygote will divide continuously, forming a blastomere (group of cells) as it proceeds toward the uterus. When zygote cleavage (mitotic division) reaches approximately 12 to

15 blastomeres (Moore & Persaud, 2003), it is termed a *morula.* The term *morula* is Latin for *morus,* meaning mulberry, because at this state the blastomere resembles the fruit on a mulberry tree. After the morula enters the uterus, it becomes a blastocyst. Approximately 6 days after fertilization, the blastocyst attaches to the endometrium, usually at the posterior wall of the uterus. During the second week, the blastocyst sinks beneath the endometrium, thus completing implantation.

If a teratogen is introduced during the preembryoic stage, death of the embryo is possible, because during this stage the substance is likely to damage all or most of the developing cells. If the teratogen damages only a few cells, the conceptus might recover and develop normally.

Weeks 3 to 8: Embryonic Period

The third through the eighth week of prenatal development is referred to as the main embryonic period. During this time, the organ systems and support systems begin to form. More specifically, the zygote forms an inner layer of cells called the **endoderm** and an outer layer of cells that are subdivided to form the **ectoderm** and the **mesoderm.** At this point the organism is referred to as an embryo. The endoderm provides the groundwork for the development of both the digestive system and the respiratory system. The ectoderm becomes the basis for the development of the nervous system, sensory receptors (eyes, ears, etc.), and skin features including nails and hair. The circulatory system, muscles, bones, excretory system, and reproductive system are all outgrowths of the mesoderm. Also during the embryonic period, the placenta (where the blood vessels between mother and embryo intertwine), umbilical cord (which connects the embryo to the placenta), and amnion (the clear fluid sack that protects the embryo) develop.

It is during the embryonic period that the embryo is most susceptible to the influences of a teratogen. Recall that this period of development is characterized by the development of the tissue and organ systems. Furthermore, it is during this time that the placenta forms, so the mother's blood sup-

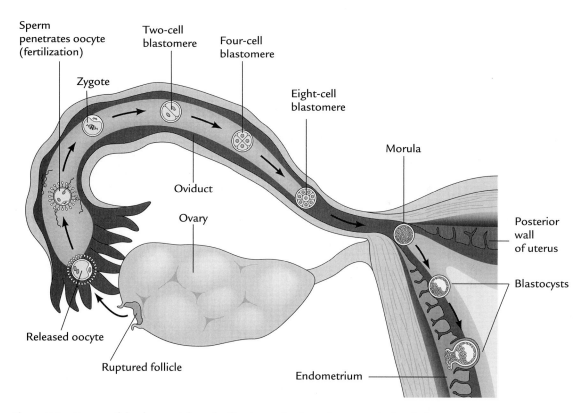

Figure 5-1   Course of development from fertilization to implantation—germinal period.

ply is now being shared with the embryo. In fact, the discovery that ***thalidomide,*** a tranquilizing drug, was the agent responsible for causing over 5000 malformed births in West Germany dispelled the myth that the maternal environment was a completely protective shelter for the developing embryo (Ferreira, Sachs, & Bombard, 2000). The thalidomide scare further illustrates how the timing of teratogen exposure affects development. For example, thalidomide had diverse effects on babies, with some babies developing malformed arms; others failed to achieve normal development of the outer ear, and some were missing a small bone in the hand. Still others were fortunate to experience no ill effects. Clearly, the thalidomide affected the tissue or organ system that was growing and developing the fastest at the time of exposure. Logically, most major congenital anomalies occur in this stage

of development. Figure 5-2 presents a detailed illustration of critical periods in human development. Pay particular attention to the dark shaded areas in Figure 5-2 as they indicate the times of greatest susceptibility.

Week 9 to Birth: Fetal Period

The fetal period begins at about 9 weeks after fertilization and continues until birth. During this period the fetus experiences rapid body growth as well as differentiation of organ systems. For example, 9 weeks after fertilization the fetus is only about 3 inches long and weighs only 1 ounce. However by birth, the average U.S. baby will be about 20 inches long and will weigh about 7 pounds.

Teratogens introduced during the fetal period generally result in relatively minor anomalies and

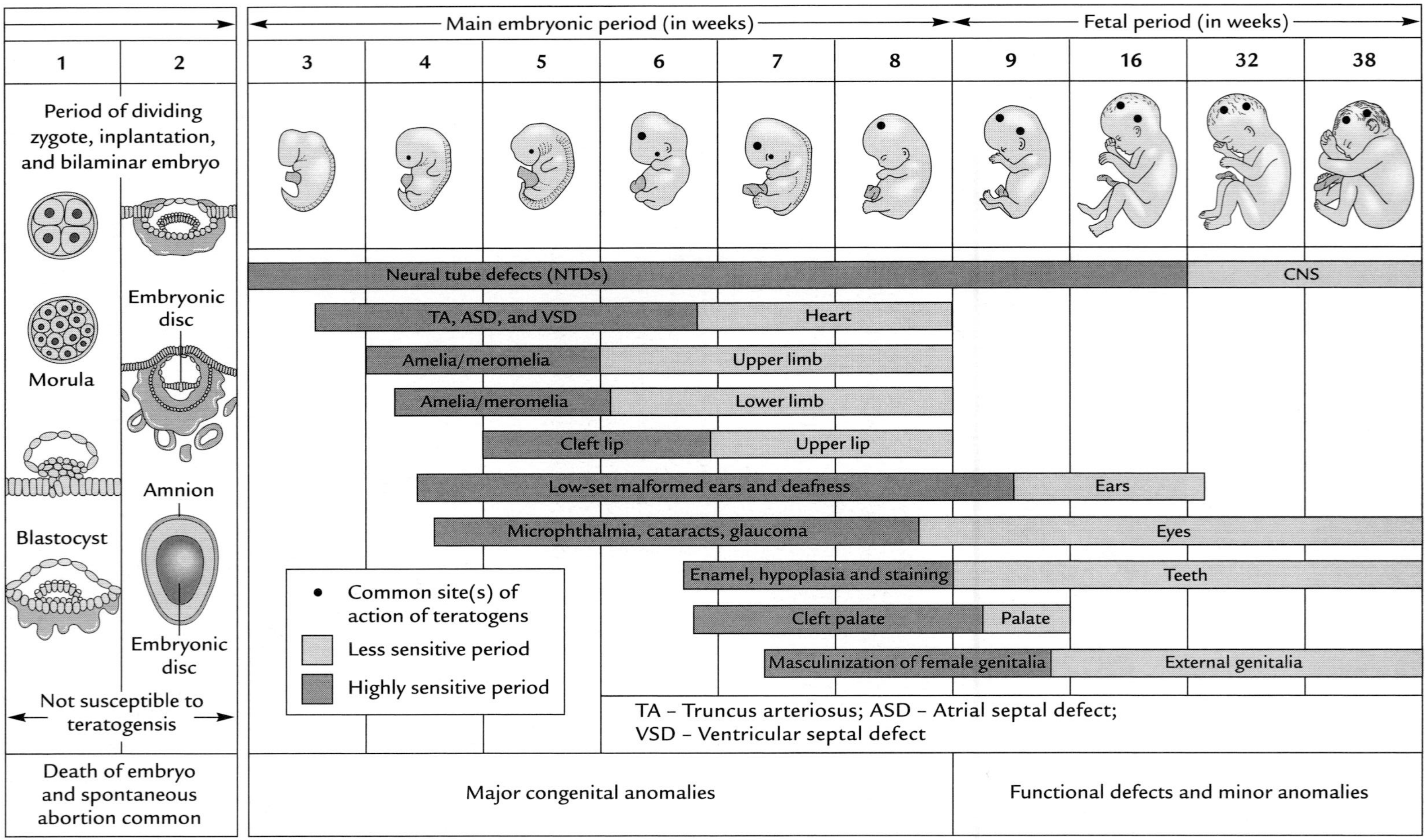

Figure 5-2 Schematic illustration of the critical periods in human development. During the first 2 weeks of development, the embryo is not usually susceptible to teratogens. During these preembryonic stages, a substance damages either all or most of the cells of the embryo, resulting in death, or it damages only a few cells, allowing the conceptus to recover and the embryo to develop without birth defects. Dark shading denotes highly sensitive periods when major defects may be produced (e.g., limb deficiencies). Lighter shading indicates stages that are less sensitive to teratogens when minor defects may be induced (e.g., hypoplastic thumbs).

SOURCE: Reprinted from Moore, K. L., and Persaud, T. V. N. (2003). *Before we are born.* 6th ed. Philadelphia: Saunders, p. 130. Copyright 2003, with permission from Elsevier.

functional defects. This is because the initial development of the tissues and organ systems has occurred and the period is mainly devoted to "building up tissues and preparing systems involved in the transition from intrauterine to extrauterine environments, primarily the respiratory and cardiovascular systems" (Moore & Persaud, 2003, p. 88).

DRUGS AND MEDICATIONS

Certain drugs and medications can enter fetal circulation and therefore should be taken by a pregnant woman only as advised by a physician. Recreational drugs, prescriptive drugs, nonprescriptive drugs, and obstetrical medications are all chemicals that can affect both the mother and the developing fetus.

Recreational Drugs

These are drugs that generally serve no medical purpose. The four most widely used recreational drugs are alcohol, cocaine, tobacco, and cannabis (marijuana).

ALCOHOL   About one in seven women aged 18 to 44 use alcohol (Centers for Disease Control and Prevention [CDC], 2003). More important, however, are findings indicating that the prevalence of any alcohol use among pregnant women is 12.9 percent. Perhaps of even greater concern is that 2.2 percent reported binge drinking (five or more drinks on any one occasion) and 3.3 percent reported frequent drinking (seven or more drinks per week or five or more drinks on any one occasion) during pregnancy (CDC, 2003). Thus the CDC estimates that more than 130,000 women in the United States consume alcohol during pregnancy at levels known to increase significantly the risk of giving birth to a baby having signs or symptoms associated with uterine alcohol exposure.

Women frequently ask, "How much alcohol can I safely drink during pregnancy?" In the opinion of the American Academy of Pediatrics (AAP, 2000) Committee on Substance Abuse and the Committee on Children with Disabilities, to date, there is no safe dose of alcohol for pregnant women. In fact, as little as one drink per day during pregnancy has been found to be associated with growth retardation (Mills et al., 1984). Because of the potential damage that drinking alcohol during pregnancy can have on the developing baby, the AAP recommends a greater societal effort to educate women of all ages about the potential dangers of drinking alcohol during pregnancy. More specifically, their recommendations include (1) the development and delivery of a mandatory curriculum for all elementary, junior high, and high school students, as well as postsecondary students attending adult education centers, (2) support of federal legislation mandating a warning label on all printed and broadcast alcohol advertisements such as "Drinking during pregnancy may cause mental retardation and other birth defects. Avoid alcohol during pregnancy," and (3) the development of state legislation that would make available information regarding the teratogenic effects of drinking alcohol during pregnancy at marriage-licensing bureaus and other public places.

These strong recommendations are necessary since the incidence of an infant developing symptoms associated with maternal alcohol consumption ranges between 6.7 per 10,000 (Henderson, 2000) to about 1 in every 300 live births. The cluster of birth defects resulting from prenatal alcohol exposure is known as *fetal alcohol syndrome (FAS)*. This condition manifests such abnormalities as altered facial features, mental retardation, attention deficit disorder with hyperactivity, and retarded physical growth in stature, weight, and head circumference. Indeed, the average birth weight of children born with FAS (2290 grams or 5 pounds, 1 ounce) is far below the average birth weight of children born without FAS (3370 grams or 7 pounds, 7 ounces) (Abel, 1990). Because of poor brain growth, FAS children attain an average IQ of only 67. Less severe symptoms are generally referred to as *alcohol-related neuro-developmental disorders (ARND)* and include such manifestations as fine motor dysfunction, clumsiness, delays in motor performance, and speech disorders, to name a few.

During the neonatal period, the child may even exhibit withdrawal symptoms known as *neonatal abstinence syndrome (NAS)*. The onset of NAS ranges from minutes or hours after birth to 14 days after birth, with most onsets occurring within

Table 5-1 Selected Outcomes of FAS and ARND		
Growth Deficiency	**Central Nervous System Dysfunctions**	**Craniofacial Anomalies**
Weight and length below 10th percentile corrected for gestational age	Poor motor coordination in 50% of infants	Epicanthic folds around eyes
Microcephaly	Weak sucking reflex	Obstruction of upper airway passages
Increased risk of congenital anomalies	IQ generally less than 70	Cleft palate
Decreased adipose tissue	Increased reaction time	
	Myopia (visual disorder)	
	Sensorineural hearing loss	
	Irritability (infancy)	
	Attention-deficit hyperactivity disorder	
	Hypotonia	
	Increased risk for seizures	
	Delayed language development	
	Fine motor impairment	

72 hours (MacGregor & Chasnoff, 1993). Symptoms generally include tremulousness, hyperactivity, and irritability. In short, few organ tissues or body systems are unaffected by alcohol consumption during the prenatal period. Table 5-1 highlights selected outcomes of FAS and ARND. Note that the abnormalities associated with FAS and ARND make up three categories: growth deficiency, central nervous system dysfunctions, and craniofacial anomalies.

COCAINE   Cocaine is the most infamous recreational drug of our time. Its use in all forms has increased dramatically in recent years. It is snorted, smoked as "crack," and injected more than ever before. Its use among pregnant women has also soared, with as many as 1 in 10 newborns being affected in some major urban areas (American College of Obstetricians and Gynecologists [ACOG], 2002). In any form, as little as one use of cocaine during pregnancy can have devastating consequences. Because cocaine is one of the most dangerous drugs to the unborn baby, the March of Dimes has strongly advised stopping use before pregnancy or delaying pregnancy until the drug can be avoided. They also advise the pregnant cocaine user to reveal her cocaine use immediately to her physician so that she can receive treatment to help her stop using the drug and so that early prenatal care can begin. Women who use co-

caine during pregnancy have a 25 percent higher incidence of preterm birth (ACOG, 2002).

One potentially devastating effect of cocaine use during pregnancy is fetal brain damage. This damage is believed to be the result of blood vessel constriction causing oxygen deprivation to the brain. This may explain why cocaine exposed babies exhibit mental retardation at a rate nearly five times greater than that observed in the general population (Singer et al., 2002). Additionally, because of brain and central nervous system damage, "cocaine babies" often score low on tests of responsiveness. For example, they perform poorly on measures of infant reflexes, often having poor sucking ability. Their attention span is also reduced considerably, making them relatively unresponsive to voices or faces. In addition, they are often "jittery" and extremely irritable, as they cry with minimal provocation. This lack of responsiveness and increase in irritability impedes the bonding process and makes the task of child rearing especially difficult for the mother. This likely contributes to later incidence of child abuse or neglect.

Other effects from maternal cocaine use include increased occurrence of miscarriage. This is often caused by uterine contractions late in pregnancy, which can result in premature labor. Cocaine also causes extreme fluctuations in the heart rate and blood pressure of the mother and the fetus. These rapid fluctuations in blood pressure can result in ruptured blood vessels of the brain, leading to stroke and contributing to the fetal brain damage mentioned earlier. Occasionally, the blood vessels to the placenta are also affected. They can be constricted to the point that the passage of nutrients to the fetus is impeded. This causes poor prenatal nutrition and increases the likelihood of a low birth weight baby who is shorter and has an abnormally small head circumference (Singer et al., 2002). Poor blood supply to the placenta can also cause the placenta to pull away from the uterine wall prematurely, causing extensive bleeding and potentially death to the mother and baby.

Finally, babies born to mothers who used cocaine excessively during pregnancy are also believed to be at greater risk of sudden infant death syndrome (SIDS) and will likely exhibit a slower rate of growth compared with the norm after birth (Rist, 1990). Slow growth rate, like the effects discussed earlier, could be prevented by not using cocaine during pregnancy.

Of particular interest to readers of this text is the influence of cocaine exposure during pregnancy on future motor development. Arendt and colleagues (1999) reported that 98 cocaine-exposed children performed significantly less well than 101 controls on both fine motor and gross motor indices as measured by the Peabody Developmental Motor Scales during a 2-year follow-up examination. Cocaine exposure independently predicted fine motor deficiencies involving eye-hand coordination and general hand usage. Significant differences in both balance and object reception and propulsion skills were noted within the gross motor scales. Thus detectable deficiencies in motor development of prenatally cocaine-exposed children remains detectable beyond 2 years of age.

TOBACCO The damaging effects of smoking tobacco during pregnancy were first recognized in 1935. However, intensive studies investigating the effects of smoking on prenatal development did not begin until the 1950s. By 1964, the adverse effects of smoking were so well documented that the Surgeon General's Report led to warning labels being placed on cigarette packages.

During this time of intensive study, over 2200 different ingredients were found in tobacco and to-

bacco smoke. Many of these ingredients were believed to have deleterious effects on the developing fetus. The major defects established included low birth weight (about 200–377 g lighter; Roche & Sun, 2003; Wang et al., 2002), higher rate of mortality at or around the time of birth, increased occurrence of miscarriage, decreased mental functioning in surviving offspring, and a twofold increase in the risk of SIDS (Haglund & Cnattingius, 1990). Postnatally, nicotine poisoning was a danger for the children of mothers who chose to breast-feed. In fact, M. S. Gold (1995) states that "a nursing mother is, in effect, giving her baby a cigarette if she smokes while nursing" (p. 182).

Today, the most studied pharmacological by-products of tobacco smoke are **carbon monoxide** and **nicotine.** Carbon monoxide is known to interfere with hemoglobin's oxygen-carrying and oxygen-releasing capabilities and therefore increases the risk of fetal hypoxia (lack of oxygen to body tissues). Nicotine also contributes to fetal hypoxia by causing the adrenals to release epinephrine, a hormone capable of constricting the placenta's blood vessels (M. S. Gold, 1995).

According to the Surgeon General's report on women and smoking (Superintendent of Documents, 2001), about 12 to 22 percent of pregnant women smoke during pregnancy. Researchers further note that these women are more likely to experience maternal complications than are their nonsmoking counterparts. Also of interest are findings that indicate that secondhand smoke also leads to these same maternal complications. Researchers have only begun to examine the effects of postnatal smoking on children's health. Initial studies have found that children who live in homes where smoking is prevalent exhibit more episodes of respiratory diseases such as bronchiolitis and pneumonia (Kandall, 1991). Table 5-2 summarizes short- and long-term risk factors associated with maternal tobacco smoking.

CANNABIS Marijuana, a mind-altering drug, is composed of more than 400 different chemicals (Turner, 1980). The most active ingredient frequently discussed is *11-hydroxy-delta-9-tetrahydrocannabinal,* commonly referred to as *THC.* Some researchers have estimated that as many

Table 5-2 Risk Factors Associated with Maternal Tobacco Smoking
Prenatal Complications
Premature rupture of membranes
Increased chance of spontaneous abortion
Higher rates of stillbirth
Intrauterine growth retardation
Postnatal Complications
Lower average birth weight
Small for gestational age
Sudden infant death syndrome (SIDS)
Long-term retardation of growth
Weight, stature, and head circumference
Respiratory disorders
Pneumonia
Bronchitis
Behavioral Effects
Reduced mental alertness
Reduced visual alertness
Mother less likely to breast-feed

as 44 percent of the female population have smoked marijuana during their reproductive years (Mac-Gregor & Chasnoff, 1993); those women who admitted using the drug during pregnancy said that they did so moderately (Fried et al., 1980). There are voluminous amounts of literature associating the detrimental effects of alcohol and tobacco use with maternal and fetal complications, but little conclusive research has examined marijuana and its effect on the human embryo or fetus (Miller & Chasnoff, 1993). For example, regular use of cannabis during pregnancy has been associated with longer, shorter, and normal gestational periods. Similarly, its use has also been associated with low birth weight and small-for-gestational-age infants. Yet, some have reported no effects at all on birth weight (MacGregor & Chasnoff, 1993). Currently, authorities are in general agreement that cannabis is associated with no known obstetric complications. Furthermore, the drug does not alter fetal growth (Queenan, 1999),

even though traces of it are detectable in the urine for up to 1 month and THC easily crosses the placenta and can accumulate in the fetal compartment. Nevertheless, doctors recommend that pregnant women refrain from the use of all recreational drugs.

Prescriptive Drugs

Many women have some sort of long-term disease that must be controlled by the continuous use of prescriptive medications, even during pregnancy. These women tend to give birth to malformed infants at a greater rate than do women who do not use prescriptive medications. There is controversy, however, as to whether the real cause of the reported malformations is the drugs or the mother's general ill health. For instance, women who control their epilepsy by using nonbarbiturate anticonvulsants tend to increase twofold their risk of giving birth to malformed offspring (Niebyl & Kochenour, 1999). However, when researchers controlled for the different degrees of the disease, they found that the incidence of malformations was no greater than what would be expected in the general population. Nevertheless, caution is advised during pregnancy when prescriptive drugs are considered, because they may damage the fetus.

Prescriptive drugs are believed to affect the fetus in two general ways. First, they may, like thalidomide, damage the body part that is growing and developing the fastest during the time of drug use. Second, they may adversely affect in the fetus that which was intended to be positively affected in the mother. For example, a mother taking prescriptive thyroid medication expects a positive effect on her thyroid gland. Though she may reap such benefits, the thyroid of the fetus may be damaged from the mother's prescriptive drug use. Table 5-3 presents popular prescriptive drugs and their possible side effects if taken during pregnancy.

Nonprescriptive Drugs

Nonprescriptive, or "over-the-counter," medications are generally assumed to be safe, because no prescription is required for them to be dispensed. While this is generally true, many nonprescriptive drugs can have dramatic teratogenic effects on the unborn

Table 5-3   Selected Prescriptive Medications and Their Possible Effects on the Developing Fetus

Medication	Use of Medication	Possible Teratogenic Effect
Anticoagulants: Warfarin	Blood clots	Central nervous system defects Miscarriage Eye defects
Lithium	Bipolar disorder	Congenital heart defects

Antibiotics:
   Tetracycline
   Streptomycin
	Infections	Underdevelopment of tooth enamel
		and tooth yellowing

Anticonvulsants: Dilantin	Seizure disorders	Mental retardation Neural tube defects Hand and face defects
Streptomycin	Tuberculosis	Hearing loss

Antithyroids:
   Propylthiouracil, Iodide,
   and Methimazole
	Overactive thyroid	Thyroid gland defects

baby. For that reason, many physicians recommend not treating such illnesses as colds with nonprescriptive drugs unless absolutely necessary. If a pregnant woman feels she needs to take such a medication, she should consult her physician before taking it.

Aspirin, one of the most common over-the-counter drugs, has been linked to postterm pregnancy and prolonged labor if taken in high doses over an extended time. It can also cause excessive bleeding within the skull of the baby and increase the mother's bleeding during delivery (Ensher, Clard, & Yarwood, 1994). Unlike most teratogens, which are particularly dangerous early in pregnancy, the greatest risk with aspirin occurs when taken within a few weeks of giving birth.

Acetaminophen (Tylenol) may be the safest substitute for aspirin, as current research has shown no prenatal damage associated with this drug. Similarly, there is no current evidence that other nonsteroidal anti-inflammatory drugs such as ibuprofen (Advil, Motrin) and naproxen (Aleve) are teratogenic, especially with short-term limited use. However, chronic use may lead to oligohydramnios (abnormally small amount or absence of amniotic fluid) and constriction of the fetal ductus arteriosus (Niebyl & Kochenour, 1999).

A problem with many over-the-counter medications is that they have been designed to treat an array of maladies. Such nonprescriptive medications should always be avoided during pregnancy because of increased risk of prenatal harm due to the variety of chemicals they contain. This is the case with many cold medications, which can also be potentially damaging if high in alcohol content. As discussed earlier in the chapter, ingesting alcohol during pregnancy can cause fetal alcohol syndrome or alcohol-related neurodevelopmental disorder. Avoiding cold medications can be particularly difficult during pregnancy, because pregnant women tend to have a lower resistance to illness and, therefore, have more colds.

Obstetrical Medications

Physicians prescribe and administer many drugs during pregnancy and delivery. It has been estimated that in one year obstetrician-gynecologists prescribe 3.7 million doses of narcotic analgesics, 1.3 million doses of barbiturate sedatives, 1.1 million doses of nonnarcotic analgesics, and 1.1 million doses of tranquilizers (Brackbill, 1979). Stewart, Cluff, and Philip (1977; cited in Osofsky, 1987) reported that, on average, 7 drugs are administered during a vaginal delivery and 15.2 drugs during a cesarean section delivery. Though health-care professionals have become more cautious concerning the effects of drugs on the unborn, just 25 years ago only 5 percent of deliveries were accomplished without anesthesia (Brackbill, 1979).

The preanesthetic medications most frequently administered to laboring women are oxytocin (to initiate and aid labor), meperidine (to relieve pain), and phenergan (to relieve anxiety). Other forms of anesthetic agents include those for general anesthesia (loss of sensation throughout the entire body—that is, sleep) and regional anesthesia (loss of sensation in a selected area of the body).

There is controversy over the use of obstetric medications because these agents are known to enter fetal circulation, exerting their effects on the child, within minutes after being administered to the mother. Brazelton (1961) has shown that the use of preanesthetic sedatives caused depressed sucking behaviors throughout the first week of life. A longitudinal investigation by Brackbill (1976) demonstrates that infants displayed the effects of being exposed to obstetrical medications just as strongly at 8 months as during the first month of postnatal life.

MATERNAL DISEASES

A host of maternal diseases can potentially exert an influence upon the developing fetus. These diseases include the following: viral diseases (rubella, HIV), parasitic diseases (toxoplasmosis), hematologic diseases (Rh incompatibility), and endocrine diseases (diabetes mellitus). In this section we examine several of the most influential maternal diseases that can affect the outcome of pregnancy.

Rubella and Congenital Rubella Syndrome

Rubella, sometimes referred to as the German measles, is a highly contagious virus characterized by swollen lymph nodes, mild fever, headache, aching joints, and a pink rash appearing on the face,

body, arms, and legs. In fact, the symptoms can be so mild that between 20 to 50 percent of infected individuals may actually fail to notice any symptoms at all. Rubella reached epidemic proportions in the United States in 1964 and 1965 when 15.5 million cases of the infection were reported. Additionally, according to the Centers for Disease Control and Prevention (2003), approximately 20,000 newborns were affected and exhibited symptoms referred to as *congenital rubella syndrome (CRS).* Unlike the mild symptoms usually experienced by the adult, the developing fetus can incur great damage. The extent of this damage depends in part on when the pregnant woman becomes infected with the virus. The most prevalent defect of CRS, occurring in 80 percent of infected children, is deafness (Alger, 2000). Other potential fetal defects include growth retardation, cataracts, bony lesions, pneumonia, hepatitis, congenital glaucoma, mental retardation, and cardiac anomalies resulting in early heart failure. The incidence of rubella and CRS defects is difficult to establish accurately, because many of the associated defects are frequently masked during infancy, surfacing only in later months or years (E. Gold et al., 1991). Fortunately, however, we do know that since the introduction of vaccines, the incidence of rubella and CRS has steadily declined (see Figure 5-3).

Human Immunodeficiency Virus

Women who carry the *human immunodeficiency virus (HIV)* risk passing this deadly virus on to their offspring. According to the Centers for Disease Control and Prevention, approximately 7000 infants are born each year to HIV-infected mothers in the United States. Until 1994, about 15 to 25 percent of these newborns acquired their mother's HIV infection (Minkoff & Burgess, 1999). Perinatal transmission is generally accomplished in one of three ways: (1) in utero from the mother to the fetus, (2) during delivery when the fetus comes in contact with infected blood or infected vaginal secretions, and (3) through breast milk.

Since 1994, oral administration of zidovudine during pregnancy, intravenously during labor and

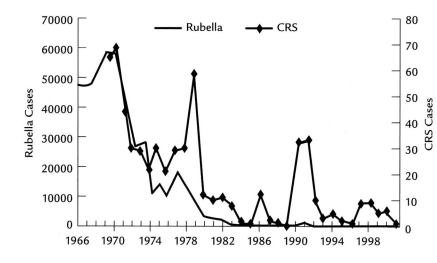

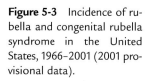

Figure 5-3 Incidence of rubella and congenital rubella syndrome in the United States, 1966–2001 (2001 provisional data).
SOURCE: Centers for Disease Control and Prevention (2003).

orally for 6 weeks to the newborn, has significantly decreased HIV infection in susceptible children to as low as 4.8 percent (Hueppchen, Anderson, & Fox, 2000). The prognosis for infants infected by HIV, however, is not bright. In fact, the median survival time from clinical onset is only 24 months. However, there does appear to be a form of HIV (static HIV), the course of which, for some reason, is not as rapid. Children who can survive past 2 years of age have a chance at prolonging life. Nevertheless, 90 percent will manifest symptoms by age 4 (Diamond & Cohen, 1992), and few will live past 13.

HIV-infected children exhibit an array of developmental disabilities. Table 5-4 lists several of the neurological complications. Many of these complications are described in a case study by Diamond and associates (1990) involving a 14-month-old white boy (J. M.) and a 6-year-old African American boy (C. P.). For example, J. M. was small and exhibited noticeable muscle wasting at 4 months of age. In addition, pervasive spasticity with truncal hypotonia and poor head control was evident. He also showed no interest in playing with small toys. C. P. was also small for his age with height and weight only at the 40th percentile. He also experienced difficulty with both fine motor and visual-motor integrative tasks and used an immature pencil grip.

When the disease becomes full-blown AIDS, the immune system generally deteriorates rapidly, and

Table 5-4   Neurological Deterioration in HIV-Infected Children
Loss of previously acquired milestones
Failure to attain developmental milestones at the expected age
Impaired brain growth
Spasticity or rigidity
Muscle weakness
Ataxia (impaired ability to control movement)
Seizures and extrapyramidal tract signs (tremor, athetosis)

SOURCE: Diamond and Cohen (1992).

death is usually caused by the body's inability to fight off infection.

Toxoplasmosis

The fetus can also be infected by protozoan parasites, of which the most common is ***Toxoplasma gondii.*** Members of the feline (cat) family are the primary hosts for this organism. Pregnant women are introduced to the organism when they are exposed to infectious oocysts present in soil contaminated by cat feces or when they ingest undercooked meats containing the active organism. This virus has frequently been called the "silent infection" because only 10 percent of infected newborns show clinical evidence of the disease at birth (Alford, Pass, & Stagno, 1983).

In cases of acute toxoplasmosis, 85 percent of live births will experience mental retardation and convulsions; 75 percent will experience abnormalities in motor abilities. Other reported abnormalities include deafness (13 percent) and visual impairments (50 percent) that may be present at birth or take many years to become detectable (Alford et al., 1983). The incidence of primary maternal toxoplasmosis in the United States has been estimated at 1 in 900 pregnancies (Sison & Sever, 1999).

Rh Incompatibility and Erythroblastosis Fetalis

Early attempts to transfuse blood from human to human and from animal to human did not succeed, because people were unaware that human blood contains many different components. At the turn of the twentieth century, the medical community discovered that human blood can be divided into four distinct groups (A, B, AB, O) and that attempts to cross-transfuse blood types stimulates the recipient's immune system to produce antibodies to destroy the donor's foreign cells.

We know now that in addition to the four major blood groups, the red blood cells of approximately 85 percent of the population contain an additional protein: the *Rh factor.* Individuals with the Rh factor have Rh-positive blood; those people lacking the blood protein possess Rh-negative blood. That all individuals do not possess an Rh factor on their red blood cells is of special concern for a selected group of parents. There is a potential problem when an Rh-positive man and an Rh-negative woman conceive an Rh-positive child. If during the course of gestation, Rh-positive blood cells escape from fetal circulation to enter maternal circulation, the mother's Rh-negative blood will view the Rh-positive cells as foreign bodies. The mother's body will then be stimulated to produce antibodies against the Rh-positive cells. These antibodies may then enter fetal circulation and destroy the fetal red blood cells.

Because maternal and fetal circulation do not mix under normal circumstances, some experts suggest that fetal blood cells may enter maternal circulation by escaping from broken vessels in the placental villi. Because the placental vessels do not generally rupture until later in pregnancy, the mother develops antibodies postnatally, sparing her first offspring. However, in order for subsequent children to be protected, the mother should receive an injection of *anti-D IgG immunoglobulin* immediately after her first delivery. Treatment within 72 hours after delivery is adequate for protection in 98 percent of cases. This form of treatment has been a major breakthrough in obstetrics, lowering the percentage of deaths from 3.9 percent in 1969 to 0.5 percent in 1986 (cited in Perry, Martin, & Morrison, 1991).

Rh-positive offspring exposed to the antibodies of their Rh-negative mother are born with a condition called *erythroblastosis fetalis,* also called congenital hemolytic disease. Characteristics of this disorder include anemia, an increased number of immature red blood cells in circulation, generalized edema, and jaundice.

The probability of a susceptible couple giving birth to an Rh-positive child depends on whether the father carries the Rh antigens on both members of his paired chromosomes (*homozygous*) or just one of the two chromosomes (*heterozygous*). If the father is a homozygous carrier, all of his children will be Rh positive; a heterozygous carrier has a 50 percent chance of producing an Rh-positive child. Approximately 12 percent of all marriages involve Rh-positive men and Rh-negative women.

Diabetes Mellitus

Infants born to mothers with *diabetes mellitus* remain a high-risk population in spite of improving management (insulin regulation and diet therapy). Complications during pregnancy are attributed to the fetus's exposure to a constantly altering metabolic environment. This metabolic environment can range from *normoglycemia* (normal blood sugar) to *hypoglycemia* (low blood sugar) to intermittent or constant *hyperglycemia* (high blood sugar). A particular problem is fetal hyperinsulinemia (excessive insulin) induced by maternal hyperglycemia. Pedersen and Pedersen (1971, cited in Luke, Johnson, & Petrie, 1993) have hypothesized that this condition may result in (1) *macrosomia* (birth weight above the 90th percentile for gestational age or greater than 4000 grams), making a vaginal delivery difficult; (2) inhibition of maturation of lung surfactant; (3) muscle weakness or cardiac arrhythmias as a result of decreased serum potassium; and (4) possible permanent neurological damage brought on by neonatal hypoglycemia. Of these four outcomes, the most frequently mentioned is macrosomia. Pedersen (1977) has advanced a theory as to the cause of this condition. Namely, during the third trimester, maternal hyperglycemia leads to increases in fetal glucose. As a result, fetal secretion of insulin from the pancreas is increased, causing fetal hyperinsulinemia. This increase in insulin production in turn leads to an increased level of glycogen in the fetal liver, thus stimulating increased triglyceride synthesis in fat (adipose) cells. As a result, there is an increase in fetal body fat.

Of particular interest to health professionals are findings that suggest that macrosomia in infants of diabetic mothers may be an important factor in accounting for obesity in later life. More specifically, it was found that all macrosomic infants were classified as obese at 7 years of age, compared with only 1 in 14 appropriate-for-gestational-age infants (Vohr, Lipsitt, & Oh, 1980). If hyperglycemia can be eliminated throughout the term of pregnancy, the perinatal mortality rate is similar to that seen in the general population. Table 5-5 highlights selected abnormalities of infants born to mothers with diabetes.

GENETIC FACTORS

Genetic factors affecting normal prenatal growth and development can take one of two forms. That is, abnormal development can be caused by a chromosomal or gene-based disorder.

Chromosomal Disorders

Every normal cell within our bodies contains 46 chromosomes, with the exception of the reproductive cells (sperm and ovum), which contain only 23 chromosomes. When the sperm and ovum join during conception, each contributes its 23 chromo-

Table 5-5   Selected Abnormalities of Infants Born to Diabetic Mothers

Central nervous system deformities
  Spina bifida
  Hydrocephalus

Cogenital anomalies
  Heart defects
  Skeletal and central nervous system defects

Macrosomia
Musculoskeletal deformities
Respiratory distress syndrome

Traumatic birth injury
  Asphyxia
  Facial nerve injury
  Brachial plexus injury
  Cesarean section due to cephalopelvic disproportion

somes, to form a new individual whose cells will also contain the usual 23 pairs of genetic material. When the sex chromosomes reproduce through cell division (meiosis), there can be problems if, during the division, a pair of chromosomes does not separate properly. This lack of chromosomal separation is called *meiotic nondisjunction,* the result of which is that one sperm or egg cell contains two members of a particular numbered chromosome while the other member contains none. If, during conception, the cell containing the extra chromosome unites with a normal sex cell, the new individual will possess 47 chromosomes. This individual is said to be trisomic, meaning that one of the chromosomes has three rather than the usual two members.

The most frequent cytogenetic defect is *Down syndrome (DS).* The technical name for this syndrome is trisomy 21, indicating that chromosome number 21 has three chromosomes instead of the usual two. As a result of meiotic nondisjunction, Down syndrome occurs at an average rate of 1 in 700 births (Eglinton & Seydel, 1999). The incidence of occurrence is greatest in children of mothers over age 35.

The most striking behavioral outcome of this syndrome is mental retardation. This population generally obtains IQ scores between 20 and 60 and functions at a maximum average mental age of 8 years. Table 5-6 lists other prominent characteristics

Table 5-6 Symptoms and Signs of Trisomy 21 (Down Syndrome)

Walking delayed 1 or more years

Speech development slow

Slow development of fine motor control

Toilet training delayed

Lower than normal birth weight

Hypotonia (too little muscle tone)

Short stature

Puberty often delayed

Prone to respiratory infections

Heart disease common

Prominent anatomical features
    Close-set eyes
    Short, thick neck
    Small, rather square head

of this genetic defect. Pay special attention to the fact that the fundamental motor pattern, walking, is generally delayed until 2 years of age, compared with 1 year of age in the normally developed child. D. A. Ulrich and colleagues (2001) discovered that infants with DS were capable of exhibiting well-coordinated, alternating stepping patterns at approximately 11 months of age when held in the upright position. Because alternating stepping movements resembled walking, the researchers believed that stepping practice in the form of parent-assisted treadmill walking could influence the onset of independent walking in children with DS. They felt that, in accordance with dynamical systems theory, assisted treadmill walking would emphasize not only neural connections, but also the training of multiple subsystems, such as muscular strength, proprioception, joint structure, motivation, and temperament, and that these subsystems are as important as the nervous system in determining specific motor behaviors (D. A. Ulrich & Ulrich, 1999). As a result of this hypothesis, D. A. Ulrich and colleagues (2001) developed an infant treadmill-walking intervention program. Subjects with DS were admitted to the study when they were capable of sitting alone for 30 seconds. The treadmill intervention program consisted of parent-assisted walking at a speed of 0.46 mph for

8 minutes per day, 5 days per week, until the infant was capable of independent walking. Analysis indicated that DS subjects assigned to the intervention group, on average, walked independently 101 days sooner than did subjects in a control group who did not participate in the intervention program.

Gene-Based Disorders

PHENYLKETONURIA   One gene-based disorder is *phenylketonuria (PKU).* Since its discovery in 1934 by Asbjorn Folling, a Norwegian doctor, PKU has been the topic of literally thousands of research papers, mainly because the discovery led to the prevention of the mental retardation associated with PKU. Mental manifestations are the most commonly reported clinical features of the disorder, but some individuals may exhibit neurological dysfunctions and extraneural symptoms, including motor impairments such as tight muscles and muscle tremors.

PKU is caused by a disturbance in amino acid metabolism as a result of inheriting a gene that suppresses the activity of the liver enzyme phenylalanine hydroxylase. This enzyme is responsible for converting dietary L-phenylalanine to the amino acid tyrosine. If there is not enough of this conversion, the body tissues accumulate dangerous levels of L-phenylalanine, causing irreversible changes in the central nervous system. The estimated occurrence of the disorder is 1 in 14,000 (Evans et al., 1991).

Unlike the other birth disorders discussed, PKU cannot be evaluated by visual inspection; blood levels of phenylalanine must be measured in the laboratory. For accurate blood level measures to be obtained, all newborns should be evaluated no sooner than 8 days after birth, because the level of phenylalanine in the blood of phenylketonuric children rises after birth until the concentration reaches a dangerous level. Screening too early may result in not diagnosing 5 to 10 percent of phenylketonuric children.

As early as the mid 1950s, the medical community demonstrated that many of the symptoms of PKU could be favorably modified and even prevented by placing the child on a low phenylalanine diet. For treatment to be most effective, the disorder should be diagnosed as soon as possible. Major significant differences have been found between early- and late-treated groups of phenylketonuric children. Steinhausen (1974) found that early-treated groups maintained normal levels of development, whereas those treated after 6 months of life remained below age-level functioning in motor and social development.

CYSTIC FIBROSIS Another gene-based disorder is *cystic fibrosis (CF).* This devastating disease affects approximately 30,000 children and adults in the United States. Approximately 1 out of every 25 Caucasians carries the gene, and 1 in every 2500 births is affected by CF (Verp, Simpson, & Ober, 1993). One-half of the individuals with CF die before age 30, while the second half will generally live into their early 40s. Characteristically, this disease causes a thick, sticky mucus to be secreted within the lungs. This mucus causes those with CF to experience reoccurring bouts of pulmonary infection. In addition, the thick mucus frequently will clog the pancreas and interfere with normal digestion. From a movement perspective, those with CF often experience shortness of breath, and they fatigue easily. With repeated bouts of lung infection, additional scar tissue within the lungs accumulates and worsens the condition. To date there is no cure for CF. However, in December 1993, the U.S. Food and Drug Administration approved the first new class of CF medication in 30 years. This new drug is an enzyme (pulmozyme) that thins the CF mucus. Researchers are now experimenting with gene therapy in an attempt to correct abnormalities within the gene.

SICKLE-CELL TRAIT AND SICKLE-CELL DISEASE *Sickle-cell trait (SCT)* describes a condition in which a person inherits a genetic abnormality of the red blood cell caused by a mutation in a parental gene for hemoglobin (Hb). The individual is said to possess the SCT if he or she possesses one normal gene (A) and one abnormal gene (S). Individuals with the SCT are generally asymptomatic (Martineaud et al., 2002) and the trait does not appear to pose a significant barrier to athletic performance (National Collegiate Athletic Association, 2001). However, a far more serious condition, *sickle-cell disease (SCD)*, occurs when the offspring inherits two defective genes (SS). In this situation, the red blood cell will change from its characteristic doughnut shape to the classic "sickle" shape—thus the name, sickle-cell disease. As illustrated in Figure 5-4, when both parents carry the SCT, their chance of producing an offspring with SCT is 50 percent; of producing an offspring with SCD, 25 percent; and of producing a normal offspring, 25 percent. Also illustrated in Figure 5-4 are the potential consequences of sickle-cell disease. Briefly, such consequences come about because of a destruction of red blood cells; a clumping of the sickle-shaped cells, which leads to circulatory problems because of the cells' inability to travel through small blood vessels; and an unusually high concentration of sickle-shaped cells in the spleen. Current treatments involve red blood cell transfusions and a new drug (hydroxyurea), which is capable of turning on the production of healthy Hb. This disease predominately affects people in Africa and those of African descent. In the United States, SCD occurs in approximately 1 in 500 African American births and in approximately 1 in 1000 to 1400 Hispanic births, while the rate of SCT is about 1 in every 12 African Americans (National Heart, Lung, and Blood Institute, 1996).

PRENATAL DIAGNOSTIC PROCEDURES

Though the list of potential teratogens seems to increase daily, most babies are born healthy. In fact, only about 4 percent will be born with abnormalities. Among those, most will have abnormalities so slight as to have minimal impact on daily function. Aiding in the battle against the small number of abnormalities that occur is an array of diagnostic tools. Though these tools are not "cures" for the prenatal abnormalities they can detect, they can alert expectant parents and health-care professionals of the need to take special precautions for the remainder of the pregnancy. For some, these tools may provide valuable information in deciding whether to continue the pregnancy.

Although medical technology is creating new diagnostic tools regularly, the four most current prenatal diagnostic tools are ultrasound, amniocentesis, chorionic villus sampling, the alpha-fetoprotein test, and

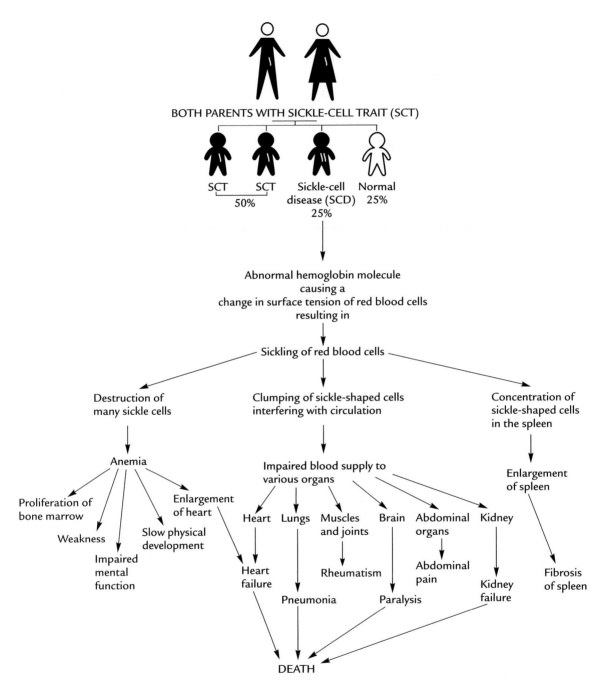

Figure 5-4 Sickle-cell incidence and outcomes

the triple marker screening blood test. These tools are especially important for women who are believed to be at risk for giving birth to a child with abnormalities. A woman might be a high-risk candidate if she

- will be over age 35 at the time of delivery
- has already given birth to (or has a partner who has had) a child with a genetic disease or birth defect
- has a family history of genetic disease or birth defects
- has a medical history of certain genetic traits (e.g., sickle-cell anemia or diabetes)

Women who are not high risk may also have these tests administered. However, these tests can be expensive and, in the case of amniocentesis and chorionic villus sampling, can pose a small risk of damaging the fetus. With the exception of the alpha-fetoprotein test, where the law in some states mandates offering the test to all pregnant women, these tests should be administered judiciously.

Ultrasound

Ultrasound, also referred to as a sonogram, is administered by placing a small transmitter on the abdomen of the pregnant woman. Typically, the abdomen is lubricated so the transmitter can be easily maneuvered into the position that enables the best picture of the fetus. The transmitter emits high-frequency sound waves that echo off the fetus. In turn, these sound waves are transformed into computer-enhanced images on a monitor. Though not producing a particularly clear image, a sonogram creates a clear enough picture to measure the head size of the baby, which can help determine the exact length of gestation (see Figure 5-5). It can also be used to examine the placement and structure of the placenta as well as detecting the baby's gender, multiple pregnancies, and some anatomical abnormalities. The advantages of an ultrasound test are that it causes no pain, no injection is required, and it takes only about 30 minutes. According to the American Institute of Ultrasound in Medicine, there are no confirmed adverse biological effects on either patients or operators (Rosen & Hoskins, 2000).

Amniocentesis

Unlike ultrasound, *amniocentesis* requires a needle to be inserted through the abdominal wall. This procedure, which was first used for fetal diagnosis in 1967, employs a thin needle to remove approximately 2 tablespoons of amniotic fluid drawn from the small amniotic sac around the fetus. This fluid contains fetal cells, which can be examined to determine the presence of some abnormalities. Because amniocentesis is an intrusive test, ultrasound is used to locate the best site for puncture, to locate the placenta, and to guide the needle safely to the best pool of amniotic fluid.

Though amniocentesis is believed to present minimum risk to the mother and fetus, the needle has been known to damage the fetus on occasion. In addition, amniocentesis has caused miscarriages in approximately 1 in 200 pregnancies (Cincinnati Children's Hospital, 2003). For those reasons, this test is generally only employed when the mother is at high risk for giving birth to a child with abnormalities. Amniocentesis is administered in the second trimester, usually between 15 and 20 weeks of gestation. With an increase in the resolution of ultrasound, some centers are now performing this procedure at the 13th or 14th week of gestation (Elias & Simpson, 2000). The process takes about 20 minutes and can detect numerous chromosomal abnormalities (e.g., Down syndrome), the gender of the baby, and neural-tube defects (e.g., spina bifida, a failure of the bony structure of the spine to close completely around the spinal cord) with a high degree (99%) of accuracy (DeVore, 2003).

Chorionic Villus Sampling

Chorionic villus sampling (CVS) is a technique that offers one major advantage over amniocentesis: It can be administered between 10 and 12 weeks of gestation, so that any abnormalities are detected earlier (Elias & Simpson, 2000). At that time, there are too few viable cells per milliliter of amniotic fluid for amniocentesis to be reliable and safe. Like amniocentesis, CVS is designed to gather cell samples for examination. However, rather than sampling the amniotic fluid, CVS is intended to take samples

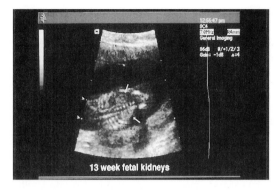

(a)

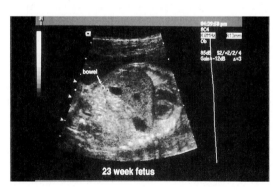

(b)

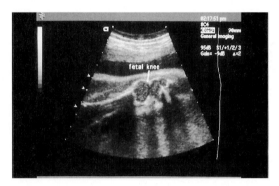

(c)

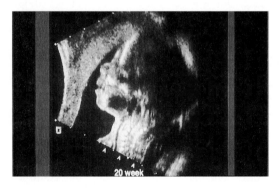

(d)

(e)

(f)

Figure 5-5 The sonogram is a valuable diagnostic tool that enables medical professionals to view the fetus. Fetal kidneys (a), fetal arm (b), fetal knee (c), 2-chamber heart < 6-week embryo (d), 20-week fetal head and neck (e), and 23-week fetal bowel (f).

SOURCE: Images courtesy of Acuson Corporation.

of the small hairlike projections of the placenta (see Figure 5-6). These projections, known as *villi,* can reveal the same information available through amniocentesis. CVS is administered by inserting a needle through the abdomen or through the cervix of the pregnant woman. Both methods employ ultrasound to guide the needle used to take the sample.

Though CVS offers the advantage of earlier administration and thus earlier detection of abnormalities, it is also potentially riskier than amniocentesis. Three times as many miscarriages are caused by CVS than by amniocentesis, with 1 in 100 CVS administrations causing problems. Therefore, CVS is recommended for only the highest-risk pregnant women. For such women, any dangers are generally believed to be outweighed by the benefit of knowing early in the pregnancy that the baby is experiencing abnormalities and may need special prenatal care.

Alpha-Fetoprotein Test

The *alpha-fetoprotein test* is a simple blood test performed at approximately 15 to 20 weeks into the pregnancy. This blood test measures the amount of alpha-fetoprotein (AFP) in the blood and can indicate the presence of neural-tube defects in the case of high AFP levels or such chromosomal disorders as Down syndrome when levels are low. In fact, high serum AFP values can identify 95 percent of anencephaly (congenital absence of part of the brain) and 80 percent of open spina bifida, while low values identify up to 25 percent of fetuses with Down syndrome (Scioscia, 1993). Because the majority of women who have abnormal AFP levels give birth to normal babies, the AFP test is usually employed as a screening device to determine if additional prenatal diagnostic testing should be done. The presence of twins or a small miscalculation in the time of gestation can cause misinterpretation of AFP levels.

Triple Marker Screening

Until recently, there were no useful tests for identifying Down syndrome in pregnant women younger than age 35. However, it is now possible to screen maternal blood serum to test for the amount of human chorionic gonadotropin, unconjugated estriol, and the previously mentioned alpha-fetoprotein. These substances, which vary in amount during the course of the pregnancy, are produced by both the mother's placenta and the fetus and as a screening package are referred to as the *triple marker* (DeVore, 2003). Unlike the risk involved in amniocentesis, the triple marker screening simply requires a small amount of blood to be drawn from the mother's arm. In most instances, the test is offered to younger mothers during the second trimester. The rate of accuracy is currently between 40 and 60 percent. While this rate of detection is acceptable for women less than 35 years of age, it is unacceptable for older pregnant women. For those older than 35, amniocentesis, with its 99 percent rate of detection, is still the preferred screening procedure.

MATERNAL NUTRITION

Adequate prenatal nutrition is essential for the well-being of the mother-to-be as well as the growing fetus. The prenatal diet must cover the increased metabolic load that accompanies pregnancy. These additional calories are needed to support the growth of the placenta and the developing fetus. Indeed, total caloric intake appears to be one of the foremost factors affecting infant birth weight. To supply the extra energy needed during pregnancy, sedentary women need to increase their caloric intake by approximately 300 calories per day, for a total of 85,000 calories over the course of the pregnancy (Worthington-Roberts, 2000). Women who continue strenuous physical activity during pregnancy must make additional adjustments. How much of an adjustment depends on the caloric cost of the activities performed. In general, the active pregnant woman should ingest additional calories equivalent to the energy expended during physical activity plus the 300 calories per day maintenance load. If weight gain falls below expected levels during the course of pregnancy, then it may be necessary to increase caloric intake further.

How much weight should a woman gain over the course of pregnancy? The answer to this question is influenced by the woman's weight prior to

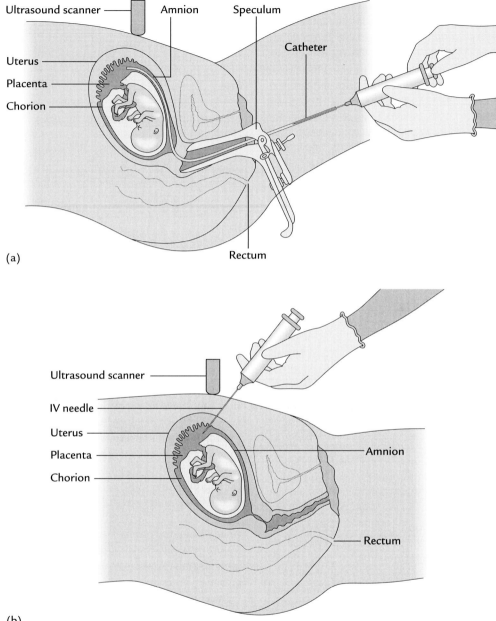

Figure 5-6   Here are two different methods employed to gather a tissue sample in chorionic villus testing. A plastic catheter is inserted through the cervix and guided by ultrasound (a). A biopsy needle is inserted through the abdominal wall and guided by ultrasound (b).

Table 5-7 Recommended Weight Gain During Pregnancy, Based on Pregravid Weight[*]				
Pregravid Weight	**1st Trimester**	**2nd Trimester**	**3rd Trimester**	**Total Recommended Gestational Weight Gain**
Ideal weight (Ideal weight for height)	3.5 lb	1 lb/wk	1 lb/wk	25–35 lb
Overweight (>20% above ideal)	2 lb	$\frac{2}{3}$ lb/wk	$\frac{2}{3}$ lb/wk	15–25 lb
Underweight (>10% below ideal)	5 lb	1.2 lb/wk	1.2 lb/wk	28–40 lb

[*]Body weight prior to becoming pregnant.

SOURCE: Luke, Johnson, and Petrie (1993).

conception, her ***pregravid weight.*** For example, if the woman's pregravid weight is appropriate for her height, then total gestational weight gain should be 25–35 pounds. In contrast, if the woman is overweight (her pregravid weight is 20 percent above her ideal), then total gestational weight gain should be 15–25 pounds. Last, the underweight woman (more than 10 percent below ideal) should gain 28–40 pounds, depending upon the severity of her low pregravid weight. Table 5-7 shows the recommended distribution of this total gestational weight gain across each of the three trimesters. Ideally, these weight gains should result in an offspring weighing approximately 7.0 to 7.5 pounds (Hughes & Noppe, 1991).

The importance of receiving an adequate supply of dietary protein during pregnancy cannot be overemphasized. Research by Rosenbaum and colleagues (1973) found that 51 mothers who experienced heavy proteinuria (loss of protein in the urine) during the last $4\frac{1}{2}$ months of pregnancy gave birth to infants who scored significantly lower on the Bayley mental scales and the Binet IQ (at age 4) when compared with infants born to mothers without proteinuria. The appearance of this deficit suggests impaired prenatal brain growth. Thus the developing fetus must receive adequate nutrition in utero, particularly because the developing brain achieves 25 percent of its mature weight prior to birth. Furthermore, poor weight gain in under-

weight women is associated with a fivefold increase in perinatal mortality (Newton, 1999). It is also important that the mother receive an adequate supply of vitamins and minerals, because deficiencies in these nutrients can cause physical and mental damage and, in some instances, fetal death. Table 5-8 presents the recommended daily allowances of selected nutrients. Pay particular attention to the recommended percent of increase in most of these nutrients as a result of pregnancy. These essential nutrients should be acquired by eating a variety of foods, and every attempt must be made to avoid "empty calories." Vitamin and mineral supplements should be taken only under the watchful eye of a physician, since an association has been found between selected supplements and neural-tube defects including spina bifida, anencephaly, and encephalocele (protrusion of the brain through a congenital defect in the skull) (Luke et al., 1993).

Potential problems stemming from undernutrition during pregnancy are severe. We have already discussed some of its effects on offspring. Potentially as severe are the effects stemming from the ***grandmother effect:*** the second- as well as the first-generation effects of poor nutrition. Even if a woman attains adequate nutrition throughout her life, she has an increased chance of giving birth to abnormal offspring if her mother was undernourished during pregnancy. This generational effect is not passed by men, because it is the mother

Table 5-8 A Comparison of Recommended Daily Allowances for Selected Nutrients Among Nonpregnant and Pregnant Women			
Nutrient	**Nonpregnant Level**	**Pregnant Level**	**Percent Change**
Protein	46 gm	71 gm	+42
Calcium	1000 mg	1000 mg	0
Vitamin A	700 IU	770 IU	+10
Vitamin D	5 IU	5 IU	0
Vitamin E	15 mg	15 mg	0
Vitamin C	75 mg	85 mg	+13
Folic Acid	400 mcg	600 mcg	+50

who provides the prenatal environment for the baby where the second-generation effects are believed to occur. Unfortunately, one of the repercussions of the first-generation damage could have been the development of faulty internal organs, jeopardizing the prenatal environment for the second-generation baby. Fortunately, this effect is not believed to go beyond two generations unless subsequent generations are also undernourished. The grandmother effect clearly alerts us to the perils of poor nutrition during pregnancy and the plight of the undernourished areas of the world. Poor nutrition, particularly during pregnancy, is a long-term problem.

BIRTH WEIGHT

Until fairly recently, the medical community considered any newborn weighing less than 2500 grams (5.51 pounds) premature. Today, standards classify infants weighing less than 2500 grams (5.56 pounds) as low birth weight (LBW) and those weighing less than 1500 grams as very low birth weight (VLBW). A newer category, extremely low birth weight (ELBW), is now being used to classify those weighing less than 500 grams at birth (Moore & Persaud, 2003).

Low birth weight is not necessarily associated with premature birth; that is, not all low birth weight newborns are premature. Further, complications associated with small full-term infants differ significantly from those a premature infant experiences. Because of this distinction, gestational age and weight are no longer used independently to describe or label an infant as premature. Instead, it must be established whether the low birth weight is from a shortened gestation period or whether the growth retardation is a result of intrauterine impoverishment. This is an important distinction because the clinical outcomes of the two conditions are quite different. More specifically, low birth weight caused by intrauterine impoverishment is associated with mental retardation, whereas spastic deplegia (cerebral palsy) is more closely associated with prematurity.

Figure 5-7 illustrates the three major diagnostic groupings of birth weight. Note that infants with a low birth weight for their gestational age can be born either full term (40 weeks) or preterm (37 weeks or less). These infants exhibit weights two standard deviations below their expected birth weight for their length of gestation and are generally termed **small for gestational age (SGA).** Excluding other congenital problems, SGA infants experience a growth retardation from inadequate nutrition in utero and are at great risk of being mentally disabled. The infant's inability to receive adequate nutrition in utero can have a devastating effect on brain development, particularly because brain cells have completed proliferation by 20 weeks in utero. Churchill writes, "The infant suffering from intrauterine impoverishment is

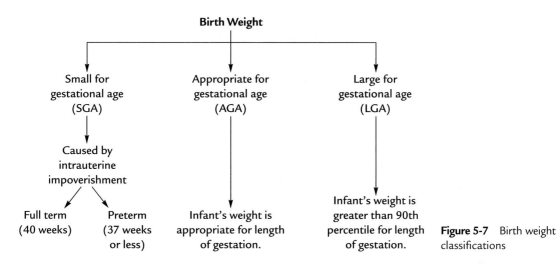

Figure 5-7 Birth weight classifications

not merely small and so of small concern: it is stunted and has a permanent warp imposed within the fabric of its brain which may be expected to impede learning processes throughout its life" (1977, p. 72).

Researchers are also interested in the long-term effects of low birth weight on later motor behavior and physiological function. Isaacs and Pohlman (1988) first compared 5- to 9-year-old children who were either low or normal birth weight babies on fundamental motor skills and reaction time. The normal body weight group performed significantly better on locomotor and object control skills, though no statistically significant differences were noted for reaction time. The researchers are careful to indicate that child-rearing attitudes of the various parents varied greatly. In fact, parents of low birth weight babies often expressed concern that their children not be involved in vigorous physical activity. This, as much as the low birth weight condition, may have accounted for the lower abilities on fundamental motor skills (Isaacs & Pohlman, 1988; Pohlman & Isaacs, 1990).

These early findings have now been extensively supported by more recent research involving children ranging in age from 2 to 13 years and representing each of the three levels of birth weight classification: LBW, VLBW, ELBW (Baraldi et al., 1991; Bareket et al., 1997; Hack et al., 1994; Johnson et al., 1993; Lie, 1994; Marlow, Roberts, & Cooke, 1989,

1993; Powls et al., 1995; Stjernqvist & Svenningsen, 1995). In short, all have reported reduced motor functioning in these populations. Falk and colleagues (1997) have reported that 5- to 8-year-olds who were born prematurely and weighed between 535 grams and 1760 grams performed below those weighing more than 2500 grams on measures of both peak mechanical power output (15-second modified Wingate Anaerobic Test) and in peak power determined through the use of a force plate vertical jump. In both instances, those classified as ELBW were the most deficient. The authors suggest that the motor deficiencies observed in these premature (low weight) children may be the result of inferior intermuscular coordination. Furthermore, they suggest that future research examine the possible underlying factors responsible for these motor deficiencies.

Infants born preterm but of a body weight *appropriate for gestational age (AGA),* particularly those weighing more than 1500 grams, tend to be at less risk than SGA infants. Preterm AGA children show developmental delays in weight, length, and head circumference at 1 year of age, but researchers have found that some catch-up growth occurs during the second year (Shennan & Milligan, 1980). Regarding the physiological function of infants of less than 1501 grams, it appears that their ability to catch up in some ways with their AGA peers is quite complete. For example, Baraldi and colleagues

Figure 5-8 Exercise during pregnancy may hold benefits for both mother and child.
Source: Ryan McVay/
Getty Images/PhotoDisc

(1991) compared VLBW children with AGA children, following them from 7 years to 12 years of age, and found the VLBW children to be comparable with AGA children on pulmonary function tests and maximum oxygen consumption. However, the SGA children did exhibit less efficiency in running.

Another birth weight classification is *large for gestational age (LGA).* The birth weight of LGA infants is greater than the 90th percentile for their given gestational age. Because of the infants' large body size, birth injuries, especially brachial plexus injuries and fractures of the clavicle, are common. Respiratory distress syndrome and developmental retardation are also characteristics of this group of infants. Infants of diabetic mothers tend to be macrosomic and are, therefore, frequently LGA (Ensher & Clard, 1994).

EXERCISE DURING PREGNANCY

In recent years, more and more women have sought to continue or begin exercise programs during pregnancy. This demand has led many qualified, and some unqualified, individuals to design exercise programs for the pregnant woman. These programs stem from the popular view that exercise holds beneficial effects for the pregnant woman (Morkved, Bo, Schei, & Salvesen, 2003) and possibly her baby (see Figure 5-8). One critical question that has yet

to be scientifically answered is whether continuation of exercise during pregnancy affects the course of the pregnancy or the outcome of pregnancy in the general population. In an attempt to shed light on this question, Mittelmark, Dorey, and Kirschbaum (1991) conducted an exhaustive review of the literature. They uncovered several consistent findings, including the following:

1. Women who exercised before pregnancy and continued to do so during pregnancy tended to weigh less, gain less weight, and deliver smaller babies than controls (by about 300–500 grams).

2. All women, regardless of initial level of physical activity, decrease their activity as pregnancy progresses.

3. No information is available to assess whether active women have better pregnancy outcomes than their sedentary counterparts. No information is available on sedentary women.

4. Physically active women appear to tolerate labor pain better. (Mittelmark, Wiswell et al., 1991, p. 228)

Only recently have sufficient data been gathered on physically trained women. One study involving 2828 women and conducted by the Missouri Department of Health concluded that level of exercise, number of hours spent at work, and specific activities undertaken during pregnancy such as carrying heavy loads, did not increase the risk of fetal demise or the incidence of low birth weight in this population of physically conditioned women (Schramm, Stockbauer, & Hoffman, 1996).

However, injuries do occur during exercise, and exercising during pregnancy is no exception. For example, in pregnancy, connective tissue becomes more lax and joints less stable, making the joints more susceptible to injury. The increased size of the uterus and breasts alters the center of gravity. This not only can cause a lordosis (extreme curvature of the lower back) and strain on the joints and lower back but can create balance problems as well. More falls and more back and hip pain can be expected (Araujo, 1997).

Maternal Response to Exercise

In pregnant women who exercise, the maternal blood volume is increased by 35 to 45 percent and cardiac output is increased while at rest (Araujo, 1997). These specific changes can persist for up to 4 weeks postpartum. Other cardiovascular changes include the diversion of blood away from the visceral organs to the working muscles during exercise. Though animal research indicates that up to 50 percent of the blood flow must be diverted from the viscera before the fetus is harmed, no such research has been conducted on humans. In other words, we do not know at what point exercise might begin to jeopardize the fetal oxygen supply.

Toward the end of the pregnancy the diaphragm is elevated, which is believed to cause discomfort and dyspnea (difficult or painful breathing). This elevation does not impair the respiratory function of the lungs, because the rib cage expands to increase the overall tidal volume of the lungs. So, low levels of exercise appear to be readily accommodated for breathing. High levels, however, tend to increase oxygen levels less than expected, indicating that, during pregnancy, the woman may not be able to maintain high activity levels as readily as normal (American College of Obstetricians and Gynecologists [ACOG], 1994).

As in the nonpregnant exerciser, body temperature rises. This is particularly true if insufficient liquid is ingested, causing dehydration. In cases of dehydration, the temperature may soar to levels that are dangerous to the health of the fetus (Drinkwater, Wissell, & Mittelmark, 1991). The fetus, being incapable of reducing body temperature through such normal means as perspiration, may be at particular risk when the mother's body temperature becomes too high (an argument against hot tub use). For this reason, some still recommend moderation in exercise and avoidance of exercise on very hot or humid days, even though research has failed to document an increase in neural-tube and other birth defects in pregnant women who continue to perform vigorous exercise during early pregnancy (ACOG, 1994).

Fetal Responses to Maternal Exercise

Little has been written regarding fetal responses to maternal exercise. It does appear, however, that various fetal systems are affected. For example, fetal heart rate (FHR) increases by approximately 10–30 beats per minute in response to maternal exercise. In addition, this elevation in FHR is sustained into recovery. In general, FHRs return to preexercise levels during the first 15 minutes of recovery in women who exercise at mild (approximately 2.5 metabolic equivalents [METS]) and moderate (approximately 5 METS) levels. In comparison, FHR remained elevated for at least 30 minutes in women who exercised at a strenuous level (approximately 8 METS) (Mittlemark & Posner, 1991). For an in-depth review of maternal and fetal responses to exercise, consult the book by McMurray and colleagues (1993) or the review article by Bell and O'Neill (1994).

Perhaps because of inconclusive research findings and differences of opinion, the role of exercise during pregnancy has been surrounded by controversy. For example, in 1985 the American College of Obstetricians and Gynecologists published guidelines concerning exercise during pregnancy and the postpartum period (*Exercise during pregnancy,* 1985). While these initial guidelines were created with the safety of the mother and the baby in mind, many believed the guidelines were conservative. Of particular concern were the recommendations that (1) exercise should last no longer than 15 minutes,

Table 5-9   Guidelines from the ACOG on Exercise During Pregnancy and the Postpartum Period

1. Choose mild to moderate exercise routines for maximum health benefits.

2. Exercise at least three times per week rather than sporadically.

3. Avoid exercising in the supine position after the first trimester, since this position is associated with decreased cardiac output in most pregnant women.

4. Avoid periods of motionless standing.

5. Modify intensity of exercise according to your symptoms.

6. Stop exercising when fatigued and do not exercise to exhaustion.

7. Choose non-weight-bearing exercises such as swimming and cycling to minimize the risk of injury and allow you to exercise further into pregnancy.

8. Avoid exercises involving the potential for even mild abdominal trauma.

9. Adapt to your body's changes. The type of exercises that can be performed during pregnancy may change as morphological developments occur such as an altered center of gravity and the subsequent potential for loss of balance.

10. Eat enough healthy food and recognize that pregnancy requires an additional 300 kilocalories per day to maintain metabolic homeostasis.

11. During the first trimester, let your body release heat. Drink enough water, wear appropriate clothing, and exercise in an optimal environment.

12. Resume prepregnancy exercise routines gradually, since the physiological and morphological changes of pregnancy persist 4 to 6 weeks postpartum.

NOTE: During pregnancy, peak rectal temperature decreases by 0.3°C at 8 weeks and continues to fall at a rate of 0.1°C per month through 37 weeks of gestation (Clapp, 1991) because of maternal physiological adaptations to pregnancy.
SOURCE: American College of Obstetricians and Gynecologists (1994).

Table 5-10   Selected Contraindications to Exercise During Pregnancy

Absolute Contraindication to Exercise

Pregnancy-induced hypertension

Preterm rupture of membranes

Preterm labor during the prior or current pregnancy or both

Incompetent cervix/cerclage

Persistent second- or third-trimester bleeding

Intrauterine growth retardation

Relative Contraindication to Exercise

Chronic hypertension

Thyroid disease

Cardiac, vascular, or pulmonary disease

Medication-controlled diabetes

Breech presentation in the third trimester

Multiple gestation

Excessive weight gain or loss

SOURCES: American College of Obstetricians and Gynecologists (1994) and Araujo (1997).

(2) maternal heart rate should not exceed 140 beats per minute, and (3) core body temperature should not exceed 38°C (100.4°F). In 1994, new guidelines regarding exercise during pregnancy and the postpartum period were published. Most notably, the recommendations regarding the establishment of limits to exercise duration and exercise heart rate were eliminated. The new guidelines stated, "There is no data in humans to indicate that pregnant women should limit exercise intensity and lower target heart rates because of potential adverse effects" (ACOG, 1994, p. 68). Instead, they suggested that, for most women, moderate exercise is appropriate for maintaining fitness during pregnancy and the postpartum period (Araujo, 1997). Table 5-9 examines in greater detail the 1994 ACOG recommendations for exercise in pregnancy and the postpartum period, while Table 5-10 lists selected contraindications to exercise during pregnancy. Any pregnant woman exhibiting any of the contraindicated symptoms should refrain from exercise until she can discuss her symptoms with her physician.

SUMMARY

Both genetic and environmental misfortunes can alter the normal fetal growth and development process.

Drugs and medications consumed during pregnancy can affect the developing fetus. They are particularly damaging at certain times during pregnancy, especially during the main embryonic period of development.

Women should not use recreational drugs during pregnancy. Cocaine is one of the most harmful drugs to the unborn child. The pregnant woman should also be cautious of prescriptive and nonprescriptive drugs; when she must take them, she must work closely with her physician to monitor any drugs used during pregnancy, for many can harm the developing fetus.

There are numerous maternal diseases that can influence the development of the fetus. These diseases take many forms, including viral, parasitic, hematologic, and endocrine diseases.

Four frequent genetic abnormalities are Down syndrome, phenylketonuria, cystic fibrosis, and sickle-cell disease. Down syndrome, a chromosome-based disorder, is caused by the presence of an extra chromosome on chromosome number 21. Phenylketonuria, cystic fibrosis, and sickle-cell disease are gene-based disorders.

Prenatal diagnostic procedures are available to detect the presence of many fetal abnormalities. Four of the most common prenatal procedures are ultrasound, amniocentesis, chorionic villus sampling, and the alpha-fetoprotein test. These tests are particularly important for women believed to be at risk for fetal abnormality because of maternal age, a previous child born with an abnormality, a family history of abnormalities, or a medical history of certain genetic traits. The triple marker test may be used for women under age 35; it is relatively new and less used than the other four.

The pregnant woman must receive adequate nutrition. Maternal weight gain can be a partial indication of the nutritional state of the fetus. How much weight should be gained during the pregnancy is a function of weight status prior to conception. With adequate nutrition, maternal weight gain should produce an offspring weighing approximately 7.0 to 7.5 pounds.

Babies born to women who did not receive adequate nutrition during pregnancy score lower than average on mental scales and can also suffer physical impairment. In some cases, because of the grandmother effect, the damage caused from poor nutrition can be passed to a second generation. The grandmother effect can occur even when the first-generation offspring has received adequate nutrition.

There are three basic birth weight classifications: small for gestational age (SGA), appropriate for gestational age (AGA), and large for gestational age (LGA). SGA babies are particularly at risk for such associated problems as mental retardation. Recent research has also shown that low birth weight babies may lag on motor skill development later in life.

Women who want to exercise during pregnancy and the postpartum period are encouraged to follow the guidelines established in 1994 by the American College of Obstetricians and Gynecologists.

KEY TERMS

alcohol-related neurodevelopmental disorders (ARND)
alpha-fetoprotein test
amniocentesis
anti-D IgG immunoglobulin
appropriate for gestational age (AGA)
carbon monoxide
chorionic villus sampling (CVS)
congenital rubella syndrome (CRS)
cystic fibrosis (CF)

diabetes mellitus
Down syndrome (DS)
ectoderm
11-hydroxy-delta-9-tetrahydrocannabinal (THC)
endoderm
erythroblastosis fetalis
fetal alcohol syndrome (FAS)
grandmother effect
heterozygous
homozygous

human immunodeficiency virus (HIV)
hyperglycemia
hypoglycemia
large for gestational age (LGA)
macrosomia
meiotic nondisjunction
mesoderm
neonatal abstinence syndrome (NAS)
nicotine

normoglycemia
phenylketonuria (PKU)
pregravid weight
Rh factor
rubella

sickle-cell disease (SCD)
sickle-cell trait (SCT)
small for gestational age (SGA)
teratogen
thalidomide

Toxoplasma gondii
triple marker
ultrasound

QUESTIONS FOR REFLECTION

1. What are three factors that determine the extent of damage caused from a teratogen? When are teratogens most dangerous and why? In your discussion, refer to each of the three prenatal stages of development.

2. Can you summarize the features of a child born with fetal alcohol syndrome regarding growth, central nervous system abnormalities, and craniofacial abnormalities?

3. A woman who is 3 months pregnant smokes an average of three cigarettes per day. Following the birth of her child, she continues smoking and breast-feeds her baby. Why might smoking have an effect on her newborn baby? Summarize the short- and long-term risk factors associated with maternal tobacco smoking.

4. What are the fetal defects associated with rubella infections in the mother during pregnancy?

5. What are the events that lead up to the development of erythroblastosis fetalis?

6. What special nutritional concerns do pregnant women have?

7. What are the potential consequences of sickle-cell disease?

8. Why does a concern exist for children who exhibit small-for-gestational-age and large-for-gestational-age birth weights?

9. What are the guidelines concerning exercise during pregnancy and postpartum put forth by the American College of Obstetricians and Gynecologists?

INTERNET RESOURCES

American Academy of Pediatrics **www.aap.org**

American College of Obstetricians and Gynecologists
  www.acog.org

Center for Motor Behavior in Down Syndrome
  www.umich.edu/~cmbds

Cystic Fibrosis Foundation **www.cff.org**

Fetal development: 1st trimester
  www.w-cpc.org/fetal1.html

Fetal development: 2nd trimester
  www.w-cpc.org/fetal2.html

Fetal development: 3rd trimester
  www.w-cpc.org/fetal3.html

March of Dimes **www.modimes.org**

Mayo HIV Clinic **www.mayo.edu/hiv/index.html**

National Down Syndrome Society
  www.ndss.org/main.html

U.S. National Library of Medicine **www.nlm.nih.gov**

ONLINE LEARNING CENTER (www.mhhe.com/payne6e)

Visit the *Human Motor Development* Online Learning Center for study aids and additional resources. You can use the study guide questions and key terms puzzles to review key terms and concepts for this chapter and to prepare for exams. You can further extend your knowledge of motor development by checking out the Web links, articles, and activities found on the site.

REFERENCES

Abel, E. L. (1990). *Fetal alcohol syndrome.* Oradel, NJ: Medical Economics Books.

Alford, C. A., Pass, R. F., & Stagno, S. (1983). Chronic congenital infections and common environmental causes for severe and subtle birth defects. In S. C. Finley, W. H. Finley, & C. E. Flowers, Jr. (Eds.), *Birth defects: Clinical and ethical considerations.* New York: Alan R. Liss.

Alger, L. S. (2000). Common viral infections. In W. R. Cohen (Ed.), *Cherry and Merkatz's complications of pregnancy.* 5th ed. Baltimore: Lippincott Williams & Wilkins.

American Academy of Pediatrics. (2000). Fetal alcohol syndrome and alcohol-related neurodevelopmental disorders (RE9948). *Pediatrics, 106,* 358–361.

American College of Obstetricians and Gynecologists. (1994). Exercise during pregnancy and the postpartum period. *International Journal of Gynaecology and Obstetrics, 45,* 65–70.

———. (2002). Pregnancy: Illegal drugs and pregnancy. American College of Obstetricians and Gynecologists Patient Education, Pamphlet AP104.

Araujo, D. (1997). Expecting questions about exercise and pregnancy? *Physician and Sportsmedicine, 25,* 85–93.

Arendt, R., Angelopoulos, J., Salvator, A., & Singer, L. (1999). Motor development of cocaine-exposed children at age two years. *Pediatrics, 103,* 86.

Baraldi, E., Zanconato, S., Zorzi, C., Santuz, P., Benini, F., & Zacchello, F. (1991). Exercise performance in very low birth weight children at the age of 7–12 years. *European Journal of Pediatrics, 150,* 713–716.

Bareket, F., Eliakim, A., Dotan, R., Liebermann, D. G., Regev, R., & Bar-Or, O. (1997). Birth weight and physical ability in 5- to 8-year-old healthy children born prematurely. *Medicine and Science in Sports and Exercise, 29,* 1124–1130.

Bell, R., & O'Neill, M. (1994). Exercise and pregnancy: A review. *Birth, 21,* 85–95.

Brackbill, Y. (1976). Long-term effects of obstetrical anesthesia on infant autonomic function. *Developmental Psychobiology, 9,* 353–358.

———. (1979). Obstetrical medication and infant behavior. In J. D. Osofsky (Ed.), *Handbook of infant development.* New York: Wiley.

Brazelton, T. B. (1961). Effects of maternal medications on the neonate and his behavior. *Journal of Pediatrics, 58,* 513–518.

Centers for Disease Control and Prevention. (2003). *Rubella.* Retrieved June 3, 2003, from www.cdc.gov/nip/publications/pink/rubella.pdf.

Churchill, J. A. (1977). Factors in intrauterine impoverishment. In K. S. Moghissi & T. N. Evans (Eds.), *Nutritional impacts on women throughout life with emphasis on reproduction.* New York: Harper & Row.

Cincinnati Children's Hospital. (2003). *High risk pregnancy test and procedures: Amniocentesis.* Retrieved from www.cincinatichildrens.org/health/info/pregnancy/procedure.

Clapp, J. K. (1991). The changing thermal response to endurance exercise during pregnancy. *American Journal of Obstetrics and Gynecology, 165,* 1684–1689.

DeVore, G. R. (2003). *The triple marker screening blood test.* Retrieved June 5 from www.fetal.com/gen_triple.htm.

Diamond, G. W., & Cohen, H. J. (1992). Developmental disabilities in children with HIV infection. In A. C. Croker, H. J. Cohen, & T. A. Kastner (Eds.), *HIV infection and developmental disabilities: A resource for service providers.* Baltimore: Paul H. Brookes.

Diamond, G. W., Gurdin, P., Wiznia, A. A., Belman, A. L., Rubinstein, A., & Cohen, H. J. (1990). Effects of congenital HIV infection on neurodevelopmental status of babies in foster care. *Developmental Medicine and Child Neurology, 32,* 999–1005.

Drinkwater, B. L., Wiswell, R. A., & Mittlemark, R. A. (1991). Heat stress and pregnancy. In R. A. Mittlemark, R. A. Wiswell, & B. L. Drinkwater (Eds.), *Exercise in pregnancy.* 2nd ed. Baltimore: Williams & Wilkins.

Eglinton, G. S., & Seydel, F. D. (1999). Screening for neural tube defects. In J. T. Queenan (Ed.), *Management of high-risk pregnancy.* 4th ed. Oxford, England: Blackwell Science.

Elias, S., & Simpson, J. L. (2000). Genetic amniocentesis and chronic villus sampling. In J. T. Queenan (Ed.), *Management of high-risk pregnancy.* 4th ed. Oxford, England: Blackwell Science.

Ensher, G. L., & Clard, D. A. (1994). *Newborns at risk: Medical care and psychoeducational intervention.* 2nd ed. Gaithersburg, MD: Aspen.

Ensher, G. L., Clard, D. A., & Yarwood, L. M. (1994). Substance use and abuse, pregnancy, and the newborn. In G. L. Ensher & D. A. Clard (Eds.), *Newborns at risk: Medical care and psychoeducational intervention.* 2nd ed. Gaithersburg, MD: Aspen.

Evans, O. B., Subramony, S. H., Hanson, R. R., & Parker, C. C. (1991). Neurologic diseases. In A. Y. Sweet & E. G. Brown (Eds.), *Fetal and neonatal effects of maternal disease.* St. Louis, MO: Mosby-Year Book.

Exercise during pregnancy and the postnatal period. (1985). Washington, DC: American College of Obstetricians and Gynecologists.

Falk, B., Eliakim, A., Dotan, R., Liebermann, D. G., Regev, R., & Bar-Or, O. (1997). Birth weight and physical ability in 5- to 8-year-old healthy children born prematurely. *Medicine and Science in Sports and Exercise, 29,* 1124–1130.

Ferreira, J., Sachs, G. S., & Bombard, A. T. (2000). Teratogenic drugs. In W. R. Cohen (Ed.), *Cherry and Merkatz's complications of pregnancy.* 5th ed. Baltimore: Lippincott Williams & Wilkins.

Fried, P. A., Watkinson, B., Grant, A., & Knights, R. M. (1980). Changing patterns of soft drug use prior to and during pregnancy: A prospective study. *Drug Alcohol Dependency, 6,* 323–343.

Gold, E., Kumar, M. L., Nankervis, G. A., & Sweet, A. Y. (1991). Viral infections. In A. Y. Sweet & E. G. Brown (Eds.), *Fetal and neonatal effects of maternal disease.* St. Louis, MO: Mosby-Year Book.

Gold, M. S. (1995). *Drugs of abuse: A comprehensive series for clinicians: Tobacco.* New York: Plenum Medical Book Company.

Hack, M., Taylor, H., Klein, N., Eiben, R., Schalschneider, C., & Mercuri-Minich, N. (1994). School-age outcomes in children with birth weights under 750 g. *New England Journal of Medicine, 331,* 753–759.

Haglund, D., & Cnattingius, S. (1990). Cigarette smoking as a risk factor for sudden infant death syndrome: A population-based study. *American Journal of Public Health, 80,* 29.

Henderson, C. E. (2000). Alcohol and substance abuse. In W. R. Cohen (Ed.), *Cherry and Merkatz's complications of pregnancy.* 5th ed. Baltimore: Lippincott Williams & Wilkins.

Hueppchen, N. A., Anderson, J. R., & Fox, H. E. (2000). Human immunodeficiency virus infection. In W. R. Cohen (Ed.), *Cherry and Merkatz's complications of pregnancy.* 5th ed. Baltimore: Lippincott Williams & Wilkins.

Hughes, F. P., & Noppe, L. D. (1991). *Human development across the lifespan.* Columbus, OH: Merrill.

Isaacs, L. D., & Pohlman, R. (1988, Oct.). Motor development and performance concerns regarding individuals of low birth weight. Paper presented at the meeting of the Motor Development Research Consortium, University of Illinois, Urbana.

Johnson, A. P., Townsend, P., Yudkin, P., Bull, D., & Wilkinson, A. R. (1993). Functional abilities at age 4 years of children born before 29 weeks of gestation. *British Medical Journal, 306,* 1715–1718.

Kandall, S. R. (1991). Drug abuse. In A. Y. Sweet & E. G. Brown (Eds.), *Fetal and neonatal effects of maternal disease.* St. Louis, MO: Mosby-Year Book.

Lie, K. G. (1994). Sensitivity of perceptual motor measures for very low birth weight (VLBW<1500 g) preschoolers. *Child Care Health Development, 20,* 239–249.

Luke, B., Johnson, T. R., & Petrie, R. H. (1993). *Clinical maternal-fetal nutrition.* Boston: Little, Brown.

MacGregor, S. N., & Chasnoff, I. F. (1993). Substance abuse in pregnancy. In C. C. Lin, M. S. Verp, & R. E. Sabbagha (Eds.), *The high-risk fetus: Pathophysiology, diagnosis, and management.* New York: Springer-Verlag.

Marlow, N., Roberts, B. L., & Cooke, R. W. I. (1989). Motor skills in extremely low birthweight children at the age of 6 years. *Archives of Disease in Children, 64,* 839–847.

———. (1993). Outcome at 8 years for children with birth weight of 1250 g or less. *Archives of Disease in Children, 68,* 286–290.

Martineaud, J. P., Samb, A., Gueel, L., Seck, D., Badji, L., & Cisse, F. (2002). Exercise performance in young subjects with sickle cell disease. *Scipta Medica, 75,* 111–117.

McMurray, R. G., Mottola, M. F., Wolfe, L. A., Artal, R., Millar, L., & Pivarnik, J. M. (1993). Recent advances in understanding maternal and fetal responses to exercise. *Medicine and Science in Sports and Exercise, 25,* 1305–1321.

Miller, W. H., & Chasnoff, I. J. (1993). Perinatal substance abuse. In T. Moore, R. Reiter, R. Rebar, & V. Baker (Eds.), *Gynecology and obstetrics: A longitudinal approach.* New York: Churchill Livingston.

Mills, J. L., Granbard, B. I., Harley, E. E., Rhoads, G. G., & Berendes, H. W. (1984). Maternal alcohol consumption and birth weight: How much drinking in pregnancy is safe? *Journal of the American Medical Association, 252,* 1875–1879.

Minkoff, H. L., & Burgess, T. (1999). HIV infection. In J. T. Queenan (Ed.), *Management of high-risk pregnancy.* 4th ed. Oxford, England: Blackwell Science.

Mittlemark, R. A., Dorey, F. J., & Kirschbaum, T. H. (1991). Effect of maternal exercise on pregnancy outcome. In R. A. Mittlemark, R. A. Wiswell, & B. L. Drinkwater (Eds.), *Exercise in pregnancy.* 2nd ed. Baltimore: Williams & Wilkins.

Mittlemark, R. A., & Posner, M. D. (1991). Fetal responses to maternal exercise. In R. A. Mittlemark, R. A. Wiswell, & B. L. Drinkwater (Eds.), *Exercise in pregnancy.* 2nd ed. Baltimore: Williams & Wilkins.

Mittlemark, R. A., Wiswell, R. A., Drinkwater, B. L., & St. Jones-Repovich, W. W. (1991). Exercise guidelines for pregnancy. In R. A. Mittlemark, R. A. Wiswell, & B. L. Drinkwater (Eds.), *Exercise in pregnancy.* 2nd ed. Baltimore: Williams & Wilkins.

Moore, K. L., & Persaud, T. V. N. (2003). *Before we are born: Essentials of embryology and birth defects.* 6th ed. Philadelphia: Saunders.

Morkved, S., Bo, K., Schei, B., and Salvesen, K. A. (2003). Pelvic floor muscle training during pregnancy to prevent urinary incontinence: A single-blind randomized controlled trial. *Obstetrics and Gynecology, 101,* 313–319.

National Collegiate Athletic Association. (2001). *NCAA guide line 3c: The student-athlete with sickle cell trait.* Indianapolis, IN: National Collegiate Athletic Association.

National Heart, Lung, and Blood Institute. (1996, Nov.). *Sickle cell anemia.* NIH publication no. 96-4057. Bethesda, MD: NIH.

Newton, E. R. (1999). Maternal nutrition. In J. T. Queenan (Ed.), *Management of high-risk pregnancy.* 4th ed. Oxford, England: Blackwell Science.

Niebyl, J. R., & Kochenour, N. K. (1999). Medications in pregnancy and lactation. In J. T. Queenan (Ed.), *Management of high-risk pregnancy.* 4th ed. Oxford, England: Blackwell Science.

Osofsky, J. D. (Ed.). (1987). *Handbook of infant development.* 2nd ed. New York: Wiley.

Pedersen, J. (1977). *The pregnant diabetic and her newborn.* 2nd ed. Baltimore: Williams & Wilkins.

Pedersen, J., & Pedersen, L. M. (1971). Diabetes mellitus and pregnancy: The hyperglycemia, hyperinsulinemia theory and the weight of the newborn baby. In R. Rodriguez &

J. Vallance-Owens (Eds.), *Proceedings of the 7th Congress of the International Diabetes Federation, Amsterdam. Excerpta Medica, 97,* 678–685.

Perry, K. G., Martin, J. N., & Morrison, J. C. (1991). Hematologic and hemorrhagic disease. In A. Y. Sweet & E. G. Brown (Eds.), *Fetal and neonatal effects of maternal disease.* St. Louis, MO: Mosby-Year Book.

Pohlman, R. L., & Isaacs, L. D. (1990). The previously low birth weight infant: Fundamental motor skill outcomes in the 5- to 9-year-old. *Pediatric Exercise Science, 2,* 263–271.

Powls, A. N., Botting, R. W., Cooke, R. W., & Marlow, N. (1995). Motor impairment in children 12 and 13 years old with a birthweight of less than 1250 g. *Archives of Disease Childfetal Neonatal Education, 73,* F62–F66.

Queenan, R. A. (1999). Substance abuse in pregnancy. In J. T. Queenan (Ed.), *Management of high-risk pregnancy.* 4th ed. Oxford, England: Blackwell Science.

Rist, M. C. (1990). The shadow children: Preparing for the arrival of crack babies in school. *Research Bulletin, 9,* 1–6.

Roche, A., & Sun, S. (2003). *Human growth: Assessment and interpretation.* Cambridge, England: Cambridge University Press.

Rosen, T., & Hoskins, I. A. (2000). Environmental and occupational hazards. In W. R. Cohen (Ed.), *Cherry and Merkatz's complications from pregnancy.* 5th ed. Baltimore: Lippincott Williams & Wilkins.

Rosenbaum, A. L., Churchill, J. A., Shakhashiri, A. A., & Moody, R. L. (1973). Neuropsychologic outcome of children whose mothers had proteinuria during pregnancy: A report from the collaborative study of cerebral palsy. In L. J. Stone, H. T. Smith, & L. B. Murphy (Eds.), *The competent infant: Research and commentary.* New York: Basic Books.

Schramm, W. F., Stockbauer, J. W., & Hoffman, H. J. (1996). Exercise, employment, and other daily activities, and adverse pregnancy outcomes. *American Journal of Epidemiology, 143,* 211–218.

Scioscia, A. L. (1993). Reproductive genetics. In T. Moore, R. Reiter, R. Rebar, & V. Baker (Eds.), *Gynecology and obstetrics: A longitudinal approach.* New York: Churchill Livingstone.

Shennan, A. T., & Milligan, J. E. (1980). The growth and development of infants weighing 1000 to 2000 grams at birth and delivery in a perinatal unit. *American Journal of Obstetrics and Gynecology, 136,* 273–275.

Singer, L. T., Arendt, R., Minnes, S., Farkas, K., Salvator, A., Kirchner, H. L., & Kliegman, R. (2002). Cognitive and motor outcomes of cocaine-exposed infants. *Journal of the American Medical Association, 278,* 1952–1960.

Sison, A. V., & Sever, J. L. (1999). Toxoplasmosis. In J. T. Queenan (Ed.), *Management of high-risk pregnancy.* 4th ed. Oxford, England: Blackwell Science.

Steinhausen, H. C. (1974). Psychological evaluation of treatment in phenylketonuria: Intellectual, motor, and social development. *Neuropaediatrie, 5,* 146–156.

Stewart, R. B., Cluff, L. E., & Philip, R. (1977). *Drug-monitoring: A requirement for responsible drug use.* Baltimore: Williams & Wilkins.

Stjernqvist, K., & Svenningsen, N. W. (1995). Extremely low-birth weight infants less than 901 g: Development and behaviour after 4 years of age. *Acta Paediatric, 84,* 500–506.

Superintendent of Documents. (2001). *Surgeon General's report: Women and smoking.* Washington, DC: U.S. Department of Health and Human Services.

Turner, C. E. (1980). Marijuana research and problems: An overview. *Pharmacology International, 7,* 93.

Ulrich, D. A. & Ulrich, B. D. (1999, March). *Treadmill training facilitates the onset of walking in infants with Down syndrome.* Paper presented at the 32nd annual Gatlinburg Conference on Research and Theory in Mental Retardation and Developmental Disabilities, Charleston, SC.

Ulrich, D. A., Ulrich, B. D., Angulo-Kinzler, R. M., & Yun, J. (2001). Treadmill training of infants with Down syndrome: Evidence-based developmental outcomes. *Pediatrics, 108,* Article e84. Retrieved June 5, 2003, from www.pediatrics.org/cgi/content/full/108/5/e84.

Verp, M. S., Simpson, J. L., & Ober, C. (1993). Prenatal diagnosis of genetic disorders. In C. C. Lin, M. S. Verp, & R. E. Sabbagha (Eds.), *The high-risk fetus: Pathophysiology, diagnosis, and management.* New York: Springer-Verlag.

Vohr, B. R., Lipsitt, L. P., & Oh, W. (1980). Somatic growth of children of diabetic mothers with reference to birth size. *Journal of Pediatrics, 97,* 196–199.

Wang, X., Zuckerman, B., Pearson, C., Kaufman, G., Chen, C., Wang, G., Niu, T., Wise, P. H., Bauchner, H., & Xu, X. (2002). Maternal cigarette smoking, metabolic gene polymorphism, and infant birth weight. *Journal of the American Medical Association, 287,* 195–202.

Worthington-Roberts, B. S. (2000). Nutrition. In W. R. Cohen (Ed.), *Cherry and Merkatz's complications of pregnancy.* 5th ed. Baltimore: Lippincott Williams & Wilkins.

6

Effects of Early Stimulation and Deprivation

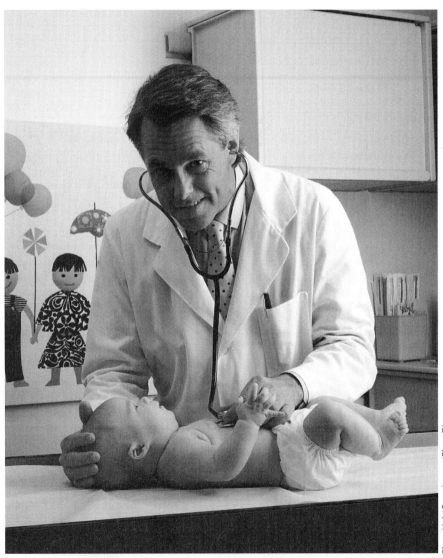

According to David Elkind (1990), the idea that "earlier is better has become an entrenched conviction among contemporary parents and educators." This trend has become so ingrained in many sectors of society that the common philosophy now states that it is "never too early to start children in reading, math, swimming, violin, or karate lessons" (p. 3). This, according to Elkind, has resulted in a confounding of the perceived need for early education and all children's need for quality child care.

Interestingly, and perhaps logically, the general philosophical trend has been that *stimulation* is always "good" and ***deprivation*** is "bad." Although we admire parents who "stimulate" their child, we often scorn parents who "deprive" their child. However, can overstimulation occur? Is deprivation ever in the child's best interest? When are the best times for stimulation or the worst times for deprivation? Is stimulation worthwhile for the acquisition of all human behaviors, or are there some behaviors that cannot be facilitated by early exposure to stimulating experiences? These are all questions that researchers have considered while examining the effects of stimulation and deprivation.

EFFECTS OF EARLY STIMULATION

In recent years, parents have been involving their children more than ever in early educational programs—everything from swimming, gymnastics, and violin lessons to the study of reading and foreign languages. The unusual aspect of these programs designed for early stimulation is that in some cases they start as early as birth. The rush to enroll children in such programs is documented in the article "Bringing up Superbaby" (Langway et al., 1983). Though this article is over 20 years old, it seems to have accurately predicted what was to come. Many of its concerns are more at issue today than they were two decades ago. For example, many of today's babies are born to parents who are older and richer than earlier generations and who are assured that any behavior they desire for their child

can be taught. The increased knowledge concerning child development and the idea that the environment influences human behavior have motivated parents to seek all possible advantages for their children. In fact, the belief that kindergarten is "too late" is increasingly prevalent. Burton White, the author of a commercially popular book titled *The First Three Years of Life* (1975), states that parents are now being considered as teachers, not merely the creators of the baby.

Glenn Doman has written several books about the teaching of such skills as reading and math to babies. Although these skills are often believed to be entirely intellectual, the fine control of eye movement, for example, emphasizes the influence of motor development on one's reading or math success. For optimal success in these skills, Doman recommends initiating instruction by using flashcards during the first few days of neonatal life. Doman does not substantiate the success of this technique by scientific evidence, and there is mixed popular opinion as to the program's value. Some children have learned to respond appropriately to flashcards; others simply play with the cards. Critics of such early programs as the one Doman prescribes question the advantage of simple recognition skills enhanced by the flashcards. They further contend that such pressure to learn at an early age may actually frighten the child from future experiences of a similar nature. Child developmentalists such as Benjamin Spock have stated that children may be "over-intellectualizing." This emphasis on achievement so early may hamper the emotional, physical, or creative aspects of the child's development. Wood Smethurst, former director of the Reading Center at Emory University, believes that too much early stimulation toward reading may actually cause reading difficulties later in the child's education.

Regardless of such opinions, parents generally believe early educational stimulation is valuable, as evidenced by the quantity and popularity of the early educational programs available today. This may be the case, but no doubt such factors as the child's age and type of stimulation as well as the parents' and child's attitudes are critical factors in the success or failure of programs involving early stimulation.

121

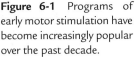

Figure 6-1 Programs of early motor stimulation have become increasingly popular over the past decade.

PROGRAMS TO ENHANCE EARLY MOTOR DEVELOPMENT

As suggested in the preceding section, early stimulation programs have become extremely popular (see Figure 6-1). Because of this popularity, new programs are evolving regularly by qualified or sometimes unqualified persons to fill the consumer demand. Despite the diversity of programs available, those that are designed to generally stimulate or optimize early motor development often fall into two categories: no programming and programming.

The *no-programming* category includes programs that do not emphasize the specific practice of future motor skills through developmental exercises, specialized equipment, or a motor curriculum. This mode of operation was originally advocated in Hungary at the National Institute for Infant Care and Education. The main advocate, Emmi Piker, believes in withholding instruction until an infant learns early body control. Piker advocates the avoidance of systematic practice of specific motor skills — that is, the practice of assisting the child into certain positions or doing anything that requires babies to perform a movement of which they are not yet capable. The no-programming mode suggests leaving infants on their backs until they themselves can change the position. Toys are placed near the child to stimulate movement activity but are not placed too near or handed to the child. This philosophy of early stimulation also advocates against placing children in a position that they cannot attain alone. Therefore, the child would not be placed in a sitting or standing position until first capable of attaining that position alone. Furthermore, a baby who could not walk without assistance would not be given a hand or external support to enable a few extra steps. This system also advocates highly nonrestrictive apparel for the baby. In addition, hard-soled shoes are discouraged until the baby can walk unassisted. Even then, shoes are advised only when necessary. These measures, Piker believes, will assist the baby in the acquisition of such early movements as rolling, creeping, sitting, and standing (Ridenour, 1978).

In the *programming* plan for early motor programs, the parent takes an active role in moving the baby or the baby's limbs during an activity. This plan encourages the use of infant walkers and bouncers because they are believed to facilitate posture and early locomotion. Programs in this category often employ manual manipulation of the limbs for infant fitness or flexibility. They also use special equipment—cushions, dolls, balls, rods, hoops, toys, and so forth—to encourage or assist babies in movement.

Unfortunately, little research has been conducted to substantiate the no-programming or the programming mode of operation for early motor stimulation. Perhaps parents should avoid programs claiming to make excessive improvements in the baby's future motor or intellectual development until more conclusive research is available. Until that time, a more appropriate focus might be creating a stimulating home environment that could facilitate the child's natural development.

Specifically concerning infant exercise programs, the American Academy of Pediatrics (AAP) has issued a policy statement with some clear views and recommendations. This group acknowledges an increase in the abundance of infant programs that tout massage, passive exercises, or even manipulation of the child through a variety of positions for several posited objectives. The AAP notes that, for infants, the "predominant" movement-related responses are reflexive and therefore intrinsic and oriented toward "self-sufficiency." While providing stimulation whereby babies touch, play, and generally interact with their environment is important, research has not demonstrated that organized programs will improve movement skills or "provide any long-term benefit to normal infants." Furthermore, children of this young age may be more susceptible to injury when parents unintentionally exceed a safe range of motion during passive exercise. The AAP recommends that structured programs not be "promoted as being therapeutically beneficial for the development of healthy infants" and that "parents be encouraged to provide a safe, nurturing, and minimally structured play environment for their infant" (AAP, 1988).

These beliefs are supported by J. M. Gardner, Karmel, and Dowd (1984), who suggest that more stimulation is not always better. In fact, they claim it may be harmful if the intensity and type of activity are not individualized to fit the infant's individual needs. Additionally, intervention may lead to false assumptions by some parents. They may think they are not offering their child enough opportunities if their child does not achieve the claims of the program. Parents not enrolled in programs may also lower their expectations of their child and create a "self-fulfilling prophecy of failure" (J. M. Gardner et al., 1984, p. 94).

Gardner and colleagues (1984) agree that too little research has been conducted on early intervention programs. Research that has been conducted is often unsupportive of the concept of early stimulation. Though most of the best research has been conducted on animals, not humans, findings are striking. Often, a seemingly beneficial early outcome later proves to be detrimental. This has been hypothesized to be a function of the disruption of the sequencing of normal central nervous system maturation. Such may have been the case with rat pups whose eyes were opened early. Though improved visual ability occurred initially, over time, deficits emerged. This has also been noted in preterm infants exposed to visual stimulation earlier than full-term babies. Eventually, preterm babies may show more variable and disorganized visual responses rather than improved vision. Clearly, additional stimulation of a specific area can be disruptive or harmful even if intended to facilitate or expedite normal function (J. M. Gardner et al., 1984).

Though little research has been conducted on programs of early stimulation, many programs conduct self-evaluations intended to determine how the child's development has been enhanced. They are seldom devised to detect any detrimental effects. Furthermore, developmental gains that are noted are often those that would have occurred anyway with a normal exposure to a stimulating home environment. This is not to suggest, however, that programs should never be considered or employed. Rather, programs that make indiscriminate claims should be avoided. We must be careful consumers by seeking qualified professionals, clean and appropriate facilities, reasonable fees, and objectives that seem appropriate for the baby or child in question.

Gymboree

Though many new programs of early motor stimulation have evolved in recent years, few have gained the attention and popularity of *Gymboree.* The first Gymboree program, designed for children from birth to 5 years, was opened in northern California in 1976 and, by 2000, had grown to over 430 franchises throughout the world. According to the founder, Joan Barnes, it was developed on the belief that the preschool years may be the most critical part of education, though it is a time when parents have the least amount of outside help in educating their child. Furthermore, the Gymboree philosophy assumes preschoolers need to be provided with certain types of play activities that are believed to be essential to their development but are not readily available at home, on the playground, or in the nursery. The environment of Gymboree is described by the developer as being safe and noncompetitive while challenging the psychomotor needs of preschoolers. Typically, a Gymboree program lasts from 9 to 13 weeks, with the child attending one session per week for approximately 45 minutes. The average cost of each session was about $11 in 2000.

According to a Gymboree marketing specialist (personal communication, August 21, 2000), Gymboree programs range from GymBabies to GymKids. GymBabies is for infants from birth to 6 months of age; the program focuses on gentle play while the parents gain supportive and useful parenting information through class lectures and discussions. GymCrawlers (6 to 12 months) is for more ambulatory infants who can "sit confidently." Focus is placed on activities that help develop balance, strength, and coordination. Then, as the name implies, GymWalkers (10 to 18 months) is for babies who can walk, at least with support. This program emphasizes the motor skills involved in climbing stairs, moving up ramps, and exploring slides, all in interaction with peers. GymRunners (14 to 28 months), for toddlers who can walk with confidence, run, and even climb, places emphasis on enhancing language skills and motor skills through play on equipment and through interaction with peers. GymExplorers (2-year-olds) employs songs, storytelling, movement, and the child's own imagination to further enhance development. Last, GymKids (3- to 4-year-olds) focuses on presport activities, such as catching and throwing, as well as cooperation in a fun environment.

Most Gymboree sessions offer a variety of colorful, scaled-down equipment for children to explore with varying degrees of guidance from their parent(s). Balance beams, balls, scooters, tunnels, rollers, hoops, and ladders are a few of the many pieces of equipment that may be available for exploration during free time. Free time is one segment of each Gymboree session. A Gymboree representative is present during each session to assist the children in using and enjoying the equipment. Usually, free time with the equipment is followed by group activity. These dancing, singing, or pantomime activities are said to emphasize sensory stimulation, coordination, and social interaction.

Gymboree proponents claim that parents benefit from participation by learning their child's needs and developing a better understanding of the child's growth and development. This, proponents say, will help parents to meet their child's needs and to encourage development in an efficient yet fun way.

In general, Gymboree claims that its participants should show improvement in balancing, performing fundamental movements (running, jumping, throwing, catching, etc.), switching from different modes of locomotion, assuming a variety of body positions, changing directions and speeds, socializing (sharing and taking turns), and expressing the imagination freely.

To assess the outcome of their programs, Gymboree surveys parents and claims that parents report benefits for themselves and their children. Specifically, parents have cited increases in undistracted, quality time with their children. They also appear to appreciate the opportunity to meet other families and exchange ideas. They further claim that their children often appeared less passive and dependent and developed better coordination and social skills after participation in a Gymboree program (Barnes, Astor, & Tosi, 1981). However, as mentioned earlier, little research exists to substantiate the claims made by programs such as Gymboree. Self-evaluations must be viewed cautiously, as there is an obvious bias on the part of the evaluator—Gymboree. Gymboree does make some lofty claims but generally tempers them. They are careful to point out that fun is paramount. Until controlled research is conducted, we shall not know whether Gymboree attains its goals or whether their participants are simply developing skills that are a normal part of the developmental process. Decisions on participating in such programs as Gymboree may need to be made on the basis of family needs, desires, and ability to pay for the sessions. As said earlier, we need to be cautious consumers.

Swim Programs for Infants and Preschoolers

Over the last decade, one of the most common forms of early motor stimulation has been swim programs for infants and preschoolers. For infants (birth to 1 year) in particular, there may be little justification for the programs designed to teach infants to swim. The American Academy of Pediatrics (2000) specifically states that infant and toddler aquatic programs do not decrease the risk of drowning and that children are generally not ready for swimming lessons until their fourth birthday. The position stated by the American Red Cross (2000) is consistent with the guidelines issued by the AAP.

In support of the assertions of both organizations, research by Blanksby and colleagues (1995) and Parker and Blanksby (1997) found that swimming skills can be achieved more readily once a child has achieved the motor development of a typical 5-year-old. Although some children may achieve these skills earlier, children younger than 4 years require longer to learn to swim and are often hampered by their developmental status. In short, beginning lessons for children at younger ages does not lead to a more rapid mastery of skill or an eventual higher level of mastery of swimming skills.

Nevertheless, the popularity of some swim programs for infants and preschoolers has too often been fueled by parents' visions of Olympic medals. Evidence about the success of early swim programs in facilitating the child's later level of success in swimming is contradictory. Some children have graduated from these swim programs and achieved considerable success in their later swimming en-

deavors, but others have left such early programs with no apparent improvement. In fact, in some cases, parents claimed that their children became more fearful of the water!

Some early aquatic programs, however, may not profess to teach swimming but rather "drown-proofing," "waterproofing," or simply making an infant water-safe. Most experts agree that these terms are inappropriate. Infant and toddler swim "programs that claim to make children safe in the water or safe from drowning are misrepresenting what is possible and are giving parents a false sense of security about their child's safety in the water" (AAP, 2000, p. 868). The American Red Cross specifically states that "many programs make claims that drown-proofing can be accomplished, but it cannot" (1988, p. 7). The YMCA (1998) recommends words like *water adjustment, readiness,* and *orientation* to describe the philosophy of their program for children under 3. Furthermore, the YMCA advises that parents be informed that aquatic programs alone do not eliminate the chance of a child drowning. Children this young need constant supervision around water, and parents who have homes with pools should install multiple barriers to inhibit the young child's unsupervised access to the water. Finally, the YMCA supports the use of child-centered programs that are developmentally appropriate, with appropriate progressions. Exploration and enjoyment in the water should be paramount at this age (YMCA, 1998).

These guidelines are somewhat similar to the guidelines for infant and preschool aquatic programs created by the American Red Cross (1988). They advise avoiding such terminology as *drown-proofing* or *waterproofing*. Like the YMCA guidelines, the Red Cross urges adult, in-water supervision. It also advises avoiding any activity that would potentially traumatize a participant, as learning to experience pleasure in the water is one of its program's main objectives. Finally, infants must have voluntary head control prior to enrolling in a Red Cross aquatic program.

Parental desire to improve the safety of the infant around water is often the impetus for involvement in infant "swimming." Interestingly, given the risks of some infant swim programs, the child's overall odds of drowning could actually be increased by participating in an early swim program (AAP, 2000). In addition, the completion of a "drownproofing" program could give parents a false sense of security, which could lead to tragic consequences.

HYPONATREMIA Another health consideration with early aquatic programs, especially those involving infants, is the condition known as *hyponatremia,* or water intoxication. Hyponatremia occurs when an individual ingests so much water that the body's electrolytes are reduced and the kidneys cannot filter the excess fluid. This condition becomes a concern in those programs that practice forced or frequent submersions or are particularly long. For these reasons, parents should be advised to monitor the quantity of water consumed by their children before, during, and after participation in a water program (YMCA, 1998).

This condition was vividly described in a case study of an 11-month-old infant who swallowed more water than usual during an infant swim lesson (Bennett & Wagner, 1983). Though she experienced no problems while in the pool, 30 minutes after leaving the water she became irritable, lethargic, and disoriented. She also vomited while going to the hospital and began having seizures once she arrived. This excess water consumption is believed to reduce serum sodium levels, causing the symptoms just described and also restlessness, weakness, and in severe cases, death. It is unknown exactly how much water must be consumed to cause hyponatremia (Bennett & Wagner, 1983), and we also have little information as to the exact number of cases of water intoxication. While hyponatremia is believed to be rare, there may be many more cases than are being reported. This lack of reporting is due to the nonspecific nature of the symptoms and the fact that symptoms may not show up until hours after the water has been swallowed. Thus, the relationship between the illness and exposure to the water often remains unestablished (Burd, 1986).

Hyponatremia can often be avoided by prohibiting participants from being totally submerged.

Nevertheless, many local swim organizations continue to place an emphasis on the need to submerge babies during infant swim programs. Experience does indicate that the quantity of water swallowed increases with a greater number of submersions (Bennett & Wagner, 1983). For that reason, the YMCA (1998) advises prohibiting total submersion of infants in aquatic programs. In addition, the guidelines from the American Red Cross state that "forced, prolonged or frequent submersion(s) . . . are not acceptable techniques" in their infant and preschool aquatic program (1988, p. 4). Bennett and Wagner (1983) also advise avoiding total submersion as well as stopping a lesson if a child ever swallows too much water or begins to exhibit any of the symptoms of hyponatremia.

GIARDIA A more common problem with infant swim programs is *giardia.* This parasite, which develops in cysts in the intestinal tract, can cause severe diarrhea and is easily transmitted to others when the cysts circulate through the pool water. The YMCA *Guidelines for Infant Swimming* (1984) recommends certain precautions for avoiding the chance of spreading giardia, including showering after class, washing off any giardia that may have been contracted through the pool water; requiring that tight-legged diapers or pants be worn in the water; and not allowing children who have been ill, especially with diarrhea, to participate.

Despite the shortcomings of some early aquatic programs, exposure to the water at an early age offers many potential benefits to the participant. Though supportive data are lacking, early aquatic programs may be valuable in developing affection for the water at a young age. It may provide an excellent, unique environment for quality parent–child interactions and may be comforting to some very young children. Unfortunately, little scientific evidence exists to assist us in substantiating any of these claims or in furthering our understanding of these programs. We need much more research on the early development of swimming skill, the effects of early exposure to the water, and hyponatremia. We also need more substantial information concerning the effects of such factors as water condition, facility

Table 6-1   American Academy of Pediatrics and YMCA Statements or Guidelines on Infant Swim Programs

1. Children are generally not ready for formal swimming lessons until after their fourth birthday (AAP, 2000).

2. Avoid total submersion or anything that would appear to be traumatic to infants in the water, because pleasure in the water should be a major objective (YMCA, 1998).

3. Provide measures for avoiding fecal contamination in the pool; have participants wear tight-legged diapers or pants and shower thoroughly after participation; do not allow children who have been ill, especially with diarrhea, to participate (YMCA, 1998).

4. More research is necessary on the issue of infant swim programs (AAP, 2000).

5. Children should never be dropped or pushed into the water; this serves no educational purpose, and such coercion or submersion should be prohibited (YMCA, 1998).

6. Babies chill easily, so programs for 6- to 12-month-olds should be limited to 15 minutes, with longer sessions as children age and their thermoregulatory systems mature (YMCA, 1998).

design, and aquatic teaching methodologies to aid in the establishment of new aquatic teaching curricula (Langendorfer, Bruya, & Reid, 1988). Clearly, we still have much to learn concerning infant and preschool aquatic programs. Specific statements and guidelines are highlighted in Table 6-1.

Suzuki Method of Playing the Violin

Another of the most popular and enduring early-stimulation programs that strongly advocates the development of appropriate parent and child attitudes is the **Suzuki method** of playing the violin. This program, which depends greatly on the early motor and intellectual capabilities of its young students, began over 50 years ago in Japan.

Before creating this program, Suzuki pondered children's ability to speak the difficult language of Japanese at 1 or 2 years. If the children could master Japanese, why not the violin? And because children learn their language by hearing the constant chatter of those around them, would a similar process work for the violin? Thus, Suzuki began the "listen and play" method of learning to play the violin.

Suzuki method practitioners advocate starting formal training at 2 to 3 years of age, though indirect approaches can begin much earlier. For example, starting as early as birth, the child simply listens to selected musical pieces. Passive modes of learning such as watching and listening are emphases of this technique and can continue even after the child receives a violin. Shinichi Suzuki believed that this type of passive musical immersion into the great performances would be similar to the effect that naturally occurs to most of us as we are immersed into the process of language acquisition. Success is enhanced by prolonged and repeated exposure. Thus, nuances of pitch, tone, and timing are gradually memorized and internalized (Coff, 2000). When the child has become accustomed to or soothed by the initial selection, other musical selections can be added. However, the key to the success of this phase of the program is the tonal quality of the music played. In other words, according to Suzuki, if the parent sings off-key to the child, the effect may be negative rather than positive.

By approximately 2 to 2 ½ years, the child begins violin lessons (see Figure 6-2). Attitude is particularly important in this phase of the program: The child must be motivated to request a violin, rather than parents making the violin and the lessons mandatory. According to the Suzuki plan, this request is developed by genuine parental interest. Suzuki believes that the child will desire that which the parents find desirable. Thus, parents are encouraged to take lessons of their own. In addition, parents attend the child's lessons and learn enough to assist the child when necessary or when requested.

Also stressed in the Suzuki method is the use of a properly sized violin. An oversized or undersized instrument restricts or inhibits the intricate movements required to play the violin capably. This general concept of correct size has been considered in a variety of other movement activities. How is a child's catching performance, for example, influenced by the size of the ball? Similar questions are discussed in Chapter 13.

Figure 6-2 The Suzuki method of learning to play the violin emphasizes listening and playing.
SOURCE: Digital Vision/Getty Images

Table 6-2 Facts About Head Start	
Percentage of children from various age groups involved in Head Start (FY 2002):	
5-year-olds and older	5%
4-year-olds	52%
3-year-olds	36%
less than 3 years old	7%
Racial/ethnic composition of children involved in Head Start programs (FY 2002):	
American Indian	2.9%
Hispanic	29.8%
Black	32.6%
White	28.4%
Asian	2.0%
Number of classrooms in FY 2002 = 49,800	
Number of centers in FY 2002 = 18,865	
Average cost per child in FY 2002 = $6,934	
Percentage of children with disabilities = 13%	

SOURCE: Head Start, Administration for Children and Families, U.S. Department of Health and Human Services (2003), www.act.hhs.gov/programs/hsb/research/2003.htm.

An additional philosophy in the Suzuki method is discouraging competition among students. Children learn and play cooperatively and do not compete for "first chair." Likewise, cooperation is strongly encouraged because more experienced children are a critical component of the education of the children newer to the program (Coff, 2000).

As is the case with most programs involving the early stimulation of children, much is unknown about the residual effects of the Suzuki method. Although some outstanding violinists began with the program, others have long since ceased their interest in the instrument. Critics of such programs contend that many children have actually been discouraged from further musical involvement by being inundated with too much violin too young.

Head Start Programs

To give financially disadvantaged children a "head start" in education, the government program known as **Head Start** was started in 1965. Current facts about Head Start are presented in Table 6-2. This program, created as part of President Johnson's war on poverty, was designed to disrupt a cycle that had become apparent in education: the disadvantaged child falling further and further behind with each school year. That child, being poorly educated, would thus foster a new generation of disadvantaged children who would suffer the same plight.

The national Head Start Bureau recently stated that the most important goal of Head Start is to "enhance the social competence of children from low-income families" (Zill, Resnick, & McKey, 1999, p. 1). *Social competence* was defined as the child's daily ability to deal with the present environment as well as school and life for the longer term. A key test of this goal is the ability to function or adjust to the demands of kindergarten and elementary school, sometimes referred to as "school readiness" (Zill et al., 1999).

The original assumption underlying Head Start was that a preschool program might actually boost the intellectual, social, and emotional behavior of the children involved. Experts presumed that the betterment of these components, which also strongly affect motor development, would enhance academic success. This assumption was found to be partially correct based on tracking 2100 Head Start children throughout their educational careers; the children were found to be 10 times more likely to complete a high school education without failure than were their socioeconomic counterparts (Begley & Carey, 1983). Although this finding appears to support strongly the idea of early education programs for children, we should be aware of the uniqueness of the group involved. Because a specific program appeared to be successful for a specific social economic group at a particular age, we cannot assume that all programs involving early education will be similarly successful.

Research examining the long-term effects of programs such as Head Start has been encouraging. The "D.C. Study" longitudinally examined how children living in poverty were affected by attendance at a preschool program. Results indicated that attending a Head Start program and various other types of preschool programs positively affected children's long- and short-term performance measures. Significant positive effects were noted in enhancing "meaningful parent" involvement that was believed to be an "immensely" important factor in a child's long-term school success. In addition, particularly positive effects were yielded concerning the child's successful transition into later grades in school (Marcon, 1996).

Other evidence concerning the efficacy of Head Start programs has evolved from the Head Start Family and Child Experience Survey (FACES), a national longitudinal study of the cognitive, social, emotional, and physical development of Head Start children. The sample includes 40 Head Start programs and 3200 children who are studied upon entry into the program, at 1 year, 2 years, and the end of kindergarten. The study is currently ongoing with only preliminary results having been reported. One critical finding was that the average educational quality of Head Start programs was "considerably" higher than many commercial or center-based programs. Structural aspects of Head Start programs, such as class size and child–adult ratios, were also favorable and exceeded existing standards. Teachers were found to be well trained and experienced, although their overall educational background was lower than that of public school teachers (Resnick & Zill, 1999).

In a second component of FACES, researchers sought to determine what children know and can do at the end of their Head Start experience. This research examined major components of social competence as well as cognitive development and early academic skills. Social skills were measured by a standardized scale completed by teachers and parents, whereas children's cognitive and academic abilities were directly measured by trained testers. Problem solving and the child's approach to learning was also examined by trained assessors.

Generally, Head Start children were found "very often" to "use their free time in acceptable ways," "follow the teacher's directions," and "help in putting materials away." However, several "things they could not do" were also determined. This included "identifying and writing letters of the alphabet," "copying complex geometric figures" (such as a parallelogram), and demonstrating "they know left or right and top to bottom in reading." By the end of kindergarten, Head Start children who were tested had shown considerable improvements in such categories as word knowledge, letter recognition, and writing skills. At the same time, recommendations stated that Head Start children might benefit from more program activities aimed at improving early literacy skills and increasing the amount of time parents spend reading and performing other literacy-related activities with their children at home. An important overall conclusion of the study was that Head Start children appeared ready for school on the basis of how much they had learned by the end of kindergarten (Zill et al., 1999).

Infant Walkers

Infant walkers (see Figure 6-3) are designed to support babies who cannot yet walk independently. They have been around for centuries, but in recent

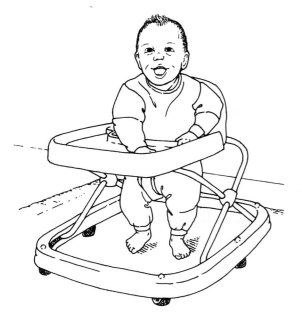

Figure 6-3 Infant walkers have become extremely popular in the last 20 years, though research suggests some danger from their use.

years they have become particularly common, with annual sales exceeding 3 million. Walkers allow the feet to touch the floor, thus permitting some mobility while the infant learns to walk. They are often equipped with built-in toys, bouncing mechanisms, a lock to keep them immobile when necessary, and the ability to be folded for storage. Studies have shown that between 55 and 92 percent of infants between 5 and 15 months of age have used walkers (AAP, 1995).

Unfortunately, questions arise as to the safety of infant walkers and their efficacy as a tool to promote early walking. Thirty-four infants died in walker-related deaths between 1973 and 1998 (AAP, 2001). Annual costs for injuries sustained to babies experiencing walker accidents have approximated $9 million (AAP, 1995). Further, as many as 10 times more injuries may occur that are insufficiently serious to warrant hospitalization or medical attention. Parent reports have indicated that as many as 12 to 40 percent of babies using walkers suffer a walker-related injury. Overwhelmingly, these injuries are caused

by falls—babies falling out of the walker as well as falling while still in the walker. Other injuries include finger or toe pinches and a smaller number of burns and poisonings (AAP, 1995).

Most of the injured babies sustained head injuries as a result of falling down stairs while in the walker. This prompted researchers to question whether the danger is from walkers or from stairs. Clearly, if more care were taken in keeping infants in walkers away from stairs, the incidence of injury would be reduced dramatically. Ridenour (1997) reports that over 70 percent of infant walker injuries requiring emergency medical care involved a fall down stairs.

Despite the controversy, parents cite many benefits to the use of walkers, though data are not supportive. Walkers are appealing for their value as a "babysitter." However, according to the American Academy of Pediatrics, they do not appear to keep babies safe. In addition, claims that they facilitate walking development are unfounded; studies indicate that they may delay the onset of independent walking while impeding crawling development. Few benefits seem to derive from walkers beyond parents' beliefs that their babies often seemed more content in the walker (AAP, 1995).

In a review of research on this issue, Burrows and Griffiths (2002) found no significant effect on the onset of walking and generally found no evidence indicating that walkers aid in the development of walking. Similarly, Siegel and Burton (1999) have suggested that walkers could be a form of deprivation in that the walker prevents infants from seeing their moving limbs. In their study examining over a hundred infants from 6 to 15 months of age, infants with walker experience sat, crawled, and walked later than infants who did not use walkers. Additionally, the infants with walker experience scored lower on assessments of mental and motor development. These findings led the authors to conclude that the benefit of using a walker is not worth the risk (Siegel & Burton, 1999).

As a result of the safety considerations regarding walkers, labeling (warning) practices have been in place since 1971. The efficacy of this practice has been called into question with the continued in-

Table 6-3 American Academy of Pediatrics Recommendations on Infant Walkers

1. Because of the risk and the lack of a clear benefit from their use, the sale and manufacture of infant walkers should be banned in the United States.

2. Education and media campaigns should be undertaken to inform parents of the hazards and lack of benefit of walkers. Special emphasis should be placed on the risk of walkers in households with stairs.

3. Community programs should be implemented to encourage the proper disposal and destruction of existing devices.

4. Licensing agencies should not permit the use of infant walkers in approved childcare centers.

SOURCE: AAP (1995).

crease of injuries, especially falls down stairs. Apparently, labeling has not deterred parents from using walkers; although labels urge parents to supervise their babies while in the walkers, some 17 percent of falls down stairs and over half of scalds and burns occur when the baby is left alone in the walker. These facts have led the American Academy of Pediatricians to publish the recommendations listed in Table 6-3 (AAP, 1995).

As of 1997, voluntary standards have been implemented for manufacturers of infant walkers. These standards include making the walker wider than 36 inches, so it cannot pass through an average doorway, and incorporating an automatic braking system when a wheel drops below the riding surface (e.g., starts to roll off a step) (AAP, 2001).

JOHNNY AND JIMMY

Back in 1935, Myrtle McGraw conducted what is now considered a classic investigation directly concerning motor development and the effects of early stimulation. In her research, McGraw closely monitored the twin brothers known as Johnny and Jimmy. She was particularly interested in determining if a child's normal progress in motor development could be altered by given conditions. Therefore, for the first 22 months of the twins' lives,

McGraw gave Johnny toys and considerable stimulation, practice, and experience in a variety of movement activities. Jimmy, however, had few toys and minimal motor stimulation.

McGraw periodically examined the effects of the varying levels of stimulation by exposing the twins to selected movement activities. For example, Johnny was given a tricycle when he was 11 months old. He was also given considerable practice and some instruction at that time. However, McGraw noted that 8 months elapsed before Johnny showed any signs of learning on the tricycle; he then proceeded to master tricycling quickly, within 2 months.

Jimmy was deprived of tricycling until he was 22 months old. However, despite his relatively low levels of stimulation, he learned tricycling much faster than Johnny. This led McGraw to conclude that a certain level of readiness is necessary for the acquisition of a motor skill. Jimmy was ready to tricycle at 22 months, but Johnny was not at 11 months. (We discuss the term *readiness* in greater detail later in this chapter.)

Using the twins as her subjects, McGraw examined many other movement activities as well. For example, Johnny was taught to roller-skate at less than 1 year of age and became skillful at the task. McGraw believed that this was facilitated by his low center of gravity, which enhanced his balance. Jimmy began skating at 22 months but never became a good skater. When their skating experiences ended, both twins' ability declined rapidly. In fact, when they were 3 years old, both twins suffered from balance difficulties. Surprisingly, Johnny, the stimulated twin, was described as having more problems skating than Jimmy, which McGraw credited to attitudinal differences that were emerging: Johnny had become somewhat reckless, whereas Jimmy maintained a much more cautious approach to movement.

Johnny and Jimmy were also observed ascending and descending slopes of varying grades. Johnny exhibited better skills at ascending the slopes than did Jimmy and also retained his ability better. Furthermore, Johnny appeared to be more clever at developing climbing strategies while being more graceful in the process. McGraw attributed this superior climbing ability to Johnny's early experience at a diversity of tasks, including slope climbing. When descending the slopes, Jimmy was particularly timid or cautious and occasionally uncooperative. Johnny rarely hesitated to descend and consistently maintained a higher level of ability.

Attitude similarly affected performances in jumping. For the jumping task, McGraw instructed the twins to jump down from a low pedestal. Frequently, Jimmy, who had far less early experience than his brother, could not be coaxed to jump. Johnny, however, jumped freely and with considerable skill.

McGraw also observed the twins while they were in the water. Both twins were given very early aquatic experiences that were abruptly halted when they were 17 months old, to be tested periodically in the future. Upon retesting when he was 6 years old, Johnny was found to be much more comfortable and skillful in the water. Although Johnny demonstrated a normal horizontal stroking position in a well-coordinated fashion, Jimmy stayed vertical and exhibited jerky swimming actions. Johnny's advanced skill was considered rather unusual, because he had never been instructed to perform the relatively sophisticated movements that he exhibited.

The contrast in levels of early stimulation for Johnny and Jimmy may have affected more than motor development. Although both Johnny and Jimmy were happy and well adjusted, Johnny was frequently favored socially. Perhaps as a result of his jealousy, Jimmy often struck Johnny and would take his toys. At other times, however, Jimmy would exhibit tremendous affection for his brother Johnny. In addition, Jimmy was more dependent on his mother and more prone to temper tantrums than was his brother.

A Rorschach (inkblot) test divulged additional information concerning the twins' personalities. Jimmy was more immature emotionally, self-centered, and dependent; Johnny more impersonal, self-confident, too brave at times, and relatively unaggressive.

McGraw's longitudinal investigation of Johnny and Jimmy was in many respects somewhat unscientific. With only two main subjects in her investigation, we might assume that the experiences of

Johnny and Jimmy were not indicative of what would happen with other subjects of a similar age. Nevertheless, McGraw is frequently credited with having had an astute and insightful ability for determining possible explanations for the differences in movement behavior between Johnny and Jimmy. For example, McGraw believed that the degree to which an activity maintains its state depends on its *level of fixity.* According to McGraw, the level of fixity is how well established a skill is when it is discontinued. This phenomenon may have accounted for the twins' maintenance of tricycling ability following a period of inactivity on the tricycle. The high level of skill that they developed upon initial exposure to tricycling facilitated their efforts when they were exposed to the same task at a later date.

McGraw also believed that practice and attitude were factors that greatly affected skill ability. Johnny's early practice in ascending and descending slopes and his willing attitude appeared to lead to his superior ability in this task. Jimmy had no previous experience to rely on and, perhaps as a result, was hampered by an uncooperative attitude concerning his ascension and descension of the slopes. Interestingly, though, this attitudinal difference may have had the reverse effect on roller-skating. Johnny was so willing to roller-skate that he became reckless and sloppy as a roller skater compared with his more conservative brother, who was extremely cautious.

Observing Johnny and Jimmy roller-skating also led McGraw to conclude that growth affected the facility with which the twins acquired movement ability. For example, as discussed, Johnny became relatively successful at the movement as early as 1 year of age. Jimmy was not introduced to the activity until he was 22 months old and never excelled at roller-skating. McGraw believed this was because the two boys had different body sizes when they were introduced to the activity: Jimmy was much taller and therefore had a higher center of gravity, making it harder for him to maintain the balance necessary for roller-skating. Johnny, although younger when he first attempted roller-skating, was also shorter, which McGraw believed was an advantage for this particular movement. Table 6-4 summa-

Factors Affecting Motor Development	McGraw's Explanation
Attitude	Johnny was successful at roller-skating when 11 months old. He became reckless soon after, causing his performance to decline. Jimmy was frequently uncooperative, which hampered his performance in descending slopes and jumping.
Practice	Johnny descended slopes much better than his brother Jimmy and developed clever strategies in the process. Jimmy, who had minimal early practice at such skills, was much less capable and very timid in his performance.
Readiness	Johnny was introduced to tricycling when he was 11 months old. He was incapable of much success at the skill until 8 months later. Jimmy was given a tricycle when he was 22 months old and tricycled immediately, despite his lack of early stimulation. According to McGraw, Jimmy exhibited a readiness for tricycling at 22 months, which Johnny did not have at 11 months.
Growth	Johnny roller-skated well when he was 11 months old but declined in his ability thereafter. This regression was attributed to his attitude and his increasing height (center of gravity), which impeded his balance.
Level of fixity	Both twins maintained their tricycling ability well, despite a period of nonparticipation. McGraw attributed this to their high levels of performance (level of fixity) at the time the skill was discontinued.

Table 6-4   McGraw's Research on Twin Brothers' Motor Development

rizes the major factors affecting Johnny's and Jimmy's motor development.

EFFECTS OF EARLY DEPRIVATION

The effects of early forms of deprivation are important to developmentalists studying all aspects of human behavior. The type, length, time, and severity of the deprivation and its subsequent effects are all variables they strive to understand. Potentially, such information may have beneficial applications for many practical situations, including education and child rearing, although investigating the effects of deprivation is difficult. Placing a baby in an intentionally deprived environment for scientific purposes is highly unethical and inhumane, so researchers have had to rely on animal research or the unusual, sometimes tragic, human cases that have occurred "naturally" in society. Therefore, there is sparse information concerning the effects of deprivation on the human being. However, certain classic studies

and cases, involving both animals and humans, have yielded important findings about the effects of various forms of deprivation early in life.

Hopi Cradleboards and Infant Development

In the 1930s, Wayne Dennis extensively studied the Hopi tribe. Much of this work culminated with the publication of his book *The Hopi Child* (1940). Of particular interest for motor development was Dennis's description of the use of infant cradleboards by the Hopis. As young as 1 month, and often until after the first birthday, babies were swaddled and tied to a board. The baby's arms were usually extended at the sides with only enough room for a slight bend. The legs were also placed in an extended position. Generally, according to Dennis, while on the board the Hopi infant was prevented from doing many movements that would be typical of babies who were not "cradled." For example, while in the cradleboard, babies could not touch their hands to the mouth, watch their hands, or kick their feet. Dennis also claimed that these infants were seldom taken from their home until about 4 months of age. When taken outside the home, the baby was usually carried in the arms of the mother or on her back while the cradleboard was left at home. By this time, babies had often become so accustomed to the board that they would cry or become restless until returned to the board. Though initially the baby was placed in the cradleboard for as long as 23 hours per day, progressively more freedom was allowed from the cradleboard starting at about 3 months of age. In addition, from 6 months the babies were not placed on their abdomens when out of the cradleboard until they were voluntarily capable of turning from a supine to a prone position. Thus, the baby was unable to practice such skills as raising the head or raising the chest off the floor when in a prone position.

As Dennis noted in his book, questions arose concerning the effect of using the cradleboard on the baby's development. Dennis maintained that, during the first few months of life, Hopi babies still assumed a flexed position when temporarily freed from the board. They also exhibited several other activities expected from babies not using a cradleboard. For example, they would play with their feet and hands. In fact, the sequence of acquisition of many voluntary movement skills seemed to follow the sequence that would normally occur without the "deprivation" of the cradleboard. According to Dennis, Hopi infants developed such skills as sitting, creeping, and walking in the usual sequence and at the same times as noncradleboard, "white American children" (Dennis, 1940).

Deprivation Dwarfism

The effects of early emotional or social deprivation are much more pervasive than were once expected. For example, infants hospitalized for a long period frequently have been found to become listless, apathetic, and depressed. Even more surprising is that infants under extended hospital care in unstimulating environments often fail to gain weight and may develop respiratory infections and fever. This condition, known as ***deprivation dwarfism,*** *psychosocial dwarfism,* or *psychosocial short stature,* can have a permanent impact on the individual.

This condition is a disorder that results in reduced or failed growth during infancy, childhood, or adolescence. It is associated with emotional deprivation or a severe psychosocial rearing environment where an unsatisfactory relationship exists between the child and the caregiver. In addition to a slowing or cessation of growth, sleep disturbance, depression, withdrawal, speech retardation, delayed cognitive abilities, and general psychomotor delay may exist. The existence of this condition can be confirmed by removing the child from the environment. Catch-up growth (discussed later) is typically demonstrated with accompanying improvements in behavior and normalization of hormonal disruptions. Catch-up occurs in varying degrees, depending on the age of the child, the severity of his or her condition, and the time of removal from their severe situation (Sirotnak, 2002).

In a 2002 study researchers examined 18 postpubertal participants who had been diagnosed with this disorder. All of the individuals had been separated from their families by the onset of the research, thus eliminating their severe psychosocial strain. The mean rate of height growth increased for all participants in the first year following the move to a more positive environment. However, less than 20 percent of the children achieved a final height greater than their "mid-parental target height." Most of the participants achieved a final height that was within the "mid-parental target range," though the mean height for the group was significantly shorter overall when compared with the mid-parental target height. Thus, some catch-up growth occurred, but patients often achieved a final height that was somewhat less than predicted under more normal circumstances (Gohlke & Stanhope, 2002).

This phenomenon was particularly well documented in Gardner's classic article, "Deprivation Dwarfism" (L. I. Gardner, 1972). Gardner described two orphanages, each directed by individuals of different temperament—one stern and uncaring, the other cheerful and loving. During one 6-month period, the relative weight gains of the children in the two orphanages were noted. The children under the care of the cheerful director at the first orphanage were larger overall relative to their respective ages. However, soon thereafter, the stern director from the second orphanage took the place of her more cheerful counterpart at the first orphanage. Ironically, this change of directors coincided with an increase of food at the first orphanage. Despite this increase in food, the emotional effect of the harsh new matron seemed to influence the growth of the children negatively: They showed reduced relative weight gain when compared with the children from the second orphanage. However, this apparent decrease in growth did not occur for all children in the first orphanage; eight children from the second orphanage who were the stern matron's favorites accompanied her to the first orphanage. They gained weight equivalently to the children in the first orphanage, the orphanage that had been directed by the more caring director. This dramatic situation illustrated the effects of adverse conditions on human growth. Although the exact operative mechanism is unclear, apparently harsh early circumstances during infancy or early childhood can lead to reduced growth.

This negative influence on human growth is apparently created by serious deprivation or adverse stimulation. Deprivation dwarfism is an emotional disturbance that is registered in the higher centers of the brain and eventually conveyed to the hypothalamus, which controls the secretion of the growth hormone somatotropin. Therefore, growth is impaired, and the likelihood of other potentially serious side effects, such as sleep disruption, increases (Schiamburg, 1985). As discussed in Chapter 7, as growth is affected, motor development may also be profoundly influenced.

Gardner described another unusual case of deprivation dwarfism. This situation involved a twin brother and sister who had grown normally for their first 4 months, at which point their mother then became pregnant with another child who was unexpected and unwanted. To complicate this situation, the father lost his job and left home, leaving the mother to care for the twins. The mother became frustrated and began to focus her hostility on the male twin. By the time he was 13 months old, the male twin was approximately the size of a 7-month-old, whereas the female twin had attained normal growth. The boy was then removed from the hostile environment and medically treated, which enabled him to regain his normal size by the age of $3\frac{1}{2}$ years (L. I. Gardner, 1972).

Anna: A Case of Extreme Isolation

Kingsley Davis (1946) described one of the most tragic of all reported cases of early deprivation. The study involved a young girl named Anna. Anna was isolated in an atticlike room of her home with minimal stimulation of any kind for almost 6 years. She was an illegitimate child who resided with her mother and grandfather. Anna was the unwitting victim of a family dispute. Her grandfather opposed having an illegitimate child living in his home while the mother argued in favor of her staying. Unfortunately, the subsequent compromise led to Anna staying in the house but living in the attic from the age of $5\frac{1}{2}$ months to approximately 6 years. In the attic, Anna received minimal care, barely enough to maintain her existence. When Anna was eventually discovered, she was in terrible condition. She showed minimal signs of intelligence, could not walk or talk, and was extremely malnourished. Davis described her legs as being "skeletonlike" and her abdomen "bloated."

Upon discovery, Anna was taken to a county home. During her stay at that institution, she showed minimal signs of improvement. She had developed motorically somewhat, as she could eat by herself and was able to walk. Her speech and intellectual abilities were still severely impaired.

Approximately 2 years after being discovered in the attic, Anna was taken to a private home for retarded children. There she continued to progress, although slowly. Her prognosis was described as unfavorable because she still showed no signs of speech other than random guttural sounds. Davis further described Anna as having an extremely poor attention span, periodically making nonpurposeful rhythmical movements, and watching her hands "as if she had seen them for the first time."

When Anna was about 8 years old, she was examined by a clinical psychologist, who found that her vision and hearing were normal and she showed progressing motor ability as she began to climb stairs. Her speech was in the babbling stage, and her mental age was determined as approximately 19 months. Her social maturity was judged roughly equivalent to a typical 23-month-old child. The examining psychologist predicted that Anna would eventually achieve the mental ability of a 6- or 7-year-old. However, he also noted that these tests were perhaps of questionable value in Anna's extreme case.

By the age of 9 years, Anna had progressed motorically. She could bounce balls and socialize somewhat. She could eat with considerable control, although her eating was confined to the use of a spoon and an eating technique typical of a much younger child. Most surprisingly, Anna had begun to speak in occasional full sentences but was still described as possessing the language abilities of a 2-year-old.

When she was 10, a final report on Anna revealed that she could string beads and build with blocks, showing evidence of progressing fine motor control. In addition, Anna walked and ran but was said to be rather clumsy. Her speech had evolved into frequent attempts at communication, although she rarely spoke in complete sentences.

Anna died at the age of 11. The case study describing Anna's conditions answered few questions concerning the effects of extreme deprivation, but it did stimulate many new thoughts and avenues of exploration concerning the effects of deprivation on the human condition. For example, how tremendous was the effect of Anna's isolation? How did Anna's actual state differ from what she would have been like in more normal circumstances? What would have happened to Anna had she been discovered earlier or later? Davis postulated that Anna's relatively early discovery may have enabled her to develop some skills that otherwise would have been impossible. Had Anna been discovered earlier, she might have had more capable communication and increased general intellectual abilities. Anna's early death was unfortunate for both humane and scientific reasons. Had she lived longer, we may have obtained partial answers to some of these questions.

The "Young Savage of Abeyron"

Throughout history, stories have arisen of children being raised in the wild. According to certain versions, some of these children were even raised by wild animals, but because of lack of documentation, most of these stories are now considered myth or folklore. However, one account that has been well documented is the case of Victor, a young boy who was found in the woods of France sometime around 1799. Victor, at what was believed to be 11 to 12 years of age, was found by three "sportsmen." Victor was immediately taken to a nearby village, where he was left in the care of a local widow. He remained there for only a week, as he soon escaped back into the nearby mountains. However, occasionally he would wander near villages, where he was once again captured and sent to a hospital and eventually to Paris for study. In Paris, Victor was placed under the care of a young physician named Itard. Dr. Itard believed Victor's condition to be a result of "lack of experience" resulting from isolation starting as early as 4 to 5 years of age. Itard immediately attempted to provide remedial experiences to help Victor catch up.

According to reports, Victor initially appeared to be "retarded." He was also "wild and shy," very impatient, and constantly seeking an opportunity to escape. He was further described as "disgustingly dirty," very inattentive, indifferent, and possessing very little affection for those around him. In fact, he was often known to bite and scratch. He moved "spasmodically" and frequently swayed back and forth. His eyes were unsteady and expressionless, and he rarely appeared to notice even loud sounds or music. Except for occasional guttural sounds, he did not speak. He appeared to have very little memory and was unable to imitate. According to Itard, "His whole life was a completely animal existence" (Itard, 1972, p. 35); he demonstrated an aversion to common foods and disliked wearing clothes and sleeping in a bed.

Victor's mode of locomotion was particularly interesting; he did not walk but tended to "trot or gallop," making walking with him very difficult. Itard also said Victor would smell anything handed to him and described Victor's chewing as being rodentlike.

The rapid action of the "incisors" led Itard to the conclusion that Victor's diet had been predominantly vegetarian. Victor's body was quite scarred. Many scars appeared to be a result of animal bites, while others were apparently the result of scratches acquired from years of living outdoors.

To determine Victor's level of intellectual ability, Itard placed food out of Victor's reach. Victor seemed to be intellectually incapable of using nearby chairs or other implements to assist him in reaching the food. Itard also placed bits of food beneath inverted cups to test Victor's memory of the location of the food. Again, Victor showed only a "feeble" capacity intellectually, though he finally began to track the cups with his eyes. Itard also attempted to show Victor how to use toys, but Victor was said to be impatient and often simply hid or broke the toys. Finally, Itard attempted to teach him to talk, though Victor appeared to achieve little verbally beyond using certain words to express pleasure. Though Victor showed moderate overall improvement over the course of his life, he never became intellectually normal. Victor died at about age 40.

CONCEPTS CONCERNING STIMULATION AND DEPRIVATION

As discussed, some fascinating and at times tragic situations have been studied to understand better the effects of stimulation and deprivation on human development. However, because such cases involved different forms of stimulation or deprivation, there are few solid conclusions. Nevertheless, many theories concerning early stimulation and deprivation have been proposed. Much of the theory to date concerns the concepts of critical periods, readiness, and catch-up (see Table 6-5). Here we define and discuss these terms and examine their relationship to early stimulation and deprivation.

Critical Periods

For years, experts have recognized that human development includes certain sensitive or critical periods. These **critical periods** are times when spe-

Table 6-5   Three Important Terms in the Study of Early Stimulation and Deprivation
Critical period: A time of particular or maximum sensitivity to environmental stimuli
Readiness: The establishment of the minimum characteristics necessary for a particular human behavior to be acquired
Catch-up: The human power "to stabilize and return" to a predetermined behavior or growth pattern "after being pushed off trajectory" (Tanner, 1978, p. 154)

cific conditions or stimuli are required for optimal, or even normal, development to ensue (Cameron & Demerath, 2002). If a child is exposed to the appropriate stimuli during this time of optimal sensitivity, a particular human behavior is likely to emerge or at least be facilitated (Newman & Newman, 1999). This term is also commonly used as a synonym for epigenetic period, which you will recall is a prenatal period during which the individual is particularly susceptible to environmental harm (Schiamburg, 1985). The prenatal factors were discussed in Chapter 5; this discussion concentrates on our first definition of the term *critical period*.

There are very few known specifics concerning this type of critical period. In fact, the idea of the existence of such periods is extremely theoretical, although there is considerable evidence to suggest their presence. Evidence is scarce, however, as to exactly how long critical periods last and which human behaviors they influence.

Also note that the idea of critical periods is that of a rather specific time in a person's life. During this time, the appropriate stimuli must be present or the potential for optimal development is lost. This concept does not indicate that total capacity for any kind of development will be squelched if the critical period is left unstimulated (Money, 1969). Therefore, even if the appropriate stimulation is not present during the critical period, mastery of a given skill may still be possible, although less than the person's genetic potential would have originally allowed.

Numerous research investigations and natural cases have led to the assumption that critical periods exist. For example, if the left hemisphere of the brain is damaged during early infancy, the right hemisphere often assumes certain functions, such as language development. However, if the left hemisphere is damaged after language has been acquired, the person may never again be capable of fluent speech, apparently because the critical period for the right hemisphere substitution has been bypassed. Perhaps the right hemisphere has been chemically or structurally altered to the point that it has become incapable of assuming left-hemisphere duties (Money, 1969).

Smiling, a fine movement, is also considered evidence that critical periods exist. A smile often occurs initially and spontaneously from approximately 5 to 14 weeks of age. At that time it can be evoked by any number of stimuli from familiar or unfamiliar individuals. For example, the sight of a human face, a touch, or a high-pitched voice frequently evokes a smile during this 9- to 10-week period early in infancy. At about 20 weeks, however, a different smiling pattern begins to emerge, in which only familiar faces elicit the smile. Children seem to lose sensitivity to the events that were once capable of causing their smiles to appear (Newman & Newman, 1999). The heightened sensitivity that existed for several weeks seems to diminish. The critical period for smiling has been further verified by studies of blind children, who smile initially at many of the same nonvisual stimuli as do sighted children but stop the behavior if it is not continually reinforced during this period of presumed sensitivity by cooing or touching (Freiberg, 1976).

Animal research has also been conducted to help fill the information void concerning critical periods. Nottebohm (1970) studied the motor task of vocalization in birds to determine if and when there was a critical period for the wild chaffinch to learn bird song. Under normal circumstances, this bird learns vocalization from adult birds and establishes a form of birdsong that is basically stable after the age of 1 year. However, Nottebohm noted that when the bird was deprived of hearing normal birdsong, its song became modified or abnormal. In fact, the more limited the bird's exposure to the necessary stimulus of hearing birdsong, the more likely the bird was to modify the vocalization to a more rudimentary form. However, if the bird was deprived of hearing birdsong after one full season of normal behavior, the deprivation seemed to have no further effect in altering the vocalization patterns. Apparently, the first 10 months to 1 year for the wild chaffinch is a critical period for the development of birdsong. If the bird acquires the appropriate ability during that time, the behavior becomes fairly stable; if the behavior is not acquired, it may never optimally develop.

These examples illustrate four of the essential elements of the idea of critical periods. First, for the environmental stimulation to be effective, the organism must have achieved a state of readiness. Second, there is a specific time limit. There may be multiple critical periods for any given behavior, but each behavior has a particular period when the stimulation is of optimal value. If the appropriate stimulation does not occur during this critical period, the opportunity for optimal development may be lost forever. Third, the effects of the stimulation during the critical period create a permanent and durable imprint. Therefore, even though an individual may temporarily discontinue a particular behavior, there may still be opportunity for optimal reestablishment as a result of the presence of appropriate stimuli during the critical period. Similarly, if appropriate stimuli were not present during the critical period, a permanent negative residue may remain. The individual would then be permanently incapable of optimally developing that behavior (Money, 1969). Finally, apparently there are critical periods for all aspects of human behavior. Although the critical period idea has been popularized in relation to cognitive skills, the critical period does appear extremely important in the development of social and motor skills as well as physical growth.

Many theories have been proposed to explain the phenomenon of critical periods. Bronson (1965) has stated that the critical period may occur as a result of the brain's neural networks attaining an optimal level of "functional significance." According to Bronson, the termination of the critical period could be a function of the decreasing sensitivity of the neural networks. This decreasing sensitivity probably occurs toward the end of a rapid structural change that is simply an aspect of the predetermined growth pattern.

Bronson's explanation is widely accepted and forms a foundation for continued consideration, but it is not specific enough to be practical. Presently there is no sufficient evidence, particularly in the area of motor development, to determine when a critical period is being experienced. Furthermore, we are not aware of the prerequisite conditions necessary for optimally preparing a child for movement acquisition (Seefeldt, 1982).

Readiness

The term **readiness** is often used in conjunction with the term *critical period*, which is sometimes defined as "a period of maximum sensitivity or readiness for the development of a particular pattern or skill" (Schiamburg, 1985, p. 638). As this definition implies, an ultimate form of readiness can be considered a critical period. However, this may not be the case, because readiness more commonly implies that the individual has become prepared, or ready, to acquire a particular behavior. In other words, the person has reached a certain point in an ongoing process that has enabled the establishment of the minimum characteristics necessary for a particular movement skill or other human behavior to be acquired. Sufficient information and ability have been accumulated and the necessary physical characteristics have been acquired so that the movement in question can be performed. Acquisition of the necessary physical characteristics implies that the person has attained a certain level of growth and that requisite neurological patterns have been created so that the new motor skill can be employed effectively. For readiness to be complete, however, the child must also be motivated to perform the behavior, implying an "internal" as well as "external" form of motivation (Kaluger & Kaluger, 1984). That is, the child must want to perform the movement skill while being appropriately encouraged from such external sources as the family.

We earlier referred to readiness in relation to McGraw's examination of the tricycling abilities of the twins Johnny and Jimmy. Johnny, who had received much stimulation and many experiences early in life, was introduced to tricycling when he was 11 months old. He was incapable of performing the skill at that time and showed no signs of learning for the next 9 months. However, Jimmy, who had received minimal stimulation as an infant, tricycled almost immediately when presented with a tricycle when 22 months old. The hypothesis proposed was that Johnny, regardless of his early stimulation, was not ready to tricycle at 11 months of age. Jimmy, at 22 months, despite his relatively deprived infancy, had acquired the physiological characteristics necessary to tricycle. Despite the varying levels of stimulation the two twins experienced, Jimmy was ready to tricycle at 22 months, whereas 11 months was too early for Johnny.

As the Johnny and Jimmy example suggests, a strict interpretation of the concept of readiness implies that early experience of or instruction in a particular movement activity prior to the achievement of readiness may not be particularly valuable (Magill, 1982). Before additional instruction can be worthwhile, the prerequisite skills must be within the child's repertoire. This belief suggests that the current trend of early educational programs may, in many cases, be fruitless.

Other researchers do not as readily accept a strict readiness theory. Bruner (1976) believes that the real burden is on the teacher or parent. Bruner stated that the child is always ready to acquire a new behavior; the key to eliciting the desired behavior from the child is determining the appropriate stimuli. Unfortunately, if Bruner's theory is accurate, the appropriate stimuli are unknown and will continue to be for years to come.

The outlook is equally disturbing for those who do subscribe to the theory of readiness, particularly regarding motor development. Currently we are unable to recognize signs that indicate that a child is ready. In fact, we really have no assurance that such signs even exist, because the concept of readiness is still a theory. Therefore, we can only estimate the most appropriate time for exposing the child to movement experiences and instruction. This is unfortunate, as recognition of the signs that indicate a state of readiness would greatly facilitate our efficiency in the instruction of movement skills. This ability, however, is not presently within our understanding of human motor development.

Catch-Up

Both stimulation and deprivation can have various effects on many aspects of human development. Depending on any number of variables, many unknown, the effects vary from one situation to the next. For example, in cases of severe deprivation, one person may exhibit permanent behavioral damage while another person exhibits only temporary effects. This may be due to the phenomenon known as catch-up. **Catch-up** is the unusual power a human being displays "to stabilize and return" to a predetermined behavior or growth pattern "after being pushed off trajectory" (Tanner, 1978, p. 154). This inexplicable phenomenon occurs in response to severe deprivation or adverse treatment, such as discussed earlier in the section "Deprivation Dwarfism." Catch-up is evidence that the human being is capable of acquiring new behavior or increasing physical growth much more rapidly than normal during a period of recovery. Figure 6-4 presents a graph that illustrates catch-up.

In a study examining catch-up growth among Filipino children from 2 to 12 years of age, just over 60 percent of the 2000 children involved in the study were "stunted" based on World Health Organization standards. Thirty percent of the two-year-olds who were stunted were no longer considered so at 8.5 years, with the percentage increasing slightly by age 12. Interestingly, low birth weight was found to be a factor that reduced the likelihood of catch-up later in childhood. Factors found to increase the likelihood of catch-up included having a taller mother, being first born, being longer at birth, having less severe growth impairment early in life, and having fewer siblings. In conclusion, this study found that some degree of catch-up growth is likely for most children during childhood. This contrasts early research suggesting that catch-up growth after age 2 was limited (Adair, 1999).

As evidenced by the preceding study, the term *catch-up* is most frequently used in conjunction

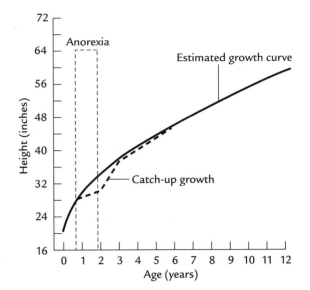

Figure 6-4   A hypothetical example of a child's catch-up growth following a period of anorexia, severe nutritional deprivation.

SOURCE: Adapted and reprinted from Prader, A., Tanner, J. M., and Von Harnack, G. A. (1963). Catch-up growth following illness and starvation. *Journal of Pediatrics, 62*, 654–659. Copyright 1963, with permission from Elsevier.

with physical growth. The term *catch-up growth* is common in the literature concerning human development. However, catch-up can also occur intellectually, socially, and motorically. Regardless of the domain of human development being directly affected, motor development is also modified to some degree. As discussed in Chapter 1, all domains of human development are reciprocally related. But whichever domain of human development appears most directly affected, the degree of recovery, or catch-up, appears to depend on the severity, the length, and the time of deprivation. Despite often remarkable recoveries, individuals who catch up will never fully realize their genetic potential, because of the time they lost during the period of deprivation and recovery (Prader, Tanner, & Von Harnack, 1963).

Anna, the victim of severe isolation, is an excellent example of catch-up and its variability. Recall that after nearly 6 years in isolation in the atticlike room of her home, Anna was incapable of most behaviors expected of the normal 6-year-old. However, with improved care and proper treatment following her discovery, Anna caught up in many of her behaviors, particularly physical size. Although she was extremely small and frail when discovered, Anna was actually described as "large for her age" in the years to follow (Davis, 1946). Similar catch-up occurred for certain gross motor skills. Anna could not walk when she was approximately 6 years old, but she was described as being capable at running, ball bouncing, and climbing in the years that followed. No doubt Anna had caught up physically and motorically. Unfortunately, her language and intellectual skills showed much less progress.

One of the most interesting examples of catch-up involves Harlow's classic studies of the rhesus monkey (Suomi & Harlow, 1978). Harlow either totally or partially isolated the monkeys from any kind of social contact for 3, 6, and 12 months. Although the total or partial isolation led to similar behavioral patterns, the longer periods of isolation created much more devastating effects. The 3-month isolates appeared to be in a state of emotional shock when allowed to interact socially. They were fearful of other monkeys and therefore avoided contact with them. This group of monkeys also exhibited the abnormal idiosyncrasies of self-clutching, self-biting, rocking, and pulling their own hair. Despite these rather unusual behaviors, the monkeys eventually recovered when allowed to play daily with a group of normal same-age monkeys.

The 6-month isolates yielded a poorer prognosis. They exhibited the same behavioral traits exhibited by the 3-month isolates, but this second group showed poorer ability to recover. They avoided their age-mates during playtime, showing social interest only in the other isolates.

As expected, the 12-month isolates exhibited even more behavioral abnormalities. Along with exhibiting the same characteristics as the other isolates, the 12-month group revealed greater apathy and were more severely withdrawn. They were extremely passive and thus defenseless to attacks from their normal age-mates.

Follow-up investigations revealed that the monkeys that were isolated 6 months or longer exhibited continued behavioral abnormalities. Social behavior during their adolescence and adulthood was considered bizarre, as exemplified by their difficulties in sexual relationships and performance. The severity of the problem with the monkeys isolated for 6 months or longer initially led Harlow to conclude that the first 6 months of social interaction may be a critical period. In other words, if social interaction were prohibited during that time of life, complete, or optimal, development of social behavior may never be possible (Suomi & Harlow, 1978).

However, in subsequent research, Suomi and Harlow found reason to doubt that initial theory. In seeking a method to rehabilitate the long-term isolates, the researchers exposed their subjects to 26 months of "therapy" with 3-month-old monkeys. Because the younger monkeys were less offensive and generally less active than the older ones, they tended to approach the isolates more cautiously. After an initial period of acquaintance, the young monkeys would even cling to the isolates. Such affection from the young "therapy monkeys" seemed to normalize the isolates' behavior to the point that they were considered recovered by the end of the 26 weeks. Thus catch-up, although normally associated with physical growth, also appears to occur with social, emotional, intellectual, and motor development (Suomi & Harlow, 1972).

SUMMARY

Programs involving early education for children have become particularly popular in recent years. However, the value of many such programs is unsubstantiated by what little research exists on early stimulation or deprivation. In fact, some research has shown that early stimulation may have long-term deleterious effects. Programs designed to stimulate or optimize early motor development have been categorized into the no-programming and the programming types. The no-programming type advocates avoidance of specific training or practice of future movements. The programming type encourages an active role in manipulating the baby in preparation for future development.

In a policy statement issued by the American Academy of Pediatrics, infant exercise programs are said to be of no known benefit for the development of healthy infants. Nevertheless, the AAP encourages parents to seek "safe, nurturing, and minimally structured" play situations for their infants.

Gymboree has been one of the most popular programs designed to enhance early motor development, though no research exists to support the claims made by the program. Infant and preschool aquatic programs are also extremely popular, though controversial, as they have been linked to water intoxication and giardia. Current interest in infant and preschool aquatic programs has led to the creation of guidelines by the American Academy of Pediatrics and the American Red Cross.

The Suzuki method of playing the violin is another popular early education program. This program is unique, as it generally requires the parent to participate with the child. Head Start programs have also catered to the preschool-age child since 1965. Research concerning the effectiveness of this early stimulation is still inconclusive.

Infant walkers have been widely used for years though research has shown a high rate of injury from infants falling down stairs in their walkers. Research has also demonstrated that walkers do not appear to enhance walking development, though parents believe they may be pleasurable for the baby.

Myrtle McGraw's research involving the twins Johnny and Jimmy yielded many valuable conclusions concerning the effects of early stimulation. McGraw concluded that readiness, practice, attitude, and physical growth were all particularly important factors that influence human movement at an early age.

During the 1930s, Wayne Dennis found that the Hopi people swaddled and tied their babies to cradleboards over the first several months of life. Though this appeared to limit some forms of early stimulation, Dennis found that the Hopi babies would often cry to return to their cradleboard, and they appeared to follow a developmental sequence and timeline that would be expected of noncradleboard babies in the acquisition of sitting, creeping, and walking.

Early deprivation also has dramatic impact on early development in all domains of human behavior. Deprivation dwarfism is the retardation of physical growth following a period of severe deprivation or adverse treatment despite sufficient levels of nutrition.

Anna, the victim of severe deprivation because of isolation, was seriously impaired as a result of her mistreatment. With improved care and special treatment, she was capable of catching up motorically, although her language and intellectual skills were extremely abnormal.

One of the most interesting cases of deprivation concerned the "young savage of Abeyron." This young boy was found at an early age after having lived in the "wild" for years. He could not talk, trotted or galloped rather than walked, chewed "like a rodent," and was delayed intellectually. Despite repeated attempts at remediation, he showed little improvement in his intellectual skills and died at the young age of 40 years.

A critical period is a time of special sensitivity to environmental stimuli. If the child is appropriately stimulated during this period, the associated behavior is most likely to emerge or be facilitated.

The term *readiness* implies that a person has achieved a certain point in an ongoing process that has enabled the establishment of the minimum characteristics necessary for a certain behavior to be acquired. Readiness depends on an adequate level of physical growth, the requisite neurological patterns, and sufficient internal and external motivation.

Catch-up is a human being's ability to return to a predetermined pattern of behavior or growth following a severe period of deprivation or mistreatment. Although normally associated with physical growth, catch-up also appears to occur with motor development.

KEY TERMS

catch-up	Gymboree	no programming
critical periods	Head Start	programming
deprivation	hyponatremia	readiness
deprivation dwarfism	infant walkers	stimulation
giardia	level of fixity	Suzuki method

QUESTIONS FOR REFLECTION

1. Describe the controversy over early-intervention motor development programs. Cite any research you can to provide detail in your explanation.

2. Describe Gymboree programs. Would you involve one of your children? What advice would you give other parents regarding these programs?

3. What is giardia? What does it have to do with programs of early motor intervention, and what would you do about it?

4. If you were in charge of an infant swim program, would you implement any guidelines? If so, what would they be, and what evidence would you cite to provide support for your decision?

5. What is the Suzuki method of learning to play the violin? What is unique about the Suzuki

method compared with other forms of early motor intervention?

6. What did Myrtle McGraw mean by "level of fixity"?

7. What did McGraw find in her research on Johnny and Jimmy? Give specific findings for the concepts of attitude, practice, readiness, growth, and level of fixity.

8. Over 200 years ago, a young boy, Victor, was found in the woods in France. He was believed to be about 12 years old and had grown up in the wild. Describe Victor's state when found. Provide specific reference to his verbal skills, his locomotor skills, and his intellectual ability.

9. What is meant by the term *catch-up*? Give at least two examples of this concept from this chapter and one from your real-life experiences.

INTERNET RESOURCES

American Academy of Pediatrics **www.aap.org**

American Academy of Pediatrics Policy Statements **www.aappolicy.aappublications.org**

American Red Cross **www.redcross.org**

Division for Early Childhood of the Council for Exceptional Children **www.dec-sped.org**

Fifty-Plus Lifelong Fitness Association **www.50plus.org**

Gymboree **www.gymboree.com**

Head Start (U.S. Department of Health and Human Services) **ww2.acf.dhhs.gov/programs/hsb**

YMCA **www.ymca.org**

ONLINE LEARNING CENTER (www.mhhe.com/payne6e)

Visit the *Human Motor Development* Online Learning Center for study aids and additional resources. You can use the study guide questions and key terms puzzles to review key terms and concepts for this chapter and to

prepare for exams. You can further extend your knowledge of motor development by checking out the Web links, articles, and activities found on the site.

REFERENCES

Adair, L. S. (1999). Filipino children exhibit catch-up growth from 2 to 12 years. *Journal of Nutrition, 129*(6), 1140–1148.

American Academy of Pediatrics (AAP). (1988). Policy statement: Infant exercise programs. *Pediatrics, 82*(5), 800.

———. (1995). Injuries associated with infant walkers. *Pediatrics, 95*(5), 778–780.

———. (2000). Swimming programs for infants and toddlers. *Pediatrics, 105*(4), 868–870.

American Academy of Pediatrics Committee on Injury and Poison Prevention (2001). Injuries associated with infant walkers. *Pediatrics, 108*(3), 790–792.

American Red Cross. (1988). *American Red Cross infant and preschool aquatic programs: Parent's guide.* Washington, DC: Author.

———. (2000). American Red Cross infant and preschool aquatic program is consistent with American Academy of Pediatrics Guidelines. Online: www.redcross.org/news/inthnews/00/4-10a-00.html.

Barnes, J., Astor, S. D., & Tosi, U. (1981). *Gymboree: Giving your child physical, mental, and social confidence through play.* Garden City, NY: Doubleday.

Begley, S., & Carey, J. (1983, Mar. 28). How far does Head Start go? *Newsweek,* 65.

Bennett, H. J., & Wagner, T. (1983). Acute hyponatremia and seizures in an infant after a swim lesson. *Pediatrics, 72*(1), 125–127.

Blankard, B. A., Parker, H. E., Bradley, S., & Ong, V. (1995). Children's readiness for learning front crawl swimming. *Australian Journal in Medicine and Sport, 27,* 34–37.

Bronson, G. (1965). The hierarchy of the central nervous system: Implications for learning processes and critical periods in early development. *Behavioral Sciences, 10,* 7–25.

Bruner, J. (1976). *The process of education.* Cambridge, MA: Harvard University Press.

Burd, B. (1986). Infant swimming: Immersed in controversy. *Physician and Sportsmedicine, 14*(3), 239–244.

Burrows, P. & Griffiths, P., (2002). Do baby walkers delay onset of walking in young children? *British Journal of Community Nursing, 7*(11), 581–586.

Cameron, N., & Demerath, E. W. (2002). Critical periods in human growth and their relationship to diseases of aging. *American Journal of Physical Anthropology,* Supplement 35, 159–184.

Coff, R. (2000). Suzuki violin versus traditional violin: A Suzuki violin teacher's view. *Musicstaff.* Online: www.musicstaff.com/lounge/article17.asp.

Davis, K. (1946). A final note on a case of extreme isolation. *American Journal of Sociology, 52,* 432–437.

Dennis, W. (1940). *The Hopi child.* New York: Appleton-Century.

Elkind, D. (1990). Academic pressures—Too much, too soon: The demise of play. In E. Klugman & S. Smilanky (Eds.), *Children's play and learning: Perspectives and policy implications.* New York: Teachers College Press.

Freiberg, S. (1976). *Insights from the blind: Developmental studies of blind children.* New York: Basic Books.

Gardner, J. M., Karmel, B. Z., & Dowd, J. M. (1984). Relationship of infant psychobiological development to infant intervention programs. *Journal of the Child in Contemporary Society, 17,* 93–108.

Gardner, L. I. (1972, July). Deprivation dwarfism. *Scientific American,* 76–82.

Gohlke, B. C., & Stanhope, R. (2002). Final height in psychosocial short stature: Is there complete catch-up? *Acta Paediatrica, 91*(9), 961–965.

Head Start (2003). Administration for Children and Families, U.S. Department of Health and Human Services. Online: www.acf.hhs.gov/programs/hsb/research/2003.htm.

Itard, J. M. G. (1972). First development of the young savage of Abeyron. In W. Dennis (Ed.), *Historical readings in developmental psychology.* New York: Appleton-Century-Crofts.

Kaluger, G., & Kaluger, M. F. (1984). *Human development: The span of life.* St. Louis, MO: Times Mirror/Mosby.

Langendorfer, S., Bruya, L. D., & Reid, A. (1988). Facilitating aquatic motor development: A review of developmental and environmental variables. In J. Clark & J. H. Humphrey (Eds.), *Advances in motor development research.* Vol. 2. New York: AMS Press.

Langway, L., Jackson, T., Zabarsky, M., Shirely, D., & Whitmore, J. (1983, Mar. 28). Bringing up superbaby. *Newsweek,* 60–66.

Magill, R. A. (1982). Critical periods: Relation to youth sport. In R. A. Magill, M. J. Ash, & F. L. Smoll (Eds.), *Children in sport.* Champaign, IL: Human Kinetics.

Marcon, R. A. (1996). The "D.C. Study": A longitudinal look at children's development and achievement under varying educational and familial conditions. Presentation made for the Head Start Third National Research Conference, Washington, DC, June 20–23.

McGraw, M. (1935). *Growth: A study of Johnny and Jimmy.* New York: Appleton-Century-Crofts. (Reprinted in 1975 by Arno Press.)

Money, J. (1969). Physical, mental, and critical periods. *Journal of Learning Disabilities, 2,* 28–29.

Newman, B. M., & Newman, P. R. (1999). *Development through life: A psychosocial approach.* 7th ed. Pacific Grove, CA: Brooks/Cole.

Nottebohm, F. (1970). Ontogeny of bird song. *Science, 167,* 950–956.

Parker, H. E., & Blankard, B. A. (1997). Starting age and aquatic skill learning in young children: Mastery of prerequisite water confidence and basic aquatic locomotion skills. *Australian Journal of Science in Medicine and Sport, 29,* 83–87.

Prader, A., Tanner, J., & Von Harnack, G. (1963). Catch-up growth following illness or starvation. *Journal of Pediatrics, 62,* 654–659.

Resnick, G., & Zill, N. (1999). Is Head Start providing high quality educational services? "Unpacking" classroom processes. Presentation made for the Society for Research in Child Development, Biennial Meeting, Albuquerque, New Mexico, April 16.

Ridenour, M. V. (1978). Programs to optimize infant motor development. In M. V. Ridenour, J. Herkowitz, J. Clark, J. Teeple, & M. A. Roberton (Eds.), *Motor development: Issues and applications.* Princeton, NJ: Princeton Book Company.

———. (1997). How effective are brakes on infant walkers? *Perceptual and Motor Skills, 84,* 1051–1057.

Schiamburg, L. B. (1985). *Human development.* New York: Macmillan.

Seefeldt, V. (1982). The concept of readiness applied to motor skill acquisition. In R. A. Magill, M. J. Ash, & F. L. Smoll (Eds.), *Children in sport.* Champaign, IL: Human Kinetics.

Siegel, A. C., & Burton, R. V. (1999). Effects of baby walkers on motor and mental development in human infants. *Journal of Developmental and Behavioral Pediatrics, 20*(5), 355–361.

Sirotnak, A. P. (2002). Child abuse and neglect: Psychosocial dwarfism. *Emedicine Journal, 3*(5), online:author.emedicine.com/PED/topic566.htm.

Suomi, S. J., & Harlow, H. F. (1972). Social rehabilitation of isolate-reared monkeys. *Developmental Psychology, 6,* 487–496.

———. (1978). Early experience and social development in rhesus monkeys. In M. E. Lamb (Ed.), *Social and personality development.* New York: Holt, Rinehart & Winston.

Tanner, J. M. (1978). *Fetus into man: Physical growth from conception to maturity.* Cambridge, MA: Harvard University Press.

White, B. L. (1975). *The first three years of life.* Englewood Cliffs, NJ: Prentice-Hall.

YMCA, Division of Aquatics. (1984). *YMCA guidelines for infant swimming.* Chicago: YMCA.

YMCA. (1998). *Y skippers: Aquatic program for children five and under.* Champaign, IL: Human Kinetics.

Zill, N., Resnick, G., & McKey, R. H. (1999). What children know and can do at the end of Head Start and what it tells us about the program's performance. Presentation made for the Society for Research in Child Development, Biennial Meeting, Albuquerque, New Mexico, April 16.

7

Growth and Maturation

What is the average height of a 5-year-old? How much taller will this child be in 1 year? What is this youngster's expected average body weight? What are the expected growth trends regarding height and weight during both middle and late adulthood? Which gender has longer legs, longer arms? What effect does exercise have on the dynamics of human growth? Is there a positive relationship between these physical characteristics and motor skill acquisition and motor skill performance? This chapter sheds light on these and other questions and explains how to measure the human body. The interrelationships between human body structure and human motor output are also discussed.

MEASURING GROWTH IN LENGTH AND STATURE

From birth to 2 years or until the child can stand without assistance, total body length (**recumbent length**) is measured while the child is supine (see Figure 7-1). A special slide ruler is used to measure the distance between the **vertex** (highest point on the skull) and the soles of the feet. The measurement should be recorded to the nearest 0.1 centimeter or $\frac{1}{8}$ inch.

When the child is capable of standing without assistance, standing height (**stature**), the distance between the vertex and the floor, is the preferred measurement of total body length (see Figure 7-2). The child should be barefoot when the measurement is taken; this measure should be recorded to the nearest 0.1 centimeter or $\frac{1}{8}$ inch. Note that a triangular headboard, which forms a right angle between the vertex and measurement scale, is used to increase accuracy.

Standard techniques for determining stature will not be accurate if the individual is not capable of standing erect or has severe spinal curvature. This is frequently the case when attempting to assess stature in elderly and handicapped populations. However, stature can be estimated from the recumbent

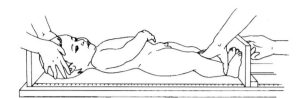

Figure 7-1 Measuring recumbent length

SOURCE: Used with permission of Ross Products Division, Abbott Laboratories Inc., Columbus, OH 43215. From *Pediatric Anthropometry*, 2nd ed., © 1983 Ross Products Division, Abbott Laboratories Inc.

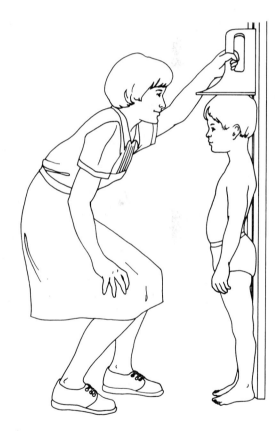

Figure 7-2 Measuring stature with the use of a triangular headboard

SOURCE: Used with permission of Ross Products Division, Abbott Laboratories Inc., Columbus, OH 43215. From *Pediatric Anthropometry*, 2nd ed., © 1983 Ross Products Division, Abbott Laboratories Inc.

measure, ***knee height.*** Figure 7-3 illustrates the technique for measuring knee height. Note that the individual bends the left knee to a 90-degree angle. The blades of the sliding caliper are then placed under the heel and over the anterior portion of the thigh. Pressure is then applied to compress the soft tissue before a reading is taken. To ensure reliability and accuracy, two consecutive measurements should be taken and both should be within 0.5 centimeter agreement. The obtained knee-height value can then be substituted into one of the following equations to estimate stature:

$$\text{Stature men} = 64.19 - (0.04 \times \text{age}) + (2.02 \times \text{knee height})$$
$$\text{Stature women} = 84.88 - (0.24 \times \text{age}) + (1.83 \times \text{knee height})$$

In solving the equation, round age to the nearest whole year and record knee height in centimeters. To convert inches to centimeters, simply multiply inches by 2.54. Conversely, if you desire to estimate stature in inches, simply divide the number derived from the equation by 2.54.

For example, if the knee height of a 75-year-old man was 50.5 centimeters, then his estimated stature would be calculated as follows:

$$64.19 - (0.04 \times 75) + (2.02 \times 50.5)$$
$$= 64.19 - (3) + (102.01)$$
$$= 61.19 + 102.01$$
$$= 163.2 \text{ cm or } 163.2 \text{ cm}/2.54$$
$$= 64.25 \text{ inches}$$

GROWTH IN LENGTH AND STATURE

Human prenatal life begins when the male sperm merges with the female egg, forming a zygote, which measures only 0.14 millimeter in diameter. During the next 38 to 40 weeks of intrauterine life, the fetus grows almost 5000 times longer. In fact, at

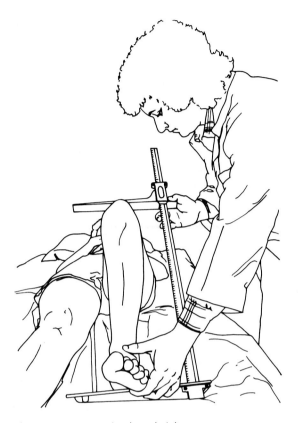

Figure 7-3   Measuring knee height

no time during the human life cycle is growth in body length greater than that which occurs during the fourth prenatal month. However, growth rapidly decelerates during the remaining prenatal period. Mean body length increases approximately 90 percent between the 10th and 14th weeks of gestation but only slightly more than 10 percent during the last 4 weeks of gestation.

Following 280 days of gestation, there is little gender difference in median birth lengths. Boys generally measure about 20 inches long (50.5 centimeters); girls generally measure about 19.75 inches long (49.9 centimeters). By the end of the first year of infancy, boys will be approximately 30 inches long, girls approximately 29.25 inches long. Thus, during the first year of postnatal life, body length can be expected to increase approximately 50 percent.

During the second year, gains in body length average 4.75 inches (12 centimeters). After age 2, stature increases at a slower rate, until the onset of the adolescent growth spurt. This growth deceleration continues during most of the elementary school years, with one exception: Some children experience a **midgrowth spurt** in height between 6½ and 8½ years. This midgrowth spurt occurs more frequently in girls than in boys (Malina & Bouchard, 1991). This unexplained deviation in growth rate is less dramatic than the adolescent spurt, and little is known about it.

The many hormonal changes known to occur during adolescence cause boys and girls to grow taller rapidly. In fact, about 20 percent of the adult stature is attained during this 2½ - to 3-year growth spurt. The onset of this milestone usually occurs in young boys at about 11 years of age with peak rate of growth occurring at about 14 years (Roche & Sun, 2003). Girls generally start their adolescent growth spurt 2 years earlier. However, some children will mature faster than others; the time of onset can vary by as much as 3 or more years. Because girls generally enter adolescence before boys, it is not at all uncommon for young girls to be slightly taller than young boys (average is 1 inch taller) between 10 and 13 years of age (Roche & Sun, 2003). During this adolescent phase of development, boys' height increases about 4 inches (10 centimeters) per year. The female spurt is somewhat slower: Girls grow about 3 inches (8 centimeters) per year. Most of the height gained during the adolescent spurt is due to a lengthening of the trunk, not a lengthening of the legs. Peak leg-length growth usually occurs 6 to 9 months earlier. "Thus a boy stops growing out of his trousers (at least in length) a year before he stops growing out of his jackets" (Tanner, 1990, p. 67).

By the time the young woman is 17.3 years old and the young man 21.2 years, most of adult height has been attained.

Stature remains stable for 15 years after age 30. At middle age (above 40), there is an apparent decrease in height, caused by intervertebral disk degeneration and decreased thickness of joint cartilage in the lower extremities. Further reductions in height are apparent in late adulthood as the vertebral column continues to degenerate, sometimes causing abnormal spinal curvature. Table 7-1 summarizes growth for various ages. Reference data for those in late adulthood (over 60) is presented in Table 7-2.

Growth in stature can be graphically illustrated. Figure 7-4 is a typical individual **distance curve** for stature. The distance curve plots accumulative growth obtained over time. In contrast, Figure 7-5 illustrates percentile velocity curves for both boys and girls on the variable stature. The **velocity curve** plots increments of change per unit of time, making the curve useful for illustrating periods of fast and slow growth. A close examination of the velocity curves will reveal the possibility of obtaining negative values. It is incorrect to interpret these negative values as representing a decrease in stature. Instead, negative values result from measurement error. For a more detailed discussion of this phenomenon, consult Roche and Himes (1980).

To determine if an individual is growing normally, compare individual data to norm-referenced data. The National Center for Health Statistics (NCHS) percentile charts have been prepared for this purpose: Figures 7-6 and 7-7 are NCHS percentile charts for stature for both boys and girls between 2 and 20 years of age (Kuczmarski, Ogden, et al., 2000, 2002) (see Figure 7-5 for NCHS velocity curves). Visual comparison of charted data to the percentile rankings can quickly alert one to growth abnormalities. Growth retardation may indicate disease, malnutrition (Roche & Sun, 2003), child abuse (Wales & Taitz, 1992), or delayed maturation, among other conditions. If growth retardation is suspected, the youngster should be referred to a physician for further screening. A complete set of growth charts recently released as part of the NHANES III national data set are presented in Appendix A.

Table 7-1   Important Growth Changes in Body Length and Stature

Age	Selected Growth Information
Conception	0.14 mm in diameter
Birth (median length)	Boys: 20 in. (50.5 cm) Girls: 19.75 in. (49.9 cm)
6 months (median length)	Boys: 26.75 in. (67.8 cm) Girls: 26 in. (65.9 cm)
Year 1 (median length)	Boys: 30 in. (75 cm) Girls: 29.25 in. (73.1 cm) Length increases approximately 50% during the first year.
Year 2	Length increases about 4.75 in.
Years 3–5	Decelerated growth rate to about 2.75 in./yr
Year 6–adolescence	Decelerated growth rate to about 2.25 in./yr
Adolescence	20% of adult stature is attained during this 2½- to 3-yr period. Approximately 4 in./yr growth for boys and 3 in./yr for girls
17.3 years	Women: median age at which growth in stature ceases
21.2 years	Men: median age at which growth in stature ceases Average adult stature of 69 in. is roughly 3.5 times larger than that of the newborn.
20–30 years	Growth of vertebral column may add another ⅛ in. (3–4 cm) to stature.
30–45 years	Stature is stable.
Above 45 years	Possible decrease in stature from disk degeneration

Table 7-2   Percentiles for Stature in cm (and in.)

	Men				Women		
Age (years)	95%	50%	5%	Age (years)	95%	50%	5%
65	181.6 (71.5)	170.3 (67.0)	159.1 (62.6)	65	171.6 (67.6)	161.0 (63.4)	153.1 (60.3)
70	181.6 (71.5)	169.9 (66.9)	158.7 (62.5)	70	169.8 (66.9)	159.1 (62.6)	151.3 (59.6)
75	181.2 (71.3)	169.5 (66.7)	158.4 (62.4)	75	167.9 (66.1)	157.3 (61.9)	149.4 (58.8)
80	180.9 (71.2)	169.1 (66.6)	158.0 (62.2)	80	166.1 (65.4)	155.4 (61.2)	147.6 (58.1)
85	180.5 (71.1)	168.8 (66.5)	157.7 (62.1)	85	164.2 (64.6)	153.6 (60.5)	145.7 (57.4)
90	180.2 (70.9)	168.5 (66.3)	157.3 (61.9)	90	162.4 (63.9)	151.7 (59.7)	143.9 (56.6)

SOURCE: Used with permission of Ross Products Division, Abbott Laboratories Inc., Columbus, OH 43215. From *Nutritional Assessment of the Elderly Through Anthropometry*, © 1984, Ross Products Division, Abbott Laboratories Inc.

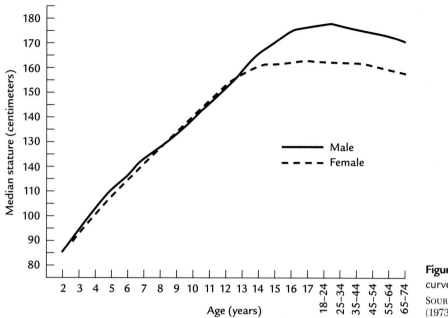

Figure 7-4 Typical distance curve for stature

SOURCE: Based on NCHS data (1973, 1979).

MEASURING BODY WEIGHT

The instrument of choice for obtaining body weight is an electronic digital scale. The scale should be calibrated in metric units, with a maximum capacity of at least 160 kilograms. The child stands in the middle of the scale with shoes and as much clothing as possible removed. If the child is fully clothed, an adjustment of approximately 1 pound is made. A platform scale should be used to measure the body weight of infants who are not capable of standing without assistance (see Figure 7-8). If the infant is crying or moving excessively, an accurate measure may be difficult to obtain. In such a case, another technique would be to weigh the parent on an adult electronic scale, repeat the process while the parent holds the infant, then subtract the parent's weight from the parent-child weight to obtain the child's weight. Most infants will be more relaxed when held by a parent in the upright position, resulting in a more accurate measurement. In addition, other types of scales are available for bedridden individu-

als or adults who cannot stand without assistance (see Figure 7-9).

GROWTH IN BODY WEIGHT

At conception, the ovum weighs approximately 0.005 milligram; it would take over 5 million of these cells to equal just 1 ounce. By the midpoint of the prenatal period (19 weeks), the mean body weight of a normally developing fetus is about 14 ounces (400 grams). At the end of the 34th week of gestation, the fetus is approximately 20 times heavier than it was at 14 weeks (5.5 pounds).

Median birth weights of boys and girls are 7.5 pounds (3.27 kilograms) and 7 pounds (3.23 kilograms), respectively. Only rarely does a newborn weigh more than 11 pounds. Weight at birth, however, tends to be more variable than length at birth. Apparently length, more than weight, is influenced by genetic makeup. Many extraneous factors have been shown to influence birth weight. For instance,

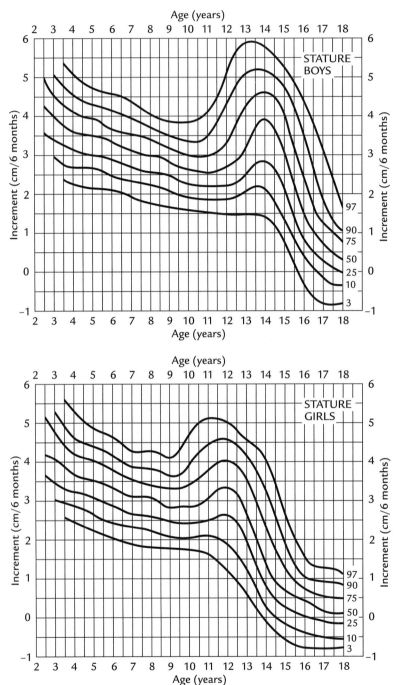

Figure 7-5 National Center for Health Statistics growth velocity charts for boys and girls on the variable stature

SOURCE: Used with permission of Ross Products Division, Abbott Laboratories Inc., Columbus, OH 43215. From data that was used in the 1981 charts from the Ross Growth and Development Program: Incremental Growth Charts — Girls and Incremental Growth — Boys, © 1981 Ross Products Division, Abbott Laboratories Inc.

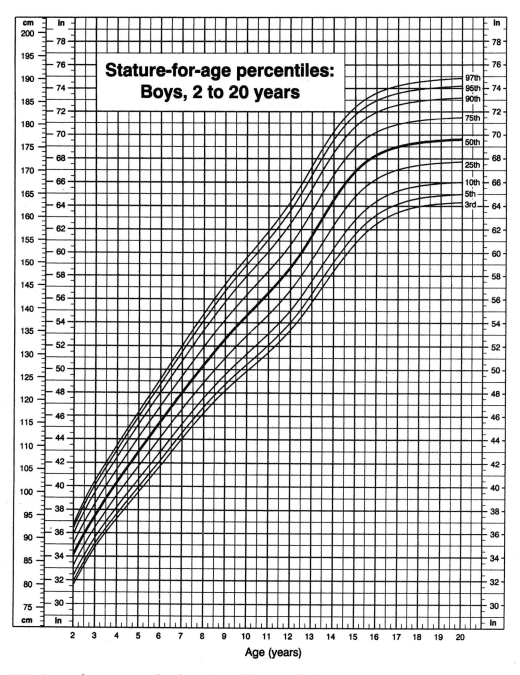

Figure 7-6 Stature-for-age percentiles, boys, 2 to 20 years, CDC growth charts: United States

SOURCES: Developed by the National Center for Health Statistics in collaboration with the National Center for Chronic Disease Prevention and Health Promotion (2000). Kuczmarski, Ogden et al., 2000, 2002.

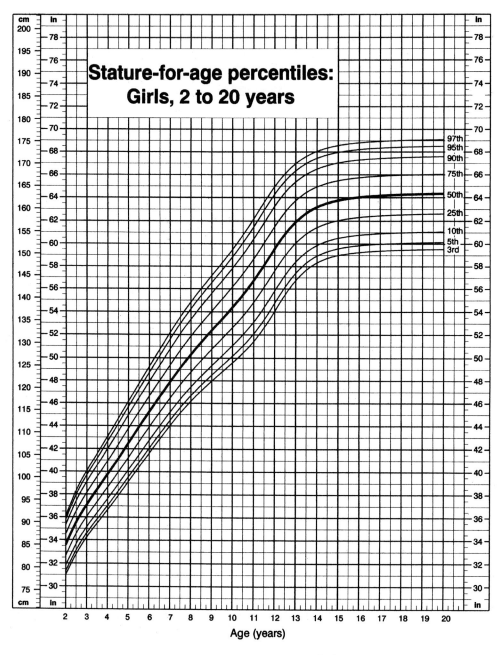

Figure 7-7   Stature-for-age percentiles, girls, 2 to 20 years, CDC growth charts: United States

SOURCES: Developed by the National Center for Health Statistics in collaboration with the National Center for Chronic Disease Prevention and Health Promotion (2000). Kuczmarski, Ogden et al., 2000, 2002.

small mothers tend to have small babies irrespective of the father's size; later-born children tend to be heavier than firstborns; mothers from low socioeconomic groups give birth to babies who are lighter than babies born to mothers from higher socioeconomic groups; and twins are roughly 1.5 pounds lighter than singletons. Thus, birth weight reflects intrauterine life to a greater degree than does birth length (Roche & Sun, 2003).

During the first 6 months of postnatal life, the infant gains about ⅔ ounce (20 grams) per day. At this rate of gain, the infant will double birth weight at 6 months. This rate of weight gain slows toward the middle and later part of the first year. At the end of the first year, boys weigh about 22.5 pounds (10.15 kilograms) and girls about 21 pounds (9.53 kilograms). Thus, birth weight can be expected to triple during the first year.

Rate of weight gain continues to decelerate during the second year of life. The average child can be expected to gain about 5.5 pounds (2.5 kilograms). This rate of gain remains steady for the next 3 preschool years, with the normally developing child averaging about 4.5 pounds (2 kilograms) per year. For the next 4 to 6 years or until the onset of adolescence, annual weight gain increases slightly to 6.5 pounds (3 kilograms) per year. Nonetheless, there is a great deal of variability. One longitudinal study found that variability in body weight tripled for girls 5 to 12½ years and nearly quadrupled for boys 5 to 14½ years (Haubenstricker & Sapp, 1980).

Adolescence can bring about sharp increases in body weight. In fact, during the first 3 years of this period, boys add about 45 pounds (20 kilograms) to their body weight, and girls add about 35 pounds (16 kilograms). Much of this added body weight is from height increases and changes in body composition. (See Chapter 8 for a discussion on the growth of adipose and muscle tissue.) Age of **peak weight velocity** (maximum rate of growth in body weight) generally occurs after peak height velocity (Beunen & Malina, 1988). Mature body weight is approximately 20 times that of birth weight.

After maturity, adults can partly control whether they add, lose, or maintain their body weight. One exception is adult weight gain following pregnancy:

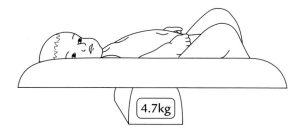

Figure 7-8   Electronic digital scale

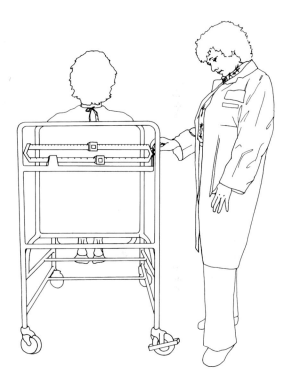

Figure 7-9   Chair scale

Women with children tend to weigh more than their childless sisters (Sinclair, 1998). Some of the weight gained during pregnancy appears to be permanent, and the amount may increase with each successive child. However, recent research has found that women who gain more weight than recommended during pregnancy are at greater risk of being obese one decade later (Rooney & Schauberger, 2002). After a person reaches adult weight, it is

Table 7-3   Important Growth Changes in Body Weight

Age	Selected Growth Information
Conception	Ovum weighs roughly 0.005 mg.
19th week of gestation	14 oz (400 g)
34th week of gestation	Fetus is 20 times heavier than at 14 weeks (5.5 lb).
Birth (median weight)	Boys: 7.5 lb (3.27 kg) Girls: 7 lb (3.23 kg)
	Small mothers tend to have small babies.
	Later-borns are heavier than firstborns (6.8 oz).
	Twins are approximately 1.5 lb lighter than singletons.
1–3 days	Weight loss is upwards of 10% of birth weight.
10 days	Weight is equal to birth weight or slightly heavier.
First 6 months	Gains about ⅔ oz (20 g)/day
	Birth weight generally doubles at 6 months.
Second 6 months	Gains decelerate to about ½ oz (15 g)/day.
Year 1	Median weight of boys: 22.5 lb (10.15 kg)
	Median weight of girls: 21 lb (9.53 kg)
	Birth weight triples during first year.
Year 2	Gains about 5.5 lb (2.5 kg)
Years 3–5	Gains about 4.5 lb (2 kg)/yr
Year 6–adolescence	Slight increase in rate of weight gain to 6.5 lb (3 kg)/yr
Adolescence	Boys add about 45 lb of body weight and girls about 35 lb of body weight during the first three years of adolescence.
Year 18 (median weight)	Men: 151¾ lb (68.88 kg) Women: 124¾ lb (56.70 kg)
	Mature body weight is approximately 20 times greater than birth weight.
Above 19 years	Weight becomes a matter of nutritional and exercise status.
	Some weight gains during pregnancy appear permanent.

difficult to interpret changes in body weight, because so much depends on the person's nutritional and exercise status. For instance, muscle and system atrophy can cause weight loss, but some sedentary but well-fed elderly people may actually gain weight. Nonetheless, older people's body composition (fat weight versus muscle weight) is markedly different from that of young adults. Table 7-3 summarizes weight changes from conception up to adulthood. Body weight reference data for individuals in late adulthood are presented in Table 7-4.

Like stature, changes in body weight can be graphically illustrated. Figure 7-10 is a typical distance curve showing differences in body weight between male and female humans. In contrast, Figure 7-11 illustrates growth velocity; Figures 7-12 and 7-13 are NCHS percentile charts for the variable body weight.

Table 7-4   Weight in kg (and lb) for Adults 50–80+ Years of Age

Men				Women			
Age (years)	85%	50%	15%	Age (years)	85%	50%	15%
50–59	100.7 (221.5)	84.1 (185.0)	72.0 (158.4)	50–59	91.6 (201.5)	71.5 (157.3)	57.2 (125.8)
60–69	98.4 (216.5)	82.4 (181.3)	67.7 (148.7)	60–69	86.9 (191.2)	68.8 (151.4)	55.4 (121.9)
70–79	93.5 (205.7)	77.9 (171.4)	64.2 (141.2)	70–79	82.1 (180.6)	64.7 (142.3)	52.9 (116.4)
80+	84.1 (185.0)	70.8 (155.8)	58.4 (128.5)	80+	72.3 (159.1)	59.7 (131.3)	47.9 (105.4)

SOURCE: Kuczmarski, Kuczmarski, and Najjar (2000).

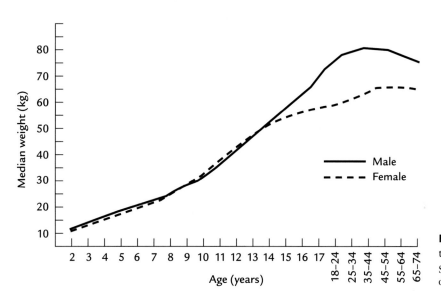

Figure 7-10 Typical distance curve for body weight
SOURCES: Based on NCHS data (1973, 1979).

COMBINING BODY WEIGHT AND HEIGHT: BODY MASS INDEX

Measures of weight and height are frequently combined to yield a measure known as the ***body mass index (BMI).*** To calculate BMI, simply divide body weight (kg) by height in meters squared (see Table 7-5) or use the BMI conversion tables located in Appendix B. According to Pietrobelli and colleagues (1998), this simple measure is valuable because it is related to body fatness and future health risks, including increased incidence of cardiovascular disease, diabetes, hypertension, hypercholesterolemia, and certain cancers (ACSM, 2000; Bray, 1992; Calle et al., 1999; Holbrook, Wingard, & Barrett-Connor, 1990). However, BMI cannot be used to determine percentage of body fat. This is because body fatness and the BMI are influenced by both age and gender. For example, for any given BMI value, women will possess more body fat than men for the same BMI value. Similarly, older individuals have more body fat than do younger individuals

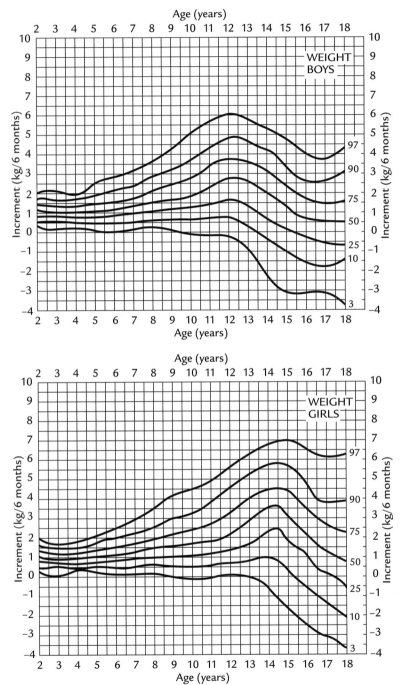

Figure 7-11 National Center for Health Statistics growth velocity charts for boys and girls on variable body weight

SOURCE: Used with permission of Ross Products Division, Abbott Laboratories Inc., Columbus, OH 43215. From data that was used in the 1981 charts from the Ross Growth and Development Program: Incremental Growth Charts—Girls and Incremental Growth—Boys, © 1981 Ross Products Division, Abbott Laboratories Inc.

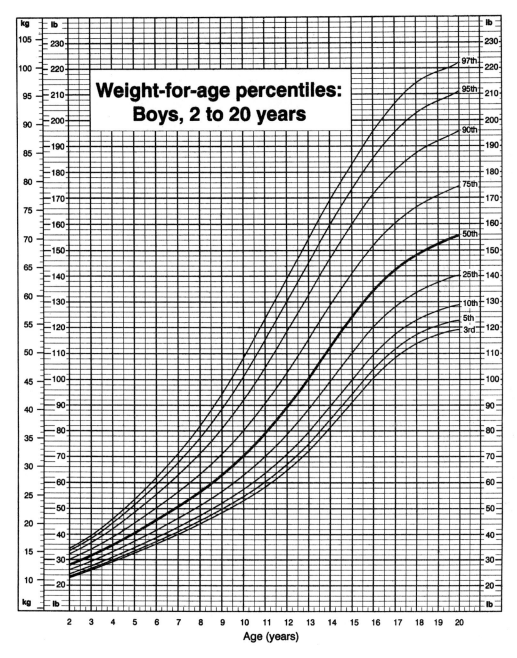

Figure 7-12 Weight-for-age percentiles, boys, 2 to 20 years, CDC growth charts: United States

SOURCES: Developed by the National Center for Health Statistics in collaboration with the National Center for Chronic Disease Prevention and Health Promotion (2000). Kuczmarski, Ogden et al., 2000, 2002.

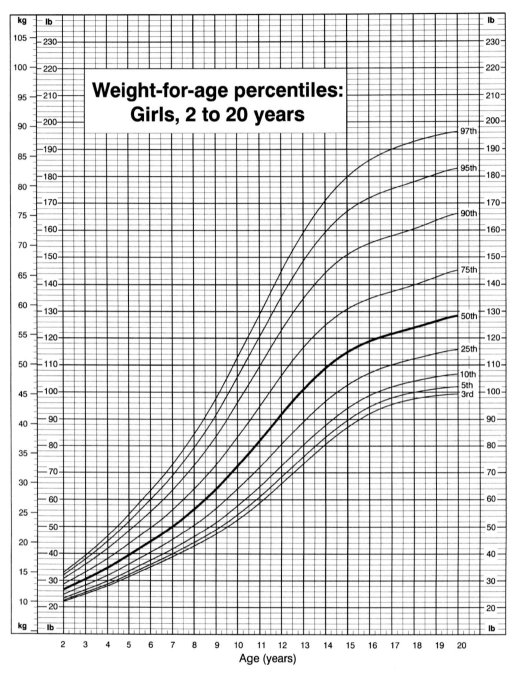

Figure 7-13   Weight-for-age percentiles, girls, 2 to 20 years, CDC growth charts: United States

SOURCES: Developed by the National Center for Health Statistics in collaboration with the National Center for Chronic Disease Prevention and Health Promotion (2000). Kuczmarski, Ogden et al., 2000, 2002.

Table 7-5   Calculating Body Mass Index (BMI)

Case: Mary is a 46-year-old woman who weighs 132 pounds and is 65 inches tall. Calculate Mary's BMI.

1. Convert pounds to kilograms by dividing pounds by 2.2:

$$\frac{132 \text{ lb}}{22} = 60 \text{ kg}$$

2. Convert height in inches to height in meters by multiplying inches by 0.0254:

$$65 \text{ in.} \times 0.0254 = 1.65 \text{ m}$$

3. Solve the BMI equation by algebraic substitution:

$$BMI = \frac{\text{weight (kg)}}{\text{height (m}^2)}$$

$$BMI = \frac{60}{1.65^2}$$

$$BMI = \frac{60}{2.72}$$

$$BMI = 22.1^\circ \text{ kg/m}^2$$

° Rounded to nearest tenth.

given identical BMI values (Gallagher et al., 1996). Thus while BMI values are used to monitor a population risk of health and/or nutritional disorders, in any given individual other data must be considered because BMI alone is not diagnostic (Willett et al., 1999).

As illustrated in both Figure 7-14 (BMI boys) and Figure 7-15 (BMI girls), BMI decreases during the preschool years and reaches a minimum around 5 to 6 years of age. Thereafter, BMI increases throughout most of adulthood, reaching a maximum velocity at about 13 years in girls and about 14 years in boys (Guo et al., 2000). During this period of rapid growth, increases in BMI are mainly due to increases in total body fat in girls and fat-free mass in boys (Maynard et al., 2001). However, BMI values regress from 60 to 80+ years of age (see Table 7-6).

The upward trend occurring after the low point on the BMI percentile curve is commonly referred to as the ***adiposity rebound.*** Researchers have re- cently discovered that the younger the child is when the adiposity rebound is encountered, the greater is the likelihood the child will have an increased BMI as an adult (Whitaker et al., 1998).

In children and adolescents BMI-for-age is best used as a guide to determine individual nutritional status (underweight, overweight). According to Himes and Dietz (1994) and the work of Kuczmarski, Ogden, and colleagues (2000), concerns regarding underweight begin when BMI-for-age is found to be at a percentile rank of less than 5 percent. When the BMI-for-age is greater than the 95th percentile, overweight is of concern. Those children exhibiting a BMI-for-age value greater than 85 percent but less than 95 percent are at risk for becoming overweight. In adults, BMI values are interpreted with one fixed number regardless of age or gender. The Centers for Disease Control (2000) guidelines for individuals are as follows: underweight — BMI less than 18.5; overweight — BMI 25.0 to 29.9; obese — BMI 30.0 or more. Thus a healthy BMI value for adults should range between 18.5 and 24.9.

Comparisons of NHANES II (1976–1980) and NHANES III Phase I (1988–1991) data for individuals between 20 and 74 years old show that the average BMI increased from 25.3 to 26.3. The mean weight of this group increased approximately 3.6 kilograms. However, during the same period, mean height increased less than 1 centimeter (Kuczmarski et al., 1994). In short, both American adults and children (Troiano et al., 1995) are becoming fatter. The prevalence of obesity and its ramifications regarding health and physiological fitness are discussed in greater detail in Chapter 8.

STATURE AND WEIGHT: INTERRELATIONSHIP WITH MOTOR DEVELOPMENT AND PERFORMANCE

In the 1930s, Shirley's classic study of 25 babies sparked interest in the relationship between length and weight at birth and the attainment of independent walking. In her study, Shirley concluded,

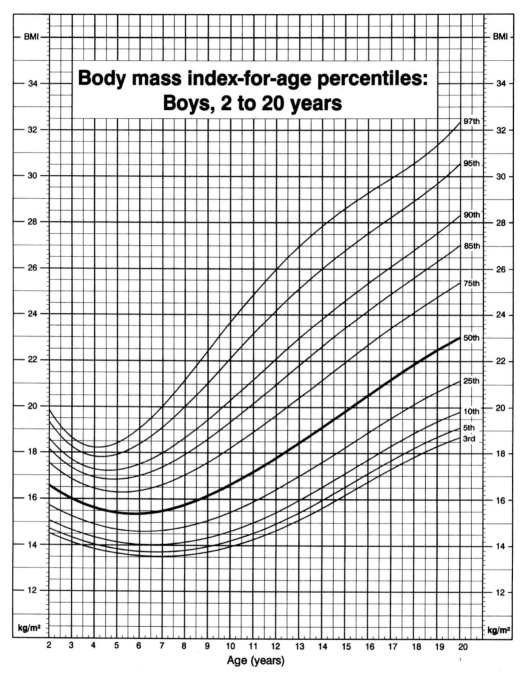

Figure 7-14 Body mass index-for-age percentiles, boys, 2 to 20 years, CDC growth charts: United States

SOURCES: Developed by the National Center for Health Statistics in collaboration with the National Center for Chronic Disease Prevention and Health Promotion (2000). Kuczmarski, Ogden et al., 2000, 2002.

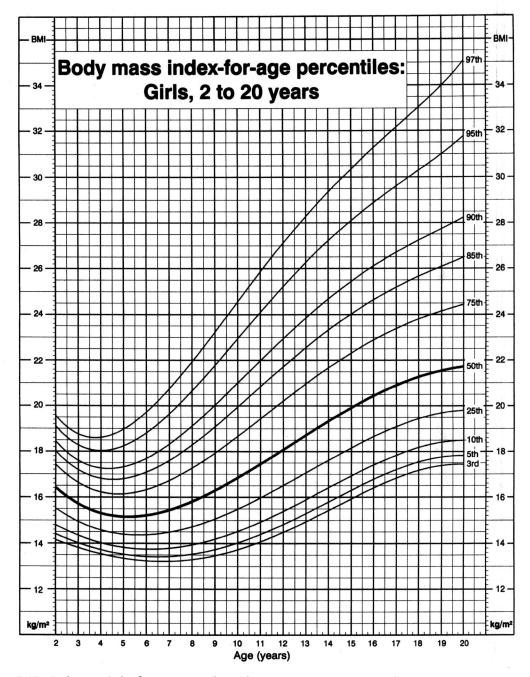

Figure 7-15 Body mass index-for-age percentiles, girls, 2 to 20 years, CDC growth charts: United States

SOURCES: Developed by the National Center for Health Statistics in collaboration with the National Center for Chronic Disease Prevention and Health Promotion (2000). Kuczmarski, Ogden et al., 2000, 2002.

Table 7-6   Mean Body Mass Index for Persons 2–80+ Years of Age*

Age (years)	Male	Female
2	16.3	16.1
3	15.9	15.6
4	15.8	15.5
5	15.6	15.6
6	16.0	15.7
7	16.0	16.1
8	16.6	16.4
9	16.8	17.5
10	18.0	17.8
11	18.7	18.9
12	18.8	19.4
13	19.6	20.1
14	20.2	21.1
15	20.8	20.6
16	22.1	21.8
17	21.7	22.3
18	22.7	22.3
19	23.0	22.5
20–29	24.9	24.1
30–39	26.1	26.4
40–49	27.3	26.7
50–59	27.2	27.2
60–69	27.1	26.6
70–79	26.1	25.9
≥80	25.0	25.0

*Pregnant women excluded.

SOURCES: National Center for Health Statistics (1987) for ages 2–19 based on NHANES II data. Kuczmarski et al. (1994) for ages 20–49+ based on NHANES III Phase I data. Kuczmarski, Kuczmarski, and Najjar (2000) for ages 50–80+ based on NHANES III data.

"In general it may be stated that thin, muscular babies and small-boned babies walk earlier than short rotund babies and exceedingly heavy babies"(Shirley, 1931, p. 126). Norval (1947) reported similar relationships. Norval stated that "it is apparent that infants who are longer for their weight walk at an ear-lier age than those who are relatively short for their weight" (p. 676). Irrespective of these findings, it is difficult to imply a cause-effect relationship between length and weight at birth and the development of independent walking. Shirley (1931) recognized this possible criticism when she wrote, "Proportionate long- or short-leggedness is by no means the all-important growth factor concomitant with walking. The concomitance of the two does not imply inter-dependence; it may mean only mutual dependence on some third factor, such as age" (p. 120).

Jaffe and Kosakov (1982) have also attempted to relate age at walking to weight and length parameters measured at the time of walking. In their study of 135 healthy infants 6 to 18 months old, they found that overweight and obese infants (Sveger, 1978) demonstrated a significant delay in motor development when compared with normal-weight infants. However, 1 year later, a follow-up examination revealed that a majority (71 percent) of the motor-delayed infants were developing normally.

During adolescence and adulthood, the interrelationship of weight and height to skilled motor performance becomes task specific. Generally, increased body weight is an asset when an external object is propelled, such as a shot put. In contrast, lighter body weight is more advantageous when the individual's body is the object propelled. Furthermore, body weight and body fatness generally exert a negative influence on performance when the task requires the body to be supported.

ADOLESCENT AWKWARDNESS

Another issue frequently addressed in the professional literature regarding performance changes during adolescence is the concept of ***adolescent awkwardness.*** This term has been used to refer to a period during the growth spurt (***peak height velocity [PHV];*** maximum rate of growth in height) that is accompanied by a temporary disruption in motor performance. According to the Fels longitudinal study, PHV occurs in boys at a mean estimated age of 13.7 years and in girls at 11.8 years (Roche & Sun, 2003). Tanner (1990) has noted a

Table 7-7 Percentage of Boys Exhibiting Declines in Motor Performance During Peak Height Velocity		
Task	**Number of Subjects**	**Percentage of Decliners**
Arm pull (static strength)	444	1.4
Plate tapping (speed of limb movement)	441	7.0
Vertical jump (explosive strength)	446	9.5
Sit and reach (flexibility)	444	18.7
Leg lift (trunk strength)	444	26.1
Bent-arm hang (strength)	446	30.5
Shuttle run (agility/speed)	445	33.5

SOURCES: Based on data reported by Beunen and colleagues (1988) and Ostyn and colleagues (1980). Adapted from Beunen and Malina (1988).

period during the growth spurt when balancing abilities may be disrupted for up to 6 months. Beunen and associates (1988) as well as Ostyn and associates (1980) also found a significant number of boys who declined in motor performance on four of seven motor tasks during peak height velocity.

Following an extensive review of the literature, Beunen and Malina (1988) concluded that this phenomenon, adolescent awkwardness, does exist, but primarily among boys. However, the phenomenon is not universal. That is, not all individuals experience a disruption in motor performance during peak height velocity. These researchers report that the percentage of boys exhibiting declines in performance during this growth spurt interval ranges from 1.4 percent to 33.5 percent. Table 7-7 illustrates their findings in more detail. Of particular interest is their finding that those boys who exhibited a decline in performance at the time of peak height velocity were generally the best performers at the beginning of peak height velocity. Moreover,

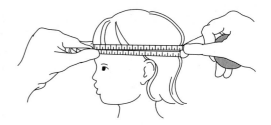

Figure 7-16 Measuring head circumference

subsequent follow-up testing during young adulthood revealed that this decline was only temporary (Beunen & Malina, 1988). For this reason, individuals responsible for motor assessments should be cautious in interpreting motor performance data that have been obtained during this critical growth period.

MEASURING CHANGES IN BODY PROPORTIONS

Relevant body proportion measures that involve the head include the relationship of head length to overall body length, as well as head circumference. As illustrated in Figure 7-16, **head circumference** is obtained by placing the measuring tape anteriorly superior to the eyebrows and posteriorly at the position of the maximum circumference. The tape should be pulled tight to compress the hair.

A second measure of proportional growth is the ratio between **sitting height** and stature (sitting height/stature × 100), which describes the contribution of the legs and trunk to total height. The person being measured should sit on a high bench so that the feet do not touch the floor; she should keep the spine erect and eyes focused straight ahead. The distance between the vertex and the sitting surface is measured.

A third measure of proportional growth is the **biacromial/bicristal ratio** (biacromial breadth/bicristal breadth × 100). Biacromial breadth, a measure of shoulder width, is the distance between the right and left acromial processes; bicristal breadth, a measure of hip width, is the distance between

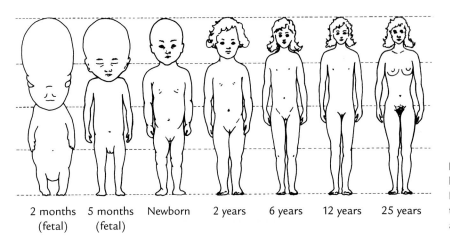

| 2 months | 5 months | Newborn | 2 years | 6 years | 12 years | 25 years |
| (fetal) | (fetal) | | | | | |

Figure 7-17 Changes in body proportions with age. Notice the great changes in the relative size of the head and the lower limbs.

the right and left iliocristales (hipbones). These distances are measured with an anthropometer, a sliding caliper, or a length caliper. The person should stand erect with arms hanging naturally by the sides while being measured.

CHANGES IN BODY PROPORTIONS

Here we describe changes in the relationship between (1) head length and total body length, (2) changes in head circumference, (3) changes in sitting height as it compares with stature, and (4) changes in shoulder width as contrasted with growth in hip width. Lastly, we describe general body shape by examining physique.

Changes in the Ratio of Head Length to Total Body Length

Figure 7-17 illustrates changes in the relationship of head length to total body length. One of the most noticeable characteristics of the newborn is the size of the head in relation to total body length. More specifically, at birth the head contributes about 25 percent to total body length, while the lower limbs contribute only 15 percent (Sinclair, 1998). Because the legs and trunk lengthen in relation to the head, the relative position of the body's mid-

point descends with age. In other words, the center of gravity slowly descends through the growing years.

As mentioned, the head, trunk, and legs do not grow proportionately; therefore, a person's center of gravity varies markedly during childhood. Although the anatomical location of the center of gravity changes with age, it remains a relatively constant proportion of total height. Most kinesiologists agree that this ratio of the center of gravity to total height is 53 to 59 percent in the adult, a range of only 6 percent. Dyson (1964) has pointed out, however, that in children the ratio of the center of gravity to total height is higher because children carry a larger proportion of their weight in their upper bodies. As a general rule, the center of gravity in the male is slightly higher than that in the female human.

At birth, the center of gravity is located approximately 20 centimeters above the trochanters. It slowly descends until it rests at approximately 10 centimeters above the trochanters at maturity. Although this shift of only 10 centimeters seems relatively small, there is a marked change in the center of gravity's anatomical location. In the newborn, 20 centimeters above the trochanters is an area in the lower level of the thoracic cavity at the xiphoid process; in the adult, 10 centimeters above the trochanters brings the center of gravity to the level of the iliac crest at the second or third sacral vertebra.

By the time children enter elementary school (6 years old), their center of gravity has dropped

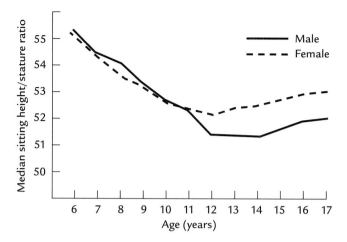

Figure 7-18 Sitting height/
stature ratio
Source: Based on NCHS data
(1974).

through the abdominal cavity and is located near
the umbilicus (Palmer, 1929). The center of gravity
then proceeds to descend at a uniform rate toward
the proximal end of the lower extremities. This uniform rate of descent is roughly proportional to the
increase in stature.

Changes in Head Circumference

The use of head circumference is considered a valuable measurement because it can reflect brain development. More specifically, during the first postnatal year, growth in head circumference reflects
increases in the number of glial cells, growth of dendrites and the establishment of synapses, and increases in myelination (Rabinowicz, 1986). As mentioned earlier, at birth the head is approximately
one-quarter of total body length. Additionally, the
head circumference is greater than chest circumference at birth. Both of these measures reflect the
advanced development of the brain at birth as compared with other body segments.

Head circumference at birth is approximately
35 centimeters (13.8 inches) and little difference
exists between boys and girls. During the course of
the first postnatal year, head circumference will increase by about 12 centimeters and will then rapidly decelerate to an increase of only 5 centimeters
during the second year. In fact, there is only about
a 5- to 6-centimeter increase in head circumference

between 3 and 20 years of age. Head circumference-
for-age percentile growth charts from the CDC for
both boys and girls between birth and 36 months of
age are located in Appendix A.

Changes in Sitting Height

At birth, sitting height accounts for 85 percent of
total body length. By 6 years of age, sitting height's
contribution to total body length has decreased to
55 percent. Typically, the sitting height's contribution to total body length in adulthood is 50 percent.
However, there are several exceptions; for example,
African American children have slightly shorter sitting heights but longer lower extremities than do
white children at all ages (Lowrey, 1986).

Until 10 years for girls and 12 years for boys,
both sexes exhibit almost the same increases in sitting height (trunk length). Given the overall stature gains during this period, it appears that 55 to
60 percent of stature gains can be attributed to leg
growth in both sexes. Usually, however, boys have
longer trunks than do girls until they are about
12 years old. Because boys are generally taller, this
means that prior to adolescence boys have relatively shorter legs than girls regarding total body
length (Haubenstricker & Sapp, 1980). During
adolescence and adulthood, however, women have
shorter legs than do men of equal stature. See
Figure 7-18.

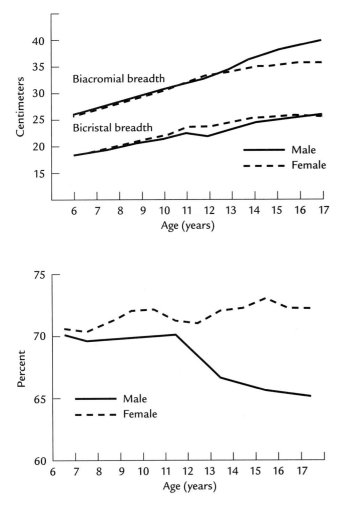

Figure 7-19 Mean biacromial and bicristal breadth

Source: Based on NCHS data reported in Roche and Malina (1983).

Figure 7-20 Bicristal/biacromial breadth × 100

Source: Based on U.S. Health Examination data reported in Roche and Malina (1983).

Growth in Shoulder and Hip Width

Even though there are sex differences in body proportions prior to adolescence, the differences are minimal. During adolescence, however, characteristic sexual dimorphisms become apparent. Perhaps the most noticeable is the relation of shoulder-width growth to hip-width growth. In fact, one of the obvious characteristics of male maturity is a widening of the shoulders. In contrast, girls grow wider through the hips in relation to their shoulder development. See Figure 7-19. The bicristal/biacromial ratio is relatively constant in both boys and girls between 6 and 11 years of age. Thereafter, the ratio declines in boys but continues to be relatively stable in girls (Malina & Bouchard, 1991). See Figure 7-20.

Physique

Thus far our assessment of growth across the lifespan has focused on specific body parts. However, it is important to understand overall body form (physique). The classification of the human form dates back to Hippocrates. More recently, Sheldon (1940) popularized his method of rating physique,

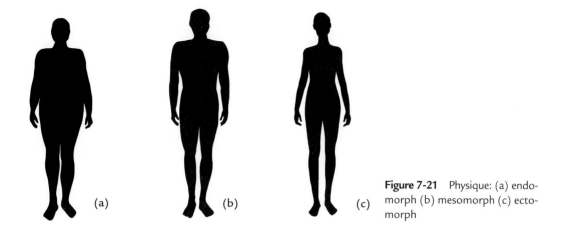

Figure 7-21 Physique: (a) endomorph (b) mesomorph (c) ectomorph

which was based on the premise that three components contribute to the conformation of the entire body. Sheldon described the three components as (1) *endomorphic* — round and soft, (2) *mesomorphic* — muscular, and (3) *ectomorphic* — tall and thin (see Figure 7-21). Each component is assessed from three standardized photographs. Each photograph is rated on a 7-point scale, with 1 representing the least expression and 7 the highest expression of the selected component of physique. For instance, an endomorphic person with a 7-1-1 physique rating is high in endomorphic qualities and low in both mesomorphic and ectomorphic qualities — in other words, a very fat person.

Heath and Carter (1967) modified Sheldon's approach to include not only photographic but also anthropometric procedures. Practically speaking, this method is most frequently employed in its anthropometric form since it eliminates the moral and ethical problems associated with obtaining nude photographs.

The Heath-Carter *somatotype* is obtained as follows: The endomorphic component is derived from summing the skinfolds taken at the triceps, subscapular, and suprailiac (anterior superior spine of the iliac crest). The mesomorphic component is adjusted for stature and is derived from biepicondylar breadth, bicondylar breadth, flexed-upper-arm circumference, and calf circumference. These latter two measurements are corrected by subtract-

ing the skinfold measurement of the mid tricep and medial calf from their corresponding circumference measurement. According to Heath and Carter, this component represents a measure of lean body mass. The final component, the ectomorphic component, is based on stature divided by the cube root of body weight. This measure is also referred to as the *ponderal index.* One major criticism of this approach is its failure to include a trunk measure because the trunk is definitely a major component making up one's physique.

Using data from the Harpenden Growth Study, Malina and Bouchard (1991) concluded that changes in physique tend to appear between 3 or 4 and 8 years of age. The physique changes at these times are a result of a redistribution of subcutaneous fat, the development of lean muscle, and a lengthening of the legs relative to stature. Changes in physique are once again noticed during adolescence as sexual dimorphisms become apparent. Nevertheless, most modifications in somatotype are minor in nature.

BODY PROPORTIONS: INTERRELATIONSHIP WITH MOTOR PERFORMANCE

Because young children are top-heavy, their high center of gravity and small base of support can limit their early motor performance. Lack of balance is a major obstacle children must overcome before they can walk. In fact, balance is an important quality necessary for performing all fundamental motor tasks. For instance, during most physical education classes, children are required to manipulate objects, most often some type of playground ball. Whenever a child holds an object such as a playground ball, the weight of the object becomes part of the child's body weight, so the youngster's center of gravity is then further displaced in the direction of the added weight. This shift in the center of gravity can influence performance. Consider a kindergarten student who is told to catch a 13-inch playground ball. This young child, who already has a relatively high center of gravity, must now maintain control of the thrown projectile while maintaining balance. As a result of the added weight, the child is apt to lose balance in a forward direction, which is most likely why some children drop objects they momentarily have control of. They catch the object but then must release it to regain their balance. Generally, Isaacs (1976) believes that a child's high center of gravity sometimes makes it difficult for the child to come to a fast, complete stop when the activity involves a fast forward or backward movement. Furthermore, Olson (1959) has suggested that this high center of gravity is why some young children have difficulty learning to perform such skills as skating and bicycling with instruction alone. Additionally, a child's relatively large head can make it difficult to perform such tumbling skills as a backward roll.

The ratio of trunk length to leg length can also potentially influence motor performance. One longitudinal investigation that examined the influences of physical growth on motor performance suggests that leg length in terms of total body height could have some impact on balance tasks and certain types of power events (Haubenstricker & Sapp, 1980). The superior balancing ability of girls may be partly due to a combination of these factors: that is, their shorter legs and broader pelvis establish a lower center of gravity, hence better balancing ability. Although these somatic characteristics can enhance balance, they are disadvantageous in other tasks. For instance, during adolescence the general struc-ture of the female pelvis places a girl at a disadvantage in both running and jumping events. In addition, Dintiman and Ward (2003) point out that leg length is one of three factors that can account for individual differences in sprinting speed. And, as mentioned earlier, male leg length is generally greater than female leg length following adolescence.

Arm length also appears to influence motor performance. Haubenstricker and Sapp (1980) note that the male's greater shoulder width and arm length could be an advantage to boys in throwing tasks. Oxendine supports this view when he writes that "after age eleven boys have greater limb lengths and thus a mechanical advantage in some activities, such as throwing and striking with force" (1984, p. 213).

Haubenstricker and Sapp (1980) note that factor analysis studies of physical growth and motor performance indicate that as much as 25 percent or more of the variance can be attributed to body size and structure. For more information regarding physical constraints and the development of motor skills, consult Newell (1984) and Kugler, Kelso, and Turvey (1982).

MEASURING SKELETAL HEALTH

In recent years, skeletal health has become an area of inquiry for many scientists. This increased interest is in part due to our aging society and the prevalence of bone diseases, especially *osteoporosis.* This disease is characterized by a loss of bone mineral to the point that it renders a bone susceptible to fracture (see Figure 7-22). Therefore, researchers interested in studying this disease are frequently concerned with accurately measuring bone mineral density (BMD), not only within the entire skeletal system, but also at susceptible sites, especially the lumbar spine region. The most frequently used instrument to measure BMD is the Lunar (see Figure 7-23) (726 Heartland Trail, Madison, Wisconsin 53717). This instrument uses a technique called *dual-energy X-ray absorptiometry (DEXA).* DEXA is a noninvasive radiologic technique capable of differentiating body weight into three compartments: lean soft tissue, fat soft tissue, and bone. In short, it can directly measure and differentiate tissue densities. Figure 7-24 shows a sample DEXA output. The printout includes the scan image, with markers defining the L1 through L4 vertebrae, the numeric BMD values, and comparison with young adult values (T-scores) and with age-matched normal values (Z-scores).

SKELETAL DEVELOPMENT

Fifteen percent of a newborn infant's body weight is due to its skeleton. Prior to birth, the skeleton is mostly cartilage. Through a process called intramembranous bone formation, the embryonic membranes begin to ossify. As early as 2 months in utero, osteoblastic activity can be observed in the upper arm and thigh at the primary ossification centers. Bone deposition occurs from these centers toward the ends so that at birth, the shaft or *diaphysis* of the long bone has begun to ossify. In fact, all the long bones (radius, ulna, humerus, femur, tibia) as well as the short bones (phalanges, metacarpals, metatarsals)

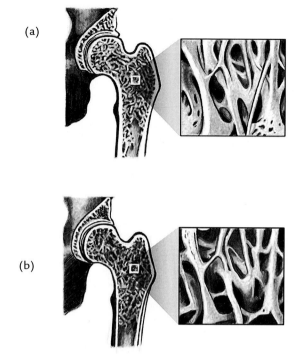

(a)

(b)

Figure 7-22   (a) normal bone and (b) osteoporotic bone

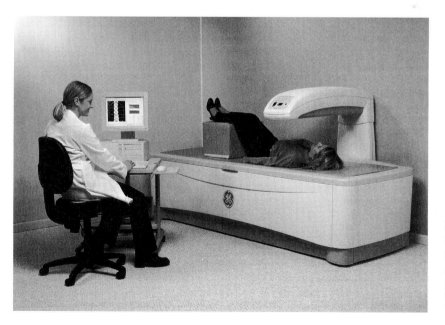

Figure 7-23 The G.E. Lunar Prodigy is the world's most advanced bone densitometer.

Source: Photo supplied by G.E. Lunar, 726 Heartland Trail, Madison, WI 53717.

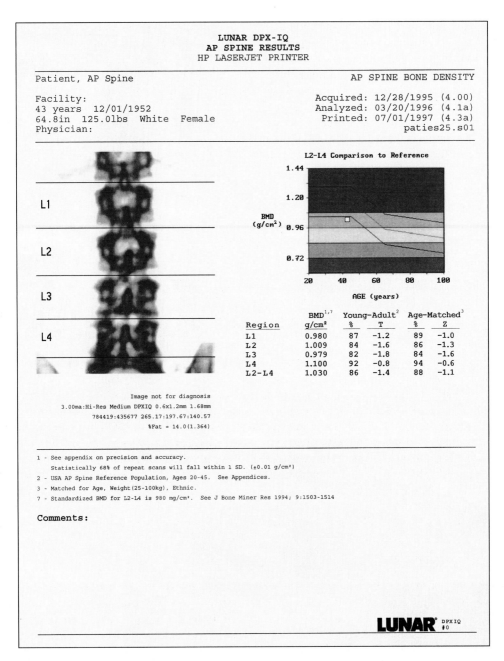

Figure 7-24 Measuring bone mineral density: dual-energy X-ray absorptiometry (DEXA) output

NOTE: The graph shows the patient's measurement plotted on the normal aging curve, with standard deviation limits. Interday reliability of 13 bone density parameters as measured by DEXA resulted in correlation coefficients ranging from $r = .90$ to $r = .99$ (Tucci et al., 1991).

SOURCE: Supplied by G. E. Lunar, 726 Heartland Trail, Madison, WI 53717.

begin to ossify prior to birth. Secondary ossification centers develop in many of the long bones near the end of the prenatal period. Over 400 ossification centers appear before birth and over 400 after birth. Chronologically, these sites emerge in girls earlier than in boys. Likewise, *epiphyseal plate* (growth plate) ossification occurs earlier in girls. For example, the median age for ossification in the head of the femur is 167 months for girls and 191 months for boys.

Two mechanisms operate in the development of bone postnatally. First, through a process called *endochondral bone formation,* the bones lengthen at the epiphyseal cartilage discs or secondary ossification centers. In the long bones, these discs are located at both ends of the bone, while in the short bones (hands and feet), these centers can be found at one end only. The primary ossification centers for the irregularly shaped bones (carpals) develop after birth. These are central ossification centers, which grow outwardly. The epiphysis is a site of *osteoblastic* (bone-building cell) activity resulting in new bone growth. It is made up of cartilage, which is eventually replaced by bone in later adolescence. Then the ossification of the diaphysis reaches the epiphysis and they fuse so that no further increase in length can occur. For most bones, by the time an adolescent is 18 to 19 years of age, the epiphyseal plates are closed. The clavicle and mandible are atypical in that they develop both intramembranously and endochondrally.

A second mechanism, *apositional bone formation,* allows the long bone to increase in diameter. Osteoblasts in the periosteum of the bone will lay down new bone on older bone while *osteoclasts* (bone-removing cells) reabsorb old bone at the same time. When the rate of deposition is greater than the rate of reabsorption, the bone will increase in diameter.

Throughout the lifespan, *bone remodeling* occurs as a function of both osteoblastic and osteoclastic activity. These two mechanisms of bone remodeling are a response to forces acting on bone, resulting in changes in the bones' size, shape, and density. To help you remember the difference between the two mechanisms, think of the "b" in osteoblast as standing for bone "building" and the "c" in osteoclast as standing for bone "chewing."

In general, bone tends to be deposited faster than it is broken down up to about 35 years of age for both men and women. However, the density increases more slowly in women than men so that, at its peak, the bone density of men exceeds that of women. After age 35, bone mineral is lost at a faster rate than it is deposited, particularly in inactive older adults and at the time of menopause in women; therefore, an osteoporosis prevention program should be started before old age. Recommendations for achieving peak bone mass are presented in Table 7-8.

EXERCISE, SKELETAL DEVELOPMENT, AND HEALTH

Most research examining the effects of exercise on bone length report little differences between the bone lengths of active and inactive children (Parizkova, 1968) as measured as a function of stature. The length of the weight-bearing long bones appears affected very little, if any, by exercise. In contrast, Buskirk, Andersen, and Brozek (1956) have reported longer forearm bones and longer dominant hand bones in seven nationally ranked tennis players when these measures were compared with the players' nondominant side. However, note that although these bones in the upper extremities were placed under much stress, they did not perform constant weight-bearing functions.

The research examining the effects of exercise on bone density is more precise. We know that exercise increases bone density (Chilbeck, Sale, & Webber, 1995), whereas inactivity is associated with bone decalcification. Bone decalcification is readily apparent following periods of inactivity, particularly in bedridden patients or people with immobilized limbs. The Gemini astronauts experienced a bone-decalcification problem: Within 4 to 14 days they lost as much as 3 percent of their bone density from being in a weightless environment (Vose, 1974). More

Table 7-8   Recommendations for Achieving Peak Bone Mass

Make a lifelong commitment to physical activity and exercise.

Weight-bearing activities are better than weight-supported activities such as swimming and cycling.

Short, intense daily activity is better than prolonged activity done infrequently.

Activities that increase muscle strength should be promoted, as these will enhance bone density.

Activities should work all large muscle groups.

Immobilization and periods of immobility should be avoided; where this is not possible (as in bed rest during sickness), even brief daily weight-bearing movements can help reduce bone loss.

In girls, abnormal delay of menarche and chronic irregular menstruation should be avoided, and natural means to restore an energy balance (reduced endurance activity and greater caloric intake) should be advocated to normalize menarche and regulate menstruation where possible. Athletes and coaches should be instructed on the potential skeletal hazards of menstrual dysfunction.

Eat a well-balanced diet that meets the recommended dietary allowance for calcium. The substitution of diet soft drinks for milk should be avoided. Soft drinks are highly acidic with a high phosphorus content that can lead to increased calcium excretion.

Teenagers should avoid cigarettes, as these are anti-estrogenic and may interfere with the attainment of normal peak bone mass.

Disordered eating patterns are destructive to the skeleton. These disorders often begin in adolescence and are frequently found in young female athletes, as well as in other adolescent females regardless of activity levels. Parents, coaches, and teachers should be alerted to the dangers of extreme eating behavior.

SOURCES: Bailey and Martin (1994, p. 343); Eastell and Lambert (2002).

recently, Russian cosmonauts have found that a reasonable level of bone health can be maintained for periods of up to 1 year when they maintain vigorous exercise in the form of treadmill walking and running (Whalen, 1991).

Without doubt, a complicated interaction exists among activity, nutrition, genetics, and lifestyle, all of which can greatly affect bone mass. For instance, if a young woman's diet is low in calcium and she has low levels of endogenous estrogen, her rate of deposition will decrease (Loucks & Horvath, 1985; Yeager et al., 1993). Additionally, calcium supplementation in the absence of mechanical loading is ineffective in bone mass maintenance. However, adequate calcium is very important when coupled with exercise to realize gains in bone mass.

A special concern regarding the relationship between exercise and bone health is a condition commonly referred to as the ***female athlete triad.*** This condition most frequently manifests itself when the female athlete attempts to lose too much body fat. It is not uncommon for the woman to develop an eating disorder, which is followed by ***amenorrhea*** (absence of menstruation) and osteoporosis (Skolnick, 1993).

The effect of exercise on bone growth is perhaps most dramatically illustrated in a case study reported by Houston and summarized by Bailey, Malina, and Rasmussen (1978). They describe a young man who had been born with one lower leg bone instead of the usual two in one extremity. Eighteen months after the small thin fibula was surgically relocated so it could bear weight, this bone took on the size, shape, and strength of the tibia, thus illustrating the effects of weight-bearing stress on bone growth.

MATURATION AND DEVELOPMENTAL AGE

The human organism spends approximately one-quarter of the lifespan in a state of physical growth. These physical changes become markedly noticeable in the developmental stage known as adolescence. ***Adolescence*** is characterized by rapid physical, biochemical, social, and emotional changes and involves 6 years, or approximately one-third, of a youngster's growing period. The onset of adolescence and the time necessary to advance from a state

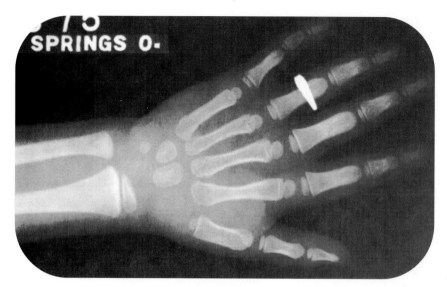

Figure 7-25 Hand-wrist X-ray of a 3-year-old

of immature to mature development varies from person to person both within and between the sexes.

Because changes during adolescence are not always discernible, **chronological age** is generally used to denote a person's level of maturity. **Developmental age,** however, is by far a better indicator of maturity than is chronological age, which simply denotes the length of time from birth but fails to address individual variation in rate of maturation. Fortunately, however, landmark parameters tied to physiological events occur in all people. These parameters share a common developmental endpoint and thus can be used for determining whether a child is lagging behind peers or springing ahead of them. Height and weight measures are inadequate, because people differ in mature stature and weight. However, a set of predictable physiological parameters can be monitored in all persons. The most frequently used parameters are skeletal maturity, dental maturity, age of menarche, and genitalia maturity.

Skeletal Maturity

Skeletal age is the most widely accepted assessment procedure for determining stage of maturation. During growth, predictable changes in bone structure, observable via radiography, enable professionals to determine skeletal age. As a child matures, primary and secondary centers of bone ossify, rendering them opaque to X-rays. The progressive enlargement of these ossified bone centers can be monitored during the growth years and compared with a set of standard films in which each film in a series represents bone development of children of a similar age. The area of the body most frequently X-rayed is the left hand and wrist (see Figures 7-25 to 7-27). The first set of standardized radiographs of the hand and wrist were developed in 1937 by T. Todd and published in the same year in the now classic text *Atlas of Skeletal Maturation*. To date, the most carefully prepared atlases have been published by Todd's colleagues at Case Western Reserve University, in particular the atlas by Greulich and Pyle (1959), which is in use today. Tanner (Tanner et al., 1975) developed a different technique of assessing skeletal maturity (Tanner-Whitehouse Method 2), but the most appropriate method for determining the skeletal age of American children today is the Fels method (Roche, Chumlea, & Thissen, 1988).

Even though the hand and wrist are the most popular assessment site, some researchers are now

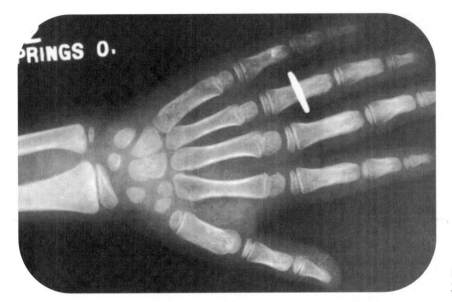

Figure 7-26 Hand-wrist X-ray of a 5-year-old

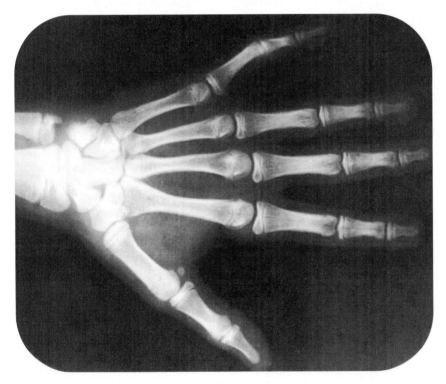

Figure 7-27 Hand-wrist X-ray of a 14-year-old

recommending other areas of the body, particularly the knee, using a method known as the Roche-Wainer-Thissen (RWT) technique (Roche, 1992). Which of the two sites offers the best assessment is still in question. Roche (1979), however, suggests that the choice should be guided by the purpose of the assessment. For instance, Roche believes the knee is the most appropriate site if information is being sought concerning stature. He also suggests using the knee up to 4 years of age and toward the end of maturation, because during this period few maturational changes are apparent in the hand and wrist.

Dental Maturity

The development and emergence of teeth also provide important information for estimating physical maturity. There are two approaches to studying dental maturation in both deciduous (temporary) and permanent teeth. The first approach is simply counting the number of teeth that have emerged. In fact, prior to the advent of the X-ray, emergence of the second molar was accepted as proof of age to work in English factories; later, dental emergence was used for determining when a child was old enough to enter school (Demirjian, 1979).

More recently, researchers have used radiographs to assess ***dental age.*** Similar to the evaluation process used for determining skeletal age, radiographs indicate stages of calcification in both the teeth and the jaw. The use of radiographs is now considered the technique of choice because they provide a permanent record and are a way to compare continuous sequences of development stages longitudinally.

Age of Menarche

Age of menarche is an important event useful for estimating maturation, even though the event does not generally occur until relatively late in puberty. In fact, female peak growth spurt in height is over at this point, so young women are in a period of maximal growth deceleration when this milestone appears. The mean age of this event within developed countries is 13.2 years (standard deviation = 1.0 yr)

although it does occur slightly earlier in American girls (Roche & Sun, 2003). The age span, however, at which menarche occurs tends to be more closely related to skeletal maturity (12 to 14½ bone-age years) than chronological age. Even though menarche signifies the attainment of mature uterine development, it does not necessarily denote mature reproductive functioning; early menstrual cycles tend to be irregular, and often an egg is not shed from the ovary.

Researchers rely on one of the three methods for determining or estimating the date of the first menstrual flow. The most reliable and accurate technique is longitudinally following a group of girls until the event occurs. Because this technique is so time-consuming, the event is most often estimated by a second technique, retrospective questioning. For instance, Beunen and colleagues (1978) asked their experimental population the following questions to determine date of onset:

1. Do you know what menstruation means?
2. Have you already menstruated?
3. Can you remember the exact date of your first menstruation?

To increase the accuracy of recall, the investigator should include questions that focus on associated events. For example, "What grade were you in?" and "Was the event close to your birthday?" The third method is statistical: calculating normative values for a large female population.

Genitalia Maturity

An ancillary method for rating maturation is evaluating by visual inspection the ***genitalia maturity,*** or stages of pubertal development. In girls this consists of assessing pubic hair and breast development. Menarche commonly occurs when pubic hair and breast development reaches a Tanner stage of 4; however, great variability is possible. In boys, pubic hair as well as changes in the size of the reproductive organs are evaluated. Tables 7-9 and 7-10 describe each developmental stage. For a complete set of standardized photographs depicting each stage of development, refer to the work of Roche and Sun (2003).

Table 7-9   Development of Pubic Hair

Female

Stage 1: There is no pubic hair.

Stage 2: There is sparse growth of long, lightly pigmented, downy hair, straight or only slightly curled, primarily along the labia.

Stage 3: The hair is considerably darker, coarser, and more curled. The hair spreads sparsely over the junction of the pubes.

Stage 4: The hair, now adult in type, covers a smaller area than in the adult.

Stage 5: The hair is adult in quantity and type.

Male

Stage 1: There is no pubic hair.

Stage 2: There is a sparse growth of long, slightly pigmented, downy hair, straight or only slightly curled, primarily at the base of the penis.

Stage 3: The hair is considerably darker, coarser, and more curled. The hair spreads sparsely over the junction of the pubes.

Stage 4: The hair, now adult in type, covers a smaller area than in the adult.

Stage 5: The hair is adult in quantity and type.

SOURCE: Used with permission of Ross Products Division, Abbott Laboratories Inc., Columbus, OH 43215. From *Children Are Different*, pp. 25–29, © 1978 Ross Products Division, Abbott Laboratories Inc.

MATURATION: INTERRELATIONSHIP WITH MOTOR PERFORMANCE

Researchers recognize that physically advanced people generally perform selected motor tasks more proficiently than their less mature counterparts. For instance, it has been shown that youth baseball success is related to skeletal maturity. More specifically, data collected during the 1957 Little League World Series indicated that 71 percent of the participants had advanced skeletal ages relative to their chronological ages, while only 29 percent of the participants were delayed in skeletal age (Krogman, 1959). Hale (1956) reported somewhat similar findings when he assessed the pubic hair development of 112 participants during the 1955 Little League World Series. Not only did he find a majority of the young participants either in puberty (37.5 percent) or postpuberty (45.5 percent), he also found that the most

important positions—pitcher, first base, and left field—were played by postpubescent individuals. In addition, the postpubescent youngsters held the all-important fourth position in the batting order. Thus, these postpubescent athletes were bigger and stronger than their prepubescent opponents. Level of maturation as determined by pubic hair assessment has been found to correlate positively with the prediction of strength in adolescent boys (Bastos & Hegg, 1984).

In studying the young male elite athlete, Malina concludes,

Early maturation, with its concomitant size and strength advantages, constitutes an asset positively associated with success in several sports. However, as adolescence approaches its termination, the maturity status of the youngsters is of less significance as the catch-up of late-maturing boys reduces the size differences so apparent in early adolescence. (1984, p. 56)

Table 7-10	Development of Female Breast and Male Genitalia

Female Breast

Stage 1: The breasts are preadolescent. There is elevation of the papilla only.

Stage 2: Breast bud stage. A small mound is formed by the elevation of the breast and papilla. The areolar diameter enlarges.

Stage 3: There is further enlargement of breasts and areola with no separation of their contours.

Stage 4: There is a projection of the areola and papilla to form a secondary mound above the level of the breast.

Stage 5: The breasts resemble those of a mature female as the areola has recessed to the general contour of the breast.

Male Genitalia

Stage 1: The penis, testes, and scrotum are of childhood size.

Stage 2: There is enlargement of the scrotum and testes, but the penis usually does not enlarge. The scrotal skin reddens.

Stage 3: There is further growth of the testes and scrotum and enlargement of the penis, mainly in length.

Stage 4: There is still further growth of the testes and scrotum and increased size of the penis, especially in breadth.

Stage 5: The genitalia are adult in size and shape.

SOURCE: Used with permission of Ross Products Division, Abbott Laboratories Inc., Columbus, OH 43215. From *Children Are Different*, pp. 25–29, © 1978 Ross Products Division, Abbott Laboratories Inc.

This is essentially what Clarke (1971) found in his now classic Medford Growth Study—namely, that the superior elementary school athlete may no longer be outstanding in junior high school and that the superior junior high school athlete may not have been outstanding in elementary school. In fact, once the late-maturing person has reached a state of postpubescent development, he is generally larger and has more athletic success simply because he has had a longer growth period.

Although early maturation may give boys an early athletic advantage, the opposite generally is true for girls. With the exception of swimming, female athletic participation is associated with delayed biological maturation. Malina and associates (1979) first suggested that delayed biological maturation may give young girls a slight competitive edge in such Olympic events as volleyball. Beunen and col-

leagues (1978) have also studied the relationship between age of menarche and motor performance in 398 Belgian school girls. They found the motor performances of late-maturing girls superior to the motor performances of early- and average-maturing girls on such tasks as trunk strength, functional strength, running speed, and speed of limb movement. Thus, "in general, motor performance is negatively related to biological maturity status in girls but positively related to biological maturity status in boys" (Beunen & Malina, 1988, p. 522).

Many professionals have tried to explain why this maturity–performance relationship is opposite that observed in boys. Espenschade and Eckert (cited in Beunen et al., 1978) propose one popular hypothesis: Because menarche denotes the peak increase in motor performance, late-maturing girls have more interest in performing motor skills for a longer time.

SUMMARY

Growth in both stature and weight rapidly decelerates after the fourth prenatal month. Stature and weight growth remain relatively constant during the childhood years, only to accelerate again in the phase of development known as adolescence. This rapid change in body size is sometimes accompanied by a period of adolescent awkwardness, especially in boys. However, this decline in motor performance is only temporary.

During childhood, children are top-heavy; that is, they have a high center of gravity. This high center of gravity can affect children's stability.

The wider shoulders and longer arms of boys and men give them an advantage in throwing events. On the other hand, women and girls are generally superior in balancing, perhaps because of their shorter legs and broader pelvis.

Growth data can be visually inspected by plotting the data on a distance curve or velocity curve. A distance curve plots accumulative growth obtained over time; a velocity curve plots the rate of change in growth per unit of time.

Physical activity affects bone density and bone width but does not influence bone length.

Developmental age is a better indicator of maturity than is chronological age. Level of maturity can be determined by skeletal maturity, dental maturity, age of menarche, and genitalia maturity.

Level of maturation can influence motor performance. In general, research indicates that postpubescent boys initially outperform prepubescent boys. However, once the late-maturing person reaches adolescence, this advantage is no longer evident. Nevertheless, although early maturation is associated with superior athletic performance for boys, the opposite is generally true for girls, except for female swimmers.

KEY TERMS

adiposity rebound
adolescence
adolescent awkwardness
age of menarche
amenorrhea
apositional bone formation
biacromial/bicristal ratio
body mass index (BMI)
bone remodeling
chronological age
diaphysis
dental age
developmental age

distance curve
dual-energy X-ray absorptiometry
  (DEXA)
ectomorphic
endochondral bone formation
endomorphic
epiphyseal plate
female athlete triad
genitalia maturity
head circumference
knee height
mesomorphic
midgrowth spurt

osteoblast
osteoclast
osteoporosis
peak height velocity (PHV)
peak weight velocity
ponderal index
recumbent length
sitting height
skeletal age
somatotype
stature
velocity curve
vertex

QUESTIONS FOR REFLECTION

1. Can you summarize changes in body length and stature, as well as changes in body weight across the human lifespan? Pay particular attention to changes that occur during the adolescent growth spurt.

2. Can you describe the difference between a distance curve and a velocity curve?

3. Can you calculate a body mass index (BMI) and state the desired BMI range associated with optimal health?

4. What is adolescent awkwardness, and what is peak height velocity? How are they related? How common is adolescent awkwardness, and what types of motor performance seem most impacted by this phenomenon?

5. What changes in sitting height occur for male and female persons from birth through adulthood?

6. Can you describe and illustrate the relative change in the body's center of gravity from 2 fetal months through adulthood?

7. What is the Heath-Carter somatotyping process, and how does this process differ from that used by Sheldon?

8. What is the interrelationship between body proportion and motor performance from childhood through adolescence?

9. Can you describe the use of dual-energy X-ray absorptiometry (DEXA) for measuring skeletal health?

10. Can you describe bone development, including discussions about the following terms: *diaphysis,*

epiphyseal plate, endochrondal bone formation, osteoblast, osteoclast, and *apositional bone formation?* Also, at what age is bone broken down faster than it is deposited?

11. What are five recommendations for achieving peak bone mass?

12. Can you describe the condition referred to as female athlete triad?

13. Can you list and explain four methods of determining physical (biological) maturity? What is Tanner's approach for determining biological maturity?

14. What differences exist between male and female persons regarding the relationship between motor performance and biological maturation?

INTERNET RESOURCES

Body Mass Index Calculator
www.cdc.gov/nccdphp/dnpa/bmi/calc-bmi.htm

Centers for Disease Control and Prevention
www.cdc.gov

CDC Growth Charts **www.cdc.gov/growthcharts**

Kid's Height Predictor
**www.webmd.com/medical_information/
health-e-tools/calculator/heighpredict**

Lunar Corporation **www.lunarcorp.com**

National Center for Health Statistics
www.cdc.gov/nchs

National Osteoporosis Foundation **www.nof.org**

Osteoporosis Society of Canada **www.osteoporosis.ca**

ONLINE LEARNING CENTER (www.mhhe.com/payne6e)

Visit the *Human Motor Development* Online Learning Center for study aids and additional resources. You can use the study guide questions and key terms puzzles to review key terms and concepts for this chapter and to prepare for exams. You can further extend your knowledge of motor development by checking out the Web links, articles, and activities found on the site.

REFERENCES

American College of Sports Medicine. (2000). *ACSM's guidelines for exercise testing and prescription.* 6th ed. Baltimore: Williams & Wilkins.

Bailey, D. A., Malina, R. M., & Rasmussen, R. L. (1978). The influence of exercise, physical activity, and athletic performance on the dynamics of human growth. In F. Falkner & J. M. Tanner (Eds.), *Human growth: Postnatal growth.* New York: Plenum.

Bailey, D. A., & Martin, A. D. (1994). Physical activity and skeletal health in adolescents. *Pediatric Exercise Science, 6,* 330–347.

Bastos, F. C., & Hegg, R. V. (1984). The relationship of chronological age, body build and sexual maturation to hand-grip strength in school boys, ages ten through seventeen years. *Proceeding of the 1984 Olympic Scientific Congress*, Eugene, OR.

Beunen, G., Beul, G., Ostyn, M., Renson, R., Simons, J., & Gerven, D. (1978). Age of menarche and motor performance in girls aged 11 through 18. *Medicine and Sport, 11*, 118–123.

Beunen, G., & Malina, R. M. (1988). Growth and physical performance relative to the timing of the adolescent spurt. In K. B. Pandolf (Ed.), *Exercise and sport sciences reviews.* New York: Macmillan.

Beunen, G., Malina, R. M., Van't Hof, M. A., Simons, J., Ostyn, M., Renson, R., & Van Gerven, D. (1988). *Adolescent growth and motor performance: A longitudinal study of Belgian boys.* Champaign, IL: Human Kinetics.

Bray, G. A. (1992). Pathophysiology of obesity. *American Journal of Clinical Nutrition, 55*, 488S–494S.

Buskirk, E. R., Andersen, K. L., & Brozek, F. (1956). Unilateral activity and bone and muscle development in the forearm. *Research Quarterly, 27*, 127–131.

Calle, E. E., Thun, M. J., Petrelli, J. M., Rodriguez, C., & Heath, C. W. (1999). BMI and mortality in a prospective cohort of U.S. adults. *New England Journal of Medicine, 341*, 1097–1105.

Centers for Disease Control and Prevention. (2000). BMI for adults. Atlanta, GA: Retrieved September 12, 2000, from www.cdc.gov/nccdphp/dnpa/bmi/bmi-adult.htm.

Chilbeck, P. D., Sale, D. G., & Webber, C. E. (1995). Exercise and bone mineral density. *Sports Medicine, 19*, 103–122.

Clarke, H. H. (1971). *Physical and motor tests in the Medford boy's growth study.* Englewood Cliffs, NJ: Prentice-Hall.

Demirjian, A. (1979). Dental development: A measure of physical maturity. In F. E. Johnston, A. F. Roche, & C. Susanne (Eds.), *Human physical growth and maturation.* New York: Plenum Press.

Dintiman, G., & Ward, R. (2003). *Sport speed.* 3rd ed. Champaign, IL: Human Kinetics.

Dyson, G. H. (1964). *The mechanics of athletics.* 3rd ed. London: University of London Press.

Eastell, R., & Lambert, H. (2002). Strategies for skeletal health in the elderly. *Proceedings of the Nutrition Society, 61*, 173–180.

Gallagher, D., Misser, M., Sepulveda, D., Pierson, R. N., Harris, T., & Heymsfield, S. B. (1996). How useful is BMI for comparison of body fatness across age, sex and ethnic groups? *American Journal of Epidemiology, 143*, 228–239.

Greulich, W. W., & Pyle, S. I. (1959). *Radiographic atlas of skeletal development of the hand and wrist.* 2nd ed. Palo Alto, CA: Stanford University Press.

Guo, S. S., Huang, C., Maynard, L. M., Demerath, E., Towne, B., Chumlea, W. C., & Siervogel, R. M. (2000). Body mass index during childhood, adolescence and young adulthood in relation to adult overweight and adiposity: The Fels Longitudinal Study. *International Journal of Obesity, 24*, 1628–1635.

Hale, C. J. (1956). Physiologic maturity of Little League baseball players. *Research Quarterly, 27*, 276–284.

Haubenstricker, J. L., & Sapp, M. M. (1980). A longitudinal look at physical growth and motor performance: Implications for elementary and middle school activity programs. Paper presented at the meeting of the American Alliance for Health, Physical Education, Recreation, and Dance, Detroit, MI.

Heath, B. H., & Carter, J. E. L. (1967). A modified somatotype method. *American Journal of Physical Anthropology, 27*, 57–74.

Himes, J. H., & Dietz, W. H. (1994). Guidelines for overweight in adolescent preventive services: Recommendations from an expert committee. *American Journal of Clinical Nutrition, 59*, 307–316.

Holbrook, T. L., Wingard, D. L., & Barrett-Connor, E. (1990). Sex-specific vs. uni-sex body mass indices as predictors of non-insulin dependent diabetes mellitus in older adults. *International Journal of Obesity, 14*, 803–807.

Isaacs, L. D. (1976). The anatomical changes of the center of gravity during development: Implications to physical education. Unpublished manuscript, University of Maryland.

Jaffe, M., & Kosakov, C. (1982). The motor development of fat babies. *Clinical Pediatrics, 27*, 619–621.

Krogman, W. M. (1959). Maturation age of 55 boys in the Little League world series. *Research Quarterly, 30*, 54–56.

Kuczmarski, M. F., Kuczmarski, R. J., & Najjar, M. (2000). Descriptive anthropometric reference data for older Americans. *Journal of the American Dietetic Association, 100*, 59–66.

Kuczmarski, R. J., Flegal, K. M., Campbell, S. M., & Johnson, C. L. (1994). Increasing prevalence of overweight among U.S. adults: The National Health and Nutrition Examination Surveys, 1960 to 1991. *Journal of the American Medical Association, 272*, 205–211.

Kuczmarski, R. J., Ogden, C. L., Grummer-Strawn, L. M., Flegal, K. M., Guo, S. S., Wei, R., Mei, Z., Curtin, L. R., Roche, A. F., & Johnson, C. L. (2000). *CDC growth charts: United States advance data from vital and health statistics.* No. 314. Hyattsville, MD: National Center for Health Statistics.

Kuczmarski, R. J., Ogden, C. L., Guo, S. S., Grummer-Strawn, L. M., Flegal, K. M., Mei, Z., Wei, R., Curtin, L. R., Roche, A. F., & Johnson, C. L. (2002). CDC growth charts: United States, 2000. *Vital and Health Statistics National Center for Health Statistics.* Washington, DC: Department of Health and Human Services.

Kugler, P. N., Kelso, J. A., & Turvey, M. T. (1982). On the control and coordination of naturally developing systems. In J. A. Kelso & J. E. Clark (Eds.), *The development of movement control and coordination.* New York: Wiley.

Loucks, A. B., & Horvath, S. (1985). Athletic amenorrhea—A review. *Medicine and Science in Sports and Exercise, 17*, 56–72.

Lowrey, G. H. (1986). *Growth and development of children.* 8th ed. Chicago: Year Book Medical Publishers.

Malina, R. M. (1984). Maturational considerations in elite young athletes. *Proceeding of the 1984 Olympic Scientific Congress,* Eugene, OR.

Malina, R. M., & Bouchard, C. (1991). *Growth, maturation, and physical activity.* Champaign, IL: Human Kinetics.

Malina, R. M., Bouchard, C., Shoup, R. F., Demirjian, A., & Lariviere, G. (1979). Age at menarche, family size, and birth order in athletes at the Montreal Olympic Games, 1976. *Medicine and Science in Sport, 11,* 354–358.

Maynard, L. M., Wisemandle, W. A., Roche, A. F., Chumlea, W. C., Guo, S. S., & Siervogel, R. M. (2001). Childhood body composition in relation to body mass index: The Fels Longitudinal Study. *Pediatrics, 107,* 344–350.

National Center for Health Statistics. (1973). Height and weight of youths 12–17 years, United States. *Vital and Health Statistics,* ser. 11, no. 124.

———. (1974). Body dimensions and proportions: White and Negro children 6–11 years, United States. *Vital and Health Statistics,* ser. 11, no. 143.

———. (1979). Weight and height of adults 18–74 years of age, United States 1971–74. *Vital and Health Statistics,* ser. 11, no. 211.

———. (1987). Anthropometric reference data and prevalence of overweight: United States, 1976–80. *Vital and Health Statistics,* ser. 11, no. 238.

———. (2000). *2000 CDC growth charts: United States.* Retrieved from www.cdc.gov/growthcharts.

National Heart, Lung and Blood Institution. (2000). Body mass index table. Retrieved September 26, 2000, from www.nhlbi. nih.gov/guidelines/obesity/bmi_tbl.htm

Newell, K. M. (1984). Physical constraints to development of motor skills. In J. R. Thomas (Ed.), *Motor development during adulthood and adolescence.* Minneapolis, MN: Burgess.

Norval, M. A. (1947). Relationship of weight and length of infants at birth to the age at which they begin to walk alone. *Journal of Pediatrics, 30,* 676–678.

Olson, W. (1959). *Child development.* Boston: Heath.

Ostyn, M., Simons, J., Beunen, G., Renson, R., & Van Gerven, D. (Eds.). (1980). *Motor development of Belgian secondary schoolboys.* Leuven, Belgium: Leuven University Press.

Oxendine, J. B. (1984). *Psychology of motor learning.* Englewood Cliffs, NJ: Prentice-Hall.

Palmer, C. E. (1929). The center of gravity in the developmental period of man. *Anatomical Records, 42,* 31.

Parizkova, J. (1968). Longitudinal study of the development of body composition and body build in boys of various physical activity. *Human Biology, 40,* 212–225.

Pietrobelli, A., Faith, M. S., Allison, D. A., Gallagher, D., Chiumello, G., & Heymsfield, S. B. (1998). Body mass index as a measure of adiposity among children and adolescents: A validation study. *Journal of Pediatrics, 132,* 204–210.

Rabinowicz, T. (1986). The differentiated maturation of the human cerebral cortex. In F. Falkner & J. M. Tanner (Eds.), *Human growth: A comprehensive treatise: Vol. 2. Postnatal growth.* 2nd ed. (pp. 385–410). New York: Plenum Press.

Roche, A. F. (1979). The measurement of skeletal maturation. In F. E. Johnston, A. F. Roche, & C. Susanne (Eds.), *Human physical growth and maturation.* New York: Plenum Press.

———. (1992). *Growth, maturation and body composition: The Fels longitudinal study 1929–1991.* Cambridge, England: Cambridge University Press.

Roche, A. F., Chumlea, W. C., & Thissen, D. (1988). *Assessing the skeletal maturity of the hand-wrist: Fels method.* Springfield, IL: Thomas.

Roche, A. F., & Himes, J. H. (1980). Incremental growth charts. *American Journal of Clinical Nutrition, 33,* 2041–2052.

Roche, A. F., & Malina, R. M. (Eds.). (1983). *Manual of physical status and performance in childhood.* Vol. 1. New York: Plenum Press.

Roche, A., & Sun, S. (2003). *Human growth: Assessment and interpretation.* Cambridge, England: Cambridge University Press.

Rooney, R. L., & Schauberger, C. W. (2002). Excess pregnancy weight gain and long-term obesity: One decade later. *Obstetrics and Gynecology, 100,* 245–252.

Sheldon, W. H. (1940). *The varieties of human physique.* New York: Harper & Row.

Shirley, M. M. (1931). *The first two years: A study of twenty-five babies.* Minneapolis: University of Minnesota Press.

Sinclair, D. (1998). *Human growth after birth.* 6th ed. New York: Oxford University Press.

Skolnick, A. A. (1993). Medical news and perspective: "Female athlete triad" risk for women. *Journal of the American Medical Association, 270,* 921.

Sveger, T. (1978). Does overnutrition or obesity during the first year affect weight at age four? *Acta Paediatica Scandinavica, 67,* 465–467.

Tanner, J. M. (1990). *Fetus into man.* Cambridge, MA: Harvard University Press.

Tanner, J. M., Whitehouse, R. H., Marshall, W. A., Healy, M. J., & Goldstein, H. (1975). *Assessment of skeletal maturity and prediction of adult height (TW 2 method).* New York: Academic Press.

Todd, T. W. (1937). *Atlas of skeletal maturation.* St. Louis, MO: Mosby.

Troiano, R. P., Flegal, K. M., Kuczmarski, R. J., Campbell, S. M., & Johnson, C. L. (1995). Overweight prevalence and trends for children and adolescents. The National Health and Nutrition Examination Surveys, 1963–1991. *Archives of Pediatric and Adolescent Medicine, 149,* 1085–1091.

Tucci, J., Carpenter, D., Graves, J., Pollock, M. L., Felheim, R., & Mananquil, R. (1991). Interday reliability of bone mineral density measurements using dual energy X-ray absorptiometry. *Medicine and Science in Sports and Exercise, 23,* S115.

Vose, G. P. (1974). Review of roentgenographic bone demineralization studies of the Gemini space flights. *American Journal of Roentgenology, 121,* 1–4.

Wales, J., & Taitz, L. (1992). Patterns of growth in abused children. In M. Hernandez & J. Argente (Eds.), *Human growth: Basic and clinical aspects.* Amsterdam: Elsevier Science Publishers.

Whalen, R. T. (1991). Preface to NASA symposium on the influence of gravity and activity on muscle and bone. *Journal of Biomechanics, 24,* v.

Whitaker, R. C., Pepe, M. S., Wright, J. A., Seidel, K. D., & Dietz, W. H. (1998). Early adiposity rebound and the risk of adult obesity. *Pediatrics, 101*(3), 462.

Willett, W., et al. (1999). Guidelines for healthy weight. *New England Journal of Medicine, 341,* 427–434.

Yeager, K., Agostini, R., Nattiv, A., & Drinkwater, B. (1993). The female athlete triad: Disordered eating amenorrhea, osteoporosis. *Medicine and Science in Sports and Exercise, 25,* 775–777.

Physiological Changes: Health-Related Physical Fitness

Within the last two decades, the emphasis on physical fitness in both the workplace and society has shifted from motor fitness or athletic ability to what is commonly referred to as health-related or physiological fitness. The primary thrust behind this movement is the popular notion that U.S. children and youth are less fit today than children of 40 years ago. In addition, results from the most recent National Health and Nutrition Examination Survey (NHANES III, 1999–2000) indicate a dramatic increase in the prevalence of obesity in both children and adults in the United States (Kuczmarski, Kuczmarski, & Najjar, 2000). This should come as no surprise, since nearly one-half of U.S. youths and more than 60 percent of U.S. adults fail to engage in a regular vigorous activity. In fact, 25 percent of all adults are not active at all (Superintendent of Documents, 1996).

Because of the links that have now been established between physical activity and health, several prestigious organizations have come forth to pronounce the importance of maintaining an active lifestyle. One such report was released in July of 1996 by the Department of Health and Human Services (see Appendix C). This landmark report summarizes the research showing the benefits of physical activity in preventing disease and, furthermore, draws conclusions as to what Americans should be doing to improve their health. In addition, the Centers for Disease Control have issued their report titled *Guidelines for School and Community Programs to Promote Lifelong Physical Activity Among Young People* (1997) (see Appendix D). While this report echoes the Surgeon General's regarding the importance of an active lifestyle, it also makes 10 recommendations, directed specifically at schools and community programs, on how to promote physical activity among young people. More recent reports from the U.S. Department of Health and Human Services titled *Physical Activity Fundamental to Preventing Disease* (2002) and *The Surgeon General's Call to Action to Prevent and Decrease Overweight and Obesity* (2001) continue to express a major concern over the health of both young and old alike. One thing is clear: Maintaining an active lifestyle is linked to good health.

The most frequently identified components that make up health-related fitness include cardiovascular endurance, body composition, flexibility, and muscular strength and endurance. This chapter examines each of these components. We look at the evolution of each, paying particular attention to how an active lifestyle affects them. In addition, both laboratory data and field-test performance data are examined.

CARDIOVASCULAR FITNESS

Cardiovascular fitness is a special form of muscular endurance. It is the efficiency of the heart, lungs, and vascular system in delivering oxygen to the working muscle tissues so that prolonged physical work can be maintained. A person's ability to deliver oxygen to the working muscles is affected by many physiological parameters, including heart rate, stroke volume, cardiac output, and maximal oxygen consumption. Here we examine changes that occur in each parameter as a result of maturation, aging, and physical training.

Heart Rate

Heart rate (HR), the number of times the heart beats each minute, is a physiological parameter that undergoes much change during the lifespan. The heart rate is first evidenced about the fourth prenatal week, when the fetal heart begins to beat. Characteristically, fetal HR is rapid and frequently irregular. Immediately following birth, HR usually decreases and often is accompanied by intermittent periods of ***bradycardia*** (slow HR). Once independent breathing and in turn adequate blood oxygenation have been established, HR again increases but remains below fetal levels.

At rest, children's HRs are consistently higher than adults'. In fact, the newborn infant averages about 130 beats per minute, ranging between 120 and 140 beats per minute. With time (age), however, this resting heart rate progressively decelerates. For example, by 1 year of age, the average resting HR will have declined an average of 40 beats per minute. This trend is evident until late adolescence, when young men exhibit an average HR of about 57 to 60 beats per minute while young women average between 62 to 63 beats per minute (Malina & Bouchard, 1991). Thus resting HR can be expected to decline by about 50 percent from birth to maturity. In young adulthood the average HR among 20-year-old men and women averages 75 to 79 beats per minute, respectively. Thereafter, there is little change in resting HR until 60 years of age, when the HR again decreases slightly.

There is a linear relationship between physical work and HR. That is, up to a point, increases in workload increase HR. During labor contractions, fetal HR frequently exceeds 200 beats per minute. Furthermore, newborn crying, a form of physical work, induces rates greater than 170 beats per minute. In preadolescent children, HR responses to submaximal work decline with age. Bouchard and colleagues (1977) found the submaximal HRs of 8-year-old subjects to be as much as 30 to 40 beats per minute faster in comparison with 18-year-old subjects, even though the workload was the same. Younger children most likely have higher HRs to compensate for their smaller stroke volume (Bar-Or, 1983).

Unlike submaximal HR, which declines with age, maximal HR does not decline until after maturity. The maximal HR of both children and adolescents is from 195 to 220 beats per minute. For young men and women, the maximal HR generally peaks at values just under 200 beats per minute. This decline in heart rate is approximately 0.8 beats/minute/year of age (Bar-Or, 1983) and is independent of gender. Rates as high as 250 to 300 beats per minute have been reported during short bursts of activity, but when the activity is sustained, rates are significantly lower (Shephard, 1994).

The following formula provides a general estimate of maximal HR in young and middle-aged adult populations:

$$\text{Maximal HR} = 220 - \text{age (years)}$$

However, recent evidence suggest that for elderly individuals, maximal HR is more accurately pre-dicted by using the following equation (Tanaka, Monahan, & Seals, 2001):

$$\text{HR max} = 208 - 0.7 \times \text{age (years)}$$

Researchers believe that this decline in HR with age is due to a decrease in sympathetic outflow and changes in the contractile properties of the cardiac muscle. Indeed, the wall of the left ventricle increases in thickness by approximately 30 percent between 25 and 80 years of age. This wall thickening probably influences the myocardial contractile properties and is most likely due to the age-related increase in systolic blood pressure (Lakatta, 1990).

Stroke Volume

With each contraction of the heart, a certain volume of blood, called *stroke volume (SV)*, is ejected from the left ventricle into general circulation via the aorta. In other words, stroke volume is the amount of blood pumped from the heart with each beat. The size of the stroke volume is limited by many factors, including heart size, contractile force of the myocardial (heart) tissue, vascular resistance to blood flow, and venous return (the rate blood is returned to the right side of the heart).

At all levels of physical work, SV is substantially lower in children than adults, most likely because of the child's smaller heart, which, as mentioned, partly explains children's need for higher HRs. At birth, SV is only 3 to 4 milliliters per ventricular contraction. This value increases tenfold by adolescence to about 40 milliliters, and it remains quite stable until the adolescence growth spurt, when it rapidly accelerates to about 60 milliliters at rest (Malina & Bouchard, 1991). In the typical untrained male adult, the SV is usually between 70 and 90 milliliters per beat. This range is significantly elevated in highly trained people. Even at rest, the aerobically trained person's SV is 100 to 120 milliliters per beat (Foss & Keteyian, 1998).

Maximal SV is achieved during submaximal work, somewhere between 40 to 60 percent ($\bar{x} = 50\%$) of aerobic power (McArdle, Katch, & Katch, 2000). A further increase in workload is not likely to increase SV significantly. During exercise, the untrained man can expect to attain an SV of 100 to 120 milliliters per beat. Conversely, the highly trained man is capable of obtaining values as high as 200 milliliters per beat, although the average values are 150 to 170 milliliters per beat. In contrast, maximal SV in untrained and trained women is generally between 80 to 100 milliliters per beat and 100 to 120 milliliters per beat, respectively (Foss & Keteyian, 1998). Nevertheless, at all levels of work, SV is higher in male than in female adults.

Like most other physiological parameters, age can affect SV. A person's SV at rest can fall as much as 30 percent between the ages of 25 and 85. During light exercise, however, elderly individuals are capable of maintaining an SV slightly less than that of a young adult. But when workloads become exhausting, SV decreases 10 to 20 percent in untrained elderly individuals (Shephard, 1981). Older individuals who perform aerobic exercise systematically can minimize this decline in SV, because regular aerobic training increases blood volume, reduces vascular resistance, and increases heart preload, all of which help maintain a more youthful SV. In fact, SV in highly trained older people may actually exceed that of much younger untrained people (Weisfeldt, Gerstenblith, & Lakatta, 1985).

Cardiac Output

Cardiac output is the amount of blood that can be pumped out of the heart in 1 minute. Thus, cardiac output is the product of heart rate and stroke volume. Cardiac output is less in children than in adults, for both resting and exercising states. Although children are capable of obtaining a higher exercise HR than adults, their elevated HR is not enough to compensate for the marked difference in stroke volume.

At rest, adults have a cardiac output of approximately 5 liters per minute. With the onset of exercise, cardiac output rises in both children and adults until it reaches a new steady state. Two of the most important factors affecting ultimate maximal cardiac output are level of physical condition and age.

The untrained adult generally achieves a maximal cardiac output of 20 to 25 liters per minute; a trained adult can achieve a maximal cardiac output 10 liters per minute greater than can the untrained adult.

Because both HR and SV decrease with age, resting cardiac output does as well. Specifically, there is a 58 percent reduction between the ages of 25 and 85 in the amount of blood the heart can pump in a given unit of time. Thus, resting cardiac output, on average, declines approximately 1 percent per year after age 25. There is a somewhat similar pattern for maximal cardiac output: Cardiac function typically declines 20 to 30 percent by age 65, but like other cardiorespiratory parameters, this decline can be minimized through regular aerobic exercise.

Maximal Oxygen Consumption

An increase in the level of physical work brings a corresponding increased need for oxygen among the active muscles. Thus, human beings' ability to sustain physical work for extended periods is directly related to their ability to transport oxygen to the working muscle tissue. The largest amount of oxygen that a human can consume at the tissue level is the *maximal oxygen consumption* (VO_2 max). This physiological measure is considered the best single measure of *physical working capacity.*

There is abundant information about VO_2 max consumption in adults and older children, but little data on children younger than 6 years. It is difficult to study this population, because it is hard to motivate young children to an all-out effort. Nevertheless, several researchers have undertaken the challenge of using subjects younger than 6 years. In Mrzena and Macek's study (1978), two groups of preschool children between 3 and 5 years of age were required to walk or run on a treadmill. Group 1 performed for 5 minutes at each of the following speeds: 3, 4, and 5 kilometers per hour. In contrast, group 2 performed at 4 kilometers per hour, but instead of increasing treadmill speed, the researchers increased the treadmill's grade 5 degrees every 5 minutes until the treadmill was at a 15-degree grade. In group 1, the highest oxygen consumption value a child attained was 22.06 ± 4.7 milliliters per kilogram of body weight per minute (ml/kg/min). Oxygen consumption was higher in the second group, where the highest value attained was 28.7 ± 4.84 ml/kg/min. This study was limited by the size of the subject pool: Group 1 contained only 4 children, and group 2 had only 10 children.

Results involving children older than 6 years are fairly consistent. The VO_2 max for boys is fairly constant during the childhood and adolescent years. Typical values for individuals 6 to 16 years old is 50 to 53 ml/kg/min (Krahenbuhl, Skinner, & Kohrt, 1985). Boys generally exhibit a spurt in maximal oxygen consumption at puberty, but it is believed that this increase is more directly related to increases in body size than to a true increase in oxygen extraction. In fact, Rowland's (1996) review of the literature uncovered information supporting the idea that maximal oxygen uptake closely parallels the dimensions of cardiorespiratory organ growth. For example, between 8 and 12 years of age, maximal aerobic capacity rises about 49 percent. However, during this same period, the average weight of the lungs increases 58 percent, lung vital capacity improves 48 percent, and left ventricular volume increases 52 percent. This phenomenon raises an interesting point: Although older children obtain higher VO_2 max values than do younger children, the discrepancy in values is no longer as great when body weight is used to standardize the measures.

This point is apparent when comparing the VO_2 max of young boys to that of young girls. When absolute values between the genders are compared without body weight being standardized, young boys evidence much higher values than do young girls. However, when body weight is introduced as a standardization factor, girls' working capacity is nearly as good as that of the young boys. On average, young girls 8 years of age exhibit VO_2 max values of 50 ml/kg/min.

Unfortunately, girls' VO_2 max declines very early in life. Krahenbuhl and colleagues (1985) note that by 12 years of age the VO_2 max in girls declines to approximately 45/ml/kg/min and will decline further to approximately 40 ml/kg/min by 16 years of

age. This is 32 percent lower than the VO_2 max for 16-year-old boys. Rutenfranz and colleagues (1981) report similar findings. In their longitudinal research, they found the decline most evident beyond 12 to 13 years of age (cited by Cunningham, Paterson, & Blimkie, 1984). This early decline is most likely caused by the female increase in body fat at maturation, lower blood hemoglobin concentrations at puberty, and lesser degree of large-muscle development in the lower extremities.

With age, the body's ability to acquire and deliver oxygen to the working tissue is altered, reducing physical work capacity. The rate of decline in VO_2 max is just slightly less than 1 percent per year after 20 years of age (McArdle, et al. 2000). Thus a 70-year-old's physical work capacity is only one-half of what a person 50 years younger can attain. This loss of aerobic power is caused by many factors, including increase in fat tissue and a subsequent decrease in lean muscle tissue, decreased cardiac output, and a decrease in physical activity (which so often accompanies retirement). Later in the chapter we discuss how an active lifestyle can alter or delay the decline in VO_2 max.

Physical Activity and Cardiovascular Fitness in Childhood

Our understanding of the effects of physical activity on cardiovascular fitness in young children is both fragmented and limited. Also, many findings are frequently contradictory, most likely because different conditioning protocols between studies and a host of methodological factors have been used. For instance, when long-term training is used, the researcher must distinguish between training effects and those effects caused primarily by the natural growth and maturation process. Authorities have recognized that many of the reported changes following physical training occur naturally through maturation; for example, lower resting and submaximal HRs are known to be by-products of physical training. But this physiological parameter naturally declines with age. Because of this predicament, Bar-Or (1983) suggests that research data be viewed as occurring with conditioning and training, not necessarily as a result of conditioning or training.

Rowland (1985) critically analyzed the research literature regarding aerobic responses to endurance training in preadolescent children. After reviewing 14 studies, Rowland excluded 5 because they had not used training regimens known to alter fitness in adult populations. Of the remaining 9 studies, 8 examined the influence of endurance training on VO_2 max; 6 of these 8 studies reported gains in VO_2 max ranging from 7 to 26 percent, with mean gains of 14 percent. The data from these studies appear to indicate that adult training protocols are effective in improving aerobic capacity. Recently, Mandigout and colleagues (2002) came to this same conclusion when they found that 13 weeks of aerobic training for two sessions per week for 15–20 minutes at an intensity of 80 percent failed to improve VO_2 max in prepubertal children 10–11 years of age. However, when frequency (3 days per week) and duration (25–35 minutes) were increased to be more in line with adult recommendations, an average enhancement of 7 percent occurred in VO_2 max.

A growing amount of evidence questions the benefit of endurance training for improving aerobic capacity in preadolescent children. This controversy is apparent in both short-term (Stewart & Gutin, 1976) and long-term (Ekblom, 1969) training studies. In the 1976 Stewart and Gutin study, 13 boys aged 10 to 12 years trained 4 days per week for 8 weeks at an average intensity of 90 percent maximal HR. Following the experimental program, no significant improvement in VO_2 max was noted. The researchers concluded that the already high VO_2 max of children is difficult to improve, particularly in light of their already active lifestyle. Ekblom (1969) reports similar results in his longitudinal study, which required 11- to 13.6-year-old boys to train for 6 and 32 months. VO_2 max rose 10 per-cent after 6 months and 15 and 18 percent after 32 months. However, these values were not significantly different from the values of a control group. Thus, these improvements are thought to be a result of growth, not training.

Payne and Morrow (1993) performed a meta-analysis on the professional literature in an attempt to shed light on this important question regarding the effects of exercise on VO_2 max in children. Their findings were based on the analysis of 28 studies resulting in 70 effect sizes. Data was also analyzed according to research design (cross-sectional and pretest/posttest). The authors concluded that findings from the cross-sectional studies must be interpreted with caution because the effect sizes calculated on these subjects may have been a reflection of "self-selection." In other words, these subjects could have been attracted to their sport because of their preexisting physiological predisposition to successful play. Those subjects who were part of a pretest/posttest design improved VO_2 max by only about 2 ml/kg/min, or only a 4 percent improvement. Results indicate that changes in VO_2 max in children are small to moderate and are a function of the experimental design used.

Even though mounting evidence questions the value of endurance training in preadolescent children, some experts argue that training does improve performance. Most believe that training can improve product performance by improving mechanical efficiency. For example, training can improve mechanical aspects of running style without an associated rise in aerobic capacity, with the end result being better run times.

Can endurance training improve aerobic capacity in preadolescent children? The answer remains unclear and must await the findings of better-controlled scientific research.

Cardiovascular Endurance Field-Test Data on Children and Adolescents

While a maximum treadmill test is the preferred method for determining cardiovascular efficiency (VO_2 max), this laboratory procedure is not practical when a large number of individuals must be assessed. Instead, a more practical alternative is the use of some type of **field test.** Currently, the most popular field test of cardiovascular endurance is a timed distance run.

In the two most recent large-scale studies called the National Children and Youth Fitness Studies (NCYFS) I and II, two different timed distance

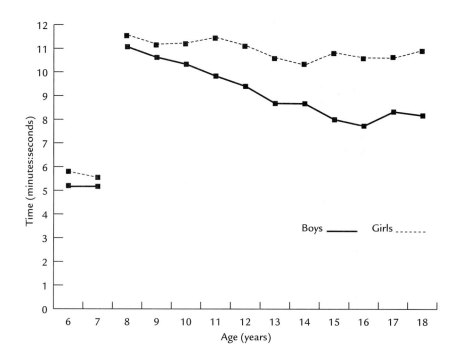

Figure 8-1 Average distance walk/run times for boys and girls based on findings of the National Children and Youth Fitness Studies I and II. Ages 6–7: ½ mile; ages 8–18: 1 mile.

SOURCES: As reported by Ross and Gilbert (1985) and Ross and Pate (1987).

events were used as a measure of cardiovascular endurance. Children between 6 and 7 years of age ran ½ mile while those between 8 and 18 years of age ran 1 mile. The average run times as reported in the NCYFSs (Ross & Gilbert, 1985; Ross & Pate, 1987) are reported in Figure 8-1. With age comes a steady improvement in run-time performance. Boys were found to peak at 16 years of age and girls at 14. Performance tends to level off after these ages, with boys running the mile in slightly over 8 minutes (range: 7:44–8:20) and girls running the mile in slightly over 11 minutes (range: 10:42–11:14). On average, boys run faster than girls at all ages.

Pate and Shephard (1989) have noted that it is incorrect to assume that the yearly improvement in run-time performance indicates an improved weight-relative VO_2 max. Instead, this improvement in performance can in part be explained by a decrease in the weight-relative oxygen cost of running that results from increased leg length. Furthermore, as noted earlier, improved running technique and a better understanding of "pace" can also contribute to improved performance times.

Physical Activity and Cardiovascular Fitness in Adulthood

The effects of aerobic exercise on the cardiovascular system of young and middle-aged adults are well documented. Authorities generally agree that to attain beneficial effects, a person must perform large-muscle activities 3 to 5 days per week for 20 to 60 minutes at an HR intensity of 60 to 90 percent of maximum (American College of Sports Medicine, 2000). Such a program will increase physical work capacity. During submaximal work, SV will increase and HR will decrease, cardiac output will increase, HR recovery following physical work will be faster, and VO_2 max will increase.

Less is known about the effects of physical training in late adulthood. Frequently asked questions regarding exercise training and the elderly include "What effect does a physical exercise training program have on the physical work capacities of elderly people?" "Can long-term training offset the decline in physical work capacity that sedentary people exhibit?"

| Table 8-1 | Selected Winning Times for Men and Women at the Senior Olympics, 2003 |

	50–54	55–59	60–64	65–69	70–74	75–79	80–84	85–89	90–94	95–99
Road Race	36:26	38:20	38:37	45:57	46:59	56:35	59:45	1:14.43	1:31.18	–
10K	(45:30)	(52:22)	(49:57)	(51:11)	(57:25)	(1:09.39)	(1:31.18)	(1:39.57)		
1500 Meter	4:44	4:51	5:18	5:15	6:11	7:16	7:59	10:24	10:27	14:12
Run	(5:33)	(6:24)	(6:47)	(6:51)	(7:20)	(8:35)	(14:01)	(15:28)	(13:07)	
100 Meter	12.06	12.89	13.30	12.85	13.83	15.01	16.30	18.39	20.03	38.36
Dash	(13.70)	(14.13)	(15.60)	(15.57)	(17.47)	(17.97)	(21.43)	(21.46)	(35.77)	

Female performance values appear in parentheses.

SOURCE: U.S. National Senior Sports Association (2003).

After reviewing several longitudinal studies, Shephard (1978) concluded that the rate of decline in VO_2 max in male athletes was about 0.60 mL/kg/min per year. "In absolute terms, the rate of loss seems similar in active and in sedentary individuals, but because the athlete starts with a large working capacity, his relative loss is substantially smaller" (Shephard, 1978, p. 245). The rate of decline in the general adult population has been established as about 1 percent per year beyond 25 years of age (Whitbourne, 1996). Therefore, one could expect a 40 percent decline between 25 and 65 years of age.

Obviously, not all individuals age at the same rate. Take, for example, the athletic feats that are shown in Table 8-1. These performances were accomplished by individuals participating in the U.S. National Senior Sports Association's Senior Olympics held in Hampton, Virginia, in 2003 (U.S. National Senior Sports Association, 2003).

What makes these individuals so different from the general population? Most authorities believe it is their active lifestyle. It has been suggested that as much as 50 percent of the functional declines that mediate physical performance are due to disuse rather than aging (Spirduso, 1995). For example, in one longitudinal study (Kasch et al., 1990), researchers found only a 13 percent decline in VO_2 max in men 45–68 years old who had maintained an active lifestyle over the previous 18 years. However, a somewhat similar group of men (52–70 years

old), who did not exercise, showed a 41 percent decline in maximal oxygen consumption during the period under study. This finding mirrors the results reported by Marti and Howald (1990), who found that formerly highly trained runners exhibited decreases in aerobic capacity and an increased level of body fat if they did not continue to train. Similarly, Pollock (1974) found that endurance runners over 70 years of age had a maximum aerobic capacity that was 14 percent greater than that of their sedentary counterparts who were 20 to 30 years younger.

Similar findings have been reported in short-term studies (Pollock et al., 1976), which should be of particular interest to older individuals who wonder whether it is too late to establish a regimen of aerobic activity. Shephard "has projected that commencement of regular fitness training at the time of retirement may delay the age at which environmental demands exceed physical capabilities (i.e., the age of dependency) by as much as 8 years" (cited in Stones & Kozma, 1985). Furthermore, Shephard (1987) suggests that if an older individual increases her or his VO_2 max by approximately 20 percent, it "offers the equivalent of 20 years of rejuvenation— a benefit that can be matched by no other treatment or lifestyle change" (p. 5). In summary, those who can maintain an active lifestyle throughout middle and late adulthood can slow down the rate of deterioration and, in some cases, even improve on their aerobic capacity. The physical activity pyra-

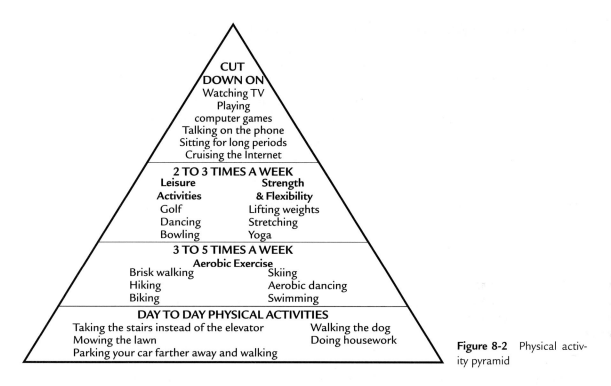

CUT DOWN ON
Watching TV
Playing
computer games
Talking on the phone
Sitting for long periods
Cruising the Internet

2 TO 3 TIMES A WEEK

Leisure Activities	**Strength & Flexibility**
Golf	Lifting weights
Dancing	Stretching
Bowling	Yoga

3 TO 5 TIMES A WEEK
Aerobic Exercise

Brisk walking	Skiing
Hiking	Aerobic dancing
Biking	Swimming

DAY TO DAY PHYSICAL ACTIVITIES

Taking the stairs instead of the elevator	Walking the dog
Mowing the lawn	Doing housework
Parking your car farther away and walking	

Figure 8-2 Physical activity pyramid

mid presented in Figure 8-2 offers suggestions as to how to maintain an active lifestyle.

MUSCULAR STRENGTH

Minimal **muscular strength** is important because the contraction of skeletal muscle makes human movement possible. We use the term *minimal muscular strength,* but researchers to date have not been able to qualify this term. In fact, to do so is nearly impossible because each human movement requires different degrees of strength. For instance, the 14-month-old toddler possesses enough lower-extremity strength to walk but lacks the strength needed to propel the body through space, a requirement of running. People, regardless of age, who lack the necessary strength needed to launch the body from a supporting surface are said to be **earth-bound.** This inability to project the body through space limits the number of ways a person can move in the environment, which is why earthbound chil-dren's ability to acquire many of the fundamental movement patterns is frequently delayed. Furthermore, older children and adults whose movement freedom is restricted by inadequate levels of muscular strength generally find themselves leading a sedentary life. In brief, muscular strength is needed for the execution of all motor tasks.

Defining and Measuring Muscular Strength

Strength is the ability to exert muscular force. This muscular force can be exerted under various conditions. A muscular force exerted against an immovable object, with no or very little change in the length of the exercised muscle, is called **static** or **isometric.** A muscular force exerted against a movable object, with a change in the length of the exercised muscle, is called **dynamic.** Attempting to push down a wall is an example of static force; lifting a barbell is a dynamic force.

Special instruments called dynamometers and tensiometers are used to measure static muscular force.

With these instruments, the variable of interest is not minimal strength but maximal strength production.

The use of these specialized instruments for mass assessment is not always feasible. Instead, when large numbers of individuals must be assessed in a short period, the most feasible approach is to use one or more field tests. The two most frequently employed field tests of muscular strength (and endurance) are the pull-up test (upper-body strength/endurance) or chin-up test (upper-arm strength/endurance) and a modified or bent-knee sit-up test (abdominal strength/endurance).

In the next two sections, we describe in detail age-related changes in muscular strength development and performance in both laboratory and field-test situations.

Age-Related Changes in Muscular Strength: Laboratory Tests

Few data are available regarding strength in preschool children. However, many investigators have examined this component of fitness in populations older than 6 years. Most frequently, the dependent variable in these studies has been grip strength. This measure of static force production is used more frequently than any other test of muscular strength because it is easy to administer and is reliable.

Studies examining changes in grip strength during the childhood and adolescent years are consistent in their findings. A review of the literature by Keogh and Sugden (1985) revealed that the grip strength in boys increased 393 percent from 7 to 17 years of age. This figure compares favorably with the values observed over 50 years ago. More specifically, Metheny found grip strength in girls increased 260 percent; Meredith reported that grip strength in boys increased 359 percent between 6 and 18 years of age (cited in Metheny, 1941).

Shephard (1981) and, more recently, McArdle and colleagues (2000) found that changes in the strength curve closely resembled changes in body weight, at least for young boys. Moreover, Shephard (1981) states that "the strength spurt lags at least a year behind the height spurt, and there is thus a sense in which boys outgrow their strength just

prior to puberty" (p. 219). This finding partly explains why some boys experience a brief period of clumsiness during puberty: They have not yet acquired the muscular strength necessary to handle their larger bodies (see the discussion in Chapter 7 on adolescent awkwardness). According to Bar-Or (1989), under normal growth conditions, boys' fastest increase in muscular strength occurs approximately 1 year after peak height velocity, whereas in girls the strength spurt generally occurs during the same year as peak height velocity. In general, prior to puberty boys are about 10 percent stronger than girls (McArdle et al., 2000).

Gender differences in muscular strength become most apparent after puberty. In boys, puberty is associated with the introduction of the male sex hormones, which in turn influence muscularity. During this time of development, boys become leaner and young girls begin to develop more body fat. Prior to adolescence, muscle weight is about 27 percent of total body weight, but after sexual maturity, muscle development is increased to about 40 percent of total body weight (Malina & Bouchard, 1991; Vrijens, 1978). In adulthood, even when body size is taken into consideration, women are not as strong as men. The degree of difference in strength between the genders is a function of the muscle being measured and the type of muscle contraction being employed. In general, absolute upper-body strength in women is about 50 percent less than men, while women's lower absolute body strength is approximately 20 to 30 percent below values achieved by men. Overall, women's total maximal absolute body strength is about 63.5 percent of men's strength (McArdle et al., 2000). The interested reader is referred to the work of Fleck & Kraemer (2004, pp. 264–272) for a detailed analysis of gender differences in both absolute and relative strength.

During early and middle adulthood, grip strength remains relatively constant. Men between 25 and 45 years exhibit an average grip strength of 54 kilograms. However, during the next 20 years, it declines by 20 percent (Shephard, 1981). Precise measures are difficult to interpret, since it appears that both muscular strength and muscular endurance are a function of age and activity level. Nevertheless, the association of aging with loss of muscle mass, and therefore muscle strength, appears to occur in two stages. First, a rather slow regression in muscle mass of about 10 percent occurs between 25 and 50 years of age. Thereafter, the rate of loss accelerates between 50 and 80 years of age, resulting in an additional loss of about 40 percent. Thus, as much as one-half of muscle mass is lost by 80 years of age (McArdle, Katch, & Katch, 2001; Powers & Howley, 2001).

Age-Related Changes in Muscular Strength/Endurance: Field Tests

Popular field tests are not capable of assessing muscular strength in the absence of muscular endurance. This is because whenever repeated muscular contractions are performed under a workload that is less than maximal, an element of muscular endurance is introduced. As mentioned previously, most popular fitness batteries incorporate the use of a chin-up test (palms of hands face toward the performer) or a pull-up test (palms face away from the performer) and some type of modified sit-up test in order to assess muscular strength/endurance within a field setting. Both assessment tests require repeated muscular contractions. For example, in both National Children and Youth Fitness Studies (NCYFS), children were allowed 60 seconds to perform as many bent-knee sit-ups as possible. Likewise, both the chin-up test administered in the first NCYFS and the modified pull-up test administered in the second NCYFS required the children to perform as many repetitions as possible. Presumably, the timed bent-knee sit-up test reflects the ratio of abdominal strength/endurance to upper-body mass (Pate & Shephard, 1989), whereas the chin-up test reflects the ratio of upper-body strength/endurance to total body mass. This latter point has been confirmed in an investigation by Pate and colleagues (1993). This investigation sought to test the validity of five popular field tests of muscular strength and endurance (pull-ups, flexed arm/hand, push-ups, New York modified pull-ups, and Vermont modified pull-ups). The researchers concluded that upper-body strength and endurance as measured by these instruments were not significantly correlated with laboratory measures of absolute muscle strength and endurance in 9- to 10-year-old children. However, the test performances were moderately related to measures of muscular strength relative to body weight, indicating that body weight is a natural confounding factor in these field tests.

Figures 8-3 and 8-4 illustrate average scores for boys and girls between 6 and 18 years of age on the muscular strength/endurance items included within the NCYFS test battery. Little difference exists between boys' and girls' abdominal strength/endurance scores between 6 and 9 years of age. However, from 10 through 16 years of age, the gap in performance widens, with boys always scoring higher than girls. Performance for both boys and girls tends to level off and remain constant between 16 and 18 years of age.

Upper-body strength/endurance performance as reported in the first NCYFS is discouraging. Thirty percent of the boys (between 10 and 11 years) failed to perform one chin-up. For this reason, a modified pull-up test was employed in the second NCYFS to help overcome the zero performance score problem exhibited in the first NCYFS (Pate et al., 1987). Figure 8-5 depicts the special apparatus that is employed in the administration of the modified pull-up test. A complete description of this test is presented in Chapter 17. As the median scores indicate, little difference in upper-body strength exists between the genders at 6 to 9 years of age (as measured by the modified pull-up test). After 10 years of age, boys show consistent improvement in their ability to perform chin-ups, whereas on average girls could not perform any chin-ups.

Muscular Strength Training

Any discussion regarding the value of resistance training on the development of muscular strength must account for the differences in training outcomes as a function of maturity level. For this reason, our discussion on trainability will be divided into three sections: prepubescent, adolescence/early and middle adulthood, and late adulthood.

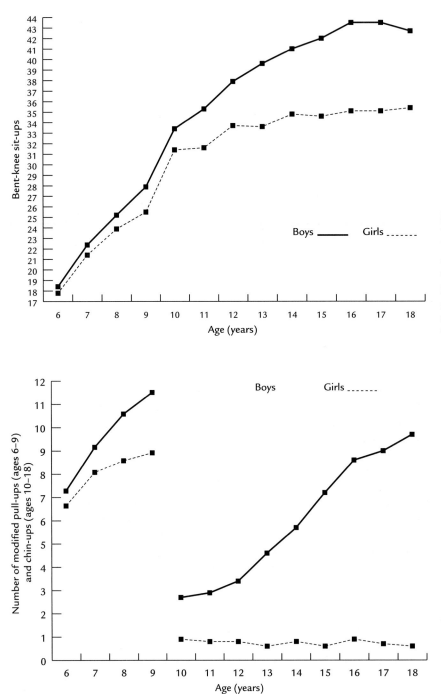

Figure 8-3 Average scores for boys and girls on bent-knee sit-ups (60 sec) based on findings of the National Children and Youth Fitness Studies I and II

SOURCE: As reported by Ross and Gilbert (1985) and Ross and Pate (1987).

Figure 8-4 Average scores for boys and girls on modified pull-ups and chin-ups based on findings of the National Children and Youth Fitness Studies I and II

SOURCES: As reported by Ross and Gilbert (1985) and Ross and Pate (1987).

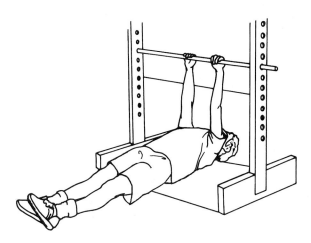
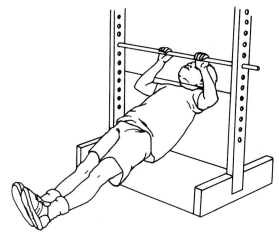

Figure 8-5 Modified pull-up apparatus

PREPUBESCENCE Much controversy exists regarding the use of resistance training for the purpose of developing muscular strength in prepubescent populations. According to strength-training specialists (Micheli, 1988; Sale, 1989), this controversy exists in regard to three questions. First, can prepubescent children significantly increase their muscular strength through participation in a resistance-training program? Second, if gains in muscular strength are possible, does this increase in strength enhance skilled athletic performance? Last, does the benefit of increased strength outweigh the potential of sustaining injury during participation in a resistance-training program?

The first question is posed because popular belief suggests that without a sufficient level of circulating *testosterone,* significant gains in muscular strength are not possible. This belief was reinforced when Vrijens (1978) found no significant strength gains in 16 prepubescent individuals following an 8-week training program. However, most recent studies have reported significant strength gains following participation in resistance-training programs (Faigenbaum et al., 1993, 1996, 2000, 2002; Falk & Mor, 1996; Isaacs, Pohlman, & Craig, 1994; Ozmun, Mikesky, & Surburg, 1994; Servidio, Bartels, & Hamlin, 1985; Sewall & Micheli, 1986; Stahle et al., 1995).

Unfortunately, most of these studies incorporated very small sample sizes. Because small sample sizes can greatly influence the chance of finding significant effects, researchers have analyzed the prepubescent strength-training literature by using meta-analysis. Recall that this technique is a quantitative approach for analyzing the conclusions drawn from a large number of studies for the purpose of reducing information and making generalizations (Hyllegard, Mood, & Morrow, 1996). For example, Falk and Tenenbaum (1996) reviewed the professional literature regarding resistance training in girls and boys under age 12 and 13, respectively. Of the 28 studies identified, only 3 reported nonsignificant effects following resistance training. Unfortunately, because of missing data, only 9 studies yielding 10 effect sizes (ES) could be used in the meta-analysis. A majority of the studies included in the analysis found increases in strength, following a resistance-training program, in the range of 13.7–29.6 percent. More recently, Payne and colleagues (1997) identified 28 studies yielding 252 effect sizes, in their meta-analysis regarding resistance training in both children and youth. Like Falk and Tenenbaum, Payne and colleagues concluded that children and youth can acquire a significant increase in both muscular strength and endurance as a result of participating in resistance training. With few exceptions, effect sizes ranged from .65 to .83. Of particular interest was the finding that the average effect size of the younger children (boys < 13 years; girls < 11 years; ES = .75) was very similar to that obtained for the older participants (boys at 16+ years; girls at 14+ years; ES = .69). This further supports the idea that resistance training is as beneficial to young children as it is to adolescents. Interestingly, the mean effect size for girls (.81) was larger than that found for boys (.72). This finding is likely the result of girls being further from their strength potential than were the boys.

While most recent studies point to the value of resistance training, other basic physiological questions regarding resistance training must be addressed before professionals can wholeheartedly recommend resistance training to prepubescent individuals. Namely, what is the effect of resistance training on flexibility, blood pressure, aerobic fitness, anaerobic fitness, and body composition?

Because most of the recent professional literature suggests that prepubescent individuals are capable of significantly increasing strength following resistance training, the next logical question is whether or not these strength gains are accompanied by improved athletic performance. Following an extensive review of the literature, the National Strength and Conditioning Association (NSCA, 1996) has concluded that resistance training is effective in improving both motor fitness skill and sports performance. Skills that showed improvement include both the long jump and the vertical jump (Falk & Mor, 1996; Weltman et al., 1986) as well as running speed and agility (Williams, 1991). However, the greatest improvements appeared in activities for which the children trained (Nielsen et al., 1980). Therefore, it seems that the training adaptations witnessed in children are often specific to the movement pattern engaged in, the velocity of the movement, the contraction type, and the force of contraction (Hakkinen, Mero, & Kavhanen, 1989).

As mentioned previously, there has been much concern regarding the safety of strength training among prepubescent individuals. This concern has prompted such prestigious organizations as the American Academy of Pediatrics (AAP, 2001), and the NSCA (1996), to publish position statements regarding prepubescent strength training.

Within their position statement, the AAP (1990, 2001) makes a clear distinction among weight training, weight lifting or power lifting, and body building. **Weight training** involves the use of various resistance exercises to enhance physical fitness or to increase muscular strength, muscular endurance, and power for sports participation. In contrast, **weight lifting** and **power lifting** are considered sports that involve maximum lifts including the snatch, clean and jerk, squat, bench press, and dead lift. **Body building** is also considered a competitive sport in which participants use resistance training to develop muscle size, symmetry, and muscle definition. All three associations now recognize that weight training can benefit the prepubescent individual if conducted within the framework of other established guidelines (see Table 8-2). In fact, Blimkie (1993) contends that weight training is no riskier than other youth sports or recreational activities in terms of incidence and severity of musculoskeletal injury. As an added precaution, Micheli (1988) suggests that young weight trainers not be allowed to perform full squats and that no standing lifts be allowed. None of the three associations recommend prepubescent weight lifting, power lifting, or body building, because of their association with injury.

An examination of Table 8-2 reveals one particularly important point—namely, young children should not train with maximum lifts. This guideline leads one to then question, "At what age is training with maximal lifting acceptable?" The United States Weight and Power Lifting Federations recommend maximal lifting at 14 years of age. Yet, the answer to this question is not so simple, since chronological age is not an acceptable indicator of biological maturity. Rather than using chronological age, it has been suggested that boys and girls not be allowed to perform maximal lifts until reaching a Tanner stage 5 level of development (see Chapter 7). At this level of developmental maturity, peak height velocity will have occurred; therefore, there will be a smaller likelihood of injury to the epiphyses

Table 8-2   Selected Weight-Training Guidelines

1. Before beginning a strength program, the child should have a physical examination if he or she is not already apparently healthy.

2. The child must be emotionally mature enough to follow directions from a coach.

3. The program should be supervised by someone knowledgeable in strength training, with a student–teacher ratio no greater than 10 to 1.

4. Fifty to 80 percent of the child's training should be in activities other than strength training.

5. The exercise session should include 5 to 10 minutes of general warm-up exercises, followed by one or more light to moderate specific warm-up sets on the chosen resistance exercises. A 15-minute cooldown should follow each session.

6. The session should start with one set of several upper- and lower-body exercises that focus on the major muscle groups. Single- and multijoint exercises should be included in the training program. Beginning with relative light loads (e.g., 12 to 15 RM) will allow for appropriate adjustments to be made.

7. After 15 repetitions can be accomplished in good form, weight can be increased by 5 to 10 percent.

8. Progression may also be achieved by gradually increasing the number of sets, exercises, and training sessions per week. Depending on the goal of the training program (e.g., strength or local muscular endurance), 1 to 3 sets of 8 to 15 repetitions performed on 2 or 3 nonconsecutive days a week is recommended.

9. The child should receive instruction regarding correct lifting technique, training guidelines, and spotting procedures. Whenever a new exercise is introduced, the child should start with a relatively light weight, or even a broomstick, in order to learn the correct technique.

10. All exercises should be carried out through the full range of motion.

11. Emphasis should be on dynamic concentric contractions.

12. The concept of *periodization* (variation in training volume and intensity) should be taught.

13. The child should use only appropriately sized equipment.

14. No maximum lifts are allowed prior to reaching physical and skeletal maturity.

SOURCES: Position Statements of the American Academy of Pediatrics and the National Strength and Conditioning Association (1996).

(growth plates). However, recent research has found that 1 RM (repetition maximum) testing in young boys and girls (6.2–12.3 years of age) is safe when conducted under appropriate adult supervision (Faigenbaum, Milliken, & Westcott, 2003).

ADOLESCENCE/EARLY AND MIDDLE ADULTHOOD Less controversy surrounds the use of resistance training in adolescent and adult populations. Authorities agree that programs of progressive resistance training will result in improved muscular strength/endurance within these two populations. Gains in muscular strength/endurance, however, are contingent on adhering to established principles of training. The American College of Sports Medicine (ACSM, 2000) recommends that the healthy adult perform approximately 8 to 10 exercises involving the body's major muscle groups. These resistance-training exercises should be performed a minimum of two times per week. Each exercise should consist of a minimum of one set with 8 to 12 repetitions. According to the ACSM, these minimal standards are based on two findings. First, while more intense training will result in greater strength gains, training sessions lasting longer than 1 hour per session are associated with higher drop-out rates. Second, it has been established that the extra amount of strength gained as a result of increasing frequency of training and intensity of training is relatively small. As a general rule, 60 percent of one repetition maximum is a reasonable starting intensity. The length of each training session (duration) is not as important as it is for cardiovascular efficiency, and will vary depending on the number of exercises employed and the amount of rest between exercises. Micheli's review of the literature has led him to conclude that "there is good evidence that the adolescent male makes strength gains in much the same pattern as the adult male when placed on a properly designed progressive resistive strengthening program" and that "adolescent girls will also gain strength in response to progressive resistive training although the response is less dramatic than that seen in boys" (1988, p. 100).

Even though near maximal and maximal lifts are acceptable for adolescents (beyond Tanner stage 5) and young adults, there is still a need to educate these two populations about proper lifting technique. It is particularly important that these individuals understand the importance of proper breathing during the performance of resistance training (Tanner, 1993). In short, breath holding or straining with a closed glottis (Valsalva maneuver) can cause a "blackout" and should therefore be avoided.

One additional concern is the use of **anabolic steroids,** sometimes referred to as androgens (Joyner, 2000). Recall that the primary androgen, testosterone, aids in the development of muscle mass. Because of this, some athletes believe that taking anabolic steroids will lead to better athletic performance. However, the use of synthetic anabolic steroids is not confined just to athletes. A growing number of nonathletic youth are taking steroids as a means of improving physique (O'Neil, 1993). In fact, one national survey found that 7 percent of high school seniors had used or were using anabolic steroids (Buckley et al., 1988).

When women are administered anabolic steroids, they may develop various male characteristics such as more upper-body muscularity, facial hair, a deeper voice, and a reduction of body fat, especially in the breasts and hips. In contrast, when administered to young boys, steroids accelerate puberty and make possible the premature closure of the growth plates of the long bones (Friedl, 1994).

Individuals attempting to spot anabolic steroid use should be on the lookout for individuals exhibiting rapid changes in body size and weight, a sudden change in behavior, and the appearance of severe acne.

LATE ADULTHOOD   For those in late adulthood, the paramount question is whether strength training is capable of altering, delaying, or even allowing one to avoid some of the physiological deterioration believed to be associated with aging. A study of female master swimmers by Dummer and associates (1985) found that although competitive swimming training positively influenced strength, it did *not* prevent age-related declines in this parameter. Nevertheless, the physically active women in the study were able to maintain a relatively high degree of grip strength into the eighth decade of life. Dummer further noted that her subjects who were older than 60 exhibited grip strengths equivalent to those possessed by less active women in their 20s and 30s. Thus we conclude that even though decreases in muscular strength can be expected with age, the rate of decline can be significantly retarded. In fact, a recent investigation by Lemmer and colleagues (2000) found that when older men and women (65–75 years) trained for 9 weeks, not only did both genders significantly improve strength, but the women maintained strength above baseline after 12 weeks of detraining. Most impressive was the finding that the older men maintained strength above baseline even after 31 weeks of detraining.

Munnings (1993) has uncovered convincing evidence that suggests that it is never too late to start a resistance-training program. Her belief is predicated on the findings of a study that reports significant gains in both strength and balance in a population of individuals between 67 and 91 years of age (Parsons et al., 1992). These senior citizens performed 15 resistance exercises using free weights, three times a week for 24 weeks. The fact that strength and balance was improved may not be that unusual, however; of the 17 subjects, all were taking medication for hypertension, 3 had undergone cancer surgery, 4 were diabetic, 5 had significant coronary artery disease, and 1 had undergone quadruple bypass surgery. Also in line with this finding is the conclusion drawn by McArdle and colleagues (2001) following their review of the literature re-

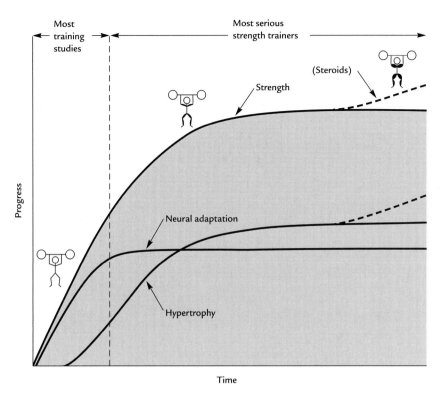

Figure 8-6 The relative roles of neural and muscular adaptation to strength training. In the early phase of training, neural adaptation predominates. This phase also encompasses most training studies. In intermediate and advanced training, progress is limited to the extent of muscular adaptation that can be achieved, notably hypertrophy; hence the temptation to use anabolic steroids when it becomes difficult to induce hypertrophy by training alone.

SOURCE: Sale, D. G. (1988). *Medicine and Science in Sports and Exercise, 20,* s135–s145. Used with permission of Lippincott, Williams & Wilkins.

garding the influence of a resistance-training programs on strength gains in individuals greater than 60 years of age. More specifically, they found improvements in strength to range from 1.9 to 132 percent. Perhaps most important are findings indicating that improvements in muscular strength and muscular endurance following resistance training positively influence the activities of daily living, thus leading to a better quality of life (Vincent et al., 2002).

Another study has demonstrated that resistance training can benefit individuals well into the 10th decade of life (Fiatarone et al., 1990). More specifically, the frail institutionalized men and women of this study improved quadriceps strength by 31 percent and muscle cross-sectional area by 8 percent following an 8-week resistance-training program. Clinically, these individuals exhibited significant improvement in walking speed, a functional index of mobility. This and the previous study both indicate that it is the intensity of the training and not the initial level of fitness that determines the response to training (Rogers & Evans, 1993). Furthermore, resistance training reduces the number of falls experienced by elderly individuals (Brown, Sinacore, & Host, 1995; Judge et al., 1995; Wolfson et al., 1995) and helps them maintain skills of daily living (Brill et al., 2000; Carmeli et al., 2000).

Mechanisms of Increasing Muscular Strength

Even though our review thus far indicates that individuals of all ages can improve strength by following a program of progressive resistance, the mechanisms responsible for change may differ among the various age groups. Voluntary muscular strength can be improved in two main ways: (1) by increasing the size of the muscle (**hypertrophy**) and the specific tensions that can be exerted within the muscle and (2) by neural adaptations that result in an increased ability of the nervous system to activate more muscle tissue. Figure 8-6 illustrates the interplay between neural and muscular adaptations (Sale, 1988). Following an extensive review of the literature, Sale concluded that the present evidence indicates that children may have more difficulty than older age groups in increasing muscle mass. On the other hand, adaptations within the nervous system are similar to or even greater in children than in older groups (1989, p. 211).

Why prepubescent children have difficulty in increasing muscle mass is not clear at this time. One possible explanation is their low level of circulating **androgens** (sex hormones). Indeed, with the introduction of higher levels of circulating testosterone, which occurs in boys at around 13 to 14 years of age, there is a corresponding increase in muscle hypertrophy and muscular strength, even in the absence of resistance training. Nevertheless, this circulating androgen-level theory cannot be totally accurate, because young adult women, with their low androgen levels, can increase their muscle mass. Thus the answer to why prepubescent individuals have difficulty in increasing muscle mass must await further study.

Potential mechanisms of muscle deterioration within the elderly are many. For example, age brings a decrease in both the size and the number of muscle fibers (Isaacs, 1989; Spirduso, 1995). Furthermore, muscular deterioration tends to affect the **Type II**, fast-twitch, muscle fibers more than the **Type I**, slow-twitch, fibers (Powers & Howley, 2001; Rogers & Evans, 1993). Because of this reduction in fast-twitch fibers, elderly individuals frequently experience a reduction in speed of muscular contractions. This may in part help explain why falls are so frequently incurred by elderly people. Even when a loss of postural balance is recognized, it may be of little value if muscles in the lower extremity are not capable of contracting quickly and with sufficient force to regain postural stability. Furthermore, those fibers that are not lost and do not atrophy tend to fatigue more quickly. This is believed to be caused by degenerative changes involving energy metabolism.

FLEXIBILITY

The abilities to ambulate and perform such daily tasks as bending over to pick up an object, tying shoes, rising out of a chair, and even eating all have one thing in common: Each task requires the bending of various parts of the body. Smooth functioning of the body's joints makes these bending movements possible. The range of movement within these joints, **flexibility,** is regionally specific. In other words, there is little relationship between the flexibility of each of the body's joints. For example, a person with flexible shoulders does not necessarily have a flexible back. Thus, few physical-fitness test batteries include flexibility among the test items, because it is impossible to determine the one best flexibility test that would estimate total body flexibility. Nevertheless, when a flexibility test is included, it is generally a test of hamstring, back, and hip flexibility — the **sit-and-reach test** (see Figure 8-7) or the back saver sit-and-reach test (see Figure 8-8). Our study of flexibility is further complicated because researchers have not yet been able to determine how much flexibility is needed for optimal health. The next section examines the general course of flexibility across the lifespan.

Flexibility: Performance Trends

Surprisingly, there is little empirical information on flexibility and joint mobility. However, what literature there is is consistent in its findings. More specifically, when the sit-and-reach test is used to measure hamstring, hip, and back flexibility, the data illustrate that peak flexibility is achieved in the late teens or early 20s. Thereafter, range of motion decreases. This trend is most apparent in NCYFS I and II (Ross & Pate, 1987). In these studies, norms were established for a nationally represented sample of youngsters 6 through 18 years of age (see Figure 8-9). Generally, the data from these studies show a yearly increase in range of motion during these childhood and adolescent years. Furthermore, gender differences are apparent in that girls attained better scores than did boys across all ages and across all percentile ranges. This finding is also consistent with the sit-and-reach data obtained from studies of Canadian children (Docherty & Bell, 1985). Docherty and Bell also note that across the four age groups examined (6, 9, 12, and 15 years), the relative difference in flexibility between the genders widened with age.

Figure 8-7 Sit-and-reach test

Figure 8-8 The back saver sit-and-reach test evaluates flexibility on one side at a time. This technique places less stress on the lower back.

Using 378 sedentary women between ages 14 and 76, Alexander, Ready, and Fougere-Mailey (1985) also report decreases in sit-and-reach performance with age. However, decreases in flexibility were gradual up to age 49, whereupon significant drops occur with age.

Declining Flexibility and Aging: Causes and Therapy

Because flexibility is known to decrease with age, we wonder what causes this decline in our range of motion. This decrease in joint mobility is partly caused by physiological changes to the structures that make up the joint: tendons, ligaments, muscle, synovial fluid, and cartilage. With age, the joint's connective structures become less resilient and crack and fray. Synovial fluid becomes less viscous, and cartilage is frequently damaged from both injury and everyday wear and tear. Degenerative joint disease such as osteoarthrosis also contributes to loss of joint functioning. About 80 percent of the population between 55 and 64 years have signs of osteoarthrosis in at least one joint. Furthermore, although joint degeneration is usually associated with aged populations,

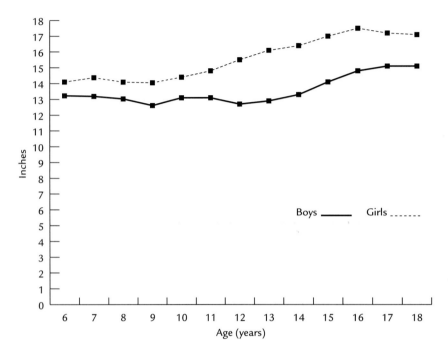

Figure 8-9 Average sit-and-reach scores for boys and girls based on findings of the National Children and Youth Fitness Studies I and II

The zero point was located at 12 inches.

SOURCES: As reported by Ross and Gilbert (1985) and Ross and Pate (1987).

the degenerative process actually begins prior to skeletal maturity (Whitbourne, 1996). Further research is needed to separate those processes that are age related and those that are pathological.

Even though researchers have not been able to ascertain to what extent joint changes are caused by age-related processes or by pathological changes, one fact is clear: Physical activity is necessary to maintain joint mobility. Moreover, joint flexibility can be improved with moderate to light activity. This finding was illustrated in Munns's study (1981), in which 20 experimental and 20 control subjects between 65 and 88 years of age volunteered to take part in a 12-week exercise and dance program to determine its effect on joint flexibility. At the conclusion of the experiment, subjects in the experimental group showed significant improvement in all six joints measured: neck, shoulder, wrist, hip and back, knee, and ankle. Range of motion improved from a low of 8.3 percent in the shoulder to a high of 48.3 percent in the ankle. In contrast, control subjects showed decreased flexibility in the same six joints, from 2.7 percent in the knee to 5.1 percent in both the shoulder and the ankle.

Controlling for level of activity, Germain and Blair (1983) found that shoulder flexibility decreases after 10 years of age. However, this decrease was minimal in people who were active.

BODY COMPOSITION

We live in a technological society—a society that is relying increasingly on special machinery to perform daily tasks. The use of robotics in the workforce has improved productivity, but we are paying a price for this technology. Some experts believe that this price is an increasingly sedentary lifestyle. Accompanying this lifestyle is a corresponding increase in the number of overweight and overfat people. Adipose (fat) tissue serves many useful and important functions: It insulates the body, it can be a source of energy reserve, and it is also a protective cushion for internal organs. Unfortunately, mounting evidence suggests that excess fat in relation to total body composition may have serious health consequences, including high blood lipid levels, elevated blood pressure, and many other physiological parameters associated with cardiovascular and metabolic disease.

Defining Overweight and Obese

The term **obese** is difficult to define with precision because so many different definitions have been offered, which partly explains why scientists have difficulty establishing an ideal level of fatty tissue. An acceptable level as defined by one definition may describe an unacceptable level according to another. Three popular definitions take a social, a statistical, and an operational approach. The major thesis of the social definition is appearance. If a person looks as if he is extremely overweight, then he is considered obese, even though no sophisticated measurements are taken. The statistical definition is based on estimates established from normative studies. For instance, a person weighing 50 to 100 pounds above her desired weight is classified as extremely obese. Or a man falling above the 85th to 95th percentile on whatever criteria is being used may be classified as obese. The operational definition is based on criteria tied to rates of mortality and morbidity. For example, the operational definition receiving the most attention is body mass index (BMI). Recall from Chapter 7 that BMI is a measure of weight relative to height (weight in kg/height in meters^2: See page 161). While the ideal BMI should range between 18.5 kg/m^2 to 24.9 kg/m^2, obesity is defined as a BMI $\geq$ 30 kg/m^2. BMI values between 25.0 kg/m^2 and 29.9 kg/m^2 indicate an **overweight** condition. Also gaining in popularity is the gender-neutral value for waist circumference. Irrespective of body weight and height, one is classified as obese when waist circumference exceeds 100 centimeters.

Researchers subscribe to the statistical definition, where norms for proposed ideal body fat are based on descriptive data. Nevertheless, descriptive data are population-specific. That is, observed levels of body fat differ, depending on many factors. For instance, gender, race, lifestyle, and many geographical factors can all influence **body composition.** In other words, how much of the body is made up of fat and how much is composed of **lean body tissue** such as muscle and bone?

Because of these apparent problems, during the Sixth Ross Conference on Medical Research (Newman, 1985), Roche suggested that we no longer use the terms *standard* or *ideal* to describe body composition. He stated that "standard and ideal imply values that are fixed for all time, with biologic interpretations of what ought to be. However, these reference data change from one survey to the next" (p. 4). Therefore, in the following section, when we describe changes in body composition across the life-span, keep in mind that we are simply highlighting general trends and that these trends are population-specific. This helps explain the wide range of values reported in different studies.

General Growth Trends of Adipose Tissue

Subcutaneous adipose tissue first appears toward the end of the second trimester and rapidly develops during the last 2 months of gestation (Moore & Persaud, 2003). At birth, the amount of fat present is about 11 percent in boys and 14 percent in girls. This fat is stored in about 5 billion adipocytes (fat cells). The number of fat cells continues to increase during childhood. For example, during the next 12 months, the percentage of body fat can rise to about 26 percent in boys and 28 percent in girls (Butte et al., 2000). This increase in fat tissue during the first year of life is one of the two rapid growth spurts of adipose tissue. The second spurt occurs during puberty in boys and during both prepuberty and puberty in girls. The result of this second spurt is a greater fat mass in girls than in boys. On the average, the young but mature female adolescent can have a body-fat content 50 percent greater than that of her male counterpart of the same age (Rowland, 1996). Authorities believe that the number of adipocytes does not increase following puberty. Instead, changes in fat's contribution to overall body composition depend on the size of each fat cell, not the number of fat cells.

There appears to be one period early in the life-span when body fat declines: at the onset of independent walking. It ends somewhere between 6 and

Figure 8-10 The prevalence of obesity is increasing among both adults and children.

8 years of age; at this time, body fat is about one-half of what it was at 1 year of age (Sinclair, 1998).

A body-fat content 1 or 2 standard deviations above the mean lies outside the normal range recommended for optimal health. Foss and Keteyian (1998) believe that body-fat content should be 10 to 25 percent in men and 18 to 30 percent in women. However, for optimal fitness, body-fat content must be reduced to approximately 12 to 18 percent in men and 16 to 25 percent in women. In comparison, most male athletes possess a body-fat content of 5 to 13 percent, with most female athletes at 12 to 22 percent. Because fat is an essential body component, it should not drop below 1 to 5 percent in men and 3 to 8 percent in women. Often, slightly higher levels of essential fat are recommended for women in order to avoid amenorrhea.

Body weight per se is not an appropriate indicator of body composition. Body weight tends to reach its peak at about 45 years of age; during the next 15 years, body weight generally decreases or remains constant. A decrease in body weight implies a reduction in adipose tissue, but generally this is not the case. For instance, skinfold thicknesses do not change during this period, so this reduction in body weight is due to a reduction in lean body mass,

not fat mass. The increasingly sedentary lifestyle that generally accompanies aging partly explains this reduction in lean body mass.

Prevalence of Overweight and Obesity

The prevalence of overweight and obesity in the U.S. population continues to escalate (see Figure 8-10). The most recent NHANES (1999–2000) data indicate that the percentage of young children and adolescents between 6 and 19 years of age who are overweight continues to increase; as of 2000, 15 percent are overweight (Figure 8-11). Most alarming is the finding that the number of overweight children between 6 and 11 years of age has almost doubled during the last 20 years and has almost tripled for adolescents between 12 and 19 years of age.

The prevalence of overweight and obesity is even greater among adults over 20. More specifically, approximately 64 percent of United States adults are either overweight or obese (Flegal et al., 2002). Compare this figure with the one established in the late 1970s when 47 percent of United States adults were either overweight or obese (U.S. Department of Health and Human Services, 2001, 2002). Figure 8-12 illustrates the

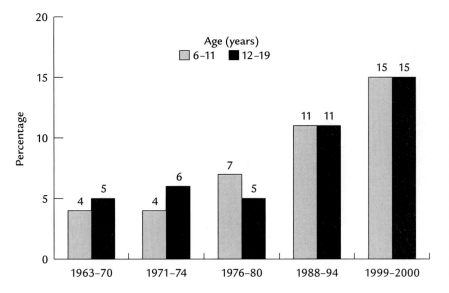

Figure 8-11 Prevalence of overweight in children and adolescents aged 6–19

NOTES: Excludes pregnant women starting with 1971–1974. Pregnancy status not available for 1963–65 and 1966–1970. Data for 1963–1965 are for children 6–11 years of age; data for 1966–1970 are for adolescents 12–17 years of age, not 12–19 years.

SOURCES: CDC/NCHS, NHES, and NHANES.

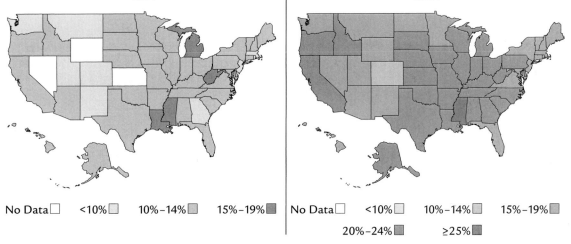

Figure 8-12 These two figures demonstrate the increasing prevalence of obesity (30 pounds overweight) among U.S. adults.

NOTE: BRFSS uses self-reported height and weight to calculate obesity: self-reported data may underestimate obesity prevalence.

SOURCE: Behavioral Risk Factor Surveillance System (BRFSS).

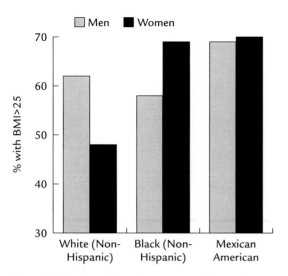

Figure 8-13 Age-adjusted prevalence of overweight or obesity in selected groups, 1988–1994

Source: *Surgeon General's Call to Action to Prevent and Decrease Overweight and Obesity.* Washington, DC: U.S. Government Printing Office. Stock no. 017-001-00551-7.

surfacing epidemic of obesity among adults within the United States.

Figure 8-13 summarizes the prevalence of overweight and obesity among men and women of selected racial and ethnic groups. In general, Mexican American and black non-Hispanic women exhibit higher rates of overweight and obesity than do white non-Hispanic women. In contrast, Mexican American men exhibit a higher prevalence of overweight and obesity than do non-Hispanic blacks and non-Hispanic whites. The prevalence of overweight and obesity among non-Hispanic men is slightly greater in whites than in blacks (U.S. Department of Health and Human Services, 2002).

Also interesting is the prevalence of overweight and obesity among individuals within both low socioeconomic status groups (income ≤ 130 percent of the poverty level) and high socioeconomic status groups (income > 130 percent of the poverty level). While men in both groups are equally likely to become overweight and obese, the same is not true of women. When combining all racial and ethnic groups, women of low socioeconomic status exhibit

a greater prevalence of overweight and obesity than do women with high socioeconomic status (U.S. Department of Health and Human Services, 2002).

Given this data, it is obvious the United States did not meet the *Healthy People 2000* objectives of reducing the prevalence of overweight to no more than 20 percent (U.S. Department of Health and Human Services, 1990). The newer *Healthy People 2010* objective aims at lowering the incidence of overweight and obesity in adults older than 20 years of age to 15 percent and in children/adolescents between 6 and 19 years of age to only 5 percent (U.S. Department of Health and Human Services, 2000). This is surely a most challenging objective.

For detailed information on the role of physical activity in the prevention and treatment of obesity, consult the report of the American College of Sports Medicine Consensus Conference (American College of Sports Medicine, 1999) and the report titled *Physical Activity Fundamental to Preventing Disease* (U.S. Department of Health and Human Services, 2002). This latter report can be downloaded from www.fitness.gov.

Association Between Childhood and Adulthood Obesity

It is common knowledge that obesity is related to an increased risk of cardiovascular disease, diabetes, and hypertension. Because of this public health concern, scientists have recently attempted to examine the value of measures of childhood obesity—body mass index (BMI)—in predicting the likelihood of developing obesity in adulthood.

Using BMI values of >28 for men and >26 for women in defining overweight, Guo and colleagues (1994) have constructed models to predict the likelihood of being overweight in adulthood based on BMI values during childhood (see Figures 8-14 and 8-15). In general, Guo and colleagues found that children with BMI values at the 95th percentile for their age and gender have a greater than 60 percent chance of being obese at age 35. The strength of this association increases with age. Accordingly, the prediction is excellent at age 18, good at 13 years of age, and moderate at ages younger than 13 years.

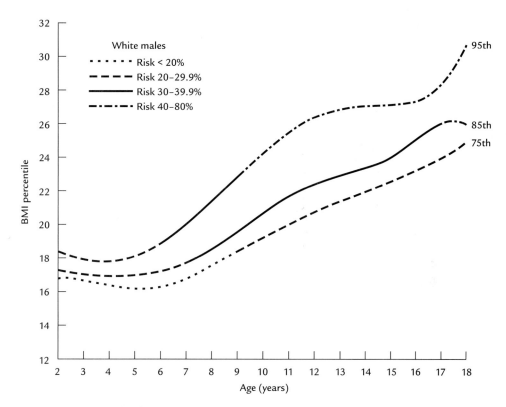

Figure 8-14   Selected percentiles for body mass index (BMI = wt(kg)/ht(m)^2) in boys from the Second National Health and Nutrition Examination Survey. Segments of the 75th, 85th, and 95th percentile lines are differentially shaded to indicate differences in the probability that BMI at 35 years will be >28.

Source: Guo, S., Roche, A. F., Chumlea, W. C., Gardner, J. D., and Siervogel, R. M. (1994). The predictive value of childhood body mass index values for overweight at age 35y. *American Journal of Clinical Nutrition, 59*, 810–819. Reproduced with permission by the *American Journal of Clinical Nutrition.* © American Society for Clinical Nutrition.

To utilize Figures 8-14 and 8-15, simply cross the child's age with her or his present BMI and note the point of intersection. Then you can determine the child's percentile rank based on national data. Additionally, pay close attention to the shading of the percentile lines. Use the key to interpret the risk of being overweight at age 35. Take for example a 10-year-old white male child who has a BMI value approaching 24. This child is at the 95th percentile. According to the shaded scale, this child has a 40 to 80 percent ($\bar{x} = 60\%$) chance of being overweight at 35 years of age. In contrast, a 9-year-old white female child with a BMI value of about 18 has a less than 20 percent risk of being overweight at age 35. This information can help identify at-risk individuals in order to start early intervention.

Laboratory-Test Measures of Body Composition

Hydrostatic weighting (HW) has long been considered the "gold standard" for determining body composition. This technique, which requires total body submersion under water, is based on Archimedes' principle (see Figure 8-16). This principle states that an object's loss of weight in water is equal

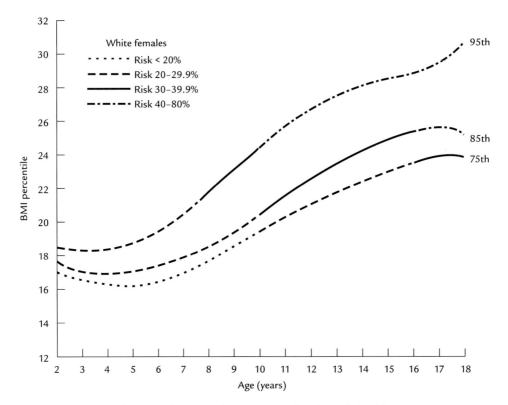

Figure 8-15   Selected percentiles for body mass index (BMI = wt(kg)/ht(m)^2) in girls from the Second National Health and Nutrition Examination Survey. Segments of the 75th, 85th, and 95th percentile lines are differentially shaded to indicate differences in the probability that BMI at 35 years will be >26.

SOURCE: Guo, S., Roche, A. F., Chumlea, W. C., Gardner, J. D., and Siervogel, R. M. (1994). The predictive value of childhood body mass index values for overweight at age 35y. *American Journal of Clinical Nutrition, 59,* 810–819. Reproduced with permission by the *American Journal of Clinical Nutrition.* © American Society for Clinical Nutrition.

to the weight of the volume of water it displaces. Equations are then used to calculate body density and to then predict percentage of body fat (see ACSM, 2000). While the error rate is less than 2 percent, the test requires a highly skilled technician to administer and is not appropriate for individuals with an aversion to water. Additionally, the test can take as long as an hour to administer.

A popular alternative to HW is the use of the **Bod Pod** (See Figure 8-17). Unlike HW, which is based on the displacement of water, the Bod Pod is based on the displacement of air (air-displacement plethysmography). All calculations are computerized, and the test lasts for only about 5 minutes. Because submersion is water is not required, the test is suitable for all populations including children and elderly or disabled persons. In fact, a recent study found air-displacement plethysmography to be more accurate than HW and dual-energy X-ray absorptiometry (DEXA, see Chapter 7) when calculating body composition in children between 9 and 14 years of age (Fields & Goran, 2000).

Figure 8-16 Hydrostatic weighting is the preferred method for determining percentage of body fat, but this technique is not practical as a field-test measure.
Source: © David Young-Woff/PhotoEdit.

Field-Test Measures of Body Composition

While HW, the Bod Pod, and DEXA are the preferred methods for estimating percent body fat, these laboratory procedures are not always practical. A more practical alternative is the use of **skinfold calipers.** Calipers are used to indirectly estimate body composition. While numerous companies manufacture skinfold calipers, the caliper of choice is manufactured by Harpenden. An appropriate, yet less expensive substitute is the caliper produced by

Lange. One should shy away from cheap plastic calipers, which have scales that are difficult to read and are not spring loaded. Using calipers that are spring loaded ensures that a constant calibrated pressure ($10g/mm^2$) is applied to the double fold of skin and fat tissue.

Skinfold calipers were used in both NCYFSs to estimate body fat in children between 6 and 18 years of age. Table 8-3 presents the findings of this study. The values for the 6- through 9-year-olds were obtained by summing the skinfold thicknesses for the tricep, subscapular, and medial calf. In contrast, values for the 10- through 18-year-olds were obtained by summing only the tricep and subscapular skinfolds. Because of the inclusion of the medial calf measure in the younger group, it is difficult to compare trends between these two age groups. In order to make comparisons across ages easier, Figure 8-18 shows changes in only the sum of tricep and subscapular skinfolds across both age groups (the medial calf measure has been removed from the younger age group). Clearly, girls possess more body fat than do boys, at all ages. In general, body fat appears to increase steadily in girls until 15 years of age. In contrast, boys exhibit a steady increase in body fat until about 10 years; thereafter, it remains relatively constant through 18 years of age. One should also note that the magnitude of difference between the genders widens significantly after 11 years of age, and this widening trend continues until about age 15. At this time, the average sum of tricep and subscapular skinfolds is nearly 10 millimeters greater in girls.

Skinfold thickness remains relatively constant between 45 and 65 years of age (Shephard, 1978) although its value can be greatly affected by both nutritional and exercise status. The data presented in Table 8-4 shows a definite decrease in tricep skinfold thickness in men between 60 and 80+ years of age and women between 50 and 80+ years of age (Kuczmarski et al., 2000). Chumlea, Roche, & Mukherjee (1984) have recognized that both obesity and malnutrition are common occurrences in late adulthood. For this reason, they recommend that body-fat changes be closely monitored in elderly individuals.

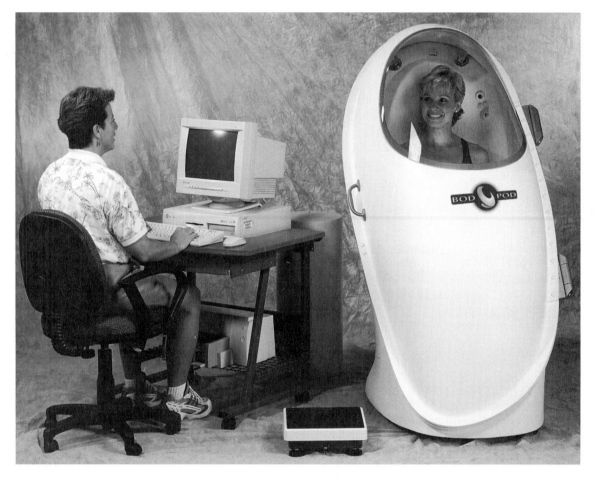

Figure 8-17 The Bod Pod uses air displacement technology to measure body composition.

Source: Image courtesy of Life Measurement, Inc.

Obesity tends to be the most common reason elderly individuals approach the 90th percentile in measures of body fat, whereas malnutrition and serious illness can cause a significant drop in body fat.

Relationship of Obesity to Motor Development and Performance

As early as 1931, Shirley noted that of the 25 babies in her study, the heavy ones evidenced more delays in walking than did the lighter ones. Jaffe and Kosakov (1982) echoed this finding in their study of the motor development of fat babies. The authors cate-

gorized 135 babies as being either of normal weight or fat. The fat babies were further classified as either overweight or obese; 29 percent of the overweight babies and 36 percent of the obese babies evidenced motor delays as measured by the Sheridan Stycar Developmental Assessment Schedules. In comparison, only 9 percent of the normal-weight babies showed any delay in their motor development.

Pissanos, Moore, and Reeve (1983) used the Sum of Skinfold Fat Test to study the influence of age, gender, and body composition on predicting children's performance on basic motor abilities and on health-related physical fitness. Subjects were 80 boys and

Table 8-3	Average Sum of Skinfolds (mm) for Boys and Girls Based on Findings of the NCYFS I and II												
Age (years)												
	6	7	8	9	10	11	12	13	14	15	16	17	18
Sum of Tricep, Subscapular, and Medial Calf Skinfolds													
Boys	24.56	26.36	28.91	32.07									
Girls	30.55	32.25	36.11	39.16									
Sum of Tricep and Subscapular Skinfolds													
Boys					20.90	21.20	21.60	20.10	20.10	20.10	19.40	20.10	20.20
Girls					22.60	24.80	25.30	26.80	27.90	30.00	28.70	30.20	28.90

SOURCES: As reported by Ross and Gilbert (1985) and Ross and Pate (1987).

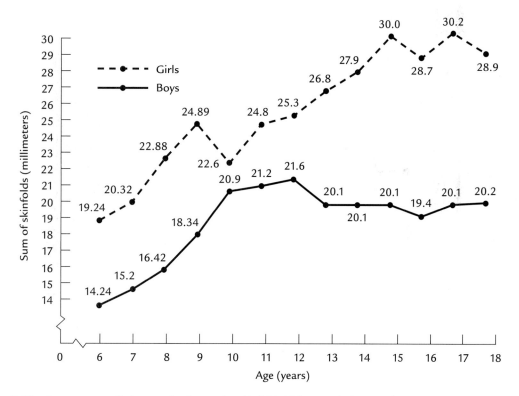

Figure 8-18 Average sum of tricep and subscapular skinfold thicknesses in boys and girls based on findings of the National Children and Youth Fitness Studies I and II
SOURCES: As reported by Ross and Gilbert (1985) and Ross and Pate (1987).

Table 8-4   Percentiles for Tricep Skinfold Thickness in Men and Women 50 Years of Age and Older Examined in NHANES III (1988–1994)

Age (years)	Men				Women			
	Mean ±SE	90th	50th	10th	Mean ±SE	90th	50th	10th
50–59	33.7 ±0.18	21.8	12.6	7.5	26.6 ±0.40	37.0	26.7	16.4
60–69	14.2 ±0.25	23.1	12.7	7.7	24.2 ±0.37	34.9	24.1	14.5
70–79	13.4 ±0.28	20.6	12.4	7.3	22.3 ±0.30	32.1	21.8	12.5
80+	12.0 ±0.28	18.0	11.2	6.6	18.6 ±0.42	28.9	18.1	9.3

SOURCE: From data compiled by Kuczmarski et al. (2000).

girls 6 years 8 months to 10 years 3 months old. This study found that body composition was the best predictor of cardiovascular performance, as measured by a step test, and power, as measured by the standing long jump. The authors conclude that "large amounts of subcutaneous fat [are] negatively related to activities in which the body is projected through space" (p. 76). This position is supported by Isaacs and Pohlman's (2000) findings that for every kilogram increase in body fat there is a corresponding decrease in vertical jump performance of 0.65 centimeters (¼ inch) among a group of elementary school-age children between 7 and 11 years of age. Slaughter, Lohman, and Misner (1977) also reported that the 7- to 12-year-old subjects in their study who had large amounts of body fat ran more slowly in the mile and 600-yard run than did the leaner subjects. Additionally, Watson (1988) found, in a group of adolescent boys, that for every 1 percent increase in body fat there is, on average, a 46-yard decrement in distance covered during a 12-minute walk/run test. Similar findings have been reported by Chatrath and colleagues (2002). More specifically they required children between 4 and 18 years of age to take part in an endurance exercise test (the Bruce treadmill protocol). Results revealed that 61 percent of the boys and 81 percent of the girls performed below the 25th percentile. A strong negative correlation was found between BMI and endurance performance, suggesting that obesity contributed greatly to decreased aerobic fitness.

Treatment of Overweight and Obesity

A logical extension of our discussion on overweight and obesity is to develop a treatment plan for safely losing weight. The algorithm presented in Figure 8-19 summarizes our discussion regarding the identification and classification of overweight and obesity based on BMI and waist circumference (National Heart, Lung, and Blood Institute, 2002). Note that once the identification and classification has been made, this algorithm can be consulted to provide information regarding potential treatments and follow-up maintenance programs.

GENDER DIFFERENCES IN HEALTH-RELATED PHYSICAL FITNESS

Uncovering gender differences in health-related physical fitness was the subject of an investigation by Thomas, Nelson, and Church (1991). The study

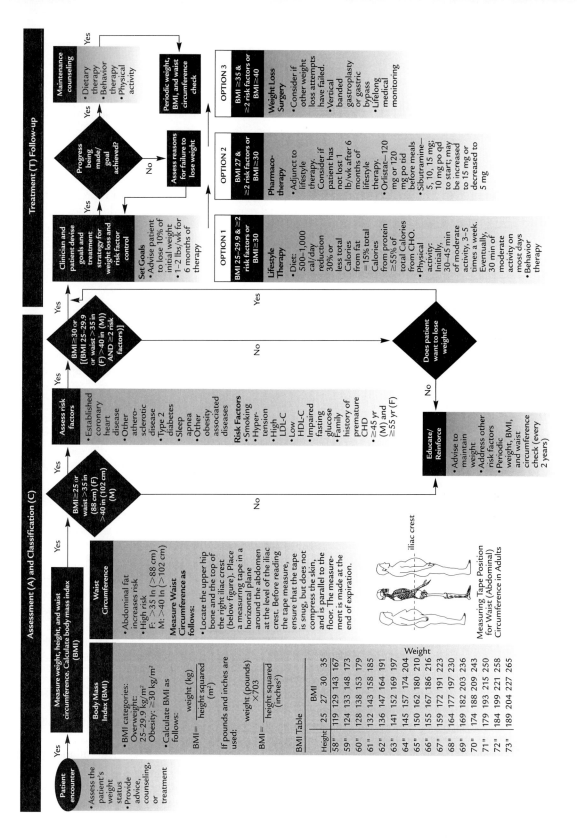

Figure 8-19 Identification, evaluation, and treatment of overweight and obesity in adults

SOURCE: National Heart, Lung, and Blood Institute (2002).

involved a secondary analysis of the physical and environmental variables measured in the National Children and Youth Fitness Study I and II. Across all ages examined (6–18 years), boys outperformed girls in three (distance run, chin-up, and sit-up) of the four health-related fitness components. The only event where girls consistently outperformed boys was the sit-and-reach test. The pattern of difference between the genders was similar for all three events. Namely, a gradual increase during the elementary school years followed by a more rapid acceleration in differences after puberty in favor of the boys. Gender differences were then adjusted for physical and environmental factors. This analysis found the most important factors prior to puberty to be predominately skinfolds, while after puberty the major factors to reduce the gender differences were both skinfolds and the amount of exercise outside of school time. In fact, compared with the girls, boys consistently reported involvement in higher intensity activities from about 9 or 10 years of age.

FACTORS ASSOCIATED WITH PHYSIOLOGICAL FITNESS IN CHILDREN AND ADOLESCENTS

One of the major objectives of both NCYFSs was to attempt to uncover factors that could influence a child's performance on physiological-fitness test items. In general, children who performed best on tests of physiological fitness tended to participate in more community-based activities, watch less television, receive their physical education instruction from a specialist, experience more activities over the course of a year, and come from a family that was active and willing to spend time exercising with its children (Dotson & Ross, 1985; Pate & Ross, 1987).

Regarding exercise intensity, approximately 59 percent of the subjects reported participating in moderate- to high-intensity physical activity. Blair and associates (1989) recommend that physical activity be of such an intensity to result in an energy expenditure of 12.6 kJ/kg/day in order to derive

health benefits. Over 75 percent of the children surveyed in the NCYFS exceeded this standard (very active: >16.8 kJ/kg/day). This is an important finding since some suggest that activity levels exhibited during childhood may influence adult level of activity (Armstrong, 1992; Dennison et al., 1988; Janz, Dawson, & Mahoney, 2000). If future research were to support this finding, it would represent an additional reason to encourage active lifestyles during childhood.

POINTS OF CONTROVERSY AND CONCERN

One reason so much importance has been placed on the attainment of acceptable levels of physiological fitness is its alleged association with optimal health. That is, we assume that children who obtain acceptable fitness standards will evade serious health problems. Unfortunately, researchers have not been able to support this assumption with empirical evidence. According to Blair and associates, "Childhood exercise habits are probably not associated with adult health status. . . . Thus, adult exercise has a much greater beneficial effect on adult health status than does childhood exercise" (1989, p. 402). This point of view has been substantiated by Brill and colleagues, who report that "athletic participation in youth is not associated with coronary risk factor status in middle age in Cooper Clinic patients" (cited in Blair et al., 1989). More recently, Kemper and colleagues (2001) attempted to find whether physical fitness in adolescence predicted adult activity. This longitudinal study, which followed 400 boys and girls for 20 years, concluded that between the ages of 13 and 33 years, physical fitness in adolescence is only weakly related to physical activity in adulthood.

Motor developmentalists, physical educators, and curriculum specialists are currently debating what should be emphasized in today's curriculum: motor skill development or physiological fitness. Once again, the debate will continue until we can obtain an acceptable answer to our original question: What are the exact performance standards needed in order to obtain optimal health?

At the other end of the age continuum is our concern regarding the maintenance of an active lifestyle throughout the entire lifespan. While it is true that life expectancy is improving, one must also consider the quality of these additional years. For example, Barry, Rich, and Carlson (1993) noted that while life expectancy in Quebec has increased to 70.3 years in men and 78.2 years in women, that disability-free life expectancies are only 59 and 60 years, respectively. In other words, we may be living longer, but we need to find ways to remain independently functional during the latter years of life. Randomized controlled clinical trials have indicated that exercise training in the elderly is an effective means of remaining functionally independent (Fujita et al., 2003). As should be evident from the information presented in this chapter, physical activity can contribute greatly toward maintaining functional independence.

SUMMARY

Cardiovascular fitness is the ability to deliver oxygen to the working muscle tissues. Increased workloads involve a corresponding increase in cardiac output, the amount of blood pumped through the heart in 1 minute. This increased blood flow is made possible by an increase in the heart's rate of contraction and stroke volume, the amount of blood ejected with each beat. Aging affects each of these parameters; for instance, HR, SV, and cardiac output all decrease with age.

The largest amount of oxygen the body can consume at the tissue level is called VO_2 max. Generally, VO_2 max remains fairly constant during the childhood and adolescent years. Boys may exhibit greater values than girls, but the differences are not as great when variations in body size are considered. The influence of aging on this parameter first becomes evident as early as 12 years of age, when girls experience a reduction in VO_2 max. In general, the rate of decline is between 9 and 15 percent between 45 and 55 years of age; thereafter, the rate of decline accelerates.

A growing amount of evidence questions the benefit of aerobic training for improving aerobic capacity in preadolescent children.

Strength is the ability to exert force. Static force is produced when there is no change in the length of the exercised muscle; dynamic force is produced when the exercised muscle does change its length. Most studies examining strength changes across the lifespan use grip strength as the dependent variable. Boys increase their grip strength by 393 percent between the ages of 7 and 17. Girls improve their grip strength about 260 percent between the ages of 6 and 18. Between age 25 and 45 years, men lose about 20 percent of their grip strength, and active women between 30–39 and 60 years of age lose about 16 percent of their grip strength.

Most authorities now agree that resistance training can improve muscular strength in prepubescent individuals, especially if approved guidelines are followed. To date, the American Academy of Pediatrics and the National Strength and Conditioning Association have published position statements and guidelines for prepubescent resistance training.

Flexibility is the range of motion of a joint. Yearly increases in sit-and-reach flexibility are apparent during childhood and adolescence. Thereafter, decreases in joint mobility become evident. Girls are usually more flexible than boys, and this gender difference widens with age.

Body composition is the ratio of fat tissue to lean muscle mass. There are two growth spurts of fat tissue, the first during the first year of life and the second during puberty in boys and both prepuberty and puberty in girls. Following this second spurt, girls possess more body fat than do boys throughout the lifespan.

The prevalence of obesity in the United States continues to increase. The most recent NHANES (1999–2000) data set reveals that the number of overweight children between 6 and 11 years of age has almost doubled during the last 20 years and has almost tripled for adolescents between 12 and 19 years of age. Even more shocking is the finding that approximately 64 percent of adults are either overweight or obese. Researchers have found a positive correlation between childhood obesity and adulthood obesity.

Large amounts of body fat are negatively related to activities in which the body is projected through space.

KEY TERMS

anabolic steroids
androgens
Bod Pod
body building (sport)
body composition
bradycardia
cardiac output
cardiovascular fitness
dynamic force
earthbound
field test

flexibility
heart rate (HR)
hydrostatic weighing (HW)
hypertrophy
lean body tissue
maximal oxygen consumption
muscular strength
obese
overweight
periodization
physical working capacity

power lifting (sport)
sit-and-reach test
skinfold calipers
static, or isometric, force
stroke volume (SV)
subcutaneous adipose tissue
testosterone
Type I muscle fibers
Type II muscle fibers
weight lifting (sport)
weight training

QUESTIONS FOR REFLECTION

1. What are the typical VO_2 max values in children between 6 and 16 years of age?

2. Can you describe trends in cardiac output after 25 years of age?

3. A child improves in run-time performance of the 1-mile run from a test taken in September and one in March of the same school year. What are the primary factors, as reported by Pate and Shephard (1989), that contribute to this improvement?

4. What is the ACSM's position regarding the duration, frequency, and intensity of exercise needed to obtain an improvement in cardiorespiratory fitness?

5. What are the age of peak distance run times as uncovered in the National Children and Youth Fitness Studies I and II?

6. Can you describe gender differences in muscle strength in both relative and absolute terms?

7. Can you distinguish between weight training, weight lifting (power lifting), and body building as defined by the AAP?

8. Can you describe pull-up performance for both boys and girls according to the findings of the National Children and Youth Fitness Studies I and II? Note ages of peak performance.

9. What is the one main difference, regarding test administration, between the NCYFS I and the NCYFS II? Why was this change in test administration employed?

10. Can you summarize Payne and colleagues' (1997) meta-analysis regarding resistance training in both children and youth?

11. Can you summarize the weight-training guidelines established by AAP and the NSCA?

12. What is the position of the U.S. Weight and Power Lifting Federation regarding maximum lifting during resistance training?

13. Can you describe potential mechanisms of muscle deterioration, paying particular attention to changes in selective fiber type deterioration? Can you also describe the role of this deterioration in potential falls by elderly persons?

14. What mechanisms are responsible for increases in muscular strength?

15. What are the causes of declining flexibility with age?

16. Why is obesity so prevalent in the U.S. population?

17. What is the association between childhood obesity and the probability of adult obesity?

18. What is the relationship between body composition and both motor development and motor performance?

19. Can you summarize the *Surgeon General's Report on Physical Activity and Health?* (See Appendix C.)

20. Can you summarize the CDC's guidelines for school and community programs promoting lifelong physical activity? (See Appendix D.)

INTERNET RESOURCES

American College of Sports Medicine **www.acsm.org**

American Heart Association **www.americanheart.org**

Healthy People 2010 **www.health.gov/healthypeople**

National Center for Health Statistics
www.cdc.gov/nchs

National Heart, Lung, and Blood Institute
www.nhlbi.nih.gov

National Senior Games Association (Senior Olympics)
www.nsga.com

National Strength and Conditioning Association
www.nsca-lift.org/menu.asp

North American Association for the Study of Obesity
www.naaso.org

President's Council on Physical Fitness **www.fitness.gov**

ONLINE LEARNING CENTER (www.mhhe.com/payne6e)

Visit the *Human Motor Development* Online Learning Center for study aids and additional resources. You can use the study guide questions and key terms puzzles to review key terms and concepts for this chapter and to prepare for exams. You can further extend your knowledge of motor development by checking out the Web links, articles, and activities found on the site.

REFERENCES

Alexander, M. J., Ready, A. E., & Fougere-Mailey, G. (1985). The fitness levels of females in various age groups. *Canadian Journal of Health, Physical Education, and Recreation, 51,* 8–12.

American Academy of Pediatrics. (1990). Strength training, weight and power lifting, and body building by children and adolescents. *Pediatrics, 86,* 801–802.

———. (2001). Strength training by children and adolescents. *Pediatrics, 107,* 1470–1472,

American College of Sports Medicine. (1999). Physical activity in the prevention and treatment of obesity and its comorbidities. *Medicine and Science in Sports and Exercise, 31,* S497–S667.

———. (2000). *ACSM's guidelines for exercise testing and prescription.* 6th ed. Baltimore: Lippincott Williams & Wilkins.

Armstrong, N. (1992). Are American children and youth fit? Some international perspectives. *Research Quarterly for Exercise and Sport, 63,* 449–450.

Bar-Or, O. (1983). *Pediatric sports medicine for the practitioner.* New York: Springer-Verlag.

———. (1989). Trainability of the prepubescent child. *Physician and Sportsmedicine, 17,* 65–82.

Barry, H. C., Rich, B. S. E., & Carlson, R. T. (1993). How exercise can benefit older patients: A practical approach. *Physician and Sportsmedicine, 21,* 124–140.

Blair, S. N., Clark, D. G., Cureton, K. J., & Powell, K. E. (1989). Exercise and fitness in childhood: Implications for a lifetime of health. In C. V. Gisolfi & D. R. Lamb (Eds.), *Perspectives in exercise science and sports medicine: Youth, exercise, and sport.* Indianapolis, IN: Benchmark.

Blimkie, C. (1993). Resistance training during preadolescence: Issues and controversies. *Sports Medicine, 15,* 389–407.

Bouchard, C., Malina, R. M., Hollmann, W., & Leblanc, C. (1977). Submaximal working capacity, heart size and body size in 8 to 18 years. *European Journal of Applied Physiology, 36,* 115–126.

Brill, P. A., Macera, C. A., Davis, D. R., Blair, S. N., & Gordon, N. (2000). Muscular strength and physical function. *Medicine and Science in Sports and Exercise, 32,* 412–416.

Brown, M., Sinacore, D., & Host, H. (1995). The relationship of strength to function in the older adult. *Journals of Gerontology, 50A,* 55–59.

Buckley, W. E., Yesalis, C. E., Friedl, K. E., Anderson, W. A., Streit, A. L., & Wright, J. E. (1988). Estimated prevalence of anabolic steroid use among male high school seniors. *Journal of the American Medical Association, 260,* 3441–3445.

Butte, N. F., Hopkinson, J. M., Wong, W. W., O'Brian-Smith, E., & Ellis, K. J. (2000). Body composition during the first 2 years of life: An updated reference. *Pediatric Research, 47,* 578–584.

Carmeli, E., Reznick, A. Z., Coleman, R., & Carmeli, V. (2000). Muscle strength and mass of lower extremities in relation to functional abilities in elderly adults. *Gerontology, 46,* 249–257.

Centers for Disease Control. (1997). Guidelines for school and community programs to promote lifelong physical activity among young people. *Morbidity and Mortality Weekly Report, 47,* Pub no. RR-6.

Chatrath, R., Shenoy, R., Serratto, M., & Thoele, D. G. (2002). Physical fitness of urban American children. *Pediatric Cardiology, 23,* 608–612.

Chumlea, W. C., Roche, A. F., & Mukherjee, D. (1984). *Nutritional assessment of the elderly through anthropometry.* Columbus, OH: Ross Laboratories.

Cunningham, D. A., Paterson, D. H., & Blimkie, C. J. (1984). The development of the cardiorespiratory system with growth and physical activity. In R. A. Boileau (Ed.), *Advances in pediatric sport sciences.* Champaign, IL: Human Kinetics.

Dennison, B. A., Straus, J. H., Mellits, E. D., & Charney, E. (1988). Childhood physical fitness tests: Predictor of adult physical activity levels? *Pediatrics, 82,* 324–330.

Docherty, D., & Bell, R. D. (1985). The relationship between flexibility and linearity measures in boys and girls 6–15 years of age. *Journal of Human Movement Studies, 11,* 279–288.

Dotson, C. O., & Ross, J. G. (1985). Relationships between activity patterns and fitness. *Journal of Physical Education, Recreation, and Dance, 56,* 86–89.

Dummer, G. M., Clarke, D. H., Vaccaro, P., Vander Velden, L., Goldfarb, A. H., & Sockler, J. M. (1985). Age-related differences in muscular strength and muscular endurance among female masters swimmers. *Research Quarterly for Exercise and Sport, 56,* 97–110.

Ekblom, B. (1969). Effects of physical training in adolescent boys. *Journal of Applied Physiology, 27,* 350–355.

Faigenbaum, A. D., Milliken, L. A., Loud, R. L., Burak, B. T., Doherty, C. L., & Westcott, W. L. (2002). Comparison of 1 and 2 days per week of strength training in children. *Research Quarterly for Exercise and Sport, 73,* 416–424.

Faigenbaum, A. D., Milliken, L. A., & Westcott, W. L. (2003). Maximal strength testing in healthy children. *Journal of Strength and Conditioning Research, 17,* 162–166.

Faigenbaum, A., O'Connell, J., Glover, S., Loud, R. L., & Westcott, W. (2000). Comparison of different resistance training protocols on upper body strength and endurance development in children. *Medicine and Science in Sports and Exercise, 32* (5 Supplement), S278.

Faigenbaum, A., Westcott, W., Micheli, L., Outerbridge, A., Long, C., LaRosa-Loud, R., & Zaichkowsky, L. (1996). The effects of strength training and detraining on children. *Journal of Strength and Conditioning Research, 10,* 109–114.

Faigenbaum, A. D., Zaichkowsky, L. D., Westcott, W. L., Micheli, L. J., & Fehlandt, A. F. (1993). The effects of a twice-a-week strength training program on children. *Pediatric Exercise Science, 5,* 339–346.

Falk, B., & Mor, G. (1996). The effects of resistance and martial arts training in 6–8-year-old boys. *Pediatric Exercise Science, 8,* 48–56.

Falk, B., & Tenenbaum, G. (1996). The effectiveness of resistance training in children: A meta-analysis. *Sports Medicine, 22,* 176–186.

Fiatarone, M. A., Marks, E. C., Ryan, N. D., Meredith, C. N., Lipsitz, L. A., & Evans, W. J. (1990). High intensity strength training in nonagenarians: Effect on skeletal muscle. *Journal of the American Medical Association, 263,* 3029–3034.

Fields, D. A., & Goran, M. I. (2000). Body composition techniques and the four-compartment model in children. *Journal of Applied Physiology, 89,* 613–620.

Fleck, S. J., & Kraemer, W. J. (2004). *Designing resistance training programs.* 3rd ed. Champaign, IL: Human Kinetics.

Flegal, K. M., Carrol, M. D., Ogden, C. L., & Johnson, C. L. (2002). Prevalence and trends in obesity among U.S. adults, 1999–2000. *Journal of the American Medical Association, 288,* 1723–1727.

Foss, M. L., & Keteyian, S. J. (1998). *Fox's physiological basis for exercise and sport.* Boston: WCB/McGraw-Hill.

Friedl, K. E. (1994). Performance-enhancing substances: Effects, risks, and appropriate alternatives. In T. R. Baechle (Ed.), *Essentials of strength training and conditioning.* Champaign, IL: Human Kinetics.

Fujita, K., Nagatomi, R., Hozawa, A., Ohkubo, T., Sato, K., Anzai, Y., Sauvaget, C., Watanabe, Y., Tamagawa, A., & Tsuji, I. (2003). Effects of exercise training on physical activity in older people: A randomized controlled trial. *Journal of Epidemiology, 13,* 120–126.

Germain, N. W., & Blair, S. N. (1983). Variability of shoulder flexion with age, activity and sex. *American Corrective Therapy Journal, 37,* 156–160.

Guo, S., Roche, A. F., Chumlea, W. C., Gardner, J. D., & Siervogel, R. M. (1994). The predictive value of childhood body mass index values for overweight at age 35y. *American Journal of Clinical Nutrition, 59,* 810–819.

Hakkinen, K., Mero, A., & Kavhanen, H. (1989). Specificity of endurance, sprint, and strength training on physical performance capacity in young athletes. *Journal of Sports Medicine and Physical Fitness, 29,* 27–35.

Hyllegard, R., Mood, D. P., & Morrow, J. R. (1996). *Interpreting research in sport and exercise science.* St. Louis, MO: Mosby.

Isaacs, L. D. (1989). The role of an active lifestyle in maintaining movement proficiency. *Journal Times, California Association for Health, Physical Education, Recreation, and Dance, 51,* 7–8.

Isaacs, L. D., & Pohlman, R. L. (2000). Effectiveness of the stretch-shortening cycle in children's vertical jump performance. *Medicine and Science in Sports and Exercise, 32* (5 Supplement), S278.

Isaacs, L. D., Pohlman, R., & Craig, B. (1994). Effects of resistance training on strength development in prepubescent females. *Medicine and Science in Sports and Exercise, 26* (5 Supplement).

Jaffe, M., & Kosakov, C. (1982). The motor development of fat babies. *Clinical Pediatrics, 21,* 619–621.

Janz, K. F., Dawson, J. D., & Mahoney, L. T. (2000). Tracking physical fitness and physical activity from childhood to adolescence: The Muscatine study. *Medicine and Science in Sports and Exercise, 32,* 1250–1257.

Joyner, M. J. (2000). Over-the-counter supplements and strength training. *Exercise and Sport Science Reviews, 28*(1), 2–3.

Judge, J., King, M., Whipple, R., Clive, J., & Wolfson, L. (1995). Dynamic balance in older persons: Effects of reduced visual and proprioceptive input. *Journals of Gerontology, 50A,* M263–M270.

Kasch, F. W., Boyer, J. L., Van Camp, S. P., Verity, L. S., & Wallace, J. P. (1990). The effects of physical activity and inactivity on aerobic power in older men: A longitudinal study. *Physician and Sportsmedicine, 18,* 73–83.

Kemper, H. C., de Vente, W., van Mechelen, W., & Twisk, J. W. (2001). Adolescent motor skill and performance: Is physical activity in adolescence related to adult physical fitness? *American Journal of Human Biology, 13,* 180–198.

Keogh, J., & Sugden, D. (1985). *Movement skill development.* New York: Macmillan.

Krahenbuhl, G. S., Skinner, J. S., & Kohrt, W. M. (1985). Developmental aspects of maximal aerobic power in children. *Exercise and Sport Science Review, 13,* 503–538.

Kuczmarski, M. F., Kuczmarski, R. J., & Najjar, M. (2000). Descriptive anthropometric reference data for older Americans. *Journal of the American Dietetic Association, 100,* 59–66.

Lakatta, E. G. (1990). Changes in cardiovascular function with aging. *European Heart Journal, 11,* 22–29.

Lemmer, J. T., Hurlbut, D. E., Martel, G. F., Tracy, B. L., Ivey, F. M., Metter, E. J., Fozard, J. L., Fleg, J. L., & Hurley, B. F. (2000). Age and gender responses to strength training and detraining. *Medicine and Science in Sports and Exercise, 32,* 1505–1512.

Malina, R. M., & Bouchard, C. (1991). *Growth, maturation, and physical activity.* Champaign, IL: Human Kinetics.

Mandigout, S., Melin, A., Lecoq, A. M., Courteix, D., & Obert, P. (2002). Effect of two aerobic training regimens on the cardiorespiratory response of prepubertal boys and girls. *Acta Paediatric, 91,* 403–408.

Marti, B., & Howald, H. (1990). Long-term effects of physical training on aerobic capacity: Controlled study of former elite athletes. *Journal of Applied Physiology, 69,* 1451–1459.

McArdle, W. D., Katch, F. I., & Katch, V. L. (2000). *Essentials of exercise physiology.* 2nd ed. Philadelphia: Lippincott Williams & Wilkins.

———. (2001). *Exercise physiology.* 5th ed. Philadelphia: Lippincott Williams & Wilkins.

Metheny, E. (1941). The present status of strength testing for children of elementary school and preschool age. *Research Quarterly, 12,* 115–130.

Micheli, L. J. (1988). Strength training in the young athlete. In E. W. Brown & C. F. Branta (Eds.), *Competitive sports for children and youth.* Champaign, IL: Human Kinetics.

Moore, K. L. & Persaud, T. V. N. (2003). *Before we are born: Essentials of embryology and birth defects.* 6th ed. Philadelphia: Saunders.

Mrzena, B., & Macek, M. (1978). Use of treadmill and working capacity assessment of preschool children. In J. Borms & M. Hebbelinck (Eds.), *Pediatric work physiology.* New York: Karger.

Munnings, F. (1993). Strength training: Not only for the young. *Physician and Sportsmedicine, 21,* 133–140.

Munns, K. (1981). Effects of exercise on the range of joint motion in elderly subjects. In E. Smith & R. Serfass (Eds.), *Exercise and aging.* Hillside, NJ: Enslow.

National Heart, Lung, and Blood Institute. (2002). *The practical guide: Identification, evaluation, and treatment of overweight and obesity in adults.* Bethesda, MD: NIH publication no. 00-4084. Also at www.nhlbi.nih.gov.

National Strength and Conditioning Association (NSCA). (1996). Youth resistance training: Position statement paper and literature review. *Strength and Conditioning, 18,* 62–75.

Newman, S. L. (1985). Clinical assessment of adipose tissue in youth. In A. Roche (Ed.), *Body-composition assessments in youth and adults.* Columbus, OH: Ross Laboratories.

Nielsen, B., Nielsen, K., Behrendt-Hansen, M., & Asmussen, A. (1980). Training of functional muscular strength in girls 7–19 years old. In K. Berg & B. O. Eriksson (Eds.), *Children and exercise IX.* Champaign, IL: Human Kinetics.

O'Neil, M. S. (1993). Body image distortion, athletic participation and steroid use by high school students in southwestern Ontario. Unpublished master's thesis, University of Windsor, Canada.

Ozmun, J. C., Mikesky, A. E., & Surburg, P. R. (1994). Neuromuscular adaptions following prepubescent strength training. *Medicine and Science in Sports and Exercise, 26,* 510–514.

Parsons, D., Foster, V., Harman, F., Dickinson, A., Oliva, P., & Westerlind, K. (1992). Balance and strength changes in elderly subjects after heavy-resistance strength training. *Medicine and Science in Sports and Exercise, 24* (5 Supplement), S21.

Pate, R. R., Burgess, M. L., Woods, J. A., Ross, J. G., & Baumgartner, T. (1993). Validity of field tests of upper body muscular strength. *Research Quarterly for Exercise and Sport, 64,* 17–24.

Pate, R. R., & Ross, J. G. (1987). Factors associated with health-related fitness. *Journal of Physical Education, Recreation, and Dance, 58,* 93–95.

Pate, R. R., Ross, J. G., Baumgartner, T. A., & Sparks, R. E. (1987). The modified pull-up test. *Journal of Physical Education, Recreation, and Dance, 58,* 71–73.

Pate, R. R., & Shephard, R. J. (1989). Characteristics of physical fitness in youth. In C. V. Gisolfi & D. R. Lamb (Eds.), *Perspectives in exercise science and sport medicine: Youth, exercise and sport.* Indianapolis, IN: Benchmark.

Payne, V. G., & Morrow, J. R. (1993). Exercise and VO₂ max in children: A meta-analysis. *Research Quarterly for Exercise and Sport, 64,* 305–313.

Payne, V. G., Morrow, J. R., Johnson, L., & Dalton, S. N. (1997). Resistance training in children and youth: A meta-analysis. *Research Quarterly for Exercise and Sport, 88,* 80–88.

Pissanos, B. W., Moore, J. B., & Reeve, T. G. (1983). Age, sex, and body composition as predictors of children's performance on basic motor abilities and health-related fitness items. *Perceptual and Motor Skills, 56,* 71–77.

Pollock, M. L. (1974). Physiological characteristics of older champion track athletes. *Research Quarterly, 45,* 363–373.

Pollock, M. L., Dawson, G. A., Miller, H. S., Ward, A., Cooper, D., Headley, W., Linnerud, A. C., & Nomier, M. (1976). Physiologic responses of men 49 to 65 years of age to endurance training. *Journal of the American Geriatrics Society, 24,* 97–104.

Powers, S. K., & Howley, E. T. (2001). *Exercise physiology: Theory and application to fitness and performance.* 4th ed. Boston: McGraw-Hill.

Rogers, M. C., & Evans, W. J. (1993). Changes in skeletal muscle with aging: Effects of exercise training. In J. O. Holloszy (Ed.), *Exercise and sport sciences reviews.* Vol. 21. Baltimore: Williams & Wilkins.

Ross, J. G., & Gilbert, G. G. (1985). The national children and youth fitness study: A summary of findings. *Journal of Physical Education, Recreation, and Dance, 56,* 45–50.

Ross, J. G., & Pate, R. R. (1987). The national children and youth fitness study II: A summary of findings. *Journal of Physical Education, Recreation, and Dance, 58,* 51–56.

Rowland, T. W. (1985). Aerobic response to endurance training in prepubescent children: A critical analysis. *Medicine and Science in Sports and Exercise, 17,* 493–497.

———. (1996). *Developmental exercise physiology.* Champaign, IL: Human Kinetics.

Rutenfranz, J., Anderson, K. L., Seliger, V., Klimmer, F., Berndt, I., & Ruppel, M. (1981). Maximum aerobic power and body composition during the puberty growth period: Similarities and differences between children of two European countries. *European Journal of Pediatrics, 136,* 123–133.

Sale, D. G. (1988). Neural adaptation to resistance training. *Medicine and Science in Sports and Exercise, 20,* S135–S145.

———. (1989). Strength training in children. In C. V. Gisolfi & D. R. Lamb (Eds.), *Perspectives in exercise science and sport medicine: Youth, exercise, and sport.* Indianapolis, IN: Benchmark.

Servidio, F. J., Bartels, R. L., & Hamlin, R. L. (1985). The effects of weight training using Olympic style lifts on various physiological variables in pre-pubescent boys. *Medicine and Science in Sports and Exercise, 17,* 288.

Sewall, L., & Micheli, L. J. (1986). Strength training for children. *Journal of Pediatric Orthopedics, 6,* 143–146.

Shephard, R. J. (1978). *Human physiological work capacity.* London: Cambridge University Press.

———. (1981). Cardiovascular limitations in the aged. In E. L. Smith & R. C. Serfass (Eds.), *Exercise and aging.* Hillside, NJ: Enslow.

———. (1994). *Aerobic fitness and health.* Champaign, IL: Human Kinetics.

Shirley, M. (1931). *The first two years: A study of twenty-five babies.* Minneapolis: University of Minnesota Press.

Sinclair, D. (1998). *Human growth after birth.* 6th ed. Oxford, GB: Oxford University Press.

Slaughter, M. H., Lohman, T. G., & Misner, J. E. (1977). Relationship of somatotype and body composition to physical performance in 7- to 12-year-old boys. *Research Quarterly, 48,* 159–167.

Spirduso, W. W. (1995). *Physical dimensions of aging.* Champaign, IL: Human Kinetics.

Stahle, S., Roberts, S., Davis, B., & Rybicki, L. (1995). Effect of 2 versus 3 times per week weight training programs in boys 7 to 16. *Medicine and Science in Sports and Exercise, 27,* S114.

Stewart, K. J., & Gutin, B. (1976). Effects of physical training on cardiorespiratory fitness in children. *Research Quarterly, 47,* 110–120.

Stones, M. J., & Kozma, A. (1985). Physical performance. In N. Charness (Ed.), *Aging and human performance.* New York: Wiley.

Superintendent of Documents. (1996). *Surgeon general's report on physical activity and health.* Washington, DC: U.S. Department of Health and Human Services.

Tanaka, H., Monahan, K. D., & Seals, D. R. (2001). Age-predicted maximal heart rate revisited. *Journal of the American College of Cardiology, 37,* 153–156.

Tanner, S. M. (1993). Weighing the risks: Strength training for children and adolescents. *Physician and Sports-medicine, 21,* 105–116.

Thomas, J. R., Nelson, J. K., & Church, G. (1991). A developmental analysis of gender differences in health related physical fitness. *Pediatric Exercise Science, 3,* 28–42.

U.S. Department of Health and Human Services. (1990). *Healthy people 2000: National health promotion and disease prevention objectives.* Pub. No. (PHS) 90-50212. Washington, DC: U.S. Department of Health and Human Services.

———. (2000). *Healthy people 2010: Leading health indicators.* Retrieved August 15, 2003, from www.health.gov/healthypeople.

———. (2001). *The Surgeon General's call to action to prevent and decrease overweight and obesity.* Rockville, MD: U.S. Department of Health and Human Services.

———. (2002, June). *Physical activity fundamental to preventing disease.* Washington, DC: U.S. Department of Health and Human Services.

U.S. National Senior Sports Association. (2003). *U.S. National Senior Sports Association: The Senior Olympics—2003.* Baton Rouge, LA: Author. Retrieved July 1, 2003, from www.nsga.com.

Vincent, K. R., Braith, R. W., Feldman, R. A., Magyari, P. M., Cutler, R. B., Persin, S. A., Lennon, S. L., Gabr, A. H., & Lowenthal, D. T. (2002). Resistance exercise and physical performance in adults aged 60 to 83. *Journal of the American Geriatric Society, 50,* 1100–1107.

Vrijens, J. (1978). Muscle strength development in pre- and postpubescent age. In J. Borms & M. Hebbelinck (Eds.), *Pediatric work physiology.* New York: Karger.

Watson, A. W. (1988). Quantification of the influence of the body fat content on selected physical performance variables in adolescent boys. *Ireland Journal of Medical Science, 157,* 383–384.

Weisfeldt, M. L., Gerstenblith, G., & Lakatta, E. G. (1985). Alterations in circulatory function. In E. L. Bierman & W. R. Hazaard (Eds.), *Principles of geriatric medicine.* New York: McGraw-Hill.

Weltman, A., Janney, C., Rians, C. B., Strand, K., Berg, B., Tippett, S., Wise, J., Cahill, B. R., & Katch, F. I. (1986). The effects of hydraulic resistance strength training in prepubescent males. *Medicine and Science in Sports and Exercise, 18,* 629–638.

Whitbourne, S. K. (1996). *The aging individual: Physical and psychological perspectives.* New York: Springer.

Williams, D. (1991). The effect of weight training on performance in selected motor activities for preadolescent males. *Journal of Applied Sport Science Research, 5,* 170

Wolfson, L., Judge, J., Whipple, R., & King, M. (1995). Strength is a major factor in balance, gait, and the occurrence of falls. *Journal of Gerontology, 50A,* 64–67.

9 Movement and the Changing Senses

We all embody many complicated communication channels that allow us to respond to the multitude of stimuli we encounter, primarily during our waking hours. This communicative link between the human organism and the environment is in part made possible by a group of senses: vision, proprioception, touch, taste, smell, and hearing. Information we receive from these senses enables us to describe our environment.

Without doubt, we rely on vision more than on any other sense to describe our environment and to react to environmental stimuli. In fact, most movement tasks are initiated as a result of receiving visual information. Vision provides the needed information for us to adjust our bodies to intercept moving objects. Furthermore, we rely on vision not only to emulate the movements of others but also to find our way around our visually oriented world.

Even though vision is the sensory modality of choice, nonvisual sensory modalities are also known to influence motor development and motor performance. Therefore, this chapter will end with a brief discussion of the nonvisual sensory modalities and the role they play in both directly and indirectly influencing both motor development and motor performance.

UNDERSTANDING THE MECHANICS OF VISION

The photographic camera and the human eye share many common structural features. For a sharp photograph to be obtained, the lens of the camera must be focused so that light rays converge on its light-sensitive material, the photographic film. Similarly, for a clear visual image, light entering the eye must converge on the eye's light-sensitive tissue, the *retina.*

The retina is composed of two types of photoreceptors: *rods,* which make colorless night vision possible, and *cones,* which make color vision and acuity possible. Cones are predominantly concentrated in a region of the retina known as the *macula;* the rod cells are located in the periphery and thus make peripheral vision possible.

Exactly how does light enter the eye and get focused on the retina? Again, the similarities between a camera and the human eye can illustrate this point. At one time or another you took a photograph that came out blurred, perhaps because light entering the camera did not properly converge onto the camera's film, causing the image to be out of focus. You should have changed the refractory power of the camera's lens by rotating it either clockwise or counterclockwise. Similarly, the ocular refractory power of the human eye can be adjusted by changing the shape of the eye's lens. The lens of the human eye changes shape whenever the *ciliary muscle* is contracted. This process that enables a clear retinal image to be maintained in the presence of varying light conditions is called *accommodation.* Sharp vision is possible whenever light properly converges on the macula. Figure 9-1 illustrates the major structures of the human eye.

PHYSICAL DEVELOPMENT OF THE EYE

The eye develops as an outgrowth of the forebrain and is an inseparable component of the central nervous system. Of the 12 cranial nerves, 6 play a role in vision. The eye, like the brain, achieves most of its growth prior to birth. For instance, at birth the anteroposterior diameter of the eye is 17 millimeters; 3 years later it measures about 22.5 millimeters—just 1.5 millimeters short of adult size. Because the eye is shorter at birth than it will be at maturity, the infant's eye is *hyperopic;* that is, light entering the eye focuses behind the retina. Nevertheless, sharp vision is possible because of accommodation.

The eye's cornea also increases its diameter 2 millimeters during the first year of life and at adulthood is 12 millimeters. Thereafter, the cornea does not grow but does change its curvature to become less spherical.

The retina is also fairly well developed at birth, even though it is thicker than an adult retina and contains mostly rod cells. During the first postnatal month, as the retina thins and cone cells begin to squeeze between the rod cells, the macula becomes

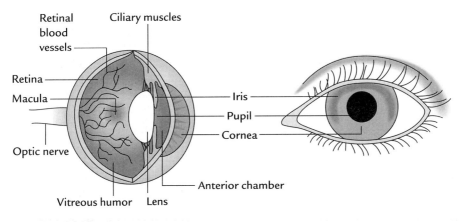

Figure 9-1   Diagram of the human eye

more differentiated. By 8 months of age, the macula is histologically mature.

The muscles that control eye movements and the dilator muscles of the pupil are perhaps the slowest structures to develop. Ciliary muscle cells are first present in the eye at about the fifth prenatal month. Thus, except for the macular and dilator muscles of the pupil, by the end of the sixth prenatal month, all eye parts are present and presumably able to function (Smith, Gallie, & Morin, 1983).

DEVELOPMENT OF SELECTED VISUAL TRAITS AND SKILLED MOTOR PERFORMANCE

Despite the relatively advanced size of the eye in utero, the eye is still immature at birth, because optimal vision requires good central and peripheral function of the retina, the ability to gauge depth, and the ability to track moving objects. Here, we describe postnatal changes within these selected visual attributes, paying special attention to the influence of these changes on skilled motor performance.

Visual Acuity

Visual acuity is the degree of detail that can be seen in an object. The fine details of objects are blurred for a person with poor visual acuity.

To better appreciate changes in visual acuity across the lifespan, we must first describe how this measure of visual sharpness is determined. With the most common technique, a person resolves the smallest letters possible on the *Snellen eye chart* (see Figures 9-2 and 9-3). Visual acuity determined by the Snellen eye chart is called *static visual acuity* because both the target and the performer are stationary. Normal distance visual acuity is expressed in fractional notation. Thus, a person with 20/20 vision can clearly see an object placed 20 feet away in the same manner that other people with normal vision can see objects placed 20 feet away. An example of less-than-normal static acuity is a person with 20/100 vision: this person can clearly see objects placed 20 feet away, whereas people with normal vision can see the same objects 100 feet away. Use of the Snellen eye chart is not recommended before 3 years of age.

Developmentally, improvement in static visual acuity occurs during the first 4 to 5 years of life. However, there is much variability in reported acuity measures both within and across different ages. For instance, at birth, visual acuity has been estimated as between 20/200 and 20/400 (Haith, 1990). By 6 months, visual acuity has improved to 20/200; by 12 months, to 20/50. Normal static distance acuity (20/20) is generally attained sometime during the fourth or fifth year (Rosenblith, 1992). At first glance, it may appear that the infant has very low quality

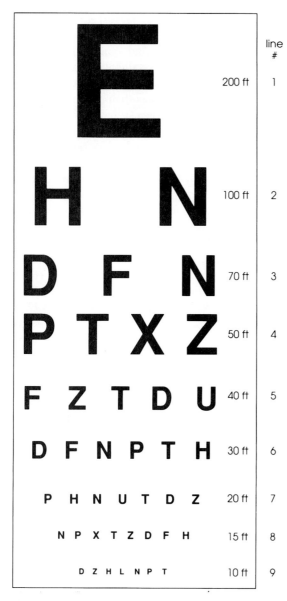

Figure 9-2 This Snellen eye chart is used to determine static visual acuity for individuals who are old enough to recognize letters.

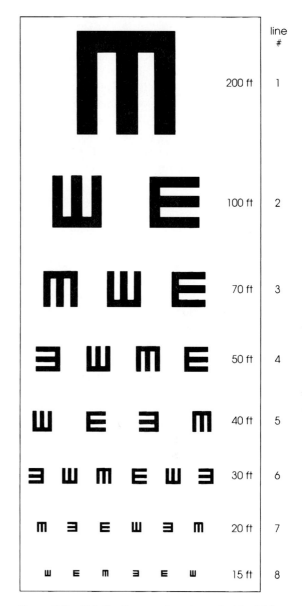

Figure 9-3 This Snellen eye chart is used with children in grades K–1 who may not be capable of letter recognition. The child must point in the direction that the "E" symbol faces or state that the symbol faces up, down, right, or left.

functional vision. In reality, however, infants are capable of handling most of the static visual tasks they confront. For example, the acuity level of a 1-month-old infant is adequate for resolving facial expressions when the baby is held close to a person. Similarly, the acuity level of a 6-month-old infant is adequate for stimulating the visual curiosity that is needed to elicit reaching for small objects as grasping skills begin to develop. In other words, static acuity is adequate for the major visual tasks that an infant confronts.

A second type of visual acuity is called **dynamic visual acuity,** which is the ability to see the detail in moving objects. Dynamic visual acuity reflects the ability of the central nervous system to estimate an object's direction and velocity and the ability of the ocular-motor system "to catch" and "to hold" an object's image on the eye's fovea (center posterior part of the retina) long enough to permit resolution of the object's detail.

According to Morris (1977), dynamic visual acuity improves between 6 and 20 years of age. Therefore, static visual acuity matures before dynamic visual acuity. The most significant changes in dynamic visual acuity occur between 5 and 7 years, 9 and 10 years, and 11 and 12 years (Williams, 1983). Decreases in this visual attribute start at about 25 years. In general, dynamic visual efficiency decreases as the object of interest increases in speed (Morris, 1980).

VISUAL ACUITY AND MOTOR PERFORMANCE Both static and dynamic visual acuity correlate with specific motor performance tasks. Thus this visual attribute may play a key role in motor task performance. For example, correlations as high as 0.76 have been found between measures of dynamic visual acuity and basketball field-goal shooting percentage during a competitive season (Beals et al., 1971). Similar results were reported by Morris and Kreighbaum (1977), who found that high-percentage basketball field-goal shooters showed less variability in selected dynamic visual acuity scores than did a group of low-percentage field-goal shooters. Results from these two investigations suggest that shooting from the field in basketball may highly depend on dynamic visual acuity. Studies by Sanderson and

Whiting (1974, 1978) also suggest a possible relationship between dynamic visual acuity and task performance. Sanderson and Whiting found a significant relationship between dynamic visual acuity and performance on a ball-catching task. This explains why people with less-than-desirable degrees of dynamic visual acuity may have to use special equipment when playing ball-skill activities. For instance, fleece balls and whiffle balls travel through space more slowly than do baseballs, thus giving participants more time to process visual information.

VISUAL ACUITY AND EXERCISE Exercise generally influences visual acuity. Russian physiologists have reported as much as 45 percent visual acuity improvement in 73 percent of the participants, following a 1000-meter race (Graybiel, Jokl, & Trapp, 1955). Vlahov also noted improved visual acuity following both bicycle ergometer exercise bouts (1977b) and participation in the Harvard Step Test (1977a). Even participation in table tennis for 10 minutes can temporarily improve visual acuity (Whiting & Sanderson, 1972). Improvements in acuity have lasted as long as 2 hours after the exercise ended (Graybiel et al., 1955). This increase in acuity is probably caused by the increased blood flow in and subsequent oxygenation of the eye.

EFFECTS OF AGING ON VISUAL ACUITY Age-related eye diseases (AREDs) are a leading cause of loss of visual acuity and, if left untreated, can sometimes lead to blindness. In fact, approximately 47,000 Americans become blind each year. The four major AREDs are age-related macular degeneration, glaucoma, cataracts, and diabetic retinopathy. Let's examine each.

Age-related macular degeneration (AMD) is one of the most prevalent causes of loss of visual acuity in the elderly. This serious condition, which affects as many as 30 percent of individuals over age 75 (Wu, 1995), is the result of many anatomical changes that occur in the retina with age. AMD can take one of two forms, dry AMD or wet AMD (National Eye Institute, 2000). Dry AMD is the most prevalent, affecting approximately 90 percent of all AMD cases. This form of AMD is the result of a breakdown of the light-sensitive cells in the macula.

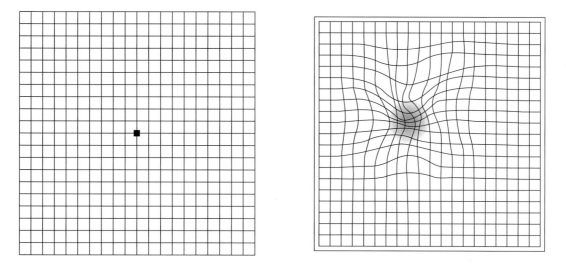

Figure 9-4   On the left is an Amsler grid; on the right is how it might look to someone with AMD.
SOURCE: National Eye Institute (2000).

Because the breakdown occurs in the macula, this disease affects central vision. Therefore, although the elderly with dry AMD are not capable of driving and may find reading difficult, they are still capable of general mobility. While dry AMD cannot be medically treated, it progresses so slowly that most affected people will not lose total central vision. The most devastating form of AMD is wet AMD. With wet AMD, new blood vessels grow behind the retina, and these new vessels tend to be very fragile and oftentimes will leak. This leakage causes a rapid deterioration of the macula. While only 10 percent of AMD cases are of this form, it is responsible for 90 percent of all AMD blindness.

Visual acuity in people affected with AMD ranges anywhere from 20/50 to 20/100 to total central vision blindness. Several tests are available to detect AMD. First, the eye-care professional administers a test of visual acuity with the pupils chemically dilated. Pupil dilation allows for a closer visual inspection of the retina. One of the earliest signs of AMD is the presence of **drusen,** small yellow deposits in the retina. The patient may also be asked to take an **Amsler grid** examination (see Figure 9-4), a test associated with wet AMD. If wet AMD is suspected, a fluorescein angiography will be performed. Here a special dye is injected into an arm

vein, and pictures of the inner eye are taken in an attempt to look for retinal blood vessel leakage. Laser surgery is frequently performed in an attempt to stop or reduce this leakage.

Glaucoma, a leading cause of loss in visual acuity and blindness, affects approximately 2 million Americans (Garnett, 1999). In the healthy eye, fluid constantly circulates in and out of the eye's anterior chamber. For some unknown reason, this chamber sometimes becomes plugged, so that the fluid can no longer freely circulate and causes pressure to rise within the eye. This eye disease is first manifested by a loss in peripheral vision; if left untreated, it can rapidly progress to where central visual acuity is affected and the optic nerve is damaged.

Cataracts are the most common cause of loss in visual acuity, which results from the clouding of the eye's lens. Like glaucoma, cataracts generally cause no pain or initial symptoms. However, as the condition progresses, frequent complaints include glare, faded colors, and an increased need for additional light when reading. Alcohol use, smoking, and long-term exposure to the sun's ultraviolet rays are believed to increase the risk for developing cataracts. Accordingly, the American Academy of Ophthalmology (2000) recommends the use of sunglasses that block at least 99 percent of ultraviolet radiation.

Cataracts are not to be confused with senile miosis, which also limits the amount of light that enters the eye. With **senile miosis,** the restriction of light is caused by a decrease in the pupil's resting diameter. Typically, there is a linear decline in the amount of light reaching the retina between 30 and 60 years of age. In fact, the amount of light that reaches the retina at age 60 is only one-third the amount that reached the retina at age 20 (Weale, 1963).

Diabetic retinopathy is a complication of diabetes. Diabetes is known to cause abnormal changes in all of the body's blood vessels, including those in the retina. As with AMD, this disease can cause the vessels of the retina to hemorrhage. This hemorrhage in turn discolors the eye's normally clear interior gel (vitreous humor). To complicate matters further, these blood vessels tend to contract as they heal and oftentimes will detach the retina (Garnett, 1999). For these reasons, it is critical that diabetics control their blood sugar in order to slow the onset and progression of diabetic retinopathy. Figure 9-5 shows, through simulated photos, how individuals with age-related eye diseases may see the same subject.

By approximately 40 years of age, we begin to lose the ability to accommodate near objects. For instance, print can be brought into focus from 10 centimeters at age 20, 18 centimeters at age 40, 50 centimeters at age 50, and 100 centimeters at age 70 (Shephard, 1978). Not specially classified as an ARED, this inability to focus clearly on near objects is clinically known as **presbyopia.** Because presbyopia does not affect distance vision, some of its symptoms can be overcome with bifocal lenses. These special lenses contain the person's normal prescription in the top half of the eyeglasses; the bottom half has a different prescription that allows for more normal near vision.

Binocular Vision and Depth Perception

As mentioned, the ocular muscles that control eye movements are not fully developed at birth. As a result, the newborn frequently moves each eye at random; the newborn has **strabismus,** misaligned eyes. Strabismus is common at birth but should not persist beyond the first year. Usually, the degree of strabismus greatly diminishes during the first week of life, and by the end of the third month, most normal infants move both eyes in a coordinated manner. Approximately 2–5 percent of preschool children exhibit strabismus (Catalano & Nelson, 1994).

Coordinated eye movements are important because they are the basis of **binocular vision,** which occurs when both eyes move in unison so that each eye focuses the desired image on its macula. Because each eye views the object from a different angle, there is a slight disparity between the two macular images. The human brain is capable of fusing and comparing this disparity and using this information as a primary cue for judging depth. Thus, although binocular vision is contingent on a properly functioning visual system, depth perception is a cerebral function.

Gibson and Walk's (1960) classic **visual cliff** study (see Figure 9-6) was one of the first to demonstrate that infants are capable of organizing depth clues during the first year of life. The researchers constructed a platform that was raised several feet off the ground. They laid plastic glass across a checkerboard pattern; on one side the pattern was directly under the glass, and on the other side the pattern was on the floor, thus creating a visual drop-off or cliff. Infants 6 to 14 months old were placed in the middle of the platform. When mothers called their infants from the side of the visual cliff, nearly all the babies backed off and cried, refusing to cross the apparent cliff. However, when mothers coaxed their infants from the other side, all ventured over the apparent shallow area. This finding implied that infants could detect the differences in depth between the two sides.

One question that has interested researchers for many years is whether depth perception is innate or develops with time. There are arguments for both positions, but mounting evidence indicates that some form of depth recognition is possible early in life. Nevertheless, even though depth perception begins to develop early in life, it is slow to mature, as evidenced by toddlers frequently bumping into things that they apparently see. In any case, depth perception is usually mature by 6 years of age.

Figure 9-5 Simulated photos of a single subject as it might be seen by people with various age-related eye diseases.

SOURCE: Garnett (1999). Courtesy of the National Eye Institute (2001).

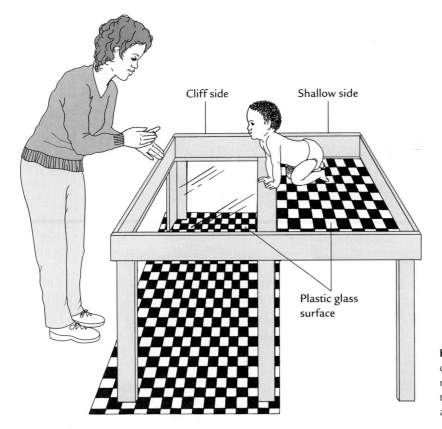

Cliff side   Shallow side

Plastic glass
surface

Figure 9-6 An illustration
of the visual cliff. Note the
mother attempting to coax
the infant into crossing the
apparent deep (cliff) side.

The accurate judgment of depth is an important visual attribute for skilled motor performance. Nevertheless, the research literature presents conflicting viewpoints regarding the relationship between depth perception and sporting success. Attempts at correlating measures of depth perception with basketball shooting both from the field (Beals et al., 1971; Shick, 1971) and from the free throw line failed to produce high-positive correlations. Conversely, earlier studies reported that 30 tennis players perceived depth better than did 122 football players and that the more skillful athlete perceived depth better than the average athlete (Graybiel et al., 1955). One might speculate on the basis of these findings that accurate depth perception is task specific. In addition, most likely the central nervous system uses secondary cues (shadows, ball texture, projectile size) to perceive depth, which explains how some athletes maintain a high level of performance without the aid of stereo vision.

Field of Vision

According to Sage, "field of vision refers to the entire extent of the environment that can be seen without a change in fixation of the eye" (1984, p. 133). Two frequently studied aspects of field of vision are lateral and vertical **peripheral vision.** Normal adult lateral peripheral vision is usually just over 90 degrees from straight ahead, resulting in a visual field slightly over 180 degrees. In contrast, normal adult vertical peripheral vision is approximately 47 degrees above the visual midlines and approximately 65 degrees below the visual midline (Sage, 1984). Consequently, adults are capable of detecting movements that significantly deviate from central vision.

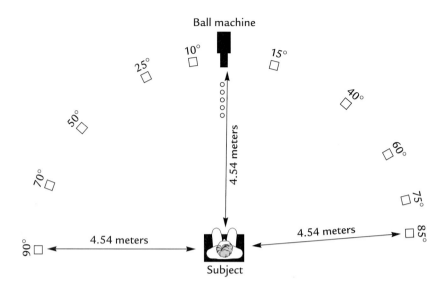

Figure 9-7 Davids's 1987 experiment examining peripheral vision processing during the performance of a catching task

In comparison, the infant's field of vision is extremely limited. For example, when fixating on a light located in their central field of vision, infants younger than 2 months will not refixate on a second light introduced until it is within 15 degrees laterally. When the second light is allowed to blink, the neonate's lateral peripheral vision enlarges to 25 degrees, and at 7 weeks of age to 35 degrees (Macfarlane, Harris, & Barnes, 1976).

Davids (1987) has expressed concern that reported functional peripheral vision values have predominantly been collected in laboratory situations and as a result lack ecological validity. He believes it is important to measure the development of peripheral vision in more ecologically valid settings because such measurement may influence our expectations of children's performance in ball games in which peripheral vision is used. According to Davids, the problem with laboratory assessments is their failure to include an appropriate central task during the peripheral vision assessment. Indeed, earlier work has noted that the presence of a central task can significantly affect peripheral vision performance (Ikeda & Takevchi, 1975).

Davids (1987) examined peripheral vision processing capabilities in both children and adults (age groups: 9-, 12-, 15-year-olds and adults). The uniqueness of his study was that peripheral vision processing was assessed not only by itself (single task similar to most laboratory tasks) but also in ecologically valid settings where subjects were presented peripheral information during the performance of a ball-catching task (dual-task performance; see Figure 9-7). An analysis of the data revealed that 9-year-old subjects made significantly more catching errors during the dual task than did subjects in the other three age groups. This finding is particularly interesting when one considers that, during the single-task performance, there was no difference in peripheral visual sensitivity between the 9-year-olds and the adults.

Davids's findings suggest that earlier laboratory estimates regarding the size of the functional visual field have been overestimated in children. Only the adult subjects (over 18 years) were capable of effectively coping with the dual processing demands presented in this study. It therefore appears that the size of the functional peripheral visual field is reduced when the child performer is confronted with a real-world central task such as catching a ball. According to Davids (1987):

The implications for teachers and coaches of ball games are that due consideration must be given to the central task when instructing young athletes to respond to peripheral visual cues such as gaps in the field, positioning of players, and location of boundaries and targets. (p. 283)

The role of peripheral vision in monitoring limb movements in infancy and childhood is not clear. However, a group of studies that Graybiel and associates (1955) reported illustrate the importance of peripheral vision to skilled motor performance in an adult population. Central and peripheral vision were systematically occluded during performance in various track and field events and in gymnastics and skiing events. In all cases, the championship athletes reported that the elimination of peripheral vision affected their performance more than did the exclusion of central vision. Common complaints included a loss of precision and timing, difficulty in judging distances, and clumsiness of movements. It appears that when carrying out skills at high speeds, performers have to rely on peripheral vision for essential spatial orientation cues.

Obviously, performers in some sport activities rely on peripheral vision to deceive opponents. Without doubt, basketball is one activity in which an increased field of vision is an asset. Most people would agree that a ball handler must utilize peripheral vision to avoid the mistake of "telegraphing" the pass. This assumption is supported by the work of Hobson and Henderson (1941), who found that a group of proficient basketball passers had a lateral visual perception 15 degrees greater than that of other ball players. Furthermore, the team's two best shooters had a vertical visual field that was 10 degrees greater than normal.

Effects of Aging on Depth Perception and Field of Vision

Many of the changes associated with AMD also affect the size of a person's field of vision. Retinal cells lost are lost not only in the area of the macula but also in the retina's periphery. Burg (1968) found that a person's lateral field of vision is at its greatest at about age 35; thereafter, the size of the functional field of vision gradually decreases until about age 60, whereupon changes occur more rapidly (Wolf & Nadroski, 1971). Anatomical and physiolog-ical changes within the visual system itself are not the only causes of decreased field of vision. Changes in facial structure can also reduce the size of the visual field. For instance, with age the upper eyelid may droop, a clinical condition known as **senile ptosis.** This condition can significantly limit vertical peripheral vision. Furthermore, loss of fat tissue around the orbital sockets can make the eyeball sink, restricting vision in all directions (Shephard, 1978).

Eye Dominance

It is well known that humans show a dominance for handedness, and within the last decade much has been written about right versus left hemispherical brain dominance. A lesser-known fact regarding human makeup is *eye dominance,* which refers to the ability of one eye to lead the other in tasks involving visual tracking and visual fixation.

The development of eye dominance is believed to be established early in life. About 75 percent of children will develop a dominant eye by 3 years of age, and by 5 years the percentage of children who have developed a dominant eye increases to about 95 percent (cited in Whiting, 1971).

The most frequently used test to determine eye dominance is the "hole-in-card" test. To administer this test, one simply cuts a $\frac{1}{4}$-inch (diameter) hole in the middle of a sheet of cardboard measuring 11 inches square. Standing 7 feet from a blackboard, the individual is to hold the cardboard at arm's length and, while keeping both eyes open, to look through the hole and locate a $\frac{1}{2}$-inch (diameter) dot that is drawn on the blackboard. The individual then closes one eye. If the dot remains in view, then the open eye is the dominant eye. If the dot disappears, then the eye that was closed is the dominant eye.

Most studies examining the association between eye dominance and motor performance have included handedness as an additional variable. Individuals who are right-eyed and right-handed or left-eyed and left-handed are said to possess *unilateral dominance,* which means their dominant eye is on the same side of the body as their dominant hand. In contrast, *crossed-laterals* are either right-eyed and left-handed or left-eyed and right-handed.

A majority of the studies investigating this topic have found unilaterals to be superior to crossed-laterals in a variety of tasks (Christina et al., 1981; Payne, 1988). Nevertheless, a great deal of speculation exists among baseball coaches, suggesting that the crossed-lateral performer may have a distinct advantage in such tasks as batting. It is believed, among baseball coaches, that this purported advantage is due to the fact that the dominant eye of the crossed-lateral hitter is closer to the pitcher. Moreover, this leading eye is not restricted by having to look across the bridge of the batter's nose. Indeed, it appears that crossed-lateral dominance is a trait that is represented to a greater degree among baseball players than in the general population. Teig, an optometrist, found more than half of the 250 major league baseball players he examined to exhibit crossed-lateral dominance. By contrast, only 20 percent of the general population exhibit this trait (cited in Oxendine, 1984).

While an overwhelming majority of the research has reported superior performance among unilaterals, Sage (1984) cautions that crossed-laterals also perform well in a variety of activities and therefore recommends that no attempts be made to switch a performer from a crossed-lateral to a unilateral technique.

Tracking and Object Interception

To gain control over a projectile, the performer must visually track the object to be intercepted. The primary purpose of *tracking* the object is to gain important information regarding the object's flight. Thus, a properly functioning ocular-motor system is needed to track the object, and a properly functioning motor system is needed to act on the object.

The ocular-motor system is composed of two eye-movement systems. First, the smooth pursuit system is capable of matching eye-movement speed with the speed of the projectile, to maintain a stable retinal image. Second, the saccadic eye-movement system detects and corrects differences between projectile location and eye fixation. When objects are traveling faster than 24 to 33 meters per second, the saccadic system is primarily used (Yarbas, 1967), whereby the eye makes jerky movements.

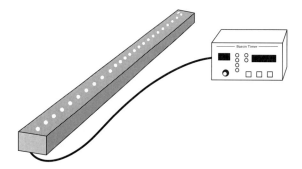

Figure 9-8 The Bassin anticipation timer

Developmentally, the infant is not capable of freely moving the eyes across an arc of 180 degrees until sometime between 40 and 52 weeks of age (Corbin, 1980), which explains why tracking is first accomplished primarily by head movements and then through a series of eye-head movements. By 5 or 6 years of age, children can efficiently track objects moving in the horizontal plane. When children are between 8 and 9 years of age, they can track balls that travel in an arc (Morris, 1980). As dynamic visual acuity improves, so does the ability to track fast-moving objects, because whenever an object is moving at an angular velocity at which smooth eye movements are no longer possible, the pursuit task becomes a function of dynamic visual acuity (Sanderson, 1972).

The coordinated interception of a moving object is a task frequently studied in research laboratories. This process involving object interception is commonly referred to as *coincidence-anticipation.* Most frequently, the Bassin anticipation timer (Lafayette Instrument Company, Model 50-575) has been selected as the instrument of choice to measure coincidence-anticipation (see Figure 9-8). The apparatus consists of one yellow warning light and two runways attached end to end. Each runway consists of 16 red LEDs (light-emitting diodes) that are 0.6 centimeters in diameter and spaced 4.5 centimeters apart. The sequentially lighted LED lamps are designed to give the appearance of a moving stimulus. Most often, the objective of the task is to depress a button placed at the end of the runway so that one's response coincides with the lighting of the last runway lamp. In order to succeed at this task, one must initiate the response one reaction time and one movement time before the lighting of the target lamp.

Many factors can influence how well a person can make a motor response coincide with the arrival of an external object, including object speed, object predictability, viewing time, gender, and age (Magill, 2004; Shea, Shebilske, & Worchel, 1993). Briefly, coincidence-anticipation improves with age and is greatly influenced by practice. Interestingly, Kuhlman and Beitel (1997) found that practice as reflected by sport participation and video game experience may be a better predictor of coincidence-anticipation than is age. It also appears that boys perform more accurately than girls (Isaacs, 1983) and that both very slow- and very fast-moving objects cause greater performance error. This finding led Wade (1980) to speculate that both children and adults may respond most accurately to speeds that they confront in their everyday world.

Based on these findings, one can speculate that a slowly projected ball may not necessarily always be the easiest to catch. Furthermore, when a child is first learning to catch, the teacher should consistently toss the ball directly toward the child instead of using an arched delivery. This may explain why Isaacs (1984) found that young T-baseball players missed 85 percent of all fly balls.

Isaacs (1987, 1990) has described a procedure whereby two independent Bassin anticipation timers are interfaced, making it capable of measuring a type of coincidence-anticipation involving the estimation of intersection of two converging targets.

Teachers of motor skills should also be aware that each visual trait described in this chapter may be improved with visual training. Seiderman and Schneider's (1983) book *The Athletic Eye* describes in detail a visual-training program.

MOTOR DEVELOPMENT OF CHILDREN WITH VISUAL IMPAIRMENTS

Chapters 10 through 14 discuss at length the acquisition of selected reflexes and motor skills. This section describes the development of selected motor acts in visually impaired children. Indeed, the effects of blindness on the motor development and motor performance of children is far more devastating than that of other sensory disabilities such as hearing impairments (Dummer, Haubenstricker, & Stewart, 1996).

The general public considers **blindness** a total loss of vision, but this is a misconception. The official definition of blindness is based on distance vision as measured by the Snellen eye chart and does not take into consideration near vision. Thus, a legally blind person may be capable of considerable vision when objects are placed close to the eyes. In general, residual vision in legally blind people can range from total blindness, where light is not perceived, to a Snellen distance vision of 20/200, which is the equivalent of an 80 percent loss of vision. Therefore, whenever we speak of blindness, we also should specify the degrees of residual vision remaining, if any.

The effects of blindness on a person's motor development also depend on the age of onset. Those people who are congenitally blind or who become blind before they are 5 years old do not retain a workable visual imagery (Lowenfeld, 1981). Thus, congenitally blind people must adjust to the visual world without the advantage of working from an established visual reference point. Conversely, those individuals who lose their sight later in life are more capable of dealing with life's demands, because they have experienced vision and are capable of remembering it. Obviously, blindness exerts its most devastating effects on motor development and motor performance when the newborn experiences total blindness (that is, 0 percent residual vision). The following sections discuss the specific influence of congenital blindness on early motor development.

Head and Trunk Control

Several weeks after birth, sighted infants attempt to raise their head off the crib mattress; soon thereafter the back is arched and the chest elevates. Because of visual curiosity, the infant elevates the trunk for increasingly longer periods. Thus, for the sighted infant, visual curiosity elicits the movements that aid in the development of head, neck, and trunk control. Nonsighted infants, however, tend to cry and fuss in the prone position. Parents often place them on their back, in an attempt to pacify, but this position does not help the development of head and upper-body control, because the practice environment is not conducive to it. And even when such infants stay in the prone position, they arch the head and neck less frequently than do sighted infants, because there is little or no vision to initiate purposeful movement at this young age.

Independent Sitting

Somewhere between 4 and 8 months of age, most sighted infants are capable of sitting alone. Nonsighted infants are also capable of sitting alone at this time if their parents have adequately prepared them for this milestone. However, if these infants have spent prolonged periods of time supine, they will not have had the opportunity to develop the necessary head, neck, and trunk control to sit alone.

Creeping

By approximately 10 months of age, sighted infants are capable of supporting themselves on their hands and knees, thus making creeping possible. Visual curiosity entices the sighted infant to creep toward objects that are in sight but out of reach. Obviously, such visual curiosity is absent in the nonsighted infant. If this infant is to develop normally, a sensory modality other than vision must be used to instigate infant creeping and exploration of the unseen environment. Parents of such infants should stimulate their children's curiosity by enticing them to move toward noise-making toys; this audiomotor coordination ability is conceptualized by about 1 year of age (Jan, Freeman, & Scott, 1977).

Independent Walking

Both sighted and nonsighted children are capable of standing and walking with support at approximately the same time. Nevertheless, the achievement of independent walking is significantly delayed in the latter (Adelson & Fraiberg, 1976). In fact, children with partial vision tend to walk sooner than totally blind children or those who possess only

light perception. When independent walking is achieved, the blind child characteristically exhibits an insecure gait consisting of a wide base of support, flat-footed contact with the supporting surface, and toeing out. These characteristics describe the expected sequence of events in sighted children, but some nonsighted individuals exhibit these immature characteristics throughout the lifespan.

Prehension

Prehension, the ability to grasp and seize objects with the hands, is an important aspect of a child's motor development. Prehensile abilities enable a child to gather information about the environment in new ways. Increased and varied exploration is possible because of the child's ability to seize and manipulate objects with the hands. This new mode of exploration lets the child discover properties of objects and allows the child to use objects as implements in achieving goals (Bower, 1982).

Vision is important for the development of prehension for three reasons. First, the initial phase of self-directed reaching is visually evoked; that is, the child reaches upon viewing some object in the environment. This form of reaching is an improvement over the random grasping that occurs earlier in the child's life. Second, vision is used to facilitate hand closure around an object once the child has manual contact with the desired object. Third, during the act of visually guided reaching, vision enables the child to correct errors throughout the reach.

Thus, for the nonsighted child the primary modality for stimulating prehensile skills is absent (Troster & Brambring, 1993). Because reaching for sound-producing objects generally will not occur until the last quarter of the first year of life, it is important that parents encourage their nonsighted child to manipulate objects that have been placed in her or his hand. In addition, manual guidance by the parents is important; it is imperative that finger dexterity and sensitivity be acquired early in development because they establish a readiness for Braille instruction at school age.

An investigation by Adelson and Fraiberg (1976) compares the gross motor achievements of 10 congenitally blind infants with those of normally sighted

Table 9-1 Comparison of Sighted and Unsighted Children on Selected Bayley Scale Items

	Median Age (months)	
Item	Sighted	Nonsighted
Elevates self by arms, prone	2.1	8.75
Sits alone momentarily	5.3	6.75
Rolls from back to stomach	6.4	7.25
Sits alone steadily	6.6	8.00
Raises self to sitting position	8.3	11.00
Stands up using furniture (pulls up to stand)	8.6	13.00
Makes stepping movements (walks with hands held)	8.8	10.75
Stands alone	11.0	13.00
Walks alone, three steps	11.7	15.25
Walks alone across room	12.1	19.25°

°One child had not achieved this task by age 2 years.

SOURCE: Adapted from Adelson and Fraiberg (1976).

peers. The children were observed for 2 years, and comparisons were made in reference to selected items from the Bayley Scales of Infant Development. Table 9-1 presents the median age comparisons for sighted and nonsighted children on selected Bayley Scale items. Note that nearly all the nonsighted infants were found to be on schedule when compared with their sighted counterparts on items requiring postural control. These items include sitting alone momentarily, making stepping movements when hands are held, and standing alone. Attaining these items on schedule suggests normal development of trunk control and the ability to bear weight and perform stepping movements with support.

However, there were five items in which the nonsighted subjects showed significant delays. With the exception of elevating self by arms when prone, the remaining four items—raising self to sitting position, standing up using furniture (pulls up to stand), walking alone (three steps), and walking alone across room—all involve self-initiated mobility. Thus the authors concluded that if nonsighted children are to develop within the normal limits of their sighted peers in self-initiated mobility, they

need sound as an adaptive substitute for sight; this substitution should occur toward the end of the first year of life.

Play Behavior of Children with Visual Impairments

For the sighted child, play is a spontaneous and creative act carried out for its own sake and usually consisting of self-imposed games where new movement skills are learned and old movement skills are refined. New movement ideas are picked up from imitating the movements of other children. Thus, play is an important learning medium. In contrast, nonsighted children tend to be inactive and show little drive to explore their unseen environment. If left on their own, many engage in physical activity involving little more than body rocking, eye pressing, and finger tapping (Jan et al., 1977).

As noted earlier, even the degree of blindness can influence rate of development across all domains (motor, cognitive, affective). For example, Hatton (1995) has recently reported that children whose visual function was 20/800 experienced poorer performance in both motor and adaptive development than did children exhibiting a visual deficit as great as 20/500. Therefore, it is important—within reason—not to overprotect the nonsighted child. Such children should be given the opportunity to engage in numerous movement experiences and should be encouraged to explore their unseen world.

THE NONVISUAL SENSES

While the visual system is the predominant system of choice, it is by no means the only sensory modality that can exert an influence on motor development and motor performance. Unfortunately, less information is available on the other sensory modalities that are known to influence motor development and motor performance. This lack of information relating to the nonvisual senses has been recognized by Reisman (1987):

> To be able to consider five sensory modalities in one chapter is actually a statement about the need for further research in this area. Not only is there much work to be done in understanding changing sensitivities with age, especially in the cutaneous senses, but very little attention has been paid to the normal range of individual differences to be found in infant sensory functioning. (p. 295)

Nevertheless, in this section we describe the proprioceptive system and its accompanying vestibular apparatus as well as the auditory and cutaneous systems.

The Proprioceptive System

The **proprioceptive system** makes it possible for one to be aware of one's movements as well as the ability to perceive the location of one's body parts in space without visual reference to them. This feat is made possible by a group of sensory receptors located in the joints, muscles, tendons, and labyrinth of the inner ear. These specialized receptors are the muscle spindles, Golgi tendon organs, joint receptors, and vestibular apparatus. These sensory receptors respond to changes in joint angles, changes in the length and tension relationship of muscles,

and movements of the head. Because these receptor cells are activated by mechanical deformation, they are frequently referred to as **mechanoreceptors.** Let us briefly examine the function of each.

The **muscle spindles** are cigar-shaped structures that are attached in parallel with the muscles' largest fibers, known as the *extrafusal muscle fibers.* Contained within the spindle itself is a smaller muscle fiber known as an *intrafusal muscle fiber.* Because the fibers lie parallel to one another and are attached to the sheath of the extrafusal fibers, it is possible for the muscle spindle to gauge the amount of tension within the muscle itself. For instance, when the larger extrafusal muscle fibers are stretched, they, in turn, stretch the smaller intrafusal fibers of the muscle spindle. This stretch will cause activation of the spindle, resulting in afferent discharge. The effect of an afferent discharge is to stimulate the skeletomotor neurons, which, in turn, will cause a contraction of the muscle's larger extrafusal fibers, thus reducing the stretch on the intrafusal muscle fibers. The classical knee jerk is an example of this phenomenon.

The **Golgi tendon organs** are small stretch receptors located near the junction of the muscle and the muscle's tendon (musculo-tendinous junction). Their primary role is to detect tension in the muscle's tendon and, in fact, provide the central nervous system with continuous information regarding force development in both static and dynamic conditions. These highly sensitive organs play a major role in maintaining muscle tone.

Joint receptors are located throughout the body and, as the name implies, are located in the body's joints. More specifically, these receptors are located in the joint's capsule in those areas that are most responsive to stretch. While some joint receptors fire at specific joint angles, most fire at the joint's extreme range of motion. This has led researchers to question the early belief that these receptors were responsible for providing precise information about movement (Schmidt, 1988). Instead, some now believe that these receptors could be acting as "limit detectors." For example, "joint receptors in the hip could signal the end of the flexion phase of the step cycle; their reflex effect might help to terminate activity in the appropriate flexion muscles, and contribute to the initiation of the extension phase of the step cycle" (Tracey, 1980, cited in Sage, 1984).

The ***vestibular apparatus,*** which is located in the inner ear, is responsible for registering head motion as well as accompanying body motion. Any time the head is turned or moved through space, the vestibular receptors will be stimulated. As illustrated in Figure 9-9, the vestibular system is actually composed of two subsystems, the ***semicircular canals*** and the ***otolith organs*** (utricle and saccule). The semicircular canals are fluid-filled ducts that lie at right angles to one another. Because they are capable of registering changes in head motion, they are sometimes referred to as angular accelerometers. Unlike the semicircular canals, which primarily detect rotational motion, the otolith organs are primarily responsible for detecting linear acceleration, as they provide information concerning the body's position in relation to the force of gravity (Sage, 1984). This system is also important in some reflexive behaviors (righting reflex) and the coordination of visual fixation.

The proprioceptive system plays an important role in motor development and skilled motor performance. Briefly, proprioception contributes to the development of body awareness, spatial awareness, and directional awareness. In addition, the vestibular apparatus is critical in the development of both static and dynamic balance, a topic that is discussed at some length in Chapters 4 and 16.

The Auditory System

Auditory perception describes the process whereby auditory stimuli are received, selected, organized, and interpreted. As illustrated in Figure 9-9, the sensory organ that makes auditory perception possible is the ear. Note that the human ear is composed of three main parts: the outer, middle, and inner ear. Any source of sound sends vibrations through the air (sound waves), which are collected through the ear opening, then travel down the ear canal and onto the eardrum. The eardrum vibrations are transmitted to the inner ear's cochlea, which in turn stimulates the auditory nerve, which sends the nerve impulses to the brain for interpretation (sensation of hearing).

Prenatally, babies are capable of hearing during the last few months of pregnancy. Therefore at birth, the newborn is structurally equipped for hearing; however, hearing is generally compromised for several days as the inner canal is usually filled with fluid. Additionally, the sensory threshold is believed to be higher in newborns than in mature adults. Said differently, a louder auditory stimulus is needed to stimulate newborn auditory perception.

Auditory development during the first three months of postnatal life is characterized by an enjoyment of hearing the voice of parents. At this age, babies generally respond better to the mother's voice, as it is associated with food and comfort. This helps explain why most people will use an exaggeratedly high-pitched voice when speaking to babies.

From 4 to 7 months of age, babies begin to recognize some components of speech instead of simply recognizing tone of voice. This milestone is critical for speech development. During the seventh month, babies should be able to recognize and respond to their own name. Additionally, babbling, the baby's first attempt at speech, should be encouraged.

From 8 to 12 months, babies start to produce recognizable sounds and exhibit a more sophisticated babbling that resembles attempts at real conversation. Also during this time, babies should be capable of responding to simple verbal requests such as looking toward "Dad" when asked "Where's Daddy?" and waving "bye" upon command. Attempts to reproduce sounds made by parents should also be encouraged.

From 1 to 2 years of age, infants and toddlers continue to improve their ability to recognize and respond to commands. One can expect children of this age to respond to the names of family members and familiar objects. When children fail to exhibit the developmental milestones mentioned in this section, some hearing impairment may exist. Of the more than three million American children with hearing impairments, approximately 1.3 million are under the age of 3. It is imperative that hearing impairments be recognized early so that corrective

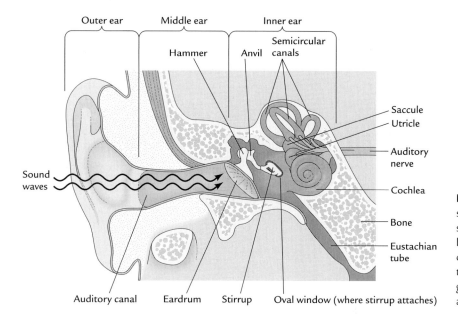

Outer ear   Middle ear   Inner ear

Hammer   Anvil   Semicircular canals

Sound waves

Saccule
Utricle
Auditory nerve
Cochlea
Bone
Eustachian tube

Auditory canal   Eardrum   Stirrup   Oval window (where stirrup attaches)

Figure 9-9 The vestibular system is composed of two subsystems: the semicircular canals and the otolith organs. The auditory system involves the other organs of the outer, middle, and inner ear.

action can be taken; this early intervention limits the impairments' effect on language and speech development.

The Cutaneous System

The **cutaneous system,** also known as tactile sensitivity, receives its information from sensory receptors located at the body's surface, the skin. Once thought of as just the sense of touch, we now know that the cutaneous system consists of at least four skin senses: pressure, coldness, warmth, and pain. Because of its sensitivity to temperature and pain, this sensory system is what alerts us to potential adverse environmental conditions.

When studying the development of the cutaneous system, researchers typically look for one of three possible responses to tactile stimulation: reflex, withdrawal, and approach. For example, the *reflex behaviors* known as the sucking reflex, the searching reflex, the Babkin reflex, and the Babinski reflex, as well as the palmar grasp and plantar grasp reflexes, are all normally elicited by tactile stimulation (see Chapter 10). *Withdrawal responses* generally manifest themselves when the infant or child attempts to

turn the head or move a limb away from the source of stimulation and may sometimes be accompanied by a facial grimace. Last, *approach behaviors* are generally exhibited by children when they show responsiveness to kisses, hugs, and playful tickling. In fact, these approach behaviors are essential for the human bonding process early in life and are also important later in life when intimacy and human sexual interactions become evident.

Which of these three possible reactions to tactile stimulation will be exhibited depends on many factors. Some of these factors include mood state (awake or sleeping), area of stimulation (body area), gender, and level of maturity. For example, an absence of the palmar, plantar, and Babkin reflexes has been noted during periods of quiet sleep but sometimes observed during active sleep, and nearly always when the infants were quietly awake. Regarding gender, girls have been found to habituate to vibrotactile stimulation at an earlier age than do boys (Leader et al., 1982). This is believed to be a result of the former's greater level of nervous system maturity.

Many believe the cutaneous system is the first functional sensory system to develop. For example,

Humphrey (1964) has demonstrated the functional capacity of this system's receptors as early as 7.5 weeks fetal age. More specifically, Humphrey notes that light stroking of the perioral area elicits a neck flexion causing the head to move away from the stimulus. Approximately 1 week later, however, the same stimulus on occasion results in the fetus turning the head toward the stimulus, accompanied by opening the mouth and swallowing. This is believed to be the precursor to the feeding reflex seen at birth (Humphrey, 1970).

Initially, sensitivity to tactile stimulation is greatest in those parts of the body that are used to explore the child's ever changing world. These regions include the mouth, lips, and tongue. One only has to observe a newborn infant for a short period to witness this fact. As soon as the child comes in contact with an object, it is generally placed into the mouth for exploration. This point is best highlighted by Lipsitt's (1978) observation:

> The importance of such tactual stimulation, and the low threshold of the newborn for response to it, can be demonstrated by rotating the finger completely around the lips in a circle, and noting the precise following of such stimulation which many newborns can demonstrate. (p. 499)

The cutaneous receptors play an important role in both motor development and motor control. For example, as mentioned previously, this sense is initially used by the infant to explore objects within its new world. (See also *haptic perception* in Chapter 12.) Nevertheless, perhaps its importance is best illustrated by persons with **Romberg's sign** disease. Individuals with this disease have varying degrees of damage to the sensory receptors, usually those in the soles of their feet. As a result, they experience difficulty in maintaining balance, especially if their eyes are closed. Furthermore, if the sensory receptors are damaged in the hands, fine motor manipulations with the hand or fingers are extremely difficult when vision is not available, and even impossible if the receptors are completely destroyed. Just think how often you have held an object in your hand only to have it start to slip. In this scenario, most individuals are capable of quickly grasping the slipping object to keep it from falling. In fact, Johansson and Westling (1988) report that our ability to recognize that an object is slipping from our grasp and then quickly to tighten our grasp only takes about 80 milliseconds. This research indicates the rapidity with which individuals can respond to cutaneous stimulation.

SUMMARY

A sharp visual image is possible whenever light entering the eye converges on the aspect of the retina called the macula. Varying light entering the eye comes to rest on the macula through the process of accommodation.

The eye develops as an outgrowth of the forebrain and remains an inseparable component of the central nervous system throughout the lifespan. Like the brain, the eye achieves most of its growth prior to birth.

The eye is functionally immature at birth. For instance, visual acuity steadily improves during the first 4 to 5 years, as do depth perception and field of vision. Furthermore, these visual attributes correlate positively with selected motor tasks.

After about 40 years of age, there are changes in functional vision. These changes become noticeable because the amount of light reaching the eye's retina is reduced and there is frequent difficulty in focusing near objects.

Because with age less light reaches the retina, it is important that elderly people perform their physical tasks in well-illuminated activity areas. In addition, activity supervisors should be aware that bifocal wearers frequently experience difficulty in both tracking and judging the speed of moving objects. Also with advancing age comes the risk of developing age-related eye diseases. The four major AREDs are age-related macular degeneration, glaucoma, cataracts, and diabetic retinopathy.

The effects of blindness on motor development depend on the age of onset and the degree of residual vision remaining, if any. Blindness exerts its most devastating effects on motor development and motor performance when the newborn is totally blind. Because visual curiosity elicits movement, the nonsighted child is not visually motivated to explore the unseen world. If the nonsighted infant is to develop normally, another sensory modality (usually sound) must be substituted for vision.

Vision is not the only sensory modality known to influence motor development and motor performance. Three other important sensory systems are the proprioceptive system, the auditory system, and the cutaneous system. The proprioceptive system receives sensory input from joint receptors, muscle spindles, and the Golgi tendon organs. Each of these specialized receptors monitors

the stretch and/or force being placed on the muscle and its tendons. Additionally, the vestibular system, an element of the proprioceptive system, provides information regarding changes in the body's position in space and the location of the body's limbs in space without visual reference to them. The primary components of the vestibular system include the semicircular canals and the otolith organs. The auditory system allows sound to be received, selected, organized, and interpreted. The cutaneous system, also known as tactile sensitivity, is a specialized system that receives information regarding pressure, temperature, and pain.

KEY TERMS

accommodation
age-related macular degeneration
  (AMD)
Amsler grid
auditory perception
binocular vision
blindness
cataracts
ciliary muscle
coincidence-anticipation
cones
crossed-laterals
cutaneous system
diabetic retinopathy

drusen
dynamic visual acuity
eye dominance
glaucoma
Golgi tendon organs
hyperopic
joint receptors
macula
mechanoreceptors
muscle spindles
otolith organs
peripheral vision
presbyopia
proprioceptive system

retina
rods
Romberg's sign
semicircular canals
senile miosis
senile ptosis
Snellen eye chart
static visual acuity
strabismus
tracking
unilateral dominance
vestibular apparatus
visual acuity
visual cliff

QUESTIONS FOR REFLECTION

1. Can you draw an illustration of the human eye and describe how the human eye is very much like a camera?

2. Can you outline the time course of development for key physical eye structures including the following: rods, cones, lens, ciliary muscles, and dilatory muscles of the pupil?

3. How are both static and dynamic visual acuity assessed in children and adults? What are the typical values of static visual acuity for individuals at birth, 1 year, and 4–5 years of age?

4. Can you describe research regarding the relationship between visual acuity and skilled motor performance?

5. What changes in vision occur with aging?

6. Can you describe and illustrate how binocular vision is needed in order to accomplish depth perception?

7. What is the typical time course leading to mature depth perception? Support your finding by describing the classical study conducted by Gibson and Walk (1960).

8. Can you identify the typical range of both lateral and vertical fields of vision in children and adults?

9. What are the meanings of eye dominance, unilateral dominance, and crossed laterals? What are the research findings associated with each of these concepts?

10. Can you identify and explain each of the two eye-movement systems?

11. Can you describe the development of eye tracking behavior, paying attention to coincidence-anticipation?

12. Can you describe the motor development of visually impaired children and contrast their play behavior with that of a sighted individual?

13. What are the specialized receptors of the proprioceptive system?

14. What are the four skin senses? How is the cutaneous system important regarding both motor development and motor performance?

15. Draw an illustration of the human ear and describe the development of auditory perception.

INTERNET RESOURCES

American Academy of Otolaryngology
www.aaohns.org

National Eye Institute **www.nei.nih.gov**

National Federation of the Blind   **www.nfb.org**
Prevent Blindness America
www.prevent-blindness.org

ONLINE LEARNING CENTER (www.mhhe.com/payne6e)

Visit the *Human Motor Development* Online Learning Center for study aids and additional resources. You can use the study guide questions and key terms puzzles to review key terms and concepts for this chapter and to prepare for exams. You can further extend your knowledge of motor development by checking out the Web links, articles, and activities found on the site.

REFERENCES

Adelson, E., & Fraiberg, S. (1976). Sensory deficit and motor development in infants blind from birth. In Z. S. Jastrzembska (Ed.), *The effects of blindness and other impairments on early development.* New York: American Foundation for the Blind.

American Academy of Ophthalmology. (2000). Sunglasses. Retrieved on September 26, 2000, from eyenet.org/public/pi/eye_health/safety/ sunglasses_fag.html.

Beals, R. P., Mayyasi, A. M., Templeton, A. E., & Johnson, W. L. (1971). The relationship between basketball shooting performance and certain visual attributes. *American Journal of Optometry and Archives of American Academy of Optometry, 48,* 585–590.

Bower, T. G. (1982). *Development in infancy.* 2nd ed. San Francisco: Freeman.

Burg, A. (1968). Lateral visual field as related to age and sex. *Journal of Applied Psychology, 52,* 10–15.

Catalano, R. A., & Nelson, L. B. (1994). *Pediatric ophthalmology.* Norwalk, CT: Appleton & Lange.

Christina, R. W., Feltz, D. L., Hatfield, B. D., & Daniels, F. S. (1981). Demographic and physical characteristics of shooters. In G. C. Roberts & D. M. Landers (Eds.), *Psychology of motor behavior and sport.* Champaign, IL: Human Kinetics.

Corbin, C. B. (1980). *A textbook of motor development.* 2nd ed. Dubuque, IA: Brown.

Davids, K. (1987). The development of peripheral vision in ball games: An analysis of single- and dual-task paradigms. *Journal of Human Movement Studies, 13,* 175–284.

Dummer, G. M., Haubenstricker, J. L., & Stewart, D. A. (1996). Motor skill performances of children who are deaf. *Adapted Physical Activity Quarterly, 13,* 400–414.

Garnett, C. (1999). Age-related eye disease doesn't have to steal your sight. The NIH Word on Health. Retrieved on September 26, 2000, from www.nih.gov/news/wordonhealth/jan99/story01.htm.

Gibson, E. J., & Walk, R. D. (1960). The visual cliff. *Scientific American, 4,* 67–71.

Graybiel, A., Jokl, E., & Trapp, C. (1955). Russian studies of vision in relation to physical activity and sport. *Research Quarterly, 26,* 480–485.

Haith, M. M. (1990). Progress in the understanding of sensory and perceptual processes in early infancy. *Merrill-Palmer Quarterly, 36,* 1–26.

Hatton, D. D. (1995). Developmental growth curves of young children who are visually impaired. Unpublished doctoral dissertation, University of North Carolina, Chapel Hill.

Hobson, R., & Henderson, N. T. (1941). A preliminary study of the visual field in athletics. *Iowa Academy of Science, 48,* 331–337.

Humphrey, T. (1964). Some correlations between the appearance of human fetal reflexes and the development of the nervous system. *Progress in Brain Research, 4,* 93–133.

———. (1970). The development of human fetal activity and its relation to postnatal behavior. In H. Reese & L. Lipsitt (Eds.), *Advances in child development and behavior.* Vol. 5. New York: Academic Press.

Ikeda, M., & Takevchi, T. (1975). Influence of foveal load on the functional visual field. *Perception and Psychophysics, 18,* 255–260.

Isaacs, L. D. (1983). Coincidence-anticipation in simple catching. *Journal of Human Movement Studies, 9,* 195–201.

———. (1984). Players' success in T-baseball. *Perceptual and Motor Skills, 59,* 852–854.

———. (1987). Modifying the Bassin anticipation timer. *Journal of Human Movement Studies, 13,* 461–465.

———. (1990). Effects of angle of approach on coincidence-anticipation timing within a two-target display. *Journal of Human Movement Studies, 19,* 171–179.

Jan, R. E., Freeman, R. D., & Scott, E. P. (1977). *Visual impairment in children and adolescents.* New York: Grune & Stratton.

Johansson, R. S., & Westling, G. (1988). Programmed and triggered actions to rapid load changes during precision grip. *Experimental Brain Research, 71,* 72–86.

Kuhlman, J. S., & Beitel, P. A. (1997). Development/ learning of coincidence-anticipation. NASPSPA Abstracts. *Journal of Sports and Exercise Psychology, 19,* S76.

Leader, L., Baillie, P., Bahia, M., & Elsebeth, V. (1982). The assessment and significance of habituation to repeated stimulus by the human fetus. *Early Human Development, 7,* 211–219.

Lipsitt, L. P. (1978). Sensory and learning processes of newborns: Implications for behavioral disabilities. *Allied Health Behavior Science, 1,* 493–522.

Lowenfeld, B. (1981). *Berthold Lowenfeld on blindness and blind people.* New York: American Foundation for the Blind.

Macfarlane, A., Harris, P., & Barnes, I. (1976). Central and peripheral vision in early infancy. *Journal of Experimental Child Psychology, 21,* 532–538.

Magill, R. A. (2004). *Motor learning: Concepts and applications.* 7th ed. Boston: McGraw-Hill.

Morris, G. S. (1977). Dynamic visual acuity: Implications for the physical educator and coach. *Motor Skills: Theory into Practice, 2,* 15–20.

———. (1980). *Elementary physical education: Toward inclusion.* Salt Lake City, UT: Brighton.

Morris, G. S., & Kreighbaum, E. (1977). Dynamic visual acuity of varsity women volleyball and basketball players. *Research Quarterly, 48,* 480–483.

National Eye Institute. (2000). Information for patients: Age-related macular degeneration. Retrieved September 26, 2000, from www.nei.nih.gov/publications/armd-p.htm.

Oxendine, J. B. (1984). *Psychology of motor learning.* 2nd ed. Englewood Cliffs, NJ: Prentice-Hall.

Payne, V. G. (1988). Effects of direction of stimulus approach, eye dominance, and gender on coincidence-anticipation timing performance. *Journal of Human Movement Studies, 15,* 17–25.

Reisman, J. E. (1987). Touch, motion, and proprioception. In P. Salapatek & L. Cohen (Eds.), *Handbook of infant perception: From sensation to perception.* Vol. 1. New York: Academic Press.

Rosenblith, J. F. (1992). *In the beginning: Development from conception to age 2.* 2nd ed. London: Sage.

Sage, G. H. (1984). *Motor learning and control: A neuropsychological approach.* Dubuque, IA: Brown.

Sanderson, F. H. (1972). Perceptual studies: Visual acuity and sporting performance. In H. T. A. Whiting (Ed.), *Readings in sport psychology.* Lafayette, IN: Balt.

Sanderson, F. H., & Whiting, H. T. A. (1974). Dynamic visual acuity and performance in a catching task. *Journal of Motor Behavior, 6,* 87–94.

———. (1978). Dynamic visual acuity: A possible factor in catching performance. *Journal of Motor Behavior, 10,* 7–14.

Schmidt, R. A. (1988). *Motor control and learning: A behavioral emphasis.* 2nd ed. Champaign, IL: Human Kinetics.

Seiderman, A., & Schneider, S. (1983). *The athletic eye.* New York: Hearst Books.

Shea, C. H., Shebilske, W. L., & Worchel, S. (1993). *Motor learning and control.* Englewood Cliffs, NJ: Prentice-Hall.

Shephard, R. J. (1978). *Physical activity and aging.* Chicago: Year Book Medical Publishers.

Shick, J. (1971). Relationship between depth perception and hand-eye dominance and free-throw shooting in college women. *Perceptual and Motor Skills, 33,* 539–542.

Smith, C. G., Gallie, B. L., & Morin, J. D. (1983). Normal and abnormal development of the eye. In J. S. Crawford & J. D. Morin (Eds.), *The eye in childhood.* New York: Grune & Stratton.

Troster, H., & Brambring, M. (1993). Early motor development in blind infants. *Journal of Applied Developmental Psychology, 14,* 83–106.

Vlahov, E. (1977a). Effect of the Harvard step test on visual acuity. *Perceptual and Motor Skills, 45,* 369–370.

————. (1977b). The effects of different workload varying in intensity and duration on resolution acuity. Unpublished doctoral dissertation, University of Maryland.

Wade, M. G. (1980). Coincidence-anticipation of young normal and handicapped children. *Journal of Motor Behavior, 12,* 103–112.

Weale, R. A. (1963). *The aging eye.* London: Lewis.

Whiting, H. T. A. (1971). *Acquiring ball skill: A psychological interpretation.* Philadelphia: Lea & Febiger.

Whiting, H. T. A., & Sanderson, F. H. (1972). The effect of exercise on the visual and auditory acuity of table-tennis players. *Journal of Motor Behavior, 4,* 163–169.

Williams, H. G. (1983). *Perceptual and motor development.* Englewood Cliffs, NJ: Prentice-Hall.

Wolf, E., & Nadroski, A. S. (1971). Extent of the visual field—Changes with age and oxygen tension. *Archives of Ophthalmology, 86,* 637–642.

Wu, G. (1995). *Retina: The fundamentals.* Philadelphia: Saunders.

Yarbas, A. L. (1967). *Eye movements and vision.* New York: Plenum Press.

Infant Reflexes and Stereotypies

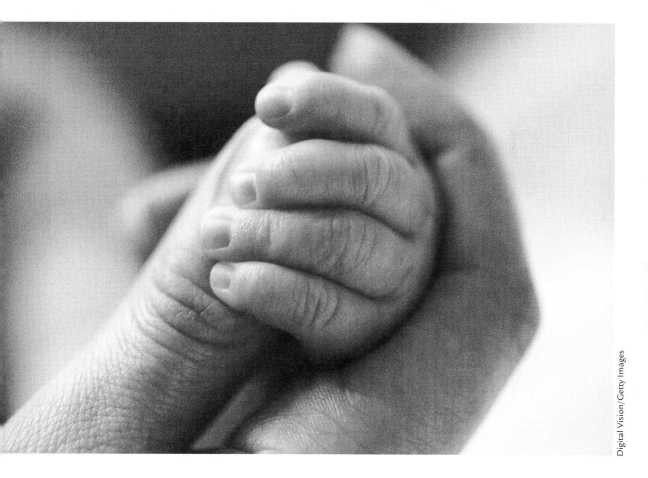

Infancy is one of the most interesting of all periods of life to study. This time is particularly fascinating because of two types of movements characteristic of the first several months of life: infant reflexes and stereotypies. This chapter describes these movements and their importance in the developmental process.

IMPORTANCE OF THE INFANT REFLEXES

During the last 4 months of prenatal life and the first 4 months after birth, a human being's movement repertoire includes movements that are reflexive; that is, each movement is an involuntary, stereotyped response to a particular stimulus. As an example, when a stimulus, such as touching the palm of the infant's hand, is applied, the stimulated hand closes in a routine or stereotypical response—each time the appropriate stimulus is applied, the same, or a highly similar, response occurs. Perhaps even more interesting is the fact that the reflexes are involuntary; these movements are a result of an unconscious effort by a person, unlike later, more familiar voluntary movements. Most reflexes also occur **subcortically,** which literally means "below the level of the cortex of the brain." A more understandable description is "below the level of the higher brain centers," because some reflexes are processed in such lower brain areas as the brain stem (Fiorentino, 1963). Reflexive movements are therefore produced without direct involvement of the higher brain centers. The electrical impulse the stimulus creates travels to the central nervous system. From there, the information is integrated and the appropriate movement message is issued to the muscles involved in the response. This simple method of movement production seems appropriate for producing certain reflexes such as the palmar grasp. However, the production of the more involved reflexes (discussed later) is one of the many phenomena of human motor development.

Infant Versus Lifespan Reflexes

In normal, healthy infants, the infant reflexes typically do not last much beyond the first birthday (the downward, sideward, and backward parachuting reflexes are exceptions; see Table 10-1). However, some reflexes persevere much longer. In fact, in normal, healthy individuals, several reflexes last throughout the lifespan. For example, most of us have personally experienced the knee-jerk reflex; while we were seated, the physician taps our patellar tendon directly below the patella and our lower leg "jerks," creating a rapid, partial extension. The flexor withdrawal reflex is another example. It exists during infancy yet does not typically cease at the end of the first year of life. In the flexor withdrawal reflex, the arm abruptly flexes upon touching a sharp or hot object. Obviously, this reflex is often quite useful in protecting us from injury. All reflexes that endure throughout the lifespan in normal healthy individuals are called **lifespan reflexes.** Because this chapter emphasizes the infant reflexes, the lifespan reflexes will not be discussed here.

Role of the Reflexes in Survival

The infant reflexes are an interesting and important aspect of human development (see Table 10-2). A human being is born with few voluntary capabilities and limited mobility. Human neonates are basically helpless and therefore highly dependent on their caretakers and their reflexes for their protection and survival. The infant reflexes used predominantly for protection, nutrition, or survival are the **primitive reflexes.** The primitive reflexes are those that appear during gestation or at birth and are suppressed by 6 months of age. They occur in all normal newborns (Barnes, Crutchfield, & Heriza, 1984).

The *sucking reflex* is one of the best-known primitive reflexes; it is characterized by an oral sucking action when the lips are stimulated. A neonate is born without the voluntary capacity to ingest food, so the sucking reflex enables the baby to ingest by involuntary means, taking in the nutrients essential for survival. This reflex is discussed in greater detail later in the chapter.

Table 10-1   Expected Time of Occurrence of Selected Infant Reflexes

	Age (months)												
	B	1	2	3	4	5	6	7	8	9	10	11	12
Primitive													
Palmar grasp	°▬▬▬▬▬▬												
Sucking	°▬▬▬▬												
Search	°▬▬▬▬												
Moro	°▬▬▬▬			– – – –									
Startle							– – – – – –						
Asymmetric tonic neck	°▬▬▬ – –												
Symmetric tonic neck	▬▬▬▬												
Plantar grasp	▬▬▬▬▬▬▬▬▬▬▬▬												
Babinski	▬▬▬▬▬												
Palmar mandibular	▬▬▬▬												
Palmar mental	▬▬▬▬												
Postural													
Stepping	▬▬▬▬▬▬ – –												
Crawling	▬▬▬▬ – –												
Swimming	2 weeks ▬▬▬▬▬												
Head-righting	▬▬▬▬▬												
Body-righting	▬▬▬▬▬▬												
Parachuting down	▬▬▬▬▬▬▬▬ +												
side	▬▬▬▬▬▬ +												
back	▬▬▬ +												
Labyrinthine	– – ▬▬▬▬▬▬▬▬												
Pull-up	▬▬▬▬▬▬▬▬▬▬												

°Also thought to exist for some weeks prenatally

Table 10-2   Why Study the Infant Reflexes?

1. During the last 4 months prenatally and the first 4 months postnatally, reflexive movement is such a dominant form of movement that the human being has been labeled a "reflex machine" (Wyke, 1975, p. 27).

2. In nourishing and protecting, the primitive reflexes are critical for human survival.

3. The postural reflexes are believed to be basic to more complex, voluntary movement of later infancy.

4. Though the age of appearance and disappearance of infant reflexes is somewhat variable, reflexes can be an important step in diagnosing infant health and neurological maturation.

Also important in maintaining sufficient nourishment for the infant is the *search* or *rooting reflex*, which functions in conjunction with the sucking reflex. The search reflex is elicited when the area of the cheek close to the lips is stimulated. The infant's head turns in the direction of the stimulation. This reflex enables the immobile newborn baby to seek nourishment when stimulated by the mother's breast.

The *labyrinthine reflex* is a slightly different protective reflex that is also crucial for survival. If an infant is placed in a prone position, breathing may be inhibited to the point of suffocation. The helpless neonate has insufficient voluntary capabilities to raise or turn the head to improve breathing. However, the involuntary labyrinthine reflex enables the infant to "right" or elevate the head, thus restoring the head to a position more conducive to breathing and allowing the baby to survive. Although the labyrinthine reflex is a protective function, it is best known for its relationship to the development of upright posture, as discussed in more detail later in the chapter.

Role of the Reflexes in Developing Future Movement

Reflexes related to the development of later voluntary movement are known as *postural reflexes.* Postural reflexes are thought to be a basis for future movements that, unlike the reflexes, emanate from a stimulation initiated by the higher brain centers. Some reflexes are believed to be directly integrated, modified, and incorporated into more complex patterns to form voluntary movements (Fiorentino, 1981). The *walking reflex* is one of the most obvious examples of a postural reflex facilitating later voluntary movement. If an infant 1 or 2 months old is held upright with the feet touching a supporting surface, the pressure on the feet stimulates the legs to perform a walking action. This movement is, of course, reflexive; the infant makes no conscious effort to produce this movement—the movement occurs involuntarily and subcortically. This early, involuntary, walkinglike movement is a critical antecedent to optimal development of voluntary walking, which appears in the months to follow.

The purported link between certain infant reflexes and later voluntary movement is questionable. As Bower (1976) describes, these reflexes, believed to be linked to voluntary behavior, often disappear before the onset of the "related" voluntary movement. This is what happens with the walking reflex. The walking reflex is noticeable soon after birth, but around the sixth month of life the reflex ceases. Application of the appropriate stimulus no longer evokes the walkinglike actions in the legs; 4 to 8 months may then elapse before the child can walk voluntarily. "How can something that disappears be critical for subsequent development?" (Bower, 1976, p. 39). Because a rather long time

passes between the offset of the reflex and the onset of the related voluntary movement, the role of the infant reflexes in the development of later voluntary movements is in question.

The overwhelmingly prevalent view, however, is that the reflexes "provide automatic movement that is a form of practice for aiding in the attainment of future movements" (Coley, 1978, p. 43). They "blend into voluntary patterns of movement . . . and are necessary for beginning movement and the development of muscle tone" (Lord, 1977, p. 89). Furthermore, the reflexes "play a dominant role in the regulation of degree, strength, balance, and distribution of muscular tone" (Fiorentino, 1981, p. 26). This muscular tone is critical to the performance of future voluntary movements.

Further research has been conducted to gain more scientific insight into this controversy. In one study, infants whose walking reflex was regularly stimulated began to walk at an earlier age than their nonstimulated counterparts (P. Zelazo, 1976). This research was undertaken with the assumption that if stimulation of the walking reflex preceding the disappearance phase affects the rate of emergence of voluntary walking, there must be a link between the pre- and postdisappearance movements. Bower (1976) conducted a similar study in which infants were subjected to "intensive practice" in reaching movements during the involuntary phase of reaching behavior. As in the Zelazo study, Bower found that the predisappearance stimulation expedited the emergence of the postdisappearance voluntary movement. In fact, in some cases, those children who were given practice experienced no disappearance phase whatsoever (Bower, 1976). "Such results pointed to the possibility that the reason abilities disappear is that they are not exercised" (p. 40). More important, these results can be interpreted as demonstrating a link between the predisappearance involuntary reaching and grasping and the postdisappearance voluntary reaching and grasping movements.

In more recent work, N. A. Zelazo and associates (1993) examined the effects of practicing reflexes on 32 male infants 6 weeks of age. After only 7 weeks of practice, infants who received elicitation of the stepping reflex stepped more on their own than did a control group of infants who received no extra practice. The researchers speculated that this occurs as a result of several factors. The practice may facilitate the ability of the baby to initiate the stepping pattern, or it may indirectly facilitate the baby's equilibrium. Yet another explanation posited by the researchers was that it could have enhanced the baby's muscle strength. Regardless of the explanation, the researchers believed that demonstrating this practice effect is important, because it will caution us to use care in interpreting established norms for motor achievement. Clearly, from this research, babies who are in homes where more practice may occur might not fall within normal ranges of development, rendering the charts somewhat fallible. In addition, this study determined that even small amounts of practice caused significant effects. This may contradict claims that early physical therapy will have only minimal effects on neuromotor development of children at this age (N. A. Zelazo et al., 1993).

The Reflexes as Diagnostic Tools

The infant reflexes are crucial for the infant's survival and for the development of future voluntary movements. These early, involuntary forms of movement behavior are also important in determining the infant's level of neurological maturation (Zafeiriou, Tsikoulas, & Kremenopolous, 1995). Pediatricians commonly use many reflexes as diagnostic tools. Although the age at which each infant reflex emerges and disappears varies with each child, knowledge of the normal timeline can help in diagnosing problems. Severe deviations from the normal time frame may indicate neurological immaturity or dysfunction. If the reflex in question is lacking, excessively weak, asymmetrical, or persisting past the normal age of offset, the examining health professional is alerted to a need for additional testing or for intervention to correct the dysfunction.

According to Blasco (1994), treatment and prognosis for maladies such as cerebral palsy are linked to and determined by several factors. These include

the infant's performance on classic neural exams, which motor milestones they have achieved at a given age, and their performance on various primitive reflexes. Therefore, pediatricians should possess a fundamental knowledge of these reflexes when examining infants. Clinical facility with infant reflexes is relatively easily acquired, easy to incorporate into exams, and quite useful in diagnosis (Blasco, 1994).

Reflexes should be tested carefully and only by trained professionals. Some parents become frantic when they cannot elicit a particular reflex, assuming that their child has an impaired neurological system when, in fact, the parents' incorrect application of the stimulus or the baby's temporary behavioral state is responsible for the lack of response. Normally, for any infant reflex to be elicited, there must be a state of quiet. If the baby is restless, crying, sleepy, or distracted, she may not respond to the applied stimulus; this lack of response certainly should not be considered an indication of a neurological aberration.

Many infant reflexes are tested during normal physical examinations of the baby. One of the most commonly used to detect neurological dysfunction is the Moro reflex, which may signify a cerebral birth injury if it is lacking or asymmetrical (appearing more forcefully on one side of the body than the other). The asymmetric tonic neck reflex is another common infant diagnostic tool. If this reflex perseveres past the normal time of disappearance, cerebral palsy or other neural damage could be indicated. These reflexes, described in more detail later, are two examples of the many infant reflexes that help health-care professionals determine the infant's neurological state.

The Milani Comparetti Neuromotor Developmental Examination is an evaluation instrument that uses several infant reflexes. This test was designed to evaluate the neurological maturity of children from birth to 24 months of age. This standardized method of examining reflexive movement presents an opportunity to inspect visually children's motor patterns and the patterns' appropriateness for the children's age. The overall objective of the test is to develop a profile of children's movement in relation to what is normally expected for children of a specific age. This examination is useful in monitoring motor function during normal checkups and is especially valuable for use with children suspected of a motor delay (Frankenburg, Thornton, & Cohrs, 1981).

A more recent tool designed to examine the status of the infant reflexes is the ***Primitive Reflex Profile*** (Capute et al., 1984). This scale was developed to enable quantification of the level of presence or strength of primitive reflexes such as the asymmetric tonic neck, the symmetric tonic neck, and the Moro reflexes. The authors of this profile believe that this tool is necessary because all previous reflex evaluation systems have noted only the presence or absence of the reflex, not the degree of strength. This system is also believed to enable a uniform grading system that assists in charting findings and facilitates communication of the results. Primitive reflexes are emphasized because of the major role they play in enabling normal motor function as they become suppressed throughout the first year of life. In fact, according to the authors of the profile, the primitive reflexes may be the most sensitive indicators of early motor abnormality. As mentioned earlier, if these reflexes persist past their expected time of occurrence, some dysfunction may be indicated.

To enable quantification of the reflexes, the Primitive Reflex Profile employs a five-point classification system. When a reflex is totally absent, a 0 is assigned, a 1 indicates a reflex that is only sufficiently present to create a small change in muscle tone. When the reflex is physically present and readily visible, a 2 is assigned, while a 3 indicates the same but with more noticeable strength or force. When the reflex is so strong that it dominates the individual, a 4 is assigned.

PINPOINTING THE NUMBER OF INFANT REFLEXES

The total number of infant reflexes is difficult to determine, for at least two reasons. First, various experts often use different terms to refer to the same reflex. For example, the rooting reflex is also called the search reflex or the cardinal points reflex because stimulation of the cardinal points—the four quadrants of the mouth—elicits a searching response.

Second, the reflexes themselves are often poorly defined. The components, as well as the name, of a certain infant reflex may vary, depending on the source. For example, the palmar grasp reflex generally is considered as consisting of the four fingers closing when the palm is stimulated. Twitchell (1970) has proposed that this reflex may in fact be much more complex. According to Twitchell, multiple stimuli and multiple responses are involved in the reflexive grasping. Along with the familiar closing of the four fingers, Twitchell describes a "synergistic flexion" response of the fingers as well as every joint of the arm when the appropriate muscles of the shoulders are stretched. This stretching, often referred to as a *traction response,* may occur when the palm of the hand is stimulated or even when there is a slight tug on the arm. In addition, Twitchell describes what he calls "local reactions." If specific areas of the hand are stimulated, there may be specific responses, depending on the infant's age or neurological maturity. For example, between the ages of 4 and 8 weeks, a stimulation between the thumb and forefinger elicits a flexion of just those two digits. During the following weeks, a similar response can be elicited for each finger individually if the surface of the palm near the base of that finger is stimulated. Are these local reactions distinct infant reflexes, or are they all part of the palmar grasp? Twitchell infers that these specific stimuli and responses are all a part of the development of the palmar grasp and eventually voluntary reaching and grasping behavior. Some sources differentiate between the palmar grasp reflex and the traction response; others cite only the palmar grasp. There is such confusion with other reflexes as well, complicating attempts to number and organize the infant reflexes accurately.

PRIMITIVE REFLEXES

Here we discuss the stimulus, response, approximate age of emergence and disappearance, and various points of interest concerning many infant primitive reflexes. This section is not an all-inclusive list of the

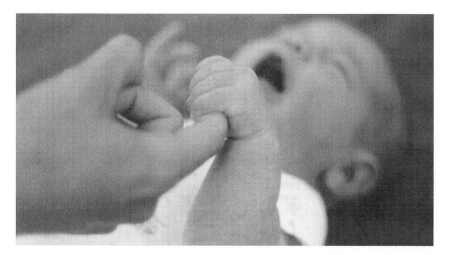

Figure 10-1 The palmar grasp reflex is one of the most noticeable reflexes to emerge.

infant reflexes; it discusses those reflexes considered the most interesting, important, or exemplary.

Palmar Grasp Reflex

The *palmar grasp reflex,* one of the most well known of all infant reflexes, may also be one of the first to emerge (see Figure 10-1). The palmar grasp reflex normally appears in utero, as early as the fifth month of gestation. As mentioned earlier, evidence indicates that this reflex may be much more complex than generally believed. However, the basic palmar grasp reflex is a response to tactile stimulation of the palm of the hand. When the palm is stimulated, all four fingers of the stimulated hand flex or close. Although the thumb does not respond to this stimulus, the grasping response of the reflex can be surprisingly forceful. For example, if an adult simultaneously stimulates both of an infant's palms, the infant may respond with a grasp sufficiently forceful to enable the adult to lift the infant completely off the supporting surface. The palmar grasp reflex normally endures through the fourth month. A grasping action of the hand will likely persist past that time, but it will be voluntary, not reflexive. In fact, the palmar grasp reflex is believed to play an important role in the acquisition of early forms of voluntary reaching and grasping (Twitchell, 1970).

Interestingly, researchers recently found that we may be able to predict handedness in adulthood by using the palmar grasp reflex. Tan and Tan (1999) measured grip strength in both the right and left hands during the palmar grasp response of several infants. The percentage of babies who were significantly stronger in the right hand versus the left paralleled the percentage seen in adults. This led the researchers to conclude that those babies who were consistently stronger in the right or left hand may well be stronger in that hand as an adult. The authors further speculated that, for those babies who showed no significant tendencies early on, handedness may change as it is influenced developmentally and socioculturally (Tan & Tan, 1999).

In a recent study of over 800 infants, Futagi, Suzuki, and Goto (1999) found that all the normal infants tested had a positive palmar grasp within the first 6 months of life. These researchers also determined that a negative palmar grasp (one that failed to appear) is highly indicative of neurological abnormality, especially for spasticity. They therefore recommended that infants with a negative palmar grasp response be observed carefully for neurological disorder.

Sucking Reflex

Another reflex that appears very early in life is the *sucking reflex,* which is normally present prenatally. In fact, babies are often born with "sucking blisters" on their lips. These minor, self-inflicted lesions, which may appear on one or both sides of the lips, result from the baby sucking in utero.

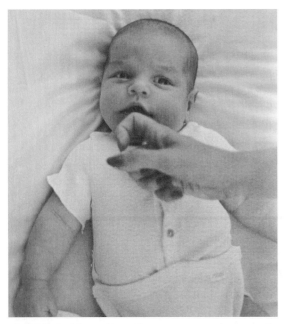

Figure 10-2   The sucking reflex occurs pre- and postnatally.

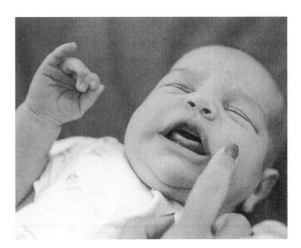

Figure 10-3   The search reflex helps the baby locate nourishment. The baby turns the head toward the food source when part of the cheek near the mouth is gently stimulated.

Recognition of these blisters is important to avoid excess anxiety by the baby's family or physician upon the baby's birth (Libow & Reinmann, 1998). The sucking response is elicited by the lips being stimulated, such as by the touch of the mother's breast or a finger (see Figure 10-2). This stimulation actually evokes two sucking-related responses. The first and most obvious response is the creation of a negative intraoral pressure as the sucking occurs. Second, the tongue applies a positive pressure; it presses upward and slightly forward with each sucking action. Thus, following the appropriate stimulation, there is a series of sucking movements, each movement consisting of the simultaneous application of negative and positive pressure. This movement normally remains a reflex through the third month of infancy; thereafter, it will be voluntary.

Search Reflex

The **search reflex** is often considered in conjunction with the sucking reflex, a logical approach because both reflexes are functionally linked to obtaining food. The search reflex helps the infant locate the source of nourishment, and then the sucking reflex

enables the baby to ingest the food. This reflex, however, contributes to more than the baby's nourishment, as the rotation of the neck often elicits other reflexes including the head- and body-righting reflexes. Also, failure or persistence of this reflex may be a sign of central nervous system or sensorimotor dysfunction. Asymmetrical appearance may mean an injury has occurred in a facial nerve or muscle or in one side of the brain (Barnes et al., 1984).

Like the sucking reflex, the search reflex is believed to exist for some weeks prenatally and persist through the third month of infancy in most instances. The search reflex normally can be elicited by softly stroking the area of the face surrounding the mouth. The corresponding response is the infant's head turning in the direction of the stimulus (see Figure 10-3). The sensitive area surrounding the mouth is sometimes referred to as the cardinal point, so the search reflex is also called the cardinal points reflex (and as mentioned earlier, the rooting reflex).

Moro Reflex

As mentioned, the **Moro reflex** is one of the most useful for diagnosing the infant's neurological maturation (see Figure 10-4). This reflex often exists at

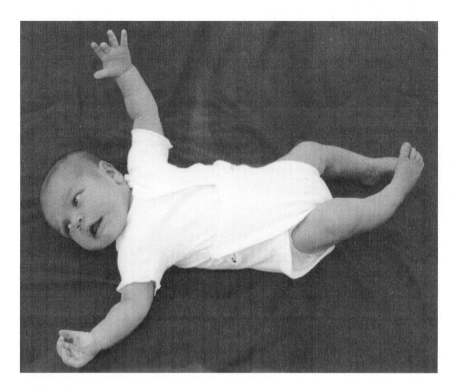

Figure 10-4 The Moro reflex is elicited by the same stimuli that induce the startle reflex. The Moro, however, precedes the startle and causes the arms and legs to extend immediately rather than flex.

birth and endures until the infant is approximately 4 to 6 months old.

The Moro reflex can be elicited in many ways. One stimulus is to place the palm of the hand under the baby's head and then suddenly but gently lower the head a few inches. This stimulus causes the baby's arms, fingers, and legs to extend. The same response occurs if the entire baby is held and suddenly lowered 3 or 4 inches. Also, if the surface on which the baby is lying is struck with the palm of the hand, normally the Moro reflex will occur. There is, however, some disagreement concerning the role of the legs in the Moro reflex. Most experts agree that the legs extend unless they were already extended, in which case they flex. Both of these situations may lead to a slight tremor or shaking of the legs (Barnes et al., 1984). Interestingly, the disappearance of this reflex depends on the type of stimulus used; the "head drop" Moro disappears sooner than the other two types. Furthermore, researchers have determined that there is a developmental trend related to how quickly the reflex responds to the stimulus—a form of reaction time. The shortest reaction time was found in 1-month-old

infants, with the time increasing through 2 and 3 months of age (Iiyama, Miyajima, & Hoshika, 2002).

Failure to acquire the Moro reflex by birth may indicate a central nervous system dysfunction. Persisting past the expected time of suppression may indicate a sensorimotor problem. In addition, persistence will delay voluntary sitting, head control, and other motor milestones. Asymmetry of the Moro, as we have seen with other reflexes, may indicate an injury to one side of the brain (Barnes et al., 1984).

Startle Reflex

Similar in many ways to the Moro reflex, the **startle reflex** can be elicited by a rapid change of head position or striking the surface that supports the baby. However, whereas the Moro causes the limbs to extend immediately, the startle reflex causes the arms and legs to flex immediately. Furthermore, the Moro normally disappears at 4 to 6 months of age, but the startle may not appear until 2 to 3 months after the Moro disappears. The startle reflex in this form is normally suppressed by 1 year of age, although

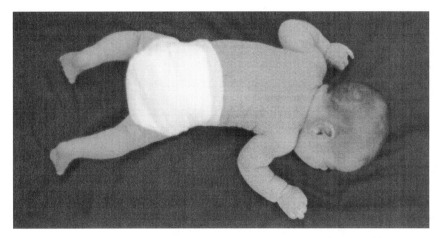

Figure 10-5 The asymmetric tonic neck reflex causes flexion on one side and extension on the other.

less-severe startle responses are elicited throughout the lifespan.

Asymmetric Tonic Neck Reflex

The *asymmetric tonic neck reflex,* sometimes referred to as the bow and arrow or fencer's position, is commonly seen in premature babies but may not be noticeable in full-term infants. This reflex can be elicited when the baby is prone or supine. When the head is turned to one side or the other, the limbs on the face side extend while the limbs on the opposite side flex (see Figure 10-5). The asymmetric tonic neck reflex is rare in the newborn (van Kranen-Mastenbroek et al., 1997) but occasionally can be elicited in infants up to 3 months old. This reflex is believed to facilitate the development of an awareness of both sides of the body as well as help develop eye-hand coordination (Lord, 1977).

Symmetric Tonic Neck Reflex

In the asymmetric tonic neck reflex, the right-side limbs respond differently from the left-side limbs, but this is not the case in the *symmetric tonic neck reflex.* As the term implies, the limbs in this reflex move symmetrically. This symmetrical response can be elicited by placing the baby in a supported sitting position. If the infant is tipped backward far enough, the neck eventually extends, which is the stimulus for a corresponding extension

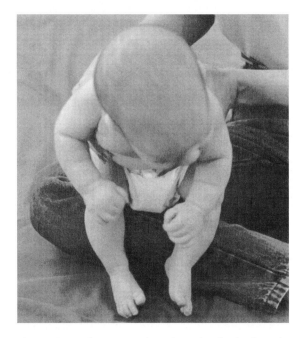

Figure 10-6 The symmetric tonic neck reflex is often observable during the first few months of life.

of the arms and flexion of the legs. However, if the baby is tipped forward until the neck is fully flexed, the arms flex, and the legs extend (see Figure 10-6).

Like the asymmetric tonic neck reflex, the symmetric tonic neck reflex is often noticeable from birth through approximately 3 months of age. Also

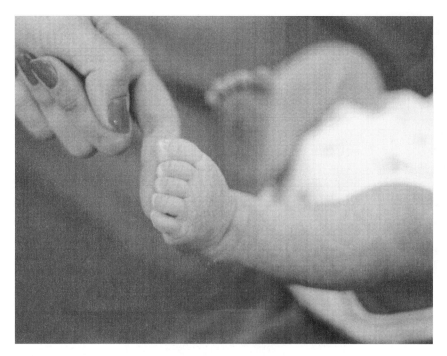

Figure 10-7 In the plantar grasp reflex, the toes appear to be attempting to grasp.

like the asymmetric tonic neck reflex, persistence in this reflex can cause serious problems. For example, persistence may impede voluntary head raising when the infant is in a prone or supine position. It will also inhibit reaching and grasping, unsupported sitting, balance for walking, and virtually all major motor milestones. Finally, spinal flexion deformities may occur as well (Barnes et al., 1984).

Plantar Grasp Reflex

From birth through the first year of infancy, the *plantar grasp reflex* normally can be elicited. This reflex is evoked by applying slight pressure, usually with the fingertip, to the ball of the foot, causing all the toes of that foot to flex. The toes curl around the stimulating object as if attempting to grasp, as in the palmar grasp reflex of the hand (see Figure 10-7).

The plantar grasp must be suppressed before the child can stand erect, stand alone, or walk. Parents will also have difficulty in putting shoes on a child who still exhibits an active plantar grasp reflex (Barnes et al., 1984).

Babinski Reflex

The year 1996 marked the 100th anniversary of the description of the *Babinski reflex* by Joseph Francois Felix Babinski (Gasecki & Hachinski, 1996). Like the plantar grasp reflex, the Babinski reflex is normally evident from birth. It remains present for the first several months of life. To elicit a response, the bottom or lateral portion of the foot is stroked (see Figure 10-8), resulting in a downward turning of the great toe and sometimes all the toes of the stimulated foot (van Gijn, 1996). The Babinski reflex, or "sign" as it is sometimes called, is believed to be a "faithful" test of the pyramidal tract that would be an indicator of our ability to perform conscious or voluntary movement (Barraquer-Bordas, 1998).

Palmar Mandibular Reflex

The *palmar mandibular reflex,* or Babkin reflex, is another infant reflex normally present at birth. The Babkin is elicited by applying pressure simultaneously

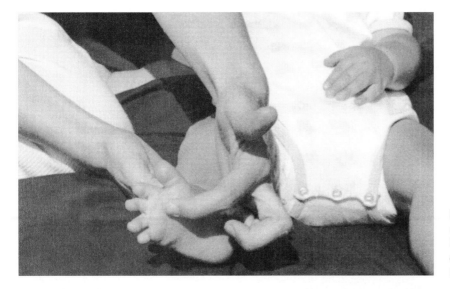

Figure 10-8 The Babinski reflex is elicited by a stimulus somewhat similar to that of the plantar grasp reflex, but the response is different.

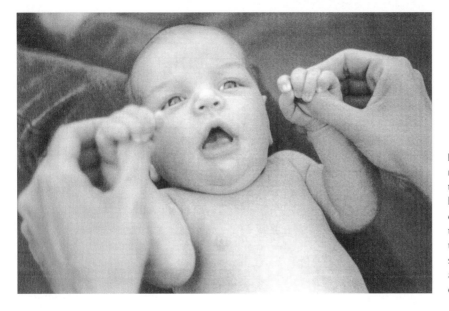

Figure 10-9 The palmar mandibular reflex is one of the most unusual reflexes because it makes the eyes close, the mouth open, and the head tilt forward. Here, the infant has begun to respond by opening his mouth and is about to close his eyes.

to the palm of each hand, eliciting all or one of the following responses: the mouth opens, the eyes close, and the neck flexes, tilting the head forward (see Figure 10-9). The Babkin response also occurs if the hand of a human neonate is lightly stimulated by hair. The Babkin reflex normally disappears by age 3 months. Interestingly, some experts believe that this reflex links the human to animals lower on the phylogenetic scale, because it often helps young animals cling to their mothers when feeding.

Palmar Mental Reflex

The **palmar mental reflex,** like the Babkin, elicits a facial response when the base of the palm of either hand is scratched; this scratching causes the

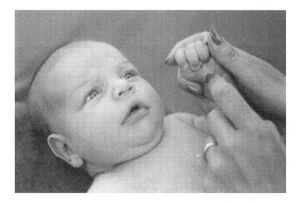

Figure 10-10   The palmar mental reflex is elicited by scratching the base of either palm.

lower jaw to open and close (see Figure 10-10). The actual response is thus a series of contractions of the jaw muscles. Like the Babkin, the palmar mental reflex is first observable at birth and normally ceases by the third month.

POSTURAL REFLEXES

Here we discuss the details of the postural reflexes. As with the primitive reflexes, the discussion is not meant to be comprehensive, but it does highlight important points about these reflexes.

Stepping Reflex

The *stepping reflex* (or walking reflex) is an essential forerunner to an important voluntary movement, walking. The stepping reflex is elicited by holding the infant upright with the feet touching a supporting surface; the pressure on the bottom of the feet causes the legs to lift and then descend (see Figure 10-11). This leg action often occurs alternately and therefore resembles a crude form of walking. Although this reflex is also called the walking reflex, there is none of the hip stability or accompanying arm movement that occurs with voluntary walking. The stepping—or walking—reflex generally can be elicited within the first few weeks

following birth and persists through the fifth or sixth month.

Interestingly, researchers have observed developmental changes across the first several months of this reflex. These include excessive coactivation or simultaneous contraction of the mutual antagonist muscles during the stance phase of the pattern (when both feet are touching the ground) during the first month (Okamoto, Okamoto, & Andrew, 2001). However, during the second month of existence, the contraction patterns become more cooperative or reciprocal, despite the continuing existence of a somewhat "squatted posture and a forward lean" during the "walk." The researchers believe these changes to be a function of gradual improvements in balance, postural control, and strength that ultimately lead to the phasing out of the reflex as complete voluntary control of walking sets in.

Crawling Reflex

The *crawling reflex* is another example of an infant reflex considered a precursor to later voluntary movement. This reflex can be observed from birth through the first 3 to 4 months. To elicit this reflex, the baby is placed prone on the floor or table. The soles of the feet are stroked alternately, causing the legs and arms to move in a crawlinglike action (see Figure 10-12). The crawling reflex disappears about 3 months before more voluntary creeping begins. This reflex is believed essential for furthering development of sufficient muscular tone for future voluntary creeping.

Swimming Reflex

One of the most unusual infant reflexes is the *swimming reflex.* Involuntary swimminglike movements can be elicited days after birth. The baby is held horizontally over a solid surface, such as a tabletop or a floor, over the surface of water, or in the water. The response to the stimulus is the arms and legs moving in a well-coordinated swimming-type action (see Figure 10-13). These movements are observable as early as the second neonatal week and normally endure through the fifth month of

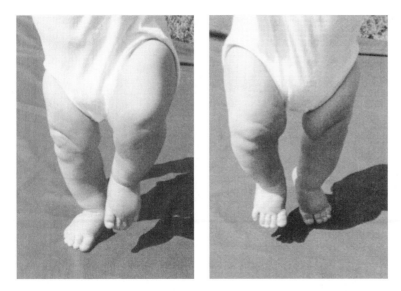

Figure 10-11 The stepping reflex can be elicited within the first few weeks following birth, even though unassisted voluntary walking may not occur until the first birthday.

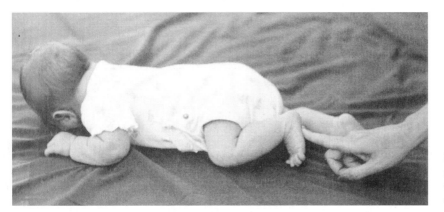

Figure 10-12 The crawling reflex is believed essential to the development of future voluntary creeping.

infancy. Recognition of this reflex has contributed substantially to the popularity of infant swim programs. Proponents of such programs assume that early stimulation of this reflex will positively affect voluntary swimming later in life. Presently, as discussed in Chapter 6, there is no scientific evidence to support this view.

Head- and Body-Righting Reflexes

The **head- and body-righting reflexes** are two similar infant reflexes believed related to the attainment of voluntary rolling movements. The head-righting reflex can be observed as early as the first month of infancy. This reflex is elicited by turning the baby's body in either direction when the infant is supine. The head responds by "righting" itself with the body; in other words, the head returns to a front-facing position relative to the shoulders (see Figure 10-14). This reflex normally disappears by the age of 6 months.

In contrast to the head-righting reflex, the body-righting reflex involves the head turning and the body "righting" itself. If the infant is placed supine and the head gently turned to one side or the other, the body follows. That is, the body rotates in the direction the

Figure 10-13 The swimming reflex is characterized by the baby's swimminglike movements when held in a horizontal position.

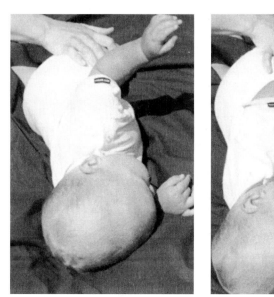

Figure 10-14 In the head-righting reflex, the head "rights" itself with the body when the body is turned to one side.

head is turned to regain the front-facing relationship between the head and the shoulders. This rotation of the body is not segmental; the body responds by rotating as a single unit (Fiorentino, 1963). Unlike the head-righting reflex, the body-righting reflex may not be evident until the fifth month of infancy. It frequently lasts throughout the first year of life.

Parachuting Reflexes

The *parachuting reflexes* (or propping reflexes) appear related to the attainment of upright posture. These reflexes occur when the infant is tipped off balance in any direction. Being off balance when in an upright position stimulates a protective movement

Figure 10-15   Parachuting reflexes appear to occur consciously in an effort to break a potential fall, but like all reflexes, they are really subcortical.

in the direction of the potential fall. For example, when the infant is tilted forward, the arms make a propping movement, extending toward the front as the fingers extend and separate. This reflex occurs as early as 4 months of age. These propping movements appear to be conscious attempts to break a fall, but like all infant reflexes, they are involuntary. See Figure 10-15.

These propping movements can also occur downward, sideward, and backward. The downward parachuting reaction can be elicited as early as 4 months if the child is suddenly lowered 2 to 3 feet when held upright. The infant's legs suddenly extend and spread, and the feet rotate slightly outward. The sideward propping movements are observable after approximately 6 months of age and are most easily elicited by placing the infant in a sitting position and then gently tilting him to either side. As in the

forward parachuting reflex, the arms and fingers extend, in this case toward the side of the potential fall. The backward propping may not occur until 10 months of age and, like the other parachuting reflexes, normally causes a propping movement in the direction of the fall. However, the backward propping reflex may also cause the body to rotate, apparently to avoid falling backward. All the propping reflexes frequently persist past the first year of life.

In a study conducted specifically on the parachuting and lateral propping reflexes of preterm infants, researchers determined that these reflexes existed in approximately 8 percent of babies at 6 months, but nearly 90 percent by 9 months of age. As a result, these researchers concluded that lateral and parachuting reflexes can be assessed in preterm children and may be viable markers of neurological development (Ohlweiler, da Silva, & Rotta, 2002).

Labyrinthine Reflex

The *labyrinthine reflex* generally appears at approximately 2 to 3 months of age and lasts throughout the first year of life. This reflex, like the parachuting reflexes, may be critical to the attainment of upright posture. The labyrinthine is characterized by the head tilting in a direction opposite the direction the body is tilted (see Figure 10-16). For example, if the infant is held at the waist and tilted forward, the neck extends to enable the head to maintain its original upright position. If the baby is tilted backward, the neck extends to enable the head to maintain the upright position. A similar response occurs when the baby is tilted to either side.

Pull-Up Reflex

The *pull-up reflex* may also be related to the attainment of upright posture. Furthermore, like the labyrinthine reflex, the pull-up reflex may not be observable until the third month of infancy. This reflex is most easily elicited by placing the infant in a supported standing position. Holding the baby's hands, one carefully tips her in any direction; this stimulus makes the supporting arm(s) flex or extend in an apparent effort to maintain the upright posi-

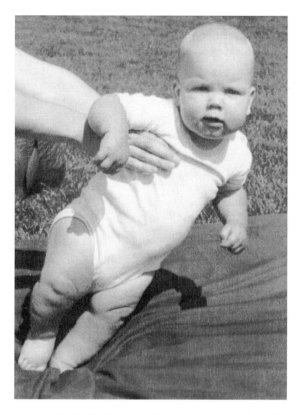

Figure 10-16 The labyrinthine reflex endures throughout most of the first year and apparently is related to the attainment of upright posture.

tion (see Figure 10-17). For example, if the baby is tipped backward, the arms flex to pull her toward the supporting person and back into an upright position. If the infant is tipped forward, the arms extend to push her away from the supporting person and back toward the initial upright position. The pull-up reflexes generally disappear by the first birthday.

STEREOTYPIES

The infant reflexes are the most studied form of human movement during the first few months of life. Much less attention has been paid to another group of movements also characteristic of infancy. These

movements, known as ***stereotypies,*** were studied over a half century ago by Lourie (1949). In examining the rhythmic patterns of over 100 normal children, Lourie established several hypotheses about their function. He believed that these somewhat unusual movements are inherent and crucial to the life of a healthy child, as he found increasing numbers of stereotypies in children who had less than normal control over their movement. Among their purposes, Lourie posited, was to decrease tension and anxiety, as he noticed increasing amounts of stereotypies during periods of higher anxiety. The stereotypies seemed to calm the child. He also believed that these movements provide stimulation for further development while they offered considerable sensory stimulation, and may even be the bridge to eventual development of more advanced voluntary movement. Thus, Lourie (1949) encouraged these movements as beneficial to later development.

In the more recent work by Thelen (1979), stereotypies were described as rhythmical, patterned, seemingly centrally controlled movements. They are believed to be relatively intrinsic, because they do not appear to be behaviors infants learn by imitation. In addition, these stereotyped movements do not seem to serve a purpose and are often invariant (Lewis et al., 1996; Sprague & Newell, 1996), as they are not regulated by the sensory system. They generally represent movements that are among the most simple, patterned actions for the muscle group involved. Stereotypies are often simple flexions, extensions, or rotations that are repeated in nearly identical, often alternating, fashion. While some may view stereotypies as inaccurate forms of movement, Piek and Carman (1994) have proclaimed them to be "partial" responses. Regardless, because these behaviors are seen in most human infants, their study is certainly warranted.

Interestingly, this type of movement is common among insects, birds, and fish. Among primates, such as zoo animals, repetitive, patterned movements are often considered pathological. Even for the human being, during any other time of life such movement would be considered abnormal; indeed,

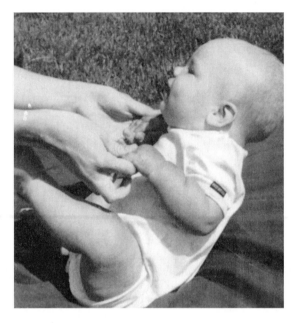

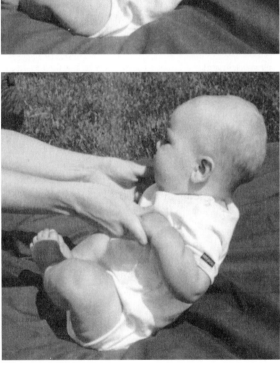

Figure 10-17 In the pull-up reflex, when the baby is tipped backward, an arm flexes in an effort to maintain the upright position.

such behavior is often seen in people with mental or emotional problems. In the human infant, however, stereotypies are considered normal behavior that is evidence of functional maturation of the neurological system. However, they are not a sign of voluntary, goal-oriented movement behavior.

In her research, Thelen (1979) observed many different stereotypies. She also found that all 20 infants she observed exhibited stereotypies. In fact, during the periods when stereotyping behavior was most common, the infants often spent as much as 40 percent of each hour exhibiting stereotypies.

Stereotypies of the legs and feet were one of the most common and first forms of rhythmical and patterned behavior Thelen observed. Rhythmical kicking was the first noticed and was evident for months to follow. These stereotypies of the legs and feet most commonly occurred when the babies were prone or supine. Examples of the leg and feet stereotypies Thelen observed were simultaneous leg kicking, alternate leg kicking, feet rubbing together, single leg kicks of various kinds, and a sharp flexing of the backs of the legs. Stereotypies of the legs were the most common form of stereotyped movement noted. They also began earlier than the other types, as early as 4 weeks of age. These rhythmical, patterned movements of the legs and feet seemed to reach their peak occurrence at around 24 to 32 weeks of age, becoming much less common by 44 to 52 weeks.

Thelen found that the legs and feet were not the only parts of the body to become involved in stereotyped movement. She categorized other stereotypies by their location of occurrence: Several stereotypies occurred in the region of the hands and arms, including arm waving while holding an object, and one arm, as well as two arms, banging against a surface. Thelen also noted several patterned, repetitive hand movements such as total hand flexion and rotation as well as individual finger flexion. The peak occurrence for arm and hand stereotypies was 34 to 42 weeks. However, the arm stereotypies generally appeared as early as 4 to 12 weeks, whereas the hand movements typically were not evident until 14 to 22 weeks. The finger stereotypies, like the movements of the arms, occurred as early as 4 to 12 weeks but reached their peak at 24 to 32 weeks.

Thelen placed another group of stereotypies into what she termed the "torso" category. Included were such movements as arching the back and rocking when in an "all fours" or a creepinglike position, rocking and bouncing when in an unsupported sitting position, and bouncing while standing. In general, these movements often reached their peak later than the movements of the legs and feet and the arms and hands, although they first appeared as early as 14 to 22 months of age.

Thelen's final category of stereotyped movement of infancy was the head and face. This grouping included some of the most interesting stereotypies. Compared with other such movements, the stereotypies in this category were considered somewhat rare. Examples of head and face stereotypies were head nodding, head shaking as if indicating "no," in and out tongue protrusions, and nonnutritive sucking. Thelen also noted small rhythmical mouthing movements.

The most common stereotypies were the single leg kick, two-leg kick, alternate leg kick, arm wave, arm wave with an object, arm banging against a surface with and without an object, and finger flexion. Thelen concluded that these, as well as the other stereotyped forms of behavior she noted, are apparently developmentally significant. She reached this conclusion on noticing that, for example, stereotyped kicking precedes voluntary use of the legs and stereotyped finger flexion precedes voluntary attempts at grasping. However, stereotypes have not been absolutely determined to be precursors of more mature motor behavior.

The number of different stereotypies increases throughout the first year. The frequency of occurrence also increases throughout the first year, peaking at approximately 24 to 42 weeks of age. Throughout the first year, many stereotypies cease and new ones emerge. There is then a major decline in the occurrence of stereotypies during the last 2 to 3 months of the first year.

SUMMARY

During the last 4 months in utero and the first 4 months of postnatal life, infant reflexes and stereotypies are the dominant form of human movement. An infant reflex is an involuntary and routine response to a particular stimulus.

The infant reflexes are extremely important to human development for several reasons. Many of the reflexes are protective; the sucking reflex, for example, enables babies to ingest food. Other reflexes help the baby avoid injury.

The infant reflexes are considered crucial for the development of subsequent voluntary movements. Reflexes such as crawling, labyrinthine, palmar grasp, and stepping are essential to the normal attainment of voluntary crawling, upright posture, voluntary grasping, and voluntary walking, respectively.

Other infant reflexes are important for neurologically examining the infant and diagnosing any abnormality. The ages of onset and offset of the infant reflexes normally follow a predictable timeline. Deviations from that timeline sometimes indicate neurological damage. Also, an excessively weak, lacking, asymmetrical, or persistent reflex can indicate a variety of neurological problems.

Stereotypies are another form of movement observable during infancy. These movements are characterized by patterned, stereotyped, highly intrinsic, and apparently involuntary movements of the legs and feet; arms, hands, and fingers; torso; and head and face. Like reflexes, stereotypies are believed important in the development of more advanced voluntary movements in later life.

KEY TERMS

asymmetric tonic neck reflex
Babinski reflex
crawling reflex
head- and body-righting reflexes
labyrinthine reflex
lifespan reflexes
Moro reflex
palmar grasp reflex

palmar mandibular reflex
palmar mental reflex
parachuting reflexes
plantar grasp reflex
postural reflexes
Primitive Reflex Profile
primitive reflexes
pull-up reflex

search reflex
startle reflex
stepping reflex
stereotypies
subcortical
sucking reflex
swimming reflex
symmetric tonic neck reflex

QUESTIONS FOR REFLECTION

1. What is a reflex?
2. What is the difference between primitive and postural reflexes?
3. Is there any practical value in knowing and understanding the infant reflexes? Give three examples.
4. What are the characteristics of a primitive reflex? Give five examples of a primitive reflex and concisely explain each.
5. What are the differences between a startle and a Moro reflex?
6. Explain five different postural reflexes with emphasis on how each would be elicited.
7. How would one elicit the search reflex? Can you think of any reasons why this reflex is important to human development?
8. What are the differences between asymmetric and symmetric tonic neck reflexes?
9. What is a stereotypie? How does it differ from and how is it similar to a reflex? Give five examples of stereotypies.

ONLINE LEARNING CENTER (www.mhhe.com/payne6e)

Visit the *Human Motor Development* Online Learning Center for study aids and additional resources. You can use the study guide questions and key terms puzzles to review key terms and concepts for this chapter and to prepare for exams. You can further extend your knowledge of motor development by checking out the Web links, articles, and activities found on the site.

REFERENCES

Barnes, M. R., Crutchfield, C. A., & Heriza, C. B. (1984). *The neurophysiological basis of patient treatment:* Vol. 2. *Reflexes in motor development.* Atlanta, GA: Stokesville.

Barraquer-Bordas, L. (1998). What does the Babinski sign have to offer 100 years after its description? *Neurological Review, 154*(1), 22–27.

Blasco, P. A. (1994). Primitive reflexes: Their contribution to the early detection of cerebral palsy. *Clinical Pediatrics, 33*(7), 388–397.

Bower, T. G. R. (1976, Nov.). Repetitive processes in child development. *Scientific American,* 38–47.

Capute, A. J., Palmer, F. B., Shapiro, B. F., Wachtel, R. C., Ross, A., & Accardo, P. J. (1984). Primitive Reflex Profile: A quantifation of primitive reflexes in infancy. *Developmental Medicine and Child Neurology, 26,* 375–383.

Coley, I. L. (1978). *Pediatric assessment of self-care activities.* St. Louis, MO: Mosby.

Fiorentino, M. R. (1963). *Reflex testing methods for evaluating C.N.S. development.* Springfield, IL: Thomas.

———. (1981). *A basis for sensorimotor development: The influence of the primitive, postural reflexes on the development and distribution of tone.* Springfield, IL: Thomas.

Frankenburg, W. K., Thornton, S. M., & Cohrs, M. E. (1981). *Pediatric developmental diagnosis.* New York: Thieme-Stratton.

Futagi, Y., Suzuki, Y., & Goto, M. (1999). Clinical significance of the plantar grasp response in infants. *Pediatric Neurology, 20*(2), 111–115.

Gasecki, A. P., & Hachinksi, V. (1996). On the names of Babinski. *Canadian Journal of Neurological Science, 23*(1), 76–79.

Iiyama, M., Miyajima, T., & Hoshika, A. (2002). Developmental change of Moro reflex with a three-dimensional motion analysis system. *No to Hattatsu, [Brain and Development] 34*(4), 307–312.

Lewis, M. H., Gluck, J. P., Bodfish, J. W., Beauchamp, A. J., & Mailman, R. B. (1996). Neurobiological basis of stereotyped movement disorder. In R. L. Sprague & K. M. Newell (Eds.), *Stereotyped movements: Brain and behavior relationships* (pp. 37–67). Washington, DC: Hafner.

Libow, L. F., & Reinmann, J. G. (1998). Symmetrical erosions in the neonate: A case of neonatal sucking blisters. *Cutis, 62*(1), 16–17.

Lord, L. (1977). Normal motor development in infants. In M. J. Krajicek & A. I. Tearney (Eds.), *Detection of developmental problems in children.* Baltimore: University Park Press.

Lourie, R. S. (1949). The role of rhythmic patterns in childhood. *American Journal of Psychiatry,* 653–660.

Ohlweiler, L., da Silva, A. R., & Rotta, N. T. (2002). Parachute and lateral propping reactions in preterm children. *Arquivos de Neuro-psiquiatria, 60*(4), 964–966.

Okamoto, T., Okamoto, K., & Andrew, P. D. (2001). Electromyographic study of newborn stepping in neonates and young infants. *Electromyographic and Clinical Neurophysiology, 41*(5), 289–296.

Piek, J. P., & Carman, R. (1994). Developmental profiles of spontaneous movements in infants. *Early Human Development, 39,* 109–126.

Sprague, R. L., & Newell, K. M. (1996). *Stereotyped movements: Brain and behavior relationships.* Washington, DC: American Psychological Association.

Tan, U., & Tan, M. (1999). Incidence of asymmetries for the palmar grasp reflex in neonates and hand preference in adults. *Neuroreport, 10*(16), 3253–3256.

Thelen, E. (1979). Rhythmical stereotypies in normal human infants. *Animal Behavior, 27,* 699–715.

Twitchell, T. E. (1970). Reflex mechanisms in the development of prehension. In K. J. Connolly (Ed.), *Mechanisms of motor skill development.* New York: Academic Press.

van Gijn, J. (1996). The Babinski sign: The first hundred years. *Journal of Neurology, 243*(10), 675–683.

van Kranen-Mastenbroek, V. H., Folman, K. B., Kaberg, H. B., Kingma, H., Blanco, C. E., Troost, J., Hasaart, T. H., & Vles, J. S. (1997). The influence of head position and head position changes on spontaneous body posture and motility in full term AGA and SGA newborn infants. *Brain Development, 19*(2), 104–110.

Wyke, B. (1975). The neurological basis of movement: A developmental review. In K. Holt (Ed.), *Movement and child development.* Philadelphia: Lippincott.

Zafeiriou, D. I., Tsikoulas, I. G., & Kremenopolous, G. M. (1995). Prospective follow-up of primitive reflex profiles in high risk infants: Clues to an early diagnosis of cerebral palsy. *Pediatric Neurology, 13*(2), 148–152.

Zelazo, N. A., Zelazo, P., Cohen, K. M., & Zelazo, P. D. (1993). Specificity of practice effects on elementary neuromotor patterns. *Developmental Psychology, 29*(4), 686–691.

Zelazo, P. (1976). From reflexive to instrumental behavior. In L. P. Lipsitt (Ed.), *Developmental psychobiology: The significance of injury.* Hillsdale, NJ: Erlbaum.

11 Voluntary Movements of Infancy

As discussed in Chapter 10, reflexive movement is the first dominant form of human movement. The reflex is a unique form of movement that is involuntary and subcortical; it is performed without conscious effort and without stimulation from the higher brain centers. At about the fourth week of life, however, cortically controlled *voluntary movement* begins to appear (Wyke, 1975). The first signs of voluntary movement are slight: movements of only the head, neck, and eyes. Nevertheless, after these first cortically controlled movements appear, the voluntary movements become increasingly prevalent and instrumental in enabling children to move in their environment. As you know, a child during the first year of life has been described as a "reflex machine" (Wyke, 1975, p. 27), but cerebral cortical control slowly assumes command of movement production as the subcortically produced reflexes gradually disappear. The diameters of the nerve dendrites, which carry the electrical stimulation to induce movement, slowly increase, accelerating the velocity of the stimulation and thus more efficiently facilitating the motor nerve cell activity necessary for producing voluntary movement.

According to Hershkowitz (2000), the disappearance of the early reflexes occurs at a time when the brain's cortex is beginning to inhibit reflexes from the lower brain areas, such as the brain stem—a major behavioral event in the first year of life. The process of the higher brain center slowly assuming command is gradual, but by the end of the first year, there is almost complete voluntary control of movement. A few of the infant reflexes discussed in Chapter 10 may endure past the first year of life, but most disappear. Voluntary movement, "the ultimate expression in the striated muscle of the integrated effects of a host of cortical and subcortical facilitory and inhibitory influences" (Wyke, 1975, p. 27), becomes the dominant source of human movement midway through the first year of life.

The voluntary movements of infancy are commonly called rudimentary movements (Gallahue & Ozmun, 2002) because they are the "rudiments" of future, more advanced movement forms. These early voluntary movements are the first, slight beginnings of the more advanced movements that normally follow.

Through a sequential, predictable, generally universal sequence of movement acquisition, the early voluntary movements gradually progress into the more readily recognizable movements of later life. For example, the first year brings major changes in a baby's ability to position the body. This new ability eventually frees the hands to enhance voluntary reaching and grasping movements. Another example is the achievement of upright posture, which enables the child to accomplish the most popular motor landmark of early life: walking. These progressions are discussed in greater depth throughout this chapter.

CATEGORIZING THE VOLUNTARY MOVEMENTS OF INFANCY

For ease of organization and discussion, the voluntary movements of infancy are often grouped into three major categories. Depending on the source, the terminology for the three categories varies somewhat. According to Gallahue and Ozmun (2002), the three major categories of early voluntary movement are stability, locomotion, and manipulation. *Stability* includes a wide range of voluntary movements, from head control to the eventual attainment of upright posture. *Locomotion* includes such movements as creeping and crawling and all their variations. Finally, *manipulation* involves the voluntary use of the hands, such as the entire progression of movements leading to the attainment of a mature reaching, grasping, and releasing ability. These and all the other important voluntary movements of infancy are discussed on the following pages, in the order of their appearance when possible. This pattern cannot be followed absolutely, however, because often the infant acquires more than one motor ability simultaneously.

HEAD CONTROL

Because the human being typically develops movement ability cephalocaudally, acquisition of the ability to make voluntary movements begins at the head.

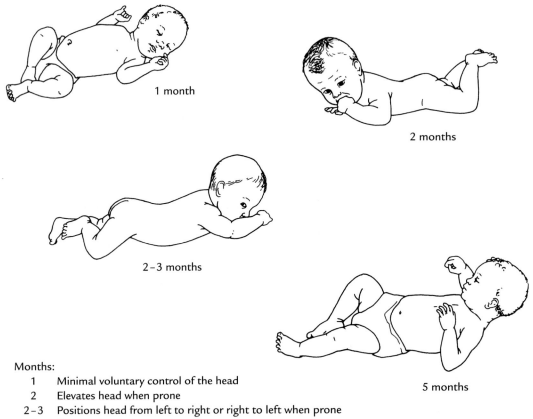

1 month

2 months

2-3 months

5 months

Months:
1   Minimal voluntary control of the head
2   Elevates head when prone
2-3 Positions head from left to right or right to left when prone
5   Elevates head when supine

Figure 11-1 Voluntary control of the head

When born, a baby has virtually no voluntary control over the head or neck, although reflexive movement may be evident, as in the head-righting reflex discussed in Chapter 10 (when the body is turned to one side or the other, the head rights itself with the shoulders). Conscious, cortical, or voluntary control over the head or neck may gradually become apparent by the end of the first month of life (Hottinger, 1980). This progression continues until 5 months, at which time the child normally exhibits relatively good muscular control over this region of the body. Figure 11-1 depicts this general sequence of head movements, which is initiated by the child elevating the head when placed prone. This seemingly simple act is often evident at approximately 2 months of age. Soon thereafter, at 2 to 3 months of age, the child can position the head from left to right or right to left when prone. When 3 months old, a child normally is capable of maintaining the head erect and upright when held in an upright sitting or standing position. Finally, at approximately 5 months of age, the child can raise the head when supine. This movement, as well as those described earlier, may seem insignificant, but vision is initially the only means of exploring the environment. Control of the head enables infants to scan their surroundings thoroughly while initiating the complex process of attaining upright posture.

BODY CONTROL

In the cephalocaudal pattern of development, control of the uppermost areas of the body follows attainment of head control. Then gradually, lower areas of the body also gain voluntary control. This cephalocaudal progression in body control begins at about 2 months of age, when the child gains the ability to elevate not only the head but the chest as well. The infant executes this maneuver by applying pressure to the supporting surface with the upper arms. This does not indicate particularly useful control of the arms, however, because the forearms and hands play a minimal role in this effort. Control of the arms, hands, and fingers is more thoroughly discussed later in the chapter.

Gaining voluntary control of body movement is particularly important during the first few months of life, because these early forms of movement are crucial for attaining more advanced movements. For example, one of the most important forms of body control evident after chest elevation is the child's attempt to roll from a supine to a prone position. The acquisition of this movement skill at approximately 6 months enables the child to attain the proper position for crawling. A form of rolling generally is noticeable earlier in life, but that movement is reflexive, not voluntary. The voluntary back-to-front rolling action is initially rigid, but gradually the movement becomes "segmented," with the head turning first, followed by the shoulders, trunk, and hips (Zaichowsky, Zaichowsky, & Martinek, 1980). By approximately 8 months, the infant can roll from front to back as well as from back to front.

Another important voluntary movement that indicates children's constantly expanding repertoire of movement is the attainment of upright posture. Upright posture is important because it frees the hands for more selective reaching, grasping, and releasing (see Figure 11-2). While supine or prone, the child has limited use of the arms and hands. In fact, these body parts are often occupied with maintaining or changing the horizontal body position and therefore are unavailable for selective attempts to obtain or manipulate objects in the child's environment. If as-

Figure 11-2 Ability to maintain upright posture frees the hands and arms for reaching and grasping.

sisted, infants can sit as early as 3 months of age. Because infants have very little lumbar control at that time, a helpful hand is necessary for supporting the lower back and abdomen. This sitting skill evolves into the ability to sit without such support by 5 months of age, because lumbar control has increased substantially. Nevertheless, the child may not have complete control of the lower back and abdomen, so the sitting position is characterized by an acute forward lean. Furthermore, the child's ability to balance is still inadequate, so infants at 5 months need to stabilize themselves by holding an external object, such as a piece of furniture. By 7 months, the child has gained sufficient movement ability to attain this self-supported sitting position from either a prone or a supine position. Finally, by approximately 8 months, most children can sit without assistance or support.

Attainment of upright body posture, like sitting, is clearly a major achievement of early development. Sitting alone offers many benefits to the infant, including its possible effect on the achievement of other abilities. For example, Rochat (1992) has studied the impact of an infant's ability to "self-sit" on the development of early eye-hand coordination. Rochat's subjects were two groups of infants 5–8 months old. Half were able and half were unable to sit on their own. Each infant was presented with a variety of displays while in four different positions: seated, reclined, prone (75 degrees to the floor), and supine. Overall, nonsitters contacted the objects in the display 89 percent of the time, while sitters made contact 98 percent of the time. All infants were found to have the least amount of success while in the supine position. Furthermore, nonsitters exhibited significantly more two-handed reaches overall. However, when seated, the nonsitters' incidence of two-handed responses decreased, compared with other positions. Overall, sitters tended to reach more with one hand in all positions, while the nonsitters tended to use one hand only when seated. Rochat believes these findings demonstrate the importance of self-sitting on early eye-hand coordination. Specifically, infants' ability to sit appears to be linked to the use of the hands in reaching activities (Rochat, 1992).

The progression in attaining upright posture does not end with sitting. One of the most popular movement landmarks is achieving complete upright posture, an unsupported standing position. This movement ability, like the others discussed earlier, is critical to future development. An upright posture enables children to walk; walking lets children expand their exploratory range and therefore facilitates cognitive, social, and motor development. The onset of the standing progression generally occurs at about 9 months, when the child begins to exhibit an ability to pull from a sitting to a standing position. For the child to attain the standing position, an external object such as a piece of furniture is required for support. Following a period of experimentation to "test" the balance, the child can stand beside furniture, occasionally reaching out for support. This standing position is characterized by a wide base of support and a "high guard" arm position. In other words, the feet generally are a considerable distance apart and the hands held high. By the age of 1 year, the child often can stand unas-

sisted (see Figure 11-3). Walking, which soon follows in the motor development progression, is discussed in Chapter 13.

In a longitudinal study on the development of crawling (Adolph, Vereijken, & Denny, 1998) 28 babies were followed from their first attempt to crawl until they began to walk. The researchers focused specifically on how age, body dimensions, and experience affected crawling development. Major findings are summarized in Table 11-1. Generally, however, these researchers found that "each subsequent posture marked a small triumph over gravity in an orderly march toward erect locomotion" (p. 1299). Gradual, continuous improvement in both crawling proficiency and speed were noted as most babies, but not all, displayed "stages" on their way to walking. Some babies skipped a stage completely, while several were found to "straddle" stages. For example, nearly half of the babies skipped belly crawling altogether. Nevertheless, notable individual patterns in the developmental sequence included lifting the head and chest off the ground, pivoting in circles while on the belly, pulling forward with the abdomen dragging on the ground, hopping forward on the belly with the belly alternately on and off the ground, and rhythmical rocking on the hands and knees.

While strict stages were not found to exist, a consistent trend did occur. For example, all babies studied demonstrated at least one "clumsy" precursor to prone progression before actually beginning hands and knees creeping. This included movements like pivoting and rocking. All in all, 25 unique combinations of body parts were used for propulsion and balance with all involving both arms and at least one leg (Adolph et al., 1998).

PRONE LOCOMOTION

As mentioned, the acquisition of body control during infancy facilitates the development of other movements. Locomotion evolves from children gaining the ability to position their bodies for movement from one location in space to another. Initially, children position themselves prone. From the

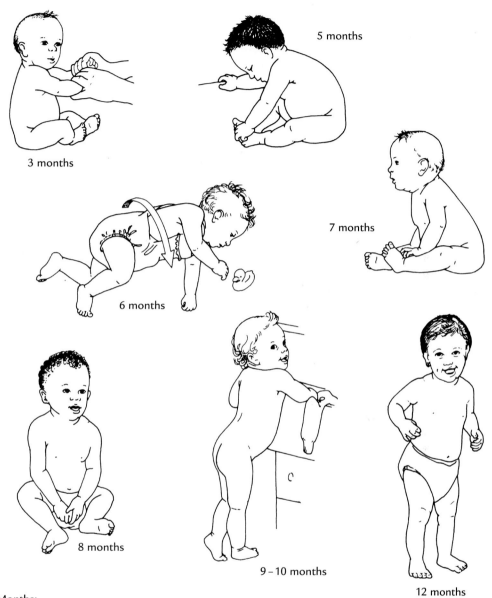

Months:
3   Tries to roll from supine to prone position; maintains sitting position when assisted
5   Sits when holding external supporting object
6   Rolls from supine to prone position; maintains standing position when assisted
7   Achieves sitting position from prone or supine position
8   Sits alone; rolls from prone to supine position
9–10 Pulls self to standing position, briefly maintains stand while holding external supporting object
12   Stands unassisted

Figure 11-3   Voluntary control of the body

Table 11-1	Keys in Learning to Crawl

1. "No strict progression of obligatory, discrete stages" (p. 1299) appears to exist in the development of prone locomotion.

2. Multiple crawling postures are often exhibited in the development of crawling/creeping.

3. While many babies crawl on their bellies prior to hands and knees, many skip belly crawling and proceed directly to hands and knees.

4. The amount of experience in early forms of crawling seems to predict the speed and efficiency of later forms of crawling/creeping.

5. Babies who belly crawl are more proficient on their hands and knees.

6. The first form of mobility for many babies is often a belly-dragging form of crawling.

7. Smaller, slimmer, more naturally proportioned babies crawl earlier than do larger, chubbier babies.

8. Hands and knees creeping or shifting from a prone position to sitting is always the last milestone preceding walking.

SOURCE: Adolph, Vereijken, and Denny (1998).

onset of voluntary attainment of the prone position to the end of the first year of life, there are several transformations in a child's prone locomotion. Semblances of crawling occur prior to 7 months of age, but these movements are reflexively rather than voluntarily controlled. The next 6 months of life are the main concern in voluntary locomotion, because during this time the child becomes adept at movements in the prone position. This is a valuable movement acquisition, because locomotion, even in the prone position, enables the child to explore the surrounding environment more thoroughly.

Like all the voluntary movements of infancy, locomotion develops in a somewhat predictable progression. However, although the progression generally is similar for all children, the rate at which these movement skills are acquired may vary considerably. The rate of acquisition for *all* voluntary movements during infancy may vary, but there is an even greater difference among children for attaining prone locomotor movements.

Creeping and *crawling* are the two locomotion movements that have received the most attention among both the general populace and motor developmentalists. Unfortunately, there is some confusion as to the specific meaning of the two terms. To many parents and lay people, creeping denotes a precrawling movement consisting of inefficient, highly variable arm and leg movements intended to propel the body forward. According to many contemporary references, however, that description is more accurate for crawling. Crawling actually precedes creeping in the progression of movement acquisition for prone locomotion (Gallahue & Ozmun, 2002). Although some experts disagree with this terminology (Cratty, 1986), most current texts involving motor development cite crawling as the antecedent to creeping. For our purposes here, crawling is considered the less mature of the two forms of locomotion, regardless of the popular use of the term.

Crawling normally begins between approximately 7 and 8 months of age (this rate may vary considerably, depending on the child and the environment). In the first attempts at locomotion, the trunk is minimally elevated off the supporting surface. The infant tries to travel by thrusting the arms forward and then subsequently flexing them. The flexion of the arms may eventually lead to a slight forward thrust. Initially the legs are minimally involved, although eventually they play an extremely important role in the more advanced forms of prone locomotion. Soon after the initial attempts at forward progress, a leg or legs may be flexed up to or under the body. This flexion may cause the body to move toward the rear, a backward crawling (Gesell & Ames, 1940). This somewhat counterproductive form of locomotion is short-term, however, because the child soon begins to use the legs more efficiently to help move forward. The child flexes the legs and then reextends them for propulsion. This action may initially involve both legs simultaneously extended in a vigorous motion that causes the body to move forward in short and abrupt actions.

Gradually, the infant's body is elevated from the supporting surface. As the elevation of the body increases, the legs can be flexed into a position beneath the body, increasing the infant's ability to lo-

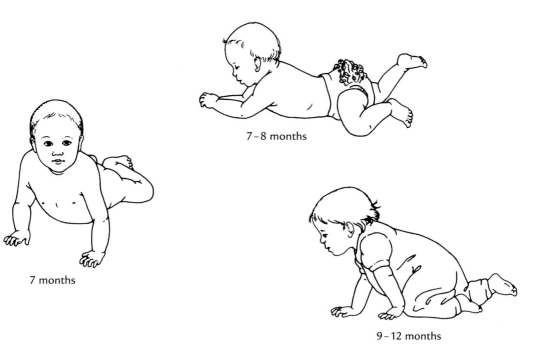

7–8 months

7 months

9–12 months

Months:
   7   Elevates trunk slightly; forward arm extension and flexion creates occasional
         forward movement; leg flexion occasionally creates backward crawling
   7–8   Initial crawling
   9–12 Creeping; creeping upstairs

Figure 11-4   Prone locomotion

comote and leading to the more sophisticated movement form known as creeping. Crawling is a form of locomotion in which the body is, in a sense, dragged or "slid" along the supporting surface, but creeping is an elevated, highly efficient form of locomotion. In fact, many children who have learned to walk often revert to creeping when they have a desire to make speedy progress. Once the body is elevated from the supporting surface, a variety of limb movements are evident in creeping. Initially, the child will move only one limb at a time (Eckert, 1973), which is obviously an inefficient, slow form of beginning creeping that has yet to be perfected.

Eventually, the child develops a ***contralateral*** or a ***homolateral*** creeping pattern. The homolateral pattern is characterized by the limbs on the same side simultaneously moving forward or backward; for example, as the right leg goes forward, so does the right arm. Most children creep contralaterally, in that the movements of the limbs oppose each other. For example, as the right leg moves forward, the right arm moves back. Rather than the arm and leg on the same side being coordinated to move simultaneously, the arm and leg on opposite body sides work together.

An efficient form of creeping, contralateral or homolateral, may begin to appear as early as 9 months of age. However, as indicated in Figure 11-4, most children do not creep efficiently until the first year of age. Once children begin to creep, they rapidly become so efficient that they can creep up stairs. This form of creeping is almost identical to creeping on a flat surface (Eckert, 1973) but initially may lead to frustration because most likely the child will be unable to descend the stairs.

UPRIGHT LOCOMOTION

Many experts consider upright locomotion, which includes walking, the culmination of the acquisition of a series of infant voluntary movements. Of obvious importance, walking is the result of the progression of movement skills described to this point. Although there is no question of the value of upright locomotion, many parents place too much significance on the age at which their offspring start walking. The acquisition of any skill—motor, cognitive, or social—is enough to excite many parents, but they often place extreme emphasis on the rate of acquisition of unassisted walking. Contrary to the beliefs of many parents, there is little evidence proving that early walking accelerates or refines skill performance later in life.

Regardless of when a child begins to walk independently, the initial upright locomotion is far from a mature walking pattern. (The more advanced forms of walking are discussed in more depth in Chapter 13.) Before a child walks unassisted, a predictable movement progression generally occurs. If assisted with considerable support, a child can walk as early as 8 months of age, although this varies considerably. In fact, children occasionally walk independently at 8 months of age, but this rarely occurs. At approximately 10 months, a child can walk with much less support. Generally, by this time a strong handhold is enough to enable the child to "cruise" laterally around furniture or other supporting objects. By 11 months, children have normally progressed to a level of proficiency enabling them to walk when led by another person. Finally, by 12 months of age, the child normally walks unassisted. See Figure 11-5.

Each step in the progression to a mature walking pattern is characterized by many extremely immature walking techniques. For example, the infant often assumes a wide stance. The knees maintain a flexed position, and the toes point out slightly. The length of the steps is highly inconsistent.

In a recent investigation of infant walking patterns, researchers compared changes in gradually increasing body dimensions with age and walking experience. Participants in the study ranged in age

from 9–17-month-old infants to 5–6-year-old children. Generally, as the participants aged, grew, and gained experience, steps lengthened, narrowed, straightened, and became more consistent. The overall findings indicated a narrowing base of support and improved overall control of the walk as the participants increased in age. Interestingly, though age and walking experience both contributed to the maturity of the walking characteristics, experience was found to be the more important indicator of a mature walking pattern (Adolph, Vereijken, & Shrout, 2003).

Interestingly, children with smaller bones (Shirley, 1931) or linear frames (Norval, 1947) are believed to walk somewhat earlier than larger-boned or larger-framed children. According to Garn (1966), larger muscle mass delays the attainment of walking skill. In fact, the child's muscle mass at 6 months of age may relatively accurately predict the onset of independent walking.

In a study examining when and if training would affect infant treadmill stepping, infants received daily training on a "fast," "slow," or stationary treadmill. When compared with a control group of infants who received no training, the treatment subjects were found to have an increased number of steps. In addition, the training proved to be more effective with infants who initially had less stable stepping patterns. The researchers believed that these early findings indicate that the infant neuromotor system is amenable to training, particularly when the initial performance is unstable (Vereijken & Thelen, 1997).

In a study examining slightly older children, Preis, Klemms, and Muller (1997) measured ground reaction forces of 1–5-year-olds during independent walking. The overall velocity of the walk and step length were found to increase with age, though step frequency remained relatively fixed. The amount of time that both feet were simultaneously touching the ground during walking also declined, with the sharpest decrease seen during the first year of walking. A ground reaction force pattern with notable heel strike and general similarity to the adult pattern was detected between the ages of 2 and 3 years. The researchers also concluded that the

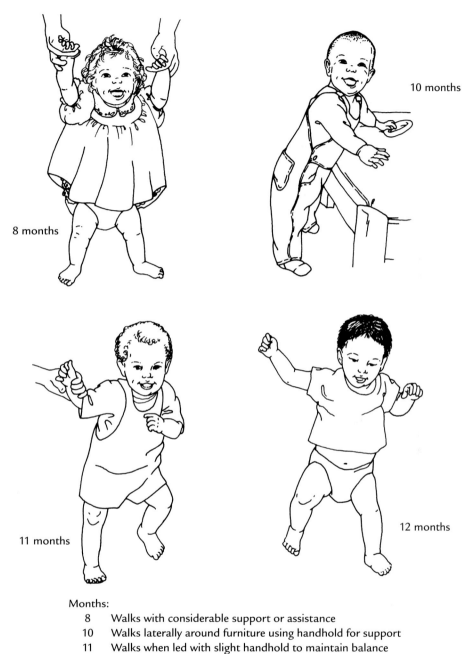

Months:
   8   Walks with considerable support or assistance
   10   Walks laterally around furniture using handhold for support
   11   Walks when led with slight handhold to maintain balance
   12   Walks unassisted

Figure 11-5   Upright locomotion

measurement of ground reaction forces appears to be a "promising tool" for the direction of gait abnormalities and, potentially, neurological disease (Preis et al., 1997).

In a 2002 study examining infant gait development, 35 infants ranging in age from 7 to 70 months were monitored for several walking-related characteristics. The stability of the walk was estimated from the lateral, or side to side, sway of the various body segments and the amount of flexion or extension in the related joint segments. Movement at the shoulder, hip, knee, and ankle were found to decrease significantly over the first few months after walking had begun and gradually thereafter. The most notable decreases began at the points of the body farthest from the midline (most distal). According to these researchers, these findings indicate the importance of lateral stability in the development of the walking pattern (Yaguramaki & Kimura, 2002).

REACHING, GRASPING, AND RELEASING

Parents and others are familiar with many of the voluntary movements of infancy discussed so far. The date of the child's first successful and unsupported stand is frequently a highlight of infancy eagerly anticipated by parents. Creeping, and especially walking, are similarly awaited. But early voluntary use of the hands generally is not as awaited as other voluntary infant movements. Parents readily cite the date of the child's first unassisted walk, but generally they are much less aware of the baby's initial attempts to reach, grasp, and manipulate a nearby object, even though prehension is an extremely important aspect of the child's motor development. Use of the hands enables children to gather information about their environment in a new way. Manipulation enables increased and varied exploration; this new mode of exploration lets the child discover properties of objects and use the objects as implements in achieving goals (Bower, 1982).

Although popular awareness concerning prehension is lacking, much has been written about this early form of manipulation. The first forms of manipulation are reflexive. The palmar grasp reflex

discussed in Chapter 10 is not intentional manipulation, but it does give the child an involuntary means of grasping an object during the first few months of life. Surprisingly, a voluntary form of reaching has also been reported as present in the newborn (Bower, 1982). The newborn reaching behaviors quickly vanish, however, as higher brain centers become more dominant in controlling movement. This initially inhibits the newborn reaching behavior until new "connections" are formed, which allow the movement to reappear (Humphrey, 1969).

This reappearance, often cited as the "first" successful reach and grasp, generally appears around 4 months of age. At this time, the movement behavior is similar in technique to that present in the newborn. In fact, the newborn reaching behavior, which lasts for about 4 weeks, and the reaching that reappears at 4 months are called ***phase I reaching*** (Bower, 1977).

This phase I reaching and ***grasping*** is characterized by several specific qualities. First, the reach and grasp occur simultaneously. As the child reaches, the hand may open and close repeatedly rather than open upon attaining the desired object. This inability to grasp accurately indicates the phase I imperfect abilities of reaching and grasping relative to the more advanced phase II. Also characteristic of phase I reaching and grasping is one-handed reaching, if the desired object is not too heavy. This is generally a mature reaching technique among older children. However, Bower believes that during early infancy this technique allows minimal success in actually attaining control of the desired object and is therefore indicative of the immature reaching characteristics of phase I.

Phase I reaching is also visually initiated. That is, children reach when they see something in their environment. This form of reaching is an improvement over the random groping that occurs earlier in the child's life. But, because the reach is only visually initiated and not controlled, the 5-month-old child may frequently fail to achieve the desired goal. At this age, the child retracts the hand upon an initial failure and completely reattempts the reach. The child is not yet capable of correcting the error during the reach.

Vision also plays an important role in the phase I grasp. Once the child makes manual contact with

Table 11-2 Bower's Phase I and II Reaching and Grasping Behavior Characteristics	
Phase I	**Phase II**
1. Simultaneous reaching and grasping	1. Differentiated reaching and grasping
2. One-handed reaching	2. Two-handed reaching
3. Visual initiation of the reach	3. Visual initiation and guidance of the reach
4. Visual control of the grasp	4. Tactile control of the grasp

Source: Bower (1977).

the desired object, vision facilitates hand closure. In other words, children decide when to grasp based on what they visually perceive to be necessary. Visually monitoring the hand upon contact enables children to determine exactly when they should close the hand around the desired object.

Phase II reaching and grasping is considerably advanced over that of phase I. Phase II generally becomes apparent by the sixth to seventh month of life. This more advanced behavior is characterized by a differentiated reach and grasp. Once the reach has been completed, the child attempts the grasp. This is a considerable advancement over the random, repeated grasping seen throughout the reach in phase I. Furthermore, in phase II, the infant uses two hands when attempting to contact and acquire an external object. Although this is not typically the mature technique an older child would select, this method is the most successful for an infant with more inaccurate manual control. Also, whereas in phase I the reach was visually initiated, in phase II the reach is visually initiated *and* visually controlled, which is why this newly acquired, more efficient movement form is often called *visually guided reaching*. This term emphasizes the important role of vision in enabling the child to correct errors throughout the reach. Children in phase II can actually visually monitor the reach to ensure that they achieve the proper destination. Table 11-2 summarizes phases I and II.

As described earlier, the infant's vision is integral to determining exactly when to close the hand in phase I reaching and grasping. Although vision becomes prominent in guiding the reach in phase II, the role of vision in the grasp diminishes. For phase II infants, the grasp is controlled by tactile stimula-

tion. The touch or feel that they perceive via their hands or fingers becomes the dominant force in making decisions concerning the grasp.

Despite Bower's claims concerning the importance of vision in early reaching and grasping behavior, recent evidence suggests that it may not be necessary. Traditionally, as Bower has suggested, we have believed that the earliest accurate forms of reaching are visually guided and, though highly variable, appear within the first few months of life. Several studies in recent years have sought to eliminate infants' view of their hands to determine the effects on the incidence and accuracy of reaching behavior (Perris & Clifton, 1988; Stack et al., 1989). If reaching in dark (where infants can see glowing objects but not their hands) and light situations begin around the same time, we would assume that proprioceptive cues are apparently providing valuable information to infants. Clifton and associates (1993) have investigated this issue. Seven infants from 6 to 25 weeks of age were videotaped reaching in light and dark situations for objects that made a sound, glowed in the dark, made a sound and glowed, and were "in conflict" as a rattle was presented on one side while a glowing object was presented on the other. The researchers found considerable individual differences among the infants. The onset of touching ranged from 7 to 16 weeks while the onset of grasping ranged from 11 to 19 weeks. Despite a relatively wide range of individual differences, touching and grasping objects in the light and dark situations emerged at the same age for individual infants. For both light and dark situations, the first signs of touching began about 12 weeks and stabilized by 16 weeks. Grasping began at about 16 weeks and stabilized at about 20 weeks. This led to the conclusion that the development of manual contact with objects is similar when the hand and target are sighted versus when only the target is sighted. In short, according to this research, infants do not appear to need to see their hands to reach. They can reach for objects that they hear but not see and see but not hear. In addition, they can do both of these with or without seeing their own hands. These relatively recent findings conflict with traditional beliefs that reaching depends on viewing the hand and the target in early reaching and grasping activities. However, as these abilities become refined, viewing one's own hand may become more important. On the basis of these findings, Clifton and associates state that the "emphasis on visual guidance of the hands . . . needs to be revised" (p. 1109). Furthermore, in future theories governing the study of infant reaching, greater emphasis needs to be placed on the role of proprioception (Clifton et al., 1993).

The metamorphosis of reaching and grasping behavior from phase I and phase II as described by Bower follows the general proximodistal rule of motor development. Recall that proximodistal is the development of movement ability from the points close to the center of the body or the midline to the distal or extreme points. Reaching and grasping behavior does exactly that. In fact, at about 4 months of life, reaching is predominantly controlled by the shoulder and elbow. These first attempts at purposeful reaching are slow and awkward but soon develop into accurate, efficient movements. By as early as 5 to 6 months, the child has developed greater wrist, hand, and finger control and can use the thumb in opposition to the other fingers. By 9 to 10 months, the child can use the thumb to oppose one finger, enabling more precise "pincerlike" control (Keogh & Sugden, 1985). However, despite the considerable improvement in reaching and grasping ability over a relatively short time span, the child may not be able to easily release an object until 18 months of age. Relaxing the muscles in the arm sufficiently to facilitate the release of an object is one of the final acquisitions in the infant reaching, grasping, and *releasing* progression.

Many, more current, studies have also been conducted to help us better understand the develop-

ment of reaching, grasping, and releasing. For example, in evaluating 54 children from 4 to 12 years old, Kuhntz-Buschbeck and colleagues (1998) asked subjects to reach repeatedly for cylinders with their dominant hand. The trajectory and magnitude of finger opening was specifically analyzed. While no significant differences were found in the velocity of the hand, the hand trajectory straightened across ages as coordination improved. The grip became smoother and more consistent by age 12, and younger graspers opened their hands wider, even when unnecessary, creating a greater margin for error. Overall conclusions suggested that the development of prehension continues to evolve until the end of the first decade of life (Kuhntz-Buschbeck et al., 1998).

In a recent investigation of 1-year-old infants and their reaching as it related to the development of walking, the participants were studied before, during, and after they began walking. The infants' reaching during this time was carefully noted while they were presented with a series of reaching tasks. Following the initiation of walking, the incidence of two-handed reaching became more prominent on all reaching tasks. Gradually, however, as the infants gained better balance and overall control of their gait, the two-handed pattern diminished. The authors believed that this indicated that the use of two hands, as it related to walking, depended on experience (Corbetta & Bojczyk, 2002).

Anticipation and Object Control in Reaching and Grasping

To achieve adultlike reaching and grasping capabilities fully, the child must master the skills just described and be able to adjust for the varying sizes, shapes, and weights of objects, which requires different reaching and grasping techniques. Mounoud and Bower (1974) carefully studied infants' awareness of the properties of objects and its effect on their reaching and grasping behavior. As is the case with many movement behaviors, they found a distinct progression. Mounoud and Bower determined that prior to 9 months of age, the application of force in the reach was unrelated to the weight of an

Table 11-3   Approximate Occurrence and Highlights of Reaching, Grasping, and Releasing

Age	Characteristics
Birth	Phase I reaching.
1 month	Phase I reaching disappears.
4 months	Phase I reaching reappears.
4–5 months	Unable to receive multiple toys.
5–6 months	Thumb used to oppose fingers in grasping.
6 months	Phase II reaching appears.
6–8 months	Receives two toys while storing one toy in opposite hand.
9 months	Adjusts arm and hand tension to object's weight after grasping the object.
9–10 months	Thumb can oppose one finger in grasping.
9–11 months	Receives three toys; stores first two toys on lap or chair.
12 months	Adjusts arm and hand tension upon repeatedly receiving the same object.
12–14 months	Receives three or more toys and crosses midline to hand toys to other person.
18 months	Releases objects with relative ease; anticipates arm and hand tension for repeated presentation of same object; expects unknown long objects to weigh more than short objects.

object. Therefore, regardless of an object's weight, the child applied the same force in both the arm movement and the subsequent grasp. The researchers determined this reaction as they observed the arms of their subjects suddenly rise or fall when presented with a series of objects of varying weights. Mounoud and Bower gained additional information by placing force transducers on the objects the infants were receiving; the transducers indicated the magnitude of the force being applied during the grasp.

By 9 months of age, most of the subjects had developed the ability to adjust to the weight of the object after they had grasped it. However, they showed limited anticipatory abilities. This inadequacy diminished by 1 year of age as the infants developed skill in adjusting their arm and hand tension when they were repeatedly presented with the same object. Errors were initially made, but if the same object was presented to the chil-

dren, errors were eliminated. However, this was true only for familiar objects—the knowledge the infants gained from the repeated application of one object did not positively affect their performance on the first few trials with new objects.

By the age of 18 months, the children exhibited anticipation. Upon repeated presentations, they displayed an awareness that the same object weighs the same. Furthermore, the subjects seemed to follow the "rule" that similar objects weigh more or less than the familiar object, based on length. Therefore, although anticipation was evident, it was not always accurate, because longer objects are not always heavier. Nevertheless, Mounoud and Bower concluded that by the age of 18 months, their subjects had developed an ability to perform two critical skills: anticipate and differentiate their reaching and grasping responses (see Table 11-3).

In another study that focused on anticipation and force and velocity of prehension development during childhood, Pare and Dugas (1999) asked children to use a precise grip to grasp several objects of varying size. Two-year-olds were found to have a negative correlation between the speed of their grasp and their grip force. In other words, as one increased, the other decreased. However, by the age of 3 years, that correlation had become positive and increasingly strong. Overall, these researchers determined that the high variability of grip force seen early on declines with age. In addition, starting at the age of about 4 years, children controlled the rate of speed of their grasp and tended to use a single "burst of speed" of grip force to grasp an object. In general, Pare and Dugas believe their research indicated that distinct developmental milestones in grasping development exist from 2 to 9 years of age, and that the anticipation of the grip is not innate, but develops over several years.

Bimanual Control

Many cognitive and psychomotor skills are necessary for optimal manual control. So far we have dealt predominantly with one-handed reaching. However, in many practical instances, movement from arms and hands must both be integrated. Bruner (1970) examined several specific manipulative circumstances, including complementary use of the hands.

In examining the progression of reaching and grasping behavior, Bruner specifically investigated infants' control of several objects simultaneously. Subjects were 4 to 17 months old. The infants were handed a second toy immediately after receiving a first toy. The second toy was handed to the side of the body that was already occupied by the first toy. If the infant did not take the toy within 15 to 20 seconds, the second toy was moved to the infant's midline. If the child took the toy at any time, he was handed a third toy (and a fourth one, if necessary).

The 4- to 5-month-old infants in the Bruner research exhibited varying abilities. Some could not reach and grasp any of the toys; others could reach and grasp the toys but were unable to maintain con-

trol thereafter. None of the subjects in this youngest of age groups could deal with more than one toy at a time.

The 6- to 8-month-old subjects displayed a more highly developed reaching and grasping ability. They easily grasped the first toy and generally received a second. To facilitate this process, they transferred the first toy to the opposite hand for storage while receiving the second toy on the side to which it was offered. Three objects, however, appeared beyond the ability level of the infants in this group.

The 9- to 11-month-old group exhibited another new skill. Most subjects at this age could receive three objects, although this task was troublesome initially. To manipulate three objects, the child frequently positioned the initial toy(s) in the lap or on a nearby chair to free the hand for receiving the next toy. By 12 months of age, the infant often handed the initial toys to an experimenter or nearby parent for safekeeping. By this age, Bruner noted, subjects could cross the midline in handing the toy to a nearby person, a skill usually not exhibited in younger age groups. In addition, the two oldest age groups, the 12- to 14-month-olds and the 15- to 17-month-olds, could all handle three or more objects successfully. However, the oldest subjects consistently used a storage method, whereas the 12- to 14-month-old group used a variety of techniques. But even among these two groups of older subjects, toys were stored on the lap, in the chair, or handed to a nearby person rather than being stored in the other arm. A major point of importance in this research was that complementary use of the two hands to achieve a purposeful goal was evident as early as 6 to 8 months by infants storing a toy in one hand to free the receiving hand for a second toy.

Bruner performed additional research to more specifically examine bimanual control. In this research, a child was exposed to a box with a visible toy inside. To obtain the toy, the child had to slide open a wooden lid, keep the lid open, and grasp and withdraw the toy with the other hand. For this research, Bruner used the same subjects who were studied in the previous investigation, with the exception of the 4- to 5-month-old group. Bruner found that although the younger groups succeeded in this endeavor only approximately 20 percent of the time, the older age groups did so 90 percent of the time. A common progression was also noted. Younger subjects often simply struck the box. A second strategy that was also unsatisfactory was closing the door immediately after opening. A successful but still single-handed approach was then used: The lid was opened and released, to free the hand for grabbing the toy. Once the lid was released, the hand was slowly slipped into the box to grasp the toy. This technique was commonly used by the subjects in the 12- to 14-month-old group and occasionally by older subjects. In approximately 16 to 17 percent of all trials, the subjects in the 12- to 14-month-old group used two hands. However, as described by Bruner, these movements were not efficient and were characterized by poor timing.

The complementary use of two hands increased in the two older age groups. In fact, two hands were used over 30 percent of the time. Bruner concluded from this research that the bimanual control necessary for success in this task was well structured and differentiated by 18 months of age but still could not be considered mastered.

SUMMARY

By the end of the first few months of life, infant reflexes have begun to be replaced by the cortically controlled voluntary movements. These voluntary movements develop in a fairly predictable sequence, although the rate of acquisition of the movement skill may vary considerably from child to child.

Voluntary movement follows a cephalocaudal pattern of development: The head is the first body part to be voluntarily controlled. This is an important movement acquisition because it enables the child to more completely visually scan the environment.

Body control is gained soon after control of the head. The upper body gains control first, with lower portions gradually acquiring voluntary movement. Control of the body enables appropriate positioning for the eventual acquisition of locomotion and allows the child to position the body in such a way as to free the hands for reaching and grasping.

Locomotion is an important contributor to the child's cognitive development because many new environments can be experienced. Initial crawling is slow, inefficient, awkward, and characterized by an extremely low-to-the-ground prone position. Soon the child develops a more elevated and efficient form of locomotion known as creeping.

Independent walking is preceded by several assisted forms of upright locomotion. Cruising laterally around furniture while maintaining a handhold for balance and assisted walking are both significant forms of locomotion because they contribute to the emergence of independent walking and running in the locomotor progression.

Reaching and grasping abilities are facilitated by the emergence of upright posture and locomotion. Upright positioning frees the hands for more frequent use; locomotion enables the child to move to objects of interest for purposes of manipulation.

According to Bower, reaching and grasping emerge in two phases. Increasing control of the arms and hands is particularly important because it allows increased manual exploration and facilitates daily routine activities.

KEY TERMS

contralateral	homolateral	phase II reaching
crawling	locomotion	releasing
creeping	manipulation	stability
grasping	phase I reaching	voluntary movement

QUESTIONS FOR REFLECTION

1. What are the three categories of voluntary movement during infancy? Describe each category and give three examples of movements within each.

2. How does infant head control evolve from birth to approximately 5 months of age?

3. How does infant upright posture evolve from birth to approximately 8 months of age?

4. Describe the body position of an infant in the early stages of standing.

5. Which occurs first, crawling or creeping? Describe

each and explain the difference between the two. What is meant by contralateral creeping?

6. What is prehension? How does it affect motor development in general during infancy?

7. Explain the characteristics associated with phase I reaching and grasping as described by Bower.

8. What does the term *proximodistal* mean? Give two examples of this phenomenon.

9. What is bimanual control? Give two examples of this concept.

ONLINE LEARNING CENTER (www.mhhe.com/payne6e)

Visit the *Human Motor Development* Online Learning Center for study aids and additional resources. You can use the study guide questions and key terms puzzles to review key terms and concepts for this chapter and to

prepare for exams. You can further extend your knowledge of motor development by checking out the Web links, articles, and activities found on the site.

REFERENCES

Adolph, K. E., Vereijken, B., & Denny, M. A. (1998). Learning to crawl. *Child Development, 69*(5), 1299–1312.

Adolph, K. E., Vereijken, B., & Shrout, P. E. (2003). What changes in infant walking and why. *Child Development, 74*(2), 475–497.

Bower, T. G. R. (1977). *A primer of infant development.* San Francisco: Freeman.

———. (1982). *Development in infancy.* 2nd ed. San Francisco: Freeman.

Bruner, J. S. (1970). The growth and structure of skill. In K. J. Conolly (Ed.), *Mechanisms of motor skill development.* New York: Academic Press.

Clifton, R. K., Muir, D. W., Ashmead, D. H., & Clarkson, M. G. (1993). Is visually guided reaching in early infancy a myth? *Child Development, 64,* 1099–1110.

Corbetta, D., & Bojczyk, K. E. (2002). Infants return to two-handed reaching when they are learning to walk. *Journal of Motor Behavior, 34*(1), 83–95.

Cratty, B. J. (1986). *Perceptual and motor development in infants and children.* 2nd ed. Englewood Cliffs, NJ: Prentice-Hall.

Eckert, H. M. (1973). Age changes in motor skills. In G. L. Rarick (Ed.), *Physical activity: Human growth and development.* New York: Academic Press.

Gallahue, D. L., & Ozmun, J. C. (2002). *Understanding motor development: Infants, children, adolescents, adults.* 5th ed. New York: McGraw-Hill.

Garn, S. M. (1966). *De genetica medica, pars II.* Edited by L. Gedda. Pp. 415–434. Rome: Gregor Mendel Institute.

Gesell, A., & Ames, L. B. (1940). The ontogenetic organization of prone behavior in human infancy. *Journal of Genetic Psychology, 56,* 247–263.

Hershkowitz, N. (2000). Neurological bases of behavioral development in infancy. *Brain Development, 22*(7), 411–416.

Hottinger, W. L. (1980). Motor development: Conception to age 5. In C. B. Corbin (Ed.), *A textbook of motor development.* 2nd ed. Dubuque, IA: Brown.

Humphrey, T. (1969). Postnatal repetition of human prenatal activity responses with some suggestions for their neuroanatomical basis. In R. J. Robinson (Ed.), *Brain and early behavior.* New York: Academic Press.

Keogh, J., & Sugden, D. (1985). *Movement skill development.* New York: Macmillan.

Kuhntz-Buschbeck, J. P., Stolze, H., Johnk, K., Boczek-Funcke, A., & Illert, M. (1998). Development of prehension movements in children: A kinematic study. *Experimental Brain Research, 122*(4), 424–432.

Mounoud, P., & Bower, T. G. R. (1974). Conservation of weight in infants. *Cognition, 3,* 229–240.

Norval, M. A. (1947). Relationship of weight and length of infants at birth to the age at which they begin to walk. *Journal of Pediatrics, 30,* 676–678.

Pare, M., & Dugas, C. (1999). Developmental changes in prehension during childhood. *Experimental Brain Research, 125*(3), 239–247.

Perris, E., & Clifton, R. (1988). Reaching in the dark toward sound as a measure of auditory localization in infants. *Infant Behavior and Development, 11,* 473–491.

Preis, S., Klemms, A., & Muller, K. (1997). Gait analysis by measuring ground reaction forces in children: Changes to an adaptive gait pattern between the ages of one and five years. *Developmental Medicine and Child Neurology, 39*(4), 228–233.

Rochat, P. (1992). Self-sitting and reaching in 5- and 8-month-old infants: The impact of posture and its development on early eye-hand coordination. *Journal of Motor Behavior, 24*(2), 210–220.

Shirley, M. M. (1931). *The first two years: A study of twenty-five babies.* Vol. 1: *Postural and locomotor development.* Minneapolis: University of Minnesota Press.

Stack, K., Muir, D., Sherriff, F., & Roman, J. (1989). Development of infant reaching in the dark to luminous object and "invisible sounds." *Perception, 18,* 69–82.

Vereijken, B., & Thelen, E. (1997). Training infant treadmill stepping: The role of individual pattern stability. *Developmental Psychology, 30*(2), 89–102.

Wyke, B. (1975). The neurological basis of movement: A developmental review. In K. Holt (Ed.), *Movement and child development.* Philadelphia: Lippincott.

Yaguramaki, N., & Kimura, T. (2002). Acquirement of stability and mobility in infant gait. *Gait and Posture, 16*(1), 69–77.

Zaichowsky, L. D., Zaichowsky, L. B., & Martinek, T. J. (1980). *Growth and development: The child and physical activity.* St. Louis, MO: Mosby.

12 Fine Motor Development

The term ***fine motor*** generally refers to those movements predominantly produced by the smaller muscles or muscle groups of the body. As discussed in Chapter 1, the terms *fine* and *gross motor* can be generally used to categorize types of movements. Running and walking are functions predominantly of the larger muscle groups of the body, so we usually think of these movements as gross motor. However, manual activity such as sewing, sculpting, drawing, and playing most musical instruments involves smaller muscle groups of the body, so such movements are therefore considered fine motor. Fine movements usually involve the use of the hands. Williams (1983) confines her definition of fine movement to just the movements of the hands and the eyes. Fine movement, she says, is "the ability to coordinate or regulate the use of the eyes and the hands together in precise and adaptive movement patterns" (p. 188). Although this definition accurately notes the "precise and adaptive" nature of fine movement, it also implies that fine movement must involve the hands and the eyes. This is generally the case, but it might not be true for a visually impaired individual who, despite no involvement of the eyes, still develops fine motor control. This definition also fails to encompass those who have developed fine motor control of another body part. A soccer player, for example, often develops exceptional fine motor control of the foot for precisely manipulating the ball around defenders.

There is little information concerning these non-hand types of fine movement, and only slightly more information about fine movement of the hands. Because the most practical information concerning fine movement involves the hand, this chapter emphasizes the development of fine hand movements critical to daily activities and to the attainment of high-level performance in many movement endeavors.

ASSESSING FINE MOVEMENT

Though many tools exist for assessing both gross and fine movement, many of these instruments do not establish clear performance criteria nor maintain complete or contemporary norms. Furthermore, some assessment tools employ norms that are incomplete or were devised from multiple sources, making review of the original sources difficult. For these reasons, norms developed by several of these instruments often disagree, which may indicate a need for research into the establishment of a more cohesive protocol for assessment (Noller & Ingrisano, 1984). With that in mind, Noller and Ingrisano (1984) examined nearly 200 healthy newborn to 6-year-old subjects on 37 motor tasks. They selected these test items on the basis of which items appeared most frequently in other assessment batteries. The times of emergence and achievement on these tasks were determined by Noller and Ingrisano. Emergence of a task was considered to have occurred when 68 percent of the subjects within a 6-month interval performed the task independently. Achievement was considered to have occurred when 95 percent of the subjects within a 6-month interval were capable of independent performance. These particular levels were selected because of their similarity to standard deviations in population statistics and their ease of comparison to other assessment tools.

The findings concerning time of emergence and achievement, as well as the norm from other popular assessment tools, are presented in Table 12-1. According to Noller and Ingrisano, the emergence times appear to be fairly similar to established norms, though achievement times were found to vary considerably from other published norms. While all of these figures are worthwhile for roughly indicating the times of attainment of certain fine motor tasks, sufficient discrepancies exist to suggest that more research is necessary concerning fine motor assessment.

CATEGORIZING MANIPULATION

Use of the hands, or ***manipulation,*** is an ability most people take for granted, even though they need to manipulate things hundreds of times a day. Because of the critical nature of hand movement, there have been efforts to categorize the many types of daily hand movements, in order to facilitate discussion and study. Traditionally, hand movement involves intrinsic and extrinsic movements. ***Intrinsic***

Table 12-1   Comparison of the Norms for the Attainment (in months of age) of Various Fine Motor Skills as Determined by Several Popular Assessment Instruments and Noller and Ingrisano's 1984 Study

					Sources		Noller/Ingrisano	
Task	Peabody	DPIYC	Bayley	Gesell	DDST	Erhardt	Emergence	Achievement
Tracking across midline								
toward right	2–3			2	2.5		B°–5	6–11
toward left	2–3			2	2.5		B–5	6–11
Tracking 180°								
toward right	2–3			4	4			6–11
toward left	2–3			4	4			6–11
Turns to sound								
turns right			3.8	6–7			6–11	
turns left			3.8	6–7			6–11	
Reach and grasp of 1-in. cube	4–5		4.6	5				6–11
Radial digital grasp of cube						8	12–17	48–53
Transfers cube	6–7	3–5	5.5	7	7.5		6–11	
Stacks a tower of cubes								
2	12–15	12–15	13.8	15	20	15	12–17	18–23
3	16–18	16–19	16.7	15				18–23
4	16–18			18	26			18–23
5	19–24			21			18–23	24–29
6	19–24	20–23	28	21			18–23	30–35
7	19–24			24				24–29
8	25–30	28–31	30	30	38			30–35
9	31–36			30			30–35	48–53
10	31–36			36			36–41	54–59
Copies cube bridge	37–48						36–41	54–59
Copies cube gate				54			30–35	54–59
Pincer grasp raisin	10–11	9–11		11	14.7			
Pincer grasp rice							18–23	36–41
Copies drawing square	37–48				60	54	54–59	
Static tripod grasp on crayon when copying square						36–48	42–47	
Formboard								
places round shape	12–15	16–19	16.8	15			12–17	18–23
places square shape	16–18	20–23	21.2	21			18–23	30–35
places triangular shape	31–36	20–23	21.2	36			18–23	24–29
Finger position		61–72					48–53	66–71

°B stands for birth.

Source: Adapted from Noller, K., and Ingrisano, D. (1984). *Physical Therapy* 64(3), 308–316. Reprinted with the permission of the American Physical Therapy Association.

movements are coordinated movements of the individual digits used to manage an object already in the hand. **Extrinsic movements** displace both the hand and the in-hand object through movements of the upper limb (Elliott & Connolly, 1984).

Intrinsic and *extrinsic* are useful terms for organizing the movements of the hand, but Elliott and Connolly (1984) found these terms somewhat general, so they have created a slightly more detailed system of categorizing the "bewildering number of hand movements." In their system, there are three categories of hand movements: **simple synergies, reciprocal synergies,** and **sequential patterns.** Although these three general categories are believed to encompass most types of hand movements, the authors state that movements involving flexion-extension movements, such as typing or piano playing, have not been categorized.

The simple synergy category involves all hand movements in which the action of all the digits, including the thumb, is similar. The digits converge on an object and sometimes alternately flex and extend. Examples of simple synergies include the action of squeezing a rubber ball, most pinching and squeezing movements, and the formation of the dynamic tripod, the grip most people use when holding a writing implement or when handwriting.

Reciprocal synergies are combinations of movements involving the thumb and other involved digits reciprocally and simultaneously interacting to produce relatively dissimilar movements. Reciprocal synergies might involve the flexion of the fingers as the thumb adducts or extends. Elliott and Connolly (1984) note that the thumb's capacity for movement, which is independent of the fingers, is often used in the production of reciprocal synergies. This category of hand movement includes many intrinsic movements such as twiddling the thumbs or rolling a pencil back and forth between the thumb and forefinger.

A major difference between sequential patterns and the other two categories is that sequential patterns are indeed sequential, not simultaneous. A systematic sequence of hand movements contributes to the attainment of a specific goal. Included in this category of movements are tying a knot, unscrewing

a lid, or squeezing a tube of toothpaste until toothpaste flows from the opening.

This system of categorizing hand movement is still relatively new but helpful for communicating or describing information concerning hand movement. It also alerts us to the extremely wide range of movement the broad term *manipulation* encompasses.

THE DEVELOPMENT OF PREHENSION

Manipulation is a general term referring to hand use and movement at any time throughout the lifespan. **Prehension** applies specifically to the act of grasping, which includes approaching, grasping, and releasing objects. Prehension is critical to the development of a multitude of hand movements used throughout the lifespan.

One of the most frequently cited studies in this area of prehension was completed over 70 years ago. Though the findings of this research have recently been called into question, the work of Halverson (1931) is often considered a classic study in the area of early manipulation because of the depth of the conclusions and the critical nature of the subject under investigation.

The purpose of the Halverson study was to examine the development of prehension, particularly the grasp, in children 16 to 52 weeks old. To examine the children's grasping ability, Halverson presented each child with a 1 inch red cube, filmed the response, and then attempted to describe the developmental progression for the grasp of the cube. Generally, Halverson noted that the total process of prehension—early reaching, grasping, and releasing behavior—involved four steps: (1) the object is visually located; (2) the object is approached; (3) the object is grasped; (4) the child disposes of the object by releasing it.

More specifically, Halverson noted that there appeared to be three basic methods of reaching. The most immature method involved sweeping the hand and arm in a backhand manner toward the object. Eventually, this mode of reaching evolved into a more mature sweeping or scooping approach. Despite the advanced nature of this method relative to the backhand style, this second method was indirect or "circuitous" and involved approaches from a variety of angles. Finally, the children in the study developed a direct reach that is common in slightly older, more motorically advanced children.

The brunt of Halverson's investigation concerned the actual grasp of the object. Overall, Halverson noted that younger children had not yet developed the ability to oppose the fingers with the thumb. He noted that when children reached for the red cube, the position of the thumb during the reach often indicated the likelihood of the thumb being used in opposition to the fingers. If the thumb was inward when the hand approached the cube, thumb opposition was likely to occur. However, a thumb positioned downward or curled under the hand indicated an upcoming grasp that was less mature than the thumb-opposition grasp.

Halverson also found a relatively specific progressive sequence of grasping behavior in his 4- to 13-month-old subjects. Initially, at 4 months of age, the children were totally incapable of making contact with the object. Next, at 5 months, children could contact crudely but could not actually acquire the object. The third step in the developmental sequence of grasping was known as the "primitive squeeze," also characteristic of children very near 5 months of age. In this case, the hand was generally thrust beyond the desired object and then scooped or corralled inward until the object was actually squeezed against the body or the other hand. The hand performed no real grasping action. In the fourth step, at approximately 6 months of age, a grasp of sorts did occur. This "squeeze grasp" was made possible by the hand approaching the object laterally until contact was made—then the fingers closed around the object and pressed it against the palm of the hand. This system of acquiring the cube was the first sign of an actual grasp and was typically clumsy and unsuccessful.

The fifth type of grasping, the "hand grasp," occurred at approximately 7 months and was somewhat similar to the squeeze grasp except that the child bridged the hand down over the cube. The child maintained the thumb in a position parallel to the fingers, which curled down over the side of the cube. Once that position was attained, the fingers pressed the cube against the heel of the hand. This form of grasp was similar to the sixth level of grasping ability Halverson noted. In the "palm grasp," the hand was again placed down over the cube. However, as the fingers curled down over the side of the cube, so did the thumb. This appeared to be an initial sign of the thumb's ability to oppose the movement of the fingers and was also common in infants at approximately 7 months.

The opposition of the thumb became increasingly apparent in the seventh level of grasping. For example, at approximately 8 months, the "superior palm grasp" was facilitated by placing the hand, radial side down, on the cube. The thumb then pressed on the near side of the cube as the first two fingers curled down onto the far side and applied opposing pressure. This system was similar to the grasp observed in level 8 at 9 months, the "inferior forefinger grasp." The thumb and forefinger opposition noted in level 8 once again was evident but was initiated by the fingers wrapping around the cube and pointing medially rather than downward. As in the seventh level, once acquired, the cube was controlled and maintained near the palm area of the hand.

At 13 months of age, in the next to the last level of grasping that Halverson observed, the cube was finally controlled and maintained by the fingertips of the first three fingers, which were opposed by the thumb. To attain this control, the hand was stabilized by the tabletop during the initial contact and grasp of the cube. This characteristic differentiated level 9, the "forefinger grasp," from level 10, the "superior forefinger grasp," which also became common among infants at approximately 13 months of age. Otherwise, the superior forefinger grasp was similar to the level 9 grasp. Table 12-2 summarizes the 10 stages of grasping development.

Generally, Halverson noted a progression that clearly evidenced the proximodistal pattern of development discussed in Chapter 1. Movement ability progressed in a direction away from the body. Although the initial efforts at obtaining an object through reaching and grasping were crude shoulder

Table 12-2   Halverson's 10 Stages of Grasping Development in Children 16 to 52 Weeks Old

Grasping Characteristic	Approximate Age of Occurrence (months)
Failure to make contact.	4
Crude contact but failure to obtain the object.	5
Object is scooped toward the body and squeezed against the body or opposite hand.	5
Following a lateral approach of the hand, the fingers close around the object and press it against the palm of the hand, the first sign of an actual grasp.	6
Hand is bridged down over the object, with the thumb parallel to the fingers; then the fingers press the object against the palm of the hand.	7
Hand is bridged down over the object, with the fingers and the thumb curling over the object, an initial sign of thumb opposition.	7
Hand is placed, radial side down, on the object; the thumb presses the near side of the object while the fingers apply pressure on the far side.	8
Fingers wrap around the object by pointing medially rather than down; once acquired, the object is maintained in the palm area.	9
Fingertips of the first three fingers oppose the action of the thumb in the grasp while the hand is stabilized on the supporting surface.	13
Fingertips oppose the action of the thumb without the hand being stabilized.	13

and elbow movements, the finer movements of the hand, and finally the fingertips, eventually attained control. In addition, Halverson noted a gradual increase in the movements' speed and efficiency as these children aged from 16 to 52 weeks. More recent research confirmed that the progression Halverson originally observed has endured throughout the years. However, these various movement abilities are likely to emerge earlier today than in previous years as a result of enhanced standards of living, improved nutrition, and greater awareness of the importance of early motor experiences (Hohlstein, 1974). The specific time the various grasping-related skills emerge continues to be extremely variable information.

Other, more specific, research on children's ability to manipulate objects has been conducted in recent years. Pehoski, Henderson, and Tickle-Degnen (1997a) examined children's ability to move small objects from their fingers to their palm and from palm to fingers, as well as their ability to rotate in-hand objects. Using children from 3 to 7 years of

age and adults, the researchers asked subjects to rotate the peg while in hand. The number of rotations performed per time period and the number of peg drops were tallied. The researchers noted no significant difference in performance between boys and girls, but that performance did change with periods of rapid developmental change. Children were less consistent and slower than the adult subjects as development of this skill was found to involve improvements in speed, the method of rotation employed, and the consistency of movement (Pehoski et al., 1997a).

In a related study, Pehoski and colleagues (1977b) asked the same age groups to pick up five pegs at a time, store them in their hand, and place them in the pegboard. Again, no significant differences appeared between boys and girls, though age was significant, with older subjects placing more pegs and using more adultlike techniques. According to the researchers, one major finding was the way in which children solved the problem of moving the peg in and out of hand. While adults used gravity to assist in moving the peg, children employed methods that allowed them to maintain contact with the peg at all times. The overall conclusion was that children take considerable time in developing an adult technique, and children were closer to adults in performance (number of pegs placed) than they were in the method employed (Pehoski et al., 1997b).

AN ALTERNATE VIEW OF THE DEVELOPMENT OF PREHENSION

As discussed in the previous section, the development of prehension as seen by Halverson (1931) has been viewed as an ordered, relatively fixed sequence of grip patterns predictably evolving with increasing age. However, according to more recent research (Newell, Scully, Tenenbaum, & Hardiman, 1989), this view may be a function of the narrow range of constraints imposed in Halverson's research. In that study, young subjects were offered cubes of only one size to grasp. Newell and his associates sought to examine the effects of using various sizes of objects that had been scaled to the hand size of the preschool-age and adult subjects. Ten cube sizes were used to examine which hand was employed, the number of fingers used with the thumb in contacting objects, depth of finger contact, or grip (side, top, etc.). Some differences were noted. For example, adults used one hand 60 percent of the time (two hands 40 percent of the time) while children used one hand 38.6 percent of the time. The object-to-hand-size ratio was found to be a significant factor related to the subject's use of one or two hands. Older subjects were also found to demonstrate slightly more use of the right hand, indicating that hand dominance may not yet be firmly established by the age of 4 years. When objects were scaled to the subject's hand size, the overall trend for grasping was quite similar for adult and child subjects. One finger and the thumb were used for small objects. Two to three fingers were used with the thumb for intermediate-sized objects, and four fingers and the thumb were used for larger objects. The size of the object that seemed to create a shift to a new pattern of grasping differed among

age groups. However, when the object was scaled to the subject's hand size, the "shifting point" was quite similar.

According to Newell and associates, over 1000 combinations of finger-thumb grips are possible, but subjects tended to use only a fraction of those. Adult subjects regularly employed 14 combinations, while children used 22. Even within preferred grips, certain choices appeared to dominate. Five grips accounted for 62 percent of the grips used by children and 89 percent of the grips used by adults (see Figure 12-1). The authors noted that eliminating the "playful behavior" of the child subjects would have increased the number of times that children use the five most common grips.

Based on the results of their research, Newell and associates have concluded that task constraints, in this case object size, play a major role in grip patterns for children and adults. Furthermore, contrary to traditional views of grip-pattern development, children and adults use similar patterns for similarly sized objects relative to their hand size. In short, developmental progressions may be considerably more "flexible" than those previously described by Halverson (Newell, Scully, Tenenbaum, & Hardiman, 1989). In fact, Halverson's work may be "a reflection of the narrow range of constraints tested rather than a rigid sequence of biological or cognitive prescriptions for action" (Newell, Scully, & McDonald, 1989, p. 819).

In a study similar to the work of Newell and associates, researchers studied both adult and 6–7-year-old participants and their reach-to-grasp movements while varying the distance of the object, the size of the target, and the amount of visual feedback during the reach (Kuhtz-Buschbeck et al., 1998). The experimental condition was scaled to the body proportions of the two participant groups. In general, children were found to open their hands wider than did adult reachers. The children did not do as good a job as the adults in adjusting their hand opening to accommodate the object size, and the children were also more variable overall in their reach-to-grasp actions. These findings and others led the researchers to conclude that the grip formation is not completely mature by 6–7 years of age, and

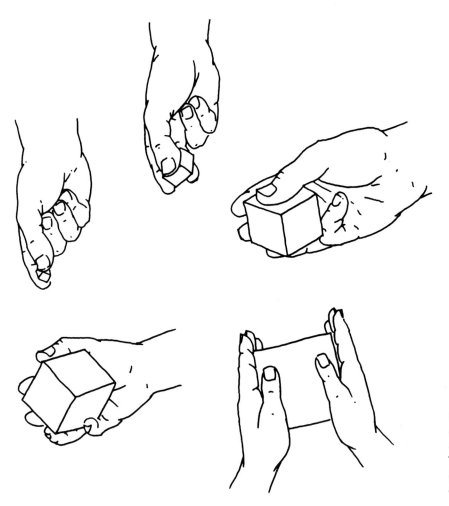

Figure 12-1 The five most common grip patterns encountered by Newell, Scully, Tenenbaum, and Hardiman (1989) in their research on child and adult grip patterns

that children rely more heavily on visual information than do adults in the performance of the reach.

To gain further insight into the development of prehension, Newell and colleagues conducted additional studies (Newell, McDonald, & Baillargeon, 1993; Newell, Scully, & McDonald, 1989) using 4- to 8-month-old infants, and in one study compared them with adult subjects. One purpose of their research was to determine if the size of the hand in relationship to the size of the object would "define" the grip patterns of children when compared with adults. Five- to 8-month-old infants were studied along with adults. All subjects were asked to grasp inverted cups that had been scaled to hand size. For

both infants and adults, the grip pattern varied systematically with the cup size. More fingers were used when the cup size increased, and when the cup was scaled to hand size, many similarities were noted in the grasping patterns of infants and adults. Subjects were generally found to use two hands more commonly with larger objects than with small. According to the authors, this indicated an ability to differentiate one- and two-handed grasps and object size as young as 4 months old. The number of fingers employed was also influenced by object shape. Of all the one-handed grasps, approximately 50 percent occurred with the right hand (or the left hand). Apparently, hand dominance had not yet begun to evolve in children this young. All subjects in this study, even the 4-month-olds, exhibited an ability to differentiate finger use based on object size. However, the younger subjects exhibited more variability in finger combinations.

As in Newell's previous research, five-finger configurations accounted for most grips. And, as we might expect from the research cited earlier, minimal age differences were noted in the grasping of 4- to 8-month-olds, though the younger subjects required more haptic information to differentiate grip configurations, while 8-month-olds were more likely to use visual information (Newell, Scully, & McDonald, 1989).

EXPLORATORY PROCEDURES AND HAPTIC PERCEPTION

Haptic perception is the "ability to acquire information about objects with the hands, to discriminate and recognize objects from handling them as opposed to looking at them" (Bushnell & Boudreau, 1993, p. 1008). Properties that we can haptically perceive include temperature, size, texture, hardness, weight, and shape (Bushnell & Boudreau, 1993). Haptic sensitivity seems to emerge in a predictable sequence. The majority of research on haptic perception has involved texture or shape distinction and infants over 6 months of age. However, evidence exists that suggests that haptic perception may evolve as early as the first few months of life. Only infants over 6 months old have been studied concerning haptic perception of temperature; however, children much younger than 6 months withdraw their hands from heat or cold. Children over 6 months can perceive and discriminate hardness, but little is known considering younger children. Children under 6 months are not believed to possess the ability to perceive texture, though during the last half of the first year, texture can be perceived. Similar findings exist for weight, though it begins a few months later, at around 9 months. Shape perception evolves later yet, around 12 to 15 months. In short, a consistent order of emergence

for haptic perception appears to exist (Bushnell & Boudreau, 1993).

In one recent study (Case-Smith, Bigsby, & Clutter, 1998) that focused on younger children, researchers examined the effect of haptic attributes of objects on infants' grasping patterns. Two- to 6-month-old infants were presented with three different objects varying in haptic characteristics. Grasping was found to vary significantly by age, and it also varied based on the haptic characteristic of the object. More mature skills were noticed in the infant when the haptic characteristic of the object was closely linked to the infant's level of skill. The overall conclusion yielded by the researchers was that haptic characteristics do impact movement patterns and the influence changes with age. This was thought to be particularly important in that grasping development could potentially be facilitated by attempting to match haptic features with the baby's skill level.

The emergence of haptic perception appears to be closely linked to one's ability to perform certain types of hand movements. These hand movements, called **exploratory procedures,** are exemplified by lateral, alternate rubbing motions across an object's surface to detect texture (Lederman & Klatzky, 1987). Another example is "unsupported holding." In this case, an in-hand object is alternately raised and lowered to assist in the perception of weight. These and other exploratory procedures are illustrated in Figure 12-2. Any restriction of these hand movements may inhibit a child's ability to learn about an object. Thus, an inability in any of the exploratory procedures may reduce certain forms of haptic sensitivity.

According to Bushnell and Boudreau (1993), infant object manipulation evolves in three phases. From birth to 3 months, babies simply clutch objects in the fist. This is largely influenced by the palmar grasp reflex, discussed in Chapter 10. At this age, the object is held with one hand, occasionally brought to the mouth or brought to the body's midline and held with both hands. Fingers may not open and close much while holding the object, but, if they do, the fingers create a kneading motion. Exploratory procedures at this age may be sufficient

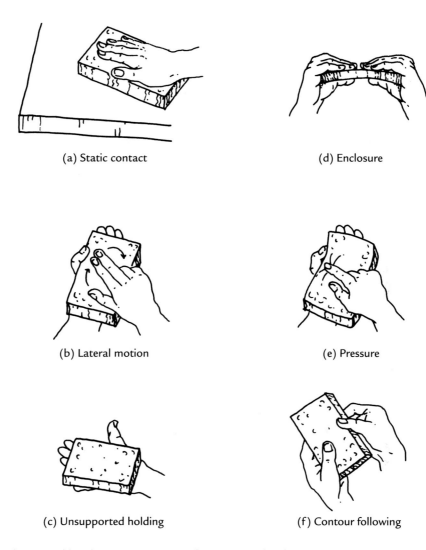

(a) Static contact

(d) Enclosure

(b) Lateral motion

(e) Pressure

(c) Unsupported holding

(f) Contour following

Figure 12-2   The optimal hand movement patterns for acquiring the object properties of temperature (a), texture (b), weight (c), volume/size (d), hardness (e), and shape (f)

SOURCE: Lederman, S. J., and Klatzky, R. L. (1987). *Cognitive Psychology, 19,* 342–368. Used with permission from Academic Press, Inc.

to detect haptic properties of temperature, size, and hardness. Interestingly, according to Bushnell and Boudreau (1993), the available research suggests that this is the order in which the ability to detect haptic properties typically emerges.

The second phase begins at approximately 4 months of age, when a wider variety of hand movements is evidenced. Visual control of manipulation and more varied and differentiated finger movements are noticeable. This includes poking, scratching, rubbing, waving, and banging objects. Infants also move the objects from hand to hand and perform some "unsupported holding" (see Figure 12-2). As indicated by Bushnell and Boudreau (1993), once these manipulatory capabilities are exhibited, the capabilities again seem to govern haptic abilities as haptic sensitivity to hardness emerges around 6 to 7 months of age. Haptic sensitivity to texture typically emerges around 6 months, while sensitivity to weight may not occur until after 9 months. In short, throughout the middle of the first year, several manipulatory capabilities emerge that appear to be similar to those necessary to perceive related haptic properties.

By 9 to 10 months, a third phase emerges when infants' ability to sit makes two-handed manipulation easier. Through "complimentary bimanual activities," one hand can position an object while the other manipulates and explores. Around this time, "contour-following" is exhibited. One hand maintains the object while the other smoothly passes over the object's outline. This gradually evolving manipulatory ability appears to contribute to the infant's ability to perceive configurational shape, which, according to Bushnell and Boudreau (1993), emerges around 12 to 15 months in most infants.

Generally, manipulatory capabilities seem to determine the order in which haptic perceptions emerge. One possible exception may be weight perception, which appears to emerge several months after the ability to perform unsupported holding (around 4 months of age). Though research is contradictory as to when the haptic ability to perceive weight emerges, Bushnell and Boudreau (1993) believe it may not be until around 9 months of age. Nevertheless, manipulation appears to be integral to the emergence of haptic ability, because object properties that correspond to exploratory procedures that have not yet evolved cannot be discriminated. Thus, an infant's manipulatory ability appears to be a constraint to the perception of certain object properties (Bushnell & Boudreau, 1993).

HOLDING A WRITING IMPLEMENT

Although fine movement has been relatively underresearched, one aspect of it that has received considerable attention is the development of technique, or the movement process, involved in handwriting or drawing. One recent study generally examined the variability in the use of writing implements by young children and adults. Studying 3- to 5-year-olds and adults, Greer and Lockman (1998) found that child subjects show a significant decrease in the number of grips used from 3 to 5 years as well as a reduction in number of overall pen positions. Compared with 3-year-olds, children who are just 6 months older use an adult pattern more often and are much less variable in their pen position relative to the writing surface.

Similarly, in a descriptive analysis of the progression of pencil and crayon grip positions in children, 3- to 7-year-olds were studied at 6-month intervals. Many of these children, at all age levels, were found to employ a mature grip. Specifically, 48 percent of the youngest subjects used the most mature grip pattern, whereas 90 percent of the oldest subjects had a mature grip pattern (Schneck & Henderson, 1990).

In a more recent investigation, researchers studied the effects of the type of the writing implement and the angle of the writing surface on children approximately 2 years of age. Fifty-one children were asked to employ a primary marker, a colored pencil, and a short crayon on an easel or a table. Children used a more mature grasp overall when using short crayons versus pencils, though no differences were found between the use of pencils and markers. Similarly, the children used a more mature grasp when the easel was used with the crayon, but did not with the marker or the pencil at the easel. The researchers believed that these findings suggest that a shorter writing implement and a vertical writing surface can influence the level of maturity in the writing or drawing process for children (Yakimishyn & Magill-Evans, 2002).

The mature grasp of the pencil or crayon is referred to as the ***dynamic tripod,*** a finger posture in which the thumb, middle finger, and index finger function as a tripod for the writing implement, enabling a child to perform small, highly coordinated finger movements. Figure 12-3 illustrates the dynamic tripod. This writing or drawing hand position normally develops from the simple tripod, in which the correct hand positioning is evident but the small coordinated movements common to the more mature dynamic tripod are lacking (Rosenbloom &

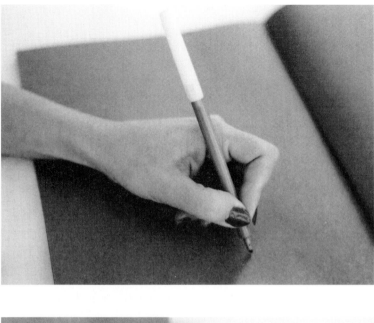

Figure 12-3 The dynamic tripod, the third and final stage of holding a writing or drawing implement. The thumb, middle finger, and index finger form a base for the implement.

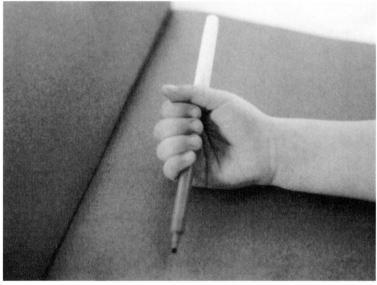

Figure 12-4 The supinate grasp, the first stage in holding a writing or drawing implement

Horton, 1971). The dynamic tripod is usually present by 7 years of age (Ziviani, 1983). Prior to the development of the dynamic tripod, the child passes through a series of rather predictable stages of handwriting technique.

In examining children who were 1½ to 7 years old, Rosenbloom and Horton (1971) determined that the earliest grasp of a writing implement usually involves the entire hand. The **supinate grasp** involves all four fingers and the thumb wrapped around the pencil to form a fist. This crude grasp, pictured in Figure 12-4, is normally replaced by the **pronate grasp,** which involves a palm-down hand position (Figure 12-5).

Figure 12-5 The pronate grasp: The hand is held with with palm down.

Once the child uses the pronate grasp, the thumb and fingers begin to play an increasingly important role in the development of the handwriting or drawing technique. For example, very young children often use their nonwriting hand to adjust the writing implement. However, as increased finger and thumb control emerge, that action becomes less important, because the children can make adjustments by using the fingers and thumb of the writing hand.

Generally, from 2 to 6 years, as children's writing ability develops, the hand moves closer to the tip of the pencil. Initially, children hold the pencil a considerable distance from the tip as the movements emanate from the shoulder. Later, the elbow produces the movement necessary to propel the pencil. Finally, in proximodistal fashion, the fingers and thumb gain sufficient control to enable improved pencil control. This improved level of movement technique, characterized by minute flexion and extension of the hand joints involved in forming the tripod, emerges in most children when they are 4 to 6 years old. In most cases, this enables the child to have developed a rather mature dynamic tripod by 7 years of age (Rosenbloom & Horton, 1971).

De Ajuriaguerra and associates (1979, as cited by Blote, 1988) have further determined that young children show clear developmental trends in handwriting. For example, posture becomes more up-right while the position of the trunk becomes more stable. This creates less need for support by distal body parts, which frees those parts for more mature writing-related movements. The hand also becomes more stable and is more commonly held below the line of writing instead of on the line as is the case with younger writers. Also increasingly prevalent is positioning the hand in line with the forearm. Generally, children were found to become more economic in their writing styles and to display a visible proximodistal trend. In other words, movements close to the body decreased in number as those movements farther from the body became more common.

Additional research on writing posture and writing movement of children from $5\frac{1}{2}$ to approximately $7\frac{1}{2}$ years of age found considerable, non-gender-related variations in children's writing development. However, as they aged, children generally tended more commonly to exhibit a mature arm and hand position. Percentages of children exhibiting specific handwriting characteristics are presented in Table 12-3. Interestingly, children were also found to increase the amount of muscle tension in writing from about $6\frac{1}{2}$ to $7\frac{1}{2}$ years. An extreme low, forward-leaning position also became prominent in many children. This position may be for improved visual inspection of the writing product and is be-

Table 12-3 Percentages of 5½- to 6½-year-old Children Performing Certain Handwriting Characteristics	
Characteristic	**Percentage**
Whole forearm on table	75
Upright body	81
Body not turned	80
Shoulders horizontal	85
Wrist in line with forearm	52
Wrist slightly extended	41
Paper perpendicular	51
Paper turned counterclockwise	30
Very low grip on pencil	53
Tripod grip	56
Proximal joint of index finger less than 90 degrees	53
Thumb opposing index finger	82
Pencil rests on:	
Third phalanx of middle finger	91
Second phalanx of middle finger	9
Tip of middle finger does not rest on shaft of pencil	87
No recurrent lifting of hand	90
No recurrent lifting of forearm	80

SOURCE: Blote, Zielstra, and Zoetewey (1987).

lieved to be related to increased effort to improve the writing. Only one characteristic was found to be significantly gender related. Excessive flexion of the index finger was more common among boys than girls (Blote & van Der Heijden, 1988; Blote, Zielstra, & Zoetewey, 1987).

CROSS-CULTURAL COMPARISON OF DEVELOPMENT OF THE DYNAMIC TRIPOD

The Rosenbloom and Horton (1971) research was conducted using British children as subjects. Saida and Miyashita (1979) similarly investigated the de-

velopment of pencil manipulation among Japanese children. The purpose of this research was to examine the development of Japanese children and to perform a cross-cultural comparison by contrasting the results with Rosenbloom and Horton's earlier findings.

The developmental sequence of the dynamic tripod in the Japanese children was found to be similar to that in the British children. For example, the Japanese children evolved through four stages of finger posture. Stage 1 was a palmar grasp of the pencil, with control of the movement emanating from the shoulder and elbow. This was similar to the supinate grasp Rosenbloom and Horton described. Stage 2 was an incomplete tripod, a transition from and a combination of the palmar grasp of the pencil and the dynamic tripod. Stage 3 involved a tripod positioning of the hand with noticeable wrist movement, although the small coordinated movements of the fingers were absent. Stage 4 was the dynamic tripod, including the highly coordinated finger movements. Over 50 percent of the Japanese boys achieved this final stage by the time they were just past 48 months old. The girls were even more advanced, with over 50 percent achieving stage 4 by as much as a year earlier. Saida and Miyashita also noted that although some generalizations could be proposed relative to age, there were marked individual differences as to when the pencil-manipulation technique was attained. One female subject first exhibited the dynamic tripod at 35 months, one male at 63 months.

In general, the Japanese children exhibited a developmental finger-posture sequence much like the British children. They also tended gradually to move their hand closer to the pencil tip as they aged. Furthermore, the average age for attaining the simple tripod was similar, with the British and Japanese children exhibiting this finger posture at 31 and 29 months, respectively.

There was a major difference between the two groups regarding the age at which the dynamic tripod emerged. The Japanese children attained it at the average age of 35 months, the British children 13 months later, at age 48 months. The authors speculated that this difference most likely occurred because of certain cultural factors. For example, Japanese children often learn to use chopsticks early in life, which may enable them to develop more advanced manipulative skills at an early age. Saida and Miyashita also speculated that any differences that do exist may begin to diminish with the continued and increased availability of convenient devices that minimize the practice of manipulative skills, such as electric toothbrushes and automatic pencil sharpeners.

THE DYNAMIC TRIPOD FROM 6 TO 14 YEARS

Thanks to studies like the ones just discussed, we have information about fine movement during childhood, but there have been few investigations into any aspect of fine motor development beyond childhood, including the study of the development of the dynamic tripod. Ziviani (1983), noting the void of information following the achievement of the dynamic tripod, did examine the refinement of this technique in children 6 to 14 years old. Subjects in this research were photographed while writing and then rated by the researchers on four characteristics. The degree of flexion of the interphalangeal joint (large knuckle) of the writing forefinger was noted—if the flexion exceeded 90 degrees, the subject was assigned a score of 1; if the angle was less than 90 degrees, a score of 2 was assigned. The angle of forearm pronation/supination was also deemed a critical factor. If the writing forearm was supinated at less than 45 degrees, the subject was assigned a 1; 2 was assigned for any other condition. Third, if more than the index finger was used on the shaft of the pencil, the subject received a 1. If the thumb and index finger gripped the pencil and the pencil rested on the radial aspect (thumb side) of the middle finger, the subject was assigned a 2. Finally, if the fingers did not form a pad-to-pad opposition around the pencil, a 1 was assigned; if they did, a 2 was assigned.

Using this method, Ziviani determined that for both index finger flexion and forearm pronation/

supination there was a significantly greater likelihood of the younger subjects scoring a 1. In other words, the younger subjects would be more likely to flex the index finger and supinate the forearm excessively. The age of changing from the immature to mature characteristics on both the finger flexion and the forearm positioning was found to be approximately 10 years. The number of fingers used on the pencil and the pad-to-pad opposition were not found to be significantly age-related. In general, Ziviani concluded that the dynamic tripod does continue to be refined between the ages of 6 and 14 years.

DRAWING AND WRITING: MOVEMENT PRODUCTS

As determined earlier in the chapter, there is a sequential development of movement technique for the manipulation of a pencil or any writing or drawing implement. This development is universal; only the rate of acquisition of the stages of movement ability varies. This movement ability is called the *movement process*. This section examines the development of the result of the movement process, the *movement product*.

Drawing: The Product

Children typically "draw" before they attempt to form the specific letters necessary for handwriting. Drawing ability has been deemed partly a function of the child's mental age. With some exceptions, evidence supports this general statement. For example, brain-injured children who function at a lower mental age than their peers of the same chronological age often have significantly greater difficulties drawing. These difficulties are manifested by an immature, exceptionally general way of mentally representing a figure. A second problem inhibiting drawing ability in children of lower mental age is their attempts at transcribing the desired image onto paper. Often the brain issues conflicting stimuli to the hand, resulting in an exceptionally immature drawing (Abercrombie, 1970).

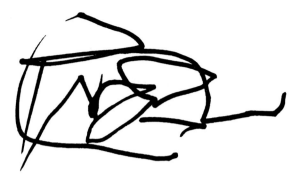

Figure 12-6   Scribbling stage: the first stage of drawing

Most children initiate their drawing development as early as 15 to 20 months by producing scribbles that have no apparent organization or intended goal. In fact, the first attempt at scribbling may occur by accident. Upon being reinforced by the resulting scribbles, the child usually does additional scribbling but often shows signs of hesitancy. Those scribbles soon become bolder as the child gains confidence. They also become less spontaneous and are drawn more slowly as the child attempts to control the movement of the hand with his or her eyes while actually pondering exactly what to create.

Following a collection and in-depth study of millions of children's paintings, Kellogg (1969) proposed that drawing is a four-step process. The *scribbling stage* is the first step to acquisition of the hand-eye coordination necessary for drawing (see Figure 12-6). Step 2, according to Kellogg, is the creation of diagrams and combinations of diagrams. This *combine stage* begins with the construction of basic geometric figures such as spirals and simple crosses (see Figure 12-7). An example of the combine stage is the 2-year-old who draws a series of spiral figures or spirals and circles. The child then slowly develops sufficient understanding and motor control to create more-precise figures, such as squares, rectangles, and triangles. Furthermore, the child becomes capable of drawing these shapes in combination with other shapes to form such things as simple houses or other familiar objects.

Step 3 in the development of the drawing product is what Kellogg refers to as the *aggregate stage* (see Figure 12-8). The child not only combines diagrams and figures but does so in combinations of three or more. Of course, the increasing number of combinations of figures enables the child to create more-complex drawings. This increasing ability culminates in the *pictorial stage* (see Figure 12-9), which is characterized by pictures drawn with increasing precision and complexity. An example of this increasing complexity is the 8- or 9-year-old child who has learned to draw the human figure with depth rather than as a stick figure, which characterized earlier artwork.

As described by Kellogg, these four major stages create a progression that most children follow, but the specific age norms for drawing are difficult to determine, because a multitude of variables tremendously affect drawing. One of the most important of these is the home environment: Children with a home environment conducive to drawing develop skills at an earlier age than average. Particularly notable components of the positive home environment are opportunities to observe other people drawing and the availability of the necessary writing implements.

Children's drawing development has been extensively examined, and much research has explored the development of a specific type of drawing by children: design copying. Typically, this type of research requires children to reproduce a particular design. For example, Birch and Lefford (1967), in one of the most comprehensive examinations of design copying, asked children 5 to 11 years old to reproduce triangles and diamonds by tracing them, drawing them on a line grid, or drawing them freehand. In each case, children improved and became more consistent with age. There was a particularly dramatic increase in ability from 5 to 6 years of age; the magnitude of improvement equaled that which occurs in most children between 6 and 11 years.

Generally, the children involved in this research found tracing to be the least difficult task. Following in order of increasing difficulty were drawing with the line grid and then freehand drawing. The

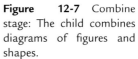

Figure 12-7 Combine stage: The child combines diagrams of figures and shapes.

Figure 12-8 Aggregate stage: The child continues to combine, but in increasing numbers of combinations.

Figure 12-9 Pictorial stage, the last stage of drawing: The child draws with more precision and complexity.

tracing of triangles and diamonds was concluded to be "mature" at 6 years of age for most subjects. Maturity in the line-grid tasks occurred at 9 years of age, and freehand drawing of the triangle continued to improve through age 9. Freehand drawing of the diamond continued to improve through age 11, which was the highest age in the research.

In a similar study of 4- to 11-year-old children, Ayres (1978) determined that ability to copy designs improved through 9 years and then plateaued, because by that age children were near the mature level. The most dramatic improvement noted, similar to Birch and Lefford's finding, fell between the ages of 5 and 7 years.

Children also display a marked sequential pattern in the way they copy and trace designs of geometric shapes. Normally, they begin at the lower left of the design and start with a vertical stroke, followed by progress to the right. In fact, children who are simply asked to point to the beginning of a letter or shape most commonly indicate the lower left aspect of the figure.

This early method of design reproduction has been hypothesized as a possible cause for children's tendencies to reverse the letter *d* more frequently than the letter *b*. This is a logical explanation, because the letter *d* requires that children reverse their usual tendency and progress to the left rather than to the right. The cause of this tendency has not been determined; however, speculation has centered on the relationship of design copying to handedness and the structure of manuscript letters (Bernbaum & Goodnow, 1974).

Handwriting: The Product

Handwriting is generally preceded by initial attempts at drawing. These initial efforts familiarize the child with the writing implement and are critical for sufficiently improving fine motor ability so that the child can form letters. Several researchers (Reimer et al., 1975; Stennet, Smythe, & Hardy, 1972) have examined the development of the ability to print letters. Through this research, experts have determined that

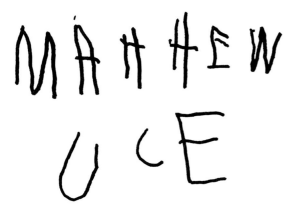

Figure 12-10   The letters a child forms when approximately 4 years old are often uppercase, large, and unorganized on the page.

children at 4 years of age are usually capable of printing recognizable numbers or letters but often fail to organize them purposefully on the page (see Figure 12-10). Typically, the letters or numbers are randomly scattered over the page; they may also be written sideways or extremely slanted.

By 5 or 6 years, however, the child has generally mastered name printing. The 5-year-old normally writes in large, irregularly shaped uppercase letters that become larger toward the end of the name. The letters of 5-year-old children generally are ½ to 2 inches high. The 6-year-old may include the surname or pertinent initials but still write in uneven uppercase letters that are occasionally reversed. The letters the 6-year-old produces continue to be large, although smaller than those most 5-year-olds produce. By age 7, the height of the letter typically has decreased to approximately ¼ inch. Children in the second grade generally master the production of uppercase letters and name printing, but the smaller lowercase letters continue to be difficult for many third-graders. Children through third grade normally find single-stroke letters, such as *I*, *c*, and *s*, easier to form than multiple-stroke letters, such as *f*, *k*, or *t*. Also, letters with horizontal and vertical strokes, such as *E*, *T*, and *H*, are easier to write than letters with slants or combined slants with vertical or horizontal strokes, such

as *K*, *B*, and *Z*. Finally, most children also find spacing letters a difficult task that often remains unmastered until they are approximately 9 years old (Cratty, 1986).

FINGER TAPPING

Most of the research on fine motor development has centered on handwriting and drawing changes during childhood. Other areas of research, however, have contributed considerably to our general knowledge of fine movement. Finger tapping, for example, is an important indicator of fine motor coordination and is often used to diagnose neurological difficulty. From research on finger tapping, investigators have determined that the increased coordination occurring over the first several years of life is highly correlated with an increase in the performance speed of the movement task. In addition, this increase in coordination and speed of movement typically plateaus at approximately 8 to 10 years on most finger-tapping tasks (Denckla, 1974).

Finger-tapping tasks are often categorized into repetitive and successive movements. *Repetitive tasks* are repetitions of the same movement, such as tapping the thumb and forefinger together as rapidly as possible. *Successive movements* are a series of similar movements performed in rapid succession. For example, a successive task that has been examined in research involving kindergarten through second-grade children is the rapid tapping of the thumb successively with each same-hand finger. In performing these kinds of tasks, young children were found to improve consistently with age. Also, girls performed better than boys at all three grades involved in the research. Interestingly, right-hand superiority was noted in these right-hand-dominant children for the repetitive but not the successive tasks; the author had not expected this finding (Denckla, 1973).

More recent research on finger tapping in children and adults examined the effects of external training on tapping speed (Dash & Telles, 2000). In this case, finger tapping was used as a measure of motor speed. Tapping speed was measured every

10 seconds for a total of 30 consecutive seconds as researchers focused on the effect of yoga training on performance. Interestingly, when compared with the control group, children demonstrated a significant increase in tapping speed after just 10 days of training; adults showed similar increases after 30 days. However, the researchers noted that increases in speed were only seen for the first 10 seconds of tapping for both child and adult subjects, indicating enhanced speed but not endurance. This appears to demonstrate the potential modifiability of our speed of performance in fine movements like finger tapping (Dash & Telles, 2000).

FINE MOTOR SLOWING IN LATE ADULTHOOD

As noted in the discussion of such fine movements as handwriting and finger tapping, most individuals' coordination and speed of performance plateau fairly early in life. From then on, few obvious changes are noticeable until regression begins late in life. Whereas the first few years of life are characterized by the central nervous system's increasing capacity and improved movement capability in a proximodistal direction, later life often involves a reversal of that process. Aging is associated with the degeneration of neurons (Bondareff, 1985). This degeneration, in conjunction with higher incidence of such chronic diseases as arthritis and osteoporosis, can reverse the proximodistal progression that occurred earlier in life. The fine motor development of the distal portions of the body, such as the fingertips, regresses. Movement can become less refined as the arm and shoulder regain control over movements that were once precisely coordinated by wrist and finger action.

Fine motor behavior may also slow as a result of the neurological degeneration associated with aging. In fact, Salthouse (1985) reviewed many movement-related studies that examine the phenomenon of slowing with age. This process of becoming slower in movement is well established. In fact, Salthouse uses phrases such as "least disputed" and "most pervasive" to describe the slowing process. However,

he also notes that this slowing trend is much more common in some types of movements than others. For example, the slowing in handwriting is much more evident than that noticed in finger-tapping research.

An interesting way to express the association of age and reduced speed for a given movement activity is with a correlation coefficient. A higher correlation coefficient indicates a higher relationship between age and time to perform the movement in question. Although Salthouse admits that this technique may occasionally be misleading, generally the coefficient gives a useful rough estimate of the magnitude of the age–speed relationship. In reviewing the research examining a variety of kinds of movement, Salthouse found the mean and median coefficients for 11 reaction-time studies to be .32 and .31, respectively. These values can be compared with the results from six movement-time studies in which the mean and median coefficients were .49 and .545. Examples of other analyzed movements were card sorting, .54; dialing a telephone, .64; zipping a garment, .64; unwrapping a Band-Aid, .48; squeezing toothpaste, .55; and using a fork, .33.

Slowing with age is believed to occur in many fine and gross movements, but Salthouse cites three major exceptions to this general rule. First, he notes that physically fit or exceptionally healthy individuals maintain their speed quite well relative to younger healthy adults. Physical activity is a means of allaying the slowing process. Second, practice also inhibits the slowing process. Older adults who consistently and regularly repeat or practice the activity in question generally show considerably less slowing than do young adults who have been uninvolved in the activity for long periods. Finally, Salthouse notes that movement involved in the creation of vocal responses shows fewer signs of slowing than does manipulative movement.

In research specifically designed to examine the effects of physical activity and aging on fine motor performance, Normand, Kerr, and Metiviei (1987) note that slowing in movement behavior is especially common with complex movements. This is particularly true of many fine movements and, as Salthouse suggested earlier, is generally believed to be strongly related to an individual's health, personal habits (e.g., physical activity), and the nature of the task. Also, while it was once believed that slowing with age was a function of decline in muscles, joints, or organs specifically related to the movement, many experts now believe that the slowing may be a function of deterioration in the central nervous system. This, of course, means that slowing could happen in cognitive processes as well as human movement. Also, because the central nervous system governs both mental and motor capacities, information gathered concerning psychomotor changes in speed may contribute to the body of knowledge concerning the central nervous system and cognitive slowing with age. Slowing reaction time, according to Normand and associates (1987), could be a function of loss of brain cells, reduction of cerebral blood flow, or the presence of disease (e.g., atherosclerosis), which may disrupt the central nervous system. They further claim, as Salthouse suggested earlier, that declining physical fitness may be a contributor to slowing with age.

To test their hypothesis, Normand, Kerr, and Metiviei (1987) studied the effects of short-term increases in physical activity level on performance of a fine motor task. The task was to rapidly and repeatedly align a steering wheel with specified target areas. Both accuracy and speed of response were important factors in the study. All of the subjects, averaging over 65 years of age, were tested before and after participating in a 10-week exercise program. Contrary to the original hypothesis and the research of others, these researchers did not find an improved level of fine motor performance on the posttest. However, periodic, informal assessments of physiological change revealed that these subjects, originally believed to be sedentary, also failed to show a physiological improvement. Perhaps, as the authors suggest, the subjects were not originally sedentary, as believed. Though none were actively engaged in a physical activity program, their daily routines of walking while shopping or doing yardwork may have been sufficient to make an improvement in physiological parameters, and therefore fine motor ability, more difficult.

This research contrasts other investigations, which have shown physical activity to enhance other forms of motor performance (Clarkson & Kroll, 1978; Spirduso, 1977). Of particular interest is the reaction- and movement-time research conducted by Spirduso (1977). In her investigation, 50- to 70-year-old active and inactive subjects were compared with their 20- to 30-year-old counterparts on simple and discriminant reaction and movement time. Though the younger adults performed better overall on these measures, activity level was a significant factor. This prompted Spirduso to conclude that "a life of physical activity appeared to play a more dominant role in simple and discriminant reaction time and movement time and age" (p. 435).

SUMMARY

Fine movement refers to those movements that are produced predominantly by the small muscles or muscle groups of the body.

Manipulation, or use of the hands, is one of the most critical of the fine movements because hundreds of manipulative movements are performed each day. Manipulation has been categorized into intrinsic movements, which involve coordinated movements of the individual digits, and extrinsic movements, which involve the management of an object that is already in hand. A more specific system of categorization includes simple synergies, reciprocal synergies, and sequential patterns.

In a frequently cited study conducted over 60 years ago, Halverson (1931) described the early reaching and grasping of 4- to 13-month-old infants. Three basic stages of development were determined for reaching, whereas grasping evolved through a 10-stage progression. Generally, a proximodistal progression was noted.

More recent research by Newell and associates has led to the questioning of the "classic" work of Halverson. Newell's research examined adult and child reaching and grasping when the object size was scaled to the size of the subject's hand. Though some differences were noted, the overall trend for grasping was quite similar for adult and child subjects. Object size was found to play a major role in grip patterns employed by children and adults.

Recent work by Bushnell and Boudreau (1993) examines the haptic perception, or the ability to glean information from objects via the hands; they found that haptic perception is apparently a function of early ability in manipulation. The emergence of exploratory procedures, like poking or unsupported "holding of an object," were found to be linked to the emergence of haptic properties of objects. Thus, any early restriction of hand movements may restrict an infant's ability to learn about an object's properties.

The development of the hand position for holding a writing implement has been one of the most widely researched areas of fine movement. The first hand position used for grasping a pencil or crayon is usually a supinate grasp: a fist around the pencil. This typically evolves into a pronate grasp, which is a palm-down position characterized by the fingers curled around the pencil, with the index finger extending the length of the pencil and pointing toward the point. Finally, usually by 7 years of age, the dynamic tripod is developed, a hand position that enables highly coordinated finger movement to occur.

Other notable developmental handwriting trends seen in young children include an increase in upright posture, a more stable trunk and hand, and an increase in the likelihood of holding the hand below the line of writing and in line with the forearm. Children were also found to increase in forward lean and muscle tension at around 7 years of age.

Extensive studies by Kellogg (1969) have led to the formulation of four major stages of drawing development as determined by the product of the act of drawing. Initially, children go through the scribbling stage, in which they simply scribble with no apparent objective in mind. In the combine stage, children create diagrams and combinations of diagrams. The third stage, the aggregate stage, is characterized by combinations of three or more diagrams or figures. Last, the pictorial stage is typified by pictures drawn with continued complexity and precision.

Handwriting can also be described developmentally by the product of the action. Researchers in this area have noted that recognizable letter writing is generally evident by 4 years of age, although there is little organization of the letters. By 5 or 6 years, children can print their names using large uppercase letters. By 7 years, children write much smaller letters and can effectively print lowercase letters.

Finger tapping is another area of fine movement that has been of interest to fine motor researchers. Through finger-tapping tests, investigators have determined that increased coordination and speed of performance occur over the first several years of life. For most finger-tapping tasks, this improvement typically plateaus at approximately 8 to 10 years.

The speed and coordination of many forms of fine movement plateau fairly early in life. No major fine motor changes are noted until the later stages of life, when a regression may occur, a reversal of the proximodistal trend in development. Fine movement may become less precise as the elbow and shoulder begin to guide the hand through movements once led by fingertip control. Slowing and decreased coordination may also occur as a result of the neural degeneration that often accompanies aging. Although slowing with age is a well-substantiated fact and inevitable for many people, physical activity and practice attenuate or even eliminate the slowing process in later adulthood.

In research designed to examine the effects of short-term increases in physical activity and aging on fine motor performance, researchers administered a rapid and repetitive fine motor task to subjects who were over 65 years of age and involved in a 10-week physical activity program. Though this investigation did not show an improved level of performance in fine movement, similar reaction- and movement-time research has shown that physical activity through adulthood may be more important than age in predicting reaction and movement time.

KEY TERMS

aggregate stage	haptic perception	reciprocal synergies
combine stage	intrinsic movements	scribbling stage
dynamic tripod	manipulation	sequential patterns
exploratory procedures	pictorial stage	simple synergies
extrinsic movements	prehension	supinate grasp
fine motor	pronate grasp	

QUESTIONS FOR REFLECTION

1. Explain the term *fine motor*. Why are fine movements of the hand emphasized in this chapter?

2. What are intrinsic and extrinsic movements of the hand?

3. Summarize the early work of Halverson. According to this researcher, how does reaching and grasping evolve over the first few years of life?

4. What is haptic perception? Describe how it evolves over the first year of life.

5. What is a dynamic tripod? How does it differ from a supinate grasp or a pronate grasp? In which order do they typically appear during the first few years of life?

6. This chapter discusses cross-cultural studies of children and their development of the dynamic

tripod. Summarize the findings as they relate to Japanese and British children. What reasons were offered for the differences found between these children?

7. Can you list three categories of hand movements and provide at least one example for each category?

8. Describe the development of drawing as proposed by Kellogg. What are the stages of drawing development, and how would you describe each stage?

9. What is the difference between the drawing product and the drawing process in the development of this ability? Give examples of each.

10. How are finger-tapping tasks categorized?

ONLINE LEARNING CENTER (www.mhhe.com/payne6e)

Visit the *Human Motor Development* Online Learning Center for study aids and additional resources. You can use the study guide questions and key terms puzzles to review key terms and concepts for this chapter and to prepare for exams. You can further extend your knowledge of motor development by checking out the Web links, articles, and activities found on the site.

REFERENCES

Abercrombie, M. L. J. (1970). Learning to draw. In K. J. Connolly (Ed.), *Mechanisms of motor skill development*. London: Academic Press.

Ayres, A. J. (1978). *Southern California sensory-motor integration test manual*. Los Angeles: Western Psychological Services.

Bernbaum, M., & Goodnow, J. (1974). Relationships among perpetual-motor tasks: Tracing and copying. *Journal of Educational Psychology, 66,* 731–735.

Birch, H. G., & Lefford, A. (1967). Visual differentiation, intersensory integration, and voluntary motor control. *Monographs of the Society for Research in Child Development, 32.*

Blote, A. W. (1988). The development of writing behavior. Personal monograph.

Blote, A. W., & van Der Heijden, P. G. M. (1988). A follow-up study of writing posture and writing movement of young children. *Journal of Human Movement Studies, 14,* 57–74.

Blote, A. W., Zielstra, E. M., & Zoetewey, M. W. (1987). Writing posture and writing movement of children in kindergarten. *Journal of Human Movement Studies, 13,* 323–341.

Bondareff, W. (1985). The neural basis of aging. In J. E. Birren & K. W. Schaie (Eds.), *Handbook of the psychology of aging*. New York: Van Nostrand.

Bushnell, E. W., & Boudreau, J. P. (1993). Motor development and the mind: The potential role of motor abilities as determinants of aspects of perceptual development. *Child Development, 64,* 1005–1021.

Case-Smith, J., Bigsby, R., & Clutter, J. (1998). Perceptual-motor coupling in the development of grasp. *American Journal of Occupational Therapy, 52*(2), 102–110.

Clarkson, P. M., & Kroll, W. (1978). Practice effects on fractionated response time related to age and activity level. *Journal of Motor Behavior, 10,* 275–286.

Cratty, B. J. (1986). *Perceptual and motor development in infants and children.* 3rd ed. Englewood Cliffs, NJ: Prentice-Hall.

Dash, M., & Telles, S. (2000). Yoga training and motor speed based on a finger tapping task. *India Journal of Psyiological Pharmacology, 43*(4), 458–462.

De Ajuriaguerra, J., Auzias, M., Coumes, F., Denner, A., Lavondes-Monod, V., Perron, R., & Stambak, M. (1979). *Children's handwriting: The development of handwriting and problems in handwriting.* Paris: Delachauz et Niestle.

Denckla, M. B. (1973). Development of speed in repetitive and successive finger movements in normal children. *Developmental Medicine and Child Neurology, 15,* 635–645.

———. (1974). Development of motor coordination in normal children. *Developmental Medicine and Child Neurology, 16,* 729–741.

Elliott, J. M., & Connolly, K. J. (1984). A classification of manipulative hand movements. *Developmental Medicine and Child Neurology, 26,* 283–296.

Greer, T., & Lockman, J. J. (1998). Using writing instruments: Invariances in young children and adults. *Child Development, 69*(4), 888–902.

Halverson, H. M. (1931). An experimental study of prehension in infants by means of systematic cinema records. *Genetic Psychology Manuscripts, 10,* 107–286.

Hohlstein, R. R. (1974). The development of prehension in normal infants. Unpublished master's thesis, University of Wisconsin, Madison.

Kellogg, R. (1969). *Analyzing children's art.* Palo Alto, CA: Mayfield.

Kuhtz-Buschbeck, J. P., Stolze, H., John, K. K., Boczek-Funcke, A., Illert, M., & Heinreichs, H. (1998). Kinematic analysis of prehension movements in children. *Behavioral Brain Research, 93*(1–2), 131–141.

Lederman, S. J., & Klatzky, R. L. (1987). Hand movement: A window into haptic object recognition. *Cognitive Psychology, 22,* 421–459.

Newell, K. M., McDonald, P. V., & Baillargeon, R. (1993). Body scale and infant grip configurations. *Developmental Psychobiology, 26*(4), 195–205.

Newell, K. M., Scully, D. M., & McDonald, P. V. (1989). Task constraints and infant grip configurations. *Developmental Psychobiology, 22*(8), 817–832.

Newell, K. M., Scully, D. M., Tenenbaum, F., & Hardiman, S. (1989). Body scale and the development of prehension. *Developmental Psychobiology, 22*(1), 1–13.

Noller, K., & Ingrisano, D. (1984). Cross-sectional study of gross and fine motor development. *Physical Therapy, 64*(3), 308–316.

Normand, R., Kerr, R., & Metiviei, G. (1987). Exercise, aging, and fine motor performance: An assessment. *Journal of Sports Medicine, 27,* 488–496.

Pehoski, C., Henderson, A., & Tickle-Degnen, L. (1997a). In-hand manipulation in young children: Rotation of an object in the fingers. *American Journal of Occupational Therapy, 51*(7), 544–552.

———. (1997b). In-hand manipulation in young children: Translation movements. *American Journal of Occupational Therapy, 51*(9), 719–728.

Reimer, D. C., Eaves, L. C., Richards, R., & Chrichton, J. (1975). Name printing as a test of developmental maturity. *Developmental Medicine and Child Neurology, 17,* 486–492.

Rosenbloom, L., & Horton, M. E. (1971). The maturation of fine prehension in young children. *Developmental Medicine and Child Neurology, 13,* 38.

Saida, Y., & Miyashita, M. (1979). Development of fine motor skill in children: Manipulation of a pencil in young children aged 2 to 6 years. *Journal of Human Movement Studies, 5,* 104–113.

Salthouse, T. (1985). Speed of behavior and its implication for cognition. In J. E. Birren & K. W. Schaie (Eds.), *Handbook of psychology of aging.* New York: Van Nostrand.

Schneck, C. M., & Henderson, A. (1990). Descriptive analysis of the development of grip position for pencil and crayon control in nondysfunctional children. *Journal of Occupational Therapy, 44*(10), 893–900.

Spirduso, W. W. (1977). Reaction and movement time as a function of age and physical activity level. *Journal of Gerontology, 30,* 435–440.

Stennet, R. G., Smythe, P. C., & Hardy, M. (1972). Developmental trends in letter printing skills. *Perceptual and Motor Skills, 34,* 182–186.

Williams, H. G. (1983). *Perceptual and motor development.* Englewood Cliffs, NJ: Prentice-Hall.

Yakimishyn, J. E., & Magill-Evans, J. (2002). Comparisons among tools, surface orientation, and pencil grasp for children 23 months of age. *American Journal of Occupational Therapy, 56*(5), 564–572.

Ziviani, J. (1983). Qualitative changes in dynamic tripod grip between seven and fourteen years of age. *Developmental Medicine and Child Neurology, 25,* 778–782.

13 Fundamental Locomotion Skills of Childhood

Children's motor repertoires greatly expand during the second year of life. At this time, children no longer have to rely on rudimentary motor behaviors to locomote, explore, and manipulate their environment. They begin to develop and use fundamental locomotion skills that include walking, running, jumping, and hopping. In addition, when several of these skills are combined, galloping, sliding, and skipping emerge. These skills can be thought of as the building blocks of the more specific skills developed later in childhood.

At the end of the first year or at the beginning of the second year, children are capable of walking without support, and soon thereafter running is evident. In turn, as soon as children are capable of momentarily propelling themselves through space, as is required in running, they will also be capable of performing some type of jumping and hopping maneuver. As strength, balance, and motor coordination improve, combination patterns will appear. These combination patterns include galloping, sliding, and skipping.

This chapter reviews the professional literature regarding the development of these fundamental skills of locomotion and explores factors that may affect this development.

WALKING

The onset of independent **walking** or **upright bipedal locomotion** is truly a glorious occasion in the lives of both infants and parents. Shortly after the birth of their offspring, many parents await the onset of this milestone with great interest and enthusiasm. However, this important event has more far-reaching ramifications for the infant. Up to this point, the infant has had to rely on the prewalking movement patterns of crawling, creeping, and locomoting with handholds. Each movement pattern is useful for getting the child from point A to point B, but they all share one major limitation: Each requires the use of the hands to perform the movement. Thus, while the child is locomoting, the hands are not free to explore the changing environment. In contrast, as soon as the infant can walk alone, his hands are free to explore.

This form of locomotion is characterized by a progressive alternation of leading legs and continuous contact with the supporting surface. The walking cycle or **gait** cycle is the distance covered by two heel strikes of the same foot and consists of two distinct phases: a **swing phase** and a stance or **support phase** (Burnett & Johnson, 1971). The swing phase begins when the foot or toes of one leg leave the supporting surface and ends when the heel or foot of the same leg recontacts the ground. The time when balance is maintained on only one foot is the support phase. Thus, while the right foot is in the swing phase, the left foot is in the support phase. When both feet are in contact with the supporting surface, the walker is in a **double support phase.**

Even though walking is one of the most highly automatized motor acts that adults perform (Bernstein, 1967), the same is not true for the walking infant. An infant's initial attempt at unsupported walking has little in common with normal adult walking, because to achieve independent walking, the infant must overcome two major obstacles. Not only must the infant have sufficient leg strength to support the body weight, but she must also be capable of maintaining a state of equilibrium. Subsequently, many of the observable characteristics of initial walking are designed to foster stability. For example, the initial movement pattern of independent walking is characterized by short, quick, rigid steps; the toes point outward, and the infant assumes a wide base of support. In addition, the infant makes a flat-footed contact with the ground instead of the heel-toe contact of an adult gait. Further attempts to maintain stability are implemented by carrying the arms in a high guard position. Also, the infant keeps the arms rigid; they do not swing freely in opposition to the legs. This independent walking pattern is apparent in most children by 12 months of age, even though the normal range is considered from 9 to 17 months. Table 13-1 summarizes certain

Table 13-1 Selected Walking Characteristics		
Characteristic	**Appearance°**	**Range°**
Heel strike	22.6	3–50
Base within lateral dimensions of trunk	17.5	5–43
Synchronous movement of upper extremities	21.6	6–43
Double knee lock	27.2	8–55

°Weeks after the onset of independent walking
SOURCE: Based on Burnett and Johnson (1971).

walking characteristics. During the next 2 to 6 years, many gradual changes occur within each gait parameter, enabling the child progressively to assume a more adultlike style of walking (Hausdorff et al., 1999).

Dynamic Base

To maintain balance during initial walking attempts, the infant places the feet apart, to widen the base of support (see Figure 13-1). As balance improves, the child brings the feet closer together. This base of support is brought within the lateral dimensions of the trunk by 17.5 weeks after the onset of independent walking (Burnett & Johnson, 1971). Bril and Breniere (1992) report that the average stepping width is 230 millimeters at the start of independent walking; this narrows to 152 millimeters 6 months later. The width continues to narrow until it reaches 111 millimeters by the end of the second year of independent walking.

Foot Angle

Foot angle is the amount of toeing-out or toeing-in. In general, the degree of toeing-out decreases during the first 4 years of life and then remains fairly stable during the teens (Engel & Staheli, 1974), although some researchers have documented increasingly narrow bases of support up to 45 years

of age (Murray, Drought, & Kory, 1964). In contrast, Engel and Staheli (1974) found toeing-in to be rare and consider this gait pattern abnormal. More specifically, they found only 6 of 130 children (4.6 percent) from 1 day to 14 years old exhibiting toeing-in gaits.

Walking Speed

Walking speed, another gait parameter, is determined by the length of the stride and the speed of the stepping movements. Each measure differs, depending on whether the walking movements are performed with or without support. In fact, when support minimizes their postural requirements, infants show well-coordinated stepping patterns months before the onset of independent walking (Thelen, 1986). Statham and Murray (1971) found both step frequency and walking speed greatest in independent walking as compared with supported walking, although there was much variability among the seven children studied. Statham and Murray found that children who were capable of walking 6 feet without support had a stepping rate of 158 steps per minute, whereas infants who walked with support attained only 107 steps per minute. While observing five children over a 2-year period, Bril and Breniere (1992) noted a threefold increase in walking speed in the first 6 months of independent walking. Furthermore, when infants first began to walk, increases in walking speed were due mostly to increased step length. This finding had been noted earlier by Phillips and Clark (1987). After 5 months of independent walking, however, the pattern reversed so that increases in walking speed were due primarily to an increased walking cadence. Keogh and Sugden (1985) reported the average footfalls per minute for babies as 180 to 200 per minute, in contrast to the average adult step frequency of 140 footfalls per minute. In short, step frequency decreases with advancing age during the childhood years.

Scrutton (1969) has studied the other component of walking speed: step length. He found that the average step length of 97 "normal" children younger

Note the high guard-arm position, wide base of support, flat-footed contact, and toeing-out in this immature walker.

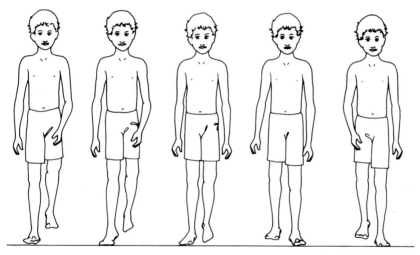

With improved balance, the base of support narrows, the arms are lowered and work in opposition to the legs, and the toes point in a more forward direction.

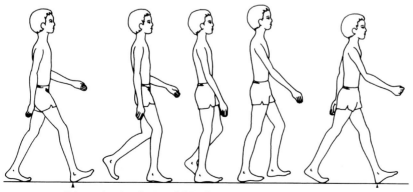

In mature walking, a heel strike is exhibited.

Figure 13-1 An illustration of selected improvements in walking

Table 13-2	Selected Walking Parameters with Advancing Age			
	Gait Parameter			
Age (years)	**Step Length (cm)**	**Stride Length (cm)**	**Steps/ Minute**	**Walking Speed (cm/s)**
1	21.6	43.0	175.7	63.7
2	27.5	54.9	155.8	71.8
3	32.9	67.7	153.5	85.5
7	47.9	96.5	143.5	114.3
Adult	65.5	129.4	114.0	121.6

SOURCE: Based on Sutherland (1984).

than 5 years old increased from 1.5 to 2 inches annually. More specifically, the average step length of the 1-, 2-, 3-, and 4-year-old children was 10, 11.5, 13, and 15 inches, respectively. In adult populations, step length is related to stature: Taller people generally have a longer step length (Murray et al., 1964).

Until the infant gains sufficient neuromuscular control, he or she must take more steps per unit of time to increase walking speed. This lack of neuromuscular control precludes any successful attempt at increasing walking speed by increasing step length (Sutherland, 1984). With age, gains in neuromuscular postural control partly contribute to longer steps.

One study that illustrates differences in step length, stride length, step frequency, and walking speed was conducted at San Diego Children's Hospital (Sutherland, 1984). Table 13-2 summarizes the findings, which are based on a subject population of 464 "normal" children 1 to 7 years old and a comparative sample of 15 adults 19 to 40 years old.

Briefly, the researchers concluded that most observable gait changes occur by 3 years of age. In fact, they found little difference between the walking patterns of 3- and 7-year-old children, with the exception of diminished stride length and a fairly high step frequency for younger children. In addi-

tion, the average 3-year-old child displayed adult-like joint-rotation characteristics. However, more resent research (Hausdorff et al., 1999) has shown that stride dynamics mature at different ages and may not be completely mature even in 7-year-old children.

Walking with External Loads

Researchers are just beginning to examine the influence of carrying an external load on changes in gait patterns in young children. This line of research has been popularized because of the increasing number of young children who have complained of back and shoulder pain as a result of carrying heavy school book bags. To examine the influence of external loading and changes in gait patterns during walking, Hong and Brueggemann (2000) required 10-year-old boys to walk on a treadmill while carrying school book bag loads of 0 percent (control), 10 percent, 15 percent, and 20 percent of their body weight. Findings indicated that the 20 percent load was responsible for inducing a significant increase in trunk forward lean, an increase in double support and stance durations, and a decrease in trunk angular motion and swing duration. In comparison, the 15 percent load only induced a significant increase in forward lean. No significant differences in gait characteristics were found between the 10 percent and the 0 percent load conditions. As a result, the researchers suggest that school book bag or backpack weight should not exceed 10 percent of body weight in these young children. This is another example of how environmental conditions can influence movement characteristics (see "Dynamical Systems Perspective" in Chapter 1).

RUNNING

Running is sometimes referred to as a natural extension of walking. This form of human locomotion is characterized by an alternate support phase and an airborne or ***flight phase.*** This flight phase is what most readily distinguishes the walk from the run. See Figure 13-2.

As with walking, children must overcome several obstacles before they can exhibit characteristics associated with minimal running form. First, and perhaps most important, children need enough lower-limb strength both to propel themselves through the air and to handle the additional force encountered when the airborne foot strikes the supporting surface. The magnitude of this impact can exceed three times the child's body weight. Second, the child needs improved motor coordination to control the rapidly moving legs.

At first, running takes on many characteristics of an immature walk: a wide base of support, arms held in a high guard position, and flat-footed contact with the supporting surface. Reverting back to this immature pattern is the child's way of temporarily improving balance while gaining confidence in performing this new movement.

On the average, most children exhibit minimal running form somewhere between 6 and 12 months after the onset of independent walking—in other words, between the 18th and 24th months of life. As children acquire increased lower-limb strength, improved balance, and finally improved motor control, their running pattern looks more adult.

Figure 13-2   Running—the flight phase

Selected Improvements in the Running Pattern

A close examination of the running pattern reveals that each running cycle consists of three phases: the support phase, the flight phase, and the recovery phase. The arms also play an important role. This section examines in greater detail certain developmental changes that occur during the running cycle.

SUPPORT PHASE AND FLIGHT PHASE   In the support phase, the leg absorbs the impact of the striking foot, supports the body, and maintains forward motion while accelerating the body's center of gravity as the leg provides thrust to propel the body forward. The inexperienced runner performs the foot strike with the full sole. As running form improves, the part of the foot hitting the ground moves closer toward the ball of the foot. Data that Fortney (1983) collected support this finding. In her study, the 2-year-old subjects' support ankle formed an angle slightly less than 90 degrees at contact with the ground. In contrast, her 4- and 6-year-old subjects attained 98 degrees ankle plantar flexion (toes pointing toward ground) at contact.

At first, the inexperienced runner is incapable of projecting the body through space for any significant distance, because the runner does not effectively use the thrust leg. The progressive developmental trend of the thrust leg calls for more involvement of the hip, knee, and ankle to provide full extension to generate maximum thrust. This increased extension of the segments of the thrust leg becomes more evident with increasing age. This is particularly apparent in Fortney's (1983) research. She noted increasing degrees of support-knee extension at takeoff among the 2- (33.67 degrees), 4- (19.25 degrees), and 6-year-old children (15.20 degrees). She also reported similar trends across ages in relation to both ankle and hip extension.

RECOVERY PHASE Once the body has been thrust into the air by the vigorous extension of the support leg, the support leg enters a phase of recovery. This leg, which has been projected backward, must be quickly brought forward to repeat its function in the next running cycle. There are obvious developmental trends in how the recovery leg is brought forward.

The experienced runner flexes the knee so the heel of the foot of the recovery leg comes very close to making contact with the buttock. The knee and thigh are then swung forward until the thigh is practically parallel with the running surface. This thigh position is usually reached the moment the support foot leaves the supporting surface. While the body is airborne, the knee of the forward leg is extended, thus allowing the foot to descend toward the running surface. The experienced runner does not place the foot so far in front of his or her center of gravity as to produce a braking effect.

In contrast, the inexperienced runner does not achieve a degree of knee flexion sufficient to bring the heel close to the buttock. Similarly, insufficient hip flexion keeps the thigh from forming a right angle with the body's trunk. In fact, because of this insufficient knee and hip flexion, the inexperienced runner frequently stumbles, because there is not adequate clearance between the foot and ground during the recovery phase. Frequently, the inexperienced runner resorts to turning the toes inward or outward to create sufficient foot-ground clearance during the forward swing of the recovery leg.

ARM ACTIONS The arms also play an important role in contributing to running form and running performance. During the child's first attempts at running, the arms are flexed in the high guard position to aid balance and do not work in opposition to the legs. In a slightly more adultlike pattern, the arms are lowered and generally hang free but still do not help running speed by working in opposition to the legs. Furthermore, when the beginning runner is observed from the front, it is evident that the arms hook or swing across the body's midline, causing undesired trunk rotation (Payne, 1985).

In contrast, the experienced runner uses the arms in opposition to the legs. The elbows are flexed at 90 degrees, and a vigorous pumping action of the arms toward but not across the body's midline fosters forward momentum.

Developmental Sequences for Running

Researchers have suggested that there are developmental sequences for running. Table 13-3 presents Roberton and Halverson's component approach analysis. Note that this approach describes changes that are expected to occur within each body segment. In contrast, Figure 13-3 illustrates the total body approach for describing the developmental sequences of running. In this approach, the "total body configuration" during performance is described. Also included in this figure is a horizontal bar graph that denotes when 60 percent of boys and girls can perform at a specific developmental level. (These values will change as data sets are updated and new data analyzed.) This graphed information can be useful to movement specialists when confronted with such questions as How close to maturity is my child's performance? or At what age should my child be expected to perform at a specific level of competence? (Branta, Haubenstricker, & Seefeldt, 1984). Furthermore, this information is also useful for comparing the "relative difficulty in achieving the various stages [developmental levels] by noting the time-span between their attainment" (Seefeldt & Haubenstricker, 1982, p. 314).

Table 13-3   Developmental Sequences for Running: Component Approach

Leg Action Component

Step 1: The run is flat-footed with minimal flight. The swing leg is slightly abducted as it comes forward. When seen from overhead, the path of the swing leg curves out to the side during its movement forward. Foot eversion gives a toeing-out appearance to the swinging leg. The angle of the knee of the swing leg is greater than 90° during forward motion.

Step 2: The swing thigh moves forward with greater acceleration, causing 90° of maximal flexion in the knee. From the rear, the foot is no longer toed-out nor is the thigh abducted. The sideward swing of the thigh continues, however, causing the foot to cross the body midline when viewed from the rear. Flight time increases. After contact, which may still be flat-footed, the support knee flexes more as the child's weight rides over the foot.

Step 3: Foot contact is with the heel or the ball of the foot. The forward movement of the swing leg is primarily in the sagittal plane. Flexion of the thigh at the hip carries the knee higher at the end of the forward swing. The support leg moves from flexion to complete extension by takeoff.

Arm Action Component

Step 1: The arms do not participate in the running action. They are sometimes held in high guard or, more frequently, middle guard position. In high guard, the hands are held about shoulder high. Sometimes they ride even higher if the laterally rotated arms are abducted at the shoulder and the elbows flexed. In middle guard, the lateral rotation decreases, allowing the hands to be held waist high. They remain motionless, except in reaction to shifts in equilibrium.

Step 2: Spinal rotation swings the arms bilaterally to counterbalance rotation of the pelvis and swing leg. The frequently oblique plane of motion plus continual balancing adjustments give a flailing appearance to the arm action.

Step 3: Spinal rotation continues to be the prime mover of the arms. Now the elbow of the arm swinging forward begins to flex, then extend during the backward swing. The combination of rotation and elbow flexion causes the arm rotating forward to cross the body midline and the arm rotating back to abduct, swinging obliquely outward from the body.

Step 4: The humerus (upper arm) begins to drive forward and back in the sagittal plane independent of spinal rotation. The movement is in opposition to the other arm and to the leg on the same side. Elbow flexion is maintained, oscillating about a 90° angle during the forward and backward arm swings.

Note: These sequences have not been validated. They were hypothesized by Roberton (1983) from the work of Seefeldt, Reuschlein, and Vogel (1972) and Wickstrom (1983).

SOURCE: Roberton, M. A., and Halverson, L. E. (1984). *Developing children—their changing movement.* Lea & Febiger. Used with permission from current copyright holder, M. A. Roberton.

Figure 13-3   Developmental sequences for running: total body approach

SOURCES: Fountain et al. (1981); Seefeldt and Haubenstricker (1982); Seefeldt, Reuschlein, and Vogel (1972). All material used with permission of Dr. John Haubenstricker.

Stage 1   The arms are extended sideward at shoulder height (high guard position). The stride is short and of shoulder width. The surface contact is made with the entire foot, striking simultaneously. Little knee flexion is seen. The feet remain near the surface.

Stage 2   Arms are carried at middle guard position (waist high). The stride is longer and approaches the midsagittal line. The surface contact is usually made with the entire foot, striking simultaneously. Greater knee flexion is noted in the restraining phase. The swing leg is flexed, and the movement of the legs becomes anterior-posterior.

Stage 3   The arms are no longer used primarily for balance but rather are carried below waist level and may flex and assume a counterrotary action. The foot contact is heel-toe. Stride length increases, and both feet move along a midsagittal line. The swing-leg flexion may be as great as 90°.

(continued)

Figure 13-3   *(continued)*

Stage 4   Foot contact is heel-toe at slow or modest velocities but may be entirely on the metatarsal arch while sprinting. Arm action is in direct opposition to leg action. Knee flexion is used to maintain the momentum during the support phase. The swing leg may flex until it is nearly in contact with the buttocks during its recovery phase.

Insufficient movements common to running patterns include inversion or eversion of the foot during the support phase. Inversion results in a medial rotation of the leg and thigh during the support phase and is characterized by an oblique rather than an anterior-posterior pattern as the leg is brought forward in the swing phase.

Eversion of the foot during the support phase results in lateral rotation of the leg and thigh. This pattern is often accompanied by an exaggerated counterrotary action of the arms in an attempt to maintain a uniform direction.

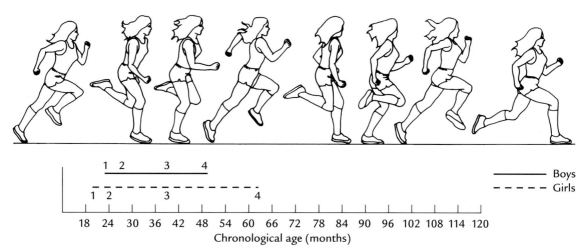

Age at which 60 percent of the boys and girls were able to perform at a specific developmental level for the fundamental motor skill of running.

Developmental Performance Trends for Running

Few investigators have studied the kinetics and kinematics of a developmental running pattern in young children. In fact, Fortney (1983) uncovered only six studies. There is, however, no lack of product performance data related to children's running speed. Unfortunately, these data are often difficult to compare because of the different distances the children were required to run and the different types of starts that were used (stationary or running), as illustrated in Table 13-4. (*Note:* Performance scores have been recalculated to reflect running velocity in order to aid comparisons.) A comparison of the data suggests overall developmental performance trends. Generally, the data indicate a fairly consistent year-to-year improvement in running speed for both boys and girls, with boys running faster than girls at all ages.

Table 13-4   Developmental Performance Trends for Running

Age (years)	Run Distance	Average Run Times (seconds)	Average Velocity (ft/sec)	Study
2.5	30 yd°	11.50 male 12.20 female	7.83 7.38	Fountain et al., 1981
3	40 ft†	3.54 male 3.96 female	11.30 10.10	Morris et al., 1982
3	30 yd°	10.20 male 10.90 female	8.82 8.26	Fountain et al., 1981
3.5	30 yd°	9.70 male 9.70 female	9.28 9.28	Fountain et al., 1981
4	40 ft†	3.26 male 3.35 female	12.27 11.94	Morris et al., 1982
4	30 yd°	8.60 male 8.80 female	10.47 10.23	Fountain et al., 1981
4.5	30 yd°	8.30 male 8.80 female	10.84 10.23	Fountain et al., 1981
5	40 ft†	2.74 male 2.88 female	14.60 13.89	Morris et al., 1982
5	30 yd	6.29 male 6.82 female	14.31 13.20	Milne, Seefeldt, & Reuschlein, 1976
5	30 yd‡	6.77 male 6.81 female	13.29 13.22	Branta, Haubenstricker, & Seefeldt, 1984
5	30 yd°	7.20 male 7.40 female	12.50 12.16	Fountain et al., 1981
6	40 ft†	2.62 male 2.76 female	15.27 14.49	Morris et al., 1982
6	10 yd	3.34	8.98	DiNucci, 1976
6	30 yd	5.54 male 5.85 female	16.25 15.38	Milne, Seefeldt, & Reuschlein, 1976
6	30 yd‡	6.02 male 6.20 female	14.95 14.51	Branta, Haubenstricker, & Seefeldt, 1984
7	10 yd	3.15	9.52	DiNucci, 1976
7	30 yd‡	5.54 male 5.61 female	16.25 16.04	Branta, Haubenstricker, & Seefeldt, 1984
7	50 yd	10.31	14.55	DiNucci, 1976
8	10 yd	2.98	10.08	DiNucci, 1976
8	30 yd‡	5.23 male 5.31 female	17.21 16.95	Branta, Haubenstricker, & Seefeldt, 1984
8	50 yd	9.66	15.53	DiNucci, 1976

(continued)

Table 13-4   *(continued)*

Age (years)	Run Distance	Average Run Times (seconds)	Average Velocity (ft/sec)	Study
9	30 yd‡	4.98 male	18.07	Branta, Haubenstricker, & Seefeldt, 1984
		5.08 female	17.72	
9–10	50 yd	8.20 male	18.29	AAHPER, 1976
		8.60 female	17.44	
11	50 yd	8.00 male	18.75	AAHPER, 1976
		8.30 female	18.07	
12	50 yd	7.80 male	19.23	AAHPER, 1976
		8.10 female	18.52	
13	50 yd	7.50 male	20.00	AAHPER, 1976
		8.00 female	18.75	
14	50 yd	7.20 male	20.83	AAHPER, 1976
		7.80 female	19.23	
15	50 yd	6.90 male	21.74	AAHPER, 1976
		7.80 female	19.23	
16	50 yd	6.70 male	22.39	AAHPER, 1976
		7.90 female	18.99	
17+	50 yd	6.60 male	22.73	AAHPER, 1976
		7.90 female	18.99	

*Subjects were allowed a 3-foot running start.

†Subjects were allowed a 12-foot running start.

‡Subjects were allowed a 15-foot running start.

On average, girls' running speed peaks at about 14 to 15 years of age, whereas boys' running speed continues to improve beyond 17 years. The running speed for boys between 9 and 17 years of age improves by 20 percent. Girls improve only about 8 percent during this time (based on average AAHPER data, 1976). Branta and colleagues (1984) report an approximate 30 percent increase in running speed in both boys and girls from 5 to 10 years of age. This finding is based on a 30-yard dash in which a 5-yard running start is allowed.

A unique approach for studying running speed in young children was conducted by Fountain and colleagues (1981). More specifically, these research-ers were in part interested in studying the relationship between developmental stage and running velocity. Data were collected for 3 years on a mixed longitudinal sample. Running speed was measured during a 30-yard dash in which a running start was employed (approximately 3 feet). Developmental running stage was assessed by the total body approach as suggested by Seefeldt and colleagues (1972). Total run times for 153 boys and 106 girls were correlated with developmental stage and yielded correlation coefficients of −.44 and −.54 for the boys and girls, respectively. Developmental stage thus accounted for 19 percent of the variance in total run times for the boys and about 29 percent of the variance in total run times for the girls. In general, the more immature the running pattern, the longer it took the children to complete the 30-yard dash.

When run times were converted to yards/second, it was found that each sex improved by 1.6 yards/second over the age range studied. By 5 years of age, the boys were running 4.2 yards/second while the girls were running 4.0 yards/second.

JUMPING

Jumping is a fundamental movement that occurs when the body is projected into the air by force generated in one or both legs and the body lands on one or both feet. Jumping can be accomplished in several ways. For example, *hopping* is a form of jumping in which the propelling force is generated in one leg and the landing is accomplished on the same leg. But if the landing occurs on the nonpropelling leg, the movement is called a *leap.*

Researchers have speculated that the downward leap while descending a step is the child's first experience with jumping (Hellebrandt et al., 1961). Keogh and Sugden (1985), however, suggested that a more sensible way to consider the beginning of jumping development is to examine jumping patterns that involve a two-footed takeoff. The two-footed jumping patterns that have received the most attention are the vertical jump and the horizontal or standing long jump. In the *vertical jump,* the body is thrust upward; in the *horizontal jump,* the body is propelled both upward and outward. Regardless of the direction the body is propelled, both two-footed jumping patterns have similar phases, including a preparatory, a takeoff, a flight, and a landing phase.

Preparatory Phase

A great deal of preparatory movement is associated with experienced two-footed jumping. Preparatory

Figure 13-4   The advanced jumper fully extends the body during the takeoff phase.

movements are necessary to ready the body to spring into action; such movements include a crouch (flexion of the hips, knees, and ankles) and a backward swing of the arms. Many of these preparatory movements are absent in the inexperienced jumper. For instance, very little if any crouch precedes the jump, and a corresponding arm swing is also absent or minimized (Payne, 1985).

Takeoff and Flight Phases

Once the preparatory movements have been accomplished, a rapid and vigorous extension of the hips, knees, and ankles along with a vigorous swing of the arms in the direction of desired travel provide the impetus for the body to become airborne. See Figure 13-4. Because the inexperienced jumper does not properly crouch, there is very little extension of the body segments. Furthermore, the inexperienced jumper is not able to integrate the arms with the lower extremities to increase the momentum of the jump. Consequently, only a short distance or height is traversed.

Angle of takeoff is also an important factor to consider. The most effective angle of takeoff in horizontal jumping is 45 degrees.

Landing Phase

During the airborne phase of the horizontal jump, the extended legs are brought forward and ahead of the body's center of gravity as the landing is anticipated. When studying college women, Felton (1960, as cited in Atwater, 1973) reported that the most successful horizontal jumpers landed with their heels 5.56 inches ahead of their center of gravity; the heels of the poorest jumpers were only 3.60 inches ahead of their center of gravity. Because inexperienced jumpers are unable to gain adequate height and forward momentum, they do not have enough time to get their feet ahead of their center of gravity.

Another obvious characteristic of the inexperienced jumper is the inability to flex the hips, knees, and ankles upon landing. This stiff-legged landing makes the landing look rigid and jolts the jumper. In contrast, the experienced jumper slowly flexes the hips, knees, and ankles to absorb the force of the jump gradually (Figure 13-5).

Developmental Sequences for the Standing Long Jump

Table 13-5 presents a hypothesized developmental sequence (component approach) for a fundamental motor skill—the standing long jump. An alternative developmental sequence (total body approach) is illustrated in Figure 13-6. This latter developmental sequence has withstood preliminary validation on a mixed longitudinal sample (Haubenstricker, Seefeldt, & Branta, 1983). This preliminary validation study included 430 preschool children (30–65 months) and 1986 primary-grade children (72–107 months) as subjects. As suggested the horizontal bar graph at the end of Figure 13-6, a developmental stage 1 pattern was found to be most prominent in children under 42 months of age (3 1/2 years). In contrast, a stage 2 jumping pattern was found to be most prevalent between 48 and 84 months of age (4 and 7 years), whereas a stage 3 jumping pattern was dominant by 96 months of age (8 years). Only about 10 percent of the older sub-

Figure 13-5 The advanced jumper absorbs the landing forces by flexing the knees, hips, and ankles at impact.

jects (102–107 months) were found to exhibit the most mature stage 4 pattern of jumping.

Developmental Sequences for the Vertical Jump

Unlike horizontal jumping, little scientific inquiry into developmental sequences for vertical jumping

---

Table 13-5   Developmental Sequences for the Standing Long Jump: Component Approach

Takeoff Phase

Leg Action Component

Step 1: Fall and catch. The weight is shifted forward. The knee and ankle are held in flexion or extend slightly as gravity rotates the body over the balls of the feet. Takeoff occurs when the toes are pulled from the surface in preparation for the landing "catch."

Step 2: Two-footed takeoff, partial extension. Both feet leave the ground symmetrically, but the hips, knees, and/or ankles do not reach full extension by takeoff.

Step 3: Two-footed takeoff; full extension. Both feet leave the ground symmetrically, with hips, knees, and ankles fully extended by takeoff.

Trunk Action Component

Step 1: Slight lean; head back. The trunk leans forward less than 30° from the vertical. The neck is hyperextended.

Step 2: Slight lean; head aligned. The trunk leans forward less than 30°, with the neck flexed or aligned with the trunk at takeoff.

Step 3: Forward lean; chin tucked. The trunk is inclined forward 30° or more (with the vertical) at takeoff, with the neck flexed.

Step 4: Forward lean; head aligned. The trunk is inclined forward 30° or more. The neck is aligned with the trunk or slightly extended.

Arm Action Component

Step 1: Arms inactive. The arms are held at the side with the elbows flexed. Arm movement, if any, is inconsistent and random.

Step 2: Winging arms. The arms extend backward in a winging posture at takeoff.

Step 3: Arms abducted. The arms are abducted about 90°, with the elbows often flexed, in a high or middle guard position.

Step 4: Arms forward; partial stretch. The arms flex forward and upward with minimal abduction, reaching incomplete extension overhead by takeoff.

Step 5: Arms forward; full stretch. The arms flex forward, reaching full extension overhead by takeoff.

(continued)

---

has been undertaken. This lack of interest is most likely due to several factors. For instance, the horizontal jump is easier to measure and is included as part of several popular tests of physical fitness. Nevertheless, following Myers and colleagues (1977), Gallahue and Ozmun (2002) described a developmental sequence for vertical jumping. As noted in Table 13-6, the mature form of vertical jumping greatly resembles that of horizontal jumping. More specifically, the mature vertical jumper prepares by taking a preparatory crouch followed by a vigorous swing of the arms upward in the

Table 13-5 *(continued)*

Flight and Landing Phase

Leg Action Component

Step 1: Minimal tuck. The thigh is carried in flight more than 45° below the horizontal. The legs may assume either symmetrical or asymmetrical configurations during flight, resulting on one- or two-footed landings.

Step 2: Partial tuck. During flight, the hips and knees flex synchronously. The thigh approaches a 20–35° angle below the horizontal. The knees then extend for a two-footed landing.

Step 3: Full tuck. During flight, flexion of both knees precedes hip flexion. The hips then flex, bringing the thighs to the horizontal. The knees then extend, reaching forward to a two-footed landing.

Trunk Action Component

Step 1: Slight lean. During flight, the trunk maintains its forward inclination of less than 30°, then flexes for landing.

Step 2: Corrected lean. The trunk corrects its forward lean of 30° or more by hyperextending. It then flexes forward for landing.

Step 3: Maintained lean. The trunk maintains the forward lean of 30° or more from takeoff to midflight, then flexes forward for landing.

Arm Action Component

Step 1: Arms winging. In two-footed takeoff jumps, the shoulders may retract while the arms extend backward (winging) during flight. They move forward (parachuting) during landing.

Step 2: Arms abducted; lateral rotation. During flight, the arms hold a high guard position and continue lateral rotation. They parachute for landing.

Step 3: Arms abducted; medial rotation. During flight, the arms assume high or middle guard positions but medially rotate early in the flight. They parachute for landing.

Step 4: Arms overhead. During flight, the arms are held overhead. In middle flight, the arms lower (extend) from their overhead flexed position, reaching forward at landing.

Note: These developmental steps have not been validated. They have been modified by Halverson from the work of Van Sant (1983).

SOURCE: Roberton, M. A., and Halverson, L. E. (1984). *Developing children—their changing movement.* Lea & Febiger. Used with permission from the current copyright holder, M. A. Roberton.

desired direction of the jump. In addition, he or she rapidly extends the hips, knees, and ankles as the body moves upward. Upon landing, the ankles, knees, and hips flex to absorb the impact forces. In general, mature process characteristics appear in the vertical jump before the horizontal jump. In fact, adultlike characteristics of the vertical jump have appeared in children as young as age 2 (Poe, 1976), with most exhibiting mature characteristics by age 5 (Williams, 1983). In comparison, mature horizontal jumping process characteristics (stage 3 and stage 4) do not predominate

Figure 13-6   Developmental sequences for the standing long jump: total body approach

SOURCES: Haubenstricker, Seefeldt, and Branta (1983); Seefeldt and Haubenstricker (1982); Seefeldt, Reuschlein, and Vogel (1972). All material used with permission of Dr. John Haubenstricker.

Stage 1   Vertical component of force may be greater than horizontal; resulting jump is then upward rather than forward. Arms move backward, acting as brakes to stop the momentum of the trunk as the legs extend in front of the center of mass.

Stage 2   The arms move in an anterior-posterior direction during the preparatory phase but move sideward (winging action) during the in-flight phase. The knees and hips flex and extend more fully than in stage 1. The angle of takeoff is still markedly above 45°. The landing is made with the center of gravity above the base of support, with the thighs perpendicular to the surface rather than parallel as in the reaching position of stage 4.

Stage 3   The arms swing backward and then forward during the preparatory phase. The knees and hips flex fully prior to takeoff. Upon takeoff, the arms extend and move forward but do not exceed the height of the head. The knee extension may be complete, but the takeoff angle is still greater than 45°. Upon landing, the thigh is still less than parallel to the surface and the center of gravity is near the base of support when viewed from the frontal plane.

(continued)

Figure 13-6   *(continued)*

Stage 4   The arms extend vigorously forward and upward upon takeoff, reaching full
extension above the head at "liftoff." The hips and knees are extended fully, with
the takeoff angle at 45° or less. In preparation for landing, the arms are brought
downward and the legs are thrust forward until the thigh is parallel to the surface.
The center of gravity is far behind the base of support upon foot contact, but at
the moment of contact the knees are flexed and the arms are thrust forward in
order to maintain the momentum to carry the center of gravity beyond the feet.

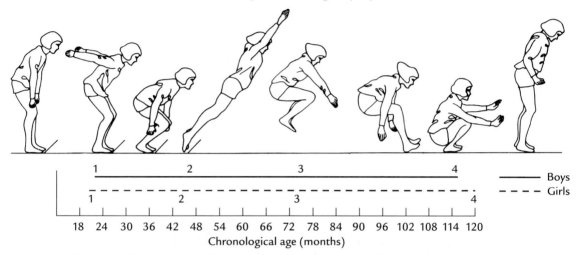

Age at which 60 percent of the boys and girls were able to perform at a specific
developmental level for the fundamental motor skills of the standing long jump.

until 8 to 9 years of age (Haubenstricker et al.,
1983).

Developmental Performance Trends for Vertical Jumping

While many studies have examined vertical jumping performance trends in adult populations (Harman et al., 1990; Hedrick & Anderson, 1996; Kraemer et al., 1996), few investigators have studied the
corresponding developmental trends in children
(Isaacs & Pohlman, 2000; Isaacs, Pohlman, & Hall,
2003; Jensen, Phillips, & Clark, 1994; Poe, 1976;
Texas Governor's Commission, 1973). This is surprising, given the role of the vertical jump in such
popular sports as basketball and volleyball. Tables
13-7 and 13-8 summarize recent vertical jump performance data collected by Isaacs and colleagues
(Isaacs & Pohlman, 2000; Isaacs et al., 2003). In
these studies, 248 boys and 232 girls aged 7–11
(grades 1–5), performed four vertical jumps with
a countermovement and four without one. In the
former condition, the child crouched and then immediately jumped vertically, while in the latter the
child had to hold the crouched position for 3 seconds before executing the vertical jump. Contrary
to findings in adult populations (Harman et al.,
1990; Hedrick & Anderson, 1996), children performed more poorly with countermovement than
with none. Apparently, these young children had

Table 13-6 Developmental Sequence for Vertical Jumping

Initial Stage

Inconsistent preparatory crouch

Difficulty in taking off with both feet

Poor body extension on takeoff

Little or no head lift

Arms not coordinated with the trunk and leg action

Little height achieved

Elementary Stage

Knee flexion exceeding 90° angle on preparatory crouch

Exaggerated forward lean during crouch

Two-footed takeoff

Entire body not fully extended during flight phase

Arms attempting to aid in flight and balance

Noticeable horizontal displacement on landing

Mature Stage

Preparatory crouch with knee flexion from 60° to 90°

Forceful extension at hips, knees, and ankles

Simultaneous coordinated upward arm lift

Upward head tilt with eyes focused on target

Full body extension

Elevation of reaching arm by shoulder girdle tilt combined with downward thrust of nonreaching arm at peak of flight

Controlled landing very close to point of takeoff

SOURCE: Gallahue and Ozmun (2002, p. 208).

not yet acquired the neural coordination needed to take advantage of the muscles' plyometric qualities. While boys performed better than girls at all ages studied, a significant difference between the genders did not appear until age 11. An examination of Table 13-7 reveals a large performance spread between the minimum and maximum vertical jump performances for each gender and age. Finally, when a target is placed overhead, vertical jump performance in young children improves (Poe, 1976).

A Variation of Jumping: Hopping

As we have seen, hopping is a form of jumping in which one foot is used to project the body into space and the subsequent landing is on the same propelling foot. This fundamental movement is considered more difficult than the two-footed jump because it requires additional strength and better balance.

Using a prelongitudinal screening technique, Halverson and Williams (1985) have provided evidence for the existence of developmental steps within both the leg and the arm components of hopping. The purpose of a prelongitudinal screening is to determine initially if the hypothesized components contain all observable behaviors and whether the steps within each component are arranged correctly (Roberton, Williams, & Langendorfer, 1980). After making some changes, the researchers were able to describe four steps within the leg component of the hop and five steps within the arm component. Table 13-9 describes each hypothesized step. There is greater extension of the propelling leg and greater involvement of the nonsupport or swing leg to assist projection. The arms are initially inactive but soon become involved by assisting the hop and by working in opposition to the legs.

Halverson and Williams concluded that 5-year-old children were at predominantly low and intermediate developmental levels and that girls were more developmentally advanced than boys. In addition, most children used less advanced developmental patterns when hopping on their nonpreferred foot.

Using the total body approach (see Figure 13-7), Haubenstricker and colleagues (1989) have produced data that agree with these earlier findings. Namely, hopping is performed better on the preferred foot as opposed to the nonpreferred foot, girls are more developmentally advanced than boys, and most 5-year-old boys and girls have not developed a mature hopping pattern. More specifically, these researchers found only 3 percent of the 5 year-old boys and 6 percent of the 5-year-old girls to exhibit a stage 4 hopping pattern (most mature stage). Furthermore, over 60 percent of these 5-year-olds were found to exhibit a stage 2 developmental

Table 13-7   Vertical Jump Performance Variables for Children Between 7 and 11 Years of Age (N = 480)*

Male	N	Mean	SD	Minimum	Maximum
7	39	10.96	1.66	8.5	14.5
8	59	11.03	1.59	8.0	15.5
9	57	11.18	1.86	6.5	15.5
10	53	11.08	2.62	4.0	18.0
11	40	11.93	2.04	7.0	16.0
Female	**N**	**Mean**	**SD**	**Minimum**	**Maximum**
7	33	10.80	1.69	7.0	16.0
8	56	10.97	1.51	8.0	14.5
9	61	10.98	2.11	6.5	16.5
10	42	10.43	2.30	6.5	16.5
11	40	10.33	2.69	5.0	16.5

°Measurement in inches.

SOURCES: Isaacs and Pohlman (2000); Isaacs, Pohlman, and Hall (2003).

Table 13-8   Selected Normative Data on Vertical Jump Performance for Children Between 7 and 11 Years of Age (N = 480)*

	Boys					Girls				
	7	8	9	10	11	7	8	9	10	11
100	14.5	14.5	15.5	18.0	16.0†	16.0	14.5	16.5	16.5	16.5
80	12.5	12.5	12.5	13.0	13.5	16.5	12.5	13.0	12.0	12.5
60	11.5	11.5	12.0	11.5	12.5	11.0	11.5	11.5	11.0	11.0
40	10.5	10.5	11.5	10.5	12.0	10.5	11.0	10.5	9.5	9.0
20	9.5	9.5	9.5	9.0	10.5	9.5	9.0	9.0	8.5	8.5

°Measurements are rounded to the nearest one-half inch.

†See "Adolescent Awkwardness," pp. 164–165.

SOURCES: Isaacs and Pohlman (2000); Isaacs, Pohlman, and Hall (2003).

level of hopping. Moreover, 10 percent of the boys and 6 percent of the girls still could not hop by 4 years of age.

In general, girls were approximately 6 months more advanced than boys. For example, the stage 1 pattern of hopping was most prevalent in 3-year-old girls, but it was not until 3½ years of age that it became the most dominant pattern in boys. Likewise, girls predominantly exhibited stage 2 characteristics by age 4, whereas boys were generally delayed until 4½ years of age (Haubenstricker et al., 1989).

Table 13-9   Developmental Steps Within Two Components of Hopping: Component Approach

Leg Action

Step 1: Momentary flight. The support knee and hip quickly flex, pulling (instead of projecting) the foot from the floor. The flight is momentary. Only one or two hops can be achieved. The swing leg is lifted high and held in an inactive position to the side or in front of the body.

Step 2: Fall and catch; swing leg inactive. Forward lean allows minimal knee and ankle extension to help the body "fall" forward of the support foot and then quickly catch itself again. The swing leg is inactive. Repeated hops are achieved.

Step 3: Projected takeoff; swing leg assists. Perceptible pretakeoff extension occurs in the support leg, hip, knee, and ankle. There is little delay in changing from knee and ankle flexion on landing to takeoff extension. The swing leg now pumps up and down to assist in projection, but range is insufficient to carry it behind the support leg.

Step 4: Projection delay; swing leg leads. The child's weight on landing is smoothly transferred along the foot to the ball before the knee and ankle extend to takeoff. The range of the pumping action in the swing leg increases so that it passes behind the support leg when viewed from the side.

Revised Developmental Sequence for Arm Action in Hopping

Step 1: Bilateral inactive. The arms are held bilaterally, usually high and out to the side, although other positions behind or in front of the body may occur. Any arm action is usually slight and not consistent.

Step 2: Bilateral reactive. Arms swing upward briefly and then are medially rotated at the shoulder in a winging movement prior to takeoff. This movement appears to occur in reaction to loss of balance.

Step 3: Bilateral assist. The arms pump up and down together, usually in front of the line of the trunk. Any downward and backward motion of the arms occurs after takeoff. The arms may move parallel to each other or be held at different levels as they move up and down.

Step 4: Semi-opposition. The arm on the side opposite the swing leg swings forward with that leg and back as the leg moves down. The position of the other arm is variable, often staying in front of the body or to the side.

Step 5: Opposing assist. The arm opposite the swing leg moves forward and upward in synchrony with the forward and upward movement of that leg. The other arm moves in the direction opposite the action of the swing leg. The range of movement in the arm action may be minimal unless the task requires speed or distance.

SOURCE: Halverson, L., and Williams, K. (1985). Reprinted with permission from *Research Quarterly for Exercise and Sport, 56*, 37–44. Copyright © 1985 by the American Alliance for Health, Physical Education, Recreation, and Dance, 1900 Association Drive, Reston, VA 20191.

Figure 13-7   Developmental sequences for hopping: total body approach

SOURCES: Haubenstricker, Henn, and Seefeldt (1975); Haubenstricker et al. (1989); Seefeldt and Haubenstricker (1974, 1982). All material used with permission of Dr. John Haubenstricker.

Stage 1   The nonsupport knee is flexed at 90° or less, with the nonsupport thigh parallel to the surface. This position places the nonsupport foot in front of the body so that it may be used for support if balance is lost. The body is held in an upright position with the arms flexed at the elbows. The hands are held near shoulder height and slightly to the side in a stabilizing position. Force production is generally limited, so that little height or distance is achieved in a single hop.

Stage 2   The nonsupport knee is fully flexed, so that the foot is near the buttocks. The thigh of the nonsupport leg is nearly parallel to the surface. The trunk is flexed at the hip, resulting in a slight forward lean. The performer gains considerable height by flexing and extending the joints of the supporting leg and by extending at the hip joint. In addition, the thigh of the nonsupport leg aids in force production by flexing at the hip joint. In the landing, the force is absorbed by flexion at the hips and the supporting knee. The arms participate vigorously in force production as they move up and down in a bilateral manner. Because of the vigorous action and precarious balance of performers at this stage, the number of hops generally ranges from two to four.

(continued)

Figure 13-7   *(continued)*

Stage 3   The thigh of the nonsupport leg is in a vertical position with knee flexed at 90° or less. Performers exhibit greater body lean forward than in stage 1 or 2, with the result that the hips are farther in front of the support leg upon takeoff. This forward lean of the trunk results in greater distance in relation to the height of the hop.

The knee of the nonsupport leg remains near the vertical (frontal) plane, but knee flexion may vary as the body is projected and received by the supporting leg. The arms are used in force production, moving bilaterally upward during the force-production phase.

Stage 4   The knee of the nonsupport leg is flexed at 90° or less, but the entire leg swings back and forth like a pendulum as it aids in force production. The arms are carried close to the sides of the body, with elbow flexion at 90°. As the nonsupport leg increases its force production, that of the arms seems to diminish.

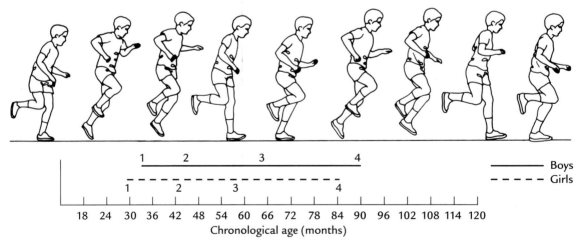

Age at which 60 percent of the boys and girls were able to perform at a specific developmental level for the fundamental motor skill of hopping.

COMBINING FUNDAMENTAL MOVEMENTS: THE GALLOP, SLIDE, AND SKIP

Fundamental motor patterns can be combined to elicit new movement patterns. The three most often described patterns are the *gallop,* the *slide,* and the *skip.* As would be expected, these more complex motor patterns do not emerge until sometime after the development of their single motor pattern counterparts.

Of these three motor patterns, the gallop is the first to be exhibited. The two basic fundamental motor patterns that make up the gallop are (1) a forward step, followed by (2) a leap onto the trailing foot. By definition, this pattern must be performed in a front-facing direction whereby the same leg always leads. Frequently, the gallop begins to emerge shortly after running has been accomplished (about 2 years of age). At this time, however, the child will be capable of leading with only the preferred leg. Galloping with the nonpreferred leg as the lead is not accomplished until several years later. Figure 13-8 illustrates and describes the developmental sequences for galloping (total body approach).

The slide is essentially the same as a gallop, with one exception. Whereas the gallop is performed forward, the slide is performed sideways. The child's difficulty in performing this more complicated motor pattern arises because the child is required to face a different direction from the line of intended movement. More specifically, the child must face straight ahead while moving in a sideward direction. As a result, early attempts at sliding frequently start off correctly, but eventually, the child begins to point the toe of the leading leg toward the direction of movement, and shortly thereafter the trunk rotates as well. At this point, the initial slide is converted into the easier motor pattern of galloping. Sliding is an extremely important motor skill to acquire, because it is used in many types of sporting activities. For example, moving along the baseline in tennis, taking a lead off of a base, and guarding an opponent in basketball all require sliding.

Of the three motor patterns described, skipping is by far the most difficult. The skip consists of a forward step followed by a hop on the same foot

Figure 13-8   Developmental sequences for galloping: total body approach
Source: Sapp (1980). All material used with permission of Dr. John Haubenstricker.

Stage 1   The pattern resembles a rhythmically uneven run with the performer often reverting to the traditional running pattern. The tempo tends to be relatively fast and the rhythm inconsistent. The trail leg crosses in front of the lead leg during the airborne phase and remains in front at contact. The trail leg is flexed at ≤45° during the airborne phase. Both feet generally contact the floor in a heel-toe pattern, although either foot may strike the surface flat-footed.

(continued)

Figure 13-8   *(continued)*

Stage 2   The pattern is executed at a slow to moderate tempo with the rhythm often appearing choppy. The trail leg moves in front of, adjacent to, or behind the lead leg during the airborne phase but is always adjacent to or behind the lead leg at contact. The trail leg is extended during the airborne phase, often causing the trail foot to turn out and the lead leg to flex at ≤45°. The feet usually contact the floor in a heel-toe/heel-toe or toe/toe combination. The transfer of weight may appear stiff and exaggerated. The vertical component is often exaggerated as the trunk extends to lift the body up.

Stage 3   The pattern is smooth, rhythmical, and executed at a moderate tempo. The trail leg may cross in front of or move adjacent to the lead leg during the airborne phase but is placed adjacent to or behind the lead leg at contact. Both the lead and trail legs are flexed at ≤45° with the feet carried close to the surface during the airborne phase. The lead foot meets the surface with heel-toe pattern followed by a transfer of weight to the ball of the trail foot.

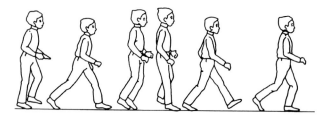

Table 13-10 Developmental Sequences for Skipping: Component Approach

Leg Action Component

Step 1: One-footed skip. One foot completes a step and hop before the weight is transferred to the other foot. The other foot just steps.

Step 2: Two-footed skip; flat-footed landing. Each foot completes a step and a hop before the weight is transferred to the other foot. Landing from the hop is on the total foot, or on the ball of the foot, with the heel touching down before the weight is transferred (flat-footed landing).

Step 3: Two-footed skip; ball of the foot landing. Landing from the hop is on the ball of the foot. The heel does not touch down before the weight is transferred to the other foot. Body lean increases over that found in step 2.

Arm Action Component

Step 1: Bilateral assist. The arms pump bilaterally up as the weight is shifted from the hopping to the stepping foot and down during the hop takeoff and flight.

Step 2: Semi-opposition. The arms first swing up bilaterally. During the hop on the right foot, the right arm moves down and back only slightly while the left arm continues to move backward until the step on the left foot. Then, both arms again move forward and upward in a new bilateral pumping action. Now, however, the left arm moves back only slightly while the right arm moves backward until the step on the right foot. Although the arm action has the beginnings of opposition, at some time in the arm cycle both hands are in front of the body.

Step 3: Opposition. The arm opposite the stepping leg swings upward and forward in synchrony with that leg and reverses direction when the stepping leg touches the floor. The arm on the same side as the stepping leg moves backward and down in opposition to the stepping leg. At no time are both hands in front of the body.

Note: These sequences, hypothesized by Halverson, have not been validated.
SOURCE: Roberton, M. A., and Halverson, L. E. (1984). *Developing children—their changing movement.* Lea & Febiger. Used with permission from the current copyright holder, M. A. Roberton.

(uneven rhythmical pattern). In addition, there is alternation of the leading leg. Unlike the gallop and slide, skipping requires both motor tasks (step and hop) to be accomplished on the same foot before the body's weight is transferred onto the other foot. Obviously, being required to perform dual tasks on a single leg is more difficult than performing a single task per leg as in galloping or sliding. The child may experience difficulty in maintaining balance when first attempting to skip. If this balance problem is severe, the child should skip in place while holding on to the back of a chair. With this arrangement, the child can maintain balance while still being afforded the opportunity to learn this more complex motor pattern. Table 13-10 describes both the leg action and the arm action component of the skip as presented from the component approach perspective. Figure 13-9 illustrates and describes the developmental sequences for skipping from the total body approach perspective. As indicated by the bar graph that accompanies Figure 13-9, girls are generally more advanced than boys. In fact, girls were found to exhibit the more mature developmental level (stage 3) about 6 to 7 months before young boys. On average, young boys and girls generally start to skip sometime between their sixth and seventh birthdays.

Figure 13-9   Developmental sequences for skipping: total body approach

Sources: Sapp (1980); Seefeldt and Haubenstricker (1974, 1982). All material used with permission of Dr. John Haubenstricker.

Stage 1   A deliberate step-hop pattern is employed, an occasional double hop is present, there is little effective use of the arms to provide momentum, an exaggerated step or leap is present during the transfer of weight from one supporting limb to the other, and the total action appears segmented.

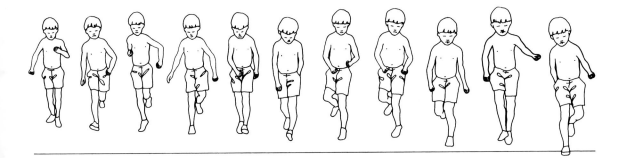

Stage 2   There is rhythmical transfer of weight during the step phase. Increased use of arms in providing forward and upward momentum is seen, as is an exaggeration of vertical component during the airborne phase — that is, while executing the hop.

(continued)

Figure 13-9   *(continued)*

Stage 3   There is rhythmical transfer of weight during all phases and reduced arm action during the transfer of weight phase. The foot of the supporting limb is carried near the surface during the hopping phase.

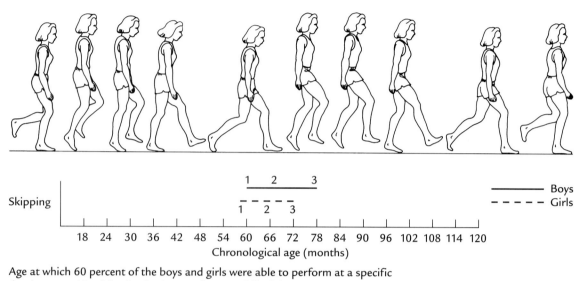

Age at which 60 percent of the boys and girls were able to perform at a specific developmental level for the fundamental motor skill of skipping.

SUMMARY

Walking is a fundamental movement in which there is an alternation of leading legs and continuous contact with the ground. To maintain balance during initial walking attempts, the child spreads the feet, points the toes outward, and carries the arms in a high guard position. Most children are capable of independent walking by 12 months, although the normal range is from 9 to 17 months.

Running is different from walking in that there is a momentary phase of suspension during which neither foot is in contact with the ground. Most children exhibit minimal running form between 18 and 24 months of age.

Jumping is propelling the body into the air from force generated in one or both legs and landing on one or both feet. Hopping, vertical jumping, horizontal or long jumping, and leaping are all variations of jumping. Each jumping variation consists of four phases: preparatory, takeoff, flight, and landing. Most children are capable of some form of jumping shortly after acquiring the ability to run.

After learning to walk, run, jump, and hop, children begin to perform several of these skills in combination. As a result, new movement skills emerge; namely, the gallop, slide, and skip. The gallop is a front-facing movement where a step is taken onto the forward leg and is followed by a leap onto the rear foot. In galloping, the same leg always leads. Sliding is similar to galloping except that the movement is performed sideways. This skill is more difficult than the gallop because, when sliding, the child must face in one direction (to the front) while moving in a different direction (sideways). Once again, the same leg always leads. The most difficult of the three combination skills is the skip. The skip is a step-hop combination where both movements are performed on the same leg before the body's weight is transferred onto the other leg. This dual movement results in an alternation of leading legs. The skipping pattern is generally exhibited in both boys and girls sometime between their sixth and seventh birthday. However, girls are about 6 or 7 months more advanced than boys.

Table 17-3 summarizes many of the fundamental locomotor skills of childhood when the total body approach is utilized (Haubenstricker, 1990).

KEY TERMS

double support phase
flight phase
gait
gallop
hopping
horizontal jump

jumping
leap
running
skip
slide
support phase

swing phase
upright bipedal locomotion
vertical jump
walking

QUESTIONS FOR REFLECTION

1. What three phases make up the walking gait cycle?

2. Can you distinguish between mature and immature foot mechanisms during walking?

3. Can you identify the normal range of time in which the onset of independent walking is exhibited?

4. What are the major phases of running? Identify the normal range of time in which running is exhibited.

5. What key observational characteristics distinguish mature and immature runners for each of the following bodily components: foot strike, heel-buttock relationship, thigh-ground relationship, arm coordination?

6. What is the difference between the two evaluation systems known as the component approach and the total body approach?

7. What is the overall developmental performance trend in running speed for both boys and girls? Identify age ranges associated with the attainment of peak running speed in both boys and girls.

8. What is the association between developmental stage and running speed in both boys and girls?

9. What are the phases associated with horizontal jumping? How do hopping and leaping differ from horizontal jumping?

10. What key observational characteristics distinguish mature and immature horizontal jumpers?

11. How is a countermovement useful during the execution of a vertical jump? In your answer, distinguish between mature and immature vertical jump performers.

12. Can you compare and contrast the gallop and the slide? Why is skipping more difficult than galloping and sliding?

13. Can you compare and contrast general skipping performance in young boys and girls? Identify the age range in which most young boys and girls begin to skip.

INTERNET RESOURCES

Gait and Locomotion: Biomechanics
   **www.per.ualberta.ca/biomechanics/
   sections.htm#loco**

Gait & Posture Journal   **www.elsevier.nl/inca/
publications/store/5/2/5/4/4/2**

ONLINE LEARNING CENTER (www.mhhe.com/payne6e)

Visit the *Human Motor Development* Online Learning Center for study aids and additional resources. You can use the study guide questions and key terms puzzles to review key terms and concepts for this chapter and to

prepare for exams. You can further extend your knowledge of motor development by checking out the Web links, articles, and activities found on the site.

REFERENCES

American Alliance for Health, Physical Education, and Recreation (AAHPER). (1976). *Youth fitness test manual.* Washington, DC: AAHPER.

Atwater, A. E. (1973). Cinematographic analysis of human movement. In J. H. Wilmore (Ed.), *Exercise and sport sciences reviews.* Vol. 1, pp. 217–257. New York: Academic Press.

Bernstein, N. (1967). *The coordination and regulation of movements.* New York: Pergamon Press.

Branta, C., Haubenstricker, J., & Seefeldt, V. (1984). Age changes in motor skills during childhood and adolescence. In R. L. Terjung (Ed.), *Exercise and sport sciences review.* New York: Macmillan.

Bril, D., & Breniere, Y. (1992). Postural requirements and progression velocity in young walkers. *Journal of Motor Behavior, 24,* 105–116.

Burnett, C. N., & Johnson, E. W. (1971). Development of gait in childhood: Part II. *Developmental Medicine and Child Neurology, 13,* 207–215.

DiNucci, J. M. (1976). Gross motor performance: A comprehensive analysis of age and sex differences among children ages six to nine years. In J. Broekhoff (Ed.), *Physical education, sports and the sciences.* Eugene, OR: Microform Publications.

Engel, G. M., & Staheli, L. T. (1974, Mar.–Apr.). The natural history of torsion and other factors influencing gait in childhood. *Clinical Orthopaedics and Related Research,* pp. 12–17.

Felton, E. A. (1960). A kinesiological comparison of good and poor performers in the standing broad jump. Unpublished master's thesis, University of Illinois, Urbana.

Fortney, V. L. (1983). The kinematics and kinetics of the running pattern of two-, four-, and six-year-old children. *Research Quarterly for Exercise and Sport, 54,* 126–135.

Fountain, C., Ulrich, B., Haubenstricker, J., & Seefeldt, V. (1981). Relationship of developmental stage and running velocity in children 2½ to 5 years of age. Paper presented at the Midwest District convention of the American Alliance for Health, Physical Education, Recreation, and Dance, Chicago.

Gallahue, D. L., & Ozmun, J. C. (2002). *Understanding motor development: Infants, children, adolescents, adults.* 5th ed. Boston: McGraw-Hill.

Halverson, L., & Williams, K. (1985). Developmental sequences for hopping over distance: A prelongitudinal screening. *Research Quarterly for Exercise and Sport, 56,* 37–44.

Harman, E. A., Rosenstein, M. T., Frykman, P. N., & Rosenstein, R. M. (1990). The effects of arms and countermovement on vertical jumping. *Medicine and Science in Sport and Exercise, 22,* 825–833.

Haubenstricker, J. (1990). Summary of fundamental motor skill stage characteristics: Motor performance study—MSU. Unpublished materials, Michigan State University, East Lansing.

Haubenstricker, J., Branta, C., Seefeldt, V., Brakora, L., & Kiger, J. (1989). Prelongitudinal screening of a developmental sequence for hopping. Paper presented at the annual convention of the American Alliance for Health, Physical Education, Recreation, and Dance, Boston.

Haubenstricker, J., Henn, J., & Seefeldt, V. (1975). Developmental sequence of hopping. Rev. ed. Unpublished materials, Michigan State University, East Lansing.

Haubenstricker, J., Seefeldt, V., & Branta, C. (1983). Preliminary validation of a developmental sequence for the standing long jump. Paper presented at the annual convention of the American Alliance for Health, Physical Education, Recreation, and Dance, Minneapolis, MN.

Hausdorff, J. M., Zemany, L., Peng, C. K., & Goldberger, A. L. (1999). Maturation of gait dynamics: Stride-to-stride variability and its temporal organization in children. *Journal of Applied Physiology, 83,* 1040–1047.

Hedrick, A., & Anderson, J. C. (1996). The vertical jump: A review of the literature and a team case study. *Strength and Conditioning, 18,* 7–12.

Hellebrandt, F. A., Rarick, G. L., Glassow, R., & Carns, M. L. (1961). Physiological analysis of basic motor skills: Growth and development of jumping. *American Journal of Physical Medicine, 40,* 14–25.

Hong, Y., & Brueggemann, G. (2000). Changes in gait patterns in 10-year-old boys with increasing loads when walking on a treadmill. *Gait and Posture, 11,* 254–259.

Isaacs, L. D., & Pohlman, R. L. (2000). Effectiveness of the stretch-shortening cycle in children's vertical jump performance. *Medicine and Science in Sports and Exercise, 32*(5 Supplement), S278.

Isaacs, L. D., Pohlman, R. L., & Hall, T. (2003). Vertical jump performance standards in children: An update. *Strategies, 16,* 33–35.

Jensen, J. L., Phillips, S. J., & Clark, J. E. (1994). For young jumpers, differences are in the movement's control, not its coordination. *Research Quarterly for Exercise and Sport, 65,* 258–268.

Keogh, J., & Sugden, D. (1985). *Movement skill development.* New York: Macmillan.

Kraemer, W. J., Bush, J. A., Bauer, J. A., Triplett-McBride, N. T., Paxton, N. J., Clemson, A., Koziris, L. E., Mangino, L. C., Fry, A. C., & Newton, R. U. (1996). Influence of compression garments on vertical jump performance in NCAA Division I volleyball players. *Journal of Strength and Conditioning Research, 10,* 180–183.

Milne, C., Seefeldt, V., & Reuschlein, P. (1976). Relationship between grade, sex, race, and motor performance in young children. *Research Quarterly, 47,* 726–730.

Morris, A. M., Williams, J. M., Atwater, A. E., & Wilmore, J. H. (1982). Age and sex differences in motor performance of 3 through 6 year old children. *Research Quarterly for Exercise and Sport, 53,* 214–221.

Murray, M. P., Drought, A. B., & Kory, R. C. (1964). Walking patterns of normal men. *Journal of Bone and Joint Surgery, 46-A,* 335–360.

Myers, C. B., et al. (1977). Vertical jumping movement patterns of early childhood. Unpublished paper, Indiana University.

Payne, V. G. (1985). *Teaching elementary physical education: Recognizing stages of the fundamental movement patterns* (videotape). Northbrook, IL: Hubbard Scientific Publications.

Phillips, S. J., & Clark, J. E. (1987). Infants' first unassisted walking steps: Relationship to speed. In B. Jonson (Ed.), *International series on biomechanics.* Champaign, IL: Human Kinetics.

Poe, A. (1976). Description of the movement characteristics of two-year-old children performing the jump and reach. *Research Quarterly, 47,* 260–268.

Roberton, M. A. (1983). Changing motor patterns during childhood. In J. Thomas (Ed.), *Motor development during childhood and adolescence.* Minneapolis, MN: Burgess.

Roberton, M. A., & Halverson, L. E. (1984). *Developing children — their changing movement.* Philadelphia: Lea & Febiger.

Roberton, M. A., Williams, K., & Langendorfer, S. (1980). Prelongitudinal screening of motor development sequences. *Research Quarterly for Exercise and Sport, 51,* 724–731.

Sapp, M. (1980). The development of galloping in young children: A preliminary study. Unpublished master's project, Michigan State University, East Lansing.

Scrutton, D. S. (1969). Footprint sequences of normal children under five years old. *Developmental Medicine and Child Neurology, 11,* 44–53.

Seefeldt, V., & Haubenstricker, J. (1974). Developmental sequence of hopping. Unpublished materials, Michigan State University, East Lansing.

———. (1982). Patterns, phases, or stages: An analytical model for the study of developmental movement. In J. A. S. Kelso & J. E. Clark (Eds.), *The development of movement control and coordination.* New York: Wiley.

Seefeldt, V., Reuschlein, P., & Vogel, P. (1972). Sequencing motor skills within the physical education curriculum. Paper presented at the American Association for Health, Physical Education, and Recreation, Houston, TX.

Statham, L., & Murray, M. P. (1971, Sept.). Early walking patterns of normal children. *Clinical Orthopaedics and Related Research,* pp. 8–24.

Sutherland, D. H. (1984). *Gait disorders in childhood and adolescence.* Baltimore: Williams & Wilkins.

Texas Governor's Commission on Physical Fitness. (1973). *Physical fitness–motor ability test.* Austin, TX: Author.

Thelen, E. (1986). Treadmill-elicited stepping in seven-month-old infants. *Child Development, 57,* 1498–1506.

Van Sant, A. (1983). Development of the standing long jump. Unpublished paper, Motor Development and Child Study Laboratory, Department of Physical Education and Dance, University of Wisconsin, Madison.

Wickstrom, R. L. (1983). *Fundamental motor patterns.* 3rd ed. Philadelphia: Lea & Febiger.

Williams, H. G. (1983). *Perceptual and motor development.* Englewood Cliffs, NJ: Prentice-Hall.

Fundamental Object-Control Skills of Childhood

As soon as the child can ambulate without assistance, the hands become free to explore the ever-changing environment more effectively. With time, experience, and practice, both eye-hand and eye-foot coordination dramatically improve. At this time, the child will begin to exhibit a category of skills commonly referred to as **object-control skills.** These skills include overarm throwing, both one- and two-handed catching, and striking things both with and without an implement. Implements that might be used with these object-control skills are racquets and bats. Sport actions that employ these skills without the use of an implement are those such as dribbling, place kicking, and punting.

OVERARM THROWING

Of the fundamental movements discussed in this chapter, *throwing* is perhaps the most complex. There are many different throwing patterns (underarm, sidearm, overarm), but this discussion is limited to one of the most common forms—the one-handed overarm throw. This throw can be conveniently divided into three phases: (1) The preparatory phase consists of all movements directed away from the intended line of projection. (2) The execution phase consists of all movements performed in the direction of the throw. (3) The follow-through phase consists of all movements performed following the release of the projectile (Langendorfer, 1980). Understanding these three phases will facilitate your understanding of the following information on throwing.

Developmental Stages of Throwing

Monica Wild (1938) is generally credited with setting the standards for the study of developmental throwing stages. Her classic study over 65 years ago in part attempted to uncover age and gender characteristics of throwing in 32 boys and girls 2 to 12 years old. As a result of this research, Wild described four developmental overarm throwing stages; Table 14-1 summarizes each stage.

Within these four developmental stages, two developmental trends are evident. First, movement progresses from an anterior-posterior plane to a horizontal plane; second, the base of support changes from a stationary to a shifting position (McClenaghan & Gallahue, 1978).

Researchers originally from the University of Wisconsin–Madison (now at Bowling Green State University) attempted to improve on Wild's pioneering work. Langendorfer (1980), for example, studied age-related changes in the arm action components during the preparatory phase of a forceful overarm throw. Using over 1000 trials recorded on 16mm film from both cross-sectional and longitudinal data, he proposed a motor development sequence consisting of four hypothesized steps.

Step 1 is best described as a lack of any preparatory backswing. Once the ball is grasped, it is moved directly forward. In step 2, the ball is brought up beside the head by upward humerus flexion and exaggerated elbow flexion. Step 3 is subdivided into one of three options. Option 1 is a circular overhead preparatory movement with the elbow extended. Option 2 is a preparatory movement characterized by a lateral swing backward. Option 3 is a simple vertical lift of the throwing arm. Step 4, the most advanced preparatory sequence, is a circular arm action in which the arm moves down and back. Figure 14-1 depicts each step.

To test this hypothesized sequence, Langendorfer (1980) analyzed 228 throwing trials of children followed from grade 1 to 6. When the data were analyzed by observing each child's progression through the hypothesized order, it was found that of the 65 subjects analyzed, only 1 omitted step 3 and only 4 transposed the hypothesized order. Even stronger support for this hypothesized sequence was obtained when the data were analyzed according to group rather than individual progress through the entire sequence. In short, with advancing age, an increasing percentage of the sample used more advanced preparatory movements. There were drastic differences, however, between the two sexes. By

Table 14-1   Wild's Four Developmental Stages of Throwing

Stage 1 (2- and 3-Year-Olds)	Stage 2 (3½- to 5-Year-Olds)	Stage 3 (5- and 6-Year-Olds)	Stage 4 (6½ Years and Older)
Throw is arm dominated. Preparatory arm movements involve bringing the arm sideways-upward or forward-upward. Thrower faces the direction of intended throw at all times. No rotation of trunk and hips is evident. Feet remain stationary during the entire throwing act.	Body moves in a horizontal plane instead of an anterior-posterior plane. Throwing arm moves in a high oblique plane or horizontal plane above the shoulder. Throwing is initiated predominantly by arm and elbow extension. Feet remain stationary, but rotary movement of the trunk is observable.	Forward step is unilateral to the throwing arm. Arm is prepared by swinging it obliquely upward over the shoulder with a large degree of elbow flexion. Arm follows through forward and downward and is accompanied by forward flexion of the trunk.	Forward step is taken with the contralateral leg. Trunk rotation is clearly evident. Arm is horizontally adducted in the forward swing.

SOURCE: Based on findings from Wild (1938).

the second grade, boys predominantly used step 4 characteristics, whereas girls had just begun to exhibit this most advanced movement pattern.

Roberton (1978) has studied other components related to the forceful overarm throw. She presented longitudinal evidence for developmental stages within the humerus, the forearm, and the trunk components of the forceful overarm throw. Of particular interest is this finding.

> Development within component parts may proceed at different rates in the same individual or at different rates in different individuals. For instance, one child might move ahead a stage in his trunk action while another child moved ahead a stage in his arm action. Thus two individuals going through the same stages within each component could look quite different at any one time. (1977, p. 55)

Table 14-2 presents Roberton's developmental sequences.

Seefeldt, Reuschlein, and Vogel (1972) have also hypothesized a developmental sequence for the fundamental motor skill of throwing. Their sequence, which appears in Figure 14-2, has with-

stood preliminary validation with the use of a mixed longitudinal sample (Haubenstricker, Branta, & Seefeldt, 1983). A close examination of the horizontal bar graph accompanying Figure 14-2 makes apparent the large gender difference in throwing development (Seefeldt & Haubenstricker, 1982). More specifically, note that the age at which 60 percent of the boys exhibited a stage 5 throwing pattern (most mature) was 63 months (slightly past 5 years of age). In contrast, 60 percent of the girls studied were not capable of exhibiting stage 5 characteristics until 102 months of age (about 8½ years). The data used to construct the horizontal bar graph were collected in the latter half of the 1970s. More recent data collected and analyzed by the same group of researchers have yielded somewhat different findings. More specifically, 58 percent of the boys aged 90 to 95 months were found to exhibit a stage 5 developmental level of throwing, but only 12.4 percent of the girls in this same age group exhibited stage 5 throwing characteristics. In fact, only 24.4 percent of the girls in the oldest age group studied (102–107 months) exhibited the most mature pattern of throwing, whereas 77.3 percent of the boys

Figure 14-1   The four steps of Langendorfer's hypothesized developmental sequence of the preparatory arm action of the overarm throw. Read all steps from left to right.

Step 1

Step 2

Step 3: Option 1

Step 3: Option 2

(continued)

Figure 14-1   *(continued)*

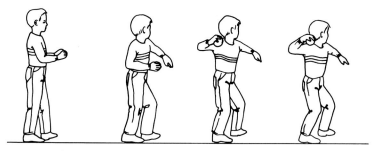

Step 3: Option 3

Step 4

in this oldest age group exhibited a stage 5 developmental level of performance (Haubenstricker, Branta, & Seefeldt, 1983).

Developmental Performance Trends for Overarm Throwing

Three techniques have been used to study changes in children's throwing performance. The most frequently used technique is the throw for distance, followed by the throw for accuracy and the measure of the velocity of the throw. Irrespective of the technique, both genders show annual improvement; in addition, boys and men perform more successfully than girls and women at all ages (Baker, 1993; Butterfield & Loovis, 1993; Halverson, Roberton, & Langendorfer, 1982; K. R. Nelson, Thomas, & Nelson, 1991; Rehling, 1996; Roberton et al., 1979; Van Slooten, 1973).

Most throwing studies that have used throwing distance or throwing accuracy as a criterion have collected the data cross-sectionally. One excep-

tion is the work of Roberton and colleagues, who have longitudinally examined changes in children's overarm ball-throwing velocities. For example, Roberton et al. (1979) studied changes in ball-throwing velocities of 54 children from kindergarten through second grade. The researchers found that the boys' throwing velocities on average increased 5.04 feet per second per year (ft/s/yr) (range: 5–8 ft/s/yr), whereas the girls' throwing velocities on average increased only 2.94 ft/s/yr (range: 2–3 ft/s/yr). In a follow-up study, 22 boys and 17 girls of the original 54 subjects were reassessed when they had reached seventh grade. One purpose of this second study was to determine how well the predicted longitudinal units of change would hold up over time. The results supported the earlier prediction regarding annual units of change for the boys' ball-throwing velocities, but the girls' unit of change had to be increased to 2–4.5 ft/s/yr.

Most recently, Runion, Roberton, and Langendorfer (2003) examined 50 13-year-old boys and girls for the purpose of comparing them with a

> **Table 14-2   Roberton's Developmental Sequence for the Trunk, Backswing, Humerus, Forearm, and Foot Action in the Overarm Throw for Force*: Component Approach**

Trunk Action

Step 1: No trunk action or forward-backward movements. Only the arm is active in force production. Sometimes, the forward thrust of the arm pulls the trunk into a passive left rotation (assuming a right-handed throw), but no twist-up precedes that action. If trunk action occurs, it accompanies the forward thrust of the arm by flexing forward at the hips. Preparatory extension sometimes precedes forward hip flexion.

Step 2: Upper trunk rotation or total trunk "block" rotation. The spine and pelvis simultaneously rotate away from the intended line of flight and begin forward rotation, acting as a unit or "block." Occasionally, only the upper spine twists away, then toward the direction of force. The pelvis then remains fixed, facing the line of flight, or joins the rotary movement after forward spinal rotation has begun.

Step 3: Differentiated rotation. The pelvis precedes the upper spine in initiating forward rotation. The child twists away from the intended line of ball flight and then begins forward rotation with the pelvis while the upper spine is still twisting away.

Preparatory Arm-Backswing Component

Step 1: No backswing. The ball in the hand moves directly forward to release from the arm's original position when the hand first grasped the ball.

Step 2: Elbow and humeral flexion. The ball moves away from the intended line of flight to a position behind or alongside the head by upward flexion of the humerus and concomitant elbow flexion.

Step 3: Circular, upward backswing. The ball moves away from the intended line of flight to a position behind the head via a circular, overhead movement with elbow extended, or an oblique swing back, or a vertical lift from the hip.

Step 4: Circular, downward backswing. The ball moves away from the intended line of flight to a position behind the head via a circular, down, and back motion, which carries the hand below the waist.

Humerus (Upper Arm) Action Component During Forward Swing

Step 1: Humerus oblique. The humerus moves forward to ball release in a plane that intersects the trunk obliquely above or below the horizontal line of the shoulders. Occasionally, during the backswing, the humerus is placed at a right angle to the trunk, with the elbow pointing toward the target. It maintains this fixed position during the throw.

Step 2: Humerus aligned but independent. The humerus moves forward to ball release in a plane horizontally aligned with the shoulder, forming a right angle between humerus and trunk. By the time the shoulders (upper spine) reach front facing, the humerus (elbow) has moved independently ahead of the outline of the body (as seen from the side) via horizontal adduction at the shoulder.

Step 3: Humerus lag. The humerus moves forward to ball release horizontally aligned, but at the moment the shoulders (upper spine) reach front facing, the humerus remains within the outline of the body (as seen from the side). No horizontal adduction of the humerus occurs before front facing.

(continued)

Table 14-2	(continued)

Forearm Action Component During Forward Swing

Step 1: No forearm lag. The forearm and ball move steadily forward to ball release throughout the throwing action.

Step 2: Forearm lag. The forearm and ball appear to "lag," i.e., to remain stationary behind the child or to move down or back in relation to the child. The lagging forearm reaches its farthest point back, deepest point down, or last stationary point before the shoulders (upper spine) reach front facing.

Step 3: Delayed forearm lag. The lagging forearm delays reaching its final point of lag until the moment of front facing.

Action of the Feet†

Step 1: No step. The child throws from the initial foot position.

Step 2: Homolateral step. The child steps with the foot on the same side as the throwing hand.

Step 3: Contralateral, short step. The child steps with the foot on the opposite side from the throwing hand.

Step 4: Contralateral, long step. The child steps with the opposite foot a distance of over half the child's standing height.

°Validation studies (Halverson, Roberton, & Langendorfer, 1982; Roberton, 1977, 1978; Roberton & DiRocco, 1981; Roberton & Langendorfer, 1980) support these sequences for the overarm throw, with the exception of the preparatory arm backswing sequence that Roberton and Langendorfer (1983) hypothesized from the work of Langendorfer (1980). Langendorfer (1982) felt that the humerus and forearm components are appropriate for overarm striking.

†This sequence was hypothesized by Roberton (1983) from the work of Leme and Shambes (1978); Seefeldt, Reuschlein, and Vogel (1972); and Wild (1938).

Source: Roberton, M. A., and Halverson, L. E. (1984). *Developing children—their changing movement.* Lea & Febiger. Used with permission from the current copyright holder, M. A. Roberton.

similar cohort of 13-year-olds from 1979. The researchers were particularly interested in determining if the overarm ball-throwing velocity of boys and girls had changed over 20 years. Findings indicated that the difference in ball-throwing velocity between the boys and girls had not narrowed during this period. This is surprising, given that in 1979 it was hypothesized that these and other male-female differences in skilled motor performance would narrow because of the passage of Title IX, by which girls and women would be afforded more opportunity to partake in skilled motor prac-

tice and play. Because of this finding, it appears that the forceful overarm throw data reported by Halverson, Roberton, and Langendorfer in 1982 is still valid today.

Factors That Influence Overarm Throwing Performance

In this section, we describe factors that have been found to influence throwing performance. Accounting for gender differences in overarm throwing will be addressed in the following section.

Figure 14-2   Developmental sequences for throwing: total body approach

SOURCES: Haubenstricker, Branta, and Seefeldt (1983); Seefeldt and Haubenstricker (1976, 1982); Seefeldt, Reuschlein, and Vogel (1972). All material used with permission of Dr. John Haubenstricker.

Stage 1   The throwing motion is essentially posterior-anterior in direction. The feet usually remain stationary during the throw. Infrequently, the performer may step or walk just prior to moving the ball into position for throwing. There is little or no trunk rotation in the most rudimentary pattern at this stage, but children at the point of transition between stages 1 and 2 may evoke slight trunk rotation in preparation for the throw and extensive hip and trunk rotation in the follow-through phase. In the typical stage 1, the force for projecting the ball comes from hip flexion, shoulder protraction, and elbow extension.

Stage 2   The distinctive feature of this stage is the rotation of the body about an imaginary vertical axis, with the hips, spine, and shoulders rotating as one unit. The performer may step forward with either an ipsilateral or contralateral pattern, but the arm is brought forward in a transverse plane. The motion may resemble a "sling" rather than a throw because of the extended arm position during the course of the throw.

(continued)

Figure 14-2 *(continued)*

Stage 3   The distinctive pattern in stage 3 is the ipsilateral arm-leg action. The ball is placed into a throwing position above the shoulder by a vertical and posterior motion of the arm at the time that the ipsilateral leg is moving forward. This stage involves little or no rotation of the spine and hips in preparation for the throw. The follow-through phase includes flexion at the hip joint and some trunk rotation toward the side opposite the throwing arm.

Stage 4   The movement is contralateral, with the leg opposite the throwing arm striding forward as the throwing arm is moved in a vertical and posterior direction during the wind-up phase. There is little or no rotation of the hips and spine during the wind-up phase; thus, the motion of the trunk and arm closely resembles the motions of stages 1 and 3. The stride forward with the contralateral leg provides for a wide base of support and greater stability during the force production phase of the throw.

(continued)

Figure 14-2   *(continued)*

Stage 5   The wind-up phase begins with the throwing hand moving in a downward arc and then backward as the opposite leg moves forward. The concurrent action rotates the hip and spine into position for forceful derotation. As the contralateral foot strikes the surface, the hips, spine, and shoulder begin derotation in sequence. The contralateral leg begins to extend at the knee, providing an equal and opposite reaction to the throwing arm. The arm opposite the throwing limb also moves forcefully toward the body to assist in the equal and opposite reaction.

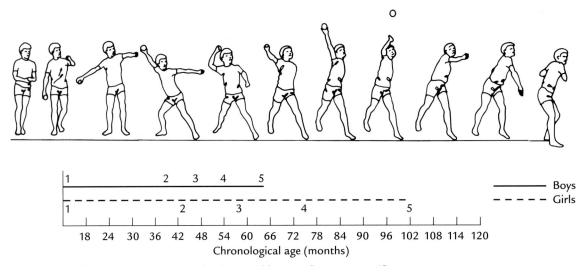

Age at which 60 percent of the boys and girls were able to perform at a specific developmental level for the fundamental motor skill of throwing.

INSTRUCTION   A basic question in recent years has been whether instruction can facilitate developmental changes or whether the year-to-year improvement in many fundamental skills is due more to age than to instruction. To investigate this question, Halverson and associates (1977) administered a movement program that included 120 minutes of guided practice in overarm throwing to 24 kindergarten students. A second group of 24 kindergarten students received the same movement program but no exposure to throwing instruction. A third group received neither program. Following the 8-week instructional program, no significant changes were found in the children's ball-throwing velocities. In a follow-up study, Halverson and Roberton (1979) used the same research design but measured developmental changes in movement components instead of developmental changes in ball-throwing velocity. An analysis of the data indicated that instruction significantly influenced throwing technique. Of the seven movement components examined, the experimental subjects used more advanced form in forearm lag, trunk action, stepping action, and range of spinal rotation. From these two studies, the researchers concluded that instructions significantly affect changes in throwing technique but not greater horizontal ball velocities. Halverson and Roberton recommend that ball-throwing velocity not be used as the sole index when investigating overarm throwing development in children.

Similarly, Luedke (1980) administered a specially designed throwing-instruction program to 144 second- and fourth-grade boys and girls. This special program focused on increasing the range of motion in each of the following throwing components: stride length, arm retraction, side facing, trunk rotation, preparatory leg recoil, arm patterns, and stride opposition. Following the 6-week experimental program, increased motion instruction significantly affected the throwing patterns of both the second- and fourth-grade boys and girls. This form of instruction was most effective in increasing the stride length component of the overarm throw.

Walkwitz (1989) found that a 6-week training program that emphasized throwing pattern was effective in improving girls' foot action and pelvic-spine rotation. However, Walkwitz noted no significant gains for arm action or distance the ball was thrown. This study, supported by the work of K. R. Nelson and colleagues (1991), suggests that the throwing pattern improvement of girls does not correspond to greater throwing distance. Thus, it appears that throwing pattern development may develop before the elements of the pattern can be appropriately and sequentially timed. Thomas, Michael, and Gallagher (1994) write,

> A major component of the mature throwing pattern is timing of segmental rotation and arm action. If coordination of body segment rotation is not appropriately linked with arm action to develop maximal velocity of the hand (and therefore the ball) at release, the pattern might look appropriate, but no gain in ball velocity will be achieved. (p. 70)

KNOWLEDGE Declarative knowledge appears to be an important factor affecting the throwing performance of young children (unlike catching, discussed later in the chapter). Using the object manipulation subtest of the Test of Gross Motor Development, Schincariol (1995) identified 25 talented and 25 awkward throwers. Using a verbally administered questionnaire, the researcher examined declarative knowledge of the one-handed overarm throw. Results indicated that the awkward throwers possessed significantly less declarative knowledge

than did the talented throwers. When analyzing each question, Schincariol found that significant differences existed for questions relating to ball size, stepping forward with the opposite foot, throwing low, and the ability to recognize correct form from a side view.

INSTRUCTIONAL CUES Because knowledge of throwing can influence throwing performance, the identification of critical cues regarding the act of throwing should facilitate both product- and process-oriented performance (Adams, 1994; Fronske, Blakemore, & Abendroth-Smith, 1997). For example, Fronske and colleagues (1997) examined the use of multiple action cues on the throwing performance of third- through fifth-grade students. Students had to throw 318 balls over five instructional days. The verbal cues emphasized were (1) Take a big step toward the target with the opposite foot of your throwing arm; (2) Take your arm straight down, then stretch it way back; and (3) Release the ball when you see your fingers. A control group received an equal number of throws but no verbal cues. The researchers concluded that the group receiving verbal cues showed significant improvement in both process (arm action, foot action) and product (distance) variables. The foot action component reflected the greatest improvement, which in turn resulted in an improved throwing distance of 78 inches for the group receiving cues and only 4.35 inches for the control group. This should be expected, since as much as 47 percent of ball velocity comes from the stepping-forward action and accompanying trunk rotation (Toyoshima et al., 1974).

On review of their findings, Fronske and colleagues (1997) recommended modifying the three critical clues to read (1) Take a *long* step toward the target with the opposite foot of your throwing arm; (2) Take your arm straight down, then stretch it way back *to make an "L" with the arm* (keep ball away from head); and (3) *Watch the target and* release the ball when you see your fingers. Miller (1995) has also stressed the importance of an instructional cue geared to the timing of finger opening. Based on these findings, the authors suggest that "teaching skill techniques using proper cues should be impressed upon preservice teachers as well as experienced practitioners" (Fronske et al., 1997, p. 93).

BALL SIZE As will be described later in this chapter, numerous studies have examined the influence of ball size on young children's catching ability, but only recently have researchers begun to examine its influence on throwing performance. Burton, Greer, and Wiese-Bjornstal (1992) examined the influence of ball size on the throwing performances of 40 children (aged 5–6, 7–8, 9–10) and 20 adults (aged 19–33). The subjects were required to throw six different-sized Styrofoam balls (1.9, 4.1, 5.8, 7.8, 9.6, and 11.6 inches in diameter) as hard as possible toward a wall that was 6.7 meters away. Styrofoam was chosen to minimize the effect that ball weight might have on throwing performance. Each throwing trial was evaluated using Roberton's component approach model, which was described earlier in this chapter. This study found throwing technique to be quite stable. More specifically, stable patterns of performance were exhibited 88.4 percent of the time within a selected ball diameter. When patterns of throwing performance became unstable, it marked the beginning of a transition to a new component level 70.6 percent of the time. In addition, the researchers hypothesized that whenever the ball diameter was scaled up, a transitional point would be reached where performers would resort to a less mature throwing pattern. This hypothesis was supported, but only for the backswing (53.3 percent) and forearm (61.3 percent) components. No significant differences were found among the other three components (humerus, 25 percent; trunk, 0 percent; and feet, 2.5 percent).

In a second study, Burton, Greer, and Wiese-Bjornstal (1993) sought to examine the influence of ball size on grasping patterns as well as throwing patterns among 104 subjects who were equally distributed among five age categories (5–6, 7–8, 9–10, 13–14, and 19–33 years). The performance task was essentially identical to that reported in the first study. The researchers witnessed a transition from one-handed grasping to two-handed grasping as the diameter of the ball increased, with adults switching at a significantly larger diameter compared

with younger subjects. However, when hand size was taken into consideration, younger subjects switched from a two-handed grasping pattern to a one-handed grasping pattern significantly later than did adults. Furthermore, there was no significant difference in the relative ball diameter at which boys and girls switched from a one- to a two-handed grasp. Regarding throwing pattern, two-handed throwing was exhibited less than 25 percent of the time and was mostly found among the 5- and 6-year-old girls. These two studies point out the importance of considering both ball size and the relationship between ball size and hand width when assessing throwing performance.

ANGLE OF BALL RELEASE One kinematic parameter influencing overarm throwing performance is the angle of ball release. When examining the overarm throwing of 15- to 30-month-old boys and girls, Marques-Bruna and Grimshaw (1997) noted that those children using arm-dominated action patterns tended to release the ball too early, resulting in an upward trajectory. Ball release in this group of arm-dominated throwers averaged 49 degrees. In comparison, the few who exhibited a more mature pattern of throwing (sequentially linked) exhibited a ball release angle of 15 degrees. With much older children (8 years of age), the angle of ball release was 25 and 28 degrees for girls and boys, respectively. According to Burton and colleagues (1993), the lack of a coordinated ball release may be a function of a poor grasp in very small children and may also be influenced by both ball weight and ball size. Thus, when working with small children, the instructor should manipulate both ball weight and size to identify the most appropriate combination for a more mature ball release.

DEVELOPMENTAL LEVEL One new line of inquiry into factors influencing throwing performance is the study of the relationship between developmental level of maturity and the product of performance. In other words, does improvement in movement process (technique) affect the outcome of performance? Using longitudinal data (6, 7, 8, and 13 years of age) collected over a 7-year period,

Roberton and Konczak (2001) found that changes in the five components making up the developmental sequence of overarm throwing (see Table 14-2) accounted for 65 to 85 percent of the variance in children's ball-throwing velocity. While the components that best predicted ball velocity changed over time, the humerus and forearm action components accounted for a significant portion of the change within the first three age groups studied. Among the oldest subjects (13 years), the greatest amount of variance was accounted for in the stride length (stepping) component. This finding confirms earlier findings that suggest that advanced throwers step a distance of 80 percent or more of their standing height (Escamilla et al., 1998). As addressed earlier in the chapter, teachers should attempt to develop and use instructional cues that may influence these developmental components.

Accounting for Gender Differences in Overarm Throwing

Anyone who works regularly with young children will tell you that there is a vast difference between the overarm throwing abilities of young boys and young girls. In fact, using meta-analysis to examine gender differences among 20 motor performance tasks, Thomas and French (1985) found the greatest gender differences among the skills examined, to be for throwing. This finding has led researchers to develop a series of studies designed to uncover why such gender differences exist. Researchers have speculated that such differences could be accounted for by heredity and sociocultural factors. This view was supported when J. D. Nelson and colleagues (1986) found that the throwing performance of 5-year-old girls was just 57 percent of that of similar-age boys. However, when the scores were adjusted for joint diameters, shoulder/hip ratio, forearm length, and arm and leg muscle mass, the throwing performance of girls improved to 69 percent of that found for boys.

In a 3-year follow-up study involving 26 of the original 100 children (K. R. Nelson et al., 1991), boys' throwing distance was positively associated with a heredity factor (arm muscle mass) and one sociocultural factor: the presence of a male adult in the home. In contrast, girls who weighed more and had more body fat along with greater joint diameters and more estimated arm and leg muscle mass threw farther than their smaller and weaker female counterparts. Nevertheless, the performance of these larger and stronger girls still lagged behind that of their male peers. Specifically, over this 3-year period boys had improved their throwing distance by 11 meters while girls improved by only 4.6 meters. Thus, by 9 years of age, girls threw only 49 percent as far as boys. Baker (1993) reported that differences in the ability to throw for distances can be accounted for by differences in grip strength, height, and upper-body strength as measured by a push-up test.

When using "throwing technique" as the variable of interest, K. R. Nelson and colleagues (1991) noted that, over this period, girls' trunk rotation and foot action did not improve as much as those of the boys. In fact, by third grade, most boys exhibited mature throwing form, while the girls still used block rotation and failed to take a long, vigorous step on the contralateral foot. The authors speculated that sociocultural factors such as lack of encouragement and therefore lack of practice time for the young girls could partially explain why the developmental level of their movement pattern did not significantly change over the 3 years.

In a study specifically designed to examine the effects of selected sociocultural factors on the overarm throwing performance of children in kindergarten through grade 3, the authors concluded that "the orderly development of fundamental movement patterns is essential and is predicated to a large extent upon appropriate nurture experiences provided within the sociocultural milieu of the child" (East & Hensley, 1985, p. 126). This conclusion is based on their finding that as much as 25 percent of the variance could be attributed to the stereotypical father figure who directed the daughter's play experiences away from sports and physically competitive situations. It was also noted that in every instance, amount of time spent watching television was negatively correlated with throwing performance. In other words, children who watched the most television tended to exhibit poorer throwing performance than did children who watched less television.

Carlton (1989) investigated how gender-mediated environmental factors affect differences in boys' and girls' throwing. Using Roberton's five-part component model, Carlton evaluated children aged 3–5. Parents were required to complete an environmental factors questionnaire designed to probe for differences in such factors as parents' engagement with children in gross motor play, provision for the use of gross motor toys, participation in recreational activities, attitudes regarding sport participation, participation in movement programs, and the presence of an older brother or sister. The author concluded that the best predictors of throwing development in girls were participation in sport and movement programs and the presence of an older brother in the household. In turn, the best predictors for throwing development in boys was fathers' sport involvement and father–son skill play. As such, social factors appear to be an important factor in accounting for differences in throwing development between boys and girls.

Thomas and Marzke (1992) pose an interesting question: Can gender differences in throwing be accounted for by factors involving human evolution? The authors build their argument on an examination of throwing behaviors believed to be exhibited in early humans and chimpanzees. It is believed that throwing was more prevalent among men and was probably used during defensive encounters and for hunting. The authors write, "Circumstantial evidence from antiquity suggests a potential connection" (p. 73).

CATCHING

Catching is the action of bringing an airborne object under control by using the hands and arms. In contrast to throwing research, there has been little process-oriented research into developmental stages associated with this fundamental movement pattern. In fact, none of the process-oriented studies conducted has validated its hypothesized stages through

longitudinal study (Deach, 1950; Gutteridge, 1939; Wellman, 1937). Nevertheless, these studies do allow us to make several generalizations concerning the development of catching.

Developmental Aspects: Two-Handed Catching

Usually, a child's first attempts at stopping or controlling a moving object occur when the child is seated on the floor with the legs spread apart. At first, the child will be successful in stopping a rolled ball by trapping the ball against the legs. With practice, the child will soon be able to trap the ball against the floor by using only the hands, with the palms facing the floor.

A child's first attempts at catching an airborne ball are generally passive. That is, the child stands facing the tosser, who attempts to project the ball into the child's outstretched arms so the child can trap the ball against his body. The palms of the hands face upward, and the child makes no attempt to adjust his body or arms to the oncoming ball.

As their visuoperceptual systems improve, children attempt to adjust their hands and arms to the ball's changing flight characteristics. The palms of the hands are now adjusted to face one another instead of upward, and the elbows are slightly bent so that the hands are in front of the face. Still, in most instances, the ball will make initial contact with the arms or body as the arms are brought up toward the face. When the ball is retained, it is done so by being hugged or trapped against the body. At this stage of development, some children may exhibit fear when the projected ball approaches them (see Figure 14-3). Negative reactions to the tossed ball include turning the head away from the ball; leaning backward, away from the ball; and closing the eyes (Deach, 1950). Seefeldt (1972a) noted these fear reactions in children 4 through 6 years of age but found no such negative reactions to a projectile in children between $1\frac{1}{2}$ and 3 years. Based on this finding, Seefeldt speculated that fear of the projectile may be a conditioned response from earlier failures at the task, not a natural phenomenon.

Figure 14-3 This 6-year-old child is showing fear in reaction to the thrown ball.

At the most advanced level of catching development, the performer adjusts the entire body so as to control the projectile with only the hands. In addition, the mature catcher "gives with the catch": The momentum of the projectile is absorbed by flexing the elbows at the moment of hand-ball contact; in effect, the elbows are shock absorbers.

These developmental characteristics are evident in Kay's (1970) comparative film analysis of the catching styles of 2-, 5-, and 15-year-old children. Kay describes the 2-year-old child as approaching the task without any general strategy. The child

tends to maintain a static position throughout the entire task and focuses her eyes on the tosser, not the ball. In short, this young child reacts too late. As Kay states, "For the most part she is doing something after it has happened, often very long after, as when she eventually turns to fetch the ball that has fallen" (p. 144).

In contrast, the 5-year-old child can anticipate some of the ball's changing flight characteristics and focuses her eyes on the thrower, the ball, and even her own hands. This child's poor timing and coordination limits her ability to retain the ball. Her movements are correct but appear to be carried out in slow motion.

Finally, the 15-year-old child is capable of predicting the ball's flight characteristics, and he carries out preparatory responses well in advance of the ball's arrival. "The overall impression is one of smoothness and ease. The eyes are concentrated upon the ball; they do not watch the hands, which are controlled entirely from the boy's own awareness of the position of his limbs" (Kay, 1970, p. 145).

Developmental Sequences for Two-Handed Catching

Table 14-3 presents Roberton and Halverson's component analysis for the fundamental motor skill of catching. Figure 14-4 illustrates the developmental sequences for catching based on the total body approach. This latter approach has withstood preliminary validation within a mixed longitudinal sample (Haubenstricker, Branta, & Seefeldt, 1983).

A close inspection of the horizontal bar graph at the end of Figure 14-4 indicates little difference in the developmental level of catching between boys and girls prior to 48 months of age (4 years). However, 1 year later, 60 percent of the girls exhibited a stage 4 developmental level of performance whereas a majority (60 percent) of the boys did not achieve this level of development until approximately 6 years of age. Also note that according to this data, collected in the latter half of the 1970s (but reported by Seefeldt and Haubenstricker in 1982), girls obtained the most mature

Table 14-3   Developmental Sequences for Catching: Component Approach

Preparation: Arm Component

Step 1: The arms are outstretched with elbows extended, awaiting the tossed ball.

Step 2: The arms await the ball toss with some shoulder flexion still apparent, but flexion now appears in the elbows.

Step 3: The arms await the ball in a relaxed posture at the sides of the body or slightly ahead of the body. The elbows may be flexed.

Reception: Arm Component

Step 1: The arms remain outstretched and the elbows rigid. There is little to no "give," so the ball bounces off the arms.

Step 2: The elbows flex to carry the hands upward toward the face. Initially, ball contact is primarily with the arms, and the object is trapped against the body.

Step 3: Initial contact is with the hands. If unsuccessful in using the fingers, the child may still trap the ball against the chest. The hands still move upward toward the face.

Step 4: Ball contact is made with the hands. The elbows still flex but the shoulders extend, bringing the ball down and toward the body rather than up toward the face.

Hand Component

Step 1: The palms of the hands face upward. (Rolling balls elicit a palms-down, trapping action.)

Step 2: The palms of the hands face each other.

Step 3: The palms of the hands are adjusted to the flight and size of the oncoming object. Thumbs or little fingers are placed close together, depending on the height of the flight path.

Body Component

Step 1: There is no adjustment of the body in response to the flight path of the ball.

Step 2: The arms and trunk begin to move in relation to the ball's flight path.

Step 3: The feet, trunk, and arms all move to adjust to the path of the oncoming ball.

NOTE: These sequences have not been validated. They were hypothesized by Harper (1979).

SOURCE: Roberton, M. A., and Halverson, L. E. (1984). *Developing children — their changing movement.* Lea & Febiger. Used with permission from the current copyright holder, M. A. Roberton.

level of performance several months before boys did. An analysis of a more recent data set has yielded different findings: Using a mixed longitudinal sample, Haubenstricker, Seefeldt, and Branta (1983) found that approximately 60 percent of the boys exhibited the most mature catching pattern (stage 5) somewhere between 90 ($n = 174$) and 96 ($n = 210$) months of age. In contrast, the percentage of girls exhibiting stage 5 catching characteristics was only about 40 percent (90 months, $n = 177$; 96 months, $n = 175$). Furthermore, approximately 70 percent of the male subjects within the oldest

Figure 14-4   Developmental sequences for catching: total body approach

Sources: Haubenstricker, Branta, and Seefeldt (1983); Seefeldt (1972a); Seefeldt and Haubenstricker (1982). All material used with permission of Dr. John Haubenstricker.

Stage 1   The child presents his arms directly in front of him, with the elbows extended and the palms facing upward or inward toward the midsagittal plane. As the ball contacts the hands or arms, the elbows are flexed and the arms and hands attempt to secure the ball by holding it against the chest.

Stage 2   The child prepares to receive the object with the arms in front of the body, the elbows extended or slightly flexed. Upon presentation of the ball, the arms begin an encircling motion that culminates by securing the ball against the chest. Stage 2 also differs from stage 1 in that the receiver initiates the arm action prior to ball-arm contact in stage 2.

(continued)

Figure 14-4 *(continued)*

Stage 3   The child prepares to receive the ball with arms that are slightly flexed and extended forward at the shoulder. Many children also receive the ball with arms that are flexed at the elbow, with the elbow ahead of a frontal plane.

> *Substage 1:*   The child uses his chest as the first contact point of the ball and attempts to secure the ball by holding it to his chest with the hands and arms.

> *Substage 2:*   The child attempts to catch the ball with his hands. Upon his failure to hold it securely, he maneuvers it to his chest, where it is controlled by hands and arms.

Stage 4   The child prepares to receive the ball by flexing the elbows and presenting the arms ahead of the frontal plane. Skillful performers may keep the elbows at the sides and flex the arms simultaneously as they bring them forward to meet the ball. The ball is caught with the hands, without making contact with any other body parts.

(continued)

Figure 14-4 *(continued)*

Stage 5 The same upper segmental action is identical to stage 4. In addition, the child is
required to change his stationary base in order to receive the ball. Stage 5 is
included because of the apparent difficulty that many children encounter when
they are required to move in relation to an approaching object.

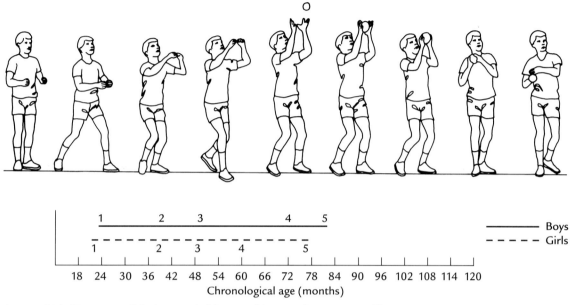

Age at which 60 percent of the boys and girls were able to perform at a specific
developmental level for the fundamental motor skill of catching.

age group studied (102–107 months) exhibited a
stage 5 developmental level of catching, whereas
only about 49 percent of the girls in this oldest age
group performed at the highest level. These more
recent data suggest that boys reach the most mature
level of catching development before girls do.

Developmental Aspects: One-Handed Catching

While there is a wealth of information regarding the
development of two-handed catching in young boys
and girls, little scientific evidence exists regarding children's ability to catch with one hand. One of
the first studies to examine one-handed catching in

young children was conducted by Fischman, Moore,
and Steel (1992). The authors were interested in
determining performance trends and gender differences in the one-handed catching ability of 240
children between age 5 and 12 years. In addition,
they were also interested in studying how the location of the ball toss affects hand orientation. A tennis ball was tossed from a distance of 9 feet to one
of four locations: waist height, shoulder height, above
the head, and out to the side at waist level. Similar
to two-handed catching, performance improved with
age for both boys and girls. The success rate among
the boys ranged from 17.2 percent at 5 years of
age to 95.8 percent at 12 years. Girls were less proficient, with success ranging from 4.2 percent to

92.2 percent at 5 and 12 years of age, respectively. While the authors concluded that by age 12 the skill appeared to be essentially mastered, one could offer an alternate hypothesis; namely, the task may have been too easy for the older children. This was not the case for the younger children. Of the 294 "no-contacts" (no part of the body contacted the ball), 269 occurred among the 5- to 8-year-old children. One could speculate that such poor performance is caused by immature temporal and spatial organization.

Ball location was also found to be an important factor. Balls tossed above the head and out to the side elicited the use of correct hand orientation. Even though the fewest number of balls was caught when the ball was tossed toward the waist, appropriate hand orientation was nevertheless exhibited. This finding suggests that even the youngest children may be capable of perceptually orienting the hand in line with the oncoming ball but experience difficulty in executing the closure of the fingers around the ball.

J. G. Williams (1992a) compared the one-handed and two-handed catching performances of young children between 4 and 10 years of age. Catching attempts were classified as being a "cradle" (hand is flexed to form a cradle into which the ball will passively fall and is then trapped against the body), a clamp (hand moves toward the ball, palm facing inward, but as the ball approaches the hand moves underneath the falling ball, which is grasped with the palm of the hand), or a grasp (hand reaches for oncoming ball with the palm facing the ball allowing the flexed fingers to grasp the ball well in front of the body). One-handed catching was only one-half as successful as two-handed catching. While grasping (the most mature technique) was the prominent movement strategy for catching with two hands, the prominent movement strategy for catching with one hand was the cradling technique (least mature). In fact, grasping declined from 66 percent to 26 percent when one-handed catching was required. This is further evidence that environmental constraints can contribute to changes in movement patterns.

Factors That Influence Catching Performance

There has been no shortage of studies designed to examine factors that may influence catching performance. Unfortunately, it is difficult to compare and contrast these studies, because they vary as to type of ball and speed of ball projection, distance of projection, color of ball and background, angle of projection, and type of evaluation system used. Nevertheless, an awareness of these findings can aid future investigative research.

BALL SIZE   The effects of ball size on an individual's catching ability have received much research attention (Isaacs, 1980; McCaskill & Wellman, 1938; Payne, 1985a; Payne & Koslow, 1981; Strohmeyer, Williams, & Schaub-George, 1991; Victors, 1961; Warner, 1952; Wickstrom, 1983). Initial studies consistently concluded that larger balls improve young children's catching performance. These conclusions were often based on the premise that young children are farsighted and would thus profit from using the larger ball, which would be easier to track visually (Smith, 1970). Also, based on neurological considerations, the young child was assumed to have insufficient fine motor control for grasping the smaller object. Most early studies, however, evaluated the child's catching attempts on a pass-fail basis: The child either did or did not retain control of the ball. Human error was a major consideration, because balls were often simply tossed to the subject by the experimenter, allowing for considerable variability of tosses.

More recently, researchers have attempted to eliminate some of the shortcomings of the earlier research by implementing more-sophisticated statistical analyses, mechanically projecting ball tosses to reduce human error, and using weighted rating scales to evaluate catching performance beyond the simple pass-fail. These recent investigations, however, have led to a sharp dissimilarity in findings.

Some research has found small balls to be more conducive to successful catching (Isaacs, 1980). Such research employed a rating scale designed to evaluate the maturation level children displayed in their catching technique. As discussed in Chapters 1 and 17, this is a process-oriented means of evaluation. Table 14-3, Figure 14-4, and the scale that follows are all examples of process-oriented ratings for the skill of catching.

0. Initial body contact; subject makes no attempt to contact the ball.

1. Arm and/or body contact, miss: Initial attempt to contact is made on the arms and/or body, and the ball is missed.

2. Arm and/or body contact, save: Initial contact is on the arms and/or body, and the ball is retained.

3. Hand contact, miss: Initial contact is made by the hands, but the ball is then dropped immediately or dropped following arm or body contact.

4. Hand contact, assisted catch: Initial contact is made by the hands. The ball is juggled but retained by using arms and/or body for assistance.

5. Hand contact, clean catch: The ball is contacted and retained by the hands only. The ball may be brought into the body on the follow-through after control is gained by the hands.
                    (Hellweg, 1972; Isaacs, 1980)

Research employing this scale was based on the premise that future success in catching depends on the early development of a mature technique. Generally, a smaller ball tended to elicit a more mature hand catch rather than an arm/chest trap. This research also determined that as the ball size increased, the maturity level in the catching technique regressed. In other words, the child would be more likely to resort to the more immature chest-trap method of catching (Isaacs, 1980; Victors, 1961; Wickstrom, 1983).

Studies finding children to be more successful using larger balls generally employed rating scales designed to evaluate the level of control that the child maintained over the ball, regardless of the maturity of the catching technique, a product-oriented

evaluation. An example of a product-oriented rating scale is as follows:

1. Failure to react

2. One hand contacts, ball dropped

3. Two hands contact, ball dropped

4. Uncontrolled catch (bobbled)

5. Controlled catch
            (Payne, 1985a; Payne & Koslow, 1981)

This research was based on the premise that children's ability to control the ball, regardless of the maturity of their technique, would make them feel successful in the movement and inspire them to try again (Payne, 1985a; Payne & Koslow, 1981).

Clearly, we need more information on this topic. In particular, we need to know what is the critical issue in teaching this or any motor skill. Should we place the premium on early acquisition of a mature technique or on early success in terms of simply controlling the ball (Payne, 1982)? Unfortunately, little scientific information is presently available to answer this question, which is so critical to the optimal teaching of motor skills to children.

BALL AND BACKGROUND COLOR   Manipulation of both ball color and background color may be another way to improve catching performance (Gavnishy, 1970; Ghosh, 1973). In studying the effects of ball and background color on young children's catching performances, Morris (1976) found that blue and yellow balls were caught significantly better than white balls. Furthermore, children attained their highest catching scores when blue balls were projected against a white background.

Data that Isaacs (1980) obtained indicate that a child's preferred color may also influence catching performances. Before being administered a criterion catch test, subjects were required to choose their favorite colored ball. Results of this study indicated that irrespective of ball color, both the boys and the girls tended to catch their preferred-color ball significantly better than their nonpreferred-color balls. Isaacs speculates that because the children in this study focused their selective attention on the ball for a longer time when catching their preferred-color ball, they were able to obtain more critical information concerning the ball's flight.

BALL VELOCITY   Ridenour (1974) has determined that ball speed also influences children's ability to predict accurately the direction in which a projectile is moving. Subjects in Ridenour's study were not required to catch the ball, but it can be generalized that prediction of an object's direction is necessary in a catching task. This was evident in Bruce's (1966) investigation. With 7-, 9-, and 11-year-old subjects, he found that the catching performances of the 7- and 9-year-old children declined as ball speed increased from 25 feet to 33 feet per second.

TRAJECTORY ANGLE   Variations in trajectory angles were also a major feature in Bruce's (1966) investigation. The balls were projected at either a 30- or a 60-degree angle. An analysis of the data indicated that angle of projection did not significantly affect a child's catching ability. On the other hand, H. G. Williams (1968) used nine skilled and nine unskilled catchers in an attempt to determine the effects of trajectory angle on judging speed and placement of a moving object. Results of Williams's study indicate that the unskilled catchers performed better when balls were projected at a 34-degree angle, whereas the group as a whole performed better when the balls were projected at a 44-degree angle.

VISION AND VIEWING TIME   Without a doubt, the catcher must rely on visual information to form a strategy that will lead to a successful catch. Research indicates that as viewing time decreases, so does proficiency in retaining the projectile (Nessler, 1973; Whiting, Gill, & Stephenson, 1970). Thus, the teacher should use a ball that moves slowly through space (e.g., beach ball, whiffle ball, sponge ball) when working with inexperienced catchers.

INSTRUCTION   To date, only one study has examined the influence of catching instruction on children's one-handed catching ability. Using a single-subject design, J. G. Williams (1992b) trained an 8-year-old boy. Training consisted of four assessment sessions and three instruction plus practice

sessions administered alternately on 7 successive days. Each instruction and practice session lasted 30 minutes. Following the third instruction and practice session, significant changes were observed in both percentage of successful catches and level of maturity (technique) used to retain the projected ball. Williams noted that by the end of the study, this 8-year-old boy's catching ability had progressed from that of a typical 8-year-old to that of subjects who are 2 years older.

KNOWLEDGE AND EXPERIENCE   In Chapter 2, we described in some detail the positive relationship between an individual's knowledge of a specific sport and subsequent sport performance. Recent research has suggested that knowledge regarding the specific task of catching may influence catching performance. For example, Kourtessis (1994) studied the influence of procedural and declarative knowledge (see Chapter 2) of ball catching in children (6–12 years old), both with and without physical disabilities. Procedural knowledge, as measured by a 15-task ball-catching hierarchy, was found to be higher in the nondisabled than the disabled populations. Furthermore, the ambulatory children with physical disabilities scored higher than their nonambulatory physically disabled peers. Declarative knowledge, however, did not differ significantly among the various groups. Thus, it appears that declarative and procedural knowledge do not develop at the same rate and that catching experience may foster the acquisition of procedural knowledge, even though a deficit in declarative knowledge may be evident. Similarly, Lefebvre (1996) reported that experience (in catching) is a crucial factor in a child's ability to predict the flight of a thrown ball. This preliminary research suggests that providing the opportunity to catch a thrown ball is, in and of itself, an important instructional strategy.

CATCHING ON THE RUN   Catching involves adjustments of not only the hands and arms but also the entire body when the ball is projected away from the child. Understandably, balls projected directly toward the child are easier to catch than those requiring the child to move to a new location to intercept the ball (Keegan, 1989). Therefore, teachers should use caution in, or avoid, pairing up an inexperienced thrower with an inexperienced catcher. The inexperienced thrower's inability to throw the ball directly to the inexperienced catcher will differently increase the difficulty of the catching task.

CATCHING WITH A GLOVE In one-handed catching, the performer must not only position the hand in the path of the oncoming ball, but also correctly time the closure of the fingers around the ball. Regarding these two phases, it appears that the use of a glove alters the nature of errors typically observed in bare-handed catching. In fact, initial research suggests that the use of a glove improves catching success by reducing the precision of limb-hand positioning and by removing the temporal grasping component (Fischman & Mucci, 1989; Fischman & Sanders, 1991). In other words, glove catching is easier because the ball moves toward a larger target and is grasped with a larger surface area. We have all seen instances at youth baseball games where a young participant mistimes the hand closure around the ball but can still hold on to it. Generally, half of the ball is in the glove and half is out. Without the glove, closing the finger too late would have resulted in a missed catch. Therefore, instructors should view one-handed glove catching as simpler than bare-handed catching. However, instructors should make sure that participants possess enough hand (grasping) strength to squeeze the glove efficiently. A new, stiff glove or one that is too large may hinder catching if the participant cannot close the glove's fingers.

STRIKING

Striking is a fundamental movement in which a designated body part or some implement is used to project an object. Propulsion skills are necessary in many sport activities and can occur in a variety of forms. For example, the bare hand is used as the striking implement in volleyball. The striking pattern can be underhanded, as in serving the volleyball, or overhanded, as in spiking the volleyball. When an implement is used, such as a racquet or bat, the striking pattern is accomplished with either

one or two hands. Regardless of the movement pattern employed, certain characteristics are readily observable. This section describes the development of striking an object with a body part (hand or foot) and with an implement (racquet or bat).

Developmental Aspects of One- and Two-Handed Striking

The child's initial attempt at striking an object with either the bare hand or some implement is very similar to the overarm throwing pattern young children exhibit. Briefly, at an inexperienced level of development, a child uses an overarm pattern that is predominantly flexion and extension of the forearm. The child usually directly faces the object to be struck and may or may not take a forward step. If the child does take a forward step, it is with the ***homolateral*** leg, the leg on the same side of the body as the striking arm. Thus, all the striking movements are accomplished in the anterior-posterior plane.

The child's upward-downward swing pattern gradually "flattens out." Flattening out the swing facilitates the child's ability to contact the ball. In most instances, this sidearm striking pattern becomes well defined by approximately 36 months (Espenschade & Eckert, 1980). Nevertheless, Espenschade and Eckert noted that when children are under stress to successfully strike a ball, they generally resort to an inexperienced overarm striking pattern.

Harper and Struna (1973) studied longitudinal changes in the one-handed striking pattern of two children filmed over 1 year. Both the 40-month-old girl and the 43-month-old boy were asked to strike a suspended ball as hard as possible toward a wall. Initially, the young girl's swing consisted purely of horizontal adduction of the striking arm. She used little backswing and did not take a forward step. Spinal or pelvic rotation was not evident. However, 3 months later, she had made much progress toward a more advanced sidearm striking pattern. The girl now took a forward step with the ***contralateral*** leg (the leg opposite the striking arm), and there was simultaneous spinal and pelvic rotation. Because the young boy already exhibited many

Table 14-4 Major Characteristics of General Striking Development	
Inexperienced Striker	**Advanced Striker**
1. Striker usually takes no step, but if the striker does, it is with the homolateral leg.	1. Striker takes a forward step with the foot opposite the striking arm or striking side.
2. Striker uses an up-down striking motion.	2. Striker uses a full backswing.
3. Striker takes little backswing with the striking arm or implement.	3. Striker swings the striking implement horizontally.
4. The striker's trunk and hips do not rotate and there is no block rotation.	4. Differentiated trunk and hip rotation is present.
5. Striker holds the arms rigid with little, if any, wrist snap when swinging a paddle or bat.	5. In the two-handed striking pattern, the striker's arms are relaxed and there is a noticeable coordinated wrist snap when swinging bat.

SOURCE: Payne (1985b).

advanced characteristics of the one-handed sidearm swing at the first filming, observable changes in his striking pattern were more subtle. Over the 1-year period, the most noticeable changes in his striking pattern were a longer stride into the ball and an increase in the preparatory backswing.

In another study, Wickstrom (1968, as cited in Wickstrom, 1983) examined the sidearm striking patterns of 33 preschool children 21 to 60 months old. His data reveal that children younger than 30 months used the overarm striking pattern when attempting to contact the suspended ball with either a bat or paddle. Children older than 30 months also used an overarm striking pattern, but they responded favorably when encouraged to use a sidearm striking pattern. Finally, Wickstrom was amazed at how close the 4-year-olds' striking pattern was to an adult pattern. Table 14-4 summarizes the major characteristics of striking development, while Figure 14-5 describes and illustrates a total body approach to the analysis of striking with a bat.

Stationary Ball Bouncing

Bouncing a ball is a fundamental movement used in many childhood and adult activities. At an advanced level of development, a person bounces a ball by using the hand to push the ball repeatedly downward, a movement called **dribbling.** At inexperienced levels of performance, a person uses one or two hands to strike instead of push the ball. Thus, striking is one of the developmental stages of ball bouncing.

Initially, the striking pattern resembles a spanking or slapping motion of the hand and wrist (see Figure 14-6). Wickstrom (1980), one of the few researchers to study the acquisition of ball-handling skills in young children, filmed 115 children in kindergarten through second grade to study developmental characteristics within this fundamental movement pattern. He noted that the inexperienced dribbler holds the fingers of the striking hand close together and sometimes slightly hyperextends the fingers at contact. Following contact with the ball, the child quickly retracts the arm, and there is little extension of the elbow. Because their eye-hand coordination is poor, young performers strike the ball in an inconsistent manner. As would be expected, young children have difficulty controlling the direction in which the ball is hit. Timing hand-ball contact is also difficult for the inexperienced performers. It is common to observe an inexperienced performer slapping at the ball when the ball is traveling down and quickly retracting the arm

Figure 14-5   Developmental sequences for striking with a bat: total body approach
SOURCE: Seefeldt and Haubenstricker (1982). All material used with permission of Dr. John Haubenstricker.

Stage 1   The motion is primarily posterior-anterior in direction. The movement begins with
hip extension and slight spinal extension and retraction of the shoulder on the striking
side of the body. The elbows flex fully. The feet remain stationary throughout the
movement with the primary force coming from extension of the flexed joints.

Stage 2   The feet remain stationary or either the right or left foot may receive the weight as the
body moves toward the approaching ball. The primary pattern is the unitary rotation
of the hip-spinal linkage about an imaginary vertical axis. The forward movement of
the bat is in a transverse plane.

Stage 3   The shift of weight to the front-supporting foot occurs in an ipsilateral pattern. The
trunk rotation-derotation is decreased markedly in comparison with stage 2, and the
movement of the bat is in an oblique-vertical plane instead of the transverse path seen
in stage 2.

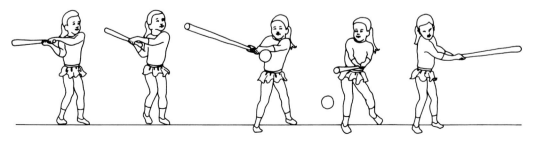

(continued)

Figure 14-5 *(continued)*

Stage 4   The transfer of weight in rotation-derotation is in a contralateral pattern. The shift of weight to the forward foot occurs while the bat is still moving backward as the hips, spine, and shoulder girdle assume their force-producing positions. At the initiation of the forward movement, the bat is kept near the body. Elbow extension and the supination-pronation of the hands do not occur until the arms and hands are well forward and ready to extend the lever in preparation to meet the ball. At contact the weight is on the forward foot.

Age at which 60 percent of the boys and girls were able to perform at a specific developmental level for the fundamental motor skill of striking with a bat.

when the ball is rebounding up, thus never making contact with the ball.

In contrast, the experienced dribbler pushes the ball toward the floor so that the elbow is nearly fully extended. The dribbling arm stays extended and recontacts the ball when it bounces, approximately two-thirds of the way up. Once hand-ball contact has been made, the hand retracts slowly, thus enabling the hand to maintain contact with the ball. The fingers are spread apart and the ball is once again pushed downward to start another dribbling cycle.

The transition from inexperienced to experienced performance becomes evident as the individual gradually extends the elbow and delays retracting the forearm. Meeting the ball before it has reached its peak height and "giving" with the ball enable the hand to maintain contact with the ball, so the ball is pushed rather than struck toward the floor.

Kicking

Kicking is another form of striking; the foot is used to give impetus to a ball. The style of kicking that we describe in this section is called place kicking. In ***place kicking,*** the ball is placed either on the ground or on a kicking tee. In its most mature form, the advanced place kicker will approach the ball from a running start. The last step taken prior to ball-foot contact involves a leap step onto the plant or support foot. Simultaneously, the kicking leg is prepared by flexing the knee and hyperextending

Figure 14-6   An illustration of inexperienced and mature dribbling

The inexperienced dribbler slaps at the ball.

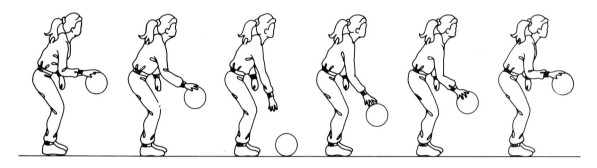

The mature dribbler fully extends the arm and when hand-ball contact is made, the arm retracts, and the hand maintains contact with the ball.

the hip. This preparatory backswing will enable the leg to be thrust forward vigorously and then to powerfully project the ball. After kicking the ball, the kicking leg continues to travel upward—the leg is allowed to follow through. The follow-through should be vigorous enough to cause the support leg to leave the ground. Simply put, a hop is performed on the support leg. During this kicking sequence, the kicker's center of gravity is displaced. To maintain balance, the advanced place kicker positions the trunk so it leans slightly backward and the arms oppose the action of the legs.

In contrast, the inexperienced place kicker lacks many of these preparatory movements. The child simply pushes the ball away with the foot. In fact, the foot barely leaves the floor, there is no at-tempted backswing of the kicking leg, the leg remains straight throughout the kicking motion, and there is no follow-through. In addition, the child holds the arms straight by the side of the body rather than using them to maintain body balance.

At an intermediate level of place-kicking development, preparatory movements are noticeable. There is less flexion of the knee and hip than in an advanced pattern, but some preparation is evident. The arms are elevated to help maintain balance but still do not work in opposition to the legs. The follow-through of the kicking leg is evident after the kick but is less than what is expected at an advanced level of kicking development. These developmental changes in place kicking are illustrated and presented in more detail in Figure 14-7.

Figure 14-7   Developmental sequences for kicking: total body approach

Sources: Haubenstricker et al. (1981); Seefeldt (1972b); Seefeldt and Haubenstricker (1975a, 1982). All
material used with permission of Dr. John Haubenstricker.

Stage 1   *Preparatory phase:* The performer is usually stationary and positioned near the ball. If the
performer moves prior to kicking, the steps are short and concerned with spatial relationships
rather than attaining momentum for the kick.

Force production: The thigh of the kicking leg moves forward with the knee flexed and is nearly
parallel to the surface by the time the foot contacts the ball. Knee-joint extension occurs
after contact, resulting in a pushing rather than a striking action. Upper extremity action is
usually bilateral but may show some opposition in older performers. (If the performer is too
far from the ball as the extremity moves to meet the ball, the knee flexes only slightly and the
leg swings forward from the hip in a pushing action.)

Follow-through phase: The knee of the kicking leg continues to extend until it approaches 180°.
If the trunk is inclined forward following contact with the ball, the performer will step forward
to regain balance. If the trunk is leaning backward, the kicking leg will move backward after
ball contact to achieve body balance.

Stage 2   *Preparatory phase:* The performer is stationary. Initial action involves hyperextension at the
hips and flexion at the knee so that the thigh of the kicking leg is behind the midfrontal
plane. The arms may move into a position of opposition in situations of extreme
hyperextension at the hips.

Force production: The kicking leg moves forward with the knee joint in a flexed position.
Knee-joint extension begins just prior to foot contact with the ball. Arm-leg opposition
occurs during the kick.

Follow-through phase: Knee extension continues after the ball leaves the foot, but the force of
the kick usually is not sufficient to move the body forward. Instead, the performer usually
steps sideward or backward.

(continued)

Figure 14-7   *(continued)*

Stage 3   *Preparatory phase:* The performer takes one or more deliberate steps to approach the ball. The support leg is placed near the ball and slightly to the side of it.

Force production: The kicking foot stays near the surface as it approaches the ball, resulting in less flexion than in stage 2. The trunk remains nearly upright, thereby preventing maximum force production. The knee begins to extend prior to contact. Arm-leg opposition is evident.

Follow-through phase: The force of the kick may carry the performer past the point of contact if the approach was vigorous. Otherwise, the performer may remain near the point of contact.

Stage 4   *Preparatory phase:* The approach involves one or more steps with the final "step" being an airborne run or leap. This permits hyperextension of the hip and flexion of the knee as in stage 2.

Force production: The shoulders are retracted and the trunk is inclined backward as the supporting leg makes contact with the surface and the kicking leg begins to move forward. The movement of the thigh nearly stops as the knee joint begins to extend rapidly just prior to contact with the ball. Arm-leg opposition is present as in the previous two stages.

Follow-through phase: If the forward momentum of the kick is sufficient, the performer either hops on the support leg or scissors the legs while airborne in order to land on the kicking foot. If the kicking foot is not vigorous, the performer may merely step in the direction of the kick.

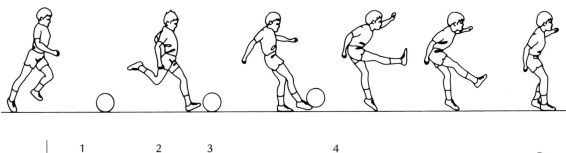

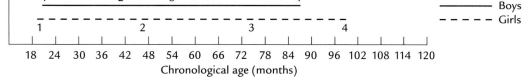

Age at which 60 percent of the boys and girls were able to perform at a specific developmental level for the fundamental motor skill of kicking.

Table 14-5   Developmental Sequences for Punting: Component Approach

Ball Release: Arm Component

Step 1: Hands are on the sides of the ball. The ball is tossed upward from both hands after the support foot has landed (if a step was taken).

Step 2: Hands are on the sides of the ball. The ball is dropped from chest height after the support foot has landed (if a step was taken).

Step 3: Hands are on the sides of the ball. The ball is lifted upward and forward from waist level. It is released at the time of or just prior to the landing of the support foot.

Step 4: One hand is rotated to the side and under the ball. The other hand is rotated to the side and top of the ball. The hands carry the ball on a forward and upward path during the approach. It is released at chest level as the final approach stride begins.

Ball Contact: Arm Component

Step 1: Arms drop bilaterally from ball release to a position on each side of the hips at ball contact.

Step 2: Arms bilaterally abduct after ball release. The arm on the side of the kicking leg may pull back as that leg swings forward.

Step 3: After ball release, the arms bilaterally abduct during flight. At contact, the arm opposite the kicking leg has swung forward with that leg. The arm on the side of the kicking leg remains abducted and to the rear.

Leg Action Component

Step 1: Either no step or one short step is taken. The kicking leg swings forward from a position parallel to or slightly behind the support foot. The knee may be totally extended by contact or, more frequently, still flexed 90° with contact above or below the knee joint. The thigh is still moving upward at contact. The ankle tends to be flexed.

Step 2: Several steps may be taken. The last step onto the support leg is a long stride. The thigh of the kicking leg has slowed or stopped forward motion at contact. The ankle is extended. The knee has 20–30° of extension still possible by contact.

Step 3: The child may take several steps, but the last is actually a leap onto the support foot. After contact, the momentum of the kicking leg pulls the child off the ground in a hop.

NOTE: These sequences, hypothesized by Roberton (1983), have not been validated.
SOURCE: Roberton, M. A., and Halverson, L. E. (1984). *Developing children—their changing movement*. Lea & Febiger. Used with permission from the current copyright holder, M. A. Roberton.

Punting

Unlike place kicking, which requires one to kick a stationary ball, **punting** involves striking an airborne ball with the foot. Obviously, the complexity of punting greatly exceeds that of place kicking.

Table 14-5 describes the hypothesized developmental sequences for punting, based on the component approach (Roberton & Halverson, 1984), while Figure 14-8 describes and illustrates this same task from the perspective of the total body approach. Many of the developmental characteristics

Figure 14-8   Developmental sequences for punting: total body approach
SOURCE: Seefeldt and Haubenstricker (1975b). All material used with permission of Dr. John Haubenstricker.

Stage 1 The performer is stationary as the hands and foot prepare for the punting action. The ball is held with both hands at waist height or higher prior to placing it in position for punting. The ball may be manipulated in a variety of ways for punting: (1) It may be held in both hands as the punting foot is lifted forward and upward with hip and knee flexion. The punting force in this situation represents a push as the ball is contacted by the plantar side of the foot when the knee extends. (2) The ball may be tossed up and forward into the air. The performer then must move forward to get the body into punting position. (3) The performer may bounce the ball and attempt to punt it as it rebounds from the surface. Whatever the mode of placing the ball into a punting position, the primary characteristics of stage 1 are a stationary preparatory position and flexion at the hip and knee of the punting leg, placing these segments in front of the midfrontal plane.

Stage 2 The performer is stationary during the preparatory phase. The ball is held in both hands and may be dropped or tossed forward or upward in preparation for punting it with the foot. The nonsupport leg is flexed at the knee, and the thigh is perpendicular to the surface or behind the midfrontal plane as the leg is placed into punting position. As the punting leg moves forward, its momentum may carry the performer forward for a step, but generally the force is upward, causing the punter to step backward after striking the ball.

(continued)

Figure 14-8   *(continued)*

Stage 3   The performer moves forward deliberately for one or more steps in preparation for punting the ball. The ball is generally released in a forward and downward direction. The knee is flexed at 90° or less, but the thigh is farther behind the midfrontal plane than in stage 2, because of the stepping action. The follow-through of the striking leg will generally carry the punter ahead of the point where the ball was contacted.

Stage 4   The punter's approach is rapid, usually comprising one or more steps, culminating in a leap just prior to contacting the ball. If the leap does not precede the punt, the forward momentum may be enhanced by taking a large step. The ball is contacted at or below knee height as a result of the ball having been released in a forward and downward direction. The momentum of the swinging leg carries the punter off of the surface in an upward and forward direction after the punt.

used in describing the place kick are also evident in punting: namely, the immature punter is generally stationary, fails to prepare the kicking leg properly, and also fails to follow through with sufficient force. With this technique, there is obviously no leap step prior to ball-foot contact and no hop on the supporting foot following ball-foot contact. In addition, the ball is held with both hands and is generally presented by tossing it upward and slightly forward.

In contrast, the mature punter will move forward rapidly, leaping onto the support foot prior to ball-foot contact. The kicking leg is prepared by hyperextending the hip and flexing the knee. Following ball-foot contact, a vigorous follow-through generally causes a forward hop on the support leg.

SUMMARY

This chapter describes the development of a group of motor skills collectively referred to as object-control skills. The specific skills described in this chapter included overarm throwing, both one- and two-handed catching, striking with an implement (racquet or bat), and striking with a body part (place kicking and punting).

One-handed overarm throwing consists of a preparatory phase, an execution phase, and a follow-through phase. Initially, throwing is arm dominated; in contrast, advanced throwing involves trunk rotation and a forward step with the contralateral leg. Thus, movement progresses from an anterior-posterior plane to a horizontal plane, and the base of support changes from a stationary to a shifting position. Gender differences in overarm throwing favor boys and men. In fact, one study that examined gender performance differences found that of the 20 skills examined, the greatest difference in performance was for throwing. It appears that both biological and sociocultural factors contribute to these performance differences between the genders.

Adultlike catching involves using only the hands to bring a moving object under control. The infant's first attempt at stopping a moving object occurs when the child is seated and traps a rolled ball against the body. Next, the child stands and attempts to trap a rolled ball against the floor. When first attempting to catch a thrown ball, some children may exhibit fear. Factors such as ball size, ball and background color, ball velocity, trajectory angle, viewing time, knowledge of catching, and using a glove can all influence children's catching performance.

Researchers are just beginning to examine the development of one-handed catching in young children. Based on the very limited amount of research available, it appears that children are only about one-half as successful when attempting to catch with one hand as with two. There is a regression in the technique used when attempting to catch with one hand. Similar to two-handed catching, boys' one-handed catching performance is generally superior to that of girls. It appears that the major difficulty factor for these young children is not hand orientation but the ability to time the closure of the fingers around the approaching ball (grasping). One study has found that instruction and practice in catching can improve one-handed catching performance.

Striking is a fundamental movement in which a designated body part or implement is used to project an object. When an implement is used, the inexperienced striker swings the implement up and down, similar to an overarm throwing pattern. In contrast, the experienced striker's swinging motion is sidearm or horizontal. Ball bouncing, place kicking, and punting are examples of fundamental movements in which a body part is used to strike a ball.

Table 17-3 summarizes many of the object-control skills of childhood when the total body approach is utilized (Haubenstricker, 1990).

KEY TERMS

catching
contralateral
dribbling
homolateral

kicking
object-control skills
place kicking
punting

striking
throwing

QUESTIONS FOR REFLECTION

1. What are the three phases associated with overarm throwing?
2. What developmental changes are exhibited across the four developmental stages of overarm throwing as presented by Wild? Compare and contrast.
3. What four steps are associated with the preparatory phase of overarm throwing? In your answer

describe the three terms that are most often used to describe the most mature technique.

4. What three techniques are used for evaluating overarm throwing performance trends? Which technique is best? Why?

5. What are the changes in ball-throwing velocity among both boys and girls, in relation to overarm throwing performance trends?

6. What factors are known to influence overarm throwing performance?

7. How do researchers account for gender differences in overarm throwing development and perform-ance? Address your answer from both biological and sociological standpoints.

8. Can you describe fear reactions to a thrown ball and identify the age range when they are most

prevalent? Why do you think these fear reactions are typically exhibited during this age range?

9. What factors are known to influence both two-handed and one-handed catching performance?

10. How does using a glove influence catching performance?

11. What are the characteristics of general striking development? Distinguish between mature and immature performance.

12. How do place kicking and punting differ? Which is more difficult and why?

13. What key observational characteristics distinguish mature and immature kickers (place kicking and punting)?

14. What key observational characteristics distinguish mature and immature ball bouncers?

ONLINE LEARNING CENTER (www.mhhe.com/payne6e)

Visit the *Human Motor Development* Online Learning Center for study aids and additional resources. You can use the study guide questions and key terms puzzles to review key terms and concepts for this chapter and to

prepare for exams. You can further extend your knowl-edge of motor development by checking out the Web links, articles, and activities found on the site.

REFERENCES

Adams, D. L. (1994). The relative effectiveness of three instruc-tional strategies on the learning of an overarm throw for force. Unpublished doctoral dissertation, Oregon State University.

Baker, R. L. (1993). The relationship between qualitative and quantitative evaluation of throwing. Unpublished master's thesis, Michigan State University, East Lansing.

Bruce, R. D. (1966). The effects of variation in ball trajectory upon the catching performance of elementary school chil-dren. Unpublished doctoral dissertation, University of Wis-consin, Madison.

Burton, A. W., Greer, N. L., & Wiese-Bjornstal, D. M. (1992). Changes in overhand throwing patterns as a function of ball size. *Pediatric Exercise Science, 4,* 50–67.

———. (1993). Variations in grasping and throwing patterns as a function of ball size. *Pediatric Exercise Science, 5,* 25–41.

Butterfield, S. A., & Loovis, E. M. (1993). Influence of age, sex, balance, and sport participation on development of throwing by children in grades K–8. *Perceptual and Motor Skills, 76,* 459–464.

Carlton, E. B. (1989). An investigation of gender-mediated fac-tors in preschool children's overarm throwing development. Unpublished doctoral dissertation, University of California, Berkeley.

Deach, D. (1950). Genetic development of motor skills in chil-dren two through six years of age. Unpublished doctoral dis-sertation, University of Michigan, Ann Arbor.

East, W. B., & Hensley, L. D. (1985). The effects of selected so-ciocultural factors upon the overhand-throwing performance of prepubescent children. In J. E. Clark & J. H. Humphrey (Eds.), *Motor development: Current selected research.* Vol. 1. Princeton, NJ: Princeton Book Company.

Escamilla, R., Fleisig, G., Barrantine, S., Zhen, N., & Andrews, J. (1998). Kinematic comparisons of throwing different types of baseball pitches. *Journal of Applied Biomechanics, 14,* 1–23.

Espenschade, A. S., & Eckert, H. M. (1980). *Motor develop-ment.* 2nd ed. Columbus, OH: Merrill.

Fischman, M. G., Moore, J. B., & Steel, K. H. (1992). Chil-dren's one-hand catching as a function of age, gender, and ball location. *Research Quarterly for Exercise and Sport, 63,* 349–355.

Fischman, M. G., & Mucci, W. G. (1989). Influence of a baseball glove on the nature of errors produced in simple one-handed catching. *Research Quarterly for Exercise and Sport, 60,* 251–255.

Fischman, M. G., & Sanders, R. (1991). An empirical note on the bilateral use of a baseball glove by skilled catchers. *Perceptual and Motor Skills, 72,* 219–223.

Fronske, H., Blakemore, C., & Abendroth-Smith, J. (1997). The effect of critical cues on overhand throwing efficiency of elementary school children. *Physical Educator, 54,* 88–95.

Gavnishy, B. (1970). Vision and sporting results. *Journal of Sports Medicine and Physical Fitness, 10,* 260–264.

Ghosh, A. (1973). Ocular problems in athletics: Role of ophthalmology in sports medicine. *Journal of Sports Medicine and Physical Fitness, 13,* 111–118.

Gutteridge, M. (1939). A study of motor achievements of young children. *Archives of Psychology, 244,* 1–178.

Halverson, L. E., & Roberton, M. A. (1979). The effects of instruction on overhand throwing development in children. In G. Roberts & K. Newell (Eds.), *Psychology of motor behavior and sport—1978.* Champaign, IL: Human Kinetics.

Halverson, L. E., Roberton, M. A., & Langendorfer, S. (1982). Development of the overarm throw: Movement and ball velocity changes by seventh grade. *Research Quarterly for Exercise and Sport, 53,* 198–205.

Halverson, L. E., Roberton, M. A., Safrit, M. J., & Roberts, T. W. (1977). Effect of guided practice on overhand-throw ball velocities of kindergarten children. *Research Quarterly, 48,* 311–318.

Harper, C. J. (1979). Learning to observe children's motor development: Part III. Observing children's motor development in the gymnasium. Paper presented at the national convention of the American Alliance for Health, Physical Education, and Recreation, New Orleans, LA.

Harper, C. J., & Struna, N. L. (1973). Case studies in the development of one-handed striking. Paper presented at the American Alliance for Health, Physical Education, and Recreation, Minneapolis, MN.

Haubenstricker, J. (1990). Summary of fundamental motor skill stage characteristics: Motor performance study—MSU. Unpublished materials, Michigan State University, East Lansing.

Haubenstricker, J., Branta, C., & Seefeldt, V. (1983). Preliminary validation of developmental sequences for throwing and catching. Paper presented at the annual conference of the North American Society for the Psychology of Sport and Physical Activity, East Lansing, MI.

Haubenstricker, J., Seefeldt, V., & Branta, C. (1983). Preliminary validation of a developmental sequence for the standing long jump. Paper presented at the annual convention of the American Alliance for Health, Physical Education, Recreation, and Dance, Minneapolis, MN.

Haubenstricker, J., Seefeldt, V., Fountain, C., & Sapp, M. (1981). Preliminary validation of a developmental sequence for kicking. Paper presented at the Midwest District convention of the American Alliance for Health, Physical Education, Recreation, and Dance, Chicago.

Hellweg, D. A. (1972). An analysis of perceptual and performance characteristics of the catching skill in 6–7 year old children. Unpublished doctoral dissertation, University of Wisconsin, Madison.

Isaacs, L. D. (1980). Effects of ball size, ball color, and preferred color on catching by young children. *Perceptual and Motor Skills, 51,* 583–586.

Kay, H. (1970). Analyzing motor skill performance. In K. Connolly (Ed.), *Mechanisms of motor skill development.* New York: Academic Press.

Keegan, T. A. (1989). Development of ball catching skills among boys of elementary school age. Unpublished master's thesis, Temple University, Philadelphia.

Kourtessis, T. (1994). Procedural and declarative knowledge of ball-catching in children with physical disabilities. Unpublished master's thesis, McGill University, Montreal, Quebec.

Langendorfer, S. (1980). Longitudinal evidence for developmental changes in the preparatory phase of the overarm throw for force. Paper presented at the Research Section of the American Alliance for Health, Physical Education, Recreation, and Dance, Detroit, MI.

———. (1982). Developmental relationships between throwing and striking: A prelongitudinal test of motor stage theory. Unpublished doctoral dissertation, University of Wisconsin, Madison.

Lefebvre, C. (1996). Prediction in ball catching by children with a developmental coordination disorder. Unpublished master's thesis, McGill University, Montreal, Quebec.

Leme, S., & Shambes, G. (1978). Immature throwing patterns in normal adult women. *Journal of Human Movement Studies, 4,* 85–93.

Luedke, G. C. (1980). Range of motion as the focus of teaching the overhand throwing pattern to children. Unpublished doctoral dissertation, Indiana University, Bloomington.

Marques-Bruna, P., & Grimshaw, P. N. (1997). Three-dimensional kinematics of overarm throwing action of children age 15 to 30 months. *Perceptual and Motor Skills, 84,* 1267–1283.

McCaskill, C. L., & Wellman, B. L. (1938). A study of common motor achievements at the preschool ages. *Child Development, 9,* 141–150.

McClenaghan, B. A., & Gallahue, D. L. (1978). *Fundamental movement: A developmental and remedial approach.* Philadelphia: Saunders.

Miller, B. C. (1995). The cause of inaccuracy in overarm throws made with the non-dominant arm. Unpublished master's thesis, University of Western Ontario, London, Ontario.

Morris, G. S. D. (1976). Effects ball and background color have upon the catching performance of elementary school children. *Research Quarterly, 47,* 409–416.

Nelson, K. R., Thomas, J. R., & Nelson, J. K. (1991). Longitudinal change in throwing performance: Gender differences. *Research Quarterly for Exercise and Sport, 62,* 105–108.

Nelson, J. D., Thomas, J. R., Nelson, K. R., & Abraharm, P. C. (1986). Gender differences in children's throwing performance: Biology and environment. *Research Quarterly for Exercise and Sport, 57,* 280–287.

Nessler, J. (1973). Length of time necessary to view a ball while catching it. *Journal of Motor Behavior, 5,* 179–185.

Payne, V. G. (1982). Current status of research on object reception as a function of ball size. *Perceptual and Motor Skills, 55,* 953–954.

———. (1985a). Effects of object size and experimental design on object reception by children in the first grade. *Journal of Human Movement Studies, 11,* 1–9.

———. (1985b). Teaching elementary physical education: Recognizing stages of the fundamental movement patterns (videotape). Northbrook, IL: Hubbard Scientific Publications.

Payne, V. G., & Koslow, R. (1981). Effects of varying ball diameters on catching ability of young children. *Perceptual and Motor Skills, 53,* 739–744.

Rehling, S. L. (1996). Longitudinal differences in overarm throwing velocity and qualitative throwing techniques of elementary boys and girls. Unpublished doctoral dissertation, Arizona State University, Tucson.

Ridenour, M. V. (1974). Influence of object size, speed, and direction on the perception of a moving object. *Research Quarterly, 45,* 293–301.

Roberton, M. A. (1977). Stability of stage categorizations across trials: Implications for the "stage theory" of overarm throw development. *Journal of Human Movement Studies, 3,* 49–59.

———. (1978). Longitudinal evidence for developmental stages in the forceful overarm throw. *Journal of Human Movement Studies, 4,* 167–175.

———. (1983). Changing motor patterns during childhood. In J. Thomas (Ed.), *Motor development during childhood and adolescence* (pp. 48–90). Minneapolis, MN: Burgess.

Roberton, M. A., & DiRocco, P. (1981). Validating a motor skill sequence for mentally retarded children. *American Corrective Therapy Journal, 35,* 148–154.

Roberton, M. A., & Halverson, L. E. (1984). *Developing children—their changing movement.* Philadelphia: Lea & Febiger.

Roberton, M. A., Halverson, L. E., Langendorfer, S., & Williams, K. (1979). Longitudinal changes in children's overarm throw ball velocities. *Research Quarterly for Exercise and Sport, 50,* 256–264.

Roberton, M. A., & Konczak, J. (2001). Predicting children's overarm throw ball velocities from their developmental levels in throwing. *Research Quarterly for Exercise and Sport, 72,* 91–103.

Roberton, M. A., & Langendorfer, S. (1980). Testing motor development sequences across 9–14 years. In C. Nadeau, W. Halliwell, K. Newell, & G. Roberts (Eds.), *Psychology of motor behavior and sport—1979.* Champaign, IL: Human Kinetics.

———. (1983). Changing motor patterns during childhood. In J. Thomas (Ed.), *Motor development during childhood and adolescence.* Minneapolis, MN: Burgess.

Runion, B., Roberton, M. A., & Langendorfer, S. J. (2003). Forceful overarm throwing: A comparison of two cohorts measured 20 years apart. *Research Quarterly for Exercise and Sport, 74,* 324–330.

Schincariol, L. M. (1995). An examination of the declarative knowledge of physically awkward and physically talented children. Unpublished doctoral dissertation, University of New Brunswick, Fredericton, New Brunswick.

Seefeldt, V. (1972a). Developmental sequence of catching skill. Paper presented at the annual convention of the American Association for Health, Physical Education, and Recreation, Houston, TX.

———. (1972b). Developmental sequence of kicking. Unpublished materials, Michigan State University, East Lansing.

Seefeldt, V., & Haubenstricker, J. (1975a). Developmental sequence of kicking. Rev. ed. Unpublished materials, Michigan State University, East Lansing.

———. (1975b). Developmental sequence of punting. Unpublished materials, Michigan State University, East Lansing.

———. (1976). Developmental sequence of throwing. Rev. ed. Unpublished manuscript, Michigan State University, East Lansing.

———. (1982). Patterns, phases, or stages: An analytical model for the study of developmental movement. In J. A. S. Kelso & J. E. Clark (Eds.), *The development of movement control and coordination.* New York: Wiley.

Seefeldt, V., Reuschlein, P., & Vogel, P. (1972). Sequencing motor skills within the physical education curriculum. Paper presented at the American Association for Health, Physical Education, and Recreation, Houston, TX.

Smith, H. (1970). Implications for movement education experiences drawn from perceptual-motor research. *Journal of Health, Physical Education, and Recreation, 41,* 30–33.

Strohmeyer, H. S., Williams, K., & Schaub-George, D. (1991). Developmental sequences for catching a small ball: A prelongitudinal screening. *Research Quarterly for Exercise and Sport, 62,* 257–266.

Thomas, J. R., & French, K. E. (1985). Gender differences across age in motor performance: A meta-analysis. *Psychological Bulletin, 98,* 260–282.

Thomas, J. R., & Marzke, M. W. (1992). The development of gender differences in throwing: Is human evolution a factor? In R. W. Cristina & H. M. Eckert (Eds.), *Enhancing human performance in sport: New concepts and developments.* Academy Papers No. 25. Champaign, IL: Human Kinetics.

Thomas, J. R., Michael, D., & Gallagher, J. D. (1994). Effects of training on gender differences in overhand throwing: A brief quantitative literature analysis. *Research Quarterly for Exercise and Sport, 65,* 67–71.

Toyoshima, S., Hoshikawa, T., Miyashita, M., & Oguri, T. (1974). Contribution of the throwing parts to throwing performance. In R. Nelson & C. Murehouse (Eds.), *Biomechanics IV.* Baltimore: University Park Press.

Van Slooten, P. H. (1973). Performance of selected motor-coordination tasks by young boys and girls in six socioeconomic groups. Unpublished doctoral dissertation, Indiana University, Bloomington.

Victors, E. E. (1961). A cinematographical analysis of catching behavior of a selected group of seven and nine year old boys. Unpublished doctoral dissertation, University of Wisconsin, Madison.

Walkwitz, E. (1989). The effects of instruction and practice on overarm throwing patterns of preschool children. Unpublished doctoral dissertation, Louisiana State University, Baton Rouge.

Warner, A. P. (1952). The motor ability of third, fourth, and fifth grade boys in the elementary school. Unpublished doctoral dissertation, University of Michigan, Ann Arbor.

Wellman, B. L. (1937). Motor achievements of preschool children. *Childhood Education, 13,* 311–316.

Whiting, H. T. A., Gill, E. B., & Stephenson, J. M. (1970). Critical time intervals for taking in flight information in a ball-catching task. *Ergonomics, 13,* 265–272.

Wickstrom, R. L. (1968). Developmental motor patterns in young children. Unpublished film study.

———. (1980). Acquisition of a ball-handling skill. Paper presented at the Research Section of the American Alliance for Health, Physical Education, Recreation, and Dance, Detroit, MI.

———. (1983). *Fundamental motor patterns.* 3rd ed. Philadelphia: Lea & Febiger.

Wild, M. (1938). The behavior pattern of throwing and some observations concerning its course of development in children. *Research Quarterly, 9,* 20–24.

Williams, H. G. (1968). The effects of systematic variation of speed and direction of object flight and of skill and age classification upon visuoperceptual judgments of moving objects in three dimensional space. Unpublished doctoral dissertation, University of Wisconsin, Madison.

Williams, J. G. (1992a). Catching action: Visuomotor adaptations in children. *Perceptual and Motor Skills, 75,* 211–219.

Williams, J. G. (1992b). Effects of instruction and practice on ball catching skill: Single-subject study of an 8-year-old. *Perceptual and Motor Skills, 75,* 392–394.

15 Youth Sports

Researchers from the Institute for the Study of Youth Sports, Michigan State University, have described youth sports as athletic endeavors that provide children and youth with a systematic sequence of practices and contests (Seefeldt, Ewing, & Walk, 1991). Approximately 39 million children and youth now participate in non-school-sponsored sport programs (Ewing, Seefeldt, & Brown, 1996) and as many as 6.7 million youth now participate in interscholastic sports (National Federation of State High School Associations, 2003). Thus, even though participation rates are known to be overestimated because individuals participating in more than one activity are counted more than once, these figures show the number of children participating in youth sports continues to increase annually. This occurs for several reasons. First, there is a trend toward earlier participation. Not long ago, growth and development specialists shuddered to think that children as young as 5 or 6 years were participating in team activities such as T-baseball and youth football. A 4-year-old holds an age-group record for running a marathon—over 26 miles—in 6 hours and 3 seconds (Jeffers, 1980). While authorities recommend children not begin competing in sports prior to age 8 (Coakley, 1986), reports indicate that children as young as age 3 are currently involved in organized youth sport programs (Martens, 1986); see Figure 15-1.

The trend toward greater involvement extends to other age groups as well. Why is there a trend toward earlier and greater involvement? One reason is the rule changes within selected sports. For example, in T-baseball, even the youngest child can perform, because the rules allow children to strike a stationary ball instead of one delivered by a pitcher. Conversely, defensive performance is no longer required, as rule changes limit the number of players who can bat per inning. Therefore, when the defensive team is unable to get anyone out, sides at bat change simply because all offensive players have had a turn at bat.

A second factor affecting the number of participants is an increase in female involvement. In 1971, the National Federation of State High School Associations identified only 14 interscholastic sports for

Figure 15-1 When will the trend toward younger sport participation ever end?
Source: Say Cheese Company/Getty Images/PhotoDisc

girls, allowing for only 294,015 participants; in 2002, the number had risen to 41 sports, involving approximately 2.8 million female participants (National Federation of State High School Associations, 2003). Table 15-1 reports a longitudinal history of interscholastic sport participation from 1971 through 2003.

Third, U.S. children are beginning to get involved in what used to be considered nontraditional sport activities. Without doubt, U.S. children have become infatuated with baseball, football, basketball, swimming, and soccer. However, the availability of agency- and community-sponsored programs

Table 15-1   Longitudinal History of Interscholastic Sport Participation, 1971–2003*

Year	Boy Participants	Girl Participants	Total
1971–72	3,666,917	294,015	3,960,932
1972–73	3,770,621	817,073	4,587,694
1973–74	4,070,125	1,300,169	5,370,294
1975–76	4,109,021	1,645,039	5,754,060
1977–78	4,367,442	2,083,040	6,450,482
1978–79	3,709,512	1,854,400	5,563,912
1979–80	3,517,829	1,750,264	5,268,093
1980–81	3,503,124	1,853,789	5,356,913
1981–82	3,409,081	1,810,671	5,219,752
1982–83	3,355,558	1,779,972	5,135,530
1983–84	3,303,599	1,747,346	5,050,945
1984–85	3,354,284	1,757,884	5,112,168
1985–86	3,344,275	1,807,121	5,151,396
1986–87	3,364,082	1,836,356	5,200,438
1987–88	3,425,777	1,849,684	5,275,461
1988–89	3,416,844	1,839,352	5,256,196
1989–90	3,398,192	1,858,659	5,256,851
1990–91	3,406,355	1,892,316	5,298,671
1991–92	3,426,853	1,940,801	5,367,654
1992–93	3,416,389	1,997,489	5,413,878
1993–94	3,478,530[a]	2,124,755[a]	5,603,285[a]
1994–95	3,536,359[b]	2,240,461[b]	5,776,820[b]
1995–96	3,634,052[c]	2,367,936[c]	6,001,988[c]
1996–97	3,706,225[c]	2,472,043[c]	6,178,268[c]
1997–98	3,763,120	2,570,333	6,333,453
1998–99	3,832,352[d]	2,652,796[d]	6,485,148[d]
1999–00	3,861,749	2,675,874	6,537,623
2000–01	3,921,069	2,784,154	6,705,223
2001–02	3,960,517	2,806,998	6,767,515
2002–03	3,988,738	2,856,358	6,845,096

*No survey was conducted in 1974–75 or 1976–77.

[a]Total does not include 11,698 participants in coeducational sports.

[b]Total does not include 17,609 participants in coeducational sports.

[c]Total does not include 16,979 participants in coeducational sports.

[d]Total does not include 19,220 participants in coeducational sports.

NOTE: Any estimate of athletic participation will be inflated, because participants are counted more than once if they participate in more than one activity.

SOURCE: National Federation of State High School Associations (2003). This and other information pertaining to participation may be obtained at www.nfshsa.org.

in such activities as tennis, cycling, bowling, ice hockey, gymnastics, volleyball, track and field, cross-country, figure skating, downhill and cross-country skiing, and many other sports has opened the door to participation for those children not interested in the more traditional sports.

Finally, there has been a dramatic increase in the number of disabled children who now actively participate in sports. This increase is directly linked to an increase in agency- and community-sponsored programs that serve people with various degrees of disabilities, including the American Wheelchair Bowling Association, Amputee Sports Association, Handicapped Scuba Association, National Foundation of Wheelchair Tennis, National Wheelchair Softball Association, United States Quad Rugby Association, and Special Olympics. Additionally, special equipment is now available for disabled persons, further encouraging participation in sports.

Researchers have identified several potential benefits afforded youth sport participants, including improvements in academic performance (Jeziorski, 1994), physical fitness (Superintendent of Documents, 1996), and self-esteem (Horn & Hasbrook, 1987), and serving as a general deterrent to negative behaviors such as a tendency toward gang membership and violent behavior (LeUnes & Nation, 1989), to name just a few. In this chapter, we examine several factors that influence the development of children through youth sport participation.

WHERE CHILDREN PARTICIPATE IN SPORTS

Today, children have many options when it comes to selecting an avenue for youth sport participation. For example, Table 15-2 presents a list of alternative sport venues and the estimated number of participants in each. By far, the greatest number of youth sport participants are found in agency-sponsored sports and in local recreational sport programs. Furthermore, over 6.8 million children and youth now participate in interscholastic sports (National Federation of State High School Associa-

tions, 2003). Table 15-3 lists the 10 most popular interscholastic sports and their numbers of participants. This national survey continues to recognize football as the most popular sport for boys and basketball as the most popular for girls. Over the last 4 years, the number of boys now participating in outdoor track and field has greatly increased. In fact, the sport now ranks third, replacing baseball, which has dropped to fourth. Regarding female interscholastic sport participation, fast pitch softball has seen an increase of nearly 126,000 participants since 1993, with additional increases of nearly 83,000 in volleyball and 80,000 in outdoor track and field. For the first time, golf made the list of the most popular sport programs for girls with 62,159 participants.

WHY CHILDREN PARTICIPATE IN SPORTS

Often-cited reasons for children's participation in sports include the following: to improve skills, to have fun, to be with friends, to be part of a team, to experience excitement, to receive awards, to win, and to become more physically fit. Of these reasons, "to have fun" appears to be the most predominant reason children want to be involved in sport (Gill, Gross, & Huddleston, 1983; Sapp & Haubenstricker, 1978). Nevertheless, the idea of having fun can mean different things to different individuals; what is enjoyable for one may not be enjoyable for another. For this reason, researchers have begun to study the underlying factors that affect enjoyment of sport.

Take, for example, a large-scale study conducted by Wankel and Kreisel (1985). In their study, 822 soccer, baseball, and hockey participants between 7 and 14 years of age were surveyed (with a 10-item inventory) to determine why they enjoyed sports. Three sport groupings were employed, because another purpose was to determine if reasons for enjoyment differed across sports. Results indicate that the top four enjoyment factors (improving skills, testing abilities against others, excitement of the

Table 15-2 Estimated Percentage of Youth Enrolled in Specific Categories of Youth Sports*

Category of Activity	Percentage of All Eligible Enrollees[a]	Approximate N of Participants
Agency-Sponsored Sports (i.e., Little League Baseball, Pop Warner Football)	45	22,000,000
Club Sports (i.e., pay for services, as in gymnastics, ice skating, swimming)	5	2,368,700
Recreational Sport Programs (i.e., everyone plays — sponsored by recreational departments)	30	14,512,200
Intramural Sports (middle, junior, senior high schools)	10	451,000
Interscholastic Sports (middle, junior, senior high schools)	12[b] 40[c]	1,741,200 5,776,820 6,195,247[d]

*Total population of eligible participants in the 5–17 year age category in 1995 was estimated to be 48,374,000 by the National Center for Education Statistics, U.S. Department of Education, 1989.

[a]Total does not equal 100 percent because of multiple-category by some athletes.

[b]Percentage of total population aged 5–17 years.

[c]Percentage of total high-school–age population (14,510,000).

[d]Total number of interscholastic participants based on 1996–1997 National Federation of State High School Associations Survey.

SOURCE: President's Council on Physical Fitness and Sports (1997).

game, and personal accomplishment—i.e., intrinsic factors) were consistent across all three sport groups. Of moderate importance were the social factors regarding "being on a team" and "being with friends." The extrinsic factors, which included "getting awards" and "pleasing others," were consistently selected as the least important factors for sport enjoyment. Also of interest is the finding that "winning the game" was ranked eighth in the list of 10 factors.

Given these findings, Wankel and Kreisel offered the following suggestions:

Emphasis should be on involvement, skill development, and enjoyment of doing the skills. Winning and receiving rewards for playing, aspects

that are frequently given considerable emphasis by parents, coaches, and the media, are of secondary importance to the participant's enjoyment and accordingly should not be heavily emphasized. The establishment of rigid schedules and elimination play-offs to declare winners is a questionable practice if the criterion is to provide enjoyment to all participants. . . . Each child should be provided an opportunity to develop his or her skills, be provided with a reasonable challenge, and be afforded an opportunity for personal accomplishment and satisfaction. (1985, pp. 62–63)

The most comprehensive findings to date are from a study sponsored by the Athletic Footwear

Table 15-3 The 10 Most Popular Interscholastic Sports for Boys and Girls	
Sport°	**Number of Participants**
BOYS	
Football	1,023,142
Basketball	540,874
Outdoor track & field	498,027
Baseball	453,792
Soccer	345,156
Wrestling	239,845
Cross-country	191,833
Golf	162,805
Tennis	144,844
Swimming & diving	94,612
GIRLS	
Basketball	457,165
Outdoor track & field	415,602
Volleyball	396,682
Fast pitch softball	357,912
Soccer	301,450
Cross-country	163,360
Tennis	162,810
Swimming & diving	141,468
Competitive spirit squads	111,191
Golf	62,159

°Listed from most to least popular.

SOURCE: National Federation of State High School Associations (2003).

Association and conducted through the Youth Sports Institute at Michigan State University under the direction of Martha Ewing and Vern Seefeldt (Athletic Footwear Association, 1990). This survey sampled more than 10,000 youths in 11 American cities. Table 15-4 shows the 10 most important reasons children chose to participate in their favorite sports. The data, along with earlier findings, consistently show that children want to participate to have "fun" and that "winning" ranks last or nearly so.

Table 15-4 The 10 Most Important Reasons I Play My Best School Sport

1. To have fun
2. To improve my skills
3. To stay in shape
4. To do something I'm good at
5. For the excitement of competition
6. To get exercise
7. To play as part of a team
8. For the challenge of competition
9. To learn new skills
10. To win

Sample: 2000 boys and 1900 girls, grades 7–12, who identified a "best" school sport. Answers above were among 25 responses rated on a 5-point scale.

SOURCE: Athletic Footwear Association (1990). Used with permission.

PARTICIPATION: COMPETENCE MOTIVATION THEORY

Other researchers have made convincing arguments that participation motivation can be linked to existing theoretical models. One model that is frequently mentioned is Harter's model of perceived competence (Harter, 1978, 1982, 1988). According to this **competence motivation theory,** individuals are motivated to be successful in various achievement areas such as sports (physical), academics (cognitive), or human relationships (social). When performance attempts succeed, the individual experiences a positive effect. This perception of successful competence motivates the individual to continue participation. Likewise, the theory predicts that individuals low in perceived competence will discontinue participation.

Scientific studies designed to test Harter's theory within a sport context have been fairly successful. For example, G. C. Roberts, Kleiber, and Duda (1981) found that youth sport participants scored higher in both perceived cognitive and perceived physical competence than did nonparticipants. Likewise, Feltz and Petlichkoff (1983) report that current sport participants scored higher on perceived physical competence than did dropouts. However, more recent work (Ulrich, 1987) failed to find a significant relationship between children in grades K–4 and perceived physical competence as measured by Harter's Perceived Competence Scale for Children (1982). This contradictory finding may be due in part to developmental differences regarding sources of information that children and adolescents use to estimate physical competence. For example, children aged 8 and 9 tend to use such factors as game outcome and parental feedback. In contrast, children 10 to 14 years old depend more on social comparisons to peers and evaluation by peers to judge their physical competence (Horn & Weiss, 1991). Furthermore, it appears that children become more accurate in judging their physical competency as they age and that this increased accuracy may be related to the source of information used (Horn & Weiss, 1991).

Coaches and teachers should not only be aware of such developmental differences but also be attuned to the value and type of feedback that is most appropriate. For example, children should not view mistakes as failures. Instead, parents and coaches should quickly intervene and help children see other reasons why a mistake has occurred. This way, children will be less likely to view their performance as a lack of physical ability to accomplish a specific task (Ewing et al., 1996).

In summary, we can conclude that children participate in organized sports for a multitude of reasons. Unfortunately, children's most often stated reasons for participation (intrinsic reasons) do not always coincide with the program goals established by the adult leadership.

WHY CHILDREN DROP OUT OF SPORTS

Gould (1987) has estimated that about 35 percent of the millions of children who participate in a youth sport will withdraw from the program within any given year. However, contradictory to popular belief, most children do not drop out of a sport because of excessive stress. Instead, empirical evidence suggests that most sport dropouts do so because of interpersonal problems (e.g., dislike the coach) or to pursue other leisure activities (Dishman, 1989). Most often, the other activity is another sport. For example, when interviewing swimming drop-outs, Gould and colleagues (1982) noted that 80 percent of the youngsters had either reentered or planned to reenter a sport activity. Likewise, Klint and Weiss (1986) found that of 37 gymnasts who dropped out of participation, 35 reentered gymnastics or another sport (cited in Gould & Petlichkoff, 1988). For this reason, sport psychologists recommend that we use caution in interpreting the term *sport dropout* (Gould & Petlichkoff, 1988). Obviously, there is a vast difference between children who withdraw from sports permanently and those who withdraw from one sport activity only to become involved in a different one. In fact, regarding the youngest competitors, frequent withdrawal from sports may signify nothing more than the child's attempt to sample many different sports before selecting the few that best meet his or her needs.

As we mentioned earlier, when sport participation is not fun, there is a greater tendency for children to drop out (see Table 15-5). When children were asked what changes would need to be made before they would reenter their sport, both the boys and the girls ranked as most important the need to "make practices more fun" (Athletic Footwear Association, 1990). Table 15-6 presents the six most important changes that these boys and girls would make before they would be willing to reenter a sport that they had earlier dropped.

SPORT PARTICIPATION: CONTROVERSIES

Participation in sports during the childhood and adolescent years has become an American way of life. Involvement in both recreational and competitive athletics contributes significantly to the young

Table 15-5 The 11 Most Important Reasons Children Stopped Playing a Sport

1. I lost interest.
2. I was not having fun.
3. It took too much time.
4. Coach was a poor teacher.
5. There was too much pressure (worry).
6. I wanted a nonsport activity.
7. I was tired of it.
8. I needed more study time.
9. Coach played favorites.
10. The sport was boring.
11. There was an overemphasis on winning.

Sample: 2700 boys and 3100 girls who said they had recently stopped playing a school or nonschool sport. Answers above were among 30 responses rated on a 5-point scale.
SOURCE: Athletic Footwear Association (1990). Used with permission.

Table 15-6 The 6 Most Important Changes Children Would Make in a Sport That Was Previously Dropped

"I would play again if . . ."

Boys
1. Practices were more fun.
2. I could play more.
3. Coaches understood players better.
4. There was no conflict with studies.
5. Coaches were better teachers.
6. There was no conflict with social life.

Girls
1. Practices were more fun.
2. There was no conflict with studies.
3. Coaches understood players better.
4. There was no conflict with social life.
5. I could play more.
6. Coaches were better teachers.

Sample: 2700 boys, 3100 girls, grades 7–12, who said they had recently stopped playing a school or non-school sport. They rated 21 different responses on a 5-point scale.
SOURCE: Athletic Footwear Association (1990). Used with permission.

participants' physical, social, emotional, and cognitive development. But sport participation, whether competitive or recreational, is sometimes clouded by controversial issues. This section examines several of the most frequently mentioned issues. For ease of discussion, these controversial issues have been divided into two categories: medical and psychological.

Medical Issues

Potential physical danger is a major criticism of youth sport participation. But is this criticism warranted? If so, are some activities more dangerous than others? Furthermore, are the injuries incurred avoidable? To help answer these important questions, we first examine injury rates of selected sports and then discuss whether the number of injuries can be reduced.

FOOTBALL   The American Academy of Pediatrics Committee on Sports Medicine has classified football as a ***contact/collision sport.*** In general, collision sports have become synonymous with physical

injury. Obviously, whenever people are repeatedly running into one another, injuries will occur. But is this true for all ages and levels of play? To provide insight to answers to this question, Stuart and colleagues (2002) studied the prevalence of injury among 921 youth football players between 9 and 13 years of age. As illustrated in Table 15-7, rate of injury tended to increase as players matured in age and grade level. While the highest rate of injury occurred among the players from the oldest age group (8th graders), the overall injury rate was only 5.97 percent. This translates to only 8.47 injuries per 1000 player-games or 0.17 injuries per 1000 player-plays. When relative prevalence of risk for injury was examined by player position, the researchers determined that 65 percent of injuries occurred to offensive players and 35 percent to defensive players.

		% Injury Prevalence	Injuries per 1000	Injuries per 1000
Grade	N	per Season	Player-Games	Player-Plays
4	218	2.73	3.80	0.09
5	211	5.67	7.86	0.16
6	206	6.31	8.74	0.16
7	147	6.00	8.20	0.15
8	133	11.28	15.45	0.33
Overall	915	5.97	8.47	0.17

Table 15-7 Prevalence of Youth Football Injuries by Grade Level

SOURCE: Stuart et al. (2002).

Among the offensive players, the running backs were at greatest risk (33 percent) followed by the receivers (11 percent), the quarterback (11 percent), and the linemen (9 percent). Among the defensive players, the backs (13 percent) and linemen (13 percent) were found to be at a slightly greater risk of injury compared with linebackers (9 percent). Thus the rate of injury in youth tackle football is relatively low compared with that of professional football. More specifically, the National Football League has reported an average injury rate of 90 percent per year (Galton, 1980).

In one large-scale study, Goldberg and colleagues (1988) studied the injury experiences of 5128 boys between 8 and 15 years of age. Only significant injuries were studied (those restricting participation for more than 7 days). Table 15-8 highlights their findings. As in previous small-scale studies, overall injury rate was rather low (5 percent), with most injuries occurring among older and heavier participants. Unlike those in higher levels of play (college and professional), most significant injuries in youth football involved the upper extremity, particularly the hand and wrist. Because a significant number of major injuries (those restricting participation for more than 21 days) occurred to members of kickoff and punt-return teams, the researchers suggested that youth football administrators consider modifying the sport to eliminate this dangerous aspect of the game. They also recommended that steps be taken to reduce the number of injuries caused by

direct impact with the football helmet (18.4 percent). Their recommendations include requiring participants to wear helmets constructed with a soft padded top and having coaches reevaluate the instructional methods used to teach blocking and tackling. This latter recommendation had been offered earlier by Silverstein (1979), who found that **spearing,** an outlawed tackling technique in which the helmet is used as a weapon, accounted for approximately 30 percent of the injuries reported in his study. Indeed, since spearing was outlawed in 1976, the number of catastrophic injuries has been greatly reduced. This finding emphasizes the need for coaches to teach their players the correct technique for executing sport skills.

BASEBALL   Youth baseball is a relatively safe activity. However, within recent years two major concerns have surfaced: chest trauma and eye injuries. First and most serious is the concern of deaths resulting from nonpenetrating chest trauma. This injury, **commotio cordis,** is typically encountered when the batter is struck in the chest by a pitched baseball or when the catcher is struck by a foul tipped baseball. Each year two to four deaths are reported (Kyle, 1996). Additionally, when Maron and colleagues (1999) examined 70 cases from the U.S. Commotio Cordis Registry, they discovered that most of the victims were boys younger than 16 years of age. Maron and colleagues (2002) have recently confirmed this finding, noting a median

Table 15-8 Injuries in Youth Football			
Injury Rate by Weight (kg)/(years):	***N***	**% Injury Rate**	**No. of Injuries**
49.5–67.5/12–15	177	9.6	(17)
40.5–60.8/11–14	1,160	8.4	(97)
36–51.8/10–13	1,489	5.8	(86)
29.3–45/9–12	1,610	2.7	(44)
22.5–38.3/8–11	692	1.9	(13)
Overall injury rate	5,128	5.0	(257)
Most-Prone Injury Sites		**% Injury Rate**	**No. of Injuries**
Hand/wrist		27.6	
Knee		18.7	
Shoulder/humerus		11.3	
Most Common Injuries		**% Injury Rate**	**No. of Injuries**
Fractures		35.0	(90)
Epiphyseal fractures		5.1	(13)
Sprains		24.5	(63)
Contusions		16.7	(43)
Strains		7.0	(18)
Injury Rates by Position		**% Injury Rate**	**No. of Injuries**
Quarterbacks/running backs		30.4	
Defensive linemen		22.2	
Offensive linemen		12.8	
Linebackers		10.9	
Kickoff/punt-return team members		7.4	
Defensive backs		5.8	
Receivers		2.7	
Occurrence of Major Injuries°		**% Injury Rate**	**No. of Injuries**
Kickoff/punt-return team members		63.2	
Quarterback/running backs		44.9	
Causes of Injuries		**% Injury Rate**	**No. of Injuries**
No unusual occurrence		58.6	(150)
Helmet		18.4	(47)
Contact after ball whistled dead		8.6	(22)
Contact during conditioning drills		8.2	(21)

°Players restricted for over 21 days
SOURCE: Goldberg et al. (1988).

age of 14 years. In an attempt to eliminate this class of injury, a debate has emerged over the value of using a softer baseball than the standard. According to the U.S. Consumer Products Safety Commission (Kyle, 1996), the American Academy of Pediatrics (AAP, 2001b) and the work of Marshall and colleagues (2003), using a softer baseball results in fewer and less severe injuries. However, doctors are concerned that the use of a softer baseball may allow a greater portion of the ball to enter the eye's orbit, thus leading to an increase in severe eye injuries. For example, Vinger, Duma, and Crandall (1999) examined baseballs of six different hardnesses and found that the softest of the six intruded significantly into the eye's orbit. To help shed light on this debate, Little League Baseball (Physician and Sportsmedicine, 1999) undertook a 3-year study to investigate the value of all protective equipment (softer baseballs, chest protectors, batting vests, face masks, breakaway bases).

SOCCER Soccer is one of America's fastest-growing sports. In the United States, between 12 and 18 million people participate in soccer. From a more global perspective, the Soccer Industry Council's 1995 estimates suggest a soccer participation rate of more than 6 million youths under 12 years of age. Like football, soccer is also classified as a contact/collision sport (AAP, 1988). Even though we know that the overall injury rate among professional soccer players is about one injury per season, less is known about the injury rate and type of injuries to young children and adolescents. Nilsson and Roaas (1978) examined all injuries that occurred during the 1975 and 1977 Norway Cup. During these two tournaments, 25,000 players between 11 and 18 years competed in 2987 matches. The medical personnel on duty at the tournaments saw a total of 1343 injuries, including cases of illnesses not directly related to soccer participation. An analysis of data revealed that girls were twice as likely to be injured as boys. Additionally, Nilsson and Roaas noted that injury rates per 1000 hours of play were greater in the final rounds of play than during the qualifying rounds. For instance, during qualifying rounds, the rate of injury for boys and girls was 21.5 and 39.5,

respectively. However, during the final rounds of play, rate of injury increased to 27.5 for boys and 53.5 for girls. Nilsson and Roaas suspect that the girls' higher rate of injury was partly caused by their lower level of skill and training. Fortunately, most injuries were minor. Contusions (36 percent), sprains and strains (20 percent), and skin abrasions (39 percent) made up a majority of the reported injuries. Only 3.5 percent of the injuries were fractures. Because 9 out of every 10 injured players missed less than 1 day of play, the authors believed that young soccer players participate in a fairly safe activity. American studies support this contention. Shively, Grana, and Ellis (1981) report an injury rate of only 8.5 per 1000 participants among high school boys and 20 per 1000 participants among high school girls.

Kibler (1993) examined injuries to both preadolescent and adolescent boys and girls 12–19 years of age who participated in soccer. Injury data were gathered over a 4-year period from individuals participating in the Bluegrass Invitational Soccer Tournament (1987–1990). An injury was defined as any condition that required a player to be removed from the game or miss a game or caused anyone to receive treatment at the tournament's medical facility. Table 15-9 summarizes the findings from data collected over 480 games, resulting in 74,000 player hours. Over this course, there were 179 injuries reported. This number represents an injury rate of just 23.8 for every 10,000 player hours.

These results support findings from other studies that suggest that youth soccer is a relatively safe activity. In fact, 37 percent of the reported injuries required no major treatment, while 43.7 percent of injuries required some treatment. Only 11.8 percent of the injuries required hospital evaluation.

These results lend insight into ways in which soccer injuries could possibly be reduced. Because most injuries were caused by person-to-person contact, closer officiating, pregame warnings regarding inappropriate playing tactics (take downs, hacking, etc.), and coaching within the spirit of the rules should all be emphasized. In addition, researchers are just beginning to examine the potential long-term consequences of youth who repeatedly head the soccer

Table 15-9	Injuries in Youth Soccer
Site of Injury	
Thigh	21.0%
Knee	15.8%
Ankle	13.0%
Foot	12.8%
Torso	10.9%
Head & Neck	8.0%
Type of Injury	
Contusions	32.0%
Muscle strains	24.5%
Sprains	21.8%
Fractures	9.0%
Heat illness	4.5%
Concussions	1.5%
Cause of Injury	
Person-to-person contact	43.0%
Repetitive overload	20.4%
Contact with ground	17.5%
Contact with objects (goal posts, etc.)	6.5%
Effect of Injury on Playing Status	
Missed one game	38.5%
Missed remaining games	19.3%

SOURCE: Kibler (1993).

Figure 15-2 Repeated heading may have long-term medical consequences.

SOURCE: Anthony Saint James/Getty Images/PhotoDisc

ball (AAP, 2000b; see Figure 15-2). Preliminary results on adult soccer players in Norway have uncovered mild to severe deficits in attention, concentration, and memory in 81 percent of the players tested (Tysvaer & Lochen, 1991). One study reported that 49 percent of the 11.5-year-old participants complained of headaches after heading the ball (Janda, Bir, & Cheney, 2002). Furthermore, protective padding for the lower extremities (shin guards) and head as well as on goal posts and the removal of all sideline objects (chairs, benches, water coolers) should further reduce soccer injuries. Indeed, a recent study by Bir, Cassatta, and Janda (1995) reported

a reduction of as much as 77.1 percent in impact forces to the shin region when shin guards are used.

DOWNHILL SKIING Even though skiing injuries do not generally result from making contact with another person, this activity has still been classified by the AAP (1988) as a *limited contact/impact sport.* With skiing, injuries generally result when contact is made with the ground or some stationary object. To make matters worse, this contact frequently occurs at a high rate of speed. A 6-year study that Johnson and colleagues (1980) conducted suggests that there are approximately 500,000 skiing injuries per year in the

United States (cited in Blitzer et al., 1984). These injuries, however, are not equally distributed across either age or gender. For example, when Garrick and Requa (1979) studied injury patterns in children and adolescent skiers, they found that girls were more prone to injury than were boys. Furthermore, injury rate increased steadily through age 13. The lowest rate of injury was for children younger than 10 years. Rate of injury leveled off between 13 and 15 years of age and declined slightly through age 17. Of the 423 injuries reported among the 3456 participants, 51 percent of the injuries were sprains; 47 fractures (11.1 percent) were observed, and most were sustained by the 12- and 13-year-olds.

A more recent longitudinal study covering 9 years reported somewhat different findings (Blitzer et al., 1984). In this study, children younger than 11 years experienced the same rate of injury as adults. More specifically, adults obtained one injury for every 254 skier days, whereas children 10 and under obtained one injury every 253 skier days. Children between 11 and 13 years old experienced the highest rate of injury: one every 151 skier days. Although these rates of injury may initially appear excessive, they are actually not when you consider that the average number of ski days per year is only 14.

IN-LINE SKATING Currently, in-line skating is the fastest growing recreational sport in the United States. As many as 26.6 million children and adults now participate in some form of this activity. In fact, in-line roller hockey is quickly replacing ice hockey in many localities. Unfortunately, as many as 100,000 individuals received injuries severe enough to warrant emergency hospital care in 1996 (Schieber et al., 1996). While injuries from in-line skating can be caused by a host of factors, excessive speed seems the leading culprit, accounting for as much as 35 percent of all in-line skating falls that result in injury (Orenstein, 1996). While simple cruising speeds generally fall between 10 and 17 miles per hour, speeds in excess of 30 mph are not uncommon (International In-Line Skating Association, 1992). To place these speeds in perspective, consider that young children generally ride a bicycle at 9 mph and adults at 13 mph (Thompson & Rivara,

1996). While 75 percent of injuries occur to individuals between 5 and 24 years of age, 60 percent occur to youths between 10 and 14 years of age (Heller, Routley, & Chambers, 1996; Schieber, Branche-Dorsey, & Ryan, 1994).

Results of a recent investigation involving 91 hospitals participating in the National Electronic Injury Surveillance System (Schieber et al., 1996) reveal that 32 percent of the injuries requiring emergency medical attention were to the wrist and that 25 percent of all injuries were wrist fractures. This is unfortunate, since the researchers established that wearing wrist guards could have reduced the risk of injury to the wrist by slightly more than 90 percent. Surprisingly, knee and head injuries account for only 6 and 5 percent, respectively. Nevertheless, those participating in in-line skating activities should wear all available protective gear: wrist guards, elbow pads, knee pads, and a helmet (see Figure 15-3). While researchers have not completely determined why people do not use these safety items, they cite four possible barriers to use: a lack of knowledge as to the importance of wearing protective equipment, discomfort, a perceived unsightly appearance, and cost (Thompson & Rivara, 1996). Individuals who work with in-line skaters should make every attempt to help participants overcome these barriers, because one thing is clear— protective equipment significantly reduces the risk of injury.

OVERUSE INJURIES *Overuse injuries* are becoming more prevalent among America's young athletes. This should come as no surprise in light of the fact that young athletes are specializing in sports at earlier ages. Specialization generally entails intense, year-round involvement. In fact, it is not uncommon for young athletes to attend sport camps that require them to train from 4 to 6 hours per day. It has also been reported that in order to become a top junior tennis player, the young athlete must practice a minimum of 8 to 15 hours per week (Wild, 1992). Perhaps even more discouraging are reports that runners as young as 4 (Jeffers, 1980) and 6 years of age (Kozar & Lord, 1988) are successfully completing marathons.

Figure 15-3 Safety equipment significantly reduces in-line skating injuries.

Source: Lawrence M. Sawyer/Getty Images/PhotoDisc

Overuse injuries occur as a result of placing the child's muscular and skeletal system under repeated stress over long periods. "Ironically, there are child labor laws in many countries that forbid stereotype work movements and excessive loading (International Federation of Sports Medicine, 1991; Roberts, 1995), but these same restrictions do not apply to children's sports" (Ewing et al., 1996, p. 30). This class of injury should not be taken lightly, because if activity is not curtailed, permanent injury could result. In adults, overuse injuries generally involve bone (stress fractures), tendon (Achilles tendinitis), and fascia (plantar fasciitis). In children and adolescents, however, additional prone

structures include physes (growth plates), cartilage of the apophyses (a site where the tendon unites with the bone), and articular cartilage (Clain & Hershman, 1989). The two most prevalent traction apophyses include Osgood-Schlatter disease (insertion of the patellar tendon at the tibial tubercle) and Sever's disease (insertion of the Achilles tendon into the calcaneous). Both diseases are most prevalent in adolescence when skeletal growth exceeds soft-tissue elongation thus causing muscle tightness about the prone site (Clain & Hershman, 1989). For this reason, young athletes should be encouraged to stretch both before and after physical activity.

Overuse injuries involving bone can result in stress fractures. The offending culprit is often the result of an abrupt change in exercise frequency and intensity. Most often the injury site is either the lower extremity or the hip. This type of injury is being seen more frequently (Backx et al., 1991) and is difficult to diagnose without the use of sophisticated imagery (bone scan, etc.).

"Little League elbow" refers to a class of overuse injuries resulting from repeated forces being applied to the medial and lateral structures of the elbow (see Figure 15-4). Most often, the pain occurs on the elbow's medial side. As the name implies, this overuse injury is most prevalent in baseball pitchers (Gugenheim et al., 1976; Larson et al., 1976). This medical condition has led youth sport administrators to change and modify baseball rules in an attempt to protect the young athlete. Among the most important changes and modifications are the following: T-baseball, where the pitcher does not deliver the ball to the batter, is becoming more popular; some leagues no longer allow the pitcher to throw a curve ball; and most youth leagues now limit the number of innings per week that a youngster can pitch.

While Little League elbow was once the most frequently treated overuse injury among young athletes, physicians now report seeing a significant increase in another overuse injury—runner's knee (Micheli, 2000). This injury is caused by an inappropriate tracking of the kneecap during running.

Because stress injuries are caused by patterns of overuse, young children should be discouraged from

Figure 15-4　Repeated throwing stress can lead to Little League elbow—an overuse injury.

Source: PhotoLink/Getty Images/PhotoDisc

specializing in a particular sport during the childhood years. Instead, they should be encouraged to play several sports (AAP, 2000c) and even different positions within a selected sport. This way, the child is less likely to overuse a specific body part.

ARE YOUTH SPORT INJURIES AVOIDABLE?　A major challenge for organizers of youth programs is to devise methods and procedures that will curtail the number of youth sport injuries. Organizers of children's sport programs need to answer two major questions: (1) Are children's sport injuries avoidable? If they are, (2) what steps can be taken to ensure a safer and healthier environment?

Although research on children's sport-related injuries is in its infancy, initial findings suggest that many injuries are avoidable. In one study, Goldberg and colleagues (1979) found that 32 of 51 sport-related injuries could have been avoided if proper precautions had been taken. These precautions include (1) wearing properly fitting safety equipment, (2) avoiding play on wet fields where footing is poor, and (3) avoiding excessive repeated movements such as those described in the section on overuse injuries. Other experts believe that the number of injuries can be reduced if coaches are more attuned to the youngsters' physical and emotional state. For example, Williams (1980) found that children forced to participate in sports experience a higher rate of injury when compared with children who want to participate. Furthermore, because many injuries occur late in a game or practice session, coaches should be aware of their players' state of fatigue.

The literature also suggests that special precautions should be taken when working with young girls of all ages and young boys 11 to 13 years old, because these two populations appear to be at the greatest risk for injury. To reduce injuries, consider the points addressed in Table 15-10.

YOUNG ATHLETES' NUTRITIONAL REQUIREMENTS　The young athlete's nutritional requirements are essentially the same as those of any active child. The child's appetite should dictate caloric need. In general, parents should provide well-balanced meals, being sure to serve appropriate portions from the food pyramid. Unfortunately, problems arise when parents alter children's diets in an attempt to give their child a competitive edge. For example, because certain sports are organized according to weight, such as wrestling and youth football, some children have been placed on diets, even periods of fasting, so that they can compete in a lower weight class. This practice should be avoided for reasons described shortly.

Another nutritional concern is the use of dietary supplements, especially vitamins. Generally the body excretes any excess vitamins, but some vitamins are not readily excreted and can accumulate in toxic

Table 15-10   Factors to Be Considered in the Prevention of Injuries

1. Make sure young athletes have been properly conditioned prior to competing.
2. Avoid overtraining.
3. Provide qualified adult supervision.
4. Change rules to create a safer environment.
5. Require the use of appropriate safety equipment.
6. Match competitors according to body size and body weight (biological age as opposed to only chronological age or grade level).
7. Do not allow an injured child to return to competition until the area of injury has been completely rehabilitated.
8. Do not allow children to partake in questionable practices designed to create a competitive edge — i.e., rapid weight reduction to qualify for a lower weight class, steroid use, etc.
9. Use coaches who have obtained certification. These coaches tend to have a better understanding of children's growth and development characteristics and are generally more capable of teaching appropriate skill technique.

levels; vitamins A and E are two vitamins that can be harmful when taken in very large doses. Nathan Smith, a well-noted pediatrician, recently reported five cases of vitamin A poisoning. In one case, parents of a young tennis player who had experienced vitamin A poisoning repeatedly kept putting the child back on the vitamin (Barnes, 1979), believing that large doses of this vitamin would give their child a competitive advantage. Vitamin supplements are *not* necessary when the young athlete is eating balanced meals.

MAKING WEIGHT Several youth sports match teams for competition on the basis of body weight. The primary intent of using this method is to better ensure the safety of those involved and provide a well-balanced competitive athletic contest. Despite this positive intention, some adults have used unacceptable practices to give their child a competitive

edge. One such negative practice is using unacceptable means to reduce the child's body weight so the child can compete in a lower weight class. The most widely used approach is depleting the body of its water content by having the child exercise in a sauna; not letting the young athlete drink water, even to the extent of requiring the child to spit into a cup instead of swallowing; administering diuretics; and requiring the child to exercise while wearing a rubber suit. Reducing body weight through rapid dehydration is extremely dangerous and should never be done. Without adequate body fluids (water), the cells, kidneys, blood, and sweating mechanisms cannot function properly. A 3 percent weight loss of body fluids can decrease physical performance; a 5 percent loss can cause apparent signs of heat exhaustion; a 7 percent loss can cause hallucinations; a 10 percent loss can lead to heat stroke and circulatory collapse.

The young athlete also should not be encouraged to fast. Fasting withholds vital substances needed to ensure proper growth during these formative years. When fasting is carried too far, death can result. A case in point is the story of Christy Henrich. This young gymnast was told by a judge that if she failed to lose body weight she would never make the Olympic team. At this time, the 15-year-old was only 4 feet 11 inches and weighed 90 pounds. Christy basically stopped eating and 6 years later died of multiple organ failure, weighing less than 60 pounds (Ryan, 1995, as cited in Ewing et al., 1996). In short, coaches must address issues of body weight quite cautiously. When in doubt, they should refer the young athlete to a physician, especially if they suspect an eating disorder.

Psychological Issues

Critics of youth sports frequently express concern regarding the young athlete's ability to handle stressful situations. Limited amounts of stress have been shown to improve motor performance, but critics believe that too much competitive stress can lead to a multitude of negative behavioral, psychological, and even health-related outcomes. Are our young athletes being exposed to too much competitive stress? If so,

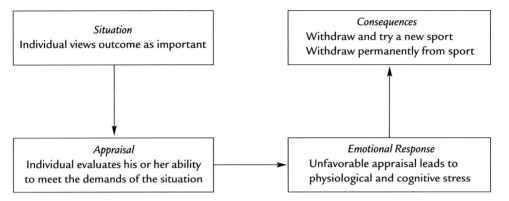

Figure 15-5   Model depicting the development of stress and potential behavioral outcomes

what are the outcomes of this competitive stress? Furthermore, if too much stress is present, how can it be reduced?

Before answering these important questions, we first define what we mean by the term ***stress.*** Stress is generally viewed as an unpleasant emotional state. Passer (1982) has developed a four-stage model that precisely illustrates how this unpleasant state is evoked (see Figure 15-5). The four stages are situation, appraisal, emotional response, and consequences. First, the stress process is evoked whenever a person is placed in a demanding situation and the person views the outcome of the situation as being important. Second, the person appraises the situation in an attempt to determine if he or she can meet its demands. A young boy may become threatened and feel anxious before the start of an athletic contest, because he wants to perform well but is not sure that he has the motor skills necessary for success. Third, whenever a person is threatened, emotional responses become evident. According to Passer, these emotional responses are made up of not only physiological components but also cognitive-attentional components. For instance, the boy may become so preoccupied with worrying about the outcome of performance that he does not pay attention to important task-related cues that are necessary for successful performance. Passer's fourth and final stage, consequences, brings us back to one of our original questions: What are the outcomes of competitive stress? As mentioned previously, when

sport participation loses its appeal, children frequently either withdraw from the disliked activity to pursue a more enjoyable activity or, in some cases, withdraw permanently from sports.

STRESS—ANOTHER VIEWPOINT   Proponents of youth sport programs do not argue with the fact that excessive stress is not beneficial. However, they do argue that youth sport participation is by no means the only stressful situation young people encounter in their lives. The proponents' view is best supported by Simon and Martens's work (1979). These two researchers examined the level of precompetitive ***state anxiety*** among 468 boys who took part in various youth sport programs and 281 boys who competed in other achievement-oriented activities, including a softball game played in a physical education class, a general school test, group competition within a band, and a band solo competition. As illustrated in Figure 15-6, the researchers found the greatest amount of precompetitive state anxiety among the band solo contestants. Furthermore, among the 11 sport and nonsport activities examined in the study, state anxiety was greatest in the individual activities. Passer writes, "This is somewhat ironic because the popular media and youth sport critics typically focus on team sports when discussing or illustrating the stressful nature of athletic competition" (1982, p. 167). In fact, on average, participating in team sports was no more stressful than taking a paper and pencil test.

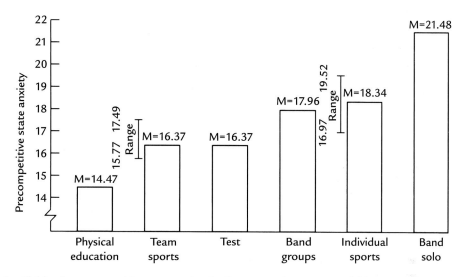

Figure 15-6 Children's precompetitive state anxiety in 11 sport and nonsport activities. The precompetitive state anxiety scale ranges from 10 to 30. "Team sports" include football, hockey, baseball, and basketball, while "individual sports" include swimming, gymnastics, and wrestling.

SOURCE: Adapted from Simon and Martens (1979).

REDUCING COMPETITIVE STRESS Undoubtedly, children will experience varying degrees of stress from participation in sports. However, steps can be taken to reduce the likelihood of this stress becoming excessive. One key is to change something about the sport so that success will occur more frequently than failure. For example, in T-baseball, the offensive demand requiring that the baseball be struck off a stationary batting tee obviously increases the probability that the young athlete will not strike out. In fact, an investigation by Isaacs (1984) found a strikeout rate of only 4 percent among young T-baseball players. Furthermore, according to Isaacs (1981), children's basketball shooting performance can be improved by lowering the basketball goal and by using a smaller basketball. In short, when children experience a fair amount of success, they develop more self-confidence about their ability to meet the demands of their sport, and in turn they feel less threatened when confronted with the demands.

A second way to instill self-confidence and thus reduce stress is by skill training. Youth sport personnel, particularly coaches, should spend more of their practice time teaching motor skills and less time scrimmaging. Furthermore, when scrimmaging is incorporated, the focus should be to reduce performance uncertainty by practicing potential situations that may arise during a competitive contest. Coaches who adhere to these two practices are helping their young players develop self-confidence in their ability not only to meet the physical demands of the sport but also to handle efficiently most situations that may occur during competitive play. Anxiety is reduced whenever the uncertainty surrounding an event is removed or reduced. Furthermore, research indicates that children who perceive themselves as competent are less threatened and actually perform better during the contest (Feltz, 1984). Thus, it is essential that the coach help the players develop an attitude of "I can do it."

To further reduce competitive stress, the outcome of the contest (winning or losing) should be placed into perspective. There should not be too much emphasis on winning the game. Recall that the stress process is evoked when the participant views the outcome of the situation as important. To a degree, when there is an increase in the importance of the outcome, there is also an accompanying increase in stress. Thus, other influential people can help young athletes by not overemphasizing winning. For instance, some young children may feel that they have disappointed their parents or coach if they have not played well. This is wrong. Parents and coaches should make it clear that the outcome of an athletic contest in no way affects their love of the child.

Finally, self-imposed stress can be reduced by helping each child set realistic goals. Realistic goals are those that motivate the young athlete to do his or her personal best and to recognize self-limitations (Martens et al., 1981). Some children set their performance goals so high that they are impossible to achieve. To keep this from happening, before the season begins, each participant should write out what she or he wants to accomplish in the upcoming season (Paulson, 1980). These objectives should focus primarily on individual improvement, not team performance. For example, one child may want to improve her batting average by 20 points over last year's average or perhaps commit five fewer errors. If team objectives are established, they should be general, such as "We'll score 15 more runs this season than we did last season." When realistic goals are established at the beginning of the season, children can still feel like winners regardless of their team's win/loss record. According to Paulson, the term *winning* needs to be redefined. "Instead of requiring that it involve beating someone else, the new definition of winning focuses on the learning and improvement an individual or team experiences in a season" (1980, p. 25).

YOUTH SPORT COACHING

Without a doubt, a youth sport program is only as good as its adult leaders. With appropriate leadership, the youth sport experience can significantly foster young children's growth and development. In this section, we examine more closely the coaching profession, paying particular attention to volunteer coaches. In addition, we address the controversial issue regarding the education and certification of coaches. Finally, guidelines for effective coaching are explored.

Who's Coaching Our Children?

Of the approximate 3.5 million coaches in the United States, about 2.5 million are volunteers (Weiss & Hayashi, 1996). While they should be commended, as many as 90 percent of these volunteers lack the necessary formal preparation to coach (Ewing et al., 1996). A question follows: Even without appropriate training, what motivates so many individuals to give their valuable time and energy to serve in this voluntary role? Researchers from the United States and Canada have attempted to design studies to shed light on this question. For example, in one Canadian study, volunteer coaches indicated that the most important reasons for their involvement included personal enjoyment, skill development of players, character development of players, and personal challenge (Hansen & Gauthier, 1988). However, some individuals involved with this Canadian study believe that an even stronger motivator was the involvement of the coach's child in the league. Indeed, 54 percent of the Canadian coaches surveyed had one or two children participating in the hockey league in which they coached. Similar trends have been reported in the United States.

Also of concern is the ratio of female-to-male coaches. In fact, one large-scale study found that 9 out of 10 youth sport coaches are men and that only half of female teams are coached by women (*Michigan Joint Legislative Study on Youth Sports*, 1978). Obviously, we need to find ways to attract more women to coaching. Ewing and colleagues (1996) speculated as to the reason why so few women volunteer to coach, particularly when such large numbers of girls now participate in interscholastic and intercollegiate sports. More specifically, they wrote,

> Societal factors may contribute to this imbalance, nearly one-half of America's young children are raised in one-parent families, most frequently by the mother. The burdens of a single parent

may be so overwhelming that the additional time needed to coach a team may be out of the question. (Ewing et al., 1996, p. 110)

Finally, safety issues arise concerning "who's coaching our kids." Parents and youth organizations need to take a more active role in screening all potential youth sport coaches, even volunteer coaches, prior to allowing these individuals to work with young children. Unfortunately, we are living in a time in which some criminals and child sex offenders use the avenue of youth sport coaching as a means of preying on young children. Fortunately, organizations now exist that are capable of quickly running criminal background checks on potential youth sport coaches. One such organization, "Safe on First," has received endorsements from such well-noted entities as the National Child Identification Program and the North American Youth Sports Institute. Safe on First is a national screening program for all youth organizations. For a small fee (about $25) a youth organization can obtain instantaneous results on criminal background checks that include a social security database search, a department of corrections database search, a search of the sex offender registry, and a search of county court records, including a search for pending charges. (To learn more about Safe on First, consult www.safeonfirst.com.)

An Increasing Need for Educating Coaches

Attempting to provide educational training to the 3.5 million coaches and particularly the 2.5 million volunteer coaches, who are mostly parents, is quite challenging. This endeavor is greatly magnified when one considers that this volunteer pool of coaches has an annual turnover rate of approximately 50 percent (Partlow, 1995). Nevertheless, Ewing and colleagues (1996) have identified three recent developments that may increase the demand for coaching education and certification.

First, we have seen a rise in the number of lawsuits directed toward youth sport coaches and organizations because of alleged negligence during practices and games. As a result, some youth sport organizations now demand that their coaches ob-

tain certification. Education and certification may offer some degree of legal protection for the sponsoring organizations. Conn and Razor (1989) argue rightly that school and youth organization administrators have both a legal and a moral responsibility to ensure that those who work with youth are qualified to do so. When unqualified individuals serve as coaches, the likelihood of litigation significantly increases. Only in those states that have established criteria for coaches has the number of injuries and subsequent lawsuits decreased (Conn & Razor, 1989).

Second, the National Standards for Athletic Coaches has recently been established (National Association for Sport and Physical Education [NASPE], 1995). Some believe these standards will change the perception and level of competence associated with youth sport coaching. These standards address eight domains: injury care and prevention; risk management; knowledge of growth and development; training, conditioning, and nutrition; the social/psychological aspects of coaching; skills, tactics, and strategies; teaching and administration; and professional preparation and development.* These standards have now been endorsed by over 140 sport organizations (NASPE, 2000).

Third, technological advances now allow educators to reach more potential youth sport coaches, who can obtain coaching education and certification online. With Americans purchasing more home computers, this service should remove many of the barriers to obtaining information and certification. Online youth sport coaching certification programs such as the one offered by the North American Youth Sport Institute (www.naysi.com) allow people to receive coaching certification through a self-paced course of instruction in their own home. This nontraditional instructional medium will likely become quite popular. However, in the coming years, researchers must also scientifically examine the effectiveness of obtaining coaching certification through online services.

*These standards are available from the National Association for Sports and Physical Education at (800) 213-7193 or www.aahperd.org/naspe.

Current Coaching Certification Programs

A growing number of organizations have been developed for the purpose of providing educational programs to prospective coaches. Graduates of these educational programs have learned how to teach motor skills to children, organize a practice, physically train children, prevent and recognize sport injuries, and communicate with and motivate young athletes. Educational information is generally conveyed through videotapes, printed materials, small-group discussions, lectures, and most recently through the Internet. The organizational names, addresses, phone numbers, and Web sites for seven of these organizations are presented in Table 15-11. Each site contains a wealth of information of interest to anyone desiring to foster the development of children and youth through youth sport participation.

Along with the increase in the number of organizations now offering coaching certification comes the need for program oversight. As a means for providing this oversight, the National Council for Accreditation in Coaching Education (NCACE) was established during its inaugural meeting held July 14–16, 2000. Facilitated by the National Association for Sport and Physical Education and the University of Southern Mississippi, this council is the first ever to be organized for the purpose of reviewing coaching education/certification programs for those organizations seeking accreditation. Accreditation standards will be based on the Guidelines for Coaching Education and the National Standards for Athletic Coaches (NASPE, 2000).

Arguments Against Mandatory Coaching Certification

As mentioned earlier, the number of children participating in both interscholastic and community/agency-sponsored youth sport programs has greatly increased. Unfortunately, this positive trend in participation has its downside. With increased participation comes a need to increase sport offerings. This in turn creates a greater demand for coaches.

Table 15-11   Organizations Dedicated to the Advancement of Knowledge Through Coaching Certification

American Sport Education Program
Box 5076
Champaign, IL 61820
(800) 747-5698
www.asep.com

Coaching Association of Canada
141 Laurier Ave. West
Suite 300
Ottawa, Ontario K1P 5J3
(613) 235-5000
www.coach.ca

National Alliance for Youth Sports
2050 Vista Parkway
West Palm Beach, FL 33411
(800) 729-2057
www.nays.org

National Association for Sports and Physical Education
1900 Association Drive
Reston, VA 20191
(800) 213-7193
www.aahperd.org/naspe

National Federation of State High School Associations
11724 N.W. Plaza Circle
Kansas City, MO 64153
(816) 464-5400
www.nfshsa.org

North American Youth Sports Institute
A Division of Paradox Group, Ltd.
4985 Oak Garden Drive
Kernersville, NC 27284-9520
(800) 767-4916
www.naysi.com

Youth Sports Institute — Michigan State University
213 IM Sports Circle Building
East Lansing, MI 48824-1049
(517) 353-6689
http://ed-web3.educ.msu.edu/ysi

In short, the demand for coaches now exceeds supply. Those who argue against mandatory coaching certification express concern that making certification mandatory would subsequently cause many volunteers to withdraw their service, thus creating a further shortage of coaches. Consequently, many youth sport programs might have to be eliminated. Others argue that to require coaching certification would be too expensive. In turn, this financial burden could force some youth sport leagues to fold. Lopiano (1986) argues that this view is shortsighted and analogous to saying that one technique of reducing the high cost of medical care would be to eliminate certification of doctors and hospitals.

Evaluating Coaching Effectiveness

Player–coach interactions can significantly influence the lives of children. In essence, the coach serves as a role model affecting not only the child's skill development but also his or her attitudes and values. For this reason, youth sport coaches need to have a better understanding of their impact on the young athlete. To this end, researchers from the University of Washington, Seattle, developed the *Coaching Behavioral Assessment System (CBAS)* (Smith, Smoll, & Hunt, 1977). This behavioral assessment instrument is designed to evaluate the behaviors of coaches in an actual game setting. Briefly, the instrument is used to assess two classes of behaviors: reactive behaviors and spontaneous behaviors. Reactive behaviors are the coach's reactions to player behaviors such as desirable performance, mistakes, and misbehaviors, while spontaneous behaviors are game-related or game-irrelevant behaviors initiated by the coach.

To use the CBAS, unannounced observers using a time-sampling procedure code the behaviors of the coach being observed. Analysis of raw data can include percentage of behaviors across all game observations or the rate of behaviors falling in each category per unit of time. The developers of the instrument suggest using the percentage measure when studying baseball coaches and the rate per unit of time measure when studying basketball coaches (Smoll & Smith, 1984).

Guidelines for Effective Coaching

Research results acquired through studies using the CBAS have proven instrumental in the development of behavioral guidelines for coaches' interactions with players. Not only are these guidelines useful to the coach, but parents of prospective young athletes can also use them as a screening device for selecting the best coach to work with their child. These behavioral guidelines are presented in Table 15-12.

PARENTAL EDUCATION: AN ATTEMPT TO CURB VIOLENCE

As described in the preceding sections, the past 20 years have witnessed much discussion and debate over the education and certification of youth coaches. Only recently has the attention shifted toward the debate over the necessity of educating parents of youth sport participants. This shift in attention has come about because of the significant increase in violent behavior that is now plaguing many youth sport programs. Take for example the 34-year-old mother who attacked a 15-year-old soccer referee because she was infuriated with him regarding her 11-year-old son's soccer game (North American Youth Sports Institute [NAYSI], 2000a). Most tragic, an all-time low was reached in August 2000 when a Massachusetts volunteer coach was beaten to death by a parent, in front of the coach's own children, following a youth ice hockey contest for 10-year-olds.

As a result of these escalating acts of violence, an increasing number of youth sport programs are requiring parental education. The primary role of this education is to provide sportsmanship training that outlines parental roles and responsibilities and clearly explains acceptable and unacceptable parental behavior. One such parental program that has received a lot of attention is the Parents Association for Youth Sports, also known as PAYS (NAYSI, 2000b). In February 2000, the Jupiter Tequesta Athletic Association (JTAA) became the first youth sport organization to mandate parental training (NAYSI, 2000b). The JTAA's view is simple:

Table 15-12   Guidelines to Enhance the Youth Sport Experience

1. Coaches' healthy philosophy of winning:
   a. Convey that winning is neither everything nor the only thing.
   b. Do not view losing a game as failing.
   c. Do not equate winning with success.
   d. Convey to children that success is found in the striving to do one's best.
2. Coaches' reactions to desirable behaviors:
   a. Be generous with positive reinforcement.
   b. Have realistic expectations of performance.
   c. Reinforce desired behaviors as quickly as possible.
   d. Reinforce effort as frequently as performance results.
3. Coaches' reactions to mistakes:
   a. Give encouragement.
   b. Give corrective instruction in a positive manner—but only if you suspect the player is not aware of the corrective information.
   c. Never punish a child for making a technical mistake.
   d. Never administer corrective instruction in a hostile manner.
4. Coaches' reactions to misbehaviors, lack of attention, and maintaining discipline:
   a. Establish team rules that are clearly understood by all.
   b. Allow player involvement in the establishment and enforcement of team rules.
   c. During the game, make sure players understand that all members are a part of the team, even those on the bench.
5. Coaches' behaviors:
   a. Set a good example as an adult role model.
   b. Encourage and reinforce both effort and progress.
   c. Encourage players to be supportive of one another and reinforce such behaviors.
   d. Always convey instruction in a positive manner.
   e. Always be patient and never expect more than a maximum effort from your athletes.
   f. Be an effective communicator.

SOURCE: Adapted from Smoll and Smith (1984).

Table 15-13   Bill of Rights for Young Athletes

1. Right of the opportunity to participate in sports regardless of ability level
2. Right to participate at a level that is commensurate with each child's developmental level
3. Right to have qualified adult leadership
4. Right to participate in safe and healthy environments
5. Right of each child to share in the leadership and decision making of his or her sport participation
6. Right to play as a child and not as an adult
7. Right to proper preparation for participation in the sport
8. Right to an equal opportunity to strive for success
9. Right to be treated with dignity by all involved
10. Right to have fun through sport

SOURCE: Thomas (1977).

In order for a child to participate in a youth sport activity, his or her parents must become a member of PAYS and attend a 30-minute training session—no exceptions. In the first 6 months following the initiation of this policy by JTAA, more than 175 other communities implemented the PAYS program (NAYSI, 2000a).

RIGHTS OF YOUNG ATHLETES

Throughout this chapter we have described and recommended various ways in which the youth sport experience can be enhanced so that all involved may experience the joy of sport to its fullest. To this end, we recommend that all youth sport leaders ascribe and uphold the principles outlined in Table 15-13. This document, ***Bill of Rights for Young Athletes,*** was written to protect young athletes from adult exploitation (Thomas, 1977).

In a further attempt to protect young athletes, various organizations have developed position statements regarding recommended practices for children's athletic endeavors. See Table 15-14 for a list of such practices.

Table 15-14   Pronouncements of Professional Organizations Regarding Youth Sports

Organization	Year	Title	Purpose/Focus
American Academy of Pediatrics	2001a	Organized Sports for Children and Preadolescents	Lists the safeguards that should accompany children's sports
American Academy of Pediatrics	2000a	Climatic Heat Stress and the Exercising Child	Documents the special problems of children when exercising in a hot and humid environment
American Academy of Pediatrics	2000d	Medical Concerns in the Female Athlete	Lists concerns relative to eating disorders, menstrual dysfunction, decreased bone and mineral density. Also describes clinical evaluation and treatments.
American Academy of Pediatrics	1988	Recommendations for Participation in Competitive Sports	Lists medical conditions that would disqualify children from athletic competition
American Academy of Pediatrics	1983	Weight Training and Weight Lifting: Information for the Pediatrician	Presents a conservative assessment of the benefits and risks of weight lifting and weight training
American Academy of Pediatrics	1982	Risks of Long-Distance Running for Children	Provides guidelines for involving children in long-distance running
American Academy of Pediatrics	1981a	Competitive Sports for Children of Elementary School Age	Updates their position statement of 1968
American Academy of Pediatrics	1981b	Injuries to Young Athletes	Presents the special problems of young athletes in competitive sports
American Academy of Pediatrics	1973	Athletic Activities for Children with Skeletal Abnormalities	Outlines the conditions under which children with specific conditions can and should not be involved in athletics
American College of Sports Medicine	1996	Exercise and Fluid Replacement	Reviews the effects of dehydration and hydration on human performance
American College of Sports Medicine and American College of Cardiology	1994	Recommendations for Determining Eligibility for Competition in Athletes with Cardiovascular Abnormalities	Provides an extensive set of papers that review the various abnormalities and makes recommendations to physicians
American College of Sports Medicine	1993	The Prevention of Sports Injuries of Children and Adolescents	Suggests that 50 percent of current injuries could be prevented with proper techniques
American College of Sports Medicine	1984	The Use of Anabolic-Androgenic Steroids in Sports	Documents the adverse effects of anabolic x steroids on the human body
American College of Sports Medicine	1982	The Use of Alcohol in Sports	Reviews the literature on the influence of alcohol on human performance
American College of Sports Medicine	1979	The Participation of the Female Athlete in Long-Distance Running	Documents that female athletes should not be denied opportunities for long-distance running

(continued)

Table 15-14 *(continued)*

Organization	Year	Title	Purpose/Focus
American College of Sports Medicine	1976	Weight Loss in Wrestlers	Warns of the dangers of personal health when excessive weight loss is incurred
American Heart Association	1986	Coronary Risk Factor Modification in Children: Exercise	Reviews ways to combat the sedentary lifestyles of children
International Federation of Sports Medicine	1991	Excessive Physical Training in Children and Adolescents	Provides guidelines and examples of activities that are to be avoided in children's training for athletic competition
Michigan Governor's Council on Physical Fitness, Health and Sports	1995	The Importance of Physical Activity for Children and Youth (Pivarnik, 1995)	Provides the scientific basis for physical activity in childhood and adolescence; advocates policies for families, communities, public health, and schools
National Strength and Conditioning Association	1996	Youth Resistance Training: Position Statement Paper and Literature Review	Presents a position statement and a review of the literature

SOURCE: Adapted from President's Council on Physical Fitness and Sports (1997).

Table 15-15   Recommendations Regarding Sponsorship and Implementation of Youth Sport Programs

Children should be exposed to a broad array of sport opportunities during their elementary years.

When possible, youth should be exposed to sports that have potential for lifetime use.

Early childhood involvement in sports should emphasize instruction more than competition.

Sport programs must reevaluate their programs and institute equitable programs that will meet the needs of all youth.

Coaches must be encouraged to teach young athletes responsibility, independence, and leadership so that they are better prepared for everyday life.

Sport organizations can provide an alternative to gang membership and violence by providing opportunities for more youth to be involved and thereby benefit from being a member of a presocial team.

Sport organizations should make a commitment to increasing the number of women and minority coaches in youth sport programs.

Public policy makers must become educated about the significance of youth sports in the nonschool lives of youth. Dedicated revenues for sport programs are an uncommon, but necessary, means to avoid the fluctuations in funding by private and public funders.

Programs must be designed so that they revitalize communities as partners in the delivery of sport programs.

(continued)

Table 15-15   *(continued)*

Communities must improve the condition and maintenance of facilities and sites so that they are attractive and safe for children and families.

A broad-based organization that unites the public/private sector of a city should be established to plan, develop, coordinate, maintain, and evaluate the municipality's comprehensive youth sport program.

Sport organizations should provide educational programs for all coaches of youth sport teams.

Sport organizations should provide education to parents about the roles of parents of youth sport participants, the use of appropriate feedback, and the positive and potentially negative aspects of participation in sports.

You can obtain a copy of the conference report, "The Role of Sports in Youth Development," by writing the Carnegie Corporation of New York, 437 Madison Ave., New York, NY 10022 or by calling (212) 371-3200.

SOURCE: President's Council on Physical Fitness and Sports (1997).

YOUTH SPORTS: ENTERING THE TWENTY-FIRST CENTURY

On March 18, 1996, a conference sponsored by the Carnegie Corporation of New York drew over 40 scholars from across the United States for the purpose of exploring the role that youth sports play in fostering many aspects of human development (Poinsett, 1996). At the conclusion of this meeting, participants generated 13 recommendations regarding the sponsorship and implementation of youth sport programs. These recommendations, presented in Table 15-15, should enhance the likelihood that youth sports will meet the needs of all children, regardless of age, gender, ethnicity, or ability.

SUMMARY

The number of young athletes participating in organized youth sport programs continues to grow for several reasons: greater participation at younger ages, greater female involvement, greater involvement in nontraditional activities, and greater participation by disabled individuals.

Children participate in sports for many reasons, but the most often cited reason is "to have fun." Researchers consistently find that children participate for intrinsic reasons (e.g., fun, to be part of a group) not extrinsic reasons (e.g., trophies).

Contrary to popular belief, most youth sport injuries are minor—primarily simple contusions, sprains, and strains. In general, girls tend to be at greater risk of injury than boys; this difference in rate of injury has been attributed to the young girls' lower level of skill and training. In an attempt to reduce the number of youth sport injuries, authorities agree that young children should be encouraged to play many different sports during their formative years. Children who do specialize in one activity year-round tend to be at greater risk for obtaining a stress or overuse injury. When special precautions are taken, many sport injuries are avoidable.

The nutritional requirements for a young athlete are the same as for any active child. Furthermore, dietary supplements such as vitamins do not give the young athlete a competitive edge.

Some experts believe that competitive stress is the agent that causes children to discontinue sport participation at an increasingly early age. However, proponents of youth sport programs point out that activities other than sports produce stress in the lives of young children. Nevertheless, both critics and proponents of youth sport programs agree that steps can be taken to ensure that the amount of stress young children encounter during sport participation is reduced. Each revolves around one central theme: Improve the child's self-confidence concerning ability to meet the demands of the selected sport.

Most youth sport coaches are in a program because of their son's or daughter's involvement in the same program. Unfortunately, most of these coaches do not have the appropriate training to foster an optimal youth sport experience. Within recent years, several organizations have been formed to provide coaching education for volunteer coaches. The Internet may make coaching education easier and more effective, though researchers will need to evaluate this new medium.

Because of an increase in violence, many programs are now requiring parental education. This training is designed to teach parents about sportsmanship and unacceptable behaviors. One such training program is the Parents Association for Youth Sports.

KEY TERMS

Bill of Rights for Young Athletes
Coaching Behavioral Assessment
  System (CBAS)
commotio cordis

competence motivation theory
contact/collision sport
limited contact/impact sport
overuse injuries

spearing
state anxiety
stress

QUESTIONS FOR REFLECTION

1. What are the five categories of youth sports? Rank them by number of participants.

2. What are the reasons for increased enrollment in youth sport programs?

3. What (in order) are the 10 most important reasons children participate in sports?

4. What (in order) are the 11 most important reasons given by children as to why they drop out of youth sport activities? In addition, what changes would both boys and girls want to see before returning to a sport that they had previously dropped?

5. What medical issues are associated with each of the following: football, baseball, soccer, downhill skiing, and in-line skating? Regarding football, which positions appear to be the most dangerous

and what changes could be made to reduce these sport-specific injuries?

6. What are the typical overuse injuries witnessed in youth sport participants?

7. What steps can be taken to reduce competitive stress within the youth sport environment?

8. What are the arguments both for and against mandatory coaching certification as well as for and against mandatory education for parents?

9. Can you describe a technique for evaluating coaching effectiveness?

10. Can you describe the Bill of Rights for Young Athletes?

11. Can you identify key professional organizations that have published pronouncements regarding youth sports participation?

INTERNET RESOURCES

American Sport Education Program **www.asep.com**
Coach Jerry **www.coachjerry.com**

Coaching Association of Canada **www.coach.ca**
International In-Line Skating Association **www.ilsa.org**

National Alliance for Youth Sports **www.nays.org**

National Association for Sports and Physical Education
www.aahperd.org/naspe

National Eating Disorders
www.nationaleatingdisorders.org

National Federation of State High School Associations
www.nfshsa.org

North American Youth Sports Institute **www.naysi.com**

Safe on First—Background Checks on Coaches
www.safeonfirst.com

Sports Parents **sportsparents.com/index.html**

Youth Sports Institute—Michigan State University
ed-web3.educ.msu.edu/ysi

ONLINE LEARNING CENTER (www.mhhe.com/payne6e)

Visit the *Human Motor Development* Online Learning Center for study aids and additional resources. You can use the study guide questions and key terms puzzles to review key terms and concepts for this chapter and to prepare for exams. You can further extend your knowledge of motor development by checking out the Web links, articles, and activities found on the site.

REFERENCES

American Academy of Pediatrics. (1973). Athletic activities for children with skeletal abnormalities. *Pediatrics, 51,* 949–951.

———. (1981a). Competitive sports for children of elementary school age. *Physician and Sportsmedicine, 9,* 140–142.

———. (1981b). Injuries to young athletes. *Physician and Sportsmedicine, 9,* 107–110.

———. (1982). Risks of long-distance running for children. *Pediatric News and Comment, 33,* 11.

———. (1983). Weight training and weight lifting: Information for the pediatrician. *Physician and Sportsmedicine, 11,* 157–162.

———. (1988). Recommendations for participation in competitive sports. *Pediatrics, 81,* 737–739.

———. (2000a). Climatic heat stress and the exercising child. *Pediatrics, 106,* 158–159.

———. (2000b). Injuries in youth soccer: A subject review (RE9934). *Pediatrics, 105(3),* 659–661.

———. (2000c). Intensive training and sports specialization in young athletes (RE9906). *Pediatrics, 106,* 154–157.

———. (2000d). Medical concerns in the female athlete. *Pediatrics, 106,* 610–613.

———. (2001a). Organized sports for children and preadolescents (RE0052). *Pediatrics, 107,* 1459–1462.

———. (2001b). Risk of injury from baseball and softball in children (RE0032). *Pediatrics, 107,* 782–784.

American College of Sports Medicine. (1976). Weight loss in wrestlers. *Medicine and Science in Sports and Exercise, 8,* 11–13.

———. (1979). The participation of the female athlete in long-distance running. *Medicine and Science in Sports and Exercise, 11,* ix–xi.

———. (1982). The use of alcohol in sports. *Medicine and Science in Sports and Exercise, 14,* ix–xi.

———. (1984). The use of anabolic-androgenic steroids in sports. *Sports Medicine Bulletin,* pp. 13–18.

———. (1993). The prevention of sports injuries of children and adolescents. *Medicine and Science in Exercise and Sports, 25,* S1–S7.

———. (1996). Exercise and fluid replacement. *Medicine and Science in Exercise and Sports, 28,* i–vii.

American College of Sports Medicine and American College of Cardiology. (1994). Recommendations for determining eligibility for competition in athletes with cardiovascular abnormalities. *Medicine and Science in Exercise and Sports, 26,* S223–S283.

American Heart Association. (1986). Coronary risk factor modification in children: Exercise. *Circulation, 74,* 1189A–1191A.

Athletic Footwear Association. (1990). *American youth and sports participation.* North Palm Beach, FL: Athletic Footwear Association.

Backx, F., Beijer, H., Bol, E., & Erick, W. (1991). Injuries in high-risk persons and high-risk sports: A longitudinal study of 1818 school children. *American Journal of Sports Medicine, 19,* 124–130.

Barnes, L. (1979). Preadolescent training: How young is too young? *Physician and Sportsmedicine, 10,* 114–119.

Bir, C. A., Cassatta, S. J., & Janda, D. H. (1995). An analysis and comparison of soccer shin guards. *Clinical Journal of Sports Medicine, 5,* 95–99.

Blitzer, C. M., Johnson, R. J., Ettlinger, C. F., & Aggebor, K. (1984). Downhill skiing injuries in children. *American Journal of Sports Medicine, 12,* 142–147.

Clain, M. R., & Hershman, E. B. (1989). Overuse injuries in children and adolescents. *Physician and Sportsmedicine, 17,* 111–123.

Coakley, J. (1986). When should children begin competing? A sociological perspective. In M. R. Weiss & D. Gould (Eds.), *Sport for children and youths.* Champaign, IL: Human Kinetics.

Conn, J., & Razor, J. (1989). Certification of coaches—a legal and moral responsibility. *Physical Educator, 46,* 161–165.

Dishman, R. K. (1989). Exercise and sport psychology in youth 6 to 18 years of age. In C. V. Gisolfi & D. R. Lamb (Eds.), *Perspectives in exercise science and sports medicine: Youth, exercise, and sport.* Indianapolis, IN: Benchmark.

Ewing, M. E., Seefeldt, V. D., & Brown, T. P. (1996, Mar. 18). Role of organized sports in the education and health of American children and youth. In A. Poinsett (Ed.), *The role of sports in youth development.* Meeting convened by the Carnegie Corporation of New York, New York, NY.

Feltz, D. (1984). Competence motivation in youth sports. Paper presented at the meeting of the Olympic Scientific Congress, Eugene, OR.

Feltz, D. L., & Petlichkoff, L. (1983). Perceived competence among interscholastic sport participants and dropouts. *Canadian Journal of Applied Sport Sciences, 8,* 231–235.

Galton, L. (1980). *Your child in sports.* New York: Franklin Watts.

Garrick, J. G., & Requa, R. K. (1979). Injury patterns of children and adolescent skiers. *American Journal of Sports Medicine, 1,* 245–248.

Gill, D. L., Gross, J. B., & Huddleston, S. (1983). Participation motivation in youth sports. *International Journal of Sport Psychology, 14,* 1–14.

Goldberg, B., Rosenthal, P. P., Robertson, L. S., & Nicholas, J. A. (1988). Injuries in youth football. *Pediatrics, 81,* 255–261.

Goldberg, B., Whitman, P., Gleim, G., & Nicholas, J. (1979). Children's sports injuries: Are they avoidable? *Physician and Sportsmedicine, 7,* 93–97.

Gould, D. (1987). Understanding attrition in children's sport. In D. Gould & M. Weiss (Eds.), *Advances in pediatric sport sciences: Behavioral issues.* Champaign, IL: Human Kinetics.

Gould, D., Feltz, D., Horn, T., & Weiss, M. R. (1982). Reasons for discontinuing involvement in competitive youth swimming. *Journal of Sport Behavior, 5,* 155–165.

Gould, D., & Petlichkoff, L. (1988). Participation motivation and attrition in youth athletes. In F. L. Smoll, R. A. Magill, & M. J. Ash (Eds.), *Children in sport.* 3rd ed. Champaign, IL: Human Kinetics.

Gugenheim, J. J., Stanley, R. F., Woods, G. W., & Tullos, H. S. (1976). Little League survey: The Houston study. *American Journal of Sports Medicine, 4,* 189–200.

Hansen, H., & Gauthier, R. (1988). Reasons for involvement of Canadian hockey coaches in minor hockey. *Physical Educator, 45,* 147–153.

Harter, S. (1978). Effectance motivation reconsidered: Toward a developmental model. *Human Development, 21,* 34–64.

———. (1982). The Perceived Competence Scale for Children. *Child Development, 53,* 87–97.

———. (1988). Causes, correlates, and the functional role of global self-worth: A life-span perspective. In J. Kolligan & R. Sternberg (Eds.), *Perceptions of competence and incompetence across the life-span.* New Haven, CT: Yale University Press.

Heller, D. R., Routley, V., & Chambers, S. (1996). Roller-blading injuries in young people. *Journal of Paediatric and Child Health, 32,* 35–38.

Horn, T. S., & Hasbrook, C. A. (1987). Psychological characteristics and the criteria children use for self-evaluation. *Journal of Sport Psychology, 9,* 208–221.

Horn, T. S., & Weiss, M. R. (1991). A developmental analysis of children's self-ability judgments in the physical domain. *Pediatric Exercise Science, 3,* 310–326.

International Federation of Sports Medicine. (1991). Position statement: Excessive physical training of children and adolescents. *Clinical Journal of Sports Medicine, 1,* 262–264.

International In-Line Skating Association. (1992). *Guidelines for establishing in-line skate trails in parks and recreational areas.* Minneapolis, MN: International In-Line Skating Association.

Isaacs, L. D. (1981, Dec.). Factors affecting children's basketball shooting performance: A log-linear analysis. *Carnegie Research Papers,* pp. 29–32.

———. (1984). Players' success in T-baseball. *Perceptual and Motor Skills, 59,* 852–854.

Janda, D. H., Bir, C. A., & Cheney, A. L. (2002). An evaluation of the cumulative concussive effect of soccer heading in the youth population. *Injury Control and Safety Promotion, 9,* 25–31.

Jeffers, P. (1980, Feb.–Mar.). A marathon runner: Thoughts on children's running. *The Main Artery,* p. 2.

Jeziorski, R. M. (1994). *The importance of school sports in American education and socialization.* Lanham, MD: University Press of America.

Johnson, R. J., Ettlinger, C. F., Campbell, K. J., et al. (1980). Trends in skiing injuries: Analysis of a 6-year study (1972 to 1978). *American Journal of Sports Medicine, 8,* 106–113.

Kibler, W. B. (1993). Injuries in adolescent and preadolescent soccer players. *Medicine and Science in Sports and Exercise, 25,* 1330–1332.

Klint, K., & Weiss, M. R. (1986). Dropping in and dropping out: Participation motives of current and former youth gymnasts. *Canadian Journal of Applied Sport Sciences, 11,* 106–114.

Kozar, B., & Lord, R. H. (1988). Overuse injuries in young athletes: A "growing" problem. In F. L. Smoll, R. A. Magill, & M. J. Ash (Eds.), *Children in sport.* 3rd ed. Champaign, IL: Human Kinetics.

Kyle, S. B. (1996). *Youth baseball protective equipment project: Final report.* Washington, DC: U.S. Consumer Product Safety Commission.

Larson, R. L., Singer, K. M., Bergstrom, R., & Thomas, S. (1976). Little League survey: The Eugene study. *American Journal of Sports Medicine, 4,* 201–209.

LeUnes, A. D., & Nation, J. R. (1989). *Sports psychology: An introduction.* Chicago: Nelson-Hall.

Lopiano, D. (1986). The certified coach: A central figure. *Journal of Physical Education, Recreation, and Dance, 57*(3), 34–38.

Maron, B. J., Gohman, T. E., Kyle, S. B., Estes, N. A. M., & Link, M. S. (2002). Clinical profile and spectrum of commotio cordis. *Journal of the American Medical Association, 287,* 1142–1146.

Maron, B. J., Link, M. S., Wang, P. J., et al. (1999). Clinical profile of commotio cordis: An underappreciated cause of sudden death in the young during sports and other activities. *Journal of Cardiovascular Electrophysiology, 10,* 114–120.

Marshall, S. W., Mueller, F. O., Kirby, D. P., & Yang, J. (2003). Evaluation of safety balls and faceguards for prevention of injuries in youth baseball. *Journal of the American Medical Association, 289,* 568–574.

Martens, R. (1986). Youth sports in the U.S.A. In M. R. Weiss & D. Gould (Eds.), *Sport for children and youths.* Champaign, IL: Human Kinetics.

Martens, R., Christina, R. W., Harvey, J. S., & Sharkey, B. J. (1981). *Coaching young athletes.* Champaign, IL: Human Kinetics.

Micheli, L. J. (2000). *Overuse injuries: The new scourge of kids sports.* Retrieved September 12, 2000, from sportsparents.com/medical/overuse.html.

Michigan joint legislative study on youth sports. (1978). Lansing: State of Michigan.

National Association for Sport and Physical Education. (1995). *National standards for athletic coaches.* Reston, VA: National Association for Sport and Physical Education.

———. (2000, July 26). Quality coaching is goal of national council for accreditation of coaching education. (Press Release). Reston, VA: Author. Retrieved September 12, 2000, from www.aahperd.org/NASPE/whatsnew-press-ncace.html.

National Federation of State High School Associations. (2003). Athletics participation survey. Kansas City, MO: Author. Retrieved on September 13, 2003, from www.nfshsa.org.

National Strength and Conditioning Association. (1996). Youth resistance training: Position statement paper and literature review. *Strength and Conditioning, 18,* 62–75.

Nilsson, S., & Roaas, A. (1978). Soccer injuries in adolescents. *American Journal of Sports Medicine, 6,* 258–361.

North American Youth Sports Institute. (2000a). Alliance outlines strategy for recreation departments to curb violence. Kernersville, NC: Author. Retrieved September 13, 2000, from www.naysi.org/html%20folder/home.html.

———. (2000b). JTAA is the first youth sports organization to mandate parents training: An interview with the JTAA president, Mr. Jeff Leslie. Kernersville, NC: Author. Retrieved September 13, 2000, from www.nays.org/article/ paysart.html.

Orenstein, J. B. (1996). Injuries and small-wheel skates. *Annals of Emergency Medicine, 27,* 204–209.

Partlow, K. (1995). *Interscholastic coaching: From accidental occupation to profession.* Champaign, IL: American Sport Education Programs.

Passer, M. W. (1982). Psychological stress in youth sports. In R. A. Magill, M. J. Ash, & F. L. Smoll (Eds.), *Children in sport.* Champaign, IL: Human Kinetics.

Paulson, W. (1980). *Coaching cooperative youth sports: A values education approach.* La Grange, IL: Youth Sports Press.

Physician and Sportsmedicine. (1999). *Getting to the heart of the softer-baseball debate.* (News Briefs). Retrieved September 18, 2000, from physssportsmed.com/issues/1999/09_99/news.htm.

Pivarnik, J. (1995). *The importance of physical activity for children and youth.* Lansing, MI: Michigan Governor's Council on Physical Fitness, Health and Sports.

Poinsett, A. (1996). The role of sports in youth development. New York: Carnegie Corporation of New York.

President's Council on Physical Fitness and Sports. (1997). Youth sports in America: An overview. *President's Council on Physical Fitness and Sports Research Digest,* ser. 2, no. 11.

Roberts, G. C., Kleiber, D. A., & Duda, J. L. (1981). An analysis of motivation in children's sport: The role of perceived competence in participation. *Journal of Sport Psychology, 3,* 206–216.

Roberts, L. (1995). Child labour: A form of modern slavery. In *The way forward: Conference on human rights.* (pp. 35–42). Verbier, Switzerland.

Ryan, J. (1995). *Little girls in pretty boxes.* New York: Doubleday.

Sapp, M., & Haubenstricker, J. (1978). Motivation for joining and reasons for not continuing in youth sports programs in Michigan. Paper presented to the national convention of the American Alliance for Health, Physical Education, and Recreation, Kansas City, MO.

Schieber, R. A., Branche-Dorsey, C. M., & Ryan, G. W. (1994). Comparison of in-line skating injuries with rollerskating and skateboarding injuries. *Journal of the American Medical Association, 271,* 1856–1858.

Schieber, R. A., Branche-Dorsey, C. M., Ryan, G. W., Rutherford, G. W., Stevens, J. A., & O'Neil, J. (1996). Risk factors for injuries from in-line skating and the effectiveness of safety gear. *New England Journal of Medicine, 335,* 1630–1635.

Seefeldt, V., Ewing, M. E., & Walk, S. (1991). *Overview of youth sports in the United States.* Paper commissioned by the Carnegie Council on Adolescent Development. New York: Carnegie Corporation of New York.

Shively, R. A., Grana, W. A., & Ellis, D. (1981). High school sports injuries. *Physician and Sportsmedicine, 9,* 46–50.

Silverstein, B. M. (1979). Injuries in youth league football. *Physician and Sportsmedicine, 7,* 105–111.

Simon, J., & Martens, R. (1979). Children's anxiety in sport and nonsport evaluative activities. *Journal of Sport Psychology, 1,* 160–169.

Smith, R. E., Smoll, F. L., & Hunt, E. (1977). A system for the behavioral assessment of athletic coaches. *Research Quarterly, 48,* 401–407.

Smoll, F. L., & Smith, R. E. (1984). Improving the quality of coach–player interaction. In J. R. Thomas (Ed.), *Motor development during childhood and adolescence.* Minneapolis, MN: Burgess.

Stuart, M. J., Morrey, M. A., Smith, A. M., Meis, J. K., & Ortiguera, C. J. (2002). Injuries in youth football: A prospective observational cohort analysis among players aged 9 to 13 years. *Mayo Clinic Proceedings, 77,* 317–322.

Superintendent of Documents. (1996). *Surgeon General's report on physical activity and health*. Washington, DC: Department of Health and Human Services.

Thomas, J. R. (Ed.). (1977). *Youth sports guide for coaches and parents*. Washington, DC: Manufacturers Life Insurance Company and National Association for Sport and Physical Education, AAHPERD Publications.

Thompson, R. S., & Rivara, F. P. (1996). Protective equipment for in-line skaters. *New England Journal of Medicine, 335*, 1680–1682.

Tysvaer, A., & Lochen, E. (1991). Soccer injuries to the brain. *American Journal of Sports Medicine, 19*, 56–60.

Ulrich, B. D. (1987). Perceptions of physical competence, motor competence, and participation in organized sport: Their interrelationships in young children. *Research Quarterly for Exercise and Sport, 58*, 57–67.

Vinger, P. F., Duma, S. M., & Crandall, J. (1999). Baseball hardness as a risk factor for eye injuries. *Archives of Ophthalmology, 117*, 354–358.

Wankel, L. M., & Kreisel, P. S. J. (1985). Factors underlying enjoyment of youth sports: Sport and age group comparisons. *Journal of Sport Psychology, 7*, 51–64.

Weiss, M. R., & Hayashi, C. T. (1996). Youth sport in North and South America: The United States. In P. D. Knop, L. Engstrom, B. Skirstad, & M. R. Weiss (Eds.), *Worldwide trends in youth sport*. Champaign, IL: Human Kinetics.

Wild, S. (1992, July–Aug.). Choosing a junior tennis program. *CrossCourt News*, p. 3.

Williams, R. (1980). Why children get hurt. *Sport Scene, 7*, 1.

Movement in Adulthood

As discussed in Chapter 1, motor development is the study of the changes in human motor behavior over the lifespan, the processes that underlie these changes, and the factors that affect them. Although this definition is widely accepted, generally it is not practically applied. The field of motor development has traditionally emphasized mainly childhood. Adolescence has been examined occasionally; movement in adulthood, seldom. Most motor developmentalists readily admit to an expertise in childhood movement but relative ignorance about the motor changes and related factors of adulthood.

The overall omission of adulthood in the study of human development has not been confined to motor development. In fact, developmentalists in general have tended to investigate children and adolescents primarily, studying adulthood only minimally or not at all. Occasional references are made to the cessation of development once adulthood is attained. And, as discussed in Chapter 2, Piaget, perhaps the most famous of all developmentalists, terminated his theory of cognitive development well before the onset of adulthood.

The traditional infatuation with the study of childhood is somewhat understandable, however. From a researcher's point of view, examining a child's rapidly changing behavior is much more immediately gratifying than observing the slower process of change that accompanies adult behavior. Additionally, although children's relatively short attention spans sometime make them less than desirable subjects, there is much more positive popular reinforcement for the child developmentalists than for those who study adulthood, no doubt partially because of ageism. As discussed in Chapter 3, ageism is the negative view many people have concerning advancing age and the elderly in general. Our own fear of the aging process may become so severe that we reject or avoid everything associated with aging, including elderly people and information about them.

Another reason for the infatuation with the study of childhood rather than adulthood is the presumption that research findings concerning children will be more practical and important than findings from the study of adult development. Many child development findings are believed to have direct practical implications for such critical areas as child-rearing practice or educational curriculum or methodology. The findings from the study of adulthood, however, have traditionally lacked such obvious potential for practical application.

However, in recent years, the awareness of the public and researchers concerning adulthood has changed drastically. The potential societal problems that "baby boomers" have created have become a public issue. Because such a large segment of the population of the United States was born between 1948 and 1964, we must prepare ourselves for the potential affects on society of the baby boomers' reaching late adulthood.

Experts estimate that approximately 12.8 percent of Americans were age 65 and older in 1995. That number is projected to rise more than 100 percent by 2030. As indicated in Chapter 1, the 65–74 group is the only group to have shown a consistent increase in numbers across the twentieth century. However, Table 16-1 and Figure 16-1 indicate the rapid increase of the 85-year-old group, who will have shown an increase in excess of 400 percent by 2050.

During the decade of the nineties, the number of centenarians nearly doubled to an estimated 70,000 today. Analysts project that this doubling-by-the-decade phenomenon may continue, with over 800,000 centenarians by 2050. Analysts are quick to indicate that this is a midrange projection for a group that is relatively hard to project because of the inaccuracy of some projection measures, such as birth records. The high-end projection for centenarians in 2050 exceeds 4 million people.

Today four-fifths of all centenarians are women, a status that is likely to continue into the future. In addition, while most centenarians today are non-Hispanic whites (78 percent), the trend is for this segment of the population to become increasingly diverse. The percentage of non-Hispanic whites is expected to decline to 55 percent by 2050; the population of African American centenarians will remain stable at about 13 percent (National Institutes of Health, 1999).

410

Table 16-1   Projections of the Population, by Age and Sex: 2000 to 2050

(Numbers in thousands. Minus sign denotes a decrease. Middle series of U.S. Bureau of the Census.)

Age Group and Year	Both Sexes			Sex		
	Number	Percentage of All Ages	Percent Increase from 1995	Male	Female	Sex Ratio°
All Ages						
2000	274,634	x	4.5	134,181	140,453	95.5
2010	297,716	x	13.3	145,584	152,132	95.7
2030	346,899	x	32.0	169,950	176,949	96.0
2050	393,931	x	49.9	193,234	200,696	96.3
55–64						
2000	23,961	8.7	13.4	11,433	12,528	91.3
2010	35,283	11.9	66.9	16,921	18,362	92.2
2030	36,348	10.5	72.0	17,441	18,907	92.2
2050	42,368	10.8	100.4	20,403	21,965	92.9
65–74						
2000	18,136	6.6	−3.3	8,180	9,956	82.2
2010	21,058	7.1	12.3	9,753	11,305	86.3
2030	37,407	10.8	99.4	17,878	19,529	91.5
2050	34,732	8.8	85.2	16,699	18,033	92.6
75–84						
2000	12,316	4.5	10.4	4,938	7,378	66.9
2010	12,680	4.3	13.7	5,363	7,317	73.3
2030	23,517	6.8	110.9	10,818	12,699	85.2
2050	25,905	6.6	132.3	12,342	13,563	91.0
85+						
2000	4,259	1.6	17.2	1,228	3,031	40.5
2010	5,670	1.9	56.0	1,771	3,899	45.4
2030	8,454	2.4	132.7	3,021	5,433	55.6
2050	18,224	4.6	401.5	7,036	11,188	62.9
65+						
2000	34,710	12.6	3.5	14,346	20,364	70.4
2010	39,409	13.2	17.5	16,887	22,522	75.0
2030	69,379	20.0	106.8	31,718	37,661	84.2
2050	78,859	20.0	135.1	36,076	42,783	84.3

°Males per 100 females.

x = not applicable

Table compiled by the National Aging Information Center.

SOURCE: U.S. Bureau of the Census (1996).

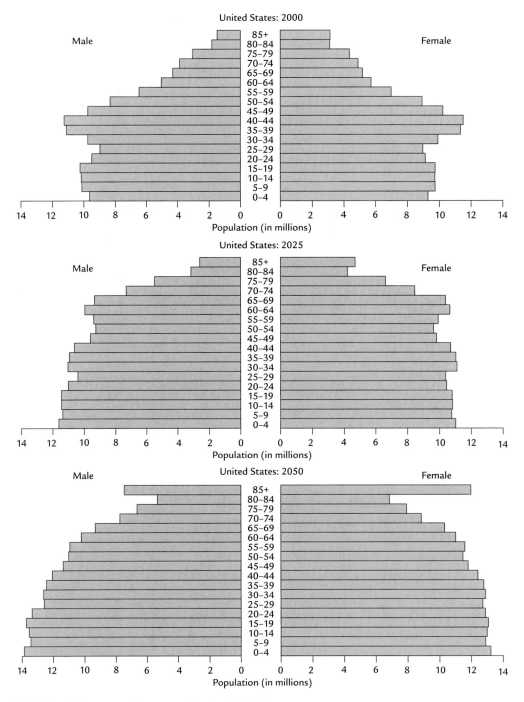

Figure 16-1 Population pyramid summary for the United States

Source: U.S. Census Bureau International Data Base.

Our preparation for this inevitable occurrence should be a logical approach to give older adults every possible chance of maintaining a quality life through their old age. Equally important, however, is our need to advance our knowledge concerning adulthood to learn to reduce both the older adult's unnecessary dependence on society and the financial drain that could result from that dependence. No doubt this vital and practical application of our knowledge of adulthood will also lead to an improved quality (and perhaps quantity) of life for everyone. Increased knowledge in all areas of development, including motor development, will help us enhance the quality of life for all ages of adults.

This chapter discusses the trends in movement behavior in adulthood, emphasizing those areas of movement in adulthood that have been investigated in some depth. As mentioned, there is much less information about adults than children. However, one area of motor development in adults that has been examined extensively involves balance, postural sway, and the incidence of falls.

BALANCE AND POSTURAL SWAY

Because many investigators believe that the incidence of falls increases with age, **balance** in adulthood has been studied considerably to determine its role in the etiology of falling among older adults. Balance, which is essential for daily tasks and most movement pursuits, gradually becomes centrally controlled during childhood. In other words, many balance behaviors become somewhat automatic as a child becomes an adult. However, this process reverses itself in late adulthood as balance gradually begins to require greater conscious effort than it had previously in life (Woollacott, Shumway-Cook, & Nasher, 1982).

Research on adults, especially older adults, and postural control are often complicated by the researcher's definition of *elderly* and the failure of researchers adequately to separate healthy older subjects from those with a pathological condition

(Woollacott, 1989). This may explain why research in this area often yields contradictory findings. For example, some studies have shown minimal change in the function of the neural substructure of postural control; others show a severe decline. Balance differences are less likely to be seen between young and older adults in research that has controlled for participants' health conditions (Woollacott, 1989).

Postural sway is a nearly imperceptible back-and-forth motion designed to assist the body in maintaining an upright or standing position. During childhood, it is gradually refined. From then until approximately the sixth decade, static control of posture generally improves. After the sixth decade, a gradual deterioration is seen (Simoneau & Leibowitz, 1996). By age 80, or shortly thereafter, postural control may look like that seen in children between the ages of 6 and 9 years. Nevertheless, older and younger adults tend to have similar automatic postural muscle responses when their balance is perturbed, though the efficiency of activating the system of older adults may decline. Further decrements are noted when older adults are deprived of certain forms of sensory information. For example, when somatosensory and visual information is incongruent with postural sway, older adults may lose balance completely. This may be a function of declining sensory systems in some older adults. Research has shown that many balance-related systems such as vision, joint position, and vestibular senses decline with age (Woollacott, 1989). However, as we noted earlier, this research must be interpreted cautiously because of potential confounding of factors.

In the study of balance in adulthood, the magnitude of a person's body sway while standing is often used to indicate balance ability (Shephard, 1978). Overstall and associates (1977) examined the body sway of subjects 60 to 96 years old. These researchers also gathered information about the frequency and type of falls the subjects experienced, for comparison with similar information gathered about younger adult subjects. Postural sway was determined to increase with age and was found to be higher in female subjects of all ages. This finding had been supported by Hasselkus and Shambes's earlier research (1975). They examined women in early and late adulthood in an upright stance and an upright forward-leaning position. According to this research, balance control probably declines as the central nervous system's capacity to control movement diminishes. Specifically, the control of balance may be impeded by the reduction of the number of cells in the cerebellum and the brain stem and a decreased capacity for using proprioceptive information. In other words, the information received about the position of various body parts is less accurate, inhibiting the ability for precise body control (Shephard, 1978). The large amount of postural sway in female subjects has been attributed to their reduced muscle mass per body weight relative to the males'. The decreasing balance ability is believed to contribute to the increasing number of falls as well as the older adults' increased inability to avoid the fall once the fall starts (Overstall et al., 1977). Balance is recovered with less speed and efficiency in later adulthood than in earlier periods of the lifespan (Woollacott et al., 1982).

In recent years, researchers have begun to study the effects of vision on postural stability. Noting the importance of postural stability and its relationship to falls in older adults, British researchers examined the effects of the visual environment on postural stability in healthy older women. Postural stability was measured by the amount of body sway detected by a force platform. The 33 participants, who ranged in age from 65 to 76 years, were asked to balance under five visual conditions: normal lighting, moderate lighting, dim lighting, eyes closed, and a repeated flashing pattern displayed on the wall. In general, as the light dimmed, the body sway increased significantly, although the repeating pattern on the wall did not significantly impede postural stability. These findings led the researchers to conclude that vision is an important factor in maintaining postural stability. Thus, conditions of poorer lighting or reduced vision may increase the chance of falling among this age group (Brooke-Wavell et al., 2002). Table 16-2 summarizes important findings regarding older adult balance, sway, and falling.

FALLS

Nothing accounts for more accidental deaths among the elderly in the United States than falls (National Institute for Occupational Safety and Health, 1992). Each year, one of every three people over 65 falls (Sattin, 1992; Tinetti & Speechley, 1989). In 1994 alone, over 7000 elderly people died because of falling (National Center for Injury Prevention and Control, 1996). For obvious reasons, falling is one of the most serious concerns of the elderly and those approaching the later years (Spirduso, 1995).

Causes of Falls

As you can see in Table 16-3, many factors contribute to the increased incidence of falls among people over 65. The causes of falls are clustered into two general categories: predispositional and situational. Predispositional causes are directly related to the inherent physiology or cognitive ability of the individual. Situational causes are linked to the environmental situation surrounding the fall (Simoneau & Liebowitz, 1996).

A prominent predispositional cause of falls is the inappropriate or excess use of medications, especially those that impair balance. For example, psychotropic medications, often used for depression, can cause such side effects as drowsiness and confusion. According to Spirduso (1995), such medications may double the chance of falling for the elderly. Compounding the problem, older people are too frequently overmedicated, a condition referred to as *polypharmacy.* This can result in a negative interaction among drugs, which in turn can lead to dizziness or difficulty in balance. A study by Kelly and associates (2003) examined the relationship between falls causing injury (requiring emergency room treatment) and the use of medication. Participants were adults 66 years of age and older living in a community of older adults. Researchers used local hospital databases to determine fall incidence and then linked that information with medication use for 30 days prior to the fall. Researchers found the fall rate to be 31.6 per 1,000 persons per year. The study determined that certain types of medica-

Table 16-2   Important Findings for Balance, Postural Sway, and Falling in Adulthood
• Postural sway increases with age (Overstall et al., 1977).
• Postural sway is higher in women than men throughout adulthood (Hasselkus & Shambes, 1975; Overstall et al., 1977).
• With increasing age, the adult receives less accurate information concerning positions of the body parts, because the number of cells in the cerebellum and brain stem decreases (Shephard, 1978).
• The number of falls increases with age (Overstall et al., 1977).
• Balance is recovered with less speed and adroitness as a person ages (Woollacott, Shumway-Cook, & Nasher, 1982).
• Reduced visual capability, increased medication, and lower foot raise during walking also contribute to the increased number of falls in adulthood.
• Falls account for more accidental deaths in the elderly than does any other factor (National Institute for Occupational Safety and Health, 1992).
• Half of the elderly who fall never regain functional walking (Spirduso, 1995).
• Fifty percent of the elderly hospitalized from a hip fracture die within a year (Rubenstein et al., 1983).
• Poor vision may increase postural sway, decrease balance, and increase the incidence of falls (Brooke-Wavell et al., 2002).
• Several simple steps and precautions, including implementing a physical activity program, can help decrease the incidence of falls among the elderly.

tions were predictors of suffering an injurious fall (Kelly et al., 2003).

Similar research was conducted on Brazilian women 60 years of age and older. All of the women studied were living in a regular community setting, and all completed a questionnaire regarding their history of falls over the previous 12 months and any medications they had taken. Participants were clustered into those who had no falls, those who had fallen one or more times, and those who had fallen two or more times. Out of the 634 women who participated, 23.3 percent reported one fall in the previous year. Slightly less, 14 percent reported two or more falls. Less than 10 percent of the women had taken no medication during the year. Over 50 percent had been taking 1–4 medications, over 34 percent had been taking 5–10 medications, and slightly less than 4 percent had been taking more than 11 medications. Those taking medications were more likely to have fallen. Specifically,

the women taking diuretics were found to be 1.6 times more likely to have fallen than were those taking no medication. Similarly, those taking beta-blockers were twice as likely to fall than were those who were not using the medication (Rozenfeld, Camacho, & Veras, 2003).

Obstacles in the environment can also contribute to increased incidence of falls. Examples of these situational causes include chairs or toilets that are too low, an absence of hand rails, uneven step height, poorly maintained rugs or carpeting, slippery surfaces, and inappropriate footwear. Approximately 1 of 10 falls occurs on stairs, usually while going down (Spirduso, 1995).

Unfortunately, half the elderly who fall never regain functional walking. Women fall more than men, but men appear to suffer worse consequences from their falls and experience a greater mortality rate from falling (Spirduso, 1995). Fear of falling can lead both men and women to avoid physical

Table 16-3   Contributors to Falls Among the Elderly

Predispositional Causes

Balance problems

Declining flexibility

Disease:

    Cardiovascular

    Parkinson's

    Dementia

    Cerebral vascular

    Arthritis

    Maladies of the feet

    Hypothyroidism

Dizziness

Fainting

Fatigue

Reduced joint mobility

Declining strength and endurance

Increased (i.e., slower) reaction time

Visual impairment

General difficulty in walking (e.g., reduced step height)

Situational Causes

Alcohol use

Improper clothing or attire

Darkness

Environmental obstacles

    Irregular walking surfaces

    Slippery surfaces

    Uneven stairs

    Cracked sidewalks

Medication

Rushing

activity. This, of course, contributes to the exercise-aging cycle we discussed in Chapter 3. Physiological parameters begin to decline with reduced activity. This initiates a downward cycle of further decreases in activity, increases in disease, and eventually death.

One of the most feared consequences of a fall for an elderly person is a fractured bone, the most serious consequence of a fall. Fractures occur in approximately 5 percent of all falls in this age group (National Center for Injury Prevention and Control, 1997). Hip fractures, occurring in about 1 percent of falls among the elderly, are considered to be the most serious of such injuries, as few victims regain previous functional ability (Spirduso, 1995). Further, of those hospitalized because of the fracture, 50 percent will die within 1 year (Rubenstein et al., 1983). The chance of breaking a hip increases 10 to 15 times from age 60–65 to age 85 and above (National Center for Injury Prevention and Control, 1997).

A study designed to examine the gait characteristics and risk factors for falling in older adults was undertaken because of the importance of falls in the mortality and morbidity of older adults. According to Pavol and associates (1999), over half of all falls at older ages are due to tripping (53 percent). In an attempt to determine if the gait pattern influences the risk of falling, 79 healthy, older adults were studied. During walking, a trip was induced with the subjects in protective harnesses. Gait patterns were carefully observed along with the likelihood of the subjects falling. The results indicated that older adults who walked faster, took faster steps, or took longer steps relative to their height had an increased chance of falling. Factors such as step width, trunk flexion, and the point during the walk at which the trip was induced were not significant factors. The authors concluded that the incidence of tripping is determined less by the walker's ability to recover than by walking characteristics, and that older adults can adjust their gait to reduce their likelihood of falling (Pavol et al., 1999).

Strategies to Avoid Falls Among the Elderly

Unquestionably, the number of falls among the elderly can be reduced. The National Institute for Occupational Safety and Health (1992) has offered several suggestions for reducing the incidence of falls at home. Table 16-4 summarizes their key recommendations. In addition to these ideas, one of the

Table 16-4 Avoiding Falls in the Home	

Floors

Avoid loose boards, slippery rugs, frayed carpets, and loose tiles.

Make sure rugs lie flat; tape their edges down if necessary.

Use rugs with nonskid backing.

Wipe up spills immediately.

Use electrical cords with caution; never run them under rugs.

Arrange furniture so everyone can move through rooms easily.

Keep floors uncluttered.

Use cleaning materials according to their instructions.

Stairs

Maintain stairs in good repair.

Keep stairs well lit and uncluttered.

Make sure lights for stairs are easily accessible.

Secure stair coverings (rugs, carpeting, runners) tightly.

Provide safe handrails.

Avoid carrying heavy loads on stairs.

Do not rush up or down stairs.

Be particularly careful in wearing high heels, slippers, or flowing clothing.

Distinguish top and bottom steps by painting them white.

Provide a rough, nonskid surface on stairs by painting them with a sand and paint mixture.

Kitchen

Keep people out of the kitchen when cleaning the floor with liquid cleansers.

Use the appropriate implement (ladder or step stool) when reaching for objects on high shelves; avoid using chairs or overreaching.

Do not rush when carrying hot foods or dishes.

Store dishes where they are easily accessible to all occupants of the house.

Bathroom

Be cautious around wet slippery surfaces.

Keep nonslip rugs on the floor.

Attach self-adhesive nonskid appliqués to the bathtub or shower floor.

Be sure that wet clothes or towels do not drip on the floor. Install night-lights.

Bedroom

Be sure traffic lanes are free of clutter.

Install night-lights.

Close drawers after use.

In General

Do not run or rush through the house.

Wear appropriate clothing (avoid long, flowing clothing) and shoes with pliable soles and low heels.

Place night-lights throughout the house.

Arrange furniture so lanes of traffic are straight and wide.

Keep furniture out of normal traffic lanes.

Keep drawers, cabinets, and closet doors closed after use.

SOURCE: Adapted and summarized from National Institute for Occupational Safety and Health (1992).

most important strategies to reduce falls among the elderly is maintenance of a physically active lifestyle. Decreasing strength, flexibility, and muscular and cardiovascular endurance all contribute to changing gait patterns and potential for falls. A physical fitness program can offset declines in these areas as well as enhance such characteristics as balance and reaction time (Spirduso, 1995). In addition, a more physically fit older adult is less likely to become ill and experience the need for medications that could cause falls. "An exercise program that significantly increases strength, maintains a body weight and composition that are efficient for locomotion, and improves balance should decrease the number of falls seen in older people" (Spirduso, 1995, p. 178).

Exercise has been determined to be one intervention that can reduce falls in older individuals. Research was designed to test the effects of year-long, weekly participation in a group exercise program with supplemental home exercises on improving balance, increasing muscle strength, reducing reaction time, improving muscle function, and preventing falls in participants over age 65 who were predisposed to falling. Participants were 163 Australians who had been assessed by standardized tests to determine their likelihood of falling. Part of the group was randomly placed in the exercise group; the remainder composed the control group. Falls were measured for the duration of the 12 months. At the end of the year, the exercise group had attended, on average, 23 exercise classes, with most performing their weekly at-home exercises regularly. Upon posttesting, the exercise group demonstrated significantly better balance on six balance tests. Most importantly, they experienced 40 percent fewer falls than did the control group, leading to the conclusion that an exercise program of this type can help reduce falls among older adults (Barnett et al., 2003).

Similar findings resulted from research conducted by Melzer, Benjuya, and Kaplanski (2003). In this study, older participants were subjected to a regular walking program and compared with a control group of nonwalkers for gait and postural disorders, postural control, static balance, and incidence of falls. The walking group demonstrated better balance, postural stability, and no falls in 6 months prior to testing. Sixteen percent of the control group experienced a fall during the same period. Interestingly, the control participants experienced more falls even though the exercise group was walking more, thus possibly increasing the opportunity for falling. The walking program therefore appeared to help stability and postural control as well as reduce the incidence of falling for the elderly exercising participants (Melzer et al., 2003).

WALKING PATTERNS OF ADULTHOOD

In comparisons of the *gait* or walking patterns of younger and older walkers, a gradual, progressive, age-related change is seen in healthy individuals. Presenile gait often starts in the seventh decade of life. It is characterized by a decrease in velocity, reduced power during the push-off phase, an increase in the time that both feet are contacting the ground

simultaneously (double support stance phase), a decrease in step length, and an increase in step width. The older walker is also more prone to making contact with the flat foot. Interestingly, many of these characteristics seem to be geared toward an attempt, conscious or unconscious, to increase the safety and stability of the walking pattern (Simoneau & Leibowitz, 1996).

Exactly why these declines occur is still unknown. However, many believe them to be a function of an age-related decline in muscle mass, skeletal changes, and declines in the central and peripheral nervous systems. Experts also indicate that behavioral changes may affect the gait pattern. Depression or fear of falling, for example, could lead to stooped posture or diminished arm swing. No doubt, increasing incidence of disease and reduced physical activity also play major roles (Simoneau & Leibowitz, 1996).

In a 2003 study of age-related walking patterns, researchers investigated the acceleration patterns of the head and pelvis in younger (22–39 years) and older (75–85 years) walkers during a walk on both level and irregular surfaces. Older participants demonstrated a more conservative pattern of walking as evidenced by slower pace, shorter steps, and an increase in the variability of the time it took to take each step. All of these characteristics were more noticeable when the walking surface was irregular. The acceleration of the head and pelvis was slower in older walkers. These findings led researchers to conclude that older walkers may adopt the more conservative pattern of walking to improve balance and reduce the chance of falling. These strategies were thought to be particularly important in light of the onset of age-related deficits in physiological function, such as reduced strength in the lower limbs (Menz, Lord, & Fitzpatrick, 2003).

In more specific research regarding walking, Aniansson (1980) determined that the norm for adult walking speed in Sweden was approximately 1.4 meters per second. However, when specifically examining adults older than 70, she noted a walking speed of 1.2 meters per second for men and 1.1 meters per second for women, an indication that older adults walk much more slowly than the norm. Step height, as mentioned earlier relative to increased rate of falling, also decreased in these older adult subjects. The women in particular had difficulty executing a 40-centimeter step; this difficulty was even more prominent when a 50-centimeter step was used.

To develop a simple, inexpensive, and reliable means of analyzing gait, Murray, Drought, and Kory (1964) conducted a more detailed investigation into the gait of adults 20 to 65 years old. These researchers also hoped that the establishment of normal ranges for several components of walking would enable future investigators to determine abnormalities in individual gait patterns.

Murray and colleagues photographed their subjects using a speed graphic camera, which takes a series of photos in a predetermined short period of time. Measurements were then taken that enabled the investigators to determine such factors as

- Duration of entire walking cycle
- Duration of stance and leg swing
- Length and width of strides and foot angles
- Amount of pelvic tipping
- Amount of hip flexion
- Amount of ankle extension

All of these characteristics were used to compare subjects by age and height. The cycle duration—the time between successive strikes of the left heel—did not vary significantly as a function of age or height, as was also true for the duration of the stance, the time each foot is in contact with the floor. However, the duration of the stance increased significantly as the overall duration of the cycle increased. The duration of the stance also seemed to relate highly to the duration of the swing, the time the foot is entirely off the floor while the opposite foot remains in contact with the supporting surface. The magnitude of the swing duration increased with the duration of the stance but was not significantly affected by age or height.

Unlike the other characteristics, stride and step length did show a significant difference according to age and height. The **stride length** is described as "the linear distance in the plane of progression

between successive points of foot to floor contact of the same foot" (Murray et al., 1964, p. 341). The **step length** is defined as "the distance between successive point of floor to floor contact of alternate feet" (p. 341). Both of these characteristics differed significantly between the youngest group of adults (20–25 years) and the oldest group (60–65 years). The authors speculate that this decreasing step and stride length reflects a restraint among older walkers that is common in much younger walkers when walking on a slippery surface. Compared with the shorter subjects, the taller subjects in this research also tended to take longer steps and strides. Foot angle, the amount of in- or out-toeing, was another significant factor. No important differences were determined according to height, but older subjects exhibited a significantly greater tendency to toe-out. Interestingly, this is a characteristic very common among immature walkers early in life. **Out-toeing** is a technique used to improve lateral stability as the ability to control balance declines in the later adult years.

Murray and associates (1964) also examined the amount of *pelvic tipping*, the forward and backward movement of the top of the pelvis (iliac crest). Although this characteristic did not vary systematically with height or age, hip flexion did. Older and shorter subjects exhibited slightly greater flexion in the hip when taking a stride. In addition, older subjects showed less ankle extension at the end of the stance, a condition that most likely contributed to the older subjects' reduced stride length.

Khattab (1980) also examined a variety of gait parameters. However, rather than using adults of varying ages, she compared adults and children. Specifically, Khattab selected subjects 4 to 25 years old. Subjects were instructed to walk across a force platform designed to determine the magnitude of the various forces as the foot struck the platform. To help the researcher describe walking techniques, subjects were filmed. Generally, Khattab found that the children in her research exhibited many adult-like walking characteristics. However, her young adult subjects had considerably fewer balance problems, because their center of gravity was relatively lower. Also, adults were more efficient, although

Table 16-5 Important Findings Concerning Adult Walking Patterns	
Early vs. Late Adulthood	**Children vs. Young Adults (Khattab, 1980)**
• Older walkers are more conservative—slower paced with shorter steps and more variability in the timing of each step (Menz, Lord, & Fitzpatrick, 2003). • Walking speed decreased (Aniansson, 1980). • Step height decreased (Aniansson, 1980). • Step and stride length were significantly shorter among older walkers (Murray, Drought, & Kory, 1964). • Older walkers had a significantly greater tendency to out-toe (Murray, Drought, & Kory, 1964). • Older adults had greater hip extension during the stride (Murray, Drought, & Kory, 1964). • Older walkers' ankle extension was reduced at the end of the stance (Murray, Drought, & Kory, 1964).	• Adults had considerably fewer balance problems, because their center of gravity was lower relative to their total height. • Adults were more efficient, less energetic walkers. • Adults took longer strides because of their longer leg length. • Adults displayed reduced hip flexion and extension during striding. • Adults required less rearward force to slow the forward momentum following a heel strike.

less energetic, walkers with longer strides. Adults displayed less flexion and extension of the hip joint in striding and required less backward force to slow their forward momentum following a heel strike. No significant differences were noted between child and adult walkers in peak vertical forces relative to body weight or in the swing/stance ratio, the length of time the leg was swinging relative to the amount of time the foot was in contact with the floor. Table 16-5 summarizes major findings from all of the gait research discussed.

DRIVING AND OLDER AGE

One of the most serious aspects of getting older is the decline in ability to drive. Up to a certain point, drivers improve in their ability. Young drivers (16–25 years old) receive more citations, are more likely to have driving privileges suspended, and are more likely to have an accident than is any other age group. Nevertheless, the number of accidents rises dramatically after the age of 75. This increase has been linked to a number of functional impairments that become more common with age with some older adults. This includes declines in vision, reac-

tion time, and some cognitive abilities, and the increase in many diseases (National Policy and Resource Center on Women and Aging, 1998).

A 1997 study conducted in Illinois examined the effects of age on driving characteristics of older drivers (Benekohal et al.). Over 850 drivers over the age of 65 years were randomly surveyed. Nearly 85 percent of the respondents were 75 or older, and several were over 90. For the purpose of analysis, drivers were divided into four age categories: 66–68, 69–72, 73–76, and 77 and older. The study determined that most older drivers use their cars regularly, but that driving frequency declined with age. Nearly half of the respondents indicated that their most recent trip was for grocery or personal shopping, though other reasons cited were personal business, recreational or social trips, and going to work or medical-related appointments. A decline in recreational or social trips was particularly notable with increasing age. The older drivers in this study indicated that they were most likely to avoid driving on ice and snow and also to avoid peak-hour travel, night driving, and driving in the rain. Twenty-six percent of the drivers surveyed indicated that they thought driving now was more difficult for them than driving 10 years ago. However, when asked about driving at night, or making left turns, many said they were having problems. Focus groups that met as a part of the research indicated that older drivers do much to compensate for or adapt to driving situations or declining abilities. Generally, the focus groups reported increased anxiety about driving and the potential loss of freedom (Benekohal et al., 1997).

Bilban (2002) claims that the elderly are unpredictable drivers who are on the roads in greater numbers than ever. Often, they drive with health problems that may impair their ability to drive safely. In addition to health concerns, differences between younger and older drivers suggest reasons for lack of safety. For example, Bilban calls younger drivers "active victims" whose main offense is driving too fast. Older drivers were found to be more passive. Thus, they may be more likely to ignore rights of way or miss important traffic signs. Based on an analysis of all traffic accidents in Slovenia from 1998 to 2000, Bilban determined that drivers over 65 years old caused three to five times more damage from their accidents than did drivers 18 to 54 years old, though the over-65 drivers were involved in fewer accidents.

The loss of driving ability or competence while driving has tremendous implications for one's opportunities to be mobile, stay engaged with society, and maintain dignity. Driving offers access to friends, family, jobs, shopping, education, culture, and religion, as well as considerable personal choice. Losing the ability to drive can be considered a major life crisis. Nevertheless, as we age, our abilities become highly variable, making any generalization about driving ability and driving age difficult if not impossible.

Driving and older age should be a topic of considerable interest for us all, as the number of older drivers is increasing dramatically. By 2030, the number of drivers over the age of 85 will be four to five times greater than today. This will likely triple the number of traffic fatalities. Nevertheless, few current cars, and our transportation system in general, have been designed with elderly drivers in mind. In addition, few alternatives exist for most elderly people, as many live in communities that are not well served by mass transit.

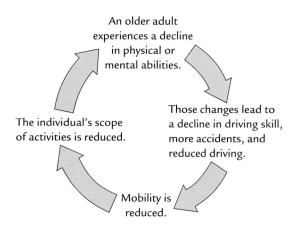

Figure 16-2   The Mobility Consequences Model
SOURCE: Adapted from Burkhart et al. (1998).

The typical, though not fixed, series of events that are associated with age-related driving changes are depicted in the **Mobility Consequences Model** (see Figure 16-2). The progression often begins with the older adult experiencing physical and/or mental changes such as reduced vision or reaction time. These changes lead to a loss of driving skill, an increase in the number of actual accidents while driving, and, inevitably, reduced driving. Less driving hampers one's general mobility, which can dramatically impact the quality of life. This process usually occurs over the course of many years, and gradually narrows a person's scope of activities. Though this scenario often occurs, it is not universal, as many older drivers do not experience the type of functional declines described here until very advanced ages. Thus, they can continue to drive safely until quite old (Burkhart et al., 1998).

For those who lose the ability or confidence to drive, alternatives must be made available. The severity of the Mobility Consequences Model becomes less apparent when alternatives exist. Obviously, increased availability of mass transit could provide some assistance. Some have suggested support groups where older drivers who have made a successful transition to no driving assist others and share ideas. Unquestionably, education and counseling are other attractive options. Of course, changing societal attitudes and eliminating the stigma of losing the privilege of driving might also help. Perhaps the most successful interventions in this area would be those that provide alternative forms of transportation along with modes to restore dignity, independence, and security. More research in this area is imperative.

ADULT PERFORMANCE ON SELECTED MOTOR ACTIVITIES

As stated earlier, with the exception of specific areas, there has been minimal research into the movement technique of adult performers. However, when studying 60-year-old women who professed to be regular exercisers, Klinger (1980) reached some interesting conclusions. These women's vertical jump pattern generally was similar to the pattern that a comparison group of college-age women used. There were major differences, however, in the older subjects' ability to achieve as much leg extension or velocity and, therefore, impulse. These women were also tested on such activities as the tennis backhand, throwing, batting, and the overhand backhand stroke. In each case, the angular velocity the college-age subject attained was greater than that of the older adults. However, in many cases the older subjects had no athletic background and had gone years without performing any of the tested movement skills. When the older subjects were subdivided into a high and a low movement ability group, the high group moved faster and with greater coordination, displayed a greater range of motion, transferred their weight more easily, and generally had a more erect posture.

Aniansson (1980) examined the functional capacity of 70-year-old men and women performing routine daily activities: Seven percent of the subjects exhibited difficulties in such routine activities as dressing and maintaining hygiene. Particularly noteworthy were decreases in flexibility, which impeded such necessary movements as touching the hand to the foot for putting on socks or tying shoes. The subjects also had problems rising from a sitting

position and performing the supination and pronation required in daily reaching activities.

Unquestionably, these kinds of declines are related to the increased inactivity that is common for most people as they age. Several investigations have been undertaken to describe the regularity with which most adults participate in leisure-time movement activity; the percentage of participants normally decreases with age. Cunningham and colleagues (1968) found the number of subjects involved in very little activity increased considerably from 40 to 69 years of age. Sidney and Shephard (1977) also found elderly men and women highly inactive, although many consider themselves just the opposite. These researchers also noted that their volunteer subjects, although inactive, were probably more active than the "normal" person of comparable age.

In a comparison study of grip force in young and elderly individuals, Kinoshita and Francis (1996) used elderly subjects. One group was 69–79 years of age, and the other was 80–93. A young adult group ranging in age from 18 to 32 was also examined. Each group gripped slippery and nonslippery weighted objects while forces were monitored. The effect of prior experience with one surface (slippery vs. nonslippery) was more pronounced in the young adult subjects, though the fingers of the elderly subjects appeared to be more slippery. The older grippers also allowed for a greater margin of error by using a wider grip when approaching the object. Overall, grip force declined with increasing age. The authors attributed some of the declines with age to more slippery skin, a decline in cutaneous sensitivity, and the decline in function of the central nervous system.

ACTIVITIES OF DAILY LIVING

One of the most dreaded aspects of older age is the loss of ability to perform one's daily functions, *activities of daily living (ADLs)* or instrumental activities of daily living (IADLs). ADLs include such activities as eating, rising from a chair, getting in

Table 16-6	Projections for People over Age 65 with ADL Limitations: 2000 to 2040			
	Number*		Percentage of Population†	
Year	Total with ADL Limitations	Severely Disabled	Total with ADL Limitations	Severely Disabled
2000	7,262	1,384	20.0	3.8
2020	10,118	1,927	19.2	3.7
2040	14,416	2,806	21.4	4.2

*Number in thousands. Based on sample data for past years.

†Base includes the institutional population.

SOURCE: Calculated on the basis of projections of the U.S. population. Table compiled by the National Aging Information Center (1989).

and out of bed, brushing one's teeth, dressing, and bathing. IADLs include such activities as cooking, shopping, doing laundry, walking, taking medications, and handling one's personal finances. The National Long-Term Care Survey conducted in 1989 (National Aging Information Center, 1989) asked people over age 65 to report any disability of theirs that lasted for 3 months or longer. A disability was considered any condition that hampered people's ability to complete the ADLs or IADLs. Over 6000 subjects met the eligibility criteria and were interviewed.

Perhaps surprising to some, just under 84 percent of subjects had no ADL or IADL limitations that lasted 3 months or longer. The majority of subjects over 85 years of age reported no limitations concerning ADLs or IADLs, though 48.7 percent claimed at least one limitation. Of these subjects, men more commonly claimed a limitation (88 percent to 81 percent for women).

Of those subjects who still resided in the community, 89 percent claimed no limitations lasting 6 months or longer. However, of those who were institutionalized, 97 percent had ADL limitations lasting 6 months or longer. This is understandable, as many institutions only admit individuals who have long-term ADL limitations.

For all community residents reporting ADL limitations, the most commonly claimed ADLs lasting more than 3 months were bathing (9.45 percent),

getting around inside (8.8 percent), and independently getting in and out of bed (5.9 percent). The most common ADL limitations lasting more than 3 months reported by institutionalized subjects over age 65 were bathing (95.6 percent), getting around (81.8 percent), and getting in and out of a bed or chair (77.9 percent). Though institutional subjects reported many more ADL limitations than did the other group, the ADL limitations fell in the exact same order for both. Table 16-6 details the number of projected ADL limitations for those over age 65 among noninstitutional subjects from the years 2000 through 2040. Most data sets show that the number of disabled older Americans will increase sharply. No doubt, this indicates the importance of pursuing additional research in lifespan motor development to determine additional methods of assuring public health, happiness, and productivity as our population continues to age.

AGE OF PEAK PROFICIENCY

In 1953, Harvey Lehman wrote *Age and Achievement*, seeking to "set forth the relationship between chronological age and outstanding performances" (p. vii). His work consisted of extensive tables detailing the ages of attainment of outstanding performances in music, art, literature, leadership, and, of course, "physical skills." Lehman carefully noted

Table 16-7   Ages at Which Individuals Have Exhibited Peak Proficiency at "Physical Skills"

Type of Skill	No. of Cases	Median Age	Mean Age
U.S. outdoor tennis champions	89	26.35	27.12
Runs batted in: annual champions of the two major baseball leagues	49	27.10	27.97
U.S. indoor tennis champions	64	28.00	27.45
World champion heavyweight pugilists	77	29.19	29.51
Base stealers: annual champions of the two major baseball leagues	31	29.21	28.85
Indianapolis-Speedway racers and national auto-racing champions	82	29.56	30.18
Best hitters: annual champions of the two major baseball leagues	53	29.70	29.56
Best pitchers: annual champions of the two major baseball leagues	51	30.10	30.03
Open golf champions of England and of the U.S.	127	30.72	31.29
National individual rifle-shooting champions	84	31.33	31.45
State corn-husking champions of the U.S.	103	31.50	30.66
World, national, and state pistol-shooting champions	47	31.90	30.63
National amateur bowling champions	58	32.33	32.78
National amateur duck-pin bowling champions	91	32.35	32.19
Professional golf champions of England and of the U.S.	53	32.44	32.14
World record-breakers at billiards	42	35.00	35.67
World champion billiardists	74	35.75	34.38

SOURCE: Lehman, H. C. (1953). *Age and achievement.* Copyright © 1953, renewed 1981 by Mrs. Harvey C. Lehman. Adapted and printed with permission of Princeton University Press.

that his work was not intended to determine the rate at which abilities "decay," nor were the ages designated for peak achievement indicative of biological factors alone. Clearly, many sociological factors contribute, and Lehman explained that simply noting the ages of peak achievement would not in any way explain the interaction of the many factors involved in the attainment of peak achievement.

Lehman's work on peak achievement in "physical skills" has been widely reprinted (see Table 16-7). In fact, his table denoting ages of peak achievement in various "physical skills" has appeared in many other motor development books (Eckert, 1987; Haywood, & Getchell, 2001), indicating considerable interest in his work. An examination of Lehman's original table explains why he concluded that more vigorous skills like "boxing, football, ice hockey, and tennis tend to deteriorate relatively early" with peak per-

formances generally occurring before the age of 30. "Other skills, such as rifle and pistol shooting, bowling, duck-pin bowling, and billiards, which require less explosive outbursts of speed and energy . . . deteriorate more slowly" (Lehman, 1953, p. 253). Interestingly, Lehman also noted that athletes born more recently may have determined how to stay better fit. Thus we might expect athletes in more recent years to be achieving peak performances later than they did prior to 1953. Unfortunately, Lehman's work culminated with the publication of his book in 1953, and by today's standards his "more recently born athletes" are not at all recent.

Recognizing that changes may have occurred in the years since Lehman's work, Degnan and Payne (1994) updated, and in some areas expanded, the work of Lehman (see Table 16-8). While information on such activities as duck-pin bowling was

Table 16-8   Ages at Which Individuals Have Exhibited Proficiency at "Physical Skills"

Type of Skill	Years of Inclusion	No. of Cases	Median Age	Mean Age
Tennis: Men				
U.S. Open	1956–92	29	25	25.6
Wimbledon	1961–90	27	24	24.48
French Open	1969–88	15	24	23.4
Australian Open	1969–91	16	27	26.88
Tennis: Women				
U.S. Open	1962–93	34	26	25.11
Wimbledon	1953–93	35	24	25.14
French Open	1969–93	22	25	24.5
Australian Open	1969–93	22	25	25.2
Baseball				
MVP	1953–88	73	29	28.79
Batting Average	1953–91	78	28	28.5
Home runs	1953–91	89	29	28.97
Stolen bases	1953–91	77	28	27.86
RBI	1953–91	82	29.5	29.14
Cy Young Award	1956–92	64	29	29.43
Boxing				
Heavyweight	1952–92	31	26	26.68
Middleweight	1953–88	39	30	30.3
Auto Racing				
Indianapolis 500	1953–93	39	35	35.59
Daytona 500	1960–94	28	36	36
Winston Cup	1964–91	25	35	34.36
Golf: Men				
U.S. Open	1953–92	32	33	33.28
PGA	1961–93	29	33	33.83
Masters	1953–93	36	32	32.5
British Open	1953–93	38	31	30.86
PGA Leading Money	1955–92	34	32	31.5
Golf: Women				
U.S. Women's Open	1958–92	33	29.455	29.46
LPGA Championship	1957–87	22	28.5	29.68
LPGA Leading Money	1954–91	33	32	31.79

(continued)

Table 16-8 *(continued)*				
Type of Skill	**Years of Inclusion**	**No. of Cases**	**Median Age**	**Mean Age**
Bowling				
American Bowling Congress: Men's Singles Champions	1959–93	36	28	30.56
Basketball				
National Basketball Association: League Leaders				
Rebounds	1953–89	37	26	27
Assists	1953–89	37	26	26.27
Scoring	1954–93	26	26.5	26.62
MVP	1956–89	34	27	26.56
Free Throw %	1953–89	36	29	29.36

SOURCE: Degnan, F., and Payne, V. G. (1994). Age and peak performance in adulthood: 1953–1993. Unpublished manuscript. Used with permission of the authors.

unavailable, Degnan and Payne were able to accumulate data on most other "physical skills" studied by Lehman. Starting in 1953, the last year of Lehman's work, Degnan and Payne more precisely subdivided many of the original "physical skills" and, in many cases, added values for female performers. As illustrated in Table 16-8, we can see that performers in the "more vigorous skills" still achieve peak performance earlier than those in activities requiring "less explosive outbursts of speed and energy." For example, in recent years, median and mean ages of peak performance for tennis ranged from approximately 24 to 26 years of age for both men and women. Baseball players achieved peak performance closer to 30 years of age, while golf and auto racing performances were achieved in the early to mid 30s, respectively. Perhaps most interesting, and somewhat surprising, Lehman's contention that "more recently born athletes" would benefit from more advanced training and "preservation" techniques to maintain their physical fitness is not generally upheld by the recent data. Both median and mean ages of peak performances are less in many athletes charted from 1953 to 1993 than those reported in Lehman's work. For example, Lehman's tennis champions were achieving

peak performances between the ages of 26 and 28. In more recent years, peak performances for both male and female tennis players have been achieved at 24 to 26 years of age. Peak performances in golf seem to have stayed about the same, while auto-racing ages have increased considerably. One group that does seem to add credence to Lehman's theory is speedway and auto-racing champions, who were achieving peak performances around age 30 prior to 1953. In the last 40 years, mean and median performances have occurred in the mid 30s.

As mentioned, these figures do not explain the underlying sociological or biological factors leading to peak performance. However, they do provide interesting bases for future research, which may someday provide some answers concerning the impact of biological and sociological factors on potential for peak performance.

ADULT PERFORMANCE DURING HIGH AROUSAL

Considerable research has been conducted on adult motor behavior during times of high arousal. In a series of studies conducted on older versus younger adults playing miniature golf, an age-related decline appeared to occur in situations of high arousal and high cognitive demand. This finding has been consistent in research with large numbers of subjects of varying skill levels and in competitions of varying levels of importance. It has also been detected in miniature golf competitions at varying locations and has been reproduced in field and laboratory settings. In every case, young adults performed better when a need arose for compensating for non-optimal levels of arousal or increased competitive distraction. Researchers have suggested this phenomenon may be a function of an age-related decline in ability to deal with the increased cognitive demands of high-arousal movement situations. Furthermore, they speculate that it could be related to a combination of physiological factors. The neuro-endocrine system, for example, may affect the action of the endocrine glands on the metabolic rate. Or, specific "target tissues" may begin to respond differently to hormonal actions as we age. If any of these hypotheses are correct, a decline in movement ability during times of high arousal would be extremely pervasive and affect many more movement activities than just miniature golf (Backman & Molander, 1989).

Fortunately, this apparent decline in motor performance during times of high arousal appears to be somewhat reversible. Drug therapy (beta andrenergic blocks) has been recommended as one source of reversal. However, the best ways for older adults to avoid performance decrements during times of high arousal are relaxation training and refocusing the attention during such times (Backman & Molander, 1989).

MOVEMENT SPEED IN ADULTHOOD

Although human beings display "incredible individual differences in many motor performances as they age" (Spirduso, 1985, p. 89), several norms have been noted concerning the speed of various adult movements. As discussed earlier, walking speed generally decreases with age, particularly in late adulthood.

The speed of many other kinds of movements, such as running, also appears to be affected.

Running Speed

The maintenance of running records and the advent of masters-age-group running programs throughout the world have facilitated examinations of running speed and age. By comparing the published records of runners from various age groups, researchers have found that the long-distance running times of the best 40-year-old runners are similar to those of world-class runners. However, by the age of 70, top runners may be only 70 percent as fast as the world-class long-distance runners. Also, for older men, the relative running speed increases as the distance increases (see Figure 16-3). Therefore, the relative sprint speed for the older person does not compare as favorably as longer distance speeds to world-class efforts, most likely a result of a general decrease in running speed with age, because such techniques as interval training for speed maintenance are fairly uncommon among older runners. Also, older runners may have increasing responsibilities in non-running activities, which impair their efforts to train. Finally, older runners may not have the peak levels of motivation that many younger runners maintain; unquestionably, such motivation is critical for optimal performance (Reigel, 1981).

Reaction and Response Time

Two measures that researchers interested in the effects of aging on movement have extensively examined are reaction time and movement time. Reaction time has been the most studied factor. As discussed in Chapter 2, reaction time has also been used to determine the status of the central nervous system for cognitive function. Specifically, **reaction time** is "the interval from presentation of an unanticipated stimulus until the beginning of the response" (Schmidt, 1991, p. 286). **Movement time** is the "interval from the initiation of the movement until its termination" (Schmidt, 1991, p. 285). The movement may be short and simple, such as pressing a button, or longer and more sophisticated, such as running.

Figure 16-3 Running speed at short distances normally declines considerably with age, but the relative running speed for longer distances is often well preserved.

According to some investigators, reaction time and movement time decline systematically in adults. In an investigation of subjects 6 to 84 years old, speed increased up to 19 years of age but decreased systematically thereafter (Hodgkins, 1962). Researchers such as Jarvik and Cohen (1973) substantiated these claims when they determined that some of the greatest declines with aging may be in the performance of speeded movement tasks. In particular, Jarvik and Cohen found that reaction time was longer and more variable in older subjects, which, they state, indicates reduced functional capability of the central nervous system, cell loss, and decreased nerve conductivity.

Considerable evidence exists indicating that activities requiring more complex processing of information will lead to a greater rate of slowing (Hertzog, 1991). In fact, Welford (1982) believes that the amount of decline in reaction time is related to how complicated the task is. According to Welford, there are slight changes from 20 to 60 years of age in repetitive and simple movements. These movements include many reaction-time tasks, such as lifting a finger off a button when presented with a certain stimulus. Slightly more complicated tasks, such as alternately tapping the hand or a pen-

cil between two targets located next to each other, also minimally decline with age. However, there is more significant change in the rate of slowing when the task becomes increasingly complex. For example, rapidly pressing a series of buttons in varied order on successive trials is more complicated and more likely to cause slower performances in older subjects.

Welford categorized the complications that typically have been most involved in research in this area as spatial transpositions and symbolic translations. **Spatial transpositions** are usually the simpler of the two complications because they involve relating one signal at one position to a response at another position. For example, releasing a button when a light stimulus appears is a spatial transposition. The **symbolic translation** requires the subject to respond to a signal by a predetermined number or code. For example, if a blue stimulus light appears, the subject must press the first in a series of buttons; if the yellow light appears, the second button in the series must be pressed. Symbolic translations generally cause disproportionate slowing in older subjects. In research combining both types of complications, older subjects' response speed has been determined to be further hampered because response becomes increasingly inaccurate as it slows.

Like many movement phenomena, reaction time appears to be affected by several variables. For example, in a recent study conducted on the effect of urgency on decision time, Reddi and Carpenter (2000) asked subjects to make quick and accurate eye movements to low-visibility targets. The results indicated that the level of urgency required for the task affected decision time. This led the authors to conclude that the urgency level seems to influence the level at which a decision signal triggers a response. Thus, reaction time would be influenced by the urgency required in the task (Reddi & Carpenter, 2000).

The phenomenon of slowing with age for relatively simple versus more complex movements generally has been explained by the *last-in-first-out hypothesis.* This hypothesis suggests that the neural and muscular capability to perform simple movement acts, such as reflexive movements or other integrated movements that fall into the category of spatial transpositions, is developed early in life and appears to somewhat resist decline with aging. However, more coordinated, goal-oriented, or complicated movements, such as the symbolic translations discussed earlier, are not developed until later in life and begin to decline in people as young as 30 (Spirduso, 1985).

Physiologically, several more specific factors are also believed to contribute to the slowing that occurs with age. The number of functional neurons and the muscle fibers they stimulate (motor units) decrease with age. At the same time, more intense neural stimulations are required because the threshold of excitation of the muscles generally declines as much as 15 to 35 percent between ages 20 and 60 years (Welford, 1982). Although more intense and "clear" neural stimulation may be required, the signal may actually decline in quality. The clarity of the signal appears to be a function of the ratio of the impulse of the neural stimulation to the extraneous "noise" or interference. With age, the decreasing capacity of the sense organs and the loss of brain cells cause reduced signal levels as noise

levels increase. Therefore, a lower signal-to-noise ratio results, requiring the person to respond with slower motor movements (Birren, Woods, & Williams, 1980).

In addition to these common physiological changes, older people also approach movement performance with a different strategy: They are willing to sacrifice speed of movement for increased accuracy, leading to the *speed/accuracy trade-off,* which may be a function of the older person's more cautious approach to movement (Schmidt & Wrisberg, 2004). The speed/accuracy trade-off is discussed in more detail later in the chapter.

Rabitt and Rogers's (1965) research lends additional support to the theory that adults are somewhat more cautious in their approach to movement. A comparison of the speed of movement of young and old adult subjects to one of two alternative end points has yielded interesting findings. The young adults were capable of pondering which was their assigned end point during the initial phase of the movement; the older subjects were incapable of such simultaneous activity, because they intently focused their attention on monitoring their movement. Rabitt and Rogers believe that this research demonstrates older adult subjects' inability to suppress the monitoring of their movement. The increased monitoring may have occurred as a result of the muscles receiving slower neural stimulation, which may have caused the subjects to become aware of the stimulus and excessively focus their attention on the movement activity. Also, the monitoring may be suppressed when the subject is assured or confident of the outcome. Rabitt and Rogers speculate that the adult subjects in their research may have lacked the assurance or confidence necessary for suppressing the monitoring.

Stones and Kozma (1981) proposed additional theories to account for the age effects that exist in many movement activities. For example, movements requiring maximal, or near-maximal, energy expenditure decline faster than those that require lesser levels of energy. Second, Stones and Kozma speculated that activities requiring explosive muscular contraction and rapid power production tend to decrease in popularity with age. To support this hypothesis, they cited decreasing numbers of older runners who interval train and the reduced popularity of power lifting among older adults. This idea is no doubt strongly related to the researchers' third hypothesis, which states that as people age, they are less motivated to train or practice activities that require a repetition of near-maximal explosive efforts. The resulting lack of training or practice causes an obvious decline in function at a faster rate than would be common in a younger performer.

IS A MOVEMENT DECLINE INEVITABLE WITH AGE?

Most adults show considerable decline in movement ability as they age. However, this decline, although inevitable for most people, does not have to begin as early or as abruptly as it does for many adults. Clearly, by taking an active role in daily habits, the evident movement regression or decline can be delayed, postponed, or possibly prevented. The decline in movement performance can be avoided by certain compensatory strategies, exercise, and practice.

Compensation for the Movement Decline

Although there is a certain amount of movement decline with age, there are many ways older adults can compensate for such phenomena as reduced speed, strength, and endurance and maintain extremely high levels of performance. For example, in longer activities where fatigue might be a factor, the older adult can learn to conserve energy by pacing: doling out energy more cautiously and avoiding unnecessary expenditures of effort. Many performers, such as distance runners, cyclists, or swimmers, consciously practice pacing, but in some older adults a certain amount of pacing occurs subconsciously as they moderate performance through a constant concern for preserving their energy. See Figure 16-4.

Figure 16-4 As Paul Spangler knew, pacing is often an effective way to compensate for speed. Until his death at age 95, Paul Spangler was still running marathons.
SOURCE: © Mark Tuschman Photography

The older adult may practice other subconscious or automatic compensatory tendencies. For example, an adult may apply more effort than would a younger person. However, this mode of compensation does not work for extended periods, because fatigue occurs more readily than with pacing. Furthermore, the long-term application of this form of compensation could lead to increased incidences of stress, ulcers, or heart problems. Experts differ as to whether older adults use this tactic more than do their younger counterparts (Welford, 1982).

Some older adults may compensate for movement deficits by long- and short-term anticipation of movement. Short-term anticipation is, for example, the racquetball player focusing on her opponent's movement so as to gain insight into proper positioning on the court. Long-term anticipation can also be useful for providing preparation through practice or for securing sufficient rest and might increase the success of performance in an upcoming movement activity. However, although some older adults effectively use compensation, they do not seem to do so any more frequently than do younger adults.

As mentioned earlier, older adults often sacrifice speed for accuracy in movement activities and occasionally may use the tactic as a form of compensation. For example, the speed/accuracy trade-off is particularly common and useful among skilled adults. However, this form of compensation, although useful in many situations, cannot fully overcome movement deficits, because the additional time the older adults gain is often insufficient to overcome the accuracy of the more youthful performers (Salthouse, 1979).

Finally, older performers may be able to compensate somewhat as a result of higher criteria or greater expectations concerning their performances. This has been found particularly true in certain memory tasks as well as tests involving sensory discrimination (Hutman & Sekuler, 1980; Potash & Jones, 1977). No doubt, having greater expectations of performance often overcomes some of the resulting movement deficit from such factors as the decrease in movement speed (Welford, 1982).

Effects of Exercise on the Movement Decline

A decline in movement performance is common as adults age, but there are means for avoiding the decline. Movement can even be maintained and improved well into late adulthood by continuing involvement in movement activities.

A 1998 position stand from the American College of Sports Medicine (ACSM) strongly supports older adults' participation in regular exercise. This position stand is based on a thorough review of the specific research related to older adulthood and exercise. According to the ACSM, exercise programs can be useful in a variety of ways. Exercise can help offset or prevent numerous functional declines that are normally seen during aging. Also, contrary to popular belief, older adults have been found to be quite trainable. In other words, they respond well to intervention programs designed to increase strength, flexibility, and cardiovascular endurance; offset loss of muscle mass; increase muscle mass in some cases; and enhance function. For example, older adults have been shown to elicit approximately the same level of increase (10–30 percent) in maximal endurance levels as young adults. Exercise programs for the older adult are also believed to decrease the risk of many diseases, including heart disease, diabetes, and osteoporosis. By reducing the incidence of disease, one can prolong one's life. Thus, exercise may actually increase life expectancy. Other factors that can be improved via exercise programs, according to the ACSM, are bone health, postural stability, and reduction in the number of falls. Psychological benefits may also result, including preservation of cognitive ability, reduction in depression, and enhanced feelings of self-control and self-efficacy. In general, the ACSM believes that regular exercise during older adulthood can help us maintain better health and maintain our independence and daily function while generally improving the quality of life. Thus, they recommend a wide-ranging exercise program that includes balance training, resistance training, and walking (ACSM, 1998).

Demonstrating support for the ACSM's position stand, Brown and colleagues (2000) examined the effects of low-intensity exercise on physical frailty in older adults. Eighty-four subjects were placed on a 3-month, low-intensity supervised exercise program. Results indicated significant positive effects on the physical frailty of the group, a physical performance test, and several indicators of frailty: flexibility, strength, gait speed, and balance. These promising results clearly indicate that physical frailty is modifiable with even a modest program of exercise. Additionally, the researchers contrasted an unsupervised home-based flexibility program, where the results were not as promising (Brown et al., 2000).

The continuation of participation in movement activity is so influential that active older adults are more similar to young active adults than to old inactive adults in performance on reaction time, choice reaction time, and response time tasks (Aniansson, 1980). The body build is also more likely to look youthful; this is simply determined by examining elderly athletes, who often have a body type similar to that of younger people (Shephard, 1978). Unfortunately, our culture often views adulthood, especially late adulthood, as a time to slow down. Adults also may be plagued by the idea that the need for exercise diminishes or that their ability is too limited for participation. In some cases older adults experience **dyspnea,** painful or difficult breathing, which can lead to a fear of overexertion. No doubt, all of these factors contribute to the increasing inactivity that often accompanies aging.

Those who do continue a regular regimen of physical activity can avoid the extremely negative cycle that frequently engulfs the aging. This cycle generally begins as activity decreases with age: The biological factors that regulate the system decline, impairing the ability to engage in movement activity. However, an active regimen of movement yields beneficial effects and breaks the cycle. In addition, even movements that seem unrelated to the experienced activity may improve (Spirduso, 1982). See Figure 16-5.

As noted earlier, reaction time has been the primary focus of researchers concerned with movement changes and aging. Those investigators who examine the effects of movement activity or exercise on movement through adulthood also have focused on reaction time. Such research has shown that exercise reduces reaction time in adult subjects, as a result of many positive biological changes that accompany chronic exercise.

Among the positive changes that accompany cardiovascular activity is increased blood flow, which may actually improve the brain's function. Exercise also tends to have an arousing effect, which may improve adults' speed of performance. However, the overall benefit from this factor is somewhat disputed because some experts believe that the additional arousal, although benefiting speed, may decrease the accuracy of performance. Another possible explanation for the beneficial effects of exercise on reaction time is that the active muscles positively influence the neural connections and the neurons that stimulate the muscle (Welford, 1982).

A multitude of other biological changes also accompany a regular exercise regimen. These factors, many of which were discussed more thoroughly in Chapter 8, include increasing work capacity, bone density, flexibility, muscle strength, coordination, and weight control. Reductions are seen in such factors as resting heart rate, total cholesterol, and blood pressure. These biological changes are accompanied by improved mental outlook and self-esteem and reduced idle time, anxiety, and loneliness (Barry, Rich, & Carlson, 1993). All of these factors greatly contribute to the quality of life and our ability to stay active. Thus, the vicious cycle created by inactivity can be slowed and, many times, even reversed.

Recent evidence has indicated that exercise can have beneficial effects in sustaining function in middle-aged adults, too. Knowing that even a young adult population is impacted by a sedentary lifestyle, Brill and colleagues (2000) studied several thousand men and women between the ages of 30 and 82. Subjects were tested for upper- and lower-body strength. Following an average of 5 years, 7 percent of the men and 12 percent of the women reported at least one functional limitation. This in-

Figure 16-5 By maintaining an active, exercising lifestyle, most adults can postpone or avoid many forms of movement decline. In fact, improvements in motor performance can frequently be elicited throughout the lifespan.

SOURCE: Steve Mason/ Getty Images/PhotoDisc

cluded decreased ability to perform recreational, household, daily-living, and personal tasks. Among the high-strength subjects, however, only slightly more than 3 percent of men and just less than 5 percent of women reported such declines. The percentages exceeded 8 percent for men and 13 per-

cent in women for the low-strength group. Though some decline with age is normally associated with old age, these researchers concluded that even middle-aged adults who do not participate regularly in strength-training programs can develop limitations (Brill et al., 2000).

Effects of Practice on the Movement Decline

Like regular physical exercise, practice of a specific movement activity is an effective way for an adult to postpone or avoid movement regression or, in many cases, improve specific movement endeavors. In fact, in examining the performance of adult subjects on reaction-time tasks, researchers have determined that practice facilitates improvement through late adulthood. Older adult subjects often show greater improvement with practice than do younger adult subjects, even though overall performance levels between the two groups may initially vary considerably (Salthouse & Somberg, 1982).

Pursuit rotor research has yielded similar findings. With the pursuit rotor device, the subject must keep a wand in contact with a moving light target as the target moves through various configurations, such as a circle. When old and young subjects were tested, there was minimal difference in the performance levels when both groups were allowed to practice before testing. The prepractice performance levels of the young surpassed those of the old, so the practice was considered more beneficial to the older than the younger adult subjects (Surburg, 1976). In general, there is little evidence to support the notion that older subjects improve any less in movement tasks following practice than do younger subjects. Despite considerable popular opinion to the contrary, adults do benefit from practice throughout life.

Physical Activity Trends in Adulthood

As indicated in the previous section, the contributions of an active lifestyle are becoming increasingly clear. Nevertheless, surveys indicate that most adults do not choose to participate in physical activity. Recent survey information from Australia, Canada, England, and the United States revealed that approximately 10 percent of the adult populations was aerobically active. *Aerobically active* meant that one "engaged in vigorous activities during leisure time

on an average of at least three occasions weekly for 20–30 minutes or more per occasion" (Stephens & Caspersen, 1994, p. 204). Clearly, sedentarism appears to be the lifestyle of choice. The number of people falling into the sedentary category (even less than moderately active) appears to range from about 25 to 33 percent in most countries surveyed. England and Finland seem to be somewhat exceptional in that their percentage of sedentary people is somewhat less. In Finland, as much as 15 percent of the 30- to 59-year-olds were believed to be highly active (Stephens & Caspersen, 1994).

In a study conducted specifically on Danish participants, the relationship between physical activity and mortality, heart attacks, hip fractures, and functional ability was examined across several decades. The cohort group of participants was first examined in 1964 at age 50. They were again examined in 1974 and for each decade thereafter until 1999 at the age of 85 years. In this population, less than one-third were found to lead a sedentary life during their leisure time. Further, physical activity clearly influenced health and mortality. Compared to less-active participants, the more-active group exhibited only 60 percent of the mortality, 70 percent of the rate of heart attacks, and 75 percent the rate of hip fractures. In addition, the physically active group was found to be more independent later in life (Schroll, 2003).

Fortunately, the incidence of sedentarism appears to be declining in many countries. The number of people exercising in the United States increased slightly from 1980 to 1990, though no change was noted in Australia and a slight decrease in the number of physically active people was noted in Canada. This increase in leisure-time physical activity is believed to be mostly sedentary people becoming moderately active rather than moderately active people becoming vigorously active. In addition, in most countries studied, men were 80 percent more likely to be vigorously active than women (Stephens & Caspersen, 1994).

In regard to developmental trends and activity levels, older adults have generally been found to be less active than are younger adults. In addition, when active, older adults often choose activities that require less energy expenditure. A slight exception to the overall general trend occurs at the end of high school, when an extreme reduction in physical activity level appears suddenly. In Canada, for example, 20- to 24-year-old subjects were found to be two times less likely to be physically active than 10- to 14-year-olds. Further into adulthood, if the intensity of the activity is considered relative to age, the expected decline across adulthood diminishes, and people at 65 years or slightly younger actually show a slight increase in activity level. In addition, in the United States, older adults increased their involvement in physical activity more than did younger adults during the 1980s, a trend that appears to be continuing. Furthermore, American men and women, 18 to 29 and 30 to 44, were the only groups not increasing their leisure-time involvement in physical activity, while 20- to 24-year-olds were the only age group not showing a similar increase in Canada. So, despite the relatively high numbers of sedentary people in many of the countries studied, some positive trends appear to exist (Stephens & Caspersen, 1994).

SPORTS-RELATED INJURIES TO BABY BOOMERS AND OLDER ADULTS

Clearly, staying active throughout adulthood can be beneficial in many ways. However, safety should always be a priority in the choices people make concerning an active lifestyle. The Consumer Product Safety Commission (CPSC, 2000) noted that sports-related injuries to baby boomers increased by over 30 percent from 1991 to 1998. According to the commission, baby boomers consist of nearly 80 million people and 30 percent of the U.S. population. This increase in injury was thought to be the result of greater participation by persons in this age range. In 1998, nearly one million sports-related injuries occurred to baby boomers. The cost of these injuries in the United States was estimated to be just

under $19 billion. Bicycling and basketball accounted for the largest numbers of injuries to this age group, with a high number of deaths related to head injuries incurred while riding a bicycle.

Seven sports showed particular increases in injuries during the 7 years studied: bicycling, golf, soccer, basketball, exercise and running, weightlifting, and in-line skating. Sports showing decreasing injury trends included skiing, tennis, and volleyball. Three sports showed a relatively large number of reported deaths during the time of review. Deaths from bicycling (290 per year) were over four times more common than the second largest number of deaths, in swimming (67 per year). The biking deaths were mostly attributable to motor-vehicle–related accidents. Skiing was the third most common source of death (7 per year).

The CPSC also noted that baby boomer deaths from bike accidents were nearly twice the rate as that seen among children. The commission purported that this difference was likely to be a function of children more commonly wearing helmets. Nearly 70 percent of children wore helmets while biking, whereas only 43 percent of the baby boomers were similarly equipped. The CPSC concluded that baby boomers are well advised to maintain their activity levels but know that safety is essential. One way of greatly reducing the most serious injuries related to physical activity is to wear protective gear, especially helmets. Other recommendations include appropriate warm-ups and increasing the intensity of exercise more gradually (CPSC, 2000).

The CPSC also studied sports-related injuries in persons 65 years of age and older (1998). Similar to the findings just discussed, the CPSC determined that a significant increase in sports-related injuries occurred in older adults from 1990 to 1996. The increase was 54 percent over the 7-year period of review. In fact, the increase in injury rate among this age group was far greater than that of any other age group. In contrast, 25–64-year-olds increased by only 18 percent. The greatest increase in injury appears to be attributable to the greater involvement in more active sports, bicycling, exercising, weight training, and skiing. The greatest single source of injuries to this age group was attributed to bicycle riding, where injuries increased nearly 75 percent over the 7 years of review. However, the greatest increase in injury occurred as a result of exercising, where a 173 percent increase was noted. Most of these injuries were from falling, tripping, and strains in the course of routine exercise.

The CPSC concluded that these increases are most likely due to increasing levels of physical activities among some older adults. As with baby boomers, the CPSC believes that using proper safety gear and taking appropriate precautions will reduce injuries in the older population. Clearly, for most Americans, avoiding physical activity is not the solution. As suggested earlier, exercise can contribute to improved health; if exercising safely, more Americans can be assured of a longer, healthier life.

TEACHING MOVEMENT SKILL TO THE OLDER ADULT

Because of the increase in the number of older adults and heightened awareness of the benefits of physical activity, many new programs emphasizing motor skill instruction for older adults have evolved. No doubt, many more will be created to meet the growing need in the years to come. Unfortunately, many of these programs will not be designed and directed by experts specifically trained for teaching movement skill to the older adult. Through the early 1980s, existing programs were most often led by volunteers or others without specific training or professional education in exercise, movement, or recreation (Heitmann, 1982). This trend has continued into the 1990s. Additionally, little research exists to assist trained professionals in designing and implementing older-adult movement instruction programs. While considerable research has been done on the adult physiological system, very little has been done on psychomotor performance. This makes it more difficult to establish a program that is congruent with the needs and objectives of the older adult.

However, according to Heitmann (1982), we do know that certain steps should be taken in formulating a program of movement instruction for the older adult. First, the existing research should be examined to increase awareness of the older adult's specific needs concerning physiological rehabilitation or maintenance. Second, the research should be used to establish a viable instructional process. Third, a program of preparation of professionals in instructing and directing programs for older adults should be implemented. According to Heitmann (1982), professionals should be well trained in the scientific bases of physical education, with specific emphasis on the older adult. They must know how to implement teaching methodologies that are specific to the elderly, thus enabling the older adult to acquire skill in the most efficient manner. These professionals also must be prepared in fitness and motor skill rehabilitation and maintenance procedures that are specific to the elderly. Heitmann (1982) suggests that the training of these professionals might parallel university teacher-credential programs. Following a 4-year specialized course of study, an internship would be prescribed. Upon successful completion of the curriculum and the internship, a specialized credential could be awarded.

Heitmann further suggests that, in designing the motor skill program for the older adult, the individual's hierarchy of needs should be heeded. The first need is physiological. Older adults may have had health problems or been sedentary for an extended period. As a result they might be poorly motivated. A major emphasis must therefore be placed on appropriately motivating the participants. A second need concerns the safety and security of the participants. Because some may have impaired vision or hearing, particular care must be taken in giving instructions. Hearing, in particular, often becomes distorted or difficult because of the echo or noise associated with a gymnasium or similar movement setting. Furthermore, Heitmann cautions against creating excess physiological and emotional stress in the participants.

Other needs that should be considered are those for belonging, affection, and identification. To assist in fulfilling these needs, Heitmann recommends the creation of a caring environment where participants feel comfortable, feel they belong, and feel they can communicate. Establishing this type of environment will also assist in meeting this last group of needs that Heitmann mentions—the need for self-esteem, success, and self-respect—which can be met by delivering positive reinforcement to the participants. When all of these needs are attained, Heitmann claims, the participant can achieve the highest level of fulfillment in the program of motor skill instruction.

Following Heitmann's advice, Anshel (1989) has examined the research specifically related to information-processing theory to establish guidelines for motor skill instruction of the older adult. Information processing is a theory we discussed briefly in Chapters 1 and 4. This theory suggests that the human being functions much like a computer in the performance of a movement skill. According to information-processing theory, we first receive environmental stimulation (suggesting that a movement is impending) through the brain's afferent (input) system. This information is organized and integrated (i.e., compared with old information about similar situations) by the brain, and a decision to move is made. Then this information is sent via the efferent (output) system to the muscles to create the desired moment. The movement occurs and is observed so relevant information can be stored for future attempts at similar movements.

Using this theory and current research, Anshel (1989) has created a series of recommendations for teaching older adults movement skill. First, to enhance the psychological readiness of the learner, a proper level of arousal must be achieved. This can be attained, according to Anshel, in several ways. One should maintain good eye contact, speak sufficiently loudly, keep a fairly close distance to participants when communicating, and address the participants by name. Finally, but equally important, one should inform the participants of the importance of learning the skill.

Anshel also recommends reducing verbal input to a minimum, because such input can slow the information-processing system. So, instructors should articulate clearly, be concise, and reduce the speed of delivery slightly. To assist the older participant further, they should make the environment conducive to learning motor skills by, for example, trying to eliminate all extraneous interference that could inhibit the participant's reception of information. Also, they should make sure lighting is adequate and the room temperature is appropriate for all.

Next, Anshel suggests teaching the participants appropriate attentional strategies. One should help them learn where to focus their attention. This requires instruction in what input they should look and listen for—and what input they should ignore. In addition, teaching the participants what sensations should accompany the movement they are learning is important.

Anshel believes that several strategies will facilitate older adults' perception and, therefore, skill acquisition. First, they must develop the proper sensory and motor "set." A *set* is the participant's readiness to employ the senses to receive relevant information. A racquetball player, for example, may watch the front wall for the positioning of the ball while listening to gain information concerning the ball's velocity. Anshel claims that these cues may be internal, rather than external as they were in the racquetball example. Imagine a diver who may need to focus on internal sensations to monitor progress during a dive. The focus of attention, whether internal or external, is the set.

Second, participants must be prepared with anticipatory strategies; that is, they must know the demands of the upcoming task in advance. An ability to predict correctly what movements might be required is particularly helpful for the elderly, who may gain speed of response or greater accuracy by their accurate anticipation.

Third, skill practice should be taught in the actual sequence in which it will happen and under circumstances that realistically simulate the task demands. At the same time, the instructor must be aware of the limitations of many older adults. For example, because they may require more time to react, the instructor should allow participants more time to receive the necessary stimulation prior to responding. Also, instructors should reduce the speed and complexity of the incoming information while allowing more time for movement alterations if necessary. During this process, they should also try to "attach old learning"—in other words, try to help the participant integrate the upcoming task with previous similar tasks. Then, once the movement has occurred, they should allow more time than usual for the participant to observe what transpired, so that this information will be available for integration on future attempts.

Anshel also notes that short-term memory deficits have been evidenced in the elderly. Recognition of this fact may also be beneficial in teaching situations. To assist older adults with any short-term memory deficits, instructors can encourage them to talk themselves through the task at a self-paced speed. This, Anshel believes, will reinforce short-term memory. Also helpful is assisting them in selecting the most meaningful movement cues that should be recognized and remembered. This might be further facilitated by the use of mental imagery, or visualization. Encouraging participants to picture themselves performing the skill is a good strategy.

Older adults have also been known to display somewhat slower recall than their younger counterparts. Recognizing this, instructors should allow participants more time to respond to stimuli, ponder their response, and store the relevant information about the movement. Situations where the older adult is rushed or extremely rapid recall is required may be discouraging. Anshel recommends establishing a slower, more constant pace initially. The pace can then be gradually speeded up.

Older performers also tend to check their actions more frequently than do younger adults. They also monitor longer after the response, which sometimes results in overanticipation on the subsequent response. This simply means that older adults should be given more time to reorganize their thoughts after performing a movement. They are frequently less capable of programming a rapid series of movements in a short period of time. For these reasons, Anshel (1989) offers several instructional strategies. First, as mentioned earlier, one should follow the actual sequence of events so the participant learns

the correct sequence. Later, more speed can be added. Second, one should have the participants focus on specific body parts or environmental information immediately before, during, and just after the movement. Asking them about the sensations associated with the movement is helpful. Third, one should provide feedback immediately following a movement, because the older performer relies heavily on it for future performances. Feedback should be precise, positive, and quantitative (e.g., "Drop your racket head about 4 inches.").

THE WORLD HEALTH ORGANIZATION HEIDELBERG GUIDELINES

Recently, experts on aging and physical activity came from all over the world to establish guidelines "for facilitating the development of strategies, policies, and both population- and community-based interventions aimed at maintaining and/or increasing the level of physical activity for all older adults" (World Health Organization [WHO] Heidelberg Guidelines, 1997, p. 2). Though the authors note that they do not specify what is meant by "older adult," they intend these guidelines to promote physical activity in the latter portion of life, with the most likely target audience being those over age 50. The authors define physical activity as "all movements in everyday life, including work, recreation, exercise, and sporting activities" (p. 2). In addition, they designed the guidelines to serve both men and women as well as a wide range of societies.

The WHO guidelines include rationales for being physically active, such as the direct social, physiological, and psychological benefits—both immediate and long-term. They further address who should undertake physical activity and sport as well as ways to promote and facilitate activity. For instance, the authors list factors that motivate people to be active as well as obstacles and barriers to achieving the desired physical activity. Table 16-9 includes an outline of the key points from this important document (WHO Heidelberg Guidelines, 1997).

Table 16-9   Key Points in the World Health Organization's Heidelberg Guidelines for Promoting Physical Activity Among Older Persons

1. EVIDENCE

    Physical activity improves health and is fun! In fact, fun is the primary reason most people undertake physical activity. Still, considerable scientific evidence attests to the value of physical activity for both daily function and health. However, for optimal benefit, the activity must be regular and continuous. Research shows that physical activity promotes general well-being, overall physical and psychological health, and independent living. In addition, it ameliorates specific diseases common in later life and reduces the impact of many disabling and painful conditions.

2. BENEFITS

    Physiological

    - Activity helps regulate glucose levels.
    - Certain hormonal levels are stimulated (e.g., adrenaline and noradrenaline).
    - Sleep improves.
    - Fitness is enhanced (e.g., aerobic endurance, muscle, strength or endurance, and flexibility).
    - Balance and coordination improve.
    - Behavioral slowing of movement decreases.

    Physiological

    - Relaxation is enhanced.
    - Stress and anxiety decrease.
    - Mood is elevated.
    - Improvements are seen in almost all psychological function following extended bouts of physical activity.
    - Depression and anxiety neuroses are improved.
    - Age-related declines in reaction time and central nervous system processing time are reduced.
    - Declines in fine and gross motor skill are reduced while new skills are learned and old ones are refined.

    Social

    - One becomes empowered to be more active in society, thereby enhancing social interactions, reducing societal withdrawal, broadening social networks, and stimulating new friendships.
    - Physical activity provides opportunities for intergenerational interaction.

3. SOCIETAL REASONS FOR PHYSICAL ACTIVITY

    - Health- and social-care costs decrease as independence increases; physical frailty and disease are delayed.
    - Productivity and active participation in society are enhanced.
    - People's view of older adults improves, enabling society to benefit from their wisdom.

4. WHO SHOULD BE ACTIVE

    - Physical activity will benefit any age group, including those with special limitations and disabilities, though they may need special adaptations to optimize the benefits.

5. PROMOTING/FACILITATING INCREASED ACTIVITY

    We can promote physical activity in all segments of the population by doing the following:

    - Influencing health policy at local, regional, national, and international levels.
    - Involving families, peers, communities, social-service providers, media, self-help groups, hospitals, nursing homes, health insurers, universities, adult education centers, rehabilitation centers, residential facilities, clubs, and or ganizations.

(continued)

Table 16-9 *(continued)*

6. MOTIVATING FACTORS

- Physical activity can be fun.
- It offers opportunities for companionship.
- Opportunities for independence can result.
- People enjoy improved health.

7. BARRIERS TO PHYSICAL ACTIVITY

- Lack of education about physical activity among participants, their families, their physicians, and society in general.
- Stereotypical depiction of older adults.
- Too little social support.
- Inadequate environmental support (e.g., transportation, architectural barriers).
- Distasteful earlier experiences in sports, exercise, physical education, etc.
- Imbalance between expected and actual gains.

8. RECOMMENDED PARAMETERS FOR PHYSICAL ACTIVITY

- It does not need to be expensive.
- One can do it in small spaces with few resources.
- Structured programs provide an excellent means for motivating continued participation.
- Both individual and group activities will work.
- Physical activity can be supervised or unsupervised.
- A simple and moderate focus is best.
- It must meet the individual's expectations.
- It should be regular (daily if possible), relaxing, and fun.

SOURCE: World Health Organization Heidelberg guidelines (1997).

SUMMARY

Traditionally, the study of adult development has been overshadowed by the study of children and adolescents. However, because of the rapidly increasing number of individuals approaching middle and late adulthood, this trend is ending as many developmentalists now focus their attention on the adult years.

As people age, balance often requires greater conscious awareness, which leads to increased body sway and an increased number of falls among older adults.

Falls cause more elderly deaths than do any other types of accidents, with nearly a third of all the elderly falling each year. Many factors, particularly a lack of phys-

ical activity and declining physical parameters, contribute to these falls. Falls can be devastating: Half of all elderly fallers never regain functional walking. Fortunately, several strategies can help people avoid falling. These include exercise programs to enhance strength, balance, and flexibility; careful screening and control of medication; and thorough analysis of the home environment to reduce factors that contribute to falling.

Although there is a paucity of research into the movement behavior of adult subjects, one area that has been studied in depth is the adult walking pattern. Such research has determined that even though many walking characteristics are retained through adulthood, some change considerably. Compared with younger adults, older adult walkers show decreased step and stride length and decreased flexion and extension of the hip joint. Perhaps as a subconscious attempt to improve stability, outtoeing increases with age.

Driving is one of the most important skills for older adults. As people age, the number of accidents they are involved in and their anxiety about driving increase while their driving frequency decreases. With the number of older adults increasing so rapidly, the number of traffic accidents among older drivers could triple within the next 30 years. The Mobility Consequences Model depicts a progression common among older drivers. Mental and/or physical changes lead to a loss of driving skill that increases accidents. Eventually, driving frequency is reduced, affecting quality of life by narrowing the scope of activities. Thus, finding safe and viable transportation alternatives for older adults is imperative.

When several selected movement activities were examined, it was found that angular velocities of body parts during movement generally decreased for 60-year-old women compared with college-age women. In addition, a small percentage of 70-year-olds exhibited difficulty in certain daily dressing and hygiene activities. Decreased flexibility was thought to be a major source of problems for these people.

An interesting way of examining motor performance in adulthood is to determine the age of "peak performance." Work conducted prior to 1953 found ages for peak performances in "vigorous skills" to be occurring before peak performances in activities requiring "less explosive outbursts of speed and energy." While that trend continues today, more recent research has determined that peak performance in many activities is occurring earlier today than 40 years ago.

ADLs are activities of daily living. Examples include eating, rising from a chair, brushing teeth, dressing, and bathing. Less than 84 percent of elderly individuals have been found to have a disability or a limitation in completing ADLs. The most commonly problematic ADLs are bathing, getting around inside, and getting in and out of bed without help. The number of Americans with ADL limitations will increase, making further study in this area particularly important.

Older adults appear to decrease performance during times of high arousal. This has been hypothesized to be a function of decreasing ability to deal with the increased cognitive demands of high-arousal movement situations. Or, it may be related to changes in the neuroendocrine system and its indirect effects on movement behavior. To some extent, this decline can be reversed by drug therapy, relaxation training, or refocusing the attention during performance.

Speed of movement typically declines with age — not only walking and running but also the more subtle kinds of movements measured in reaction-time research. Although a general slowing with age is common, the decrease is particularly pronounced in the more complicated movements known as symbolic translations. There is less decline, if any, in the simpler spatial transpositions.

The decrease in speed with age is caused by several critical factors: reduction in functional motor units, need for more intense neural stimulation, and increased caution in performance.

Declines in movement ability are extremely common for most aging people, but the decline can be postponed or, in some cases, avoided. To help maintain movement ability, several strategies may compensate for age. More important, regular practice and exercise are extremely effective in maintaining or even improving movement ability in adulthood.

Though physical activity during adulthood appears to be beneficial, trends in physical activity indicate that most adults choose to maintain a relatively inactive lifestyle. As many as a third of all people surveyed fall into the "sedentary" category. Fortunately, this number may be decreasing in many countries. In addition, men appear to be more vigorously active than women, and older adults have been increasing their activity levels more than have younger adults in recent years.

Injury rates among baby boomers and older adults during physical activity have increased in recent years. The increases are thought to be a function of greater participation. Many of these injuries could be prevented by taking simple precautions such as wearing helmets while cycling or warming up before vigorous exercise. According to the Consumer Product Safety Commission, because of the important role of exercise during aging, avoiding exercise is generally not the best solution to decreasing injury rates.

A growing population of older adults and greater interest in movement are increasing the need for quality movement-instruction programs for adults. Unfortunately, too few quality programs exist. Steps need to be taken to increase the number of professionals qualified to teach movement skills to older adults. Furthermore, these individuals need to focus on the research to ascertain the most efficient means of teaching movement skills to their clients.

The Heidelberg guidelines were developed by a panel of experts convened by the World Health Organization to help develop strategies and policies concerning physical activity for older adults. They are intended to promote physical activity for that population and include details concerning the benefits of and barriers to physical activity as well as factors that can help motivate people to be more active.

KEY TERMS

activities of daily living (ADLs)
balance
dyspnea
gait
last-in-first-out hypothesis
Mobility Consequences Model

movement time
out-toeing
polypharmacy
postural sway
reaction time
spatial transpositions

speed/accuracy trade-off
step length
stride length
symbolic translations

QUESTIONS FOR REFLECTION

1. Discuss the trend in population growth in U.S. society. What implications does this hold for the future?

2. What causes can be linked to the increasing number of falls seen in older adults?

3. What are the important findings comparing gait patterns in early versus late adulthood?

4. What are the typical trends in physical activity patterns in adulthood?

5. Can you compare and contrast the findings of Degnan and Payne (1994) to the earlier work of Lehman (1953) relative to peak proficiency in sport performances?

6. What factors might contribute to declines in running speed with age?

7. What is the difference between reaction time and movement time? Define each.

8. What do we mean by the term *speed/accuracy trade-off*? Can you provide two examples of this phenomenon?

9. How does the incidence of injury in older adulthood relate to physical activity participation?

10. What would you recommend to someone teaching movement skills to older adults? Provide at least five specific recommendations.

11. What is the relationship between aging and physical activity? Include at least five significant benefits to the aging individual.

12. Summarize the Heidelberg guidelines. What are they and what are their key points?

INTERNET RESOURCES

Fifty-Plus Lifelong Fitness Association
  www.50plus.org
*National Blueprint: Increasing Physical Activity Among
  Adults Age 50 and Older*
  www.agingblueprint.org/overview.cfm
National Center on Rural Aging
  www.ncoa.org/content.cfm?sectionID=40

National Council on Aging **www.ncoa.org**
National Institute on Aging **www.nih.gov/nia**
U.S. Bureau of the Census **www.census.gov**

ONLINE LEARNING CENTER (www.mhhe.com/payne6e)

Visit the *Human Motor Development* Online Learning Center for study aids and additional resources. You can use the study guide questions and key terms puzzles to review key terms and concepts for this chapter and to prepare for exams. You can further extend your knowledge of motor development by checking out the Web links, articles, and activities found on the site.

REFERENCES

American College of Sports Medicine. (1998). Exercise and physical activity for older adults. *Medicine and Science in Sports and Exercise, 30*(6), 992–1008.

Aniansson. A. (1980). *Muscle function in old age with special reference to muscle morphology, effect of training and capacity in activities of daily living.* Goteborg, Sweden: Goteborg University.

Anshel, M. H. (1989). An information processing approach for teaching motor skills to the elderly. In A. C. Ostrow (Ed.), *Aging and motor behavior.* Indianapolis, IN: Benchmark.

Backman, L., & Molander, B. (1989). The relationship between level of arousal and cognitive operations during motor behavior in young and older adults. In A. C. Ostrow (Ed.), *Aging and motor behavior.* Indianapolis, IN: Benchmark.

Barnett, A., Smith, B., Lord, S. R., Williams, M., & Baumand, A. (2003). Community-based group exercise improves balance and reduces falls in at-risk older people: A randomized controlled sample. *Age and Ageing, 32*(4), 407–414.

Barry, H. C., Rich, B. S., & Carlson, R. T. (1993). How exercise can benefit older patients: A practical approach. *Physician and Sportsmedicine, 21,* 124–140.

Benekohal, R. F., Michaels, R. M., Shim, E., & Resende, P. T. V. (1997). Effects of aging on older drivers. *Transportation Research Record, 1438.* Retrieved from www.usroads.com/journals/rej/9708/re97083.htm.

Bilban, M. (2002). Drivers of advanced age in traffic accidents. *Archives of Industrial Hygiene and Toxicology, 53*(4), 289–296.

Birren, J. E., Woods, A. M., & Williams, M. V. (1980). Behavioral slowing with age: Causes, organization and consequences. In L. W. Poon (Ed.), Aging in the '80s (pp. 293–308). Washington, DC: American Psychological Association.

Brill, P. A., Macera, C. A., Davis, R., Blair, S. N., & Gordon, N. (2000). Muscular strength and physical function. *Journal of Medicine and Science in Sports and Exercise, 32*(2), 412–416.

Brooke-Wavell, K., Perrett, L. K., Howarth, P. A., & Haslam, R. A. (2002). Influence of the visual environment on the postural stability in healthy older women. *Gerontology, 48*(5), 293–297.

Brown, M., Sinacore, D. R., Ehsani, A. A., Binder, E. F., Holloszy, J. O., & Kohrt, W. M. (2000). Low-intensity exercise as a modifier of physical frailty in older adults. *Archives of Physical Medical Rehabilitation, 81*(7), 960–965.

Burkhart, J. E., Berger, A. M., Creedon, M., & McGavock, A. T. (1998). Mobility and independence: Changes and challenges for older drivers. Retrieved from Administration on Aging, www.aoa.gov/research/drivers.html.

Consumer Product Safety Commission. (1998). Sports-related injuries to persons 65 years of age and older. Retrieved on February 25, 2004, from www.cpsc.gov/cpscpub/pubs/grand/aging/injury65.pdf.

———. (2000). Baby boomer sports injuries. Retrieved on February 25, 2004, from www.cpsc.gov/library/boomer.pdf.

Cunningham, D. A., Montoye, H. J., Metzer, H. L., & Keller, J. B. (1968). Active leisure time activities as related to age among males in a total population. *Journal of Gerontology, 23,* 551–556.

Degnan, F., & Payne, V. G. (1994). Age and peak performance in adulthood: 1953–93. Unpublished manuscript.

Eckert, H. M. (1987). *Motor Development.* Indianapolis, IN: Benchmark.

Hasselkus, B. R., & Shambes, G. M. (1975). Aging and postural sway in women. *Journal of Gerontology, 30,* 661–667.

Haywood, K., & Getchell, N. (2001). *Lifespan motor development.* 3rd ed. Champaign, IL: Human Kinetics.

Heitmann, H. M. (1982). Older adult physical education: Research implications for instruction. *Quest, 34*(1), 34–42.

Hertzog, C. (1991). Age, information processing speed, and intelligence. In K. W. Schaie & M. P. Lawton (Eds.), *Annual review of gerontology and geriatrics.* New York: Springer.

Hodgkins, J. (1962). Influence of age and the speed of reaction and movement in females. *Journal of Gerontology, 17,* 385–389.

Hutman, L. P., & Sekuler, R. (1980). Spatial vision and aging: II. Criterion effects. *Journal of Gerontology, 35,* 700–706.

Jarvik, L. F., & Cohen, D. (1973). A biobehavioral approach to internal changes with aging. In C. Eisdorfer & M. P. Lawton (Eds.), *The psychology of adult development and aging.* Washington, DC: American Psychological Association.

Kelly, K. D., Pickett, W., Yiannakoulias, N., Rowe, B. H., Schopflocher, D. P., Svenson, L., & Voaklander, D. C. (2003). Medication use and falls in community-dwelling older persons. *Age and Ageing, 32*(5), 503–509.

Khattab, E. (1980). The effect of aging on selected kinematic and kinetic parameters of gait. In J. M. Cooper & B. Haven (Eds.), *Proceedings of the biomechanics symposium* (pp. 348–349). Indianapolis: Indiana University; Indiana State Board of Health.

Kinoshita, H., & Francis, P. R. (1996). A comparison of prehension force control in young and elderly individuals. *European Journal of Applied Physiology, 74*(5), 450–460.

Klinger, A. (1980). Temporal and spatial characteristics of movement patterns of women over 60. Paper presented at the National Conference of the American Alliance for Health, Physical Education, Recreation, and Dance, Detroit, MI.

Lehman, H. C. (1953). *Age and achievement.* Princeton, NJ: Princeton University Press.

Melzer, I., Benjuya, N., & Kaplanski, J. (2003). Effects of regular walking on postural stability in the elderly. *Gerontology, 49*(4), 240–245.

Menz, H. B., Lord, S. R., & Fitzpatrick, R. C. (2003). Age-related differences in walking stability. *Age and Ageing, 32*(2), 137–142.

Murray, M., Drought, A. B., & Kory, R. C. (1964). Walking patterns of normal men. *Journal of Bone and Joint Surgery, 46-A,* 335–360.

National Aging Information Center. (1989). *National long term care survey.* Washington, DC: Administration on Aging.

National Center for Injury Prevention and Control. (1996). *National summary of injury mortality data, 1988–1994.* Atlanta, GA: Centers for Disease Control and Prevention.

———. (1997). *Unintentional injury fact sheet, falls and hip fractures in the elderly: Injury prevention.* Atlanta, GA: Centers for Disease Control.

National Institute for Occupational Safety and Health. (1992). *Falls in the home.* Columbus: Ohio State University Extension.

National Institutes of Health (1999). NIH news release. Retrieved from www.nih.gov/nia/news/pr/1999/06-16.htm.

National Policy and Resource Center on Women and Aging. (1998). Driving safely: Does age matter? *Women and Aging Newsletter, 3,* 1–5.

Overstall, P. W., Exton-Smith, A. N., Imms, F. J., & Johnson, A. L. (1977). Falls in the elderly related to postural imbalance. *British Medical Journal, 1,* 261–264.

Pavol, M. J., Owings, T. M., Foley, K. T., & Grabiner, M. D. (1999). Gait characteristics as risk factors for falling from trips induced in older adults. *Journal of Gerontology, 54*(11), M583–M590.

Potash, M., & Jones, B. (1977). Aging and decision criteria for the detection of tones in noise. *Journal of Gerontology, 35,* 436–440.

Rabitt, P., & Rogers, M. (1965). Age and choice between responses in a self-paced repetitive task. *Ergonomics, 8,* 435–444.

Reddi, B. A., & Carpenter, R. H. (2000). The influence of urgency on decision time. *National Neuroscience, 3*(8), 827–830.

Reigel, P. S. (1981). Athletic records and human endurance. *American Scientist, 69,* 285–290.

Rozenfeld, S., Camacho, L. A., & Veras, P. (2003). Medication as a risk factor for falls in older Brazilian women. *Revista Panamericana de Salud Publica, 13*(6), 369–75.

Rubenstein, H. S., Miller, F. H., Pastel, S., & Evans, H. B. (1983). Standards of medical care based on consensus rather than evidence: The case of routine bedrail use for the elderly. *Law and Medical Health Care, 11,* 271–276.

Salthouse, T. A. (1979). Adult age and the speed-accuracy trade-off. *Ergonomics, 22,* 811–821.

Salthouse, T. A., & Somberg, B. L. (1982). Skilled performance: Effects of adult age and experience on elementary processes. *Journal of Experimental Psychology: General, 3,* 176–207.

Sattin, R. W. (1992). Falls among the elderly: A public health perspective. *Annual Review of Public Health, 13,* 489–508.

Schmidt, R. A. (1991). *Motor learning and performance: From principles to practice.* Champaign, IL: Human Kinetics.

Schmidt, R. A., & Wrisberg, C. A. (2004). *Motor learning and performance.* 3rd ed. Champaign, IL: Human Kinetics.

Schroll, M. (2003). Physical activity in an ageing population. *Scandinavian Journal of Medicine and Science in Sports, 13*(1), 63–69.

Shephard, R. J. (1978). *Physical activity and aging.* Chicago: Year Book Medical Publishers.

Sidney, K. H., & Shephard, R. J. (1977). Activity patterns of elderly men and women. *Journal of Gerontology, 32,* 25–32.

Simoneau, G. G., & Leibowitz, H. W. (1996). Posture, gait, and falls. In J. E. Birren & K. W. Schaie (Eds.), *Handbook of the psychology of aging* (pp. 204–217). San Diego: Academic Press.

Spirduso, W. W. (1982). Physical fitness in relation to motor aging. In F. J. Pirozzolo & G. J. Maletta (Eds.), *The aging motor system.* New York: Praeger.

———. (1985). Age as a limiting factor in human neuromuscular performance. In D. H. Clarke & H. M. Eckert (Eds.), *The academy papers: Limits of human performance.* Champaign, IL: Human Kinetics.

———. (1995). *Physical dimensions of aging.* Champaign, IL: Human Kinetics.

Stephens, T., & Caspersen, C. J. (1994). The demography of physical activity. In C. Bouchard, R. J. Shepherd, & T. Stephens

(Eds.), *Physical activity, fitness, and health: International proceedings and consensus statement.* Champaign, IL: Human Kinetics

Stones, M. J., & Kozma, A. (1981). Adult age trends in athletic performances. *Experimental Aging Research, 7,* 269–279.

Surburg, P. (1976). Aging and effect of physical and mental practice upon acquisition and retention of motor skill. *Journal of Gerontology, 31,* 64–67.

Tinetti, M. E., & Speechley, M. (1989). Prevention of falls among the elderly. *New England Journal of Medicine, 320,* 1055–1059.

United States Bureau of the Census. (1996). Projections of the population, by age and sex: 1995 to 2050. Retrieved from www.aoa.dhhs.gov/aoa/stats/aging21/table1.html.

Welford, A. T. (1982). Motor skills and aging. In F. J. Pirozzolo & G. J. Maletta (Eds.), *The aging motor system.* New York: Praeger.

Woollacott, M. H. (1989). Aging, posture control, and movement preparation. In M. H. Woollacott & A. Shumway-Cook (Eds.), *Development of posture and gait across the lifespan.* Columbia: University of South Carolina Press.

Woollacott, M. H., Shumway-Cook, A., & Nasher, L. (1982). Postural reflexes and aging. In F. J. Pirozzolo & G. J. Maletta (Eds.), *The aging motor system.* New York: Praeger.

World Health Organization Heidelberg guidelines. (1997). *Journal of Aging and Physical Activity, 5,* 2–8.

17 Assessment

ertain studies suggest that many physical educators fail to assess properly their students' motor behaviors (Safrit & Wood, 1995). Leaders from several states have expressed this concern regarding the lack of teachers' ability to assess a student's motor behavior (Holland 1992; Mathieson & Herring, 1990). In fact, one study that Haubenstricker conducted (1984) found that physical educators devote little time to assessment, and when assessment does occur, it most frequently takes the form of a teacher-made test.

Why does this problem exist? Many teachers complain that tests are too difficult, too time-consuming, and too expensive to administer, but there are many valid assessment instruments that teachers in school and nonschool settings can feasibly administer. We believe the primary culprit is a lack of teacher training—many teachers simply do not fully understand the role of assessment and do not know how to select and administer tests. This chapter has been designed to help teachers and others overcome this deficiency. It describes why teachers should assess, what they should assess, how to prepare students for assessment, and how to select the assessment instrument that best meets personal needs. Various assessment instruments are also reviewed.

GUIDELINES FOR ASSESSMENT

The assessment process should not be approached haphazardly; it should be planned systematically. Following are seven important questions to consider before beginning to assess students:

1. Why do you want to assess your students?
2. What variables do you plan to assess?
3. Which tests purport to assess the important variables that you have identified?
4. How will you prepare yourself for collecting the data?
5. Do you have the statistical skills to interpret the assessment data?

6. Will you be conducting an informal or a formal assessment?
7. How, and with whom, will you share the assessment results?

Why Assess?

Many professionals assess student performance as a simple matter of course, probably because when they were in school their instructor periodically assessed their performance. But assessment of student performance should be carried out with a specific purpose in mind, such as one of the following:

1. *Screening.* Screening is a process whereby people are assessed to determine if they should be referred for further testing or whether they need a special program of instruction. Practically speaking, a physical education instructor may want to screen students at the beginning of the school year to identify children who have special needs.

2. *Program content.* Assessment results can be used to help plan the content of a program. By assessing students' incoming ability, one can write program objectives that challenge students.

3. *Student progress.* Assessment can also be used to determine how well students are proceeding toward course objectives.

4. *Program evaluation.* One can assess students' performance to determine whether a specific program of instruction is fostering their motor skill or physical fitness development.

5. *Classification.* Through assessment, it is possible to place students in homogeneous or heterogeneous groups. For example, when equating teams for competition, it is best if the two teams competing against each other have similar skills.

What Variables to Assess

Once you have determined why you need to assess, you will want to determine which variables to assess. Instructional units that are tied to specific course objectives generally indicate which variables need to be assessed; for example, in a gymnastics unit, you may want to assess balance and upper-body strength. In short, assess those variables that are part of your course objectives.

Selecting the Best Test

To select the best test, you will want to review all available tests that purport to assess the variables in question. Popular measurement textbooks contain descriptions of available tests (Burton & Miller, 1998; Kirby, 1991; Safrit & Wood, 1995; Strand & Wilson, 1993), as does the classic *Mental Measurements Yearbook* (Plake & Impara, 2001).

After consulting these references, you should be able to identify several tests that assess the variables in which you are interested. Now you must decide which test instrument best meets your needs. To help you make this decision, consider each of the following questions:

1. Is the test statistically valid, reliable, and objective?
2. If the test is norm-referenced, are the norms established on a population similar to the one you plan to assess?
3. Is the test instrument feasible to administer?
4. Do you have the training and expertise to administer the test as well as interpret the results?

CHARACTERISTICS OF IDEAL TESTS Acceptable test instruments should be valid, reliable, and objective. A valid test measures what it claims to measure. One type of validity frequently used in motor development and physical education is **content validity:** The instrument contains tasks that measure specific content of interest. This type of validity is often logically determined by a panel of experts. For example, experts have determined that the 50-yard dash is a valid indicator of running speed because it measures how fast a person runs. Other types of validity are statistically determined, and a detailed discussion of them is beyond the scope of this text. Consistency of test results is another important characteristic of a good test. A test

is reliable if student scores do not significantly vary from day to day, assuming that the students have not received additional instruction. Thus, **test reliability** is the test score's freedom from error.

The third characteristic of an ideal test is **objectivity** (sometimes called **interrater reliability**), which is the degree of accuracy to which a test is scored. Content validity is frequently determined subjectively, but both reliability and objectivity are determined statistically. Statistical determination is possible by computing a **correlation coefficient** for two sets of scores. For example, to determine objectivity, a set of ratings compiled by one scorer is correlated with the scores obtained by a second scorer. Because the resulting correlation coefficient can never be greater than 1.00, a correlation of 0.80 or 0.90 is generally deemed acceptable.

CAUTION: NORMS ARE POPULATION-SPECIFIC
Norms describe how large groups of people score in regard to selected variables. Because one large group can differ from another large group in regard to a variable of interest, norms are population-specific. An example is norms for height. Because American children are generally taller than Japanese children, it would be inappropriate to interchange normative values within these two populations. The same holds true regarding tests of motor proficiency and tests of physical fitness.

Therefore, if you decide to use a norm-referenced test, make certain that the norms were established on a population similar to the one you intend to assess.

TEST FEASIBILITY You may find several tests that meet all of the selection criteria, so the next step is to determine which of these tests are more feasible to administer. Consider the following points:

1. Which test can be administered in the least amount of time?
2. Must you administer the test individually, or can it be administered to groups?
3. Do you have the training and expertise to administer the test? Some tests require extensive training.
4. Do you have all of the supplies and equipment needed for test administration? Some tests

must be purchased as part of a test kit that may cost several hundred dollars.

5. Do you have the training and expertise to interpret the test results?

Besides referring to the publications mentioned earlier in this section, consult the test manual that accompanies most tests. Generally, the manual describes in detail how the test was developed and how it should be administered.

Preparing Students for Assessment

Without a doubt, requiring people to perform strange motor tasks, in unfamiliar surroundings, in front of strangers, while sometimes using strange-looking equipment, can produce a great deal of test anxiety. However, several steps can help reduce this uneasy feeling that frequently accompanies the administration of an assessment instrument. Horvat and Kalakian (1996) suggest that before assessing, one should consider the test environment and the participants' physical and psychological needs.

TEST ENVIRONMENT The room where the assessment is to be administered should be as comfortable as possible, and the room's temperature and lighting should be ideal. The testing area should be free of unnecessary furniture and free from distractions, such as high noise levels. Above all, the area should be free of potential hazards.

MEETING PHYSICAL NEEDS Also consider the participants' physical needs. For example, thirsty participants or those who must use the restroom will be distracted from the assessment situation. Establish a procedure whereby you ask before assessment begins whether or not the participant needs to be excused.

MEETING PSYCHOLOGICAL NEEDS The following procedures help reduce test anxiety:

1. When participants arrive, do not rush into the assessment: engage them in informal conversation for a couple of minutes. Introduce yourself, and get the participants to talk about themselves. Ask a question such as "What are some of your favorite activities?" This tech-

nique relaxes the participants by making them focus their attention on themselves instead of the assessment.

2. Tell the participants what they will be doing during the assessment. In other words, reveal the unexpected.

3. When talking with the participants, try not to use the word *test,* which can make many people nervous.

4. If equipment is to be used during the assessment, give participants an opportunity to explore it before assessment begins. For example, before requiring participants to catch a ball, let them informally play with the ball, so they can experience for themselves that the ball is soft and will not harm them.

Instructor Preparation and Data Collection

After selecting an assessment instrument and preparing your students for assessment, there is still one additional preparation—you must now be certain that you are adequately prepared to administer the assessment. To help prepare yourself, ask the following questions: Do I have the necessary equipment to administer the assessment? If administering a standardized assessment, can I deliver the standardized directions to students taking the assessment? Do I have an appropriate score sheet with extra pencils on hand? Am I adequately prepared to administer the assessment without constantly referring to the test manual? In short, you must think through and even pilot (test run) your assessment procedures prior to administering to your target population.

If your assessment requires you to observe and then rate developmental movement performance, do you possess valid observational skills? In other words, do you have a complete understanding of the developmental milestones being assessed? Are you able to recognize deviations from the norm? And, of utmost importance, have you thought through observational vantage points for each skill being assessed? For example, say that you are planning on observing an individual's stage of maturity for the fundamental locomotor skill of running. As the student performs, from what angle will you be observing? Will the runner be coming directly toward you or running away from you, or will you be observing the runner from a profile view? Obviously, the answer depends on which component of the skill is being evaluated. If you are assessing the relationship of the heel to the buttock, then a profile view would be most appropriate. However, if you are observing the runner to determine whether or not the hands are crossing the body's midline, then requiring the runner to run directly toward you is most appropriate. In other words, you should plot observational vantage points for each skill being assessed prior to assessment.

Interpreting the Assessment Data

Here is the most frequently asked question following data collection: How well did the student perform in accordance with accepted criteria or norms? To answer this question, you will need to have at least an introductory understanding of two measurement concepts: measures of central tendency and measures of variability.

Measures of central tendency include the mean, the median, and the mode. The *mean* is simply the arithmetic average. To calculate it, add all the raw scores and divide by the number of students who took part in the assessment. The *median* is actually the 50th percentile, the exact midpoint of a distribution of scores. The *mode*, the crudest measure of central tendency, is the score that appears most frequently within the distribution.

While the mean score describes the average performance within a distribution of scores, measures of variability describe the spread of the scores. The most frequently used measure of variability is the **standard deviation,** which describes the degree to which the scores vary about the mean of the distribution. The concept of standard deviation can be best illustrated by its relationship to the normal bell-shaped curve, shown in Figure 17-1. This curve is a theoretical model based on laws of chance that describe the phenomenon observed when large groups of individuals are tested. Notice that the curve consists of three positive and three negative standard deviation (σ) units. The area under the curve represents performance occurrences. That is, 68.26 percent of a normally distributed population will score somewhere between $+1\sigma$ and -1σ, while 95.4 percent will be represented somewhere between $+2\sigma$ and -2σ units. Likewise, 99.7 percent of the population tested will fall somewhere between $+3\sigma$ and -3σ units.

When analyzing assessment data, you will be interested in determining whether the raw score of interest falls above or below the mean and how far the score deviates away from the mean score. When real data are involved, σ units are transformed into actual scores. Here is an example to illustrate the point. Billy's mother is interested in how her son performed on a test measuring abdominal strength/endurance (sit-up test). Billy was able to perform 35 sit-ups. How does Billy's performance rank among his classmates or among students in a standardized population? To answer this question, you need to know the mean and σ of the distribution of scores of which Billy is a member. To complete our example, let us say that the mean of the distribution of sit-up scores is 45 and its σ is 10. With this information, we can now say that Billy's score is below the average score. Not only is his score below average, but it is -1σ below the mean. Therefore, we can say that about 84 percent of the individuals within this distribution performed better than Billy; conversely, Billy performed better than 16 percent of the individuals within this distribution.

Formal Versus Informal Assessment

We generally think of assessment as being a very detailed formal process. This formal process has been described as any situation in which the student is aware that he or she is being observed and evaluated (Sherrill, 1993). Unfortunately, many individuals become anxious and "tighten up" in these formal settings. As a result, a true performance score is probably not being obtained. For this reason, you may choose on occasion to engage in an informal assessment. When assessment is performed in an in-

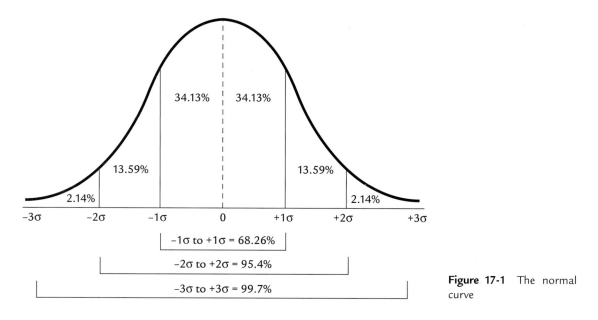

Figure 17-1 The normal curve

formal manner, the student is not generally aware that an observation is being made.

Linder (1993a; 1993b; 1996) has described a type of informal assessment known as transdisciplinary **play-based assessment.** One aspect of this type of informal assessment involves both unstructured and structured motor play. The play-based assessment is accomplished by allowing the child free play within an approved area but in the presence of an adult facilitator. At first, the facilitator simply plays along and models the child's play behavior. However, later on, the facilitator will coax the child into exhibiting new movement tasks that the child did not spontaneously initiate. During this time, but unbeknown to the child, an evaluation is being conducted. In fact, videotaping the play session is recommended.

Physical educators and other professionals are often confronted with a situation whereby they must evaluate a large group of students within a short time. If this is to be accomplished, it is important to select an assessment instrument that lends itself to this function. Two such assessment instruments are the Test of Gross Motor Development–2 as well as the Michigan State University "total body approach" of assessing basic fundamental motor skills. More will be said about these useful tools later in

the chapter. The point here is that all assessments need not be carried out in a formal manner. The nature and purpose of the assessment will, in part, dictate which instrument or method is the most appropriate to employ. As pointed out earlier, you must decide on the nature and purpose of the assessment before selecting an assessment instrument.

Sharing Assessment Results

Once test results have been analyzed and interpreted, the information should be shared with the appropriate people. Depending on the circumstances, these people are the parents, fellow teachers, the school nurse, and a host of other professionals. This information can be shared through written communication, but individual face-to-face communication is best for reviewing the written assessment. Realistically, however, individual conferences are not always possible when large groups of people are involved. Nevertheless, whether you convey assessment results individually or through written communication, the goal of the communication is the same: an explanation of why you assessed, what you assessed, and what the assessment revealed. Be careful to use terminology that the layperson will understand;

especially avoid using complicated statistical terms. Remember that parents are going to be interested in knowing what they can do to improve their child's motor or fitness abilities, so be prepared to offer program suggestions. Also, have references available to which you can refer the parents for additional program information.

TYPES OF ASSESSMENT INSTRUMENTS

After realistically considering the questions mentioned earlier, you will be in a better position to choose the type of test that will best meet your needs. This section examines the advantages and disadvantages of several assessment tools.

Norm-Referenced

Norm-referenced (NR) assessment instruments are basically ***quantitative evaluations*** designed to compare a person's skills and abilities with those of others from similar age, gender, and socioeconomic groups. Because the normative scales are derived from statistical procedures, these types of instruments are sometimes referred to as ***psychometric.*** Currently popular NR tests are the Bayley Scales of Infant Development II (Bayley, 1993), Gesell Developmental Schedules (Gesell & Ames, 1940), Bruininks-Oseretsky Test of Motor Proficiency (Bruininks, 1978), and Test of Gross Motor Development–2 (Ulrich, 2000).

ADVANTAGES   Norm-referenced tests are popular because most (but not all) are easy to administer. The examiner needs minimal training to administer the test, and scoring procedures generally are simple. The assessment score provides information as to where a person stands in relation to peers at a given point in time.

DISADVANTAGES   Because NR scales provide information concerning a person's "average" functioning, they are not precise and cannot pinpoint the cause of skill or developmental deficits. They simply supply information as to where a given person stands in comparison to people from similar backgrounds. Scores obtained from NR tests offer little insight into programming considerations.

Criterion-Referenced

Criterion-referenced (CR) assessment instruments evaluate the "quality" of a person's performance. Because development proceeds along a predictable sequence of milestones, it is possible to determine where a person lies on this continuum. Thus, one major difference between NR and CR assessments is that the latter compare people to themselves over time, whereas the former compare people to a standardized population at a given point in time. With CR tests, the examiner's primary interest, for example, is not how far a person can throw a ball but rather the technique (form) the person uses when projecting the ball. Motor development professionals frequently refer to this type of assessment as "process-oriented," which is discussed later in this chapter.

ADVANTAGES   Results from CR assessment instruments lend more insight into programming considerations than do results from NR tests. The CR test also provides for true developmental assessment — that is, comparing a person to self-performance along a continuum from immature to mature performance styles.

DISADVANTAGES   CR tests are more complicated to administer than NR tests, so much more training is needed. Frequently, the examiner must learn many functional definitions for intraskill components; confusion about them often causes scoring difficulties.

Product-Oriented Assessment

Motor development researchers in the first half of the twentieth century relied heavily on the use of ***product-oriented assessments.*** When employing this approach, the examiner is more interested in performance outcomes than the technique used to perform the task; for instance, how far or how fast a person can throw a ball. The form or technique used to throw the ball is generally of little interest to the product-oriented assessment examiner. Thus, product-oriented assessments are similar to NR assessments because both measure quantitative performance outcomes. They differ in that with NR assessments, normative data have been established for the quantitative measures. The advantages and disadvantages of product-oriented assessments are similar to those of NR assessments.

PRODUCT- VERSUS PROCESS-ORIENTED ASSESSMENT: A COMPARATIVE EXAMPLE

Pretend that you are to assess the catching ability of a 7-year-old girl. The following examples illustrate the major differences between product- and process-oriented assessment.

Product-Oriented Assessment

Without a doubt, the simplest product-oriented assessment to evaluate catching performance is the pass-fail system. The girl's performance is assessed by determining the number of thrown balls that she retains versus the number of balls she drops. To score, 1 point is awarded for each ball retained; dropped balls are recorded as 0 points.

Process-Oriented Assessment

Within the discipline of motor development, the most widely discussed *process-oriented assessments* are those Roberton and colleagues have described. Their technique is based on the idea that because development occurs at different times within different body components, assessment of motor behavior should involve a segmental or component approach. This component approach requires "the identification of developmental characteristics of body parts within a task" (Safrit & Wood, 1995, p. 303). Refer to Table 14-3, which illustrates the hypothesized developmental sequence for catching. Note that the emphasis in this type of evaluation is how each body component reacts to the oncoming projectile.

In addition, refer to Chapters 13 and 14, which present in detail the component approach for assessing running, jumping, hopping, galloping, sliding, skipping, throwing, catching, and kicking.

Roberton and Halverson, both noted for their use of process-oriented assessment, have pointed out several major drawbacks of the component approach. They feel that a comprehensive understanding of developmental steps and a prolonged period of study and practice of the techniques are required:

> Pre-observation study of the definitions of each developmental step and the decision rules for identifying that step is always necessary. . . . The ease with which successful coaches and teachers seem to spot the movement characteristics of their athletes and students comes from years of hard work. (Roberton & Halverson, 1984, pp. 53–54)

The feasibility of incorporating such an assessment approach within a large-scale school setting is questionable. Take, for example, the findings of a doctoral dissertation. Jenkot (1986) used 206 male and female students in grades K–3 in an attempt to study the feasibility of using Roberton and Halverson's component approach to assess both hopping and skipping. Table 17-1 describes the time commitment needed to train evaluators and to collect and record the data. Though Jenkot concluded that the component approach was feasible to use in a large-scale setting, we take issue with this conclusion. Given that most elementary physical education classes meet with the physical education specialist once or twice per week in 30-minute sessions, it would take nearly seven class periods simply to videotape these two simple skills. Furthermore, we believe that few physical educators are willing to devote so much "out of class" time to assess student performance. It is our belief, however, that the component approach is feasible in small-scale clinical and research settings. As mentioned earlier, assessment instruments such as Ulrich's Test of Gross Motor Development–2 (2000) and the Michigan State University "total body approach" assessments are easier and far less time-consuming to administer and therefore are more feasible to use in large-scale settings.

Table 17-1 Findings from Jenkot's 1986 Study on the Feasibility of Large-Scale Implementation of the Component Approach for Assessing Fundamental Motor Skills in Grades K–3	
Task	**Time Commitment**
Amount of time needed to train two teachers to code with 0.80 criterion agreement the two tasks of hopping and skipping	
Coder #1	9 hours 40 minutes
Coder #2	5 hours 45 minutes
Time needed to videotape 206 students performing the hop and the skip	3 hours 17 minutes
Time needed to code children's performances from the video recording	18 hours 46 minutes

SOURCE: Jenkot (1986).

SELECTED NORM-REFERENCED INSTRUMENTS

This section briefly describes four popular norm-referenced assessment instruments. In addition to the Bayley Scales of Infant Development II, the Bruininks-Oseretsky Test of Motor Proficiency, and the Basic Motor Ability Test–Revised, we also describe the Denver II.

Bayley Scales of Infant Development II

The second edition of the Bayley Scales of Infant Development (BSID-II) was released in 1993 (Bayley, 1993). This early childhood assessment instrument was renormed on a stratified random sample of 1700 children, which paralleled the 1988 U.S. Census statistics on age, gender, region, race/ethnicity, and parental education. Unlike the first edition, administered to infants 2–30 months old, the BSID-II encompasses a wider age range (1–42 months). To accommodate this increased age range, researchers created more than 100 new items. In addition, they revised the Behavior Rating Scale (formerly called the Infant Behavior Record) in both structure and content. Similar to the first edition, the BSID-II still retains the three original scales. The first is the Mental Development Index (MDI). Of particular interest is the second—the Motor Scale, which as-

sesses degree of body control, large muscle coordination, fine motor manipulatory skills involving use of the hands and fingers, dynamic movement, dynamic praxis, postural imitation, and stereognosis (perceiving and understanding the form and nature of objects by the sense of touch). Motor quality is also assessed in the third scale—the Behavior Rating Scale. New to the second edition is clinical validation information pertaining to children who were born prematurely, have HIV antibodies, were exposed to drugs prenatally, were born with asphyxia, are developmentally delayed, have frequent otitis media, are autistic, or have Down syndrome.

The complete BSID-II kit can be purchased for $975 from the Psychological Corporation, P.O. Box 708906, San Antonio, TX 78270; (800) 211-8378; www.psychcorp.com. Because the BSID-II is classified as a "level C" product, it can only be purchased by individuals with a Ph.D. in Psychology or Education or with a license or certification by an agency recognized by the Psychological Corporation in accordance with the 1985 Standards for Educational and Psychological Testing.

Bruininks-Oseretsky Test of Motor Proficiency

The Bruininks-Oseretsky Test of Motor Proficiency (BOTMP) is a norm-referenced *test battery* of eight subtests comprising 46 items. A short form,

Table 17-2 BMAT – R Test Items

Item	Purpose
Bead stringing	Eye-hand coordination and dexterity
Target throwing	Eye-hand coordination as related to throwing
Marble transfer	Finger dexterity and speed of hand movement
Back and hamstring stretch	Flexibility
Standing long jump	Strength and power of lower leg and thigh
Face down to standing	Speed and agility
Static balance	Stationary balance with eyes open and eyes closed
Basketball throw	Explosive arm and shoulder strength
Ball striking	Striking coordination
Target kicking	Eye-foot coordination
Agility run	Ability to change directions quickly

which comprises 14 items from the complete battery, can be used as a quick screening device. The battery provides both a comprehensive index of motor proficiency and individual measures of fine and gross motor skills for children 4½ to 14½ years old. The complete battery can be administered in 45 to 60 minutes; the short form takes approximately 15 to 20 minutes.

Test administration does require various pieces of equipment. The equipment can be bought for about $586 (it comes in a well-designed, well-packaged carrying case). The price includes score sheets, equipment needed to administer the complete battery, and the examiner's manual, which contains all the standardized tables needed to score the test.

The standardization procedures included a sampling of 765 children selected on the basis of age, gender, race, community size, and geographic region in accordance with the 1970 census (Bruininks, 1978). Average test-retest reliability coefficients for the complete battery and short form are 0.87 and 0.86, respectively. Haubenstricker and associates (1981) found the BOTMP useful for discriminating between "normal" children and those with gross motor dysfunction. To order, contact the American Guidance Services, 4201 Woodland Rd., Circle Pines, MN 55014-1796; (800) 328-2560.

Basic Motor Ability Test – Revised

The Basic Motor Ability Test–Revised (BMAT-R) is a norm-based test used to assess selected large- and small-muscle control responses. The original test was constructed in 1974 and revised in 1978 by Arnheim and Sinclair (1979). The battery of tests can be administered to children 4 to 12 years old. One advantage of the test is that it can be administered to a group of five children in approximately 30 minutes. Test norms were established on 1563 children of various backgrounds. The reliability for the entire test is 0.93. Table 17-2 shows the various test items.

Denver II

The Denver II (Frankenburg, Dodds, & Archer, 1990) represents a major revision and restandardization of the original Denver Development Screening Test (Frankenburg & Dodds, 1967), which was first developed over 35 years ago. The test is designed to screen children between birth and 6 years of age for developmental delays in four aspects of the child's development: (1) personal-social—the ability to perform such tasks as drinking from a cup, removing one's own garments, and washing and drying the hands; (2) fine motor adaptive—the

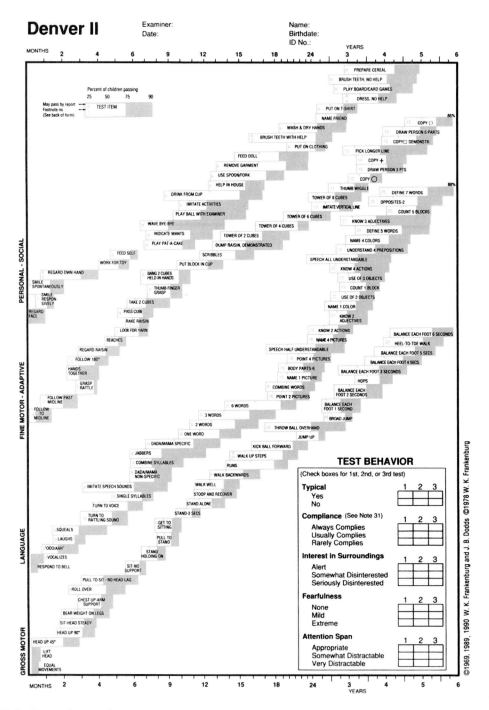

Figure 17-2   Denver II score sheet

SOURCE: Frankenburg, W. K., Dodds, J., and Archer, P. *Denver II Technical Manual, 1990.*
Denver Developmental Materials, Inc. Copyright © 1969, 1989, 1990 W. K. Frankenburg and
J. B. Dodds. Copyright © 1978 W. K. Frankenburg. Used with permission of publisher and authors.

ability to perform such tasks as passing a block from hand to hand and stacking blocks; (3) language— the ability to imitate sounds, name body parts, define words, and so forth; and (4) gross motor—such as the ability to sit, walk, jump, and throw. The entire test consists of 125 items and takes no longer to administer than the original 105-item test. The Denver II score sheet is uniquely laid out, as illustrated in Figure 17-2. Each test item is represented by a bar positioned between two age scales, one at the top and one at the bottom of the score sheet. Each bar is scaled to show when 25, 50, 75, and 90 percent of the "normal" children can accomplish a particular item. To determine which test items are to be administered, you simply locate the child's age on the age scales and draw a vertical line from the top to the bottom scale. The number of test items that you will administer varies with age. You should administer all items through which the age line passes; in addition, three items to the left of the age line should also be examined.

Each item is graded as pass, fail, refusal, or no opportunity to observe. Whenever possible, an interview with the parents should be obtained in order to determine how the child is performing within the home environment. For decision-making purposes, individual item performance is classified as either a delay, a caution, or normal. A delay represents a failure of an item that 90 percent of age group peers have passed. A caution is denoted if a child fails an item that 75 percent up to and including 90 percent of age group peers have passed. The test is suspect if a child exhibits one or more delays and/or two or more cautions.

The standardization procedures included a sampling of 2096 children from Colorado. Four types of item reliability were assessed: (1) interrater, (2) 5- to 10-minute test-retest, (3) 7- to 10-day test-retest using the same examiner and same observer, and (4) 7- to 10-day test-retest using an inter-examiner and inter-observer format. The mean percentage of agreement for each of the four types of reliability was high, ranging from 99.7 percent to 87.5 percent (Frankenburg et al., 1992).

For those interested in learning to administer this test, several training aids are now available. The aids include a self-evaluation with answers within the Denver II Training Manual, a technical manual, video instructional programs, a proficiency test, and master instructor training. The manuals, videotapes, and proficiency tests can be obtained from Denver Development Materials, Inc., P.O. Box 6919, Denver, CO 80206-0917; (303) 355-4729. Master instructor training is provided by the Denver II office at Community Child Development, 1056 East 19th Avenue, Box B215, Denver, CO 80118; (303) 831-8559 (Frankenburg et al., 1992).

SELECTED PROCESS-ORIENTED ASSESSMENT INSTRUMENTS

This section describes four popular process-oriented assessment instruments: the Ohio State University Scale of Intra-Gross Motor Assessment (SIGMA), the Developmental Sequence of Motor Skills Inventory, the Fundamental Motor Pattern Assessment Instrument, and the Test of Gross Motor Development–2.

SIGMA

The Ohio State University Scale of Intra-Gross Motor Assessment (SIGMA) (Loovis & Ersing, 1979) is a criterion-referenced assessment tool designed to evaluate the motor behavior of normal preschool and elementary school children as well as the young mentally retarded child. Each of the 11 fundamental motor skills examined (walking, stair climbing, running, throwing, catching, jumping, hopping, skipping, striking, kicking, and ladder climbing) is presented in four developmental levels. The authors state that SIGMA is unique among tests in that it can be administered in formal testing situations or in an informal free-play setting. Test administration is simplified because of a skill format sheet. Each sheet contains five sources of information to help the examiner: (1) equipment needed to administer the test, (2) directions about the test conditions, (3) criterion test performance, (4) references from which more information about the skill can be obtained, and (5) summative terms/phrases that best describe the child's performance.

SIGMA's content validity was determined by a panel of 11 experts who used a 5-point Likert-type scale to rate the test for understandability and usefulness and by documentary analysis of the literature (Sherrill, 1986). Reliability of student performance was not reported. However, 13 judges were required to rate the performance of 12 children who had been videotaped. The tape was viewed two times, 1 week apart, and the data were analyzed by Scott's *pi* statistic. Interjudge agreement ranged from 0.50 to 1.00; intrajudge agreement ranged from 0.67 to 1.00.

One unique aspect of the SIGMA is its accompanying program, the Performance Base Curriculum (PBC). The PBC is essentially an instructional program that states objectives and activities for each developmental level within each skill. The PBC is directly related to the SIGMA in that it provides a critical link between assessment and program intervention.

Developmental Sequence of Motor Skills Inventory

Despite the component analysis Roberton and colleagues used, some professionals prefer a more global analysis based on the configuration of the total body during performance of a task. This assessment technique has evolved from identification of developmental sequences within selected skills. Each sequence consists of three to five stages stated in terms of observable behaviors. The teacher's task is to observe children performing the skills and then to classify them according to their level of development. To date, the developmental sequences that have been studied are running, hopping, skipping, galloping, long jumping, throwing, catching, striking, kicking, and punting. Table 17-3 highlights the stage characteristics for each of these fundamental motor skills. These developmental sequences are the outgrowth of data collected at the Michigan State University Motor Performance Study. Remember, these skills have been presented in detail in Chapters 13 and 14.

Fundamental Motor Pattern Assessment Instrument

The Fundamental Motor Pattern Assessment Instrument was developed as an outgrowth of a 1976 doctoral dissertation by McClenaghan and later published by McClenaghan and Gallahue (1978). This observational instrument can be used to assess developmental changes over time for the following fundamental patterns: Walking, running, jumping, throwing overhand, catching, and kicking. The performer's quality of movement is scored as being in one of three stages of development: (1) initial stage — first observable attempt at performing the movement pattern; (2) elementary stage — improved coordination and the addition of maturer patterns being integrated into the movement; (3) mature stage — skilled, coordinated, adultlike performance.

Stage descriptions are accompanied by well-illustrated visuals that serve as scoring aids. The authors report test-retest reliability performance of 88.6 percent, with interrater objectivity ranging from 80 to 95 percent (McClenaghan & Gallahue, 1978).

Test of Gross Motor Development-2

The Test of Gross Motor Development–2 (TGMD–2), represents a major revision to this assessment instrument, which was first released in 1985 (Ulrich, 2000). This revised instrument can now be used to identify children between 3.0 and 10.11 years of age who may be significantly behind their peers in gross motor skill development and therefore eligible for special education services. The test assesses 12 motor skills that are divided into two subtests: locomotor skills and object-control skills. Locomotor skills measured are the run, gallop, hop, skip, horizontal jump, leap, and slide; object-control skills include striking a stationary ball, stationary dribble, catch, kick, overhand throw, and underhand roll.

TGMD–2 uses new normative data based on projected 2000 census data; normative data stratified by age relative to geography, gender, race, and residence; age norms divided by one-half-year increments; and new reliability and validity studies.

Table 17-3   Summary of Fundamental Motor Skill Stage Characteristics—MSU Motor Performance Study: Total Body Approach

Fundamental Motor Skills	Stage 1	Stage 2	Stage 3	Stage 4	Stage 5
Run	Arms—high guard Flat-footed contact Short stride Wide stride, shoulder width	Arms—middle guard Vertical component still great Legs near full extension	Arms—low guard Arm opposition—elbows nearly extended Heel-toe contact	Heel-toe contact (toe-heel when sprinting) Arm-leg opposition High heel recovery Elbow flexion	
Long Jump	Arms act as "brakes" Large vertical component Legs not extended	Arms act as "wings" Vertical component still great Legs near full extension	Arms move forward/elbows in front of trunk at takeoff Hands to head height Takeoff angle still above 45° Legs often fully extended	Complete arm and leg extension at takeoff Takeoff near 45° angle Thighs parallel to surface when feet contact for landing	
Hop	Nonsupport foot in front with thigh parallel to floor Body erect Hands shoulder height	Nonsupport knee flexed with knee in front and foot behind support leg Slight body lean forward Bilateral arm action	Nonsupport thigh vertical with foot behind support leg—knee flexed More body lean forward Bilateral arm action	Pendular action on nonsupport leg Forward body lean Arm opposition with swing leg	
Gallop	Resembles rhythmically uneven run Trail leg crosses in front of lead leg during air-borne phase, remains in front at contact	Slow-moderate tempo, choppy rhythm Trail leg stiff Hips often oriented sideways Vertical component exaggerated	Smooth, rhythmical pattern, moderate tempo Feet remain close to ground Hips oriented forward		
Skip	Broken skip pattern or irregular rhythm Slow, deliberate movement Ineffective arm action	Rhythmical skip pattern Arms provide body lift Excessive vertical component	Arm action reduced/hands below shoulders Easy, rhythmical movement Support foot near surface on hop		

(continued)

Table 17-3 *(continued)*

Fundamental Motor Skills	Stage 1	Stage 2	Stage 3	Stage 4	Stage 5
Throw	Vertical wind-up "Chop throw" Feet stationary No spinal rotation	Horizontal wind-up "Sling throw" Block rotation Follow-through across body	High wind-up *Ipsilateral** step Little spinal rotation Follow-through across body	High wind-up Contralateral step Little spinal rotation Follow-through across body	Downward arc wind-up Contralateral step Segmented body rotation Arm-leg follow-through
Catch	Delayed arm action Arms straight in front until ball contact, then scooping action to chest Feet stationary	Arms encircle ball as it approaches Ball is "hugged" to chest Feet stationary or may take one step	"To-chest" catch Arms "scoop" under ball to trap it to chest Single step may be used to approach ball	Catch with hands only Feet stationary or limited to one step	Catch with hands only Whole body moves through space
Kick	Little/no leg wind-up Stationary position Foot "pushes" ball Step backward after kick (usually)	Leg wind-up to the rear Stationary position Opposition of arms and legs	Moving approach Foot travels in a low arc Arm/leg opposition Forward or sideward step on follow-through	Rapid approach Backward trunk lean during wind-up Leap before kick Hop after kick	
Punt	No leg wind-up Ball toss erratic Body stationary Push ball/step back	Leg wind-up to the rear Ball toss still erratic Body stationary Forceful kick attempt	Preparatory step(s) Some arm/leg yoking Ball toss or drop	Rapid approach Controlled drop Leap before ball contact Hop after ball contact	
Strike	"Chop" strike Feet stationary	Horizontal push/swing Block rotation Feet stationary/stepping	Ipsilateral step Diagonal downward swing	Contralateral step Segmented body rotation Wrist rollover on follow-through	

*Same as both *unilateral* and *homolateral* — stepping forward with the foot that is on the same side of the body as the throwing arm.

SOURCE: Haubenstricker (1990). Used with permission from Dr. John Haubenstricker.

Reliability coefficients for the locomotor subtest average 0.85; for the object-control subtest the average is 0.88; and for the gross motor composite the average is 0.91. In addition, alpha coefficients for selected subgroups are all above 0.90, while time sampling reliability coefficients range from 0.84 to 0.96. Clinicians are sure to appreciate the scoring system that allows the test to be individually administered in approximately 15 to 20 minutes. For example, as illustrated in Figure 17-3, the TGMD–2 score sheet lists the "performance criteria" associated with each locomotor and object-control skill being assessed. If the child exhibits the performance criteria, a score of one is recorded. Zero is denoted for each performance criterion not exhibited. Using the manual supplied with the test kit, raw scores are used to calculate standard scores, percentile scores, age equivalents, and a Gross Motor Quotient (see Figure 17-4). The test manual is well written and easy to understand.

One recent study found that 88 percent of physical education students and 96 percent of physical education teachers could correctly classify a special education student's level of motor development following only three 50-minute training sessions with the Test of Gross Motor Development (Suomi & Suomi, 1997). This finding supports Ulrich's (1984) earlier statement that the Test of Gross Motor Development can be used with minimal training to assess accurately the motor performance of children both with and without disabilities and those with mild to moderate mental retardation. The TGMD–2 currently sells for $99 and can be purchased from Pro-Ed Inc., 8700 Shoal Creek Blvd., Austin TX, 78757-6897; (800) 897-3202.

ASSESSING THE DISABLED

Comparative studies of disabled and nondisabled populations support the contention that although individuals with selected special needs perform behind their "normal" peers, both may follow similar patterns of development (DiRocco, 1979). Unfortunately, many assessment instruments, both norm- and criterion-referenced, are geared toward the so-called normal population and so cannot be appropriately used with special populations. For instance, a child with spina bifida who must use a wheelchair may have normal motor ability in the upper extremities, but the inability to use the legs while throwing a ball makes normative performance data comparisons inappropriate (DiRocco, 1979).

Special populations pose other potential problems concerning assessment instruments geared to "normal" populations. Frequently, the developmental starting points for special children are so low that their scores are not included in the assessment materials. Clearly, there is a need for the development of more valid test instruments to assess the motor development of those with disabling conditions. However, some do exist. In the following sections, we present two popular assessment instruments frequently used by adapted physical education specialists.

Brigance Diagnostic Inventory of Early Development

The Brigance Diagnostic Inventory of Early Development (BDIED) (Brigance, 1978) is a criterion-referenced test with norms. The BDIED assesses behaviors that are divided into the 11 domains, illustrated in Table 17-4. Of the 11 domains, the first 4 are generally considered the most relevant for professionals working in the discipline of motor behavior (preambulatory motor skills and behaviors, gross motor skills and behaviors, fine motor skills and behaviors, and self-help skills). This multidomain test is designed for use with individuals between birth and 6 years of age. The test is easy to administer, and interpretation of test results is, in part, simplified by the developmental age levels accompanying each skill sequence. These developmental age levels are used to indicate roughly when a certain behavior should start to be exhibited and when that same behavior is typically mastered. Because of the wide range of skills assessed and the flexible testing format, the BDIED is very useful for assessing young individuals with severely disabling conditions (Bagnato, Neisworth, & Munson, 1997).

Preferred Hand: Right ☐ Left ☐ Not Established ☐
Preferred Foot: Right ☐ Left ☐ Not Established ☐

Locomotor Subtest

Skill	Materials	Directions	Performance Criteria	Trial 1	Trial 2	Score
1. Run	60 feet of clear space, and two cones	Place two cones 50 feet apart. Make sure there is at least 8 to 10 feet of space beyond the second cone for a safe stopping distance. Tell the child to run as fast as he or she can from one cone to the other when you say "Go." Repeat a second trial.	1. Arms move in opposition to legs, elbows bent 2. Brief period where both feet are off the ground 3. Narrow foot placement landing on heel or toe (i.e., not flat footed) 4. Nonsupport leg bent approximately 90 degrees (i.e., close to buttocks)			
					Skill Score	
2. Gallop	25 feet of clear space, and tape or two cones	Mark off a distance of 25 feet with two cones or tape. Tell the child to gallop from one cone to the other. Repeat a second trial by galloping back to the original cone.	1. Arms bent and lifted to waist level at takeoff 2. A step forward with the lead foot followed by a step with the trailing foot to a position adjacent to or behind the lead foot 3. Brief period when both feet are off the floor 4. Maintains a rhythmic pattern for four consecutive gallops			
					Skill Score	
3. Hop	A minimum of 15 feet of clear space	Tell the child to hop three times on his or her preferred foot (established before testing) and then three times on the other foot. Repeat a second trial.	1. Nonsupport leg swings forward in pendular fashion to produce force 2. Foot of nonsupport leg remains behind body 3. Arms flexed and swing forward to produce force 4. Takes off and lands three consecutive times on preferred foot 5. Takes off and lands three consecutive times on nonpreferred foot			
					Skill Score	
4. Leap	A minimum of 20 feet of clear space, a beanbag, and tape	Place a beanbag on the floor. Attach a piece of tape on the floor so it is parallel to and 10 feet away from the beanbag. Have the child stand on the tape and run up and leap over the beanbag. Repeat a second trial.	1. Take off on one foot and land on the opposite foot 2. A period where both feet are off the ground longer than running 3. Forward reach with the arm opposite the lead foot			
					Skill Score	

Skill	Materials	Directions	Performance Criteria	Trial 1	Trial 2	Score
5. Horizontal Jump	A minimum of 10 feet of clear space and tape	Mark off a starting line on the floor. Have the child start behind the line. Tell the child to jump as far as he or she can. Repeat a second trial.	1. Preparatory movement includes flexion of both knees with arms extended behind body			
			2. Arms extend forcefully forward and upward reaching full extension above the head			
			3. Take off and land on both feet simultaneously			
			4. Arms are thrust downward during landing			
					Skill Score	
6. Slide	A minimum of 25 feet of clear space, a straight line, and two cones	Place the cones 25 feet apart on top of a line on the floor. Tell the child to slide from one cone to the other and back. Repeat a second trial.	1. Body turned sideways so shoulders are aligned with the line on the floor			
			2. A step sideways with lead foot followed by a slide of the trailing foot to a point next to the lead foot			
			3. A minimum of four continuous step-slide cycles to the right			
			4. A minimum of four continuous step-slide cycles to the left			
					Skill Score	
			Locomotor Subtest Raw Score (sum of the 6 skill scores)			

Object Control Subtest

Skill	Materials	Directions	Performance Criteria	Trial 1	Trial 2	Score
1. Striking a Stationary Ball	A 4-inch lightweight ball, a plastic bat, and a batting tee	Place the ball on the batting tee at the child's belt level. Tell the child to hit the ball hard. Repeat a second trial.	1. Dominant hand grips bat above nondominant hand			
			2. Nonpreferred side of body faces the imaginary tosser with feet parallel			
			3. Hip and shoulder rotation during swing			
			4. Transfers body weight to front foot			
			5. Bat contacts ball			
					Skill Score	
2. Stationary Dribble	An 8- to 10-inch playground ball for children ages 3 to 5; a basketball for children ages 6 to 10; and a flat, hard surface	Tell the child to dribble the ball four times without moving his or her feet, using one hand, and then stop by catching the ball. Repeat a second trial.	1. Contacts ball with one hand at about belt level			
			2. Pushes ball with fingertips (not a slap)			
			3. Ball contacts surface in front of or to the outside of foot on the preferred side			
			4. Maintains control of ball for four consecutive bounces without having to move the feet to retrieve it			
					Skill Score	

Figure 17-3 TGMD–2 score sheet

SOURCE: Copyright © Pro-Ed. Used by permission.

(continued)

Skill	Materials	Directions	Performance Criteria	Trial 1	Trial 2	Score
3. Catch	A 4-inch plastic ball, 15 feet of clear space, and tape	Mark off two lines 15 feet apart. The child stands on one line and the tosser on the other. Toss the ball underhand directly to the child with a slight arc aiming for his or her chest. Tell the child to catch the ball with both hands. Only count those tosses that are between the child's shoulders and belt. Repeat a second trial.	1. Preparation phase where hands are in front of the body and elbows are flexed 2. Arms extend while reaching for the ball as it arrives 3. Ball is caught by hands only			
					Skill Score	
4. Kick	An 8- to 10-inch plastic, playground, or soccer ball; a beanbag; 30 feet of clear space; and tape	Mark off one line 30 feet away from a wall and another line 20 feet from the wall. Place the ball on top of the beanbag on the line nearest the wall. Tell the child to stand on the other line. Tell the child to run up and kick the ball hard toward the wall. Repeat a second trial.	1. Rapid continuous approach to the ball 2. An elongated stride or leap immediately prior to ball contact 3. Nonkicking foot placed even with or slightly in back of the ball 4. Kicks ball with instep of preferred foot (shoelaces) or toe			
					Skill Score	
5. Overhand Throw	A tennis ball, a wall, tape, and 20 feet of clear space	Attach a piece of tape on the floor 20 feet from a wall. Have the child stand behind the 20-foot line facing the wall. Tell the child to throw the ball hard at the wall. Repeat a second trial.	1. Windup is initiated with downward movement of hand/arm 2. Rotates hip and shoulders to a point where the nonthrowing side faces the wall 3. Weight is transferred by stepping with the foot opposite the throwing hand 4. Follow-through beyond ball release diagonally across the body toward the nonpreferred side			
					Skill Score	
6. Underhand Roll	A tennis ball for children ages 3 to 6; a softball for children ages 7 to 10; two cones; tape; and 25 feet of clear space	Place the two cones against a wall so they are 4 feet apart. Attach a piece of tape on the floor 20 feet from the wall. Tell the child to roll the ball hard so that it goes between the cones. Repeat a second trial.	1. Preferred hand swings down and back, reaching behind the trunk while chest faces cones 2. Strides forward with foot opposite the preferred hand toward the cones 3. Bends knees to lower body 4. Releases ball close to the floor so ball does not bounce more than 4 inches high			
					Skill Score	
			Object Control Subtest Raw Score (sum of the 6 skill scores)			

Figure 17-3 TGMD–2 score sheet *(continued)*

SOURCE: Copyright © Pro-Ed. Used by permission.

TGMD-2

Test of Gross Motor Development–Second Edition

Profile/Examiner Record Form

Section I. Identifying Information

Name _____

Male ☐ Female ☐ Grade _____

Date of Testing _____

Date of Birth _____

Age _____

School _____

Referred by _____

Reason for Referral _____

Examiner _____

Examiner's Title _____

Section II. Record of Scores

First Testing

	Raw Score	Standard Score	Percentile	Age Equivalent
Locomotor				
Object Control				

Sum of Standard Scores _____
Gross Motor Quotient _____

Second Testing

	Raw Score	Standard Score	Percentile	Age Equivalent
Locomotor				
Object Control				

Sum of Standard Scores _____
Gross Motor Quotient _____

Section III. Testing Conditions

A. Place Tested _____

	Interfering			Not Interfering
B. Noise Level	1	2	3	4	5
C. Interruptions	1	2	3	4	5
D. Distractions	1	2	3	4	5
E. Light	1	2	3	4	5
F. Temperature	1	2	3	4	5

G. Notes and other considerations _____

Section IV. Other Test Data

Name of Test	Date	Standard Score	TGMD-2 Equivalent

Section V. Profile of Standard Scores

Additional copies of this form (#9262) may be purchased from PRO-ED, 8700 Shoal Creek Blvd., Austin, TX 78757-6897
800/897-3202 Fax 800/397-7633

1

Figure 17-4 Profile/Examiner Record Form of the TGMD-2

SOURCE: Copyright © Pro-Ed. Used by permission.

Table 17-4	Brigance Diagnostic Inventory of Early Development: Assessment Categories

Preambulatory motor skills and behaviors

Gross motor skills and behaviors

Fine motor skills and behaviors

Self-help skills

Prespeech behaviors

Speech and language skills

General knowledge and comprehension

Readiness skills

Basic reading skills

Writing skills

Math skills

Purdue Perceptual-Motor Survey

The Purdue Perceptual-Motor Survey was constructed on the idea that perceptual-motor abilities are necessary for the acquisition of academic skills. More specifically, if certain motor generalizations are not obtained, the disabilities may be manifested in slow academic learning. This survey, which was developed by Roach and Kephart, is "not designed for diagnosis, per se, but to allow the clinician to observe perceptual-motor behavior in a series of behavioral performances" (1966, p. 11). As such, this survey should be used only as a screening device. If suspect performance is observed, further investigation would be needed before a diagnosis could be made. The survey was designed to be used with children between 6 and 10 years of age. The survey consists of 22 items subdivided into the following five categories:

1. Balance and posture
2. Body image and differentiation
3. Perceptual-motor match
4. Ocular control
5. Form perception

Each survey item is evaluated on a scale of 1 to 4. Table 17-5 lists the 22 survey items according to

Table 17-5	The Purdue Perceptual-Motor Survey
Survey Category	**Survey Item**
Balance and posture	Walking board
	forward
	backward
	sidewise
Body image and differentiation	Jumping
	Identification of body parts
	Imitation of movement
	Obstacle course
	Kraus-Weber (strength)
	Angels-in-the-snow
Perceptual-motor match	Chalkboard drawing
	circle
	double circle
	lateral line
	vertical line
	Rhythmic writing
	rhythm
	reproduction
	orientation
Ocular control	Ocular pursuits
	both eyes
	right eye
	left eye
	convergence
Form perception	Visual achievement forms
	forms
	organization

category. Test-retest reliability estimates and objectivity estimates have been reported in the range of 0.95. Nevertheless, standardization procedures are suspect, because only 200 children from one school were used in the validation process.

I CAN

Improving the quality of physical education instruction for all students is one of the primary goals of the I CAN project. This project, originally funded

Table 17-6 I CAN: Programs and Modules	
Program	**Module**
Preprimary motor and play skills	Locomotor
	Object control
	Body control
	Health fitness
	Play equipment
	Play participation
Primary skills	Fundamental skills
	Body management
	Health/fitness
	Aquatics
Sport, leisure, and recreational skills	Team sports
	Dance and individual sports
	Outdoor activities
	Backyard/neighborhood activities

by the Bureau of Education for the Handicapped, is under the direction of Janet A. Wessel.

The target population is "children whose overall developmental growth is slower than the average, as well as . . . children with specific learning disabilities, social or emotional adjustment difficulties, and/ or economic or language disadvantages" (Wessel, 1976, p. ix). Furthermore, the curriculum is designed for individuals between 3 and 25 years of age.

Currently, I CAN consists of three programs, each of which is subdivided into several instructional modules. Each module consists of a curriculum guide, assessment records, game cards, and an implementation guide. Table 17-6 illustrates the modules currently available.

Assessment is accomplished through a criterion-referenced approach. Each curriculum kit is neatly packaged and easy to administer. Once the curriculum kits have been purchased, there is no additional expense, because the assessment forms are not copyrighted and therefore may be reproduced.

Test reliability was calculated on only three skills and on the basis of percent agreement (run = 95%;

overhand throw = 89%; catch = 90%). According to the test developers, it was assumed that other test items would probably have similar reliability estimates because they were all developed using the same instructional model. Content validity has not been established and is deferred to the user (Wessel, 1976).

AIDS IN ASSESSING MOTOR SKILLS

As mentioned, one disadvantage of many tests is the need for the test examiner to learn many functional definitions describing the criterion behavior associated with each developmental level within a given skill. Checklists or reminder sheets that list key descriptive terms for each developmental level can jog the examiner's memory (see Figure 17-3). Regardless of a person's expertise with the developmental stages of selected tasks, it is still an excellent idea to have such a checklist at hand, to ensure consistent scoring.

Videotaping individual performance is another way to assess motor skills. Certain motor skills must be executed at high rates of speed, so even the experienced examiner may have difficulty denoting exactly what took place within each body segment during the performance of the task. Today's video units are capable of slow-motion playback, thus affording more-precise analysis of most motor skills. However, one motor skill that does not totally lend itself to video analysis is the overarm throw for force, because the video unit's framing rate is not fast enough to freeze the ballistic movement of the throwing arm. As a result, the throwing arm is likely to be blurred.

Another advantage of videotaping is that it decreases the number of times a child must perform a task so the examiner can evaluate the developmental level of each body segment. Within a given test session, for example, a very young child may become fatigued if required to perform a forward roll 20 times. With videotaping or filming, the child need perform only a few trials. The examiner at a later time can play back the tape or film many times while evaluating each body segment.

ASSESSING PHYSICAL FITNESS

To this point, we have focused our attention on the assessment of motor skills. There is, however, a rapidly growing body of knowledge regarding the assessment of components of physical fitness. In the sections that follow, we describe several of the most frequently used physical-fitness test batteries: the FITNESSGRAM/ACTIVITYGRAM, the President's Challenge, the National Youth Physical Fitness Program, and the National Children and Youth Fitness Studies I and II. Regarding the elderly, the Functional Fitness Assessment for Adults Over 60 Years and the Senior Fitness Test are briefly described.

The FITNESSGRAM/ACTIVITYGRAM

Developed by the Cooper Institute for Aerobics Research, the ***FITNESSGRAM/ACTIVITYGRAM*** has rapidly become the most widely used instrument for the assessment of health-related physical fitness for youth and young adults (5–25 years of age). In fact, it is currently used at more than 6000 schools around the country, and an estimated 10 million students will participate in the program (American Alliance for Health, Physical Education, Recreation, and Dance [AAHPERD], 1994). Most recently, the state of California now requires its students in grades 5, 7, and 9 to participate in the FITNESSGRAM/ ACTIVITYGRAM testing (American Fitness Alliance, 1999). This criterion-referenced instrument assesses aerobic capacity, body composition, muscular strength and endurance, and flexibility. Table 17-7 outlines tests used to assess each of these components. The FITNESSGRAM/ACTIVITYGRAM kit comes with a Test Administration Manual (Cooper Institute for Aerobics Research, 1999), FITNESSGRAM/ ACTIVITYGRAM 6.0 software on CD-ROM (Cooper Institute for Aerobics Research, 2000), and various auxiliary supplies, including plastic skinfold calipers.

Table 17-7   The FITNESSGRAM/ACTIVITYGRAM Test Battery

Aerobic capacity (select one)
- One-mile walk/run
- Pacer (a 20-meter progressive, multistage shuttle run set to music)
- Walk test (Rockport) (available for secondary students)

Body composition (select one)
- Percent body fat (calculated from tricep and calf skinfold measurements)
- Body mass index (weight in kilograms divided by height in meters squared)

Muscular strength, endurance, and flexibility
- Abdominal strength
  - Curl-up test
- Trunk-extension strength and flexibility
  - Trunk lift
- Upper-body strength (select one)
  - 90° push-up
  - Pull-up
  - Flex-arm hang
  - Modified pull-up
- Flexibility (select one)
  - Back-saver sit-and-reach
  - Shoulder stretch

New in 2003 is the Web-based version (7.0) of the program, thus allowing access to the software from any online computer (Cooper Institute for Aerobics Research, 2003). Figure 17-5 is a sample FITNESSGRAM score sheet.

The newly revised FITNESSGRAM/ACTIVITYGRAM kit costs $209 and can be purchased from Human Kinetics Publishers (800-747-4457). A reference guide describing the development of the FITNESSGRAM and its supporting research can be found at www.fitnessgram.net.

As a companion program, the new Physical Best program, developed through the AAHPERD, is

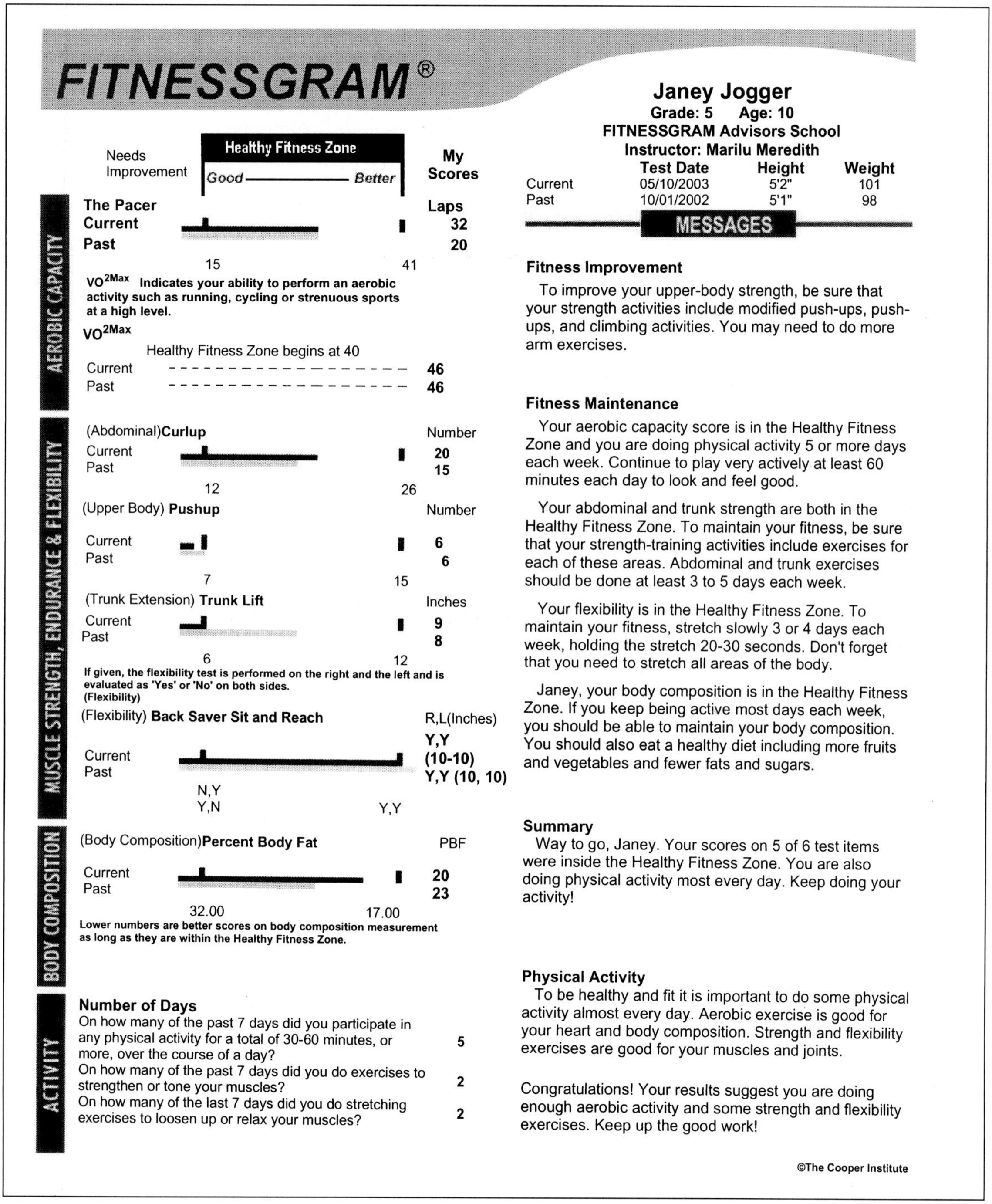

FITNESSGRAM®

Janey Jogger
Grade: 5   Age: 10
FITNESSGRAM Advisors School
Instructor: Marilu Meredith

	Test Date	Height	Weight
Current	05/10/2003	5'2"	101
Past	10/01/2002	5'1"	98

MESSAGES

Healthy Fitness Zone
Needs Improvement — Good — Better | My Scores

AEROBIC CAPACITY

The Pacer — Laps
Current ▮ 32
Past 20
15 ... 41

VO²Max Indicates your ability to perform an aerobic activity such as running, cycling or strenuous sports at a high level.

VO²Max
Healthy Fitness Zone begins at 40
Current 46
Past 46

MUSCLE STRENGTH, ENDURANCE & FLEXIBILITY

(Abdominal)**Curlup** — Number
Current 20
Past 15
12 ... 26

(Upper Body) **Pushup** — Number
Current 6
Past 6
7 ... 15

(Trunk Extension) **Trunk Lift** — Inches
Current 9
Past 8
6 ... 12

If given, the flexibility test is performed on the right and the left and is evaluated as 'Yes' or 'No' on both sides. (Flexibility)

(Flexibility) **Back Saver Sit and Reach** — R,L(Inches)
Current Y,Y (10-10)
Past Y,Y (10, 10)
N,Y / Y,N ... Y,Y

BODY COMPOSITION

(Body Composition)**Percent Body Fat** — PBF
Current 20
Past 23
32.00 ... 17.00
Lower numbers are better scores on body composition measurement as long as they are within the Healthy Fitness Zone.

ACTIVITY

Number of Days
On how many of the past 7 days did you participate in any physical activity for a total of 30-60 minutes, or more, over the course of a day? **5**
On how many of the past 7 days did you do exercises to strengthen or tone your muscles? **2**
On how many of the last 7 days did you do stretching exercises to loosen up or relax your muscles? **2**

Fitness Improvement
To improve your upper-body strength, be sure that your strength activities include modified push-ups, push-ups, and climbing activities. You may need to do more arm exercises.

Fitness Maintenance
Your aerobic capacity score is in the Healthy Fitness Zone and you are doing physical activity 5 or more days each week. Continue to play very actively at least 60 minutes each day to look and feel good.

Your abdominal and trunk strength are both in the Healthy Fitness Zone. To maintain your fitness, be sure that your strength-training activities include exercises for each of these areas. Abdominal and trunk exercises should be done at least 3 to 5 days each week.

Your flexibility is in the Healthy Fitness Zone. To maintain your fitness, stretch slowly 3 or 4 days each week, holding the stretch 20-30 seconds. Don't forget that you need to stretch all areas of the body.

Janey, your body composition is in the Healthy Fitness Zone. If you keep being active most days each week, you should be able to maintain your body composition. You should also eat a healthy diet including more fruits and vegetables and fewer fats and sugars.

Summary
Way to go, Janey. Your scores on 5 of 6 test items were inside the Healthy Fitness Zone. You are also doing physical activity most every day. Keep doing your activity!

Physical Activity
To be healthy and fit it is important to do some physical activity almost every day. Aerobic exercise is good for your heart and body composition. Strength and flexibility exercises are good for your muscles and joints.

Congratulations! Your results suggest you are doing enough aerobic activity and some strength and flexibility exercises. Keep up the good work!

©The Cooper Institute

Figure 17-5   Score Sheet of the FITNESSGRAM

SOURCE: Reprinted with permission from The Cooper Institute for Aerobics Research, Dallas, TX.

an excellent supplement to the FITNESSGRAM. This program is a comprehensive health-related fitness educational program. Materials for the Physical Best program include the Physical Best Activity Guide–Elementary Level (AAHPERD, 1999a) and the Physical Best Activity Guide–Secondary Level (AAHPERD, 1999b). Each of these texts contain more than 60 ready-to-use instructional activities that are linked with NASPE's National Physical Education Standards and references to the Surgeon General's Report on Physical Activity. Also included is the Physical Best Teacher's Guide, *Physical Education for Lifelong Fitness* (AAHPERD, 1999c). This guide presents to the teacher a framework for implementing health-related physical fitness education. Also new to the Physical Best program is an instructional video (AAHPERD, 2000). The video is currently used to teach individuals how to implement the Physical Best program and is also incorporated into certification workshops held by AAHPERD. By attending a workshop and completing a self-study examination, one can now become certified as a Health-Fitness Specialist or a Health-Fitness Instructor. For more information regarding the certification process, contact AAHPERD at (800) 213-7193, ext. 426, or e-mail physicalbest@aahperd.org. Like the FITNESSGRAM/ACTIVITYGRAM, Physical Best products can be purchased by contacting Human Kinetics Publishers (800-747-4457).

The Brockport Physical Fitness Test

The Brockport Physical Fitness Test (Winnick & Short, 1999) was specifically designed to assess the health-related fitness of youths 10–17 years old who have various disabilities. Similar to the FITNESSGRAM/ACTIVITYGRAM, the Brockport test is criterion-referenced; thus, scores are compared with carefully developed standards rather than to national averages. Criterion-referenced standards are provided for such disabilities as visual impairments, spinal cord injuries, cerebral palsy, and congenital anomalies or amputations. The test consists of 27 health-related fitness tests, and instructors can select individual items in order to create a test geared

toward a particular individual or group. This task is simplified when using the accompanying fitness challenge software that is part of the testing kit. Also included in the $175 kit is a comprehensive test manual, a training guide that will help you develop student fitness, a training video, and testing equipment needed to administer the assessment (skinfold calipers, PACER audio CD, curl-up strips). To order, contact the American Fitness Alliance at (800) 747-4457, ext. 2407.

The President's Challenge

The President's Challenge Youth Physical Fitness Program is sponsored by the President's Council on Physical Fitness and Sports (PCPFS). The program, designed for Americans aged 6 and up, allows participants to receive one of the four awards outlined in Table 17-8. The Presidential, National, and Participant awards are based mainly on normative data collected in 1985 for the PCPFS National School Population Fitness Survey and validated in 1998 with a large national sample collected in 1994 (PCPFS, 2003). Table 17-9 presents the qualifying standards for both the Presidential and the National Physical Fitness Award (PCPFS, 2003). Note that several optional events are available. For instance, participants who cannot perform one pull-up may substitute the flexed-arm hang in their attempt to secure the National Physical Fitness Award or the Participant Fitness Award.

The PCPFS also includes an alternative criterion-referenced program, the Health Fitness Award. To receive this award, participants must meet or exceed the specified health criteria established for the following five areas of assessment: partial curl-ups, 1-mile run/walk with distance options, V-sit reach or sit-and-reach option, right angle push-up or pull-up option, and the body mass index (BMI). Recall from Chapter 7 that the BMI is obtained by dividing an individual's weight in kilograms by height in meters squared. This measure is included because of the body composition's relation to physical fitness.

Regarding the accommodation of students with disabilities, the PCPFS states, "Making accommo-

Table 17-8	An Overview of Awards Offered by the President's Challenge Program
The Presidential Physical Fitness Award	Score at or above the 85th percentile on all five assessment items.
The National Physical Fitness Award	Score at or above the 50th percentile on all five assessment items.
The Participant Physical Fitness Award	For those who attempt all five assessment items but fall below the 50th percentile on one or more of the items.
The Health Fitness Award	A health criterion-referenced award offered as an alternative to the traditional physical fitness awards. Student must meet or exceed the criteria for partial curl-ups, one-mile run/walk with distance options, V-sit reach or sit-and-reach option, right angle push-ups or pull-ups option, and body mass index.

SOURCE: President's Council on Physical Fitness and Sports (2003).

dations is consistent with the goal of providing motivation for life-long physical activity through physical fitness achievement" (PCPFS, 2003, p. 19). To this end, the council has established a set of guidelines, presented in Table 17-10, for qualifying students with disabilities.

Regardless of the awards program selected, the PCPFS recommends the implementation of the assessment battery in conjunction with a physical-fitness educational program. In other words, instructors should avoid administering a physical-fitness test battery at the beginning and end of a school year. Instead, the assessment of physical fitness should be but one unit of instruction geared to the value of engaging in long-term active lifestyle. To obtain a free copy of these guidelines, contact the President's Challenge, 501 N. Morton, Suite 104, Bloomington, IN 47404; (800) 258-8146; www.presidentschallenge.org.

National Youth Physical Fitness Program

The National Youth Physical Fitness Program (YFP), sponsored by the United States Marines Youth Foundation, encourages individuals kindergarten through college age maintain a drug-free lifestyle by fostering self-respect and self-esteem through a lifelong pursuit of physical fitness (United States Marine Youth Foundation, 1997). The YFP test battery consists of the following items: push-ups, pull-ups, sit-ups, standing long jump, and 300-yard shuttle run. This battery requires a minimum amount of time, space, and equipment. As a result, one can administer the battery in inner-city or rural, poor or affluent school districts. To obtain one of the 17 available Certificates of Athletic Accomplishment (one per year), the participant must receive a composite score of at least 250 points. Students failing to do this receive a certificate of participation. Similar to the PCPFS, organizers of the YFP encourage the modification of fitness standards for people with special challenges. However, they note, "It would be impossible to set standards for all levels of physically challenged, underdeveloped, and overweight students." So, "It is left to the judgment of the physical education instructor to determine how exercises should be modified to meet an individual's needs and the appropriate scoring" (United States Marines Youth Foundation, 1997, p. 3).

The YFP is free of charge. You can obtain copies of the instructors manual as well as the full-color certificates by contacting the United States Marines Youth Foundation, Inc., 5700 Monroe Street, P.O. Box 8280, Sylvania, OH 43560; (888) 876-2348 or fax (419) 882-2906.

Table 17-9 Qualifying Standards for the Presidential and National Physical Fitness Awards

The Presidential Physical Fitness Award

In order to qualify for this award, participants must achieve at least the 85th percentile in all 5 events represented below.

Age	Curl-Ups (# one minute) OR	Partial* Curl-Ups (#)	Shuttle Run (seconds)	V-Sit Reach (inches) OR	Sit and Reach (centimeters)	One-Mile Run (min:sec) OR	Distance Options† ¼ mile (min:sec)	Distance Options† ½ mile (min:sec)	Pull-Ups (#) OR	Rt. Angle Push-Ups (#)
BOYS										
6	33	22	12.1	+3.5	31	10:15	1:55		2	9
7	36	24	11.5	+3.5	30	9:22	1:48		4	14
8	40	30	11.1	+3.0	31	8:48		3:30	5	17
9	41	37	10.9	+3.0	31	8:31		3:30	5	18
10	45	35	10.3	+4.0	30	7:57			6	22
11	47	43	10.0	+4.0	31	7:32			6	27
12	50	64	9.8	+4.0	31	7:11			7	31
13	53	59	9.5	+3.5	33	6:50			7	39
14	56	62	9.1	+4.5	36	6:26			10	40
15	57	75	9.0	+5.0	37	6:20			11	42
16	56	73	8.7	+6.0	38	6:08			11	44
17	55	66	8.7	+7.0	41	6:06			13	53
GIRLS										
6	32	22	12.4	+5.5	32	11:20	2:00		2	9
7	34	24	12.1	+5.0	32	10:36	1:55		2	14
8	38	30	11.8	+4.5	33	10:02		3:58	2	17
9	39	37	11.1	+5.5	33	9:30		3:53	2	18
10	40	33	10.8	+6.0	33	9:19			3	20
11	42	43	10.5	+6.5	34	9:02			3	19
12	45	50	10.4	+7.0	36	8:23			2	20
13	46	59	10.2	+7.0	38	8:13			2	21
14	47	48	10.1	+8.0	40	7:59			2	20
15	48	38	10.0	+8.0	43	8:08			2	20
16	45	49	10.1	+9.0	42	8:23			1	24
17	44	58	10.0	+8.0	42	8:15			1	25

The National Physical Fitness Award

In order to qualify for this award, participants must achieve at least the 50th percentile in all 5 events represented below.

Age	Curl-Ups (# one minute) OR	Partial* Curl-Ups (#)	Shuttle Run (seconds)	V-Sit Reach (inches) OR	Sit and Reach (centimeters)	One-Mile Run (min:sec) OR	Distance Options† ¼ mile (min:sec)	½ mile (min:sec)	Pull-Ups (#) OR	Rt. Angle Push-Ups (#) OR	Flexed-Arm Hang (sec)
BOYS											
6	22	10	13.3	+1.0	26	12:36	2:21		1	7	6
7	28	13	12.8	+1.0	25	11:40	2:10		1	8	8
8	31	17	12.2	+0.5	25	11:05		4:22	1	9	10
9	32	20	11.9	+1.0	25	10:30		4:14	2	12	10
10	35	24	11.5	+1.0	25	9:48			2	14	12
11	37	26	11.1	+1.0	25	9:20			2	15	11
12	40	32	10.6	+1.0	26	8:40			2	18	12
13	42	39	10.2	+0.5	26	8:06			3	24	14
14	45	40	9.9	+1.0	28	7:44			5	24	20
15	45	45	9.7	+2.0	30	7:30			6	30	30
16	45	37	9.4	+3.0	30	7:10			7	30	28
17	44	42	9.4	+3.0	34	7:04			8	37	30
GIRLS											
6	23	10	13.8	+2.5	27	13:12	2:26		1	6	5
7	25	13	13.2	+2.0	27	12:56	2:21		1	8	6
8	29	17	12.9	+2.0	28	12:30		4:56	1	9	8
9	30	20	12.5	+2.0	28	11:52		4:50	1	12	8
10	30	24	12.1	+3.0	28	11:22			1	13	8
11	32	27	11.5	+3.0	29	11:17			1	11	7
12	35	30	11.3	+3.5	30	11:05			1	10	7
13	37	40	11.1	+3.5	31	10:23			1	11	7
14	37	30	11.2	+4.5	33	10:06			1	10	8
15	36	26	11.0	+5.0	36	9:58			1	15	9
16	35	26	10.9	+5.5	34	10:31			1	12	7
17	34	40	11.0	+4.5	35	10:22			1	16	7

*Norms from Canada Fitness Award Program, Health Canada, Government of Canada with permission.

†Note: ¼ and ½ mile norms from Amateur Athletic Union Physical Fitness Program with permission.

Source: President's Council on Physical Fitness and Sports (2003, p. 18).

Table 17-10   Guidelines for Qualifying Students with Disabilities for the Presidential, National, Participant Physical Fitness, and the Health Fitness Award*

1. The instructor has reviewed the individual's records to identify medical, orthopedic, or other health problems that should be considered prior to participation in physical activities, including physical-fitness testing.

2. The individual has a disability or other problem that adversely affects performance on one or more test items.

3. The individual has been participating in an appropriate physical-fitness program that develops and maintains cardiorespiratory endurance, muscular strength and endurance, flexibility, and body composition.

4. The instructor has administered all five test items, making needed modifications or substituting alternative test items for the individual.

5. The instructor judges that the individual has been tested on all five test items and/or in each of the five fitness categories and has performed at a level equivalent to a Presidential, National, Participant Physical Fitness, or Health Fitness Award.

---

*For questions regarding these guidelines, call (800) 258-8146.

SOURCE: President's Council on Physical Fitness and Sports (2003, p. 19).

National Children and Youth Fitness Studies I and II

The National Children and Youth Fitness Study (NCYFS) was undertaken in 1985 by the Department of Health and Human Services for the purpose of describing the current fitness status of American children and youths. The first of the two fitness studies utilized items from the AAHPERD Health-Related Physical Fitness Test along with a chin-up test. Norms were developed on a national sample of 8800 participants between 10 and 17 years of age. These norms were published in the January 1985 edition of the *Journal of Physical Education, Recreation, and Dance* (Ross et al., 1985).

As an outgrowth of the first NCYFS, a second study was undertaken to describe the current fitness status of American children younger than 10 years of age. Norms were developed and broken down by age/sex (6–9 years of age) and grade/sex (grades 1–4) for each of the five fitness tests administered. The NCYFS–II differed from the first test in two ways. First, cardiovascular endurance was measured by a 1-mile run for children who were 8 or 9 years of age while a $\frac{1}{2}$-mile run was employed for children under 8 years of age. Second, instead of using a chin-up test to assess upper-body strength, a modified pull-up test was used, which required the construction of a special apparatus (see Figure 8-5) (Pate et al., 1987). Like the NCYFS–I, the NCYFS–II was developed with the use of a national sample. Norms for the NCYFS–II were published in the November/December 1987 edition of the *Journal of Physical Education, Recreation, and Dance* (Ross et al., 1987).

Functional Fitness Assessment for Adults Over 60 Years

An extremely important element of physical fitness in elderly individuals is their ability to carry out activities of daily living. For this reason, the American Association for Active Lifestyles and Fitness (AAALF), an association of the American Alliance for Health, Physical Education, Recreation and Dance, developed the Functional Fitness Assessment for Adults Over 60 Years (Osness, 1996). In accordance with the term *functional fitness*, the test contains items that are closely related to the types of normal activities generally encountered by individuals 60+ years of age.

This field-based assessment for older adults consists of five test items: a test of agility/dynamic balance, a $\frac{1}{2}$-mile walk (endurance), a test of trunk/leg flexibility (sit-and-reach), a test of muscular strength/endurance, and a soda pop coordination test. All that is needed to administer these tests is floor tape, a stopwatch, two traffic cone markers, a chair without arms, three soda pop cans, and a 4- and 8-pound weight, which can be easily made by putting sand into 1-gallon plastic milk jugs. Both the assessment manual and a 27-minute training video (Osness, 1995) can be ordered from AAALF by calling (800) 321-0789.

The Senior Fitness Test

Recently published as an outgrowth of the Human Kinetics Active Seniors program (see www.humankinetics.com), the Senior Fitness Test (Rikli & Jones, 2001) is designed to assess the major physiological components of functional capacity in elderly individuals. This assessment instrument, which meets scientific standards for reliability and validity, also contains performance norms based on testing over 7000 men and women between 60 and 94 years of age. In addition to the test manual, a 12-minute video is available that illustrates how to assess the individual fitness test items such as walking, lifting, bending, stretching, and getting up from a chair. Safety tips and scoring instructions are also offered. As an aid to tracking test scores and printing test reports, a software package is available as well. The complete Senior Fitness Test Kit consisting of the test manual, video, and software, can be purchased for $75 by calling Human Kinetics at (800) 747-4457.

SUMMARY

Psychomotor assessment should be systematically, not haphazardly, approached and based on a plan that links assessment with curricular programming.

It is difficult to select an appropriate test instrument. The instrument should be valid, reliable, objective, and feasible to administer and interpret. However, the most important characteristic is test validity. If the test fails to assess what it purports to assess, the instrument is of no value.

Norm-referenced test instruments are popular because most (but not all) are easy to administer and usually require minimal examiner training. This type of assessment provides information about a person's average functioning. On the other hand, criterion-referenced assessment instruments evaluate quality of individual performance or set a level for mastery.

The following are norm-referenced assessment instruments: the Bayley Scales of Infant Development II, the Bruininks-Oseretsky Test of Motor Proficiency, the Basic Motor Ability Test–Revised, and the Denver II.

Popular process-oriented assessment instruments include the Ohio State University Scale of Intra-Gross Motor Assessment (SIGMA), the Developmental Sequence of Motor Skills Inventory, the Fundamental Motor Pattern Assessment Instrument, and the Test of Gross Motor Development–2.

It is important not to use an assessment instrument geared to a "normal" population when assessing disabled persons. At present, there is a need for more assessment instruments to be validated with disabled populations.

Another area of interest to motor behavior specialists is the assessment of physical fitness. Popular fitness test batteries include the FITNESSGRAM/ACTIVITYGRAM, the President's Challenge, the National Youth Physical Fitness Program sponsored by the United States Marines Youth Foundation, the National Children and Youth Fitness Studies I and II, and the Brockport Physical Fitness Test. Other popular youth fitness tests can be found by consulting the work of Safrit (1995). A popular functional physical-fitness test battery for older adults continues to be the Functional Fitness Assessment for Adults Over 60 Years. In addition, the newly published Senior Fitness Test contains norms for individuals between 60 and 94 years of age.

KEY TERMS

content validity

correlation coefficient

criterion-referenced (CR) assessment instruments

FITNESSGRAM/ACTIVITYGRAM

interrater reliability

ipsilateral

norm-referenced (NR) assessment instruments

objectivity

play-based assessment

process-oriented assessments

product-oriented assessments

psychometric

quantitative evaluations

standard deviation

test battery

test reliability

QUESTIONS FOR REFLECTION

1. What are the seven guidelines for systematically preparing to perform an assessment? Explain each.

2. Can you discuss five reasons for assessing student performance?

3. Why are norms population-specific?

4. What are three areas that must be addressed when preparing students for assessment?

5. When students are assessed, they are oftentimes nervous. What steps can be taken to reduce test anxiety?

6. Can you define validity, reliability, and objectivity? Explain each and give two practical examples of each.

7. Can you draw and label the "bell-shaped" curve? Include in your illustration standard deviations and percentage area under the curve associated with each standard deviation unit.

8. What are norm-referenced assessment instruments? Can you identify the advantages and disadvantages associated with this type of assessment instrument?

9. What are criterion-referenced assessment instruments? Can you identify the advantages and disadvantages associated with this type of assessment instrument?

10. What is the difference between product-oriented assessment instruments and process-oriented assessment instruments? What are the advantages and disadvantages of each?

11. Can you describe in detail the Test of Gross Motor Development–2 (TGMD–2)?

12. How is using checklists, an observation plan, and video to aid in the process of conducting an assessment useful?

13. What popular instruments are used to assess health-related physical fitness?

INTERNET RESOURCES

Each of the Web sites listed here can be used to order assessment instruments described in this chapter.

American Alliance for Health, Physical Education and Dance **www.aahperd.org**

American Guidance Services **www.agsnet.com**

Cooper Institute for Aerobics Research
www.cooperinst.org

FITNESSGRAM **www.fitnessgram.org**

Human Kinetics Publishers **www.humankinetics.com**

Pro-Ed Inc. **www.proedinc.com**

Psychological Corporation
www.harcourt-international.com/imprints/tpc.htm

The President's Challenge
www.presidentschallenge.org

ONLINE LEARNING CENTER (www.mhhe.com/payne6e)

Visit the *Human Motor Development* Online Learning Center for study aids and additional resources. You can use the study guide questions and key terms puzzles to review key terms and concepts for this chapter and to prepare for exams. You can further extend your knowledge of motor development by checking out the Web links, articles, and activities found on the site.

REFERENCES

American Alliance for Health, Physical Education, Recreation and Dance. (1994, January 26). *Unprecedented effort between two of the nation's leading health organizations promotes youth fitness.* Press release, Reston, VA.

————. (1999a). *Physical best activity guide: Elementary level.* Reston, VA: American Alliance for Health, Physical Education, Recreation and Dance.

————. (1999b). *Physical best activity guide: Secondary level.* Reston, VA: American Alliance for Health, Physical Education, Recreation and Dance.

————. (1999c). *Physical education for lifelong fitness: The physical best teacher's guide.* Reston, VA: American Alliance for Health, Physical Education, Recreation and Dance.

————. (2000). *Physical best instructor video: Physical education for lifelong fitness.* Reston, VA: American Alliance for Health, Physical Education, Recreation and Dance.

American Fitness Alliance. (1999). *Teacher news: Three fitness education leaders join forces to encourage healthy habits by young people.* Retrieved September 14, 2000, from www.americanfitness.net/teacher-news.

Arnheim, D. D., & Sinclair, W. A. (1979). *The clumsy child: A program of motor therapy.* 2nd ed. St. Louis, MO: Mosby.

Bagnato, S. J., Neisworth, J. T., & Munson, S. M. (1997). *Linking assessment and early intervention: An authentic curriculum based approach.* Baltimore: P. H. Brookes.

Bayley, N. (1993). *Bayley scales of infant development.* 2nd ed. San Antonio, TX: Psychological Corporation.

Brigance, A. H. (1978). *Brigance diagnostic inventory of early development.* Worcester, MA: Curriculum Associates.

Bruininks, R. H. (1978). *Bruininks-Oseretsky test of motor proficiency.* Circle Pines, MN: American Guidance Service.

Burton, A. W., & Miller, D. E. (1998). *Movement skill assessment.* Champaign, IL: Human Kinetics.

Cooper Institute for Aerobics Research. (1999). *FITNESSGRAM test administration manual.* 2nd ed. Dallas, TX: Cooper Institute for Aerobics Research.

————. (2000). FITNESSGRAM 6.0. Dallas, TX: Cooper Institute for Aerobics Research.

————. (2003). FITNESSGRAM/ACTIVITYGRAM 7.0. Dallas, TX: Cooper Institute for Aerobics Research.

DiRocco, P. (1979). Physical education and the handicapped: Developmental approach. *Physical Education, 36,* 127–131.

Frankenburg, W. K., & Dodds, J. B. (1967). The Denver Developmental Screening Test. *Journal of Pediatrics, 71,* 181–191.

Frankenburg, W. K., Dodds, J., & Archer, P. (1990). *Denver II technical manual.* Denver, CO: Denver Developmental Materials.

Frankenburg, W. K., Dodds, J., Archer, P., Shapiro, H., & Bresnick, B. (1992). The Denver II: A major revision and restandardization of the Denver Developmental Screening Test. *Pediatrics, 89,* 91–97.

Gesell, A., & Ames, L. B. (1940). The ontogenetic organization of prone behavior in human infancy. *Journal of Genetic Psychology, 56,* 247–263.

Haubenstricker, J. (1984). The assessment of motor skills in grades 4 to 6. Paper presented at the ARAPCS Measurement and Evaluation Council at the AAHPERD Convention, Anaheim, CA.

————. (1990). Summary of fundamental motor skill stage characteristics: Motor performance study—MSU. Unpublished materials, Michigan State University, East Lansing.

Haubenstricker, J., Seefeldt, V., Fountain, C., & Sapp, M. (1981). The efficiency of the Bruininks-Oseretsky test of motor proficiency in discriminating between normal children and those with gross motor dysfunction. Paper presented at the Motor Development Academy at the AAHPERD Convention, Boston.

Holland, B. (1992). Adapted physical education assessment practices in Wisconsin. *Physical Educator, 3,* 160–168.

Horvat, M., & Kalakian, L. (1996). *Assessment in adapted physical education and therapeutic recreation.* 2nd ed. Madison, WI: Brown & Benchmark.

Jenkot, V. K. (1986). Feasibility of large-scale implementation of the component approach for assessment of fundamental motor skills in grades K–3. Unpublished doctoral dissertation, University of North Carolina at Greensboro.

Kirby, R. F. (Ed.). (1991). *Kirby's guide to fitness and motor performance tests.* Cape Girardeau, MS: BenOak.

Linder, T. W. (1993a). *Transdisciplinary play-based assessment: A functional approach to working with young children.* Rev. ed. Baltimore, MD: Paul H. Brookes.

————. (1993b). *Transdisciplinary play-based intervention.* Baltimore, MD: Paul H. Brookes.

————. (1996). *Observing Kassandra: A transdisciplinary play-based assessment of a child with severe disabilities* (videotape). Baltimore, MD: Paul H. Brookes.

Loovis, E. M., & Ersing, W. F. (1979). *Assessing and programming gross motor development for children.* 2nd ed. Loudonville, OH: Mohican Textbook Publishing.

Mathieson, J. A., & Herring, J. J. (1990). The status of adapted physical education in the Commonwealth of Virginia. Paper presented at the Annual Virginia Alliance for Health, Physical Education, Recreation, and Dance Meeting, Charlottesville, VA.

McClenaghan, B., & Gallahue, D. (1978). Fundamental movement: A developmental and remedial approach. Philadelphia: Saunders.

Osness, W. (1995). *Administering the functional fitness assessment video.* Dubuque, IA: Kendall/Hunt.

————. (1996). *Functional Fitness Assessment for Adults Over 60 Years.* Dubuque, IA: Kendall/Hunt.

Pate, R. R., Ross, J. G., Baumgartner, T. A., & Sparks, R. E. (1987). The modified pull-up test. *Journal of Physical Education, Recreation, and Dance, 58,* 71–73.

Plake, B. S., & Impara, J. C. (2001). *The fourteenth mental measurements yearbook.* Lincoln: University of Nebraska Press.

President's Council on Physical Fitness and Sports. (2003). *2003–2004: The new president's challenge physical activity and fitness awards program packet.* Washington, DC: President's Council on Physical Fitness and Sports.

Rikli, R. E., & Jones, C. J. (2001). *Senior fitness test manual.* Champaign, IL: Human Kinetics.

Roach, E. G., & Kephart, N. C. (1966). *The Purdue Perceptual-Motor Survey.* Columbus, OH: Merrill.

Roberton, M. A., & Halverson, L. E. (1984). *Developing children—Their changing movement.* Philadelphia: Lea & Febiger.

Ross, J. G., Dotson, C. O., Gilbert, G. G., & Katz, S. J. (1985). New standards for fitness measurement. *Journal of Physical Education, Recreation, and Dance, 56,* 62–66.

Ross, J. G., Pate, R. R., Delpy, L. A., Gold, R. S., & Svilar, M. (1987). New health-related fitness norms. *Journal of Physical Education, Recreation, and Dance, 58,* 66–70.

Safrit, M. J. (1995). *Complete guide to youth fitness testing.* Champaign, IL: Human Kinetics.

Safrit, M. J., & Wood, T. M. (1995). *Introduction to measurement in physical education and exercise science.* 3rd ed. St. Louis, MO: Times Mirror/Mosby.

Sherrill, C. (1986). *Adapted physical education and recreation: A multidisciplinary approach.* 3rd ed. Dubuque, IA: Brown.
———. (1993). *Adapted physical activity, recreation and sport: Crossdisciplinary and lifespan.* Madison, WI: Brown & Benchmark.

Strand, B. N., & Wilson, R. (1993). *Assessing sport skills.* Champaign, IL: Human Kinetics.

Suomi, R., & Suomi, J. (1997). Effectiveness of a training program with physical education students and experienced physical education teachers in scoring the test of gross motor development. *Perceptual and Motor Skills, 84,* 771–778.

Ulrich, D. A. (1984). The reliability of classification decisions made with the objectives based motor skill assessment instrument. *Adapted Physical Activity Quarterly, 1,* 52–60.
———. (2000). *Test of Gross Motor Development–2.* Austin, TX: Pro-Ed.

United States Marines Youth Foundation. (1997). *The solution to a drug-free America: National Youth Physical Fitness Program.* 6th ed. Sylvania, OH: United States Marines Youth Foundation, Inc.

Wessel, J. A. (1976). *I CAN: Implementation guide.* Northbrook, IL: Hubbard.

Winnick, J. P., & Short, F. X. (1999). *Brockport physical fitness test kit.* Champaign, IL: Human Kinetics.

Planning and Conducting Developmental Movement Programs

There is much more to organizing and conducting a developmental movement program than just having a thorough understanding of motor development principles and theories. You also need exceptional organizational and communicative skills and the ability to work well with people — these all-important satellite skills can make or break a program. This chapter presents a systematic approach for planning and implementing this special type of program. Planning and implementing such a program is a monumental task, one that takes much time, consideration, and effort.

For ease of presentation, our systematic approach is divided into three phases. In phase 1 you determine whether you have the resources to implement a quality program. For instance, can the program's aims and goals be met given the existing facilities, equipment, and personnel? Phase 2 concerns selected administrative concerns: how to advertise the program, how to register participants, and many other important procedures. Phase 3 is devoted to certain curricular issues, such as how to organize the participation aspect of the program.

PREPROGRAM CONSIDERATIONS

Before implementing a developmental movement program, you must first determine whether there is a need for such a program. If there is, you should assess whether you have the necessary facilities, equipment, and personnel for implementing the program. This section shows you how to answer these vital questions.

Philosophy

The first step in planning an effective and efficient developmental movement program is to consider two very important elements of any program. First, what will be the **program philosophy** governing its operation? What do you hope to accomplish by implementing a program? Is your objective to give the so-called normal child movement experiences necessary to foster optimal development, or is the program being designed to help children re-

mediate existing motor problems? Do you intend to cater to the highly skilled person who wants to become even more proficient in specific sport skills? In any case, you must determine the program's aims and objectives.

Second, you must consider the **program scope.** Even though most developmental movement programs are designed with young children in mind, remember that motor development and motor refinement are lifelong processes. As such, will your program cater to preschool children, elementary school children, adolescents, younger adults, or older adults? Furthermore, do you plan to include people from special populations? In other words, will you offer an **adapted program**? If so, what will be the emphasis of this program? Will it be designed for the mentally disabled, the orthopedically disabled, or individuals with some other disabling condition?

Figure 18-1 illustrates areas that could be included in a developmental movement program. Initially, you should not attempt to implement more than one area. Be patient, take your time; be certain that you can successfully implement one of these programs before you attempt to branch out into other program areas.

Facilities and Equipment

Once you have established a philosophy and defined the population you want to serve, determine whether you have the facilities and equipment needed to implement the program. The amount and type of equipment needed will depend on the scope of the program and the age groups to be served. Therefore, equipment and apparatus needs differ from program to program. This section does not list the numerous pieces of available play apparatus and equipment; it describes the differences in various types of equipment and apparatus and offers general guidelines that should help you select the most appropriate material.

TYPES OF INDOOR AND OUTDOOR PLAY APPA-RATUS There are two types of play apparatus: developmental and nondevelopmental. **Developmental apparatus** foster both organic and skill development, two objectives of most motor develop-

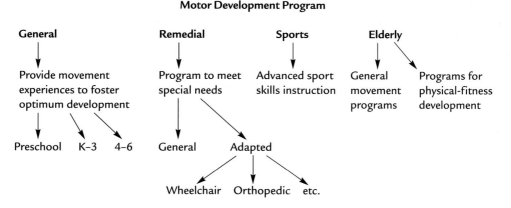

Figure 18-1   Potential areas of emphasis in a motor development program

ment programs. For example, developmental apparatus that contribute to strength development include the horizontal ladder, jungle gym, chinning bar, climbing pole, and parallel bars.

Young children especially enjoy playing on **nondevelopmental apparatus,** but this type of apparatus contributes little to the physical objectives of a developmental movement program. Nondevelopmental apparatus include sliding boards, swings, merry-go-rounds, seesaws, and spring animals. Also be aware that nondevelopmental equipment is frequently misused in such a manner as to cause bodily injury.

DEVELOPMENTALLY APPROPRIATE EQUIPMENT   Any time a person is required to perform a motor task with equipment that is not **developmentally appropriate,** performance suffers (see Figure 18-2). For example, a young child who is required to shoot a regulation-size basketball toward a 10-foot basketball goal faces a predicament. In most instances, the youngster is not capable of using the correct technique to project the ball toward the basket, because the ball is too big and too heavy and the basketball goal too high. As a result, the child uses an inappropriate shooting technique, such as an over-the-shoulder shot or an underhanded between-the-legs shot to propel the ball toward the basket. An experimental investigation that

Isaacs and Karpman (1981) conducted revealed just how unsuccessful 8- and 9-year-old children could be when required to use inappropriate equipment. In this investigation, 30 boys and 30 girls were required to shoot regulation-size basketballs, junior-size basketballs, and an even smaller and lighter Nerf basketball (soft rubber) toward 8- and 10-foot basketball goals. These young children were five times more likely to make the shot when the basketball goal was 8 feet rather than the standard 10 feet. In addition, their likelihood of missing the shot was less when they used the junior-size basketball. These findings were also supported by Haywood (1978) and Wright (1967), who found that letting children use smaller and lighter basketballs improved achievement scores on a basketball-shooting accuracy task. Also, as discussed in Chapter 14, the size of the ball influences children's throwing performance. Burton and colleagues (1992, 1993) found a critical transitional point when ball size would begin to interfere with throwing technique and the manner in which the ball is grasped. All of these studies suggest that we should take into consideration the size of the performer when recommending play equipment. In other words, the play equipment should be appropriately scaled to the size of the child.

How can you be certain that your equipment is developmentally appropriate? Furthermore, does

Figure 18-2 Failure is inevitable whenever appropriate equipment and facilities are not utilized.

your equipment take into consideration individual differences in skill ability? Little research is available to help us answer these two important questions. However, Herkowitz (1978, 1984) offers three suggestions. First, group equipment with similar functions but of different sizes. For instance, set chinning bars at different heights and be sure the diameters of the bars are different, to take into consideration differences in hand size. Similarly, construct vertical and horizontal ladders with different spacing between rungs. Second, use adjustable equipment to accommodate differences in develop-

mental levels, such as jumping hurdles, batting tees, and basketball goals, all of which can be adjusted to different heights. Last, Herkowitz suggests using a single piece of equipment constructed in such a manner that it can accommodate different developmental levels; for example, a specially constructed balance beam that is very wide at one end but progressively narrow toward the other end. These three guidelines should help you select the most appropriate equipment for your program.

PLAYGROUNDS A properly equipped and designed playground can help foster motor development. According to Siedentop, Herkowitz, and Rink, "The use of playspace over time is related to the complexity and novelty of the playspace" (1984, p. 184). For this reason, they discourage incorporating large play apparatus that by design are unchangeable, such as the nondevelopmental apparatus mentioned earlier. They recommend incorporating apparatus that can take on many different shapes. For instance, a basic piece of equipment can be embedded into the playground to which portable attachments such as ladders, stairs, and horizontal bars can be attached in different configurations. When not in use, the attachments can be kept in a storage unit located on the playground. A play environment that can take on many different looks helps eliminate boredom and encourages creative movement.

Only within recent years have we become more concerned about the number of children who sustain injury while participating on playgrounds. National surveys indicate that each year approximately 200,000 children under 15 years of age are treated in hospital emergency rooms because of injuries related to playground equipment (Tinsworth & McDonald, 2001; U.S. Consumer Product Safety Commission, 1997, 2001) and that 10 to 20 will die from their injuries (American Academy of Pediatrics, 2000). In fact, 70 percent of all playground deaths occur on home playground equipment (U.S. Consumer Product Safety Commission, 2001). As indicated in Table 18-1, the vast majority of playground injuries are caused by falling from play apparatus onto a hard surface or onto other parts of the apparatus. In fact, yard surfacing was found to

Table 18-1 Public Playground Equipment Injury Rates and Their Causes	
Primary Cause of Injury	**Percentage**
Falls resulting in contact with the underlying surface	58.0–75.0
Striking the equipment while falling	14.0
Falls resulting in contact with other equipment	2.0
Impact with moving equipment	13.1
Impact with stationary equipment	5.4
Contacting protrusions, pinch points, sharp edges, and sharp points	6.9

Source: Adapted from American Academy of Orthopedic Surgeons (1991). Based on data from the National Electronic Injury Surveillance System (NEISS) special study, April–December 1988, U.S. Consumer Product Safety Commission, Directorate Epidemiology, Division of Hazard Analysis, Washington, DC.

be inadequate in 114 of 130 playgrounds surveyed in 11 states and the District of Columbia (Duston, 1992). Inappropriate surfaces include concrete, hard-packed dirt, asphalt, and even grass. More appropriate surfaces would include sand, loosely packed pea gravel, mulch, rubber padding, and shredded tires. According to the U.S. Consumer Product Safety Commission (1997), surfaces under playground equipment should consist of shock-absorbent materials capable of significantly decreasing serious injury, especially head injury. It is believed that if, during impact, the head exceeds a peak deceleration exceeding 200 times the acceleration due to gravity (200 Gs), a life-threatening head injury is likely to occur (U.S. Consumer Product Safety Commission, 1997). Some authorities also believe that the time during which the head decelerates is another important factor contributing to serious head injury. Using a complex mathematical formula, researchers are now able to calculate a value known as the **head injury criterion** (Collantes, 1990). Using these two criteria, it is now possible to calculate a measure of **critical height,** or in other words, the maximal height that a test headform can be dropped onto a surface material yielding both a peak decel-

eration of no more than 200 Gs and a head injury criterion score of less than 1000. These two absorbency tests provide an approximation of the fall height below which a life-threatening head injury would not be expected to occur (U.S. Consumer Product Safety Commission, 1997). Table 18-2 presents critical heights for various depths of both uncompressed and compressed popular surface materials. When choosing a surface material, be sure to select one that has a critical height value of at least the height of the highest play surface (fall height). Table 18-3 presents several steps that can be taken to reduce playground injuries.

If you would like additional information on playground safety, you can obtain a free copy of the *Handbook for Public Playground Safety* (Publication Number 325) by contacting the U.S. Consumer Product Safety Commission, Washington, DC 20207; www.cpsc.gov. The *Public Playground Safety Checklist* can also be obtained by fax; call (301) 504-0051 and request document number 327. Other sources of information on playground safety can be obtained from KaBOOM (www.kaboom.org) and the National Program for Playground Safety (www.uni.edu/playground). One additional popular source of information, *Play It Safe: A Guide to Playground Safety,* can be obtained from the American Academy of Orthopedic Surgeons by calling (800) 824-BONES.

EQUIPMENT STORAGE AND TRANSPORT When acquiring equipment, give special consideration to storing and transporting it. Is there enough room for storing such apparatus as balance beams, parallel bars, and other large pieces of equipment? If so, is the storage area close to the activity area? Are these large and heavy pieces of equipment easy to assemble and disassemble? If not, chances are they will not be used frequently in the program. Ideally, the storage area should be located as close as possible to the activity area, even within the same area if possible.

Smaller pieces of equipment, such as balls, hoops, and racquets, also require much storage space. To facilitate the storage and transport of this type of small equipment, buy or make several bins to which you can attach wheels. With such a setup, you simply roll

Table 18-2   Critical Heights (in feet) of Tested Materials

| Material | Uncompressed Depth | | | Compressed Depth |
	6 inch	9 inch	2 inch	9 inch
Wood chips°	7	10	11	10
Double shredded bark mulch	6	10	11	7
Engineered wood fibers†	6	7	>12	6
Fine sand	5	5	9	5
Coarse sand	5	5	6	4
Fine gravel	6	7	10	6
Medium gravel	5	5	6	5
Shredded tires‡	10–12	N/A	N/A	N/A

°This product was referred to as *wood mulch* in previous versions of this handbook. The term *wood chips* more accurately describes the product.

†This product was referred to as *uniform wood chips* in previous versions of this handbook. In the playground industry, the product is more commonly known as *engineered wood fibers.*

‡This data is from tests conducted by independent testing laboratories on a 6-inch depth of uncompressed shredded tire samples produced by four manufacturers. The tests reported critical heights that varied from 10 feet to greater than 12 feet. It is recommended that persons seeking to install shredded tires as a protective surface request test data from the supplier showing the critical height of the material when it was tested in accordance with ASTM F1292.

Source: U.S. Consumer Product Safety Commission (1997).

out the equipment for a given instructional station, making only one trip, which is certainly more efficient than carrying two or three balls at a time, and having to make several trips before the station is totally assembled. If you cannot construct these bins, buy large rubber trash cans attached to dollies. Not only does this arrangement facilitate the speed at which a station can be set up, but it is also a valuable organizational tool because you no longer have to frantically look for equipment—you always know in which can the equipment is located.

Personnel

A motor development program accompanied by the most elaborate, versatile, and expensive equipment could nonetheless fail, because the success of any

program depends directly on the personnel available to implement the program. You must assemble a good instructional staff—a team of individuals committed to working toward the common goals of the program.

UNIVERSITY- OR COLLEGE-BASED PROGRAMS
If the program is being conducted in conjunction with a local college or university, it may be feasible to put together an instructional team of undergraduate and graduate students who want experience working with people in a movement environment. This arrangement is particularly attractive because most college students who elect to take part in the program may be available for several years, which helps eliminate the need to retrain a new instructional team every few months. Nevertheless, you should expect an influx of different personnel

Table 18-3	Factors to Consider for the Reduction of Playground Injuries

Surfaces Under Playground Apparatus

Sand surfacing should be at least 12 inches deep.

Fine pea gravel (¼ inch) surfacing should be 10–12 inches deep.

Organic materials such as mulch or shredded wood should be 10–12 inches deep.

The use of shredded tires has been found to offer improved protection.

As a rule of thumb, the surfacing under playground apparatus should be loose and deep enough to make walking on the material difficult. In other words, if you can easily walk on the material, it probably is not deep enough or loose enough to absorb the body's impact adequately.

Playground Design Considerations

Establish a "use zone" around all equipment, keeping adequate space for entering and exiting the play area.

Physically separate the most popular playground equipment to avoid overcrowding.

Establish separate play areas for younger and older children.

Install 22–38-inch-high guardrails on elevated platforms for older children and 22–26-inch-high guardrails for preschool children.

Platforms should be no higher than 8 feet above the ground.

All openings should be less than 3½ inches or greater than 9 inches to avoid potential head entrapment hazards.

Handrails and climbing bars should ideally measure 1.25 inches in diameter (safe range .95–1.55 inches).

Use developmentally appropriate equipment to ensure proper hand-grip size of bars and so forth.

Separate playgrounds from streets by fences, shrubs, or other physical barriers.

Apparatus should be accessible to wheelchair traffic.

Playground Maintenance

Inspect playground equipment regularly for rust, sharp edges, wood rot, loose bolts, bent parts, and bearing wear.

Inspect supporting surfaces and replace materials that do not meet the specifications outlined in "Surfaces Under Playground Apparatus," above.

Inspect playground for and eliminate broken glass, sharp objects, and holes.

Child Clothing

Recent changes in children's clothing fashion have resulted in an increasing number of clothing items containing drawstrings. These drawstrings can strangle a child if they become entangled with playground equipment. The American Academy of Pediatrics (2000) recently released the following recommendations regarding drawstrings:

The best advice is to choose clothing that does not have drawstrings.

Cut drawstrings to shorten the ends so that just enough is left to tie.

Sew a seam at the middle of the drawstring so that it cannot be pulled out either side.

because inevitably members of your instructional team will graduate or leave the program for some other reason.

To combat this problem, establish some type of hierarchical arrangement or ranking among instructional personnel. For example, people who have completed a series of courses in motor development and those who have had prior work experience in a clinic are assigned the position of *station leader.* Station leaders may be responsible for a variety of tasks, including (1) directing assigned activities and instruction in a given area of expertise, (2) training less experienced staff members, and (3) supervising. The less-experienced people are assistant instructors or general assistants. *Assistant instructors* are usually exercise science majors who have acquired some area of expertise but have not taken a sequence of course work in motor development. Furthermore, they generally do not have any prior teaching experience with the population involved. *General assistants,* an entry-level position, have neither experience in teaching nor an area of expertise. The primary duties of general assistants are to help carry out the directives of the station leaders and to serve as partners to the participants in the clinic. This partner or friend relationship between participant and clinician fosters a more social and relaxed atmosphere in which learning new skills can take place. Furthermore, because both participant and clinician are actively involved in participating in assigned activities under the direction of both assistant instructors and station leaders, the general assistant gains valuable experience in learning how to teach in a movement environment while slowly acquiring an area of expertise. Thus, both the motor development participant and the general assistant learn through direct participation in the program.

PUBLIC SCHOOL–BASED PROGRAMS   Not all motor programs can be developed using college students. In fact, most programs conducted in public schools are developed, organized, and carried out by one person, usually the physical education teacher. Unfortunately, one person is not usually capable of offering the one-to-one attention so often necessary when working with the people who typi-

cally attend these special programs. Thus, the physical educator's challenge is to recruit additional help, in most cases **volunteers.** Frequently, volunteers are viewed as more trouble than they are worth, but this is unfortunate, because volunteers, even those with little or no teaching experience, can perform valuable duties, enabling those with teaching experience to spend more time with program participants.

Dunn, Morehouse, and Fredericks (1985) recommend the following rules for the use of volunteers:

1. Take the time to train your volunteers. Be sure they understand their role in your program.
2. If volunteers are to be involved in teaching, be sure they are assigned teaching duties compatible with their level of training.
3. Establish a system whereby constructive feedback can be given to volunteers. Faulty performance should be corrected tactfully and proper performance praised.
4. Because there may be so little time to communicate with your volunteers, you will need to establish a simplified system of communication. Volunteers need to know what to do with given individuals, and you need to obtain from the volunteers information concerning given student performances.
5. Maintain a system of flexible scheduling.

Volunteers can be enlisted by consulting teachers, your parent-teacher association, local civic groups, private agencies, and local recreational departments. Also, do not overlook the possibility of using older students who attend neighboring schools.

ADMINISTRATIVE CONSIDERATIONS

As you think about being the director of a motor development program, you probably envision yourself spending most of your time working directly with program participants. Unfortunately, if your goal is to run a trouble-free program, you will probably be spending more time than you ever imagined handling administrative responsibilities. This section discusses the administrative tasks you are likely to confront. By following our suggestions, you should save time in handling these important duties.

Advertising the Program

Once you decide to implement a motor development program, you must then determine if there will be enough interest in the program to justify its existence. You can use one of two approaches. First, conduct a local survey to get a feel for the community's acceptance of the program. Second, you can skip this process and go directly to advertising the program and accepting applications. We recommend the latter approach—our experience has been that although the community may support the program in theory, when it comes to actually registering, the percentage of affirmative responses is often lower than the first response implied.

Depending on the scope of the program, there are different forms of advertising. If the scope of the program is limited to just one school, a simple announcement sent home in the school's newsletter suffices. In some special instances, you may want to send a personal letter to the parents of children you know will benefit from participation in the program. On the other hand, if the scope of the program is to be extended into the community, then you must establish a broader advertising base. Develop program flyers and place them in various community establishments or send them to local civic organizations. Furthermore, most local newspapers seek community-interest stories; we have found local papers an excellent way to get in-depth coverage at no expense. Simply call the local newspaper and tell them about your program. Usually, they will be glad to send someone out to interview you.

Certain essential information should be included in your advertising, whether it is in the form of a flyer or newspaper interview:

1. Tell the public the purpose of the program and how it can help them or their children.

2. Identify the age range of the participants.

3. State meeting times, meeting place, and length of program. For instance, the program will be held in Burt and Ernie Elementary School Gymnasium from 9:00 A.M. to 10:30 A.M. for eight consecutive Saturdays starting October 8, 2005.

4. Outline the registration procedures.

5. Is there a registration fee; if so, how much?

6. Include a telephone number where you can be reached if anyone has any further questions.

Remember, advertising is crucial because the best-designed program is of no value if it has no participants.

Registration

In most instances, the registration form can be a part of the advertisement flyer. Figure 18-3 is an example of a registration form. Note that the form is divided into two distinct sections. The first section contains information pertinent to the motor development program; the second section is an application for enrollment. This form serves two purposes. The bottom section, which is to be filled in by a parent or participant, is used for administrative purposes because it contains personal information about the applicant. Because the form is signed, it shows approval or consent for participation in the program. The applicant retains the top half of the form; this part contains most of the important information about the program, such as dates, meeting times, and meeting place.

When applications are received in the mail, you should get into the habit of processing each one immediately. Initially screen each application to determine if the applicant conforms to the program's philosophy and scope. For example, is the applicant within the appropriate age range that the program is to serve? Does the applicant have any physical limitations that would preclude participation in the program? If the answers to these two questions are satisfactory, then place the person's name on an official enrollment list.

Next, send the applicant a letter or postcard confirming acceptance into the program and reminding

BURT AND ERNIE ELEMENTARY SCHOOL
DEVELOPMENTAL MOVEMENT

What   During Fall 2005, the Burt and Ernie Elementary School Motor Development Clinic will again be offered to the general public. The purpose of the clinic is to improve the motor skill development and sports skills of elementary school children (Grades K–6).

How   Participants will receive individualized instruction in physical fitness, gymnastics, perceptual-motor activities, and various sports skills to include soccer, basketball, tennis, racquetball, and other individual preferences. A periodic evaluation will be performed, and parents will be provided with a written progress report. The clinic will give consideration to the first 60 applications received by September 17, 2005.

When   The clinic will be held on Saturday mornings:

Session I: 9:00–10:30 A.M.   Grades 4–6

Session II: 10:30–12:00 noon   Grades K–3

The clinic will start October 8, 2005. The fee will be $40 per child. Sessions will be held in the Burt and Ernie Elementary School gym at 1704 Virginia Avenue, Centerville, OH 45458. Enrollment will be limited to foster a low student-teacher ratio. For additional information call (937) 775-2859.

To apply for enrollment, please complete the following by September 17, 2005, and mail to Burt and Ernie Elementary School, 1704 Virginia Avenue, Centerville, OH 45458.

Payment must accompany application. Check only—made payable to:

Burt and Ernie Elementary—Motor Development Clinic

Child's name _____

Address _____

Phone _____   Sex _____   Grade _____

Parent's signature _____

Does your child have any physical limitations that require special considerations? If so, please describe. _____

Figure 18-3   Sample registration form

the applicant about the program's starting date, starting time, and location. In addition, inform the applicant of any special first-day procedures, such as what to wear.

Orientation Meeting

If the program includes young children, you have an obligation to keep all parents well informed. An *orientation meeting* can partly serve this purpose. More specifically, at the orientation meeting you disseminate important information about the operation as well as the purpose of the program. During this meeting, address each of the following issues:

1. Explain the philosophy of the program and what you hope to accomplish.
2. Explain drop-off and pick-up procedures and stress the importance of being prompt.
3. Explain cancellation procedures in the event of inclement weather.
4. Urge all participants to carry health insurance in case of an accident. If appropriate, also describe supplemental accident insurance that can be acquired.
5. Briefly preview the upcoming *parents' workshop* at which parents can learn how to teach movement skills to their children (see later section).
6. Explain your policy concerning parental observation of children during clinical sessions.
7. Have individuals fill out any consent forms.
8. Conduct an open question-and-answer session.

Send an agenda to all participants approximately 10 days before the meeting. You may want to include this agenda in your letter confirming enrollment.

First-Aid and Emergency Procedures

Motor development participants have a right to learn and play in a physically safe environment. In general, a well-thought-out and well-organized program will produce such an environment. Nevertheless, whenever people engage in movement tasks, accidents can occur. Fortunately, most accidents will be minor scrapes and bruises. However, there

Table 18-4 Blood Management Procedures

1. All activity must stop at the first sight of blood.
2. Whenever possible, the injured party should be responsible for cleaning his or her own wound.
3. Rubber gloves should always be worn when handling blood directly from an open wound or indirectly (bloody towels, clothing, etc.). The hands must be washed immediately after glove removal.
4. Anyone with blood on his or her clothing must be removed from the activity. This is not restricted to the injured party; it also applies to anyone else with blood on clothing.
5. The participant must change clothing before being allowed to return to the activity, or the bloody portion of the clothing must be cleaned and then treated with a fresh 1:100 dilution of sodium hypochlorite (bleach)—¼ cup bleach to a gallon of water.
6. Blood-contaminated surfaces must also be cleaned with a 1:100 dilution of sodium hypochlorite before activity is allowed to continue.
7. Any contaminated materials must be kept in separate biohazard containers, cleaned separately, or properly disposed of.

SOURCE: Adapted from Rasor (1994).

is a potential for more serious injury. Organizers of developmental movement programs must be prepared to handle both kinds of injury.

Who should be contacted when injuries occur? Who should administer first aid? What is the telephone number of the nearest rescue squad? In short, how should emergencies be handled? To provide a clear directive for all involved, these questions can best be addressed by establishing a set of first-aid and emergency procedures. Above all, remember that for these procedures to be effective, all personnel should be required to demonstrate their understanding of the steps to be taken when an accident occurs.

Of particular concern in recent years is the establishment of blood management procedures. This has become a special concern because of the recent spread of HIV and AIDS. Table 18-4 provides general guidelines for handling an accident where blood is present.

Cancellation Procedures

Uncontrollable circumstances, such as inclement weather, may occasionally require you to postpone a clinical session. Regardless of the reason for the postponement, you have an obligation to notify all personnel and participants as soon as possible. How would you handle the following situation?

> On Saturday mornings during the winter months, you conduct your motor development program from 10:00 to 11:30 A.M. One Saturday, at approximately 8:00 A.M., a light snow begins to fall and the temperature falls well below freezing. You are concerned about the deteriorating weather conditions, but by 8:30 you feel that weather conditions do not warrant canceling the day's program. However, during the next 15 minutes the conditions rapidly worsen. By 9:00 A.M., you decide to cancel the Saturday program. However, because of the distance that your 60 participants must travel to get to the program, you need to get the cancellation information to them within the next 15 to 20 minutes.

How can you do this? Obviously, there is not enough time for you to contact 60 families individually by telephone. The task is impossible unless you have previously thought through such a situation and developed and implemented a procedure to follow when threatening weather hits or is approaching.

The solution is simple. Because the program is being conducted in the winter months, you should have recognized the potential for inclement weather. Consequently, you need to contact a radio station that routinely announces cancellations caused by inclement weather conditions. You will not be able to simply call the radio station when you decide to cancel the day's program, because the telephone operator at the station has no way of knowing whether you are the person with the authority to make such decisions. Instead, visit the radio station well in advance. The station manager will probably require you to fill out a special form and produce positive identification. You will then be assigned an individual password. Whenever you decide to cancel the program, simply call the radio station and give them your special password; they will make the

announcement over the airwaves. Remember to discuss these procedures with the parents during the parent orientation meeting. Above all, make sure that everyone knows which stations will be making the announcement.

Drop-Off and Pick-Up Procedures

One way to increase enrollment is to make program attendance as trouble-free as possible, particularly when participants are children, because the program can be an extra burden on parents. The most troublesome aspect of movement programs, according to parents, is having to transport their child. Furthermore, because most clinical sessions seldom last longer than 1 or 1 ½ hours, parents frequently complain that by the time they return home it is time to return to pick up their child.

To combat these problems, during the orientation meeting, we suggest to the parents two possible solutions. First, parents can plan to do their grocery shopping while their child attends the program. To ensure that the parents have enough time, we have implemented an efficient drop-off and pick-up procedure. Parents of participants are given a large sign that has their child's name printed on it. Up to 15 minutes before the start of the program, parents can drive to a designated drop-off location, flash their name plate, and immediately the child's instructor comes to the car and walks the child to the activity area. Time is saved because parents never have to leave their cars. Parents especially like this procedure during inclement weather. The same procedure is followed for picking up participants. Not only is this technique efficient, but it also makes a potentially dangerous aspect of the program safer, because the children no longer have to walk to a parking lot, darting between cars.

A second solution is to provide activities for the parents while their child takes part in the movement program. A survey of parents whose children attend the Wright State University Motor Development Program resulted in the following activities: an exercise class, a television room, a quiet room reserved for reading, and a room where video movies are shown. These activities are scheduled to end approximately 15 minutes before the movement program. Parents then go to a predetermined location just outside the activity area and pick up their child.

Positive responses to these two drop-off and pick-up procedures have been overwhelming. Parents no longer feel that they waste the entire day or evening transporting their child to extracurricular activities.

Computer-Assisted Organization

As should be evident by now, organizing and conducting a motor development program can be time-consuming. You have to send out applications, advertise the program, handle registration and confirmation letters, maintain files on all participants, and perform many other administrative duties. Do not get discouraged—in this age of technology, help is available: the personal computer (PC). Most teachers now have access to PCs in their own school, and computer programs (software) are now available to handle all of the administrative activities. Visit a local computer store and tell them your needs. Using a PC to handle administrative tasks will save you time so you can get on with the task you enjoy the most: working with people in a movement environment.

CURRICULAR CONSIDERATIONS

The two previous sections showed you how to overcome many of the pitfalls frequently encountered when setting up a motor development program. For the most part, the discussion focused on philosophical and administrative considerations. One vital consideration that still needs to be addressed is how to plan and organize the participation aspect of the program. Briefly, you must become aware of each participant's level of functioning, organize a learning environment conducive to optimal learning, and devise a means of disseminating program results.

Preprogram Assessments

During the first one or two clinical sessions, you must assess each participant's incoming ability. Which abilities you will assess will differ, depending on the program philosophy and the scope of the program. For example, if the program is designed for preschool children and children in the first and second grades, you will assess children's abilities in the fundamental movement skills. But if your program philosophy is to improve adolescents' sport skills ability, your assessment will include a specific sport skills test and perhaps a measure of motor and physiological fitness. A program designed for the elderly may include a wide range of movement assessments and measures of motor and physiological fitness.

Regardless of what is assessed, keep in mind that the purpose of a preprogram assessment is to establish a baseline to which comparisons can be made in the future. And above all, these initial assessments must be linked to program content. That is, once weaknesses are evident, you must implement an individualized program designed to remediate these deficiencies. This concept was stressed in Chapter 17; refer to that chapter for ideas concerning assessment and the administration of various assessment instruments.

Instructional Organization

When designing lessons in the motor domain, you need to consider that participation is essential to the learning process. Although some researchers have found that mental rather than physical practice improves skill performance, the best way to learn new skills and refine old skills is through participation. In other words, people of all ages learn best by doing.

How you structure the learning environment can influence whether there will be maximum participation. Also, your instructional organization must provide for both maximum and individualized instruction. We have found the **stations approach** most effective for organizing instruction. In fact, this approach can offset some of the potential problems presented earlier. For instance, maximum participation requires, in most instances, that each person have a piece of equipment and that waiting time for a turn to use equipment be kept to a minimum. By dividing the group up and using stations, the number of people who need to use a specific type of equipment at a given time will be reduced, and there will obviously be less waiting for a turn.

Another advantage of the stations approach is that it allows for ability grouping or mainstreaming.

Not all participants in the program will function at the same skill level. Therefore, based on preprogram assessments, an individualized program can be written for each participant. Participants who possess similar degrees of proficiency in a given skill area can easily be grouped together for instruction. In our program, the general assistants are responsible for transporting participants to their individually assigned stations.

The amount of time that a participant should spend at any one station depends on age, interest, and attention span. In general, you can reasonably expect elementary school children to spend approximately 15 to 20 minutes at each of four stations during any clinical session. A 10-minute juice break between the second and third stations can do wonders for rejuvenating a child's level of interest.

Instructional Delivery Considerations

The best movement curriculum is of little value if the instructor cannot convey information effectively to the program participants. In this section, we address instructional points to consider and their implications. Adhering to this instructional delivery advice should foster your ability to teach motor skills.

DEMONSTRATIONS   The demonstration presents to the participants a picture of the skill to be learned, thus lending them a sense of direction. The old saying "A picture is worth a thousand words" appears to be especially true when teaching motor skills.

Because the primary purpose of a demonstration is to present to the learners a visual illustration of the task, care must be taken in selecting demonstrators. Ideally, the individual who is the most proficient at performing the selected task should be selected to demonstrate; however, many instructors feel an obligation to perform all demonstrations themselves. One advantage of the teacher demonstration appears to be the earning of students' respect. There are inherent disadvantages, however, to teacher-performed demonstrations. Students who experience difficulty in performing the selected task generally give up too early, and when reminded of the teacher demonstration, they will frequently alibi, "Sure, you can do it—you're the teacher." Such problems can be avoided by using

student demonstrations. The added peer influence from these demonstrations inspires desire and determination in practice sessions.

To find a suitable student demonstrator, you can simply ask the students to find the best method to dribble a basketball, for example. While the children are participating in this self-discovery process, be on the lookout for students who use acceptable techniques. After a short time, you will be able to point out those who are using the best methods so that other participants can watch their performance.

A word of caution: While demonstrations may be an influential factor in skill development, their use does not guarantee improved rates of learning. For demonstrations to be effective, the teacher needs to have the students' attention and in most instances should use multiple demonstrations. Remember the following two conditions for developing effective demonstrations:

1. *Condition:* The learner must be attentive to the demonstration.

   Implication: Before allowing the demonstrator to perform, care must be taken to ensure student attention. Eliminate all external distractions. If distractions occur during the demonstration, wait until the disturbances have passed.

2. *Condition:* The learner must know in advance the key elements to look for during the demonstration.

   Implication: Because most skills contain more than one key element, the ability to model behavior can be facilitated through multiple demonstrations. During each demonstration, direct the participants' attention (precue) to different aspects of the task (one cue at a time). In demonstrating the forward roll, for example, direct the participants' attention toward the initial hand position. During the second demonstration, tell the participants to focus their attention on the position of the chin during performance. Following three to five demonstration trials, students will have been exposed to the key components. Thus, multiple demonstrations tend to be more effective than a single demonstration.

Figure 18-4 Flowchart depicting cartwheel roundoff

VISUAL AIDS Recall that the purpose of a demonstration is to present to the learners a visual representation of expert performance in the hope that they will in turn model the behavior. With this in mind, you should see that any type of visual media can be utilized to represent the task visually. Common sources of visual media that may be effective include filmloops, videotapes, flowcharts, and slides and pictures.

For example, say a teacher wants students to view the positioning of the legs and ankles during the execution of a cartwheel roundoff. Nature, however, requires that this task be performed at a speed so fast that the novice performer is not likely to see clearly the body regions specified by the instructor. In this case, it would be appropriate to use a filmloop or motion picture showing someone performing this task. These media can then be shown in slow-motion and stop-action replay, which will allow the learner to follow the desired regions of observation through the entire range of the activity. For schools with budgets that do not support an extensive film library, a viable alternative is to either make or purchase a series of inexpensive flowcharts, which are actually frame-by-frame pictures or illustrations of someone performing a specific task. Figure 18-4 is an example of a flowchart depicting the cartwheel roundoff.

ATTENTION During task performance, we must direct our attention to the most important elements of the task while ignoring those elements that matter little to task performance (background noise). This concept is sometimes referred to as *selective attention*. As mentioned earlier, precuing, or telling performers where to focus their attention prior to task execution, is one technique that can be used to help ensure that students attend to the important elements of a specified task.

Many theories try to explain why we tend to lose attention. One theory suggests that we lose our ability to focus when we are required to perform in monotonous surroundings, while another theory suggests that attention is lost when we are required to respond to very infrequent signals. Thus, teachers of motor skills should make frequent changes in the physical teaching environment. For example, classes should not always be held at the same location each day, drills and activities should be limited in duration to avoid boredom, and class routines should be frequently changed. Above all, avoid teaching formations that require students to wait in long lines before getting a turn to perform.

MEMORY The terms *memory* and *forgetting* go hand in hand. Memory can be thought of as information that can be retrieved when needed, whereas forgetting generally is referred to as information that cannot be retrieved from memory. For ease of discussion, think of the structure of memory as being composed of two structures: short-term memory (STM) and long-term memory (LTM). Unlike LTM, STM is limited both in capacity—the number of items we can recall—and in duration—the length of time we can recall the items. Thus, when teaching motor skills, you must be careful not to overload the participants' memory capacity by giving them more information or instructions to attend to than necessary. Further, once information is conveyed to participants, you must organize the learning environment so that practice can begin immediately; otherwise, the students may forget what they are supposed to do. Information in STM must be acted on within 20 to 30 seconds or it will be forgotten.

LEVELS OF PROCESSING Whenever the teacher presents new information to students, it will reside in STM, provided that the students were paying attention. The job of the teacher, however, is to get the students to move this information from STM into LTM, which can be accomplished if they act on the new information. An example illustrates the point. You call the information operator to obtain a telephone number, but unfortunately you do not have a pencil to write this number down onto paper. As soon as you get the number from the operator you start to repeat it to yourself over and over again until you have successfully dialed the number. This action plan is a control process known as *rehearsal.* In other words, you have acted on the information (new telephone number) in an attempt to move it from STM to LTM. The same idea can be used in learning new motor skills. That is why it is so important to let participants begin practicing within 20 to 30 seconds following a demonstration.

ATTACHING VERBAL LABELS TO MOVEMENT Memory can also be facilitated if meaningful labels are attached to physical movements. One verbal label frequently used in physical education is the clock face. For example, instead of just demonstrating a movement such as hitting a tennis ball with a racquet, tell the student to swing the racquet from 6 o'clock to 12 o'clock. If the student can tell time, then this verbal label will probably help her establish the correct vertical swing technique. Above all, the label must be meaningful to the student; obviously, the preceding example would not help a student who could not tell time.

FEEDBACK AND KNOWLEDGE OF RESULTS Sometimes the two terms *feedback* and *knowledge of results* are used interchangeably. This is unfortu-

nate, because the terms have different definitions. **Feedback** refers to information that the performer receives through the performer's own senses (e.g., eyes, ears), whereas **knowledge of results (KOR)** refers to information that the performer receives from an external source—generally the teacher. Both feedback and KOR are useful for error correction. KOR tends to be very important during the early stages of learning a new motor skill, because at this stage of learning novice performers are not capable of knowing what feedback information they should be attending to. As a result, the teacher must point out to the student aspects of performance that need to be corrected. Once the performer is able to establish a "model of correct performance," then feedback becomes more important. A *model of correct performance* is essentially an abstract representation in the performer's mind as to what correct performance should look and feel like. This abstract representation is compared with actual performance during each performance trial, and when the two do not match up, then corrections in performance need to be made.

When KOR is conveyed to a performer, the teacher must be sure that the information is meaningful. For instance, a first grader can probably understand the direction "Move a little faster" but probably would not be able to derive much useful meaning out of the direction "You need to move 600 milliseconds faster."

A final point regarding KOR is that it should not be given after every performance trial. This is because the performer needs time to think about the KOR information. Furthermore, recall that the teacher is giving KOR in an attempt to help the performer develop a model of correct performance. When KOR is given after every performance trial, the student begins to ignore internal feedback and use KOR as a crutch.

PRIMACY-RECENCY THEORY This theory purports that we remember the first and the most recent information that is presented. Thus, during any class, the student is likely to have the most difficulty recalling the middle portion of the lesson. For this reason, the teacher should spend the last couple of minutes reviewing the lesson, paying particular attention to the middle portion of it.

Many other effective points to consider can be found in any applied textbook on motor learning. We suggest that you consult Magill (2004).

Postprogram Discussions

Following each clinical session, all personnel should gather for a brief period to discuss the day's program. During this time, encourage people to discuss and impart information that may be helpful to others. For example, someone may wish to tell the group how she successfully handled a particular discipline problem. Or perhaps someone wants additional information regarding the instructional procedures for teaching a particular skill. Or someone may have a particular problem for which he wants the advice of the entire group. In short, this concluding activity is a time when all personnel can gather to discuss problems and share ideas and other types of general information. Furthermore, now is the time to update any records.

Parents' Workshop

As mentioned, the director of the program should keep parents informed of their child's progress. We recommend a workshop for parents. During this workshop, all parents receive a copy of their child's motor development assessment and an explanation of how to interpret the assessment scores.

The parents' workshop can also be used for two other purposes. First, you receive feedback from the parents regarding their likes and dislikes about the program. We have found this information very helpful over the years for improving the service provided. Second, this time can be used to instruct parents on how to address their child's movement needs in the home environment.

SUMMARY

Before implementing a motor development program, you must develop a program philosophy. This philosophy partly describes what you hope the program will accomplish. Once you determine a philosophy, the next step is to decide whether the goals and objectives of the program can be met given the existing resources. Do you have the facilities, equipment, and personnel needed to run a quality program?

To run a trouble-free program, expect to spend much time with administrative responsibilities. In particular, you will need to develop a multitude of operational procedures, such as first aid and emergencies, cancellations, advertising and registration, and general operations. Carrying out these administrative duties can be simplified by using a PC.

Also give consideration to instructional organization. You must plan and organize the participation aspect of the program. We suggest the stations approach. Furthermore, consider program assessment and the dissemination of this information; this information can be shared with the parents in a parents' workshop.

KEY TERMS

adapted program
assistant instructors
critical height
developmental apparatus
developmentally appropriate
   equipment
feedback

general assistants
head injury criterion
knowledge of results (KOR)
nondevelopmental apparatus
orientation meeting
parents' workshop
program philosophy

program scope
rehearsal
station leader
stations approach
volunteers

QUESTIONS FOR REFLECTION

1. What steps would you take in planning and implementing a developmental movement program?

2. What is the difference between developmental and nondevelopmental playground equipment? Give three examples of each.

3. Which 10 steps can be taken to reduce playground injuries? Give specific details regarding the best surfaces on which to place playground equipment.

4. Can you list six considerations for blood management following a blood-related injury in a developmental movement program?

5. What are two important considerations in conducting an instructional demonstration?

6. What is the difference between feedback and knowledge of results? Why and how are they important to learning?

7. What is the primacy-recency theory? What implications does it have for learning?

INTERNET RESOURCES

American Academy of Pediatrics: Playground Safety
   www.aap.org/family/playgrd.htm

Happy Landing—Resilient Surfacing Systems
   www.safetysurface.com

Kaboom—Playground Safety   **www.kaboom.org**

National Program for Playground Safety
   www.uni.edu/playground/home/html

U.S. Consumer Product Safety Commission
   www.cpsc.gov

ONLINE LEARNING CENTER (www.mhhe.com/payne6e)

Visit the *Human Motor Development* Online Learning Center for study aids and additional resources. You can use the study guide questions and key terms puzzles to review key terms and concepts for this chapter and to prepare for exams. You can further extend your knowledge of motor development by checking out the Web links, articles, and activities found on the site.

REFERENCES

American Academy of Orthopedic Surgeons. (1991). *Play it safe: A guide to playground safety.* Rosemont, IL: Author.

American Academy of Pediatrics. (2000). *Playground safety.* Retrieved from aap.org/family/playgrd.htm.

Burton, A. W., Greer, N. L., & Wiese, D. M. (1992). Changes in overhand throwing patterns as a function of ball size. *Pediatric Exercise Science, 4,* 50–67.

Burton, A. W., Greer, N. L., & Wiese-Bjornstal, D. M. (1993). Variations in grasping and throwing patterns as a function of ball size. *Pediatric Exercise Science, 5,* 24–41.

Collantes, M. (1990). *Evaluation of the importance of using head injury criterion to estimate the likelihood of head impact injury as a result of a fall onto playground surface materials.* Washington, DC: U.S. Consumer Product Safety Commission.

Dunn, J. M., Morehouse, J. W., & Fredericks, H. D. (1985). *Physical education for the severely handicapped: A systematic approach to a databased gymnasium.* Austin, TX: Pro-Ed.

Duston, D. (1992, May 25). *Breaking the fall at playgrounds not just kids' stuff.* Dayton, OH: Dayton Daily News.

Haywood, K. M. (1978). *Children's basketball performance with regulation and junior-sized basketballs.* St. Louis: University of Missouri.

Herkowitz, J. (1978). The design and evaluation of playspaces for children. In M. V. Ridenour (Ed.), *Motor development: Issues and applications.* Princeton, NJ: Princeton Book Company.

———. (1984). Developmentally engineered equipment and playgrounds. In J. Thomas (Ed.), *Motor development during childhood and adolescence.* Minneapolis, MN: Burgess.

Isaacs, L. D., & Karpman, M. B. (1981). Factors affecting children's basketball shooting performance: A log-linear analysis. *Carnegie Research Papers,* pp. 29–32.

Magill, R. A. (2004). *Motor learning and control: Concepts and applications.* 7th ed. Boston: McGraw-Hill.

Rasor, D. (1994). Blood management. *Sport Pulse, 13*(1). Newsletter. Dayton, OH: St. Elizabeth Sports Medicine Center.

Siedentop, D., Herkowitz, J., & Rink, J. (1984). *Elementary physical education methods.* Englewood Cliffs, NJ: Prentice-Hall.

Tinsworth, D., & McDonald, J. (2001). *Special study: Injuries and deaths associated with children's playground equipment.* Washington, DC: U.S. Consumer Product Safety Commission.

U.S. Consumer Product Safety Commission. (1997). *Handbook for public playground safety.* Publication 325. Washington, DC: Author.

———. (2001, July). *Home playground equipment–related deaths and injuries.* Washington, DC: Author.

Wright, E. J. (1967). Effects of light and heavy equipment on acquisition of sport-type skills by young children. *Research Quarterly, 38,* 705–714.

Growth Charts: National Center for Health Statistics

Boys: Birth to 36 months
    Length-for-age and weight-for-age percentiles
    Head circumference-for-age and weight-for-
        length percentiles

Girls: Birth to 36 months
    Length-for-age and weight-for-age percentiles
    Head circumference-for-age and weight-for-
        length percentiles

Boys: 2 to 20 years
    Stature-for-age and weight-for-age percentiles
    Body mass index-for-age percentiles

Girls: 2 to 20 years
    Stature-for-age and weight-for-age percentiles
    Body mass index-for-age percentiles

Boys: Weight-for-stature percentiles

Girls: Weight-for-stature percentiles

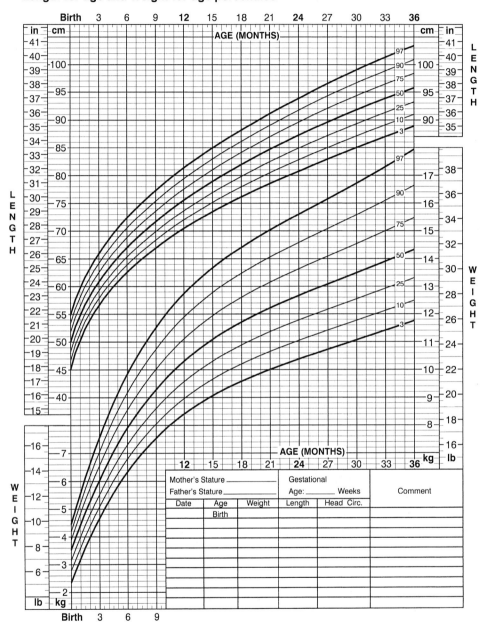

Figure A-1   Boys: Birth to 36 months. Length-for-age and weight-for-age percentiles. CDC growth charts: United States.

SOURCE: Developed by the National Center for Health Statistics in collaboration with the National Center for Chronic Disease Prevention and Health Promotion (2000), www.cdc.gov/growthcharts.

Birth to 36 months: Boys
Head circumference-for-age and
Weight-for-length percentiles

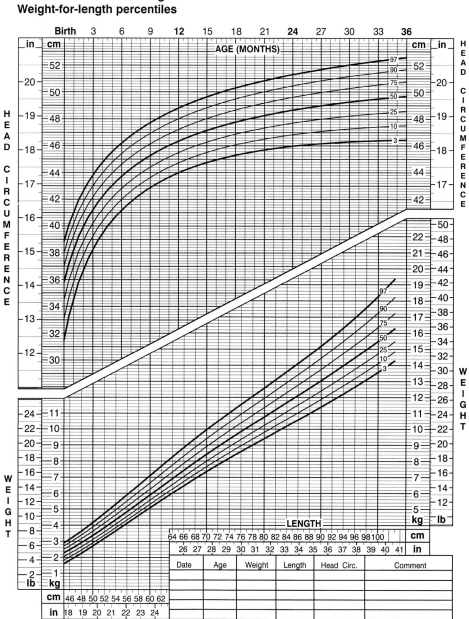

Figure A-2 Boys: Birth to 36 months. Head circumference-for-age and weight-for-length percentiles. CDC growth charts: United States.

Source: Developed by the National Center for Health Statistics in collaboration with the National Center for Chronic Disease Prevention and Health Promotion (2000), www.cdc.gov/growthcharts.

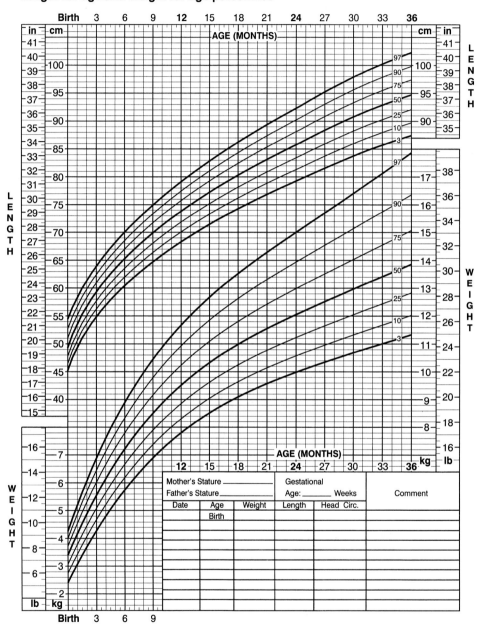

Figure A-3 Girls: Birth to 36 months. Length-for-age and weight-for-age percentiles.
CDC growth charts: United States.

SOURCE: Developed by the National Center for Health Statistics in collaboration with the National
Center for Chronic Disease Prevention and Health Promotion (2000), www.cdc.gov/growthcharts.

**Birth to 36 months: Girls
Head circumference-for-age and
Weight-for-length percentiles**

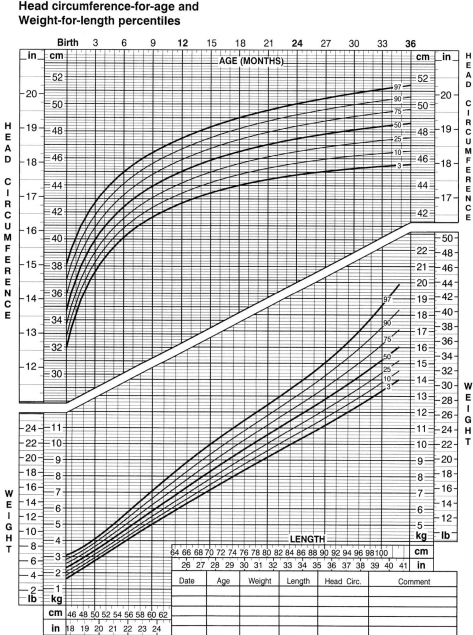

Figure A-4 Girls: Birth to 36 months. Head circumference-for-age and weight-for-length percentiles. CDC growth charts: United States.

Source: Developed by the National Center for Health Statistics in collaboration with the National Center for Chronic Disease Prevention and Health Promotion (2000), www.cdc.gov/growthcharts.

2 to 20 years: Boys
Stature-for-age and Weight-for-age percentiles

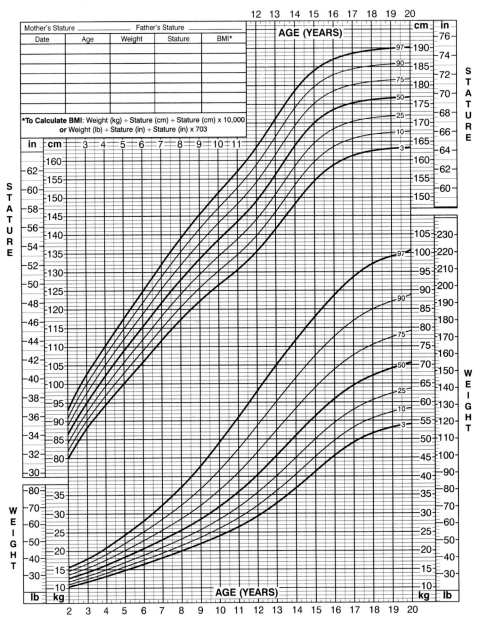

Figure A-5 Boys: 2 to 20 years. Stature-for-age and weight-for-age percentiles. CDC growth charts: United States.

SOURCE: Developed by the National Center for Health Statistics in collaboration with the National Center for Chronic Disease Prevention and Health Promotion (2000), www.cdc.gov/growthcharts.

2 to 20 years: Boys
Body mass index-for-age percentiles

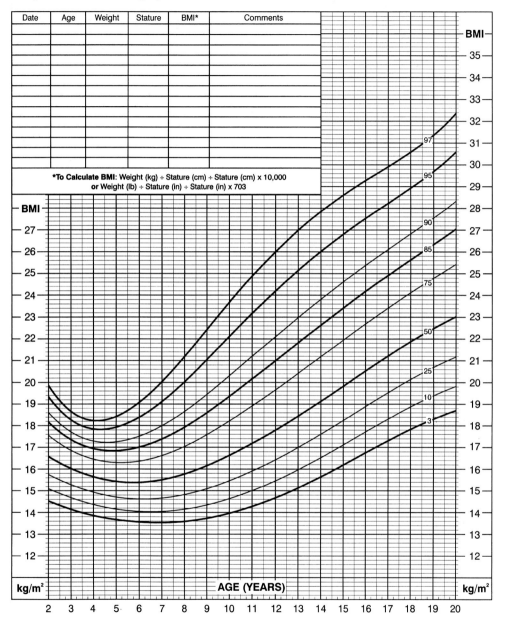

Figure A-6   Boys: 2 to 20 years. Body mass index-for-age percentiles. CDC growth charts: United States.

Source: Developed by the National Center for Health Statistics in collaboration with the National Center for Chronic Disease Prevention and Health Promotion (2000), www.cdc.gov/growthcharts.

2 to 20 years: Girls
Stature-for-age and Weight-for-age percentiles

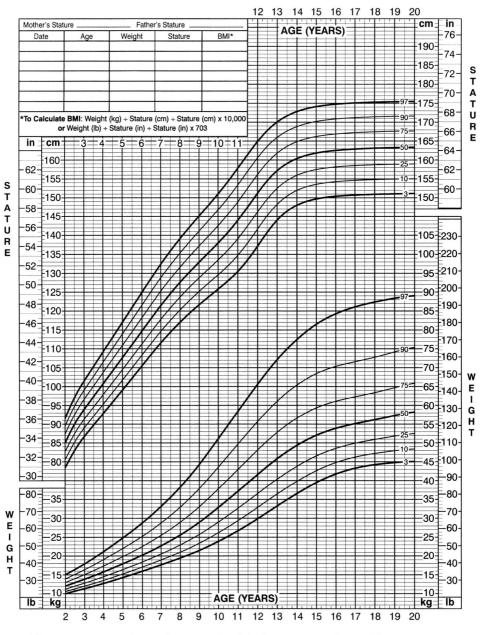

Figure A-7   Girls: 2 to 20 years. Stature-for-age and weight-for-age percentiles. CDC growth charts: United States.

SOURCE: Developed by the National Center for Health Statistics in collaboration with the National Center for Chronic Disease Prevention and Health Promotion (2000), www.cdc.gov/growthcharts.

2 to 20 years: Girls
Body mass index-for-age percentiles

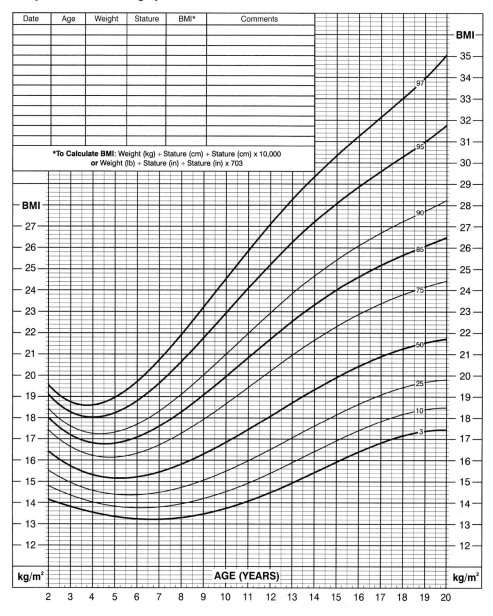

Figure A-8   Girls: 2 to 20 years. Body mass index-for-age percentiles. CDC growth charts: United States.

Source: Developed by the National Center for Health Statistics in collaboration with the National Center for Chronic Disease Prevention and Health Promotion (2000), www.cdc.gov/growthcharts.

Weight-for-stature percentiles: Boys

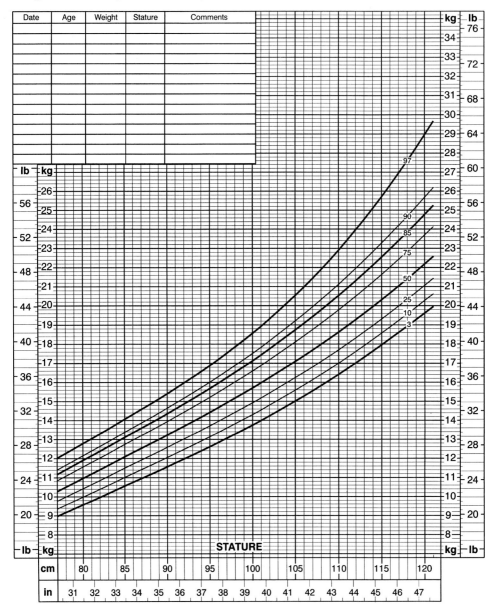

Figure A-9   Boys: Weight-for-stature percentiles. CDC growth charts: United States.

SOURCE: Developed by the National Center for Health Statistics in collaboration with the National Center for Chronic Disease Prevention and Health Promotion (2000), www.cdc.gov/growthcharts.

Weight-for-stature percentiles: Girls

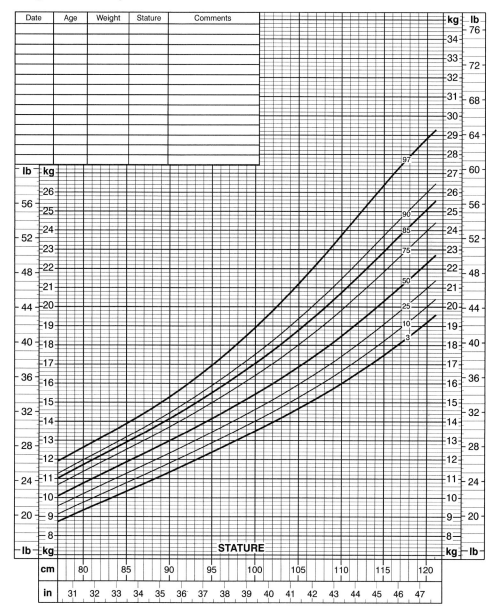

Figure A-10   Girls: Weight-for-stature percentiles. CDC growth charts: United States.

SOURCE: Developed by the National Center for Health Statistics in collaboration with the National Center for Chronic Disease Prevention and Health Promotion (2000), www.cdc.gov/growthcharts.

APPENDIX B

Body Mass Index Table

To use this table, find the appropriate height in the left-hand column. Move across to a given weight. The number at the top of the column is the BMI at the height and weight. Pounds have been rounded off.

BMI and Corresponding Body Weight (pounds)

Height (inches)	19	20	21	22	23	24	25	26	27	28	29	30	31	32	33	34	35
58	91	96	100	105	110	115	119	124	129	134	138	143	148	153	158	162	167
59	94	99	104	109	114	119	124	128	133	138	143	148	153	158	163	168	173
60	97	102	107	112	118	123	128	133	138	143	148	153	158	163	168	174	179
61	100	106	111	116	122	127	132	137	143	148	153	158	164	169	174	180	185
62	104	109	115	120	126	131	136	142	147	153	158	164	169	175	180	186	191
63	107	113	118	124	130	135	141	146	152	158	163	169	175	180	186	191	197
64	110	116	122	128	134	140	145	151	157	163	169	174	180	186	192	197	204
65	114	120	126	132	138	144	150	156	162	168	174	180	186	192	198	204	210
66	118	124	130	136	142	148	155	161	167	173	179	186	192	198	204	210	216
67	121	127	134	140	146	153	159	166	172	178	185	191	198	204	211	217	223
68	125	131	138	144	151	158	164	171	177	184	190	197	203	210	216	223	230
69	128	135	142	149	155	162	169	176	182	189	196	203	209	216	223	230	236
70	132	139	146	153	160	167	174	181	188	195	202	209	216	222	229	236	243
71	136	143	150	157	165	172	179	186	193	200	208	215	222	229	236	243	250
72	140	147	154	162	169	177	184	191	199	206	213	221	228	235	242	250	258
73	144	151	159	166	174	182	189	197	204	212	219	227	235	242	250	257	265
74	148	155	163	171	179	186	194	202	210	218	225	233	241	249	256	264	272
75	152	160	168	176	184	192	200	208	216	224	232	240	248	256	264	272	279
76	156	164	172	180	189	197	205	213	221	230	238	246	254	263	271	279	287

BMI and Corresponding Body Weight (pounds)

Height (inches)	36	37	38	39	40	41	42	43	44	45	46	47	48	49	50	51	52	53	54
58	172	177	181	186	191	196	201	205	210	215	220	224	229	234	239	244	248	253	258
59	178	183	188	193	198	203	208	212	217	222	227	232	237	242	247	252	257	262	267
60	184	189	194	199	204	209	215	220	225	230	235	240	245	250	255	261	266	271	276
61	190	195	201	206	211	217	222	227	232	238	243	248	254	259	264	269	275	280	285
62	196	202	207	213	218	224	229	235	240	246	251	256	262	267	273	278	284	289	295
63	203	208	214	220	225	231	237	242	248	254	259	265	270	278	282	287	293	299	304
64	209	215	221	227	232	238	244	250	256	262	267	273	279	285	291	296	302	308	314
65	216	222	228	234	240	246	252	258	264	270	276	282	288	294	300	306	312	318	324
66	223	229	235	241	247	253	260	266	272	278	284	291	297	303	309	315	322	328	334
67	230	236	242	249	255	261	268	274	280	287	293	299	306	312	319	325	331	338	344
68	236	243	249	256	262	269	276	282	289	295	302	308	315	322	328	335	341	348	354
69	243	250	257	263	270	277	284	291	297	304	311	318	324	331	338	345	351	358	365
70	250	257	264	271	278	285	292	299	306	313	320	327	334	341	348	355	362	369	376
71	257	265	272	279	286	293	301	308	315	322	329	338	343	351	358	365	372	379	386
72	265	272	279	287	294	302	309	316	324	331	338	346	353	361	368	375	383	390	397
73	272	280	288	295	302	310	318	325	333	340	348	355	363	371	378	386	393	401	408
74	280	287	295	303	311	319	326	334	342	350	358	365	373	381	389	396	404	412	420
75	287	295	303	311	319	327	335	343	351	359	367	375	383	391	399	407	415	423	431
76	295	304	312	320	328	336	344	353	361	369	377	385	394	402	410	418	426	435	443

SOURCE: National Heart, Lung, and Blood Institute (2000).

Summary of the Surgeon General's Report on Physical Activity and Health

CHAPTER 1: MAJOR CONCLUSIONS OF THE SURGEON GENERAL'S REPORT

- People of all ages, both male and female, benefit from regular physical activity.

- Significant health benefits can be obtained by including a moderate amount of physical activity (e.g., 30 minutes of brisk walking or raking leaves, 15 minutes of running, or 45 minutes of playing volleyball) on most, if not all, days of the week. Through a modest increase in daily activity, most Americans can improve their health and quality of life.

- Additional health benefits can be gained through greater amounts of physical activity. People who can maintain a regular regimen of activity that is of longer duration or of more vigorous intensity are likely to derive a greater benefit than are those who do not.

- Physical activity reduces the risk of premature mortality in general and of coronary heart disease, hypertension, colon cancer, and diabetes mellitus, in particular. Physical activity also improves mental health and is important for the health of muscles, bones, and joints.

- More than 60 percent of American adults are not regularly physically active. In fact, 25 percent of all adults are not active at all.

- Nearly half of American youths 12–21 years of age are not vigorously active on a regular basis. Moreover, physical activity declines dramatically during adolescence.

SOURCE: President's Council on Physical Fitness and Sports Physical Activity and Fitness Research Digest (1996, July). Series 2, No. 6 (Washington, DC: President's Council on Physical Fitness and Sports).

- Daily enrollment in physical education classes has declined among high school students from 42 percent in 1991 to 25 percent in 1995.

- Research on understanding and promoting physical activity is at an early stage, but some interventions to promote physical activity through schools, worksites, and health care settings have been evaluated and found to be successful.

CONCLUSIONS OF CHAPTER 2: HISTORICAL BACKGROUND AND EVOLUTION OF PHYSICAL ACTIVITY RECOMMENDATIONS

- Physical activity for better health and well-being has been an important theme throughout much of western history.

- Public health recommendations have evolved from emphasizing vigorous activity for cardiorespiratory fitness to including the option of moderate levels of activity for numerous health benefits.

- Experts agree that for better health, physical activity should be performed regularly. The most recent recommendations advise people of all ages to include a minimum of 30 minutes of physical activity of moderate intensity (such as brisk walking) on most, if not all, days of the week. It is also acknowledged that for most people, greater health benefits can be obtained by engaging in physical activity of more vigorous intensity or of longer duration.

- Experts advise previously sedentary people embarking on a physical activity program to start with short durations of moderate-intensity activity and gradually increase the duration or intensity until the goal is reached.

- Experts advise consulting with a physician before beginning a new physical activity program if one has a chronic disease, such as cardiovascular disease and diabetes mellitus, or if one is at high risk for these diseases. Experts also advise men over age 40 and women over age 50 to consult a physician before they begin a vigorous activity program.

- Recent recommendations from experts also suggest that cardiorespiratory endurance activity should be supplemented with strength-developing exercises at least twice per week for adults, in order to improve musculoskeletal health, maintain independence in performing the activities of daily life, and reduce the risk of falling.

CONCLUSIONS OF CHAPTER 3: PHYSIOLOGICAL RESPONSES AND LONG-TERM ADAPTATIONS TO EXERCISE

- Physical activity has numerous beneficial physiological effects. Most widely appreciated are its effects on the cardiovascular and musculoskeletal systems, but benefits on the functioning of metabolic, endocrine, and immune systems are also considerable.

- Many of the beneficial effects of exercise training—from both endurance and resistance activities—diminish within 2 weeks if physical activity is substantially reduced, and effects disappear within 2 to 8 months if physical activity is not resumed.

- People of all ages, both male and female, undergo beneficial physiological adaptations to physical activity.

CONCLUSIONS OF CHAPTER 4: THE EFFECTS OF PHYSICAL ACTIVITY ON HEALTH AND DISEASE

Overall Mortality

- Higher levels of regular physical activity are associated with lower mortality rates for both older and younger adults.

- Even those who are moderately active on a regular basis have lower mortality rates than do those who are least active.

Cardiovascular Diseases

- Regular physical activity or cardiorespiratory fitness decreases the risk of cardiovascular disease mortality in general and of coronary heart disease mortality in particular. Existing data are not conclusive regarding a relationship between physical activity and stroke.

- The level of decreased risk of coronary heart disease attributable to regular physical activity is similar to that of other lifestyle factors, such as keeping free from cigarette smoking.

- Regular physical activity prevents or delays the development of high blood pressure, and exercise reduces blood pressure in people with hypertension.

Cancer

- Regular physical activity is associated with a decreased risk of colon cancer.

- There is no association between physical activity and rectal cancer. Data are too sparse to draw conclusions regarding a relationship between physical activity and endometrial, ovarian, or testicular cancers.

- Despite numerous studies on the subject, existing data are inconsistent regarding an association between physical activity and breast or prostate cancers.

Non-Insulin-Dependent Diabetes Mellitus

- Regular physical activity lowers the risk of developing non-insulin-dependent diabetes mellitus.

Osteoarthritis

- Regular physical activity is necessary for maintaining normal muscle strength, joint structure, and joint function. In the range recommended for health, physical activity is not associated with joint damage or development of osteoarthritis and may be beneficial for many people with arthritis.

- Competitive athletics may be associated with the development of osteoarthritis later in life, but sport-related injuries are the likely cause.

Osteoporosis

- Weight-bearing physical activity is essential for normal skeletal development during childhood and adolescence and for achieving and maintaining peak bone mass in young adults.
- It is unclear whether resistance- or endurance-type physical activity can reduce the accelerated rate of bone loss in postmenopausal women in the absence of estrogen replacement therapy.

Falling

- There is promising evidence that strength training and other forms of exercise in older adults preserve the ability to maintain independent living status and reduce the risk of falling.

Obesity

- Low levels of activity, resulting in fewer kilocalories used than consumed, contribute to the high prevalence of obesity in the United States.
- Physical activity may favorably affect body fat distribution.

Mental Health

- Physical activity appears to relieve symptoms of depression and anxiety and to improve mood.
- Regular physical activity may reduce the risk of developing depression, although further research is needed on this topic.

Health-Related Quality of Life

- Physical activity appears to improve health-related quality of life by enhancing psychological well-being and by improving physical functioning in persons compromised by poor health.

Adverse Effects

- Most musculoskeletal injuries related to physical activity are believed to be preventable by gradually working up to a desired level of activity and by avoiding excessive amounts of activity.
- Serious cardiovascular events can occur with physical exertion, but the net effect of regular physical activity is a lower risk of mortality from cardiovascular disease.

CONCLUSIONS OF CHAPTER 5: PATTERNS AND TRENDS IN PHYSICAL ACTIVITY

Adults

- Approximately 15 percent of U.S. adults engage regularly (3 times a week for at least 20 minutes) in vigorous physical activity during leisure time.
- Approximately 22 percent of adults engage regularly (5 times a week for at least 30 minutes) in sustained physical activity of any intensity during leisure time.
- About 25 percent of adults report no physical activity at all in their leisure time.
- Physical inactivity is more prevalent among women than men, among blacks and Hispanics than whites, among older than younger adults, and among the less affluent than the more affluent.
- The most popular leisure-time physical activities among adults are walking and gardening or yard work.

Adolescents and Young Adults

- Only about one-half of U.S. young people (aged 12–21 years) regularly participate in vigorous physical activity. One-fourth report no vigorous physical activity.
- Approximately one-fourth of young people walk or bicycle (i.e., engage in light to moderate activity) nearly every day.
- About 14 percent of young people report no recent vigorous or light-to-moderate physical activity. This indicator of inactivity is higher among female than male youths and among female African Americans than female whites.
- Male youths are more likely than female youths to participate in vigorous physical activity, strengthening activities, and walking or bicycling.
- Participation in all types of physical activity declines strikingly as age or grade in school increases.
- Among high school students, enrollment in physical education remained unchanged during the first half of the 1990s. However, daily attendance in physical education declined from approximately 42 percent to 25 percent.

- The percentage of high school students who were enrolled in physical education and who reported being physically active for at least 20 minutes in physical education classes declined from approximately 81 percent to 70 percent during the first half of the 1990s.

- Only 19 percent of all high school students report being physically active for 20 minutes or more in daily physical education classes.

CONCLUSIONS OF CHAPTER 6: UNDERSTANDING AND PROMOTING PHYSICAL ACTIVITY

- Consistent influences on physical activity patterns among adults and young people include confidence in one's ability to engage in regular physical activity (e.g., self-efficacy), enjoyment of physical activity, support from others, positive beliefs concerning the benefits of physical activity, and lack of perceived barriers to being physically active.

- For adults, some interventions have been successful in increasing physical activity in communities, worksites, and health care settings, as well as at home.

- Interventions targeting physical education in elementary school can substantially increase the amount of time students spend being physically active in physical education class.

Summary of the CDC's Guidelines for School and Community Programs Promoting Lifelong Physical Activity

AT-A-GLANCE

Young people can build healthy bodies and establish healthy lifestyles by including physical activity in their daily lives. However, many young people are not physically active on a regular basis, and physical activity declines dramatically during adolescence. School and community programs can help young people get active and stay active.

Benefits of Physical Activity

Regular physical activity in childhood and adolescence

- Improves strength and endurance.
- Helps build healthy bones and muscles.
- Helps control weight.
- Reduces anxiety and stress and increases self-esteem.
- May improve blood pressure and cholesterol levels.

In addition, young people say they like physical activity because it is fun, they do it with friends, and it helps them learn skills, stay in shape, and look better.

Consequences of Physical Inactivity

- The percentage of young people who are overweight has more than doubled in the past 30 years.
- Inactivity and poor diet cause at least 300,000 deaths a year in the United States. Only tobacco use causes more preventable deaths.
- Adults who are less active are at greater risk of dying of heart disease and developing diabetes, colon cancer, and high blood pressure.

Physical Activity Among Young People

- Almost half of young people aged 12–21 and more than a third of high school students do not participate in vigorous physical activity on a regular basis.
- Seventy-two percent of 9th graders participate in vigorous physical activity on a regular basis, compared with only 55 percent of 12th graders.
- Daily participation in physical education classes by high school students dropped from 42 percent in 1991 to 25 percent in 1995.

This appendix and CDC's *Guidelines for School and Community Programs to Promote Lifelong Physical Activity Among Young People* can be reproduced and adapted without permission. Copies of the guidelines can be downloaded from the Internet at *www.cdc.gov.* (On the CDC home page, click on *MMWR,* select *Recommendations and Reports,* and then select March 7, 1997.) Print copies are available from: CDC, Division of Adolescent and School Health, ATTN: Resource Room, 4770 Buford Highway, Mailstop K-32, Atlanta, GA 30341-3724; (888) CDC 4NRG. CDC's Division of Adolescent and School Health also distributes guidelines for school health programs on preventing the spread of AIDS, promoting lifelong healthy eating, and preventing tobacco use and addiction.

Table D-1   How Much Physical Activity Do Young People Need?

Everyone can benefit from a moderate amount of physical activity on most, if not all, days of the week. Young people should select activities they enjoy that fit into their daily lives. Examples of moderate activity include

- Walking 2 miles in 30 minutes or running 1½ miles in 15 minutes.

- Bicycling 5 miles in 30 minutes or 4 miles in 15 minutes.

- Dancing fast for 30 minutes or jumping rope for 15 minutes.

- Playing basketball for 15–20 minutes or volleyball for 45 minutes.

Increasing the frequency, time, or intensity of physical activity can bring even more health benefits—up to a point. Too much physical activity can lead to injuries and other health problems.

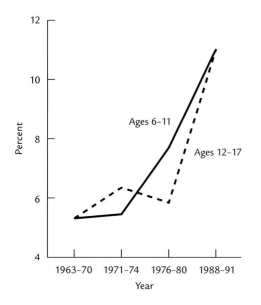

Figure D-1   Percentage of young people who are over-weight

NOTE: Overweight is defined by the age- and sex-specific 95th percentile of body mass index from National Health Examination Surveys II and III (1963–70 data).

SOURCE: National Center for Health Statistics unpublished data (age adjusted), 1998.

- The time students spend being active in physical education classes is decreasing; among high school students enrolled in a physical education class, the percentage who were active for at least 20 minutes during an average class dropped from 81 percent in 1991 to 70 percent in 1995.

(See Figures D-1, D-2, and D-3 for more on youth trends.)

CDC'S GUIDELINES FOR PROMOTING LIFELONG PHYSICAL ACTIVITY

CDC's *Guidelines for School and Community Programs to Promote Lifelong Physical Activity Among Young People* were developed in collaboration with experts from other federal agencies, state agencies, universities, voluntary organizations, and professional associations. They are based on an extensive review of research and practice.

Key Principles

The guidelines state that physical activity programs for young people are most likely to be effective when they

- Emphasize enjoyable participation in physical activities that are easily done throughout life.

- Offer a diverse range of noncompetitive and competitive activities appropriate for different ages and abilities.

- Give young people the skills and confidence they need to be physically active.

- Promote physical activity through all components of a coordinated school health program and develop links between school and community programs.

Recommendations

The guidelines include 10 recommendations for ensuring quality physical activity programs.

1. *Policy* Establish policies that promote enjoyable, life-long physical activity.

- Schools should require daily physical education and comprehensive health education (including lessons on physical activity) in grades K–12.

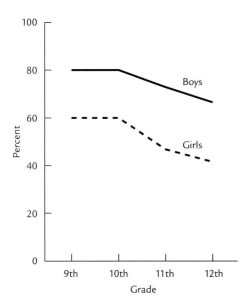

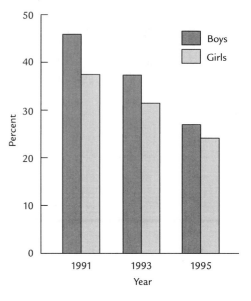

Figure D-2 Regular participation in vigorous physical activity by high school students, 1995

NOTE: Vigorous activity is defined as follows: on 3 or more of the 7 days preceding the survey, at least 20 minutes' participation in activities that made the students breathe hard and sweat.

SOURCE: CDC National Youth Risk Behavior Survey, 1995.

Figure D-3 Daily participation in physical education by high school students

SOURCE: CDC National Youth Risk Behavior Survey, 1995.

- Schools and community organizations should provide adequate funding, equipment, and supervision for programs that meet the needs and interests of all students.

2. *Environment* Provide physical and social environments that encourage and enable young people to engage in safe and enjoyable physical activity.

- Provide access to safe spaces and facilities and implement measures to prevent activity-related injuries and illnesses.

- Provide school time, such as recess, for unstructured physical activity, such as jumping rope.

- Discourage the use or withholding of physical activity as punishment.

- Provide health promotion programs for school faculty and staff.

3. *Physical Education Curricula and Instruction* Implement sequential physical education curricula and instruction in grades K–12 that

- Emphasize enjoyable participation in lifetime physical activities such as walking and dancing, not just competitive sports.

- Help students develop the knowledge, attitudes, and skills they need to adopt and maintain a physically active lifestyle.

- Follow the National Standards for Physical Education.

- Keep students active for most of class time.

4. *Health Education Curricula and Instruction* Implement health education curricula that

- Feature active learning strategies and follow the National Health Education Standards.

- Help students develop the knowledge, attitudes, and skills they need to adopt and maintain a healthy lifestyle (see Table D-1).

5. *Extracurricular Activities* Provide extracurricular physical activity programs that offer diverse, developmentally appropriate activities—both noncompetitive and competitive—for all students.

6. *Family Involvement* Encourage parents and guardians to support their children's participation in

physical activity, to be physically active role models, and to include physical activity in family events.

9. *Training* Provide training to enable teachers, coaches, recreation and health care staff, and other school and community personnel to promote enjoyable, lifelong physical activity to young people.

8. *Health Services* Assess the physical activity patterns of young people, refer them to appropriate physical activity programs, and advocate for physical activity instruction and programs for young people.

9. *Community Programs* Provide a range of developmentally appropriate community sports and recreation programs that are attractive to all young people.

10. *Evaluation* Regularly evaluate physical activity instruction, programs, and facilities.

PROMOTING LIFELONG PHYSICAL ACTIVITY AMONG YOUNG PEOPLE — HOW YOU CAN HELP

Everyone can make a difference in young people's lives by helping them include physical activity in their daily routines. If you are a parent, guardian, student, teacher, athletic coach, school administrator or board member, community sports and recreation program coordinator, or anyone else who cares about the health of young people, here are some steps you can take.

Everyone Can

- Advocate for convenient, safe, and adequate places for young people to play and take part in physical activity programs.

- Encourage school administrators and board members to support daily physical education and other school programs that promote lifelong physical activity, not just competitive sports.

- Set a good example by being physically active, making healthy eating choices, and not smoking.

- Tell young people about sports and recreation programs in their community.

- Discourage the use of physical activity as a punishment.

Parents or Guardians Can

- Encourage your children to be physically active.

- Learn what your children want from physical activity programs and help them choose appropriate activities.

- Volunteer to help your children's sports teams and recreation programs.

- Play and be physically active with your children.

- Teach your children safety rules and make sure that they have the clothing and equipment needed to participate safely in physical activity.

Students Can

- Set goals for increasing your physical activity and monitor your progress.

- Encourage friends and family members to be physically active.

- Use protective clothing and proper equipment to prevent injuries and illnesses.

- Encourage the student council to advocate for physical education classes and after-school programs that are attractive to all students.

- Take elective courses in health and physical education.

Teachers and Coaches Can

- Use curricula that follow CDC's *Guidelines for School and Community Programs to Promote Lifelong Physical Activity Among Young People* and the national standards for physical education and health education.

- Keep students moving during physical education classes.

- Ensure that young people know safety rules and use appropriate protective clothing and equipment.

- Emphasize activity and enjoyment over competition.

- Help students become competent in many motor and behavioral skills.

- Involve families and community organizations in physical activity programs.

- Refrain from using physical activity, such as doing push-ups or running laps, as punishment.

School Administrators and Board Members Can

- Require health education and daily physical education for students in grades K–12.

- Ensure that physical education and extracurricular programs offer lifelong activities, such as walking and dancing.

- Provide time during the day, such as recess, for unstructured physical activity, such as walking or jumping rope.

- Hire physical activity specialists and qualified coaches.

- Ensure that school facilities are clean, safe, and open to students during nonschool hours and vacation.

- Provide health promotion programs for faculty and staff.

- Provide teachers with in-service training in physical activity promotion.

Community Sports and Recreation Program Coordinators Can

- Provide a mix of competitive team sports and non-competitive, lifelong fitness and recreation activities.

- Increase the availability of parks, public swimming pools, hiking and biking trails, and other places for physical activity.

- Ensure that physical facilities meet or exceed safety standards.

- Ensure that coaches have appropriate coaching competencies.

- Work with schools, businesses, and community groups to ensure that low-income young people have transportation and appropriate equipment for physical activity programs.

Observation Plans

OBSERVATION PLAN FOR RUNNING

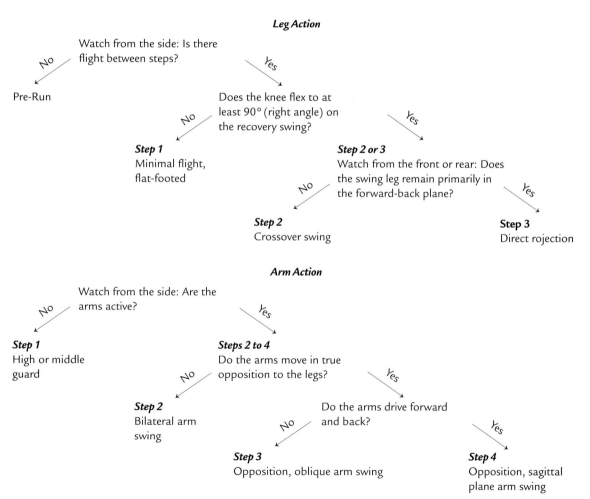

Leg Action

Watch from the side: Is there flight between steps?

No → **Pre-Run**

Yes → Does the knee flex to at least 90° (right angle) on the recovery swing?

No → **Step 1** Minimal flight, flat-footed

Yes → **Step 2 or 3** Watch from the front or rear: Does the swing leg remain primarily in the forward-back plane?

No → **Step 2** Crossover swing

Yes → **Step 3** Direct rojection

Arm Action

Watch from the side: Are the arms active?

No → **Step 1** High or middle guard

Yes → **Steps 2 to 4** Do the arms move in true opposition to the legs?

No → **Step 2** Bilateral arm swing

Yes → Do the arms drive forward and back?

No → **Step 3** Opposition, oblique arm swing

Yes → **Step 4** Opposition, sagittal plane arm swing

SOURCE: Reprinted with permission of the publisher from Haywood, K., and Getchell, N. (2001). *Laboratory activities for life span motor development.* 3rd ed. Champaign, IL: Human Kinetics.

OBSERVATION PLAN FOR THE STANDING LONG JUMP

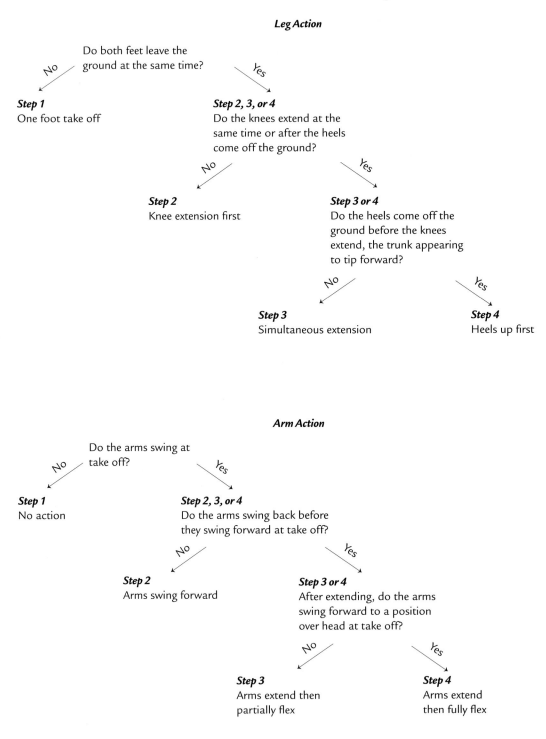

Leg Action

Do both feet leave the ground at the same time?

No → **Step 1** — One foot take off

Yes → **Step 2, 3, or 4** — Do the knees extend at the same time or after the heels come off the ground?

No → **Step 2** — Knee extension first

Yes → **Step 3 or 4** — Do the heels come off the ground before the knees extend, the trunk appearing to tip forward?

No → **Step 3** — Simultaneous extension

Yes → **Step 4** — Heels up first

Arm Action

Do the arms swing at take off?

No → **Step 1** — No action

Yes → **Step 2, 3, or 4** — Do the arms swing back before they swing forward at take off?

No → **Step 2** — Arms swing forward

Yes → **Step 3 or 4** — After extending, do the arms swing forward to a position over head at take off?

No → **Step 3** — Arms extend then partially flex

Yes → **Step 4** — Arms extend then fully flex

OBSERVATION PLAN FOR HOPPING

Leg Action

Focus on the swing leg from
the side: Is it active?

 No   Yes

Step 1 or 2
Focus on the support leg: Does
it extend at takeoff to project
the body upward?

Step 3 or 4
Does the swing leg swing behind the support leg?
Look at the support leg: Does the weight shift to the
ball of the support foot before extension at takeoff?

 No   Yes

Step 1
Momentary flight

Step 2
Fall and catch

No   Yes

Step 3
Projected takeoff

Step 4
Projection delay,
swing leg leads

Arm Action

Move to watch the arms from
the side and the front: Is arm
action bilateral or opposing?

Bilateral   Opposing

Step 1, 2, or 3
Are the arms noticeably active?

Step 4 or 5
Do both arms move in opposition
to the legs or just one?

No   Yes

Step 1
Bilateral inactive

Step 2 or 3
Do the arms pump up
and down or swing?

One   Both

Step 4
Semiopposition

Step 5
Opposing assist

 Swing   Pump

Step 2
Bilateral reactive

Step 3
Bilateral assist

OBSERVATION PLAN FOR THROWING

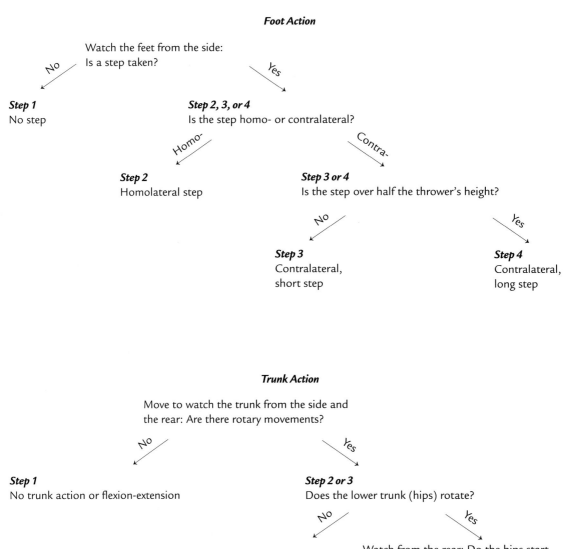

Foot Action

Watch the feet from the side: Is a step taken?

No

Yes

Step 1
No step

Step 2, 3, or 4
Is the step homo- or contralateral?

Homo-

Contra-

Step 2
Homolateral step

Step 3 or 4
Is the step over half the thrower's height?

No

Yes

Step 3
Contralateral,
short step

Step 4
Contralateral,
long step

Trunk Action

Move to watch the trunk from the side and the rear: Are there rotary movements?

No

Yes

Step 1
No trunk action or flexion-extension

Step 2 or 3
Does the lower trunk (hips) rotate?

No

Yes

Step 2
Block or
upper trunk
rotation

No

Watch from the rear: Do the hips start forward before the trunk?

Yes

Step 3
Differentiated rotation

(continued)

OBSERVATION PLAN FOR THROWING *(continued)*

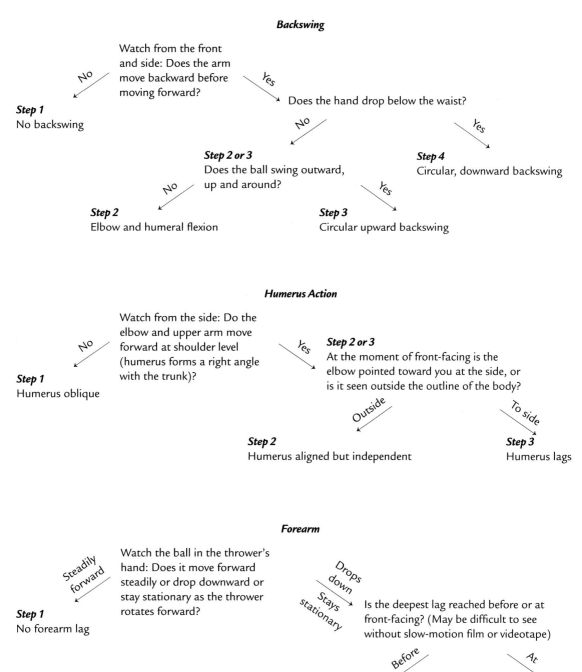

Backswing

Watch from the front and side: Does the arm move backward before moving forward?

No → **Step 1** No backswing

Yes → Does the hand drop below the waist?

No → **Step 2 or 3** Does the ball swing outward, up and around?

Yes → **Step 4** Circular, downward backswing

No → **Step 2** Elbow and humeral flexion

Yes → **Step 3** Circular upward backswing

Humerus Action

Watch from the side: Do the elbow and upper arm move forward at shoulder level (humerus forms a right angle with the trunk)?

No → **Step 1** Humerus oblique

Yes → **Step 2 or 3** At the moment of front-facing is the elbow pointed toward you at the side, or is it seen outside the outline of the body?

Outside → **Step 2** Humerus aligned but independent

To side → **Step 3** Humerus lags

Forearm

Watch the ball in the thrower's hand: Does it move forward steadily or drop downward or stay stationary as the thrower rotates forward?

Steadily forward → **Step 1** No forearm lag

Drops down / *Stays stationary* → Is the deepest lag reached before or at front-facing? (May be difficult to see without slow-motion film or videotape)

Before → **Step 2** Forearm lag

At → **Step 3** Delayed forearm lag

OBSERVATION PLAN FOR SIDEARM STRIKING

(For foot, trunk, and humerus components, use the *throwing* observation)

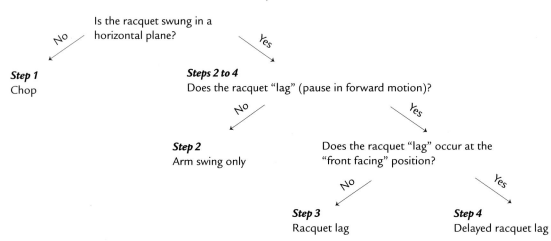

Racquet/Bat Action

Is the racquet swung in a horizontal plane?

No — **Step 1** Chop

Yes — **Steps 2 to 4** Does the racquet "lag" (pause in forward motion)?

No — **Step 2** Arm swing only

Yes — Does the racquet "lag" occur at the "front facing" position?

No — **Step 3** Racquet lag

Yes — **Step 4** Delayed racquet lag

OBSERVATION PLAN FOR CATCHING

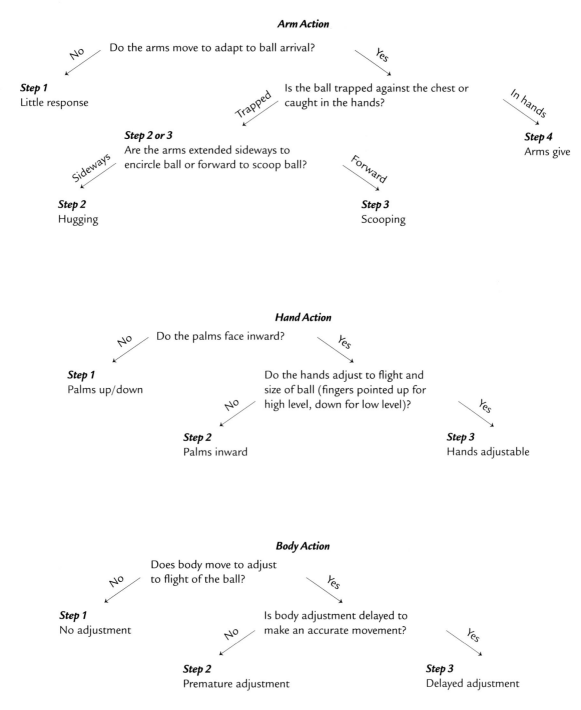

Arm Action

Do the arms move to adapt to ball arrival?

No

Step 1
Little response

Yes

Is the ball trapped against the chest or caught in the hands?

Trapped

In hands

Step 4
Arms give

Step 2 or 3
Are the arms extended sideways to encircle ball or forward to scoop ball?

Sideways

Forward

Step 2
Hugging

Step 3
Scooping

Hand Action

Do the palms face inward?

No

Step 1
Palms up/down

Yes

Do the hands adjust to flight and size of ball (fingers pointed up for high level, down for low level)?

No

Yes

Step 2
Palms inward

Step 3
Hands adjustable

Body Action

Does body move to adjust to flight of the ball?

No

Step 1
No adjustment

Yes

Is body adjustment delayed to make an accurate movement?

No

Yes

Step 2
Premature adjustment

Step 3
Delayed adjustment

List of Web Sites

A

AARP Research and Policy
www.aarp.org/research

Adult Development and Aging, Division 20 of the APA
http://aging.ufl.edu/apadiv20/apadiv20.htm

Aging: AOA Websites on
www.aoa.gov

American Academy of Otolaryngology
www.aaohns.org

American Academy of Pediatrics
www. aap.org

American Academy of Pediatrics Policy Statements
http://aappolicy.aappublications.org

American Academy of Pediatrics Research
www.aap.org/research

American Alliance for Health, Physical Education, Recreation, and Dance
www.aahperd.org

American Association for Retired Persons (AARP)
www.aarp.org

American College of Obstetricians and Gynecologists
www.acog.org

American College of Sports Medicine
www.acsm.org

American Guidance Services (publisher of assessment instruments)
www.agsnet.com

American Heart Association
www.americanheart.org

American Red Cross
www.redcross.org

American Senior Fitness Association
www.seniorfitness.org

American Sport Education Program
www.asep.com

B

Body Mass Index Calculator
www.cdc.gov/nccdphp/dnpa/bmi/calc-bmi.htm

Buros Institute — Sensory-Motor Classification
www.unl.edu/buros/index15.html

C

Center for Motor Behavior in Down Syndrome
www.umich.edu/~cmbds

Centers for Disease Control and Prevention
www.cdc.gov

Centers for Disease Control Morbidity and Mortality Weekly Report
www.cdc.gov/mmwr

Coach Jerry
www.coachjerry.com

Coaching Association of Canada
www.coach.ca

Cooper Institute for Aerobics Research
www.cooperinst.org

Cystic Fibrosis Foundation
www.cff.org

D

Division for Early Childhood of the Council for Exceptional Children
www.dec-sped.erg

F

Fetal development, 1st trimester
www.w-cpc.org/fetal1.html

Fetal development, 2nd trimester
www.w-cpc.org/fetal2.html

Fetal development, 3rd trimester
www.w-cpc.org/fetal3.html

Fifty-plus Fitness Association
www.50plus.org

FITNESSGRAM
www.fitnessgram.net

G

Gait & Posture Journal
www.elsevier.nl/inca/publications/store/5/2/5/4/4/2

Gait and Locomotion: Biomechanics
www.per.ualberta.ca/biomechanics/sections.htm#loco

Gymboree
www.gymboree.com

H

Head Start (U.S. DHHS)
www.acf.hhs.gov/programs/hsb/research/2003.htm

Healthy People 2010
www.health.gov/healthypeople

Human Kinetics Publishers
www.humankinetics.com

I

Increasing Physical Activity Among Adults Age 50
and Older
www.agingblueprint.org/overview.cfm

International In-line Skating Association
www.iisa.org

International Society for Aging and Physical Activity
www.isapa.org

J

Johns Hopkins Center for Hearing and Balance
www.bme.jhu.edu/labs/chb

L

Lunar Corporation
www.lunarcorp.com

M

March of Dimes
www.modimes.org

Mayo Clinic Vestibular Rehabilitation Program
www.mayoclinic.org/ent/vestibulalab/html

Mayo HIV Clinic
www.mayoclinic.org/infectiousdiseases-rst/
hivclinic.html

Motor Development Academy of NASPE
www.aahperd.org/naspe/specialinterest-motordev.
html

N

National Alliance for Youth Sports
www.nays.org

National Association for Self-Esteem
www.self-esteem-nase.org

National Association for Sports and Physical Education
www.aahperd.org/naspe

National Center for Health Statistics
www.cdc.gov/nchs

National Council on Aging
www.ncoa.org

National Down Syndrome Society
www.ndss.org

National Eating Disorders
www.nationaleatingdisorders.org

National Eye Institute
www.nei.nih.gov

National Federation of the Blind
www.nfb.org

National Heart, Lung, and Blood Institute
www.nhlbi.nih.gov

National Institute on Aging
www.nia.nih.gov

National Osteoporosis Foundation
www.nof.org

National Program for Playground Safety
www.uni.edu/playground/home.html

National Senior Games Association (Senior Olympics)
www.nsga.com

National Strength and Conditioning Association
www.nsca-lift.org/menu.asp

North American Association for the Study of Obesity
www.naaso.org

North American Society for the Psychology of Sports
and Physical Activity
www.naspspa.org

O

Osteoporosis Society of Canada
www.osteoporosis.ca

P

Playground Resilient Surfacing Systems — Happy
Landing
www.safetysurface.com

Playground Safety: American Academy of Pediatrics
www.aap.org/family/playgrd.htm

Playground Safety: KaBoom
www.kaboom.org

President's Challenge
www.presidentschallenge.org

President's Council on Physical Fitness
www.fitness.gov

Prevent Blindness America
www.prevent-blindness.org

Pro-Ed Inc. (publisher of TGMD 2)
www.proedinc.com

Psychological Corporation
www.harcourt-international.com

S

Safe on First (conducts background checks on coaches)
www.safeonfirst.com

U
U.S. Bureau of the Census
   www.census.gov
U.S. Consumer Product Safety Commission
   www.cpsc.gov
U.S. National Library of Medicine
   www.nlm.nih.gov

V
Vestibular Disorders Association
   www.teleport.com/veda

Y
YMCA
   www.ymca.net

Author Index

Subject Index